Memoirs Relating to European and Asiatic Turkey, and Other Countries of the East;

PREFACE.

Tⁿⁱᶜ information derived from those who visit various provinces of the Turkish empire is of a very different nature from that which is collected in travelling through parts of civilised Europe. In the former case, we not only become acquainted with a people whose habits, institutions, religion, policy, and usages, are entirely opposite to those which we find in Christian Europe; but from researches connected with the geography and natural history of these countries we are able to explain many passages of the sacred writers, as well as of other ancient authors; the customs * also and modes of life which

* Travellers who have visited parts of Syria and Egypt make frequent mention of customs and habits of life similar to those which prevailed in the time of the writers of the Old and New Testament; but no one, before Captain Light, ever pointed out a singular opinion still existing in the East, and which was common in Palestine 1800 years ago, respecting the use of saliva in certain diseases of the body. See the account in this volume, p 421., of the person at Ibrim in Nubia applying for a cure of the head-ache, and of the woman at Hermonthis in Egypt, who requested C. Light to spit on her eyes "How far spittle was accounted wholesome for weak eyes," says Lightfoot, in his Hebrew and Talmudical exercitations on John ix, "we may learn from the following tale relating to R Meir" We shall extract a part of it. " Is there ever a woman, said Rabbi Meir, among you, skilled in muttering charms over eyes? the woman said, R I am not skilled, however, saith he, do thou spit seven times on my eyes, and I shall be healed." See Mark viii. 23. and vii. 33

The passage from Capt Light's Journal should be inserted in any future edition of Harmer

still prevail in Syria and Egypt, afford occasionally excellent illustrations of the Holy Scriptures ; and coins, vases, inscriptions, throw
light on the state of the arts among the Greeks, on different parts of
their history ; and on the palæography and dialects of their language.

But no person is qualified to pay equal attention to the various
subjects which present themselves to his notice, in a journey through
European and Asiatic Turkey ; and any acquaintance with the
geography, natural history, statistics, and antiquities of these countries
is often obtained with great difficulty, even by those who are best
prepared to direct their attention to such pursuits

A selection, therefore, from the journals of different travellers,
may be the means of bringing together in a single volume a greater
variety of information than we can expect to find in the work of any
individual.

Although the publications of our countrymen, as well as of others
who have recently visited the Levant, have added many valuable
materials to those which we before possessed, relating to different
parts of the Turkish empire, yet the field of enquiry is so wide, that
much remains still to engage the notice and attention of future
travellers.   Our knowledge of these countries is necessarily acquired
by slow degrees , various circumstances occasionally interrupt the
researches of those who explore them , some provinces, in consequence
of the want of an able and efficient system of government, are exposed
to the incursions of robbers and wandering tribes ; through these the
traveller is obliged to pass in haste ; at other times, sickness, arising
from the heat of the climate or from the season of the year, impedes his
progress   The want of ready communication with the inhabitants,
together with the ignorance and jealousy so frequently displayed by
them, are obstacles to his acquiring the information which he seeks.
To these, we must add the dangers he incurs in exploring the more
uncivilised districts of the empire.

While, therefore. we are thus prevented from obtaining a more complete knowledge of these countries, it is hoped that an attempt to supply the deficiencies of it, according to the plan adopted in the present work, will be favourably received.

The observations of those whose papers are now published for the first time, are communicated either in the form of journals and letters, or detached essays. There are advantages attending each of these separate modes; in the former, the remarks of the traveller are given as they presented themselves to his mind on the spot, without any unnecessary amplification or expansion, and in adopting the latter method, the writer by subsequent reading and enquiry is able to bestow more attention on the subject than is consistent with the form of a mere narrative or journal.

There are, indeed, many subjects which have not been sufficiently illustrated, either in the present work, or in those already published, relating to the Turkish empire. Yet every information of an original kind, and drawn from authentic sources, is of importance; and if those Europeans who are settled in the great cities of the East would note down carefully their remarks, and institute enquiries on various subjects, we should soon be in possession of many new documents. A residence on the spot affords excellent opportunities for acquiring or correcting information. Materials for the valuable work of Dr. Russell were prepared in this manner; and during the twelve years which were passed by D'Arvieux in the Levant, he collected a greater number of facts respecting the Turks, their manners and customs, than Europeans in general have been able to acquire. There are many objects of research which the transient traveller, however inquisitive, cannot investigate fully; these may fall more properly under the observation of those who are resident in the country.

It is to be regretted that a plan suggested by the Editor of Russell's Aleppo, in his preface to that work, has never yet been adopted

He proposes that a collection of books on astronomy, ancient geography, and natural history, together with a few instruments, should
be placed in each of the commercial settlements in the Levant, and
that heads of enquiry under the form of queries should be adapted to
the respective stations.   There can be little doubt that a well-arranged
plan of this nature would conduce materially to our knowledge of
parts of Greece and Asia   It would stimulate enquiry, and direct
usefully some portion of that time which might be spared by persons
engaged in commercial pursuits, or by those who are resident as
consuls in some of the cities of the East.

If this plan, or one similar to it, cannot be easily carried into
effect, the Editor hopes, that at different intervals of time selections
will be made, partly from the papers of those travellers, who, although
they have been prevented by death from completing their labours,
may have left behind them remarks too valuable to be forgotten;
partly from the observations of others, who may have directed their
enquiries to new subjects, or have examined less frequented districts
of the Turkish empire.   If the journals of these travellers should be
judged by the authors of them too small to form separate publications,
still they may properly find their place in a volume, which shall in-
corporate and connect them with the remarks of others relating to the
same countries.

The Editor now proceeds to acknowledge the obligations which he
has received from those gentlemen who have communicated to him
the different papers and remarks which are published for the first
time in the present volume.

*An Account of a Journey through the District of Maina, in the
Morea*, p. 33.

THIS extract, from the papers of Mr. Morritt, relates to a part of
Greece which has seldom been explored.   Indeed an account so full

and so detailed of the character and manners of the Mainots * is no
where to be found. The district of the Peloponnesus occupied by
them is the portion of it bordering on the Messenian and Laconian
gulfs. The spirit of piracy and plunder which made them so long
the terror of the Archipelago and neighbouring seas, appears to have
been softened in some degree by commercial pursuits. A traveller
in the early part of the seventeenth century thus describes them

---

* The Mainots are called by Constantine Porphyrog κάστρου Μαίνης; οἰκήτορας, de Ad.
Imp c 50 On the eastern part of the country occupied by them they are joined by the
Tzacones descended from the ancient Laconians, and inhabiting a district of the Morea
between Nauplia and Epidaurus Limera Many Doric forms are retained by the Tzacones
in their language, some instances of which are given by Villoison They say ὀχθρὲ for
ἐχθρὲ (in Sappho we find ορπετὸν for ἑρπετον), χέρκη tor χάρτη, (the Dorians said ἄλλοχα for
ἄλλοτε), also θουγάτηρ and ψουχά They use νάυτα and προφῆτα, the Homeric nominative,
instead of νάυτη and προφήτη — See the Prolegom ad Hom xlix. and his MS notes on
Pindar, referred to by Schaefer, p 96 in Gieg de D and Leake's Researches, p. 200

We learn from Mr. Hawkins, that the names of the villages of the Tzaccaniotes are
Prasto, Castanitza, and Sitena; they have also a few hamlets or summer habitations under
the name of Kalivia All these belong to the province of Mistra, though they are situated
in the Villaéte of Agios Petros. Prasto, in respect to its Greek population, is nearly equal
to Tripolizza, containing from 800 to 1000 houses Except a few small plains on the
sea-coast, the country of Tzaccaniais entirely mountainous, and of course it is not productive of corn, but supports very numerous flocks of goats and sheep Cheese, therefore, is the
principal object of exportation, and next to this, Prino Cocci, or scarlet grains, which are
gathered from the Prinari or Quercus Ilex The inhabitants are celebrated for their skill
in draining ground, and in conducting water, and are preferred to all others in executing
works of this kind in the Ionian islands A considerable part of the whole population not
finding employment at home migrate either periodically, at particular seasons of the year,
or for a certain time. Many, for instance, visit Patras, where they are occupied in attending to the currant vineyards About three hundred leave Tzaccania every year for Zeitun
near Thermopylæ, where they are employed during three months in the cultivation of the
rice grounds. It is computed that about the same number are resident at Constantinople,
most of whom follow the occupation of Baccalides (grocers and purveyors of victuals) The
bread-sellers in that city are chiefly Armenians, but the hirelings whom they employ to
grind the corn in horse-mills and to bake the bread are Tzaccaniotes

" *Agreste et ferox genus hominum lorica induti, arcum in manibus gestant, et nullius parent imperio , sed rapinis et latrociniis assueti obscuram ducunt vitam, Christiani nomine, sed reipsa barbari et exleges plane.*" Cotovic, Itin. 61.

Remarks added to the Journal of Mr. Morritt, illustrating Part of his Route through the ancient Messenia and Laconia — from the Papers of the late Dr. Sibthorp, p. 60.*

" In the year 1784, Professor Sibthorp projected his first tour into Greece, and engaged a draftsman of great excellence, Mr. F. Bauer, to be the companion of his expedition ; they arrived in Crete in 1786 This island and many other parts of the Levant were examined by Dr. Sibthorp in that and the following year ; and he was enabled to collect a large mass of documents respecting the birds, and fishes, and plants of those celebrated countries, and to satisfy many enquiries respecting the state of agriculture and medicine among the inhabitants of them

" Dr. Sibthorp's constitution had suffered much from the fatigues and exertions undergone by him during his journey into Greece , yet sensible how much was still wanting to perfect the undertaking which he had originally designed, he determined to devote himself to the further prosecution of it, namely the botanical investigation of Greece, and especially the determination of the plants mentioned by its classical authors.

" In 1794, he again set out for Turkey ; and was joined at Constantinople by Mr. Hawkins, who had accompanied him during part of

---

* These remarks are published by the permission of Mr Hawkins, to whom the Editor is also indebted for many communications, which are properly noticed, wherever they occur, in this work.

his former tour. They visited the plain of Troy, the isles of Imbros and Lemnos, the peninsula of Athos, passed some time in Attica; proceeded on their journey to the Morea, where they spent two months, examining the most interesting parts of that province.

" They reached Zante on the 29th of April, and there Dr. S. parted from the faithful companion of his journey, whom he was destined never to see again, but in whose friendship he safely confided in his last hours. Mr. H. returned to Greece; the Professor left Zante for Otranto; on the voyage he was detained by a contrary wind at Prevesa, and visiting the ruins of Nicopolis caught a severe cold, from which he never recovered. It seems to have proved the exciting cause of that disease, which had long been latent in the mesenteric and pulmonary glands, and which terminated in a consumption. He arrived in England in 1795, and died at Bath in 1796, in the 38th year of his age.

" The posthumous benefits which Dr S. has rendered to his beloved science are sufficient to rank him among its most illustrious patrons. By his will, dated 1796, he gives a freehold estate in Oxfordshire to the University of Oxford, for the purpose of first publishing his Flora Græca, in ten folio volumes, with 100 coloured plates in each, and a Prodromus of the same work, in octavo, without plates. His executors, the Hon. T. Wenman, J. Hawkins, and T. Platt, Esquires, were to appoint a sufficiently competent editor of these works, to whom the MSS. drawings and specimens were to be confided. They fixed upon the writer of the present article, who has now nearly completed the Prodromus, and the second volume of the Flora. In preparing the latter work, the final determination of the species, the distinctions of such as were new, and all critical remarks have fallen to his lot; he has also revised the references to Dioscorides, and with Mr. Hawkins's help, corrected the modern Greek names. When these publications are finished, the annual sum of 200l.

is to be paid to a professor of Rural Economy, and the remainder of the rents of the estate above mentioned is destined to purchase books for him."*

Journey in Asia Minor — from Parium to the Troad — Ascent to the Summit of Ida — the Salt Springs of Tousla — the Ruins of Assos. — From the Papers of Dr. Hunt, p 84

IN this journey, Dr. Hunt was accompanied by the late Professor Carlyle. In their survey of the Troad, they were conducted by their guides to a part of the country which no traveller has yet visited. Of the magnificent ruins at Assos, there has been hitherto no published account; they are slightly mentioned in the Voyage Pittoresque of M. de Choiseul

The Editor acknowledges his obligations to Shute Barrington, Lord Bishop of Durham, and to George Tomline, Lord Bishop of Lincoln, for the letters of the late Professor Carlyle, addressed to them from Constantinople and other parts of Turkey, p. 152.

Various and contradictory reports had been circulated at different times, respecting the contents of the library of the Seraglio. Toderini (T. 2. Letterat. Turches) was informed that it contained many volumes in the Oriental dialects, and some manuscripts of the Greek and Latin writers. In answer to the enquiries of the Abbé Sevin, it was said, that the MSS. had been burnt. Dositheus, in his History of the Patriarchs of Jerusalem, printed in 1715, mentions the library of the Greek emperors as still existing. The late Pro-

---

* The account in the text, relating to Dr. Sibthorp, is taken, by permission of Sir J. Smith, from a more enlarged memoir printed in Rees's Cyclopædia.

fessor Carlyle was requested by Mr. Pitt and the Bishop of Lincoln to direct his attention particularly, during his residence at Constantinople, towards obtaining some satisfactory information on this subject; and one of his letters contains a very detailed and valuable statement, the result of his researches and personal enquiries.

The accuracy of the account given by Mr. Carlyle, has been strongly confirmed by the publication of some part of the journals of M. Guardin, who was ambassador from France at the Porte, in the year 1685. It appears from the enquiries that were then made, that the Greek MSS. and books in the library amounted to about 200. A renegado Italian, in the service of the Selictar, the chief officer of the Seraglio, brought away* from it many of the works at successive times; and fifteen of these volumes, written partly on vellum, partly on paper, were selected by Besnier, the Jesuit, and purchased by him for the ambassador. The remainder of the Greek works were sold at Pera; *ils ont été vendus sur le pied de* 100 *livres chacun ainsi il n'en reste plus de cette langue dans le sérail.* This account †, (with which Mr. Carlyle was entirely unacquainted,) corresponds with the statement given by him to the Bishop of Lincoln. He found in the library many works in the Oriental dialects; but none written in Greek. ‡

---

* The plunder of the library had already commenced in 1638, as we learn from a letter of Greaves " I have procured, among other works, Ptolemy's Almagest, the fairest book that I have seen, stolen by a Spahy, as I am informed, out of the King's library in the Seraglio " Vol. II. p 137.

† It was not published in the life-time of Professor Carlyle. See " Notice des MSS du Roi " T VIII.

‡ An Arabic translation of a lost work of Aristotle, πολιτεῖαι πολεών, existed at Constantinople so late as the 1089th year of the Hegira, and is quoted by Hadjee Kalfa, who lived at that time, in his Bib. Orient See Villoison, in Ac. des Inscr. xlvii. 322. The discovery of this MS would be a literary acquisition of some value.

Of the MSS. which were procured by M. Girardin, and were after-
wards brought to Paris, two were consulted by Wyttenbach and
Larcher; a manuscript of Plutarch, by the former; and one of
Herodotus, by the latter.

Mount Athos, from the Papers of Dr. Hunt, p. 198.

At the time when the capital of the Greek empire was in danger
of being attacked by the Turks, the most valuable of the manuscripts
of the learned Greeks were taken to Mount Athos, as a place of
safety. The libraries of Paris, Vienna, and Moscow, contain many
which have been brought from that peninsula* , and persons have
been sent at different times to procure others, which are preserved
in some of the convents. We have, however, no recent or authentic
account of the actual state of the monastic institutions at Athos.
Dr. Hunt and Professor Carlyle, during a residence of three weeks
there, collected much information relating to them, and examined
with particular attention the different libraries † on the Holy
Mountain.

*Remarks on Parts of Bœotia and Phocis, from the Journals of
Mr. Raikes,* p. 298.

---

* Some have supposed that the entire copy of Livy was to be found at Athos. — Gibbon's Miscell. Works, Vol. iii p 375

† Many of the MSS in these libraries were probably written by the monks who exercised the office of calligraphs, others were given as presents on particular occasions.
Maximus gave a manuscript of Chrysostom with some books to the monastery of Dionysius   Gregory, Bishop of Elasson (the ancient Oloosson in Thessaly), presented a manuscript of the Gospel of St. John to the convent of Pantocratos. — Mém. de l'Instit. 1815.

The Plain of Marathon, from the Papers of the late Colonel Squire, p 329.

IN the year 1802, Colonel Squire was engaged with Colonel Leake and Mr. Hamilton in a tour through parts of Greece ; the plain of Marathon, the defile of Thermopylæ, and the site of the battle of Platæa were particularly examined by them, and plans of these spots so celebrated in the history of Greece, were taken.

" The surveys," to use the words of Colonel Squire*, " were made from a base measured by a chain, the principal points being ascertained by angles observed with a theodolite." It is probable, that the delay of publishing these plans arose from a desire of collecting some additional details, and thus rendering them more full and perfect. The topographical sketch, which is now engraved from the papers of Colonel Squire, however incomplete, will serve to illustrate the observations made by him and his companions on the spot. More accurate geographical information respecting this and other parts of Greece, may be shortly expected from Sir W. Gell, Mr. Hawkins, and Colonel Leake, who have applied themselves with great industry, to a survey of different districts of this country. *Nos meilleurs cartes de ce pays ne sont encore que des cartes hypothétiques.* Traduction de Strabon. T. iii. 101.

---

* John Squire, late Lieutenant-Colonel in the Royal Corps of Engineers, was an officer of distinguished talents His death is sincerely lamented by his relatives, and by those who had various opportunities of being acquainted with the excellences of his heart and understanding He served his country in Egypt, South America, Holland, and Spain, and died at Truxillo during the Peninsular war, A. D. 1812, in the thirty-third year of his age, the victim of excessive fatigue and exertion.

῍Η μάλα δὴ περὶ σεῖο λύγρον πότμον ἔκλυε πάτρα.

The extracts from Colonel Squire's papers are printed by permission of the Rev. E Squire.

Observations relating to some of the Antiquities of Egypt, from the Papers of the late Mr. Davison, p. 350.

NATHANIEL DAVISON, Esq. was British consul at Algiers · he accompanied Mr Wortley Montague to Egypt, in the year 1763 ; resided eighteen months at Alexandria ; as many at Cairo ; and from that place visited frequently the pyramids of Giza *

During his stay in Egypt, he made some excursions in the vicinity of Alexandria with the Duke de Chaulnes; they afterwards embarked together on board of the same vessel for Europe. While they were performing quarantine in the Lazaretto at Leghorn, the Duke contrived by means of a false key to obtain and copy Mr. Davison's papers and drawings. † Coming afterwards to London, he advertised a publication of his own researches with drawings by Mr. Davison, whom he called his secretary ‡ The design of the work was laid aside, in consequence of a strong remonstrance on the part of Mr. Davison, conveyed in a letter to the Duke, Sept. 9. 1783, the very day on which the latter expected an engraver to wait upon him. A proposal of a joint publication was then made to Mr. D., which he declined. Two plates from Mr. Davison's drawings are engraved in Sonnini's travels, and must have been communicated by the Duke.

* Mr. D. died in 1809. His Journals, Plans, and Drawings are in the possession of his widow, Mrs Davison, of Alnwick, in Northumberland, and his nephew Dr. Yellolý, of Finsbury-square From these papers the Editor has been permitted to select the extracts now published for the first time in the present volume.

† This is stated on the authority of Mr. Meadley (the author of the life of Paley), who was well acquainted with Mr Davison

‡ This tract, in which Mr. D is called the secretary to the Duc de Chaulnes, is in the possession of Mr. Meadley.

The merit of the discovery * of the room in the great pyramid at Giza, over the chamber which contains the Sarcophagus, is due solely to Mr. Davison no traveller before or since his time has examined it, nor has any one been induced by curiosity to descend so far into another part of the same building. Very little was known of the catacombs of Alexandria before he examined them they seem to have been scarcely noticed by preceding travellers. He was the first who surveyed the whole of these extensive cemeteries; and the plan of the Necropolis among his papers, is nearly as full and complete as that which was afterwards made by the French.

Remarks on the Manners and Customs of the Modern Inhabitants of Egypt, from the Journals of Dr. Hume.

Journal of a Voyage up the Nile, between Philæ and Ibrim, in Nubia, in May 1814, by Captain Light.

On the Topography of Athens, communicated by Mr Hawkins.

On the Vale of Tempe, by the same.

On the Syrinx of Strabo, and the Passage of the Euripus, by the same.

---

* Mr D's discovery is mentioned by Niebuhr and Bruce. the former says, " Je ne fus pas assez heureux pour y découvrir une chambre, jusqu' alors inconnue, et qui fut découverte après notre départ par Mr Davison." Vol 1 p 161. The latter says, " Mr D discovered the chamber above the landing place." Vol. 1 p 41. Maillet had been forty times in the pyramid, and had no knowledge of the chamber.

Panoramic View of Athens, illustrated by Mr. Haygarth.

Letter from Mr. Morritt to Dr. Clarke, respecting the Plain of Troy.

The Architectural Inscription brought from Athens, explained and translated by Mr. Wilkins.

LIST OF THE PLATES.

GENERAL TABLE

OF

CONTENTS.

ᴀ 2

PRELIMINARY DISCOURSE.

THE CAUSES OF THE WEAKNESS AND DECLINE OF THE TURKISH MONARCHY, AND SOME REMARKS ON THE SYSTEM OF GOVERNMENT PURSUED IN THE EUROPEAN AND ASIATIC PROVINCES OF THE EMPIRE.

THE history of no country has been distinguished by conquests so rapid and extensive, as those which attended the progress of the Turkish arms from the time of Othman to the establishment of their power over the fairest parts of Asia and Europe. The Christian world viewed their successes with alarm * ; and the different states were exhorted to lay aside all mutual animosities, by the danger with which they were threatened. ┼ The nations of Europe have derived strength and security from the general improvement of human reason, and the cultivation of the arts of peace and war. In the meantime, the spirit of military enterprise has declined among the Turks , the vigorous age of their monarchy is past ; and the weakness of their empire has been exposed to their enemies, and parts of it have been invaded, or wrested from them.

---

* " The Turk," says Lord Bacon, " is the most potent and most dangerous enemy of the faith."

┼ Many treatises were written to rouse the Christian nations against the infidels " J " Reusnerus, (says Bayle,) a recueilli plusieurs volumes de ces harangues, qui ont été " publiées pour exhorter les princes Chretiens a unir leurs forces contre les infidelles " Art Mahomet. ♪ Note E

B

In examining the causes which have produced this decline, we may first advert to one deserving of more consideration, than it has generally received. We allude to the discovery of the navigation to India by the Cape of Good Hope. Before that great event took place, the Venetians had formed establishments in the ports of Syria and Egypt, to which the productions and manufactures of the East were brought; they had received various privileges of trade from the Mamelukes, which Selim the First afterwards confirmed. The valuable commodities of China and India would have continued to reach these coasts, or would have been conveyed over land to the Black Sea, and thence by a short navigation to Constantinople. It was fortunate for the security and happiness of Europe, that the communication with the East was directed at that time into a different channel, the throne of Turkey was filled by sovereigns of great energy and enterprise, and the Christian states would not have resisted that power which the increasing wealth of their enemies might have enabled them to create and maintain. But when Turkey no longer continued mistress of the commerce of that age*, her national strength began to be impaired; her armies were no longer supported by the great means which were essential to the promotion and extension of her views against the peace of the Christian world, and her importance in the political system of Europe was greatly diminished.

2. The change occasioned by this circumstance has been followed by another in the constitution of the government of equal importance. The Turkish empire could only be supported by vigour and absolute power in the centre, by a promptness and decision which should pervade the whole system of administration, by a quick communication with the remotest parts of the provinces, by an army ready

* " About the year 1620, the voyages by sea to the East Indies had so lowered the prices of Indian merchandise, that the trade between India and Turkey, by the Persian Gulph and the Red Sea, having much decayed, the Grand Signior's customs were greatly lessened." Anderson, xi. 3.

to check and subdue the first symptoms of rising independence and insurrection. The author of Oceana* considered the policy and structure of all absolute monarchies in the East, to be not only contained, but meliorated in the Turkish government; and if we reflect upon the short duration of some of the Asiatic dynasties in Persia and India; if we consider that China has been four times subject to Tartar nations since the tenth century, we have reason to conclude that an empire which has now supported itself nearly five hundred years, has not been placed on weak foundations. While the Turkish Sultans were at the head of their troops, and kept in fear and subjection the different provinces, they could enforce and establish their ordinances; they were ready to protect or punish; they were rarely disturbed by the struggle of different competitors for power; the vigour of the armies was not suffered to relax. But a due regard to the extensive concerns and interests of the empire has proved a task too great for the degenerate successors of Selim, Mahomet, and Soliman. The stability of their monarchy depends on an adherence to those principles which first formed, and afterwards maintained it. The military ardour of the people is no longer nursed by fanaticism and enthusiasm; a decrease of reputation abroad, has been accompanied by internal weakness and decay. In proportion to the want of firmness and energy which have characterised the measures of the Divan, its authority has been disregarded, and the governors of various parts of the empire have had time to form their schemes of aggrandisement. While the customary tribute has been delayed by some, under various pretences, others more or less openly, according to the opportunities which present themselves, have disclaimed all allegiance; whole tracts are wasted in the wars kindled on these occasions; and in the nature and violence of the hostilities we are frequently reminded of those which belong to the history of the feudal times in Europe.

---

* Art of Lawgiving, 368.

3. The condition of the provinces has been also affected by an alteration in the mode of appointing the governors of them. Formerly they were bestowed on slaves who had received their education in the seraglio ; who considered the Sultan as sole master of their destiny, pretended to no sovereignty over their districts but that which flowed from his good will, and were prepared to resign them at his command, and return into the obscure situation from which they had been taken.* But when the nomination to these principalities could be obtained by paying great sums to those who held power and office at Constantinople, many parts of the empire were exposed to plunder and oppression. The Turkish Pasha, like the Roman Proconsul†, is obliged to satisfy the rapacity of the officers in the capital, if the demands of the Porte increase, the provincial governor must comply with them ; the continuance in his district must be purchased by new contributions, or by sharing some part of the treasure accumulated by him for the purpose of procuring another government, upon his removal from that which he possesses. Uncertain, in the meantime, how long he may enjoy his present dignity, he is regardless of gaining the attachment or approbation of his subjects ; his time is not employed in projecting works of public utility, or forming schemes for the general improvement of the province, or for securing and facilitating the intercourse between different parts of it.

4. The labour and industry of every country, whether they are directed to agricultural or commercial pursuits, are regulated by the manner in which wealth is diffused among the inhabitants. The very unequal distribution of it in Turkey, forms a great impediment

---

* Russell's Aleppo, i. 335

† " The governors of the Roman provinces, were, if I may use the expression, the Pashas of the republic " Montesquieu, B 2 These rapacious governors acquired vast wealth. " Even Cicero," says Melmoth, " who professed to conduct himself with exemplary disinterestedness in his province, was able in the course of a single year to acquire as much as 17,600l of our money, and that too from a province by no means the most considerable of the republic's dominions."

to any advancement of prosperity or general civilization.[*] In and about the great cities of the empire, where the Pasha, Mohassil, and other officers of high situation reside, and to which manufacturers or merchants are attracted, some degree of industry and cultivation may be observed. But as we proceed through the more distant parts of many of the provinces, we find little appearance of wealth or comfort. This inequality of property is a consequence of the insecurity of the possessions of those, who are in inferior situations in life. If we except some families of feudal rank, the most opulent people in every province are the officers of government, those who hold situations under the Porte, or Pasha of the district. All of a class below them, are checked and impeded in their exertions to raise themselves. If their occupations are agricultural, they do not possess that interest in the land which would encourage them to industrious exertion, in encreasing the quantity or improving the quality of the productions of it. Their territorial assessment is nominally fixed, but they are exposed to heavy and fluctuating exactions. If their means of subsistence are derived from commercial sources [+], an incautious display of wealth would subject them to extortion and plunder. Under such a system of mischievous policy, it is not surprising that various modes of concealing property are practised. In the large towns it is not necessarily so much exposed to the eye of the government, as that wealth, which is derived immediately from the produce of the land.

Such is the favourable situation of some of the provinces of

---

* " Above all things, good policy is to be used, that the treasure and monies of a state be not gathered into few hands. For otherwise, a state may have a great stock and yet starve, and money is, like muck, not good, except it be spread." Bacon. Essay, 39.

+ " The Christians of Aleppo," says Russell, (in a remark, which admits of general application to the Christian subjects of the Turks,) " find it prudent to avoid the ostentation of wealth, from fear of attracting the attention of their rapacious governors. They are under the necessity of contributing largely to the support of the poor of their respective nations, as likewise to the payment of Avanias, or unjust exactions demanded from them." ii. 16.

Turkey, with respect to the great markets of Germany and Italy, that the merchants of this empire are enabled even in times of war, when the communication by sea is interrupted, to maintain an active commercial intercourse by land. The territorial wealth of this country is so great, the climate so various, that few parts of the world would enter into competition with European and Asiatic Turkey, if a better direction and a greater encouragement were given to the industry of the inhabitants. The activity of the Greek and Armenian merchants would extend the internal trade, and open new sources of prosperity. But the spirit of enterprise and commercial speculation, is checked by the insecurity of property, and by the defects and abuses of the administration of the affairs of the provinces. It is only in those where the Pasha exerts himself to maintain order and tranquillity, and where he feels himself secure for a time from the intrigues of the Porte, that the interests of trade or agriculture are regarded. The want of punctuality in the fulfilment of pecuniary engagements, and the difficulty of recovering debts occasion the rate of interest for money to be very high. In Constantinople, and Smyrna, it amounts to twelve *per cent.*, in many parts of the empire to twenty *per cent. per annum.* As a great portion of the commerce of the country consists in the exportation of unwrought articles, there is little encouragement given to those various occupations which in Europe excite the industry and ingenuity of the artist and mechanic. Of the sums collected by the Pashas and other powerful individuals, some part is hoarded or concealed, and thus withdrawn from general circulation, some is annually sent out of the provinces to the great officers of the Porte.

5. The transportation of goods through different districts of the empire is slow, and often obstructed by the intestine troubles of the provinces; frequent interruptions arise in parts of Syria, and the northern and eastern extremities of Asia Minor. The independent Sheiks of the tribes who frequent one of the routes from Basra to Aleppo, all maintain equal pretensions to demand from the merchant, as the price of his safety, some portion of his goods. The

caravans are obliged frequently to accept the escort which some neighbouring Sheik or Pasha offers to them, and the expences of the merchants are multiplied by the delays and obstructions which their protectors purposely occasion. (Niebuhr, i. 339.) According to the measure of their strength and force, the Arabs and other tribes resist or obey the authority of the Turks. By extraordinary energy and vigour, a Pasha may sometimes be enabled to repress the encroachments of the Arabs, and confine them within certain limits; he prevents them, until they have paid the tribute which is due, from entering the great cities for the purposes of traffic or exchanging different commodities, but the expences of raising levies and troops, active and numerous enough to watch their conduct, and threaten them with punishment are so great, that the governors, who consider their residence in the provinces as uncertain, are seldom disposed to maintain an army which can inspire the Arabs with fear and respect. The inhabitants of the villages, in the meantime, are left to a vicissitude of insult and oppression; they are kept in constant alarm by the incursion of these wandering tribes, and when the Pasha takes the field, they suffer not less injury from the vexatious insolence and disorder of the Turkish soldiers.

The internal trade of the Asiatic part of the empire has been diminished by another cause; the caravans of pilgrims or merchants, who assemble annually at the temple of Mecca, and on their return through the provinces of Asia and Syria, dispose of their various commodities and productions, are now less numerous than in former times This is to be attributed partly to a declining zeal for Mahometanism, and partly to the fear of being plundered in those routes, which have lately been frequented by the Wahabee.

The decrease of the commerce* of this part of the empire is

---

* " It is a proof of the great European commerce carried on at Aleppo about the beginning of the 17th century, that the hire only of camels to fetch and carry goods to and from Scanderoon, the port of Aleppo, amounted at least to 8000 sequins a year " See P. Texeira, quoted by Russell, ii. 3.

proved by the decline of the mercantile establishments once maintained in some of the large cities. " It is worthy of remark," says a late traveller, who directed his attention particularly to subjects of a commercial nature, " that at a period not far distant, the Turks had many articles of exportation, of which they have now scarcely a sufficiency to supply their own wants. Silk, for instance, was once exported in considerable quantities; at present, hardly enough is to be found for the manufactures of the country, and that is at six times more than its former price Every article of exportation has fallen off, the few which remain, are raised to such prices as to render exporting them a certain loss. This proceeds in a great measure from the extortion of the Agas, or governors of the provinces, and from the export goods being farmed by the rich destroyers of the state, who of course pay a small price, and prohibit the sale to any one else. Silk is at present farmed by the Reis Effendi, or minister for foreign affairs."

6. In countries, where the springs of industry and exertion are unbroken, the evils occasioned by plague, war, and famine are soon removed, but in Turkey the calamities they inflict are slowly repaired. The neglect of agriculture is one among other causes, which check the population of the country, nor is it difficult to assign the reason of the small esteem in which it is held in many parts. It is not only without any direct encouragement, but it has not that indirect assistance which an extended commerce always affords. The various tribes that wander over the deserted plains of Asia Minor and Syria, sometimes broken into small parties, at other times united in formidable numbers, remove according to the season of the year to districts where more extended pastures, or other advantages tempt them to a temporary settlement. The habits of life of all these hordes are unfavourable to a proper cultivation of the land. In addition to the Kurds and Bedoween Arabs, we may mention the Turkmans, the peculiar descendants of the Nomad Scythians, who are frequently met by travellers in Syria; we have observed their flocks, herds, and reeded tents on the western coast of Asia Minor. The

Rushwans are a tribe of wandering Kurds who inhabit the ancient Cappadocia, and in parts of the year establish themselves in the vicinity of Damascus and Aleppo. The Begdelees, a tribe of Turkmans, are described by Pococke as consisting of bodies of one thousand persons, and raising contributions on different villages. These wandering tribes increase in numbers, in consequence of the unquiet state of the country, and want of protection; peasants, Christians as well as Mahometans, being driven from the cultivation of their lands.

In policy, as in architecture, the ruin is greatest when it begins with the foundation. Under that very imperfect establishment of order and law, which prevails in some part of the European, as well as Asiatic provinces of the empire, the peasants are so depressed and interrupted in the exercise of their occupations, that the country is almost desolate. Five hundred villages are not found in the district of Mesopotamia belonging to Mardin, which once possessed sixteen hundred.[*] Cyprus before the conquest of the Turks contained 14,000 villages; in two insurrections great numbers of the inhabitants were slain, a dreadful mortality was occasioned by the plague in 1624, and in less than fifty years from that time, seven hundred villages only could be found [†] Three hundred were once comprehended in a part of the Pashalik of Aleppo, now containing less than one-third of that number.[‡] Many towns are mentioned in the history of the Caliphs, which no longer exist; the site of others may be traced on the route from Bagdad to Mosul. In consequence of the decrease of agriculture and manufacturing industry, the sums formerly paid to the government by some of its officers of revenue are diminished, 50,000l. was the amount [§] of

---

* Niebuhr, ii 320
† Rycaut State of the Greek church, p 91
‡ Russell, i 339
§ Payments of money in the Turkish empire are made in purses, each purse containing 500 piastres We find the payments made to the exchequer in the Greek empire were called ‘folles.’ Clarke on Coins, 351.

the agreement made by the Mohassil of Aleppo in D'Arvieux time with the Grand Seignior's treasury; the contract in 1769 was fixed at a much lower rate. The reservoirs and canals by which the fertility of Palestine, Syria, and Egypt, and Babylonia, under the time of the Saracens, and Mamaluke Soldans, was augmented and improved, have been neglected. The land throughout the empire is charged with a rent paid either to the Sultan himself, to the governors of provinces, or to those who farm the territorial impost, and other taxes · the amount of that levied on the Mussulman is a seventh or tenth of the produce; the Greeks on the continent and Islanders pay a fifth. But this tribute is not collected by any fixed regulations; and the inequality of exactions, and the want of just and proportioned impositions are the great political impediments to all improvements in Turkey Great *avanías* are levied occasionally on the villages of Asia Minor and Syria, and as the land owners or renters defray that part of the assessment laid on the peasants and labourers, who cannot themselves pay it, from the small portion of the fruits of the earth which they receive, a heavy debt is always due from the latter to the former In some parts, the Agas from improvident and extravagant habits of life have been unable to pay the Miri *, or territorial tax, and have been obliged to quit the lands which they had hired. A long interval of time elapses before they are again occupied, and the peasants are forced to seek in the larger towns the means of support. The great cities are filled in this manner, because they afford a certain supply of provisions, as the governors are unwilling to expose themselves to those tumults which would arise in cases of famine, or dearness of corn. In the meantime large tracts of country are deserted. A melancholy illustration of the depopulated state of them is afforded by the view of those extensive cemeteries so frequently passed by the traveller in his route. Scarcely any vestiges of the villages which

* Russell, i 339. and 342.

once flourished near them are now seen. The incursions of robbers, the calamities of war and pestilence, have compelled the inhabitants to remove to other districts. * The countries between the Tigris and Euphrates, once distinguished for their populousness, are consigned to ruin and neglect; and the inhabitants retire to villages on the banks of the rivers, where they are less harassed by the predatory attacks of the Arabs.

From the present rude and uncultivated condition of some of the provinces, we might be led to suppose that they were either barren, or incapable of affording any great produce. But nothing is wanted, except a greater number of inhabitants to draw forth by their skill and industry the productions of the soil. " If Natolia," says Hasselquist, " was well peopled, active husbandmen would certainly make the hills turn to some account; here might be planted good vineyards of the fine vines that grow around Smyrna; here numbers of sheep might feed on places that agree well with them, where the sheep's fescue grass *(festuca ovina)* grows sufficiently Goats might feed here to a much greater number than are now found, there being plenty of food for them; and if all other places, which here lie uncultivated, were turned into corn land, a careful husbandman might raise the finest crops on these hills." p. 35. From the testimonies of sacred Scripture and the writings of antiquity, we learn that great multitudes were provided with subsistence in places which now support a very small population. Two millions and a half of persons followed the Jewish legislator into Palestine.† The enumeration

---

* " As long as insulation exposes men to personal danger, we can hope for the establishment of no equilibrium between the population of towns and that of the country " Humboldt, ii. 313.

† Michaelis on the Laws of Moses, vol. 1 p. 99. Smith's translation " The men " able to bear arms somewhat exceeded 600,000, and including the Levites amounted to " nearly 620,000 If, according to the usual principle of calculation, we admit the whole " people, women and children included, to have been four times as many, we shall then " have nearly 2,500,000 souls for the amount of the population " Michaelis proceeds to shew, that within the limits of Palestine hereditary possessions and support were found for these very great numbers

of the people of Israel in the time of David, if we take the
lowest calculation, amounts, including women and children, to five
millions; but that census embraces an extensive district. The
remarks of Josephus and Tacitus respecting the fertility of parts of
this country are confirmed by the observations of a native who
examined it in the 13th century *, and by the accounts of more
recent travellers. The wealth and populousness of Syria, as well as
of Asia seem to have been considerable under the Christian emperors
of Constantinople, if we may judge from the number of archbishoprics,
bishoprics, convents, and churches which they contained. The religious faith of the actual possessors of Palestine has caused an alteration
in one branch of rural industry, the prohibition of wine, which has
now prevailed for ten centuries, has been sufficient to make a great
difference between the former and present state of a country admira-
bly adapted by nature to the growth of the grape. If we turn to
Greece, we find only 20,000 persons in Attica †, and the population
of the Peloponnesus does not exceed 350,000. The inhabitants of
Egypt are calculated to amount to two millions and a half, a small
number when we consider the resources of that country. ‡ The former civilization of many of the provinces of the empire is also proved
by the temples, theatres, and public works which strike the attention
of the traveller. A small part only of those numerous edifices can
now be discovered in their remains. Whole towns in Asia and

---

* Abulfeda   " The country about Jerusalem," he says, " is one of the most fruitful
" in Palestine." Strabo (16) informs us, "that it was unfruitful " Yet these two writers
are easily reconciled The latter alludes to the soil not being productive of grain, the
former to its great produce in wine and oil   " An acre planted with vines or olives, however arid or rocky the soil may be, will very easily be made worth ten times as much as
an acre of the richest corn land." Michaelis, iii. 138

† D'après les evaluations les plus justes Beaujour, 1

‡ This is Mr Browne's statement. Volney assigns 2,300,000, and some of the
members of the French Institute give the same number but there is a difference in the
quantity of cultivated land, the latter mention 1800 square leagues, in Volney we find
2100

Greece have been frequently destroyed by earthquakes.* Athens and other cities on the coasts of Natolia and Greece supplied Constantine, and succeeding Emperors, with materials to enrich and adorn the capital.

7. " It is a consequence of the depopulated and neglected state of
" Greece, Asia, and Syria, that there is no considerable district
" which is not exposed in some degree to the effects of a bad and
" corrupted atmosphere. The putrid miasma, arising in the summer
" and autumn from bogs and marshes and irrigated grounds, is
" attended in the north of Europe with simple agues or intermittent
" fevers ; but the Mal-aria is the scourge of the south of Europe,
" there the intermittents are of the worst description, and so violent
" and obstinate, mixed perhaps with typhus fevers, as to be fre-
" quently mortal. The spots in Greece where the mal-aria is most
" noxious are salt-works and rice grounds ; and we meet with a
" striking example of the influence of the former at Milo, where
" since the beginning of the last century, when the island was
" visited by Tournefort, four-fifths of the population have been lost
" in consequence of the establishment of a small salt-work. Patræ,
" a place celebrated in the time of Cicero for the salubrity of the air,
" has become unhealthy, because the plain around it is subject to
" irrigation. In Attica, a country once distinguished for the purity
" of its air † and climate, the effects of the disorder are felt at Ma-
" rathon; and the streams of the Cephissus, which are wholly con-
" sumed in irrigation, diffuse it through the plain of Athens."
(Mr. Hawkins) In the most flourishing periods of ancient Greece, we find the people of particular districts suffering from fevers ‡, and

---

* Quoties Asiæ, quoties Achaiæ urbes uno tremore ceciderunt ! Quot oppida in Macedoniâ devorata sunt ! Sen. Epis xci

† See the passages of Euripides and Aristides quoted by Casaub. in Athen. p 405.

‡ " The people of Onchestus in Bœotia," says Dicæarchus, " though placed on a " high spot were subject to fevers," the miasma arising from the marshy plains on the borders of the Copais may have affected, Mr. Hawkins supposes, the health of the inhabitants. The site of Sparta was insalubrious, partly from the swamps in the vicinity

disorders peculiar to marshy situations, but these were less prevalent, when industry awakened life and fertility throughout the country, than at present, when the inhabitants, living in tenements placed in unhealthy situations, nourished by scanty food, uncertain whether they can appropriate the fruits of their industry, have no motive to improvement. The climate of Egypt is affected at particular seasons by the neglect of the canals, the plain of Scanderoon was in the time of Moryson " infamous for the death of Christians," and still continues to be the most unhealthy spot on the coast of Syria; the inhabitants of Tripoli and Acre are subject to disorders arising from mephitic exhalations. In some parts of Greece the rivers, obstructed in their channels, overflow the banks, and spread into morasses. In the memory of the inhabitants of the present day new marshes have been observed in the vallies of Arcadia.* Leprous affections are becoming more frequent In Asia and Syria, as well as Greece, the inhabitants are obliged to retire at particular seasons, into the mountains to avoid the diseases of the plains, and exchange the fœculent atmosphere occasioned by stagnant moisture and putrefaction, for the dry and elastic air of more elevated regions.

8. The practice of polygamy†, so prevalent among the higher orders in this country, so contrary to the strict injunction of their law,

---

of it, partly from the great heat reflected by the mountains of Taygetus. Δυστραπελιάν τοῦ τόπου τῶν Ταυγέτου ὀρῶν ἀξιολόγον πνίγος παρεχόντων Jamblich Vit Pyth. 37 See also Plutarch *Opp Mor* " on Banishment."

   * " A face furrowed with care, a body lean with hard labour and scanty diet, represent " the portrait of a modern Arcadian The residence of a number of hungry Turks, the " vermin of the Pasha's court, continually oppresses this hapless people, and they seem " to exist only to furnish food to their lazy masters. Among the most powerful engines, " are the Codja Bashees, the treasurers of the district, or rather the collectors of the " taxes, and the bishops, whose places are all bought" From Dr. Sibthorp's MSS.

   † Four is the extreme number of wives allowed by Mahomet " Take in marriage " of such women, as please you, two, or three, or four" Koran, c iv. — For the reasons which induced Moses to tolerate polygamy, as a civil right, though he did not approve it, see Michaelis, i 277 The Jews, in the time of Solomon, did not imitate the example of their Monarch, polygamy was no longer practised.

has contributed to diminish the population of it   In the families
of that class of Turks, who abuse the permission of their legislator,
the children are found fewer than in those of Greeks, Armenians,
and Jews. " None of the women in the great Harems, (says Russell,)
speaking generally, bear so great a number of children as the
married women in the inferior ranks of life," i. 279.   The remark of
Bruce, who says that in the south and Scripture parts of Mesopotamia, Armenia, and Syria he found the proportion to be two
women born to one man, has not been confirmed by succeeding travellers.   It will probably be found by those who in their
future visits to these countries direct their attention to the question
of the numerical proportion of the two sexes, that in the cases
where the women appear to be in greater numbers than the men,
they have been brought away from the neighbouring villages to the
houses of the great and rich in towns and cities. *

The general indifference shewn by the Turks to subjects of political arithmetic, renders it very difficult to obtain satisfactory accounts of the population of the great cities of the empire   There
are only three modes by which any approximation to an accurate
estimate can be obtained.   The first is by ascertaining the weekly
or yearly consumption of corn in a city†; the second is by taking
a plan of different towns‡, and comparing them with the size and
dimensions of other places in Europe; the third is by consulting the
registers of those who pay the capitation tax, but the number of
Greeks, Jews, and Armenians only, could be obtained in this
manner.   Additional information would also be derived from knowing the amount of the duty levied on houses in some of the cities of
the empire, and from the details which the priests of different

* This is the remark of Porter, the British Ambassador at Constantinople   Philos
Trans 49.
† The calculation made by the Maronite priest of the numbers in Aleppo is partly
founded on this method   Russel, i. 362.   D'Arvieux gives the daily consumption of
grain and other articles of provision, i 6.
‡ This is the mode suggested by Niebuhr.

classes of Christians could give. The aggregate of the whole population of the empire in Europe, Asia, and Africa has been estimated at 25,330,000. * But whatever may be the realnumber, it is far below that which could be maintained in these countries, and this is to be attributed to the slow and certain operation of those measures of pernicious policy which have been long established †, and to the abuses of the provincial governments. These would have produced a greater diminution of numbers, and a more general and uniform decline of the power and resources of the empire, if they had not been modified by various circumstances. These we may now proceed to notice.

1. The exuberant fertility of the soil, and plentiful harvests of rice, corn, and maize, maintain in several districts, even under great imperfections of policy and order, a large population. In some provinces also, the territorial impost, capitation tax, and duties or customs upon commodities are farmed by the governor; but whether they are placed in his hands, or in those of any other person, an oppressive mode of levying them would be injurious to those engaged in the contracts. For the Porte is severe in demanding the fulfilment of them ‡, and if by harsh exactions, the villages are abandoned, the cultivation of the land is neglected; if any heavy imposition is laid on the merchants, the commerce of the district is lessened, and the caravans pursue a different route. In some provinces, the farmer general of these three branches of revenue, who is termed Mohassil, is a person of high situation; in the Pashalik

---

* See Humboldt, Pol. Essay on N. Spain. This is little more than half of the population of the Russian empire, which was estimated in 1805 at 40,000,000 The increase of numbers has been very great, for in 1783, the census gave 25,677,000 and in 1763, 14,726,000

† The little security there is (says a very intelligent traveller,) arises from the superior ferocity of a few Pashas, which allows of no robbery save their own The depopulation is gradual, constant, infallible, and indubitably arises from the extreme badness of the government   Browne, 418

‡ Russell mentions more than one instance of persons ruined since the year 1760, by taking the farm of the customs, capitation, and land tax

of Aleppo, he is next in the civil department to the Pasha, and under his protection those engaged in trade are more immediately placed. The Agas, also, who are renters of land, are able sometimes to defend their vassals from injuries which must, in their consequences, be prejudicial to themselves.

2. Some cities in the empire derive from their situation great facilities and advantages for carrying on an active trade. The position of Bagdad and Basra relatively to Persia and India, makes them the centre of considerable commerce. " Cairo is the metropolis " of the trade of eastern Africa."* Large caravans are constantly employed in importing various commodities from the East, to supply the wants and tastes of individuals of a high rank in Turkey; and a considerable portion of the money brought† into the Ottoman dominions from Europe in exchange for the cotton, drugs, wool and silk, and other articles, is employed by them in the purchase of the muslins, and costly and ornamental productions of India and Persia. In each of the three divisions of Asia Minor, Karaman, Roum, and Anadoli ‡, and in Syria, there are many populous cities; the various commodities which are imported from Europe are conveyed from these places to other towns of inferior note. Exclusive of the commercial relations maintained with Europe §, the different parts of

---

* Browne.

† Of the sum of 1,000,000 piastres, or 810,000l which, it has been supposed, passes annually from Europe into Asia by the Levant trade, a great part is paid to the Turks. The exportation of silver from the Austrian monarchy alone, into Turkey and the Levant, is estimated at nearly 300,000l. Humboldt, iii 412 Polit Essay.

‡ D'Anville, l'Empire Turc p 15

§ The general articles imported from Turkey into Great Britain, are, cotton-wool, carpets, madder, yellow-berries, goat's-wool, sheep's-wool, mohair-yarn, sponges, silk, cotton-yarn, safflower, gum arabic, assafœtida, opium, tragacanth, galls, whetstones, raisins, figs, valanea, emery-stones, box-wood, liquorice-root, goat-skins, sheep-skins undrest, unwrought copper

Those exported to Turkey are, muslins, calicoes, cloths, stuffs, and earthen-ware, clocks and watches, indigo, guns and pistols, hard-ware and cutlery, iron plates, sugar, tin in barrels, lead shot, red and white lead, wrought and cast iron, Brazil wood, tin-plates, lead in pigs, pepper, pimento, tar, rice, coffee

Oddy's Europ Commerce, 187

D

the Turkish empire are constantly engaged in interchanging various articles. The rice and flax of Egypt are exported to Syria, whence cotton and silk * are remitted in return. Both these provinces receive annually from 10 to 15,000 quintals of iron from Smyrna. Coffee and Indian goods are sent to Constantinople, and from this city brass and copper manufactures are carried to Egypt. The influence of a great commercial town in humanizing and improving the manners of a people is no where so evident in Turkey as on the western coast of Asia. A sense of the advantages derived from a safe and regular communication with Smyrna stimulates the governors of the different towns to a discharge of their duty. The roads are rarely infested by robbers, and travellers have little reason to complain of the manners and general conduct of the inhabitants.

3. The trade of Salonica, the second city of mercantile importance in the empire, excites a spirit of industry in the provinces of the antient Thessaly and Macedonia. The Turks at Constantinople, like the Romans under their Emperors, are so accustomed to a low and fixed price of corn †, that nothing excites murmurs and complaints in the city sooner than any rise or alteration of it. It is the business of some commissaries sent every year into parts of Greece, as well as to other provinces of the empire, to purchase wheat for supplying the granaries of Constantinople. After this, the orders of the government prohibiting the exportation of corn are without difficulty evaded; and large cargoes are sent out from different ports of Greece. This exportation ‡ encourages the Beys

---

* " This article is brought from Antioch, more silk is produced in the neighbourhood of that city, within the circuit of 30 miles than in the rest of Syria. It is sent to Aleppo, and thence exported." Parsons' Travels, 77.

† The neglect of agriculture in the vicinity of Constantinople towards the north, arises from the same cause that formerly discouraged tillage near Rome it is owing to the quantity of corn sent from the provinces. The inhabitants of Rome were supplied with corn at sixpence a peck. Adam Smith, W. of N. 1. 233.

‡ The evils which arose in consequence of a strict prohibition of the exportation of corn from parts of the Turkish empire are stated by the author of the " Essay on the " corn trade," 1766 " The Grand Vizir between 20 and 30 years ago suffered a

of Larissa and Salonica to bestow great attention on the cultivation of their lands; and in no province of the empire are the numbers of inhabitants so great as in these districts of Greece. The best peopled part of Macedonia gives 500 inhabitants to the square league. (Beaujour, vol. i.)

4. Turks, Jews, Greeks, and Armenians are associated in many cities or corporations for the purpose of watching over their separate interests, and in this manner they are frequently able to check the Pasha in the dishonest exercise of his power. By their united exertions they have been able to obtain from the government his removal. The hand of violence is always suspended over the rich in this country, as nothing is to be gained from the inferior classes of subjects; pretences therefore for seizing the wealth of the great are readily admitted; and the governor is removed or obliged to part with some of his ill-gotten treasures.

5. Throughout the empire, those who dwell in mountainous districts enjoy a security and independence which are denied to the inhabitants of the plains. This is not only true with respect to the various tribes professing the Mahometan faith, and the numerous hordes of Yesidians, who remain yet unsubdued by the Turks, but

---

quantity of corn to be exported; 300 French vessels from 20 to 200 tons were on one day seen to enter Smyrna bay, to load corn: and wheat was then sold for less than seventeen-pence English a bushel, with all the expenses of putting the same on board included. The Janissaries and people took the alarm, pretended that all the corn was going to be exported, and that they would be starved, and in Constantinople grew so mutinous, that at last the Vizir was strangled. His successor carefully avoided following his example, and suffered no exportation. Many of the farmers who looked on the exportation as their greatest demand, neglected tillage to save their rents, which in that country are paid either in kind or in proportion to their crops, to such a degree, that in less than three years, the same quantity of corn which in the time of exportation sold for not quite seventeen-pence, was worth more than six shillings, and the distress was great; and guards were placed over the bakehouses and magazines of corn. An English ship in the Turkey trade was detained from sailing some time for want of bread. The ill consequences of these proceedings were not removed for many years, and the fall of the first Vizir was regretted too late."

many Christian communities, the Nestorians and Jacobites in Mesopotamia, the Maronites of Libanus, the Sphachiots of Crete, the Mainotes of Peloponnesus protected by the fastnesses and narrow defiles of their retreats, escape the depredations and destruction which are often inflicted on the more exposed parts of the country.

6. There are many districts in Asiatic and European Turkey which are appanages of the great officers of the Porte, or part of the Imperial family. These as well as the Timars or fiefs held under the Sultans are not taxed so severely as other parts of the provinces. On the conquest of the country by the Turks, lands were appropriated to the maintenance of the church, and the ecclesiastical property of the nation since that time has been much increased. Many parts of the crown demesnes have been bestowed in this manner by different Sultans, and have become *Wakouf.* They were formerly rented by governors and nobles who were annual tenants, but in consequence of the great abuses which they committed, during their possession, an alteration took place in the mode of letting them, and they have been granted since the year 1759 on leases for lives. (D'Ohsson.) *

7. In the islands of the Archipelago, which are only visited by the Turks when the capitation money is collected, industry is not so much interrupted as in those where Turkish governors reside, and by arbitrary and injudicious regulations interfere with the employment of the inhabitants. Cyprus and Candia are ruled by Pashas; and the former is, perhaps, the most depopulated part of the empire. But in many of the islands, and indeed wherever the rigour of the Turkish government is relaxed, we find the Christian inhabitants active and laborious. The merchants of Thessaly, Macedonia, and Epirus, the islanders of Scio, the sailors of Hydra and Spezzia, the Armenians of Constantinople and Smyrna may be particularly dis-

---

* If, however, the church lands in Asia Minor are let in the exorbitant manner which regulates the leases in Egypt, the tenant of the mosque is not in a much better situation than the tenant of the government. Browne, 61.

tinguished. The religious establishments of the Christian subjects have had a very favourable influence on the agriculture of parts of the country. The cultivated state of the monastic lands of Athos, and other mountainous districts in Greece shews that the Greek priests when unmolested by the presence or interference of the Turks do not suffer themselves to be exceeded in industry by any class of their countrymen. *

8. Lastly, when a Pasha has been able to establish himself in a province for many years, to consolidate his power, and appropriate part of the neighbouring country to his family, the condition of the people is improved. He finds his own interests connected with those of his subjects; and the latter are freed from the vexatious and capricious exercise of tyranny, to which those are exposed who live under the dominion of governors desirous of amassing great wealth before they are removed to other parts of the empire, and therefore little scrupulous of sacrificing the welfare of their provinces to their immediate wants. The mountains of Albania†, and some districts of Greece afford a retreat to many bands of robbers, who still keep the country in a state of disquiet and alarm but the effects of the regulations made by Ali Pasha, during his long sovereignty, for the protection and tranquillity of it, are visible in the improved industry and wealth of many of the Greeks. On the coast of Lesser Asia, in the antient Mysia, the long established government of Kara Osman Oglu is distinguished for its mildness and moderation, and for the security of property enjoyed by those who live under it.

---

* Travellers have remarked the fruitful and well-peopled condition of the lands in the neighbourhood of the convents of the Nestorians and Jacobites in Mesopotamia, 260 Kinneir "The 200 convents," says Volney, "among the Maronites, so far from hurt-"ing population have contributed to promote it by increasing the produce of the soil"

† See Mr Hobhouse's account of Albania, and Dr. Holland's Travels, and Colonel Leake's Researches. The Albanians speak a language derived from the antient Thracian, which appears to have been the same as the Illyrian. "Utinam nobis Albaniæ linguæ "ex vetere Thracica descendentis grammaticam quispiam impertiret, videtur et Illyrica "vetus eadem ac Thracica fuisse." De Origine Linguæ, Caroli Michaeler, 178.

Such are the circumstances which affect in a great degree the prosperity and condition of the inhabitants of this empire ; and we learn from them in what manner the abuses of power are modified or corrected.   The real cause of the unequal progress of industry is to be ascribed to the fluctuating system of policy which prevents any regular, consistent, and steady attention to measures favourable to general improvement.   There can be no ground for expecting any change, while the administration of the provinces is conducted on the same principles.*   The extent of this ill-modelled and ill-balanced empire prevents any accurate inspection of the conduct of those who are placed over remote parts of it.   A large portion of the revenue of the Porte, and the great officers of it is derived from money paid by Pashas on taking possession of their government, or from occasional remittances make for the purpose of securing a continuance in their appointment.†   This money is drawn from the labour, industry, and commerce of the inhabitants of the province. If these sums are not paid, as well as those expected from the farmers of the customs, land, and capitation tax, the latter are thrown into prison, and the governors lose their Pashaliks.   If they are removed in a short time, the provinces are exposed to fresh exactions on the arrival of every succeeding Pasha.   Some districts however, have extorted from the weakness of the Porte the permission of naming their own rulers.   The Pashalik of Bagdad, since the time of Achmed, has been independent of the Sultan.‡   When the jealousy of the government is roused by any suspicion of dubious allegiance in a Pasha, or by any attempt to aspire at greater influence, different methods are adopted to check and counteract his rising power.   The

---

* " The succession of a new governor may defeat all the plans of improvement suggested or carried into effect by a former one   Sheik Daher, the predecessor of Djezzar, had raised Acre from a village to a large town, and increased the population of the district. In the time of Djezzar, the large plain near Acre was left almost a marsh."   Browne, 368.

† The Mohassil of Aleppo, in Volney's time, made his contract with the Porte for 40,000l, and paid about 4000l to the officers of the government

‡ Kinneir, 307

troops of some neighbouring province are compelled to march against him; the Pasha of Kurdistan was instigated by the Porte in 1810 to take arms against the Pasha of Bagdad; and the latter was defeated and put to death. Sometimes the government proceeds in a more summary manner, the lives of these refractory Satraps are taken from them by officers sent expressly from Constantinople.* In no part of the empire has the authority of the Porte been more disputed than in Egypt; and while the Mamelukes remained unsubdued, the Pasha of Cairo was able to exercise a very limited power in the country. Since the year 1791 a small part only of the revenue due to the Sultan had been remitted.† A proposal had been once made at Constantinople to massacre some of the most distinguished leaders among the Mamelukes, and thus put an end to all fear of future disobedience. The plan was at that time rejected; but in the year 1811 the measure was carried into execution, attended with circumstances of perfidy and cruelty not to be paralleled in the most barbarous and ferocious part of the Turkish annals. Bad as the government of the Mamelukes might be, the inhabitants of Egypt will find that they have derived no benefit from the exchange of‡ rulers. Whatever was taken by the former from this exhausted province was at least expended in it; more injury will be done by a succession of rapacious governors sent by the Porte, than if the same swarm of

---

* The officers of the Porte are not always able to execute their commission. The Grand Signior sent down more than one to take the life of Achmed, Pasha of Bagdad, but Achmed had his agents at Constantinople, who gave him timely intelligence. Nub 2 Mustapha, the father of Selim. wished to take away the life of a Pasha of Bagdad, and sent a Capigee or officer for that purpose. The Pasha cut off the Capigee's head, and sent it back to the Sultan. De Tott. 1. Some of the Capigees who were sent to take Djezzar's life, died suddenly of the cholic. Volney, 2.

† See Hamilton's Ægyptiaca, p 425.

‡ See the remarks of Raige, Reynier, and Girard, on the nature of the different tenures by which property is held in Egypt, and on the impediments which exist to a further improvement of the agriculture of the country. Mémoire de S. de Sacy. Mem de l'Instit 1815. t. 1 Classe D'Histoire.

bloodsuckers had continued. Ἐὰν δὲ τούτους νυνοραιστὰς ἀφέλη ἕτεροι ἐλθόντες πεινῶντες ἐκπιοῦνται μου τὸ λοιπὸν αἶμα. Arist. Rhet. lib. 11.

The causes of that great change in the situation of some of the states of Europe, during the three last centuries, are to be found in the commercial spirit by which they have been actuated, and the propagation of knowledge by means of the press. The intercourse with the Christian states must be very much enlarged before the condition of the Asiatic part of the empire can be affected by the former, and any alteration introduced by means of the latter will proceed by slow degrees. The little proficiency made by the Turks in subjects of a mathematical, geographical, and political nature, arises from the want of encouragement on the part of the government. Law and theology ᶜ alone occupy the attention of the students in the colleges or Médressés. Acquisitions of knowledge are not discouraged by the Koran. "The ink of the learned," said Mahomet, "and the blood "of martyrs are of equal value in the sight of Heaven." But the general improvement of the empire has been retarded by the custom of confining within the walls of the Seraglio the hereditary Princes of the Turkish throne, and thus secluding them from the world, and shutting out the means of acquiring knowledge. Literature seems to have met with more encouragement and protection from the Sultans of former ages "Be the support of the Faith, and protector of "the Sciences†," were among the last words of Osman the First, to his successor Orkhan. In the sermon entitled Koutbe, a divine benediction is implored on the orthodox Caliphs who were endowed with learning, virtue, and sanctity. There are thirty-five public libraries

---

* "Theology and jurisprudence, comprehending scholastic divinity and the voluminous " commentaries on the Koran and the Sonna, constitute the principal object of Moham- " medan study." Russell's Aleppo, ii

† " It is a ridiculous notion which prevails among us," says Sir W Jones, "that igno- " rance is a principle of the Mohammedan religion, and that the Koran instructs the " Turks not to be instructed." Discourse on History of the Turks, p 501. " Mahom- " med not only permitted but advised his people to apply themselves to learning." Id. See Lord Teignmouth's Life of Sir W. Jones, p. 501

in Constantinople, none of them containing less than 1000 manuscripts[*]; in many are found more than 5000. The collection in the two libraries of the Seraglio exceeds 15,000 volumes. At the time when the Greeks were driven by their conquerors from Constantinople, the latter might certainly be ranked among barbarous and uninformed nations; but the Greeks of the nineteenth century are not warranted in applying the contemptuous expressions of their ancestors to the Turks of later times, who have cultivated some parts of literature, particularly those relating to their own history, with great success, and have probably more real merit than many of the Byzantine writers. The use of the press was first introduced in Constantinople in the reign of Achmet the Third (in 1727), but in the interval of time which has since elapsed, the copies of few works of distinction and name have been multiplied by it. This is owing, according to the opinion of Sir William Jones [†], to the difficulty of understanding the classical writings of the Turks, without more than a moderate knowledge of Persian and Arabic. Manuscript volumes are also preferred to printed works. The French were accustomed to send to them books published in oriental types, but only a small number was purchased. Characters formed in writing are considered as more pleasing to the eye [‡], and as capable of being connected and combined in a more beautiful manner, than in printing. There are, it may be added, many hundred scribes and copyists [§], who would lose all means of support, if books could be circulated at a cheap rate by the press. In order that knowledge should be diffused through the

---

* D'Ohsson Tableau General

† Teignmouth's Life of Sir W. Jones, p. 501

‡ " Il est constant," (says Galland, in his Discourse prefixed to the Bib. Orient. of D'Herbelot,) " que ces nations ne trouvent point d'agrément dans l'impression   Les " Mahometans ne voulurent pas recevoir les exemplaires qu'on leur porta.   En effet, ils " craignoient que dans la suite, on ne leur introduisit l'alcoran imprimé, ce qui auroit été " regardé chez eux comme la plus grande profanation que pouvoit arriver à ce livre "

§ Niebuhr, i 188   " Une infinie des personnes qui subsistent parmi eux en copiant " des livres, auroient été reduits à la mendicité par cette nouveauté "   Galland

E

empire, it is not only necessary that the Sultans themselves should be favorably disposed to it, but the Oulemáh, the body of lawyers and ecclesiastics, should also lend their assistance. In the mean time, whatever may be the real obstacles, it is probable that the general ignorance, and want of curiosity in the people contribute, in some degree, to the support of the religious, as well as civil constitution of the country. " For let us suppose that learning* prevailed there, as " in these western nations, and that the Koran was as common to " them as the Bible to us, that they might have free recourse to " search and examine the flaws and follies of it, and withal, that " they were of as inquisitive a temper as we, who knows, but as there " are vicissitudes in the government, so there may happen also the " same in the temper of a nation. If this should come to pass, " where would be their religion? Let every one judge whether the " *Arcana Imperii et Religionis* would not fall together." South's Sermons, i. 144.

The different symptoms of the decline of the empire could not have escaped the attention of the Sultans who have filled the Ottoman throne during the last century. Yet none of them, if we except Mustapha the Third, and the late Emperor Selim, made any endeavours to strengthen the foundation of their power, or were excited by the dangers of their situation to correct the vices and abuses of the government. Something would have been done towards repairing the breaches occasioned by the neglect and indolence of his predecessors, if Selim had lived to see his plans digested into order ; but the exertions of this monarch were vain and unavailing. In the revolu-

---

* If little regard is paid to the literature of their own country by the orientals, it is not probable that the works of European writers will much excite their attention   Nor will this be a matter of regret, if such works only are circulated among them, as those which have been translated from the French into Arabic, by Basil and Elias Fakher, two persons employed in the French consulates in Egypt   " Il est fâcheux que leur choix ne soit pas ' toujours tombé sur des ouvrages dignes d'être propagés par la voie de traductions   Le " Contrat Social de Rousseau, et quelques pamphlets de Voltaire contre la religion, sont-ils " donc les premiers besoins des orientaux ?" Mag Encyclop Janv 1811

tion which preceded his death, the Janissaries destroyed the mathematical school instituted by him. The prejudices and ignorance of these troops lead them to resist all plans of improvement; the endeavours of Bonneval and De Tott to introduce European discipline in the Turkish armies were opposed by them; and they have viewed with jealousy alterations suggested even by their own countrymen. Experience has confirmed the truth of this observation made by Harrington, " that the wound in the monarchy, incured and incurable, " is the power which the Janissaries * have of exciting sedition." It is a power the more dangerous, as it is without controul; and while they continue to exist, the state contains in itself a source of weakness and decay.

The only method by which the Sultan of this empire could reestablish his authority in the capital and the provinces, check the incursions of those numerous hordes and tribes which infest them, and inspire the rebellious governors with respect, would be by the formation of an army †, modelled on the European system, and kept in constant pay. " There should always," says Montesquieu, " be a " trusty body of troops around the despotic Prince, ready to fall in- " stantly upon any part of the empire that might chance to waver." But the number of the Janissaries in the capital, and of those who in the different cities of the empire are enrolled in that militia is so great, that, as they might reasonably dread a diminution of their influence, they would continue to oppose such an establishment. The governors who are aiming at independence, unwilling to see themselves stripped

---

* Murad the Third, dared not go out of the Seraglio for two years, on account of the constant sedition of the soldiers D'Ohsson " Il n'y a point de nation au monde, qui " parle plus avantageusement de ses monarques, et de l'obéissance qui leur est due, " que les Turcs, et néanmoins, si nous consultons l'histoire, nous trouverons qu'il n'y a " point de monarques, dont l'autorité soit plus fragile, que celle des Empereurs Ottomans." Bayle. Dict Art Osman Note B

† " Whoever examines with attention the improvements which Peter the Great introduced into the Russian empire, will find, that they almost all resolve themselves into the establishment of a well-regulated standing army " Adam Smith's W of N vol III. p. 68

of the power which they have acquired by profiting of the weakness
of the monarchy, would also resist it.   New taxes must be imposed
for the purpose of maintaining the new troops, and a spirit of discon-
tent would be thus excited.   Lastly, the Oulemâh, whose property
has been hitherto deemed inalienable and sacred, apprehensive that
the Sultan might demand a portion of it, on occasions of great emer-
gency, would add the weight of their authority, and interpose and
obstruct the execution of such a scheme.

The causes, then, to which the feebleness and decay of this
empire may be attributed, are the existence of a military government in the capital, the want of salutary regulations in the administration of its revenues [*] ; the interruption of the peaceful habits
of industry by the numerous tribes and hordes of robbers; the
difficulty of attending to all parts of this over-grown monarchy; the
national and religious prejudices which continue to operate on the
great body of the people, the weakness displayed by the Porte
towards the different Pashas, who defy its power, the indolence,
ease, effeminacy, which, according to the Turks themselves have
been exchanged by their countrymen for the hardier and more manly
qualities of their ancestors, and lastly, the indifference to science and
art, and the little intercourse maintained by them with the civilized
states of Europe.

While the habits, manners, and situation of the Asiatic provinces
continue the same, a great alteration has taken place in the condition

---

[*] Mr Rich, in his Memoir on the Ruins of Babylon, has given a curious document
respecting the annual receipts of the governor of Hellah, p 12.   After stating the sums,
he adds, "he must fee the most powerful members of the Porte from time to time, and
yet be able to lay by a sufficiency not only for his own reimbursement, but also to pay the
mulct that is invariably levied on governors when they are removed, however well they
may have discharged their duty   And, when it is considered that his continuance in
office seldom exceeds two or three years, it may well be imagined that he has recourse to
secret methods of accumulating wealth, and that the inhabitants of his district are propor-
tionally oppressed   The regulation of this petty government is a just epitome of the
general system which has converted some of the finest countries of the world into savage
wastes and uninhabitable deserts."

of part of the subjects of the European division of the empire The improved state, and increased intelligence of the Greeks of the present day may be ascribed to their commerce and communication with the various countries of Europe. The extension of trade has been the instrument of much benefit to the nation, it furnishes employment to many thousand sailors, distinguished for activity and industry. The Turkish governors are induced from motives of interest to protect the Greek merchants; and these, again, by their wealth are enabled to defray more easily the demands made upon them. The weight of that yoke "which neither they nor their fathers have been " able to bear," is in some degree lightened; and they have the power of promoting a great and valuable object, the institution of schools for the instruction of their countrymen

We are reminded in some measure of the better days of Greece. when we contemplate the physical character of the modern inhabitants of that country. *This*, at least, has not been altered by the political degradation to which they have long been exposed. If the white complexion and long flaxen hair of the Vandals may be still discovered in the heart of the Moorish tribes, (Shaw); if the inhabitants of Normandy still resemble the Danes, whose ancestors, ten centuries ago, were fixed in that part of France, (Volney); if the Copts, though they have been mixed with other nations, still retain* the Egyptian conformation of face, we may reasonably suppose that the features and physiognomy of the modern Greeks bear a resemblance to those of the ancient inhabitants of the country. The steps which have been taken to diffuse education and literature among them must be attended with great benefits, but, after all, it is not mere instruction that can do much; the advantages to be derived from it must at present be confined within narrow limits. The character of man is formed by civil institutions, and any great national improvement is incompatible with the actual situation of the Greeks. Their political condition forbids the full exercise of those

* Browne, p. 72

moral and social relations comprehended in the term, country. They may be considered as presenting themselves to our notice under two general classes; the one, engaged in trade; the other, including many of the lower order of ecclesiastics, employed in the labours of agriculture. The path of commerce is distinctly pointed out to them by their situation under the Turkish empire, it is their necessary employment, for the same reason that it became the occupation of the Christians in the persecuting time of Diocletian, and is now that of the Jews in every quarter of the globe. The Greeks can receive in their present state no encouragement to direct their attention to objects of liberal pursuit; the finer arts, the arts of sculpture, architecture, eloquence, poetry, only flourish where a greater degree of liberty is enjoyed, than they can obtain. There is no walk of honourable ambition open to them. The very offices of trust and power which they hold enable the Turks to wrest by their means more easily from their oppressed subjects the fruits of their industry. The Greek clergy may be better instructed, and become better qualified to discharge the duties of their stations; but the cupidity and rapacity of the Porte[*] must be satisfied. The Turks will continue to expose the high offices of the Greek church to sale; and simony, and the arts of low intrigue, will be the means of procuring those of an inferior degree. Even if we should suppose that literature might be generally diffused among the Greeks, we need not necessarily conclude that they will attract the attention of the enlightened part of Europe by their exertions in any branch of it. In the reigns of Vespasian and Nero, learning was common in the Roman empire but we meet with no advancement or perfection of knowledge in those ages. In

---

[*] " The sport which they make of the miserable dignities of the Greek church, the little factions of the Harem to which they make them subservient, the continual sale to which they expose and re-expose the same dignity, and by which they squeeze all the inferior orders of the clergy, are nearly equal to all the other oppressions together, exercised by Musulmen over the unhappy members of the oriental church." Burke on the Penal Laws against the Irish Catholics, p 537.

accounting for the literary degeneracy of the modern Greeks, it is not sufficient to state, that the form of government under which they live is arbitrary and despotic, there is another cause to which great influence is to be ascribed; the Greeks can never be blended with the Turks. When the Tartar nations invaded the empire of China, they adopted the habits and manners of their subjects, when the Goths took possession of the provinces they had subdued, they became associated with the inhabitants by customs, marriages, and laws; but since the subjugation of Greece by the Turks, a broad line of separation has been drawn between the conquered and the conquerors, by the difference of religion and language; and the reciprocated feelings of aversion and dislike have been increased by the influence of the former. No country in a condition similar to that of modern Greece has ever exerted itself in letters or the fine arts. The Hindoos since the era of the Mahometan conquest have been inferior in philosophy to their ancestors. No literary production of note appeared in Spain while it was under the dominion of the Moors. In England no Anglo-Saxon composition was produced in the course of a century after the Norman conquest; but under Henry the Second the Normans and English were blended, and about this time, some poetry was composed in the English, or at least the Anglo-Norman dialect. The most eminent works of modern Italy, France, and Germany were produced by writers living under various forms of government; none, however, of these individuals were placed with respect to the rest of the community in that distinct and separate situation which the Greeks now hold under the dominion of the Turks.

NOTE, respecting the Massacre of the Mamelukes (mentioned in page 23) by the Turks, in the year 1811   Extracted from a Letter written by a Gentleman in Cairo to the Hon Frederic North, on the very day on which the event happened.

" Nothing can be imagined more dreadful than the scene of the murder.   The Mamelukes had left the Divan, and were arrived at one of the narrow passages in their way to the gate of the citadel, when a fire from 2000 Albanians was poured in upon them, from the tops of the walls and in all directions   Unprepared for any thing of the sort, and embarrassed by the want of room, they were capable of scarcely any resistance, a few almost harmless blows were all they attempted, and those who were not killed by the fire, were dragged from their horses, stripped naked, with a handkerchief bound round their heads, and another round their waists, they were led before the Pasha and his sons, and by them ordered to immediate execution   Even there the suffering was aggravated, and instead of being instantly beheaded, many were not at first wounded mortally, they were shot in different parts of their bodies, with pistols, or stuck with daggers, many struggled to break loose from those who held them, some succeeded, and were killed in corners of the citadel, or on the top of the Pasha's harem   Others, quite boys of twelve or fourteen years, cried eagerly for mercy, protesting with very obvious truth that they were innocent of any conspiracy, and offering themselves as slaves to the Pasha   all these, and in short every one, however young, and incapable of guilt, or however old, and tried in his fidelity, the most elevated and the most obscure, were hurried before the Pasha, who sternly refused them mercy, one by one, impatient until he was assured the destruction was complete.   Here, then, is an end of the Mamelukes   and this is the Pasha who piques himself on his clemency.   I know nothing in the whole of this miserable scene more distressing than the situation of the wives of the Beys, for to distinguish in every particular this tumult from all others, even the harems have not been respected, and these unfortunate women, driven from their apartments which they thought a kind of sanctuary, and stripped of nearly all their clothes, deprived of every refuge, are still wandering, without a protector, without a home, and even without bread.

" They say, six or seven hundred are already killed, and a proclamation has been cried through the town, enjoining every one to deliver up any Mameluke, who may be concealed in his house, under pain of death, and the confiscation of his property."

TRAVELS

IN

TURKEY.

ACCOUNT OF A JOURNEY

THROUGH

THE DISTRICT OF MAINA, IN THE MOREA.

THAT part of the ancient Laconia, now called Maina, though often incidentally mentioned by earlier travellers, had been scarcely, if ever, visited by any of them, when the course of my tour led me thither in the spring of 1795. The independence which the Mainiots had long maintained against the Pashas of the Morea, and the agents of the Porte, the jealousy with which they guarded their frontier from the intrusion of every stranger, who travelled under Turkish protection, the nature of that frontier, and their predatory incursions into the territory of their enemies the Turks, had not only opposed real difficulties to the intercourse of a traveller with the country, but had invested their character with so much terror, that it was almost impossible to ascertain from the report of their neighbours whether they could be visited with safety under any circumstances of precaution. Certainly they were described to us as robbers, whom no

F

consideration of hospitality could bind from the exercise of their profession, and the stranger who ventured within their frontier was
taught to expect the loss of liberty, or even of his life, unless he re-
deemed them by a heavy ransom.   Such were the representations of
the Turkish governors in the Morea, which were echoed by the Greek
merchants of Livadea and Napoli.   It was easy to perceive much
exaggeration in these accounts ; for sometimes we had met with small
vessels commanded or manned by natives of Maina, who carried on
a coasting trade with other parts of the Levant, though not without
the imputation of occasional piracy ; and we learnt from them that
it was their policy to keep up as much as possible the alarming reputation which the fears and hatred of the Turks had conferred upon
them   We determined on approaching the south of the Morea to
use every means of procuring accurate information of the state of this
almost unvisited district, and the result was that we not only passed
its boundaries, but received great gratification in witnessing from the
hospitality of its inhabitants a state of society very remote from that
which falls under the observation of a traveller in other parts of the
Levant.   It should be remembered that I am describing Maina, as
it existed in 1795, when many of its inhabitants had never seen a
foreigner, and while they strictly adhered to their institutions and
customs, on which they had founded their freedom and independence.

The Maina, as is well known to every traveller in Greece, included
at the time I was there that part of Laconia between the gulphs of
Messene and Gythium, bounded on the north by the highest ridge of
Taygetus, from whence a chain of rugged mountains descends to
Cape Matapan, the southern termination of the country.   We entered
it from the Messenian side, after visiting Calamata, a small but populous town, inhabited principally by Greeks who were subject to the
Pasha of the Morea   It was at this place that we procured the necessary intelligence respecting our further progress, and as there are
some objects of classical interest in the vicinity of this little town,
which have hitherto been imperfectly described, and the geography

of the ancients respecting this part of the Messenian territory admits of further elucidation, I shall begin the extracts from my journal from our arrival at Calamata on the 7th of April.

This town is situated not far from the sea on the eastern side of the beautiful and extensive plain of Messenia. This plain is watered by the Pamisus*, and extends along the shore for about fifteen miles from Ithome and the mountains that separate Messenia from Triphylia to Taygetus. Cotylus and Lycæus are the boundaries to the north-east and north, whence the Pamisus rolls its waters to the sea. Its sources are mentioned by Pausanias in the way which led from Thuria into Arcadia. Notwithstanding the slowness of its course it is the largest river in the Peloponnesus, and divides itself into three or four considerable streams, encircling small islands in its progress between the foot of Mount Ithome † and the sea. The whole plain is naturally fertile, and the eastern part of it near Calamata is a scene of rich and beautiful cultivation. The fields are divided by high fences of the Cactus or prickly pear, and large orchards of the white mulberry tree, the food of silk-worms (of which the inhabitants of this part of the plain rear great numbers), are interspersed with fields of maize, olive grounds, and gardens almost worthy of Alcinous himself. Among these the small town of Calamata stands, consisting of perhaps three hundred houses scattered amidst the gardens and along the banks of the rivulet that now bears its name. This rivulet descends from Taygetus, and was anciently the Nedon described in Strabo, lib. viii. p 360., as falling into the sea near Pheiæ, or Pharæ. It has every character of a mountain torrent, an inconsiderable stream in summer, and even when we were there (in spring) it was almost lost in a bed of large stones and gravel of about one hundred yards in

* Now called Pirnatza. Mr. M. confirms the words of Strabo, who says " it is the largest river (meaning the broadest, for in length the Eurotas and Alpheus exceed it) within the isthmus" Lib viii

† Now called Mount Vulkano , the ruins of Messene are near a spot named Mavromathia. See the French edition of Strabo, and Gell's Itinerary of the Morea.

width, brought down by its violence in the winter months. It falls into
the sea at the distance of about a mile from Calamata, and the same
devastation marks its course through the plain Its banks are covered
with brushwood, and its progress is interrupted by little islands of
copse   Amongst these fringes of its banks, we sought in vain for the
ruins of the town of Pheræ, which, according to Pausanias, stood at
six stadia from the sea, in the way from Abia to Thuria, consequently
at no great distance, and probably on the very situation of the modern
town of Calamata.   This last derives its name from Calamæ, a village
mentioned by Pausanias, lib. iv.; which still exists and retains its
ancient name, and is situated at the distance of about two miles from
Calamata, and more inland.   The cultivation of the plains, and the
modern buildings there, during the period when the Venetians possessed this fertile country, have tended to obliterate the inconsiderable
remains of antiquity which might be expected to have come down to
us from the age of Strabo and Pausanias.

   The modern town is built on a plan not unusual in this part of the
Morea, and well adapted for the defence of the inhabitants against
the attacks of the pirates that infest the coast.   Each house is a separate edifice, and many of them are high square towers of brown stone,
built while the Venetians had possession of the country.   The lower
story of their habitations serves chiefly for offices or warehouses of
merchandize, and the walls on every side are pierced with loop-holes
for the use of musketry, while the doors are strongly barricadoed.   A
small Greek church stands near the Nedon in front of Calamata, and
behind the town a ruined Venetian fortress rises on a hill over the
gardens and dwellings of the inhabitants.   The Greeks who lived
there were rich and at their ease; the fields in the vicinity of the
town belonged to them, and they had also a considerable trade, the
chief articles of which arose from their cultivation of silk and oil.
They were governed by men of their own nation and appointment,
subject only to the approval of the Pasha of the Morea, who resided
at Tripolizza, and to the payment of a tribute which was collected
among themselves, and transmitted by a Turkish Vaivode, who, with

a small party of Janissaries was stationed here for that purpose, and for the defence of the town against the Mainiots.

While preparations were making for our journey into Maina, we proceeded to examine the different objects of antiquity in the vicinity of Calamata. We mounted our horses, and proceeded northward along the plain to Palæo-castro, where from the name of the place we expected the ruins of an ancient city, and from the distance and direction those of Thuria. " Phaiæ is at the distance of six " stadia from the sea. From hence the city of Thuria is at the dis- " tance of eighty stadia, to a traveller who is proceeding to the inland " part of Messenia. It is supposed to be the same city which in " Homer's poem is called Anthea. The inhabitants of Thuria leav- " ing their city, which had originally been built upon an eminence, " descended into the plain and dwelt there. They did not however " entirely abandon the upper city, but the ruins of the walls remain " there, and a temple of the Syrian goddess The river Aris flows " near the city of the plain." * Strabo says that the ancient name of Thuria was Aipeia, a name derived from its lofty situation, though he also mentions the fact that some topographers placed Anthea here, and Aipeia at Methone

Leaving Calamata we passed the village of Kutchukmaina, and skirting the mountain of Taygetus which rose on our right hand, we came in about an hour to the ruin of ancient baths, of which the buildings that remain are very considerable. The construction is of brick, and the principal entrance to the south. This leads into a large vaulted hall with groined semi-circular arches, on each side of the entrance are rooms which had rows of pipes in the walls for the conveyance of hot water, of which pipes the fragments still remain. The hall has a large arch on each side, and extends beyond the arches to the east and west extremity of the building. An arched passage between other bath-rooms corresponding with the entrance leads from the north side of the hall into a spacious saloon, the ceiling of which

---

* Pausan lib. iv c 31

is also vaulted with groined arches, and the aspect to the north.   In
these bath-rooms remain contrivances for heating the apartments,
and in one the wall is cased with tiles, perforated for the admission
of steam.   A small bath is at the end of the eastern suit of rooms,
which has been lined with stucco.   This has been supplied with hot
water from the pipes.   The water used here appears from the sediment near the pipes and on the walls to have been impregnated with
sulphur.   A detached semi-circular reservoir, still traceable to the
east of the building, supplied the water for its use.   The rooms to
the north east are in ruins; the rest, though stripped of the marble
ornaments which once adorned them, remain entire.   The bricks are
of the size and texture of the Roman bricks, and probably the building itself must be referred to that people.   I find no mention of it in
any ancient author, but from the style of the construction could not
refer it to any more recent period; though it appears to have been
used long after the decline of Roman dominion.

From hence we continued our journey to Palæo-castro, a village
still inhabited, and surrounded with the ruins of an ancient city.
They cover the space of nearly the circuit of two miles, and parts of
the ancient wall of Thuria may be traced by the foundations that remain.   These are all upon a hill at the foot of Taygetus, which retains
many vestiges of the former town.   Amongst them lie scattered
several marble tympana of fluted columns of the Doric order; probably the remains of the temple dedicated to the Syrian goddess, of
which at least we found no other indication.   There is a large oblong
cistern or tank hewn in the rock, and coated with a cement that still
adheres to many parts of its sides, which we found on measurement
to be twenty-three yards long and sixteen broad.   The depth of it is
now about fourteen feet   much soil having fallen into it.   The walls
are not so distinctly traceable as to enable us to ascertain the exact
extent of this ancient city; the vestiges of that which was subsequently
inhabited in the plain are far more indistinct.   The soil there is rich
and deep, and broken into platforms and angles of very singular appearance, by the waters from the mountains.   Some of these are so

regular, as to present almost the appearance of a modern fortification.
Here, however, the Aris, an inconsiderable stream, still flows to the
Pamisus, and, while the ancient ruins are visible on the hill, the ferti-
lity of the plain has obliterated the more recent habitations of the
Thurians.

> Deep harvests bury all their pride has plann'd,
> And laughing Ceres re-assumes the land

We returned to Calamata through other villages nearer to the
mountain than the baths by which we had come before, and through
a country the cultivation of which attested the comfort of the inhabitants. The Greek proprietors of this little district could so easily
remove themselves and their property into Maina, that the dominion the Turks exercised over them was more limited in its nature,
than in most other parts of the Levant; and content with the annual
payment of a sum of money, and occasional bribes to himself and his
officers, the Pasha allowed them in peace to cultivate their estates, and
sell the produce unmolested by the petty agents of despotism, who,
as Agas and Vaivodes, exercised a subordinate tyranny through the
rest of the Morea.

April 11th.—From Calamata our journey conducted us eastward
round the end of the bay of Corone, and then in a southerly direction
along the shore. We soon came to several copious salt-springs,
which gush out from a low rock; below them are two or three mills
whose wheels are turned by their stream. These were anciently between the cities of Pheræ and Abia, and now divide the district of
Calamata from Maina. Abia is still pointed out on the shore to the
south of the salt-springs. Near the mills we came to a square stone
tower, the residence of a Mainot chief. As I shall have frequently
occasion to mention similar towers and their inhabitants, a general
explanation of the government and state of Maina at the time I saw
it will best enable the reader to understand the occurrences which I
shall have to relate.

The government of Maina at the time I visited it, resembled in
many respects the ancient establishment of the Highland clans in

Scotland. It was divided into smaller or larger districts, over each
of which a chief, or Capitano, presided, whose usual residence was a
fortified tower, the resort of his family and clan in times of peace,
and their refuge in war. The district they governed belonged to
their retainers, who each contributed a portion (I think, a tenth) of
the produce of his land to the maintenance of the family under whom
he held. Each chief, besides this, had his own domain, which was
cultivated by his servants and slaves, and which was never very
considerable. They were perfectly independent of each other; the
judges of their people at home, and their leaders when they took the
field. The most powerful Capitano of the district usually assumed
the title of Bey of Maina, and in that name transacted their business
with the Turks, negotiated their treaties, or directed their arms against
the common enemy. In the country itself his power rested merely
on the voluntary obedience of the other chiefs, and his jurisdiction
extended in fact only over his own immediate dependants. The
Turkish court, to preserve at least a shadow of power over this
refractory community, generally confirmed by a ferman the appointment of the Bey, whose own power or influence enabled him to
support the title. The population of Maina is so great in proportion
to its fertility, that they are obliged to import many of the common
necessaries of life. For these they must occasionally trade with the
Turkish provinces, and exchange their own oil and silk and domestic
manufactures for the more essential articles of wheat and maize, and
provisions. To obtain these, they had recourse sometimes to smuggling, and sometimes to a regular payment of the Charatch, and ac-
knowledgment of the supremacy of the Porte. This they again threw
off, when a favourable year, or any extraordinary sources of supply rendered their submission unnecessary; and by such rebellion had more
than once drawn upon them the vengeance of their powerful neighbour. The contest had been repeatedly renewed, and as often the
Turks had been repulsed or had fallen victims to the determined
resistance of the Mainiots, and the inaccessible nature of their
country.

The coast indented with small creeks, containing the row-boats used universally in piratical excursions, is every where surrounded by rocks and exposed to winds which render it unsafe for transports and ships of burden. On the arrival of an enemy, their villages and towers along the shore were deserted, and the people retired to the mountains, the steep ridges of Taygetus, that rise from the shore, where other villages and securer valleys afforded them a temporary shelter from the storm of invasion. Should a body of troops be landed, and wreak their vengeance on the deserted habitations, the first rising gale cuts them off from all hopes of assistance from their fleet. A hardy people, well acquainted with every path of their native mountains, armed to a man with excellent rifles, dispersing easily by day, and assembling as easily every night, would distress them every hour they staid, and harass them at every step, if they advanced. The very women, well acquainted with the use of arms, have more than once poured ruin from the walls of some strong-built tower, or well-situated village, on the assailants, from whom they had nothing to expect but slaughter or captivity, if conquered. The country admits not of the conveyance of artillery, and their towers, ill calculated as they may seem for the improved warfare of more polished nations, offered a powerful means of resistance against the efforts of the Turks, and had more than once materially delayed their progress.

Should the Turks attack them by land, their frontier to the north is still more impenetrable. The loftiest and most inaccessible rocks, and the highest summits of Taygetus occupy the whole line, leaving only two roads that are shut in by the mountain on one side, and the sea on the other. The passes of the interior part of the country are known only to the natives, and to penetrate along the coast, while the Mainiots are in possession of the mountains, would require courage and discipline very superior to such as are generally displayed by the Turkish soldiery. In the war conducted by Lambro, with Russian money, the Mainiots were found so troublesome to the Turks, that a combined attack was made upon their country by the fleet under the

Capoudan Pasha, which landed troops upon their coast, and the forces of the Morea, which marched at the same time from Misitra. The number of these two armies, probably exaggerated, was rated by the Mainiots at 20,000 men. The result of the attack by sea was pointed out to me near Cardamyle; a heap of whitening bones in a dell near the town, the remains of the Turks, who, after suffering the severest privations, were not so fortunate as the rest in finding a refuge in their fleet. The attack by land was equally disastrous. After a fruitless attempt to advance, and burning a few inconsiderable villages, their army was obliged to retire, harassed by the fury of the people, while another party of the Mainiots burst into the plain of the Eurotas, drove off whatever they could plunder, and in the flames of Misitra, a considerable Turkish town, expiated the trifling mischief they had sustained at home.

Such are the stories at least which I heard repeated by their chiefs, and which the common people no less delighted to tell. Though easily united, when threatened by the Turk, yet frequent feuds, and petty warfare, too often arose between their chiefs at home; these feuds, however, preserved alive the martial spirit of the people, and they were, perhaps, on this account more successful in their resistance than they would have been if their government was more settled, and they had enjoyed a more uninterrupted peace. By sea their warfare was still more inextinguishable They infested with their row-boats every corner of the Cyclades and Morea, and made a lawful prize of any vessel that was too weak for resistance; or entered by night into the villages and dwellings near the shore, carrying off whatever they could find. Boats of this sort, called here Trattas, abounded in every creek; they are long and narrow like canoes; ten, twenty, and even thirty men, each armed with a rifle and pistols, row them with great celerity, and small masts with Latine sails are also used when the winds are favourable. Every chief had one or more of these, and all exercised piracy as freely, and with the same sentiments, as appeared to have prevailed among the heroes of the Odyssey and early inhabitants of Greece.

Habits like these, it may well be supposed, had a correspondent effect on the national character. Their freedom, though turbulent and ill regulated, produced the effects of freedom; they were active, industrious, and intelligent. Among their chiefs, I found men tolerably versed in the modern Romaic literature, and some who had sufficient knowledge of their ancient language to read Herodotus and Xenophon, and who were well acquainted with the revolutions of their country. Their independence and their victories had given them confidence, and they possessed the lofty mind and attachment to their country which has every where distinguished the inhabitants of mountainous and free districts, whether in Britain, Switzerland, or Greece. The robbery and piracy they exercised indiscriminately in their roving expeditions they dignified by the name of war; but though their hostility was treacherous and cruel, their friendship was inviolable. The stranger that was within their gates was a sacred title, and not even the Arabs were more attentive to the claims of hospitality. When we delivered our letters of recommendation to a chief, he received us with every mark of friendship, escorted us every where while we staid, and conducted us safely to the house of his nearest neighbour, where he left us under the protection of his friend; there we again staid a short time, and were forwarded in the same manner to a third. To pass by such a chief's dwelling without stopping to visit it, would have been deemed an insult, as the reception of strangers was a privilege highly valued. While a stranger was under their protection, his safety was their first object; an insult to such a person would have aroused in their breasts the strongest incitements to revenge; his danger would have induced them to sacrifice even their lives to his preservation, as his suffering any injury would have been an indelible disgrace to the family where it happened.

The religion of the Mainots is that of the Greek Christian church, with its usual accompaniments of saints, holy places, and holy pictures. Their churches were numerous, clean, and well attended; their superstition was great, as may be supposed from the adventurous and precarious life I have described. Hence their fondness for amulets and charms, and faith in them: but I know not whether they carry these to a greater height than the rest of their nation.

A more pleasing feature in their character, was their domestic intercourse with the other sex. Their wives and daughters, unlike those of most other districts in the Levant, were neither secluded, corrupted, or enslaved. Women succeeded in default of male issue to the possessions of their fathers, and partook at home of the confidence of their husbands, the education of their children, and the management of their families. In the villages they shared in the labours of domestic life, and in war they even partook of the dangers of the field. In no country were they more at liberty, and in no country were there fewer instances of its abuse than in Maina at this period. Conjugal infidelity was extremely rare, and indeed as death was sure to follow detection, and might even follow suspicion, it was not likely to have made much progress. The dress and appearance of these heroines will be described in the course of my relation, they were very different indeed from what the Amazonian nature of their habits and accomplishments would lead the reader to suppose.

To return, then, to the tower of Myla, so called from the mills I have mentioned on the salt streams which are described by Pausanias near Abia. The Capitano who received us invited us to his house, and set before us a repast, of which he partook himself, the usual symbol of hospitality, but here the pledge of safety. He assured us of the security with which we might proceed, his own possessions were inconsiderable, and his followers not numerous, but his house, though small, was neat and well appointed. After eating with us, he attended us with a large train on foot to Abia, the ruins of which are on the shore at the distance of above a mile from the salt-springs, in a southerly direction. one old piece of wall, of massive masonry, of a circular form, and the remains of a Mosaic pavement in the floor of a modern Greek church, are all the vestiges of antiquity that ascertain the spot where Abia stood, except the platform, and marks on the ground which indicate that other buildings formerly existed. In the tradition of the country the circular ruin had been a bath. however, on asking our conductor by what authority he asserted this, his answer was, " My father received it from his father, who heard the same " from his, if they were all mistaken, so am I " Our friend here took leave of us, sending with us to Kitrees, one of his armed follow-ers, who walked on before our party. The road lies along the shore

From Myla the mountains of Taygetus rise in high ridges to the east, and descend in rocky slopes to the sea The country is barren and stony beyond conception, and yet the earth, which is washed by the rains and torrents from the higher parts is supported on a thousand platforms and terraces, by the indefatigable industry of the inhabi-tants, and these were covered with corn, maize, olives, and mulberry trees, which seemed to grow out of the rock itself Through such a country we arrived at Kitrees, a small hamlet of five or six cottages, scattered round another fortress, the residence of Zanetachi Kutu-phari, formerly Bey of Maina, and of his niece Helena, to whom the property belonged. The house consisted of two towers of stone, exactly resembling our own old towers upon the borders of England and Scotland, a row of offices and lodgings for servants, stables, and open sheds, inclosing a court, the entrance to which was through an arched and embattled gateway. On our approach, an armed retainer of the family came out to meet us, spoke to our guard who attended us from Myla. He returned with him to the castle, and informed the chief, who hastened to the gate to welcome us, surrounded by a crowd of gazing attendants all surprised at the novelty of seeing Eng-lish guests. We were received, however, with the most cordial wel-come, and shewn to a comfortable room on the principal floor of the tower, inhabited by himself and his family; the other tower, being the residence of the *Capitanessa*, his niece, for that was the title which she bore.

Zanetachi Kutuphari was a venerable figure, though not above the age of fifty-six. His family consisted of a wife and four daughters, the two youngest of which were children. They inhabited the apart-ment above ours, and were, on our arrival, introduced to us. The old chief, who himself had dined at an earlier hour, sat down however to eat with us according to the established etiquette of hospitality here, while his wife and the two younger children waited on us, notwithstanding our remonstrances, according to the custom of the country, for a short time, then retired, and left a female servant to attend us and him. At night, beds and mattresses were spread on the floor, and pillows and sheets, embroidered and composed of broad stripes of muslin and coloured silk, were brought in. These articles, we found, were manufactured at home by the women of the family ; as the Greeks themselves invariably wear their under garments when they sleep, the inconvenience of such a bed is little felt.

April 12.—As the day after our arrival at Kitreés was Easter Sunday, we of course remained there, and had an opportunity of witnessing and partaking in the universal festivity which prevailed not only in the castle, but in the villages of the country round it. In every Greek house a lamb is killed at this season, and the utmost rejoicing prevails. We dined with Zanetachi Kutuphari and his family at their usual hour of half-past eleven in the forenoon, and after our dinner were received in much state by his niece Helena in her own apartments. She was in fact the lady of the castle, and chief of the district round it, which was her own by inheritance from her father. She was a young widow, and still retained much of her beauty ; her manners were pleasing and dignified. An audience in form from a young woman accompanied by her sister, who sat near her, and a train of attendant females in the rich and elegant dress of the country, was a novelty in our tour, and so unlike the customs which prevailed within a few short miles from the spot where we were, that it seemed like an enchantment of romance. The Capitanessa alone was seated at our entrance, who, when she had offered us chairs, requested her sister to sit down near her, and ordered her attendants to bring coffee and refreshments. We were much struck with the general beauty of the Mainiot women here, which we afterwards found was not confined to Kitreés ; we remarked it in many other villages ; and it is of a kind that from their habits of life would not naturally be expected. With the same fine features that prevail among the beauties of Italy and

Sicily, they have the delicacy and transparency of complexion, with the brown or auburn hair, which seems peculiar to the colder regions. Indeed, from the vicinity to the sea, the summers here are never intensely hot, nor are the winters severe in this southern climate; the same causes in some of the Greek islands produce the same effect, and the women are much more beautiful in general than those of the same latitude on the continent. The men, too, are a well proportioned and active race, not above the middle size, but spare, sinewy, and muscular.

The Capitanessa wore a light blue shawl-gown, embroidered with gold; a sash tied loosely round her waist; and a short vest without sleeves of embroidered crimson velvet. Over these was a dark green velvet Polonese mantle, with wide and open sleeves, also richly embroidered. On her head was a green velvet cap, embroidered with gold, and appearing like a coronet, and a white and gold muslin shawl fixed on the right shoulder, and passed across her bosom under the left arm floated over the coronet and hung to the ground behind her.

Her uncle's dress was equally magnificent. He wore a close vest with open sleeves of white and gold embroidery, and a short black velvet mantle with sleeves edged with sables. The sash which held his pistols and his poignard was a shawl of red and gold. His light blue trowsers were gathered at the knee, and below them were close gaiters of blue cloth with gold embroidery, and silver gilt bosses to protect the ancles When he left the house, he flung on his shoulders a rich cloth mantle with loose sleeves, which was blue without and red within, embroidered with gold in front and down the sleeves in the most sumptuous manner. His turban was green and gold; and, contrary to the Turkish custom, his grey hair hung down below it. The dress of the lower orders is in the same form, with the necessary variations in the quality of the materials and absence of the ornaments. It differed considerably from that of the Turks, and the shoes were made either of yellow or untanned leather, and fitted tightly to the foot. The hair was never shaved, and the women wore gowns like those of

the west of Europe, instead of being gathered at the ancles like the
loose trowsers of the East.

In the course of the afternoon we walked into some of the neighbouring villages; the inhabitants were every where dancing and
enjoying themselves on the green, and those of the houses and little
harbour of Kitreés with the crews of two small boats that were moored
there, were employed in the same way, till late in the evening. We
found our friend Zanetachi well acquainted with both the ancient and
modern state of Maina, having been for several years the Bey of the
district. From him I derived much of the information to which
I have recourse in describing the manners and principles of the Mainiots. He told me that in case of necessity, on an attack from the
Turks, the numbers they could bring to act, consisting of every man
in the country able to bear arms, amounted to about 12,000. All of
these were trained to the use of the rifle even from their childhood,
and after they grew up were possessed of one without which they
never appeared; and, indeed, it was as much a part of their dress as
a sword formerly was of an English gentleman. Their constant fami-
liarity with this weapon had rendered them singularly expert in the
use of it; there are fields near every village where the boys practised
at the target, and even the girls and women took their part in this
martial amusement.

April 13.—We left Kitreés, not without regret on our part, or the
kind expression of it on that of our hospitable friends, who supplied
us with mules, and sent with us an escort to conduct us to Cardamoula, the ancient Cardamyle. It is not above ten miles from
Kitreés, where we were detained to a late hour by the kindness and
hospitality of our hosts. Below the castle is a small harbour sheltered
from the south by a rocky promontory, which runs out westward to
the sea, and is about half a mile in length. On leaving the village we
ascended by a winding road in a south easterly direction until we
came to the top of this stony ridge, and looked down on a valley enclosed by mountains still more to the east. Several little villages and
churches are scattered over the vale and on the sides of the hills that

surround it Behind them rose a high, black, and barren range of
mountains, the summits of which were covered with snow In one
of these villages we were shown, on inquiring after antiquities, an
old ruined tower, of a construction more recent than the Grecian age,
and we thought it probably was of Venetian workmanship. The
valley itself and the lower hills were cultivated like a garden, and
formed a scene of great beauty. The principal villages in this tract
are Dokyes, Barussa, and Zarnata, and among these may perhaps
be discovered the traces of some of the ancient towns of the Eleuthero-
Laconians, enumerated by Pausanias near Gerenia.

We were amused in passing through several of these little hamlets
with the simple curiosity of the people. The men who escorted us
requested with great submission that we would stop on the road,
until they could apprise their friends of our arrival, because most of
them had never seen a stranger, and none of them an Englishman.
The word was no sooner given, than off they ran, and as the tidings
spread, and shouts were heard and answered from the fields, labour
stood still, and men, women, and children flocked round us on our
approach. Their appearance was such as I have described; the men
well-formed and active, the women in general fairer than the other
Greeks, and very beautiful. The men in succession shook us cordi-
ally by the hand, and welcomed us to their country, and crowds followed us as we proceeded on our journey. The road from hence led
us in a southerly direction over a most stony and barren ridge to the
shore, and afterwards continued along the sea, until our arrival at
Cardamyla. The country round it, though cultivated in the same
laborious manner, was still more stony and barren than at Kitices;
even in the small fissures of the rock, olives and mulberries were
planted, and spots of only a few feet in diameter were dug over, and
sown with corn and maize. On the hills there were many apiaries,
and the produce is of the finest sort of honey, equal almost to that of
Hymettus, but of a paler colour.

Cardamyla is now a small village, in which were three or four
towers, the property of chieftains who possessed the country round it.

We had letters to them from Zanetachi Kutuphari, and from the merchants of Calamata, and a dispute again arose for the pleasure of
receiving us.   At last we were shown to the largest of these towers,
and treated with all possible hospitality.   The whole village flocked
to our house, and we found that nearly every man was a relation of
the chiefs, and of each other, as in these districts families seldom
migrated, and the different branches of the clan remained with the
principal stock, in whose house there was a collection of brothers, and
nephews, and cousins, to a remote degree of affinity, who, as they
became too numerous, settled themselves on the land in other houses,
but seldom at a distance from the family.

Behind the town is a small rocky eminence, on whose summit were
a few vestiges of the ancient acropolis of Cardamyla.   Just enough
remained to point out the situation ; the rock itself was split by a deep
chasm, ascribed by tradition to an earthquake.   At the foot of this
rock was seen a heap of bones, the monument of Turkish invasion.
These were pointed out to us with all the enthusiasm of successful
liberty, such as I had witnessed and remembered among the Swiss on
showing the monuments of their former glory, before they yielded
their independence and their feelings to the thraldom of France.
Here, amid the scenes of slavery that surrounded us, the contrast was
still more striking.   Below the acropolis were several caves, and the
remains of ancient sepulchres.   We were shown the spot where the
children of the village are taught the use of the rifle, and found that
they practised it at ten, and even eight years of age.   A groupe of
girls and women on the village green were slinging stones and bullets
at a mark, and seemed very expert.   Their figures were light and
active, but neither these nor their faces were more coarse or mascu-
line than those of their languid and enervated countrywomen.   The
chief of Cardamyla assured us, that in their petty wars, they had more
than once followed their fathers and brothers to the field, and that
the men were more eager to distinguish themselves before the eyes
of their female companions, and partakers in the danger.   Dances

on the green succeeded in this season of festivity to these female gymnastics, until the evening closed on our gaiety.

April 14.—We remained great part of the day at Cardamyla in compliance with the wishes of our host and of his neighbours, and partook of the amusements on the green After dining with him and his family, he attended us in his boat, the inland road being scarcely passable from the stony rugged hills that it surmounts. We viewed the situation of Leuctra, a small hamlet on the shore still retaining its ancient name, but found there few and inconsiderable traces of antiquity. About two miles and a half from hence we came to the little creek of Platsa, shut in by the rock of Pephnos, near which was a tower, the residence of the Capitano Christeia, a chief to whom we were recommended.

We had sent our letters to this chief by a messenger from Cardamyla, in consequence of which he met us at the port on our landing, attended by a large train of followers. We took leave of our friends of Cardamyla, who paid us a compliment at parting, not unusual in this country, by firing all their rifles over our heads. As this was not very carefully or regularly performed, and the pieces were always loaded with ball, the ceremony was not altogether agreeable. The tower of Capitano Christeia was at a small distance from the port, and adjoining to it were out-buildings and a long hall of entertainment as at Kitrees.

Here, according to Pausanias, was formerly the little town of Pephnos, the situation of which is now only marked by the rocky islet of the port. The place was at that time inconsiderable, and the island contained nothing, except two small bronze figures of Castor and Pollux, which were, however, miraculously immovable, even by the winter's storm and the sea which beat upon them. The miracle is no longer performed, and the statues are gone.

We walked from the shore with our host to his castle; Capitano Christeia, the owner of it, was one of the most powerful, and at the same time the most active and turbulent chieftain in this district. He had paid the price of the renown he had acquired, for he bore the

marks of three bullets in the breast; the scars of two more upon his
face, besides slighter wounds in his legs and arms. in fact his
life was a constant scene of piracy by sea and feuds at home.   He was
about forty-five years of age, and showed us with much satisfaction
the spoil he had amassed in his expeditions   He was friendly and
hospitable to us, and lively and intelligent in his conversation.   He
had recently captured at sea a small French merchant ship, and related with just indignation the following trait of the captain who commanded it.   After seizing on the men, money, and merchandize,
which the vessel contained, he told the captain he would land him on
the shore of the Morea, and offered him at his request any favour he
might ask, out of the prize.   The captain, regardless of the freedom
of his men, or the property consigned to him, solicited only an ena-
melled snuff-box, with a lady's hair on the outside, and a very indecent design within the lid.   Christea, who, though a pirate, was
enraged at his unmanly and heartless levity, retracted his offer, and
left the captain with only a shirt and a pair of trowsers in the boat, to
shift for himself.   He set the crew on shore, and brought his prize
to Platsa, where he showed us the snuff-box with great satisfaction.
He had also been engaged the year before we were there in hostilities
with a neighbouring chief, and had taken the field with a company of
eighty men, and thirty women, of whom his sister had the command.
A peace had been since made after several skirmishes, but not until
some of his Amazons had fallen, and his sister had been wounded
as well as himself.   In the tower to which we were shown, we lived in
a neat and comfortable room, but the walls were thick and strong,
the windows barricadoed with iron bars, and barrels of gunpowder
were arranged along the shelves below the ceiling.   The men who
attended in the castle had an air of military service, and the whole
place bore in its appearance the character of the master.

April 15.—We staid a day at this singular mansion, and were
prevented in the morning by a heavy rain from extending our rambles
beyond the castle.   We dined with the family at twelve o'clock, and
after dinner went to the great room of the castle.   In it, and on the

green before it, we found near a hundred people of both sexes and of all ages assembled, and partaking of the chief's hospitality. They flocked from all the neighbouring villages, and were dancing with great vivacity. The men during the dance, repeatedly fired their pistols through the windows, as an accompaniment to their wild gaiety; and the shouts and laughter and noise were indescribable. Among other dances, the Ariadne, mentioned in De Guy's Travels, was introduced, and many which we had not yet seen in Greece. The men and women danced together, which was not so usual on the continent as in the islands. On my complimenting the Capitano on the performance of his lyrist, who scraped several airs on a three-stringed rebeck, here dignified with the name of λυγ̑, a lyre, he told me with regret, that he had indeed been fortunate enough to possess a most accomplished musician, a German, who played not only Greek dances, but many Italian and German songs; but that in 1791 his fiddler, brought up in the laxer morals of western Europe, and unmindful of the rigid principles of Maina, had so offended by his proposals the indignant chastity of a pretty woman in the neighbourhood, that she shot him dead on the spot with a pistol. As evening approached, the strangers departed to their homes after a rifle salute, in the manner and form observed to us on our leaving the boat the day before. We again passed the night at Christeia's house, and set out for Vitulo the next morning.

April 16.—We left Platsa on mules, attended by a strong escort of armed men, sent with us by the chief's direction. We first proceeded eastward up a narrow rocky vale, and then turning to the south, ascended by a winding road up a high ridge of crags. We past some villages with scanty spots of cultivation round them, and keeping high along the side of Taygetus came in about two hours to the verge of Christeia's territory. Here our escort left us, and a guard belonging to one of the chiefs of Vitulo took charge of us, and conducted us down the southern side of the promontory of Platsa to their master's, which is at two hours' distance.

The whole of this tract is as barren as possible. The mountain of Taygetus is a continuance of naked crags; the cultivation disappeared as we proceeded, and the coast which lay before us towards Cape Grosso, seemed more bare and savage than any we had passed. The villages seemed poorer, and the people less attentive to comforts and cleanliness from the extreme poverty of the country. Still in the scanty spots where vegetation could be produced at all, their industry was conspicuous. Not a tree or bush is seen. We found many specimens of variegated marble in the mountains, and passed by some ancient quarries. * We at last came to Vitulo, formerly Œty-los, a considerable town in this desolate country, built along a rocky precipice. Below it is a narrow deep creek, that winds inland from the sea, and is the haven to the town. A mountain torrent falls into it through a deep and gloomy glen that is barely wide enough to afford a passage for its waters. On the opposite rocks that bound this glen to the south is another village with a square Venetian fortress. Our guides conducted us through a street, filled with gazing crouds, to the house of a chief, to whom we brought letters of recommend-ation. We found the master of the house was absent, but were hospitably received by his family, and remained there until the next day.

In the afternoon we examined the situation and environs of Vitulo for the remains of the ancient town of Œtylos. We found in the streets several massive foundations and large hewn stones still left, supporting the more slight buildings of modern times. We went to the church, which, in most places built on the situation of the old Grecian cities, contains the fragments of ancient architecture. We found there a beautifully fluted Ionic column of white marble, supporting a beam at one end of the aisle. To this beam the bells were hung. Three or four Ionic capitals were in the wall of the church, employed for building it together with common rough stone work.

---

* For the quarries in Taygetus, see Strabo, lib. viii. 367.

The volutes and ornaments were freely and beautifully executed : and different in some degree from any I have elsewhere seen. The cord which encircles the neck of the column is continued in a sort of bow-knot round the scroll of the volutes at each side of the capital, and is very freely carved. On the outside of the church are seen the found-ations of a temple, to which these ornaments in all probability belonged.

Œtylos as well as Leuctra was, in the time of Pausanias, a city of the Eleuthero-Lacones, who possessed by virtue of a grant from Augustus some of the maritime towns of Laconia, of these, nine were on the promontory of Taygetus, to the south and west of Gythium, which also belonged to them. The names were Teuthrone, Las, Pyrrhichus, on the eastern side ; Cænepolis near the point of Tænarus (at Cape Grosso), Œtylos, Leuctra, Thalamæ *, Alagonia, and Gerenia. The rest were beyond the Laconian gulph on the Malean promontory. Cardamyle, a city as ancient as the days of Homer, had, by Augustus, been taken from the Messenians and an-nexed to the dominion of Sparta. Gerenia appears to me to have been situated near Kitries ; the small town of Alagonia and Tha-lamæ are now lost among the numerous villages of the district. Leuctra, Cardamyle, and Pephnos, we were enabled to fix by un-doubted remains of antiquity, or coincidence of situation at Leutro, Cardamoula, and Platsa. Œtylos was at Vitulo, and the temple of which we found the remains was probably that of Serapis, this, with a statue of Apollo, is mentioned by Pausanias as the objects most worthy of observation at Œtylos. † The name of this town is as ancient as the æra of Homer (Iliad, ii. 585), but in the dialect of the country the present pronunciation appears to have prevailed even in the time of Ptolemy the geographer, who enumerates Bitula among the

---

* Meletius and the geographers who place Thalamæ at Calamata, forget that it was only eighty stadia from Œtylos, and consequently between Platsa and Vitulo. M.

† Some formerly pronounced it Tylos, lib. viii. Strabo but they must have read the verse of Homer, καὶ οἱ Τύλον ἀμφενέμοντο

towns of Laconia, and as the Greeks pronounce the B like our V, the name given it by Ptolemy is the same with that now used, except the feminine termination..

We had been very desirous of pursuing our survey of Maina to Cape Matapan, and visiting the situation of the ancient Tænarus We found that from Vitulo the road by land was impassable even for mules, and the country round Tænarus in so disturbed a state that none of the chiefs could undertake to conduct us thither in safety. There are, as we were told, considerable remains of an ancient city on Cape Grosso, agreeing, as far as we could ascertain the distances, with Pausanias' description of Cænepolis Cape Matapan, the Tænarian promontory, is south of Cape Grosso Of the ancient cave and temples there we could get no consistent accounts. We abandoned with great reluctance our farther researches, and resolved to proceed from hence to Marathonisi, the modern capital of Maina.

April 17. — We left Vitulo early in the morning attended by an escort of sixteen Mainiots, and proceeded eastward towards Marathonisi, leaving the sea-port behind us. A very steep and rugged road descends into the little glen below Vitulo, and continues winding along the banks of the torrent for several miles, shut in by rocky and wooded precipices. Emerging from these defiles we came to a more open and fertile tract of country, covered with groves of oak and a few scattered villages. The chief at whose house we had been at Vitulo was in one of these, and our guards gave him notice of our arrival by a discharge of all their rifles. Their salute was answered from the village by a similar discharge, and the Capitano issued immediately with about sixteen armed followers, and welcomed us in the plain. He then with this additional escort went forwards with us to Marathonisi. We had come about ten miles, and had nearly the same distance to proceed. The country grew more open and better cultivated, as we approached the eastern shore of Maina. We came in about an hour within sight of the sea, and then in a north-east direction pursued our journey through several villages, in one of which was a square Venetian fortress, until we arrived at Marathonisi.

This town was the residence of the Bey, and the capital of Maina, though it consists of little more than a single street along the shore, in front of which is a small road-stead formed by the island of Marathonisi, the ancient Cranae of Homer. The Bey of Maina, Zanet Bey, had a large and strong castle within half a mile of the place, but received us at a house in the town, where he was resident at this time, with great kindness and cordiality. We found he was of a character more quiet and indolent than many of the subordinate chiefs we had visited. This, as Christea told us, was the reason why they had chosen him in the room of Zanetachi Kutuphari, the more intelligent and enterprising chieftain of Kitries. After an early dinner he retired to his siesta, and we went to view the situation and ruins of the ancient Gythium, which stood a little to the north of the present town

What vestiges remain of Gythium appeared to me to be chiefly of Roman construction, and the buildings of earlier date are no longer traceable The situation is now called Palaeopolis, but no habitation is left upon it. The town has covered several low hills which terminate in rocks along the shore, on one of which we found a Greek inscription, but so defaced as to be nearly illegible. A salt stream that rises near the shore out of the rocks was probably the ancient fountain of Æsculapius. The temples and other monuments enumerated by Pausanias are now no more. Marble blocks and other remnants of antiquity are still found occasionally by the peasants who cultivate the ground, and the pastures in the neighbourhood are even now famous for their cheeses, which were in the time of the Spartan government an article of trade much esteemed in the rest of Greece

The rock near the salt-springs which I have mentioned, is cut smooth, and marks remain in it of beams which, with the roof that they supported, have disappeared There are two large tanks lined with stuccoed brick-work, once vaulted over, and cut in the rocky hill, divided by cross walls into two or three separate reservoirs, for the supply of water. Beyond these are two adjoining oblong buildings of brick, with niches for urns, containing the ashes of the dead, exactly similar to the Colombaia, now so well known in Italy. The doors at the end of the buildings are their only entrances. There are also near the shore ruins of baths, much like those of Thuria, but far less perfect, on which, however, we found a scallop-shell ornament in stucco still remaining in one of the niches. There are other ruins on the shore, of which a part is now under water; but a floor of Mosaic work may be still seen. Rubbish and old walls, many of which are of brick, cover great part of the ancient Gythium, but we sought in vain for the temples or any antiquities of value.

April 18.—This day was spent in examining those parts of the old city which we had not previously visited. The island Cranae is rather to the south of Gythium; and secured the port. It is low and flat, and at a distance of only a hundred yards from the shore. The ruined foundation of a temple supports at present a Greek chapel.

April 19.—On this day we were to leave Maina, and proceed to Mistra by the vale of the Eurotas, through a country over which the Turks maintained a very unsettled government, and where the protection of the Mainiots could avail us no longer. Desirous to render every assistance, the Bey gave us to the charge of five Albanians who were at Marathonisi, and who, having transacted their business there, were returning to Mistra. His boat conveyed us and our Albanian escort across the bay to the mouth of the Eurotas, it flows here through marshes bounded by a rich and fertile plain, once the patrimony of the unfortunate Helots, whose name it still retains. Our guides conducted us on foot to a village called Prinico, where we passed the night in a small cottage. Our Albanians, for reasons best known to themselves, retained the Bey's letter to the Greek Primate, of which we had no intelligence until the next morning

April 20.—We now discovered, what assuredly was not known to the Bey of Marathonisi, the very suspicious character of the guides to whom his confidence had entrusted us. We were so much in their power that we were involved by them in a thousand difficulties for procuring the horses to convey us forward, and had good reasons to suspect their intentions. What made our situation less secure was, that from hence until we arrived at Mistra the country was in the possession of the Bardouniots, a tribe of lawless vagabonds, whose villages we must pass through, and against whom our only or at least our chief protection, was the strength of our party. We resolved not to stop again on the road, until we were securely lodged at Mistra; a resolution in which we persevered, and to which we probably owed our safety, though our guides endeavoured repeatedly to frustrate our intention. In consequence of their conduct, it was noon when we left the village where we passed the night We crossed the plains to Helos, called Helios in the corrupted language of the district, the rich but defenceless country of the ancient Helots. Soon after we came to the Eurotas, and continued along its banks through a beautiful and varied vale, in some parts so narrow as to resemble a defile, at others wide and fertile, abounding in woods and varied scenery, but every where rude and uncultivated, except a few fields immediately near the villages, where a scanty and negligent culture ill provided for the wants of the inhabitants. The villages are the habitations of Albanese peasants, and were dangerous to the traveller, as every crime was easy, and the people were in the habit of marauding with impunity. The plain and mountains were infested alternately by the roving Mainiots, and the Turkish or Albanese borderers, and we soon found that to oblige us to stop in some of the villages was the determined wish of our guides. We resisted all their solicitations to that effect, and, though carried by their artifices by a circuitous route in order to persuade us that Mistra was more distant than in fact it was, yet we continued our journey until we arrived there in safety.

REMARKS ILLUSTRATING PART OF THE PRECEDING JOURNAL

[EXTRACTED FROM THE LATE DR SIBTHORP'S PAPERS]

APRIL, 1795.—Kutchuk Mama contains about one hundred and fifty houses. The town was surrounded by groves of mulberry trees, fenced in by the Indian fig, whose thorny coats form an impenetrable fence. The Morea contains a number of fertile plains; but this of Messenia * in richness of soil was superior to the rest. We were told in our evening conversation at the Aga's, that in certain spots it returned thirty-fold the seed that was sown; that the peasant sometimes reaped two crops of corn in the same year; and that the Calamboki, sown in May, when the wheat was cut, was reaped in August.

Sunday, April 12.—I was awakened early by the cry of the Sacristan, κοπιάσετε εἰς τὴν ἐκκλησίαι, which called up the whole village to celebrate the festival of the Paschal Lamb I rose an hour before sun-rise, and accompanied the Consul to church, whence we proceeded, in order, to celebrate the service in the open air " Christ is risen from the dead," was frequently repeated; the tapers were raised, and the villagers crossed themselves with much devotion The service being finished, a general salutation took place, the men kissed the men, the women, the women The congregation, who had languished with a long fast felt with impatience the desire of animal food, and many withdrew to their rustic hearth to enjoy the feast of

---

* The fertility of this district of the Morea is praised by the ancient Greeks see Plutarch in Agesi. and Strabo's quotation from Euripides, in his account of Messenia

the paschal lamb. So general is the sacrifice on this day, that no peasant is so poor, who does not find the means of procuring a lamb.

April 11 — Silk and figs are the chief objects of attention in the district of Kutchuk Maina; wine, strong and well-flavoured, is also made there, cotton, Indian corn and millet are cultivated. The silk-worm is fed on the leaves of the white mulberry tree, which is distinguished from the black; the one is called Μέϊα, the other συκαμία. The figs are sold in strings; a string, τζχαὶ consists of sixty figs; and one thousand of these strings will sell for seventy piastres. Caprification is constantly practised; without it the figs would fall off, and not ripen well.

April 15.—We had a favourable passage from Calamata to Cardamoula, a distance of six leagues; on our landing at the latter place, Panayotti, nephew of the chief who, by the popularity of his manners had gained the affections of his clan, came down with a number of his followers to receive us, we were struck at the contrast of the figure of the Mainots and the Greeks whom we had hitherto seen. The nature of man seemed here to recover its erect form, we no longer observed the servility of mind and body which distinguishes the Greeks subjugated by the Turks. We were conducted by Panayotti to his tower-like castle, a narrow entrance and dark winding staircase brought us into a chamber which, from the form of its structure, and the loop-holes in its walls, was well calculated for defence on a sudden attack. Panayotti was acquainted with the vulgar names, and supposed medicinal virtues, and economical uses, of a great number of plants. I was, soon after my arrival, presented with a root, the top, I was told, possessed the extraordinary power of acting as an emetic; while the bottom was a cathartic. I immediately recognized the root of the Euphorbia Apios *, and found my Dioscorides illustrated. In our evening walk, we observed, among the corn, a quantity of Lolium,

---

* The passage to which Dr S alludes is in the 4th Book, c 177 We may add also the words of Pliny, "Aiunt superiorem partem ejus vomitione biles extrahere, inferiorem per alvum." Lib xxvi c. 8

which our host colled ἄιρα, and added that the seeds of it, when mixed
with the corn, occasioned giddiness.* With the Lolium grew our
orobanche, which he called λύκος, from its destructive qualities; he
commended the flavor of it when young, and boiled as asparagus.
The dry stony rocks of Cardamoula, exposed to the sea air, abounded
with the wild thyme, the favorite food of the bees; and, on our return, we were served with a plate of honey, to which even that of
Hymettus yielded in point of flavor and pureness, being of a trans-
parent amber colour. We were served also with some φασκομηλιὰ,
sage apples, the inflated tumor formed upon a species of sage, and
the effect of the punctuie of a cynips.

April 16.—Panayotti had given notice to his followers of our intention to visit Mount Taygetus; and having procured mules we set
out, attended by him and an escort; our road led us along a torrent-
bed, walled in by stupendous masses of rock, fragments of the cliff
that had fallen from the precipice frequently interrupted our route.
We consigned ourselves not without fear to our mules, while, with
wonderful address, they stepped from rock to rock. We continued
to wind along the torrent side, and were saluted with the fire of musketry from the followers of Panayotti, who had collected above on
parts of the mountain to secure our passage. We saw several occasional dwellings excavated in these rocks in situations almost inaccessible, where the Mainots concealed their property on the invasion of
the Turks, or in their battles with each other. We had proceeded
about six hours, and had advanced two-thirds of the way up the
mountain, when we halted, our guides agreed, that from the snow,
and from the distance of the summit, it would be impossible to reach
it and return to Cardamoula before night. The insecurity of the
place and the early season of the year forbade us sleeping in the open
air. I looked with feelings of disappointment towards the summit of
Taygetus, and regretted the necessity of our return. I had collected
several rock plants, and though we had reached the region of the

---

* See the remark on Lolium T. in the list of the plants of Greece in this volume.

Silver Fir, we were not sufficiently advanced to find those Alpine plants which the height of the summit promised. We dined under a rock, from whose side descended a purling spring among violets, primroses, and the starry hyacinth, mixed with black Satyrium, and different coloured Orches. The flowering ash hung from the sides of the mountain, under the shade of which bloomed saxifrages, and the snowy Isopyrum, with the Campanula Pyramidalis; this latter plant is now called χαρισόνη, it yields abundance of a sweet milky fluid, and was said to promote a secretion of milk, a quality first attributed to it under the doctrine of signatures. Our guides made nosegays of the fragrant leaves of the Fraxinella; the common nettle was not forgotten as a pot herb, but the Imperatoria seemed to be the favorite sallad. Among the shrubs I noticed our gooseberry tree, and the Celtis Australis grew wild among the rocks.

April 18.—The passage to Mistra was difficult from the craggy nature of the road, and dangerous from the robbers who infested the mountains. We were now on the confines of Panayotti's territory; and it was thought advisable that we should take five of his men well armed, and five from the next captain. Our road was lengthened by the circumstance of a bridge which was broken down, and we were obliged to make a considerable *détour*, we had frequently occasion to alight and climb precipices, where our mules, with difficulty, followed us. The day was remarkably cold, and there had been a fall of snow while we were passing the ridge of the mountains. The sea pine, which grew here, had quite another appearance; it arrived at a large size, and, from the bark covered with lichens, the trees seemed of a great age. Vegetation was yet slowly advancing: the flowers of the vernal crocus, and the two-leaved squill were just appearing. I noticed the dried skeleton of the Morina Persica, and the Onopordum; a Marrubium, and a fragrant Nepeta that I had found on Parnassus. Taygetus would afford a rich field of enquiry to the botanist, but the unsettled state of the country would not allow him to examine it with care.

PARNASSUS,

AND

THE NEIGHBOURING DISTRICT

[FROM THE MANUSCRIPTS OF THE LATE DR SIBTHORP.]

Nov. 16. 1794.—We left Athens, and came by the usual road to the monastery of Daphne; having passed it, an agreeable view opened through the defile into the Saronic gulf. We coasted along its shore, having on our right a salt-marsh, with pools and water-mills, the marsh was covered with Salicornia herbacea, and different species of Tringa flew along the pools; I shot the Tringa Erythropus. We advanced towards Eleusis, when leaving the town about a mile on our left, we crossed over a rich and fertile plain towards the Cephissus; we passed the bed of it, which was narrow and filled with stones, brought down by the winter torrents from the mountains. We entered into the forest of Sarando Potamo, and having traversed it for four hours arrived at Condoura. We passed through the defiles of the forest covered with Pinaster, wild olives, the Kermes oak, Phillyrea, and some carob trees. The village of Condoura is not unpleasantly situated on a rising hill, extending into a verdant valley, watered by a narrow stream flowing from the mountain. The houses, covered with pantiles, consist of a single room, with a door-way in the middle; the area is divided into two parts, the one serves for the stable, the other, which rises a foot higher, is tenanted by the peasant and his family; in the centre is the fire-place, the smoke passing through apertures made in the roof. This place is eight hours distant from Athens, and six from Thebes.

Nov. 18.—We left Condoura in the morning, and ascending the mountain traversed some deep ravines, and crossed Cithæron, now

Eláteas. We left the summit of the mountain, near which we distinguished clumps of the silver fir Ελάτη, at the distance of about two hours, and through a narrow pass, commanded by the ruins of Gypto-chorio, descended, after a ride of three hours, into the fertile plains of Bœotia. In two hours more we arrive at Pyrgos, a small village situated on a rising ground, with the remains of an old tower, worked up with the ruins of Grecian buildings. About two miles to our left was Coela, anciently Platæa, the soil, rich and light, was in many places turned up by the moles. Leaving Pyrgos, we advanced along the plain to Eremo-castro ; in our road we observed droves of pigs tearing up the ground for the roots of the Cuckow pint *(arum maculatum)*, which was called by the swine-herd δρακοντιό. Flocks of sheep, whose fleeces were of remarkable blackness, were feeding in the plain, the breed was considerably superior in beauty and size to that of Attica. It was almost evening when we ascended the hill of Eremo-castro, three hours distant from Pyrgos, passing some fountains, and a brook choked up with sedges.

Nov 19.—The morning view from Eremo-castro was particularly striking and picturesque ; the eye extended over a rich plain walled in by rough and lofty mountains, Cithæron, Helicon, and Parnassus, with its summit covered with snow; as were also Olono and the higher tracts of land in the Peloponnesus. Descending from Thespiæ we proceeded along the plain towards Livadea ; after an hour's ride we passed a small rivulet fringed with plane trees, and a village; on our right was a marsh with the Lake Topoglias, the ancient Copais ; the greater portion of it overgrown with reeds ; the plain beyond was shut in by the high land above Talanda, and the ridge of rocky ground on the east coast of Bœotia. We saw a great number of vultures soaring over the mountains ; and the moor buzzard flew along the marshy tract of the Copais, pursuing the Scolopax, and other Grallæ. Great quantities of Saccharum Ravennæ grew by the roadside, and the peasants were employed in gathering it for covering their Callivia. After riding six hours we arrived at Livadea.

K

Nov. 20.—The river Hercyna flowed with a noisy course through stupendous rocks, whose fallen fragments often impeded its stream, and formed so many natural cascades ; in winter its torrent, swelled with rains, sometimes overflowed the bridge. Four species of fish are found at Livadea in the Hercyna; all, I suspect, of the genus Cyprinus ; in the morning two of these species were brought to us, one of which was called σαρνιόψαρο, the same with our chub; the other πασκοβόυσα was distinguished by a dark golden stripe along the sides, and was a species of Cyprinus unknown to me. *

We walked out to examine the town of Livadea. A grotto or rather a cavern was shown us as the grotto of Trophonius ; this, from the description of Pausanias, I should rather suppose to have been the place where the image of the god was kept. The suppliant proceeded to the grotto, which was probably a cavern in the rock above in the opposite side, where there is a Greek chapel. Near to this place we observed frequent stumps of laurel, probably remains of the wood which Pausanias describes as being under the grotto. The hole excavated below the rock, where we suppose the image of the god to have been kept, was too shallow to have been the grotto ; near it are to be seen the two springs of Lethe and Mnemosyne · these contribute to swell the river Hercyna.

June 28.—In the morning we ascended to the castle ; its state of defence arises from the natural situation. The cannon are dismantled, and the fortifications neglected. After dinner I walked out with a shepherd's boy to herborise ; my pastoral botanist surprised me not a little with his nomenclature ; I traced the names of Dioscorides and Theophrastus, corrupted, indeed, in some degree by pronunciation, and by the long *series annorum* which had elapsed since the time of these philosophers ; but many of them were unmutilated, and their virtues faithfully handed down in the oral traditions of the

* The extracts which follow, are selected from a part of Dr. Sibthorp's Journals describing another visit to this district of Greece.

country. My shepherd boy returned to his fold not less satisfied with some Paras that I had given him than I was in finding in such a rustic a repository of ancient science.

June 29.—We set out from Livadea about ten o'clock. In the hedges on the side of the road we observed the Cotinus, the Mastic, the Terebinth, the Coronilla, the Colutea, the Spanish broom, the myrtle. On our leaving the plain, we gradually mounted into a wild rocky country. On our arrival at Arachova, some Greeks, who kept the guard, refused to admit us within their houses; but on producing a letter from the Vaivode, they received us with much respect. Wandering parties of Albanians keep these villages in continual alarms. We slept in the guard-house, in the walls of which were loop-holes to repel sudden attacks. As we were here only four hours distant from the summit of Parnassus, we resolved to attempt the ascent.

June 30.—At day-break we set out with four of our guides; others soon joined us; the ascent was at first easy, leading by a path which conducted us up the mountain without difficulty. Our guides stopped at a fountain in the outskirts of the town, crossed themselves with much devotion, and proceeded on with cheerfulness. After mounting somewhat more than an hour, we left the road, and scrambling over steep and rough precipices arrived at a patch of snow which had collected itself in the fissures of the rock. The summit of the mountain, naked and bare, was at a considerable distance. We reached with some difficulty a Mandra or goat-stall; here we refreshed ourselves with milk, and our strength being recruited, we continued our ascent, and gained the summit. Below us extended a sheet of snow, on which I shot the Emberiza nivalis. I collected many curious plants on the sides of the precipices, though I found few which could be strictly called Alpine; those of the highest region would only be regarded as Sub-Alpine. From the top of the mountain we commanded a most extensive view of the sea of Corinth, the mountains of the Morea on the one hand, and the fertile plains of Bœotia on the other; of Attica and the island of Eubœa. An eagle

K 2

hovered over us, and the Cornix graculus, the Cornish chough, flew frequent among the rocks. Having dined on a roasted lamb, which we with difficulty had brought up to the summit, and drank our wine tempered in the crystallized snow, we descended, soon leaving the higher parts of the mountain, into a forest of pine trees. We then entered upon the plain of Callidia; the place consists of a few empty houses frequented only at certain seasons by armed Greeks, who come here to sow and reap their harvests. The corn was yet green, and promised them a thin and distant crop.

July 1. — At two in the morning we struck our tent, and passing over the plain of Callidia, descended by the steep precipices of Delphi. Our descent was difficult and dangerous; we dismounted our horses, which, though accustomed to mountainous tracks, were unable from the rocky nature of the road to keep their feet. They fell frequently, and our baggage suffered considerable damage. We arrived in three hours, much fatigued, at the convent of Delphi.

July 2 — The ruins of Delphi * are still sufficient to mark its site, placed on a rising ground, and screened by high cliffs to the north. The fountain of Castalia, excavated in a rock of marble, still exists, though choked up with weeds and stones. The only use the present Delphians, the inhabitants of Castri, draw from it, is to season their casks; some barrels, with other rubbish, served to choke up and interrupt its source. Behind it were the remains of an arched passage, hollowed in the rock. The cleft, on the east side of which was the fountain, widened at its mouth, and rising to a considerable height, ended in two points. Above the fountain were the waters of Cassotis, which still murmured. On the rocks of Delphi I observed some

---

* Some of the antiquities of Delphi are described in the MS. of San Gallo, in the Barberini Library at Rome. " In Delphis civitate, ubi magna ex parte diruta sunt vetusta atque nobilissima mœnia, diversaque sunt arte architectorum conspicua, exinde collapsum undique rotundum Apollinis templum, et amphitheatrum, juxta admirandum, magnorum lapidum gradibus xxxiii et in sublimi civitatis arce, altissimis sub rupibus ornatissimum gradibus marmoreis hippodromum DC pedum longitudinis." Broken statues, inscriptions, and " rupes incisæ arte mirabili," are mentioned.

curious plants; a new species of Daphne, which I have called Daphne Castaliensis, afforded me singular pleasure. Several birds, the Aves rupestres, inhabited these rocks; a species of Sitta different from the Europea, the Promethean vulture, the solitary sparrow, the sand martin, the rock pigeon, a small species of hawk, called Kurkenasi, and numerous jackdaws. Having dined in the monastery, and drank some meagre wine, whose flavour was not heightened by a large admixture of tar, we left Delphi, and proceeded on our route to Distomo, five hours distant from Castri, and arrived at sun-set.

July 3.—From Distomo we pursued our route to the monastery of St. Luke, where we arrived in little more than an hour. The Quercus coccifera abounds through the whole of this tract of country; one of our guides brought me a coccus adhering to a small branch of the tree, which, squeezed between my fingers, gave out a most beautiful scarlet dye. The coccus generally deposits itself on the leaves and the branches of the oak, seldom on its fruit, as Pausanias affirms (lib. x.) In our way we passed through Stiris. The monastery of St. Luke has been styled the glory of Hellas, as a Gothic structure superior to most of those that exist at present in Greece. It is greatly inferior to those magnificent piles of building, which the superstition of the early ages raised in the low countries. Chandler speaks of some curiously inlaid stones; there were beautiful large slabs of Verd-antique, which still remain in the chapel; we observed, also, in the gallery, large pieces of Phengites, probably the same mentioned by Pliny, aptly disposed to favour the notion of miracles in a place of so much reputed sanctity as the monastery of St. Luke. This sanctity was not, however, sufficient to protect it from the plunder of the Albanians, who laid it under considerable contribution. On mounting our horses we drank of the fountain which was in the court of the monastery; this seems to have escaped the notice of Chandler, who asserts that the monks fetch their water from Stiris. We descended from the monastery of St. Luke over a rough and steep road, and by dangerous precipices, to a small monastery

belonging to the convent, near the sea, about an hour distant from
the port of Asprospiti.

July 4.—I engaged a small boat belonging to the monastery, with
some Caloyers, to carry me to the islands of Didascalo and Ambelia, in
the sea of Corinth, about ten miles distant from the bay of Asprospiti.
In Didascalo there had been formerly a school. The whole island
scarcely exceeded a mile in circumference, and was covered with
ruins; at present uninhabited, except by wild pigeons, the Hirundo
Melba, and a large species of bat. Innumerable flights of the Melba
almost darkened the air, and made the island their breeding place.
We caught several of their young in the holes of the rocks. The
Hirundo Melba, mentioned as rare by Linnæus, is one of the most
frequent species of the swallow tribe in Greece. I observed it flying
over the summits of Parnassus. The Phoca vitulina we found sleeping within pistol-shot, but my gun not going off disappointed my
hopes of shooting it. The skins of these seals, our Caloyers assured
me, were sometimes sold for fifty piastres, a price much greater than
they bear in the northern climates. The vegetable productions of
the island were burnt and scorched by the sun. From Didascalo I
went to Ambelia, about half a mile distant; we discovered here no
traces of ruins; among the rocks flew immense flights of falcons,
which pursued the large owl, Strix Bubo, with shrill piercing cries;
one of these falcons was shot it proved to be the F. peregrinus of
Linnæus. I returned late to my companions; we set off for Asprospiti, anciently Anticyra, and Distomo, but could discover no trace
either of the black or white hellebore. The immediate environs of
Asprospiti present a dry sun-burnt soil. The hellebores were probably brought from the higher and colder regions of Parnassus, or
cultivated by the physicians of Anticyra in gardens.

July 5. — At six in the morning we departed for Liacoura, and
mounted gradually towards Parnassus. After a ride of somewhat more
than three hours, we arrived at the convent of Jerusalem. I wished
to ascend Parnassus a second time, and taking with me two Caloyers,
as my guides, I quitted the monastery, and then passed through a

fine forest, composed of the Pinus Picea. In somewhat more than an hour I reached some snow, lying sheltered in the chasms of the rock. Several curious plants grew here. The approach of night, the distance of the summit, and the apprehensions of banditti which alarmed my Caloyers, prevented me from proceeding further. I descended from the second summit, and reached the convent at sun-set.

July 6. — A monk of the cloister, famous for his knowledge in simples, arrived the preceding evening. I had been told of his reputation at Delphi. I walked out into the wood with him at day-break, a venerable octagenarian. I learnt from him more than one hundred names of the plants growing in the environs of the monastery; many of them were barbarous, yet most of them were significative ; some remained unaltered and uncorrupted, the ancient names of Theophrastus and Dioscorides. To all he attributed some medical virtue, some superstitious use. I regret much that the infirmities of his age would not permit me to carry him along with me to Livadea. I had offered rewards on my arrival at the convent for procuring different birds. A short time before my departure a Caloyer arrived, making a triumphant entrance, followed by two men supporting an immense vulture. I do not find it mentioned by Linnæus, though frequent in the Greek mountains. It is called ὄρνεο and λυκόρνεο ; it measured, the wings expanded, from tip to tip eight feet, and from the tip of the beak to the extremity of the tail three feet nine inches, and weighed nine okes, or twenty-two pounds and a half.

———————

In Dr. Sibthorp's Journals there is an account of his attempt to ascend Parnassus a third time. It is here inserted, being connected with some of the preceding remarks.

Sept. 11.— Soon after day-break, with two Caloyers for my guides, I began my third ascent of Parnassus, and winding along the north-east side, in about four hours reached a very high summit.   A thick fog and very deep mist obscured our view.   I saw now no snow, and was assured by the Caloyers that there was none at present on the mountains; the perennial snows, therefore, mentioned by Wheler and Chandler, are hyperbolical expressions.   I had examined Parnassus on every side, and found its vegetable productions very various. I met with several plants I had not noticed before on other parts of the mountains.   The thick mist and severe cold prevented me from continuing long on the summit, and we descended over steep precipices and torrent beds, covered with loose stones, with danger and difficulty, down the east side of the mountain.

OBSERVATIONS ON NATURAL HISTORY,

RELATING

TO PARTS OF GREECE, AND TO THE ISLAND OF CYPRUS

[FROM THE PAPERS OF THE LATE DR SIBTHORP.]

WE had observed a small number of wild animals in Cyprus, but the heights of Parnassus, and the mountains of Hymettus and Pendeli furnish a retreat to many, and considerably encrease the list of Grecian Mammalia. My enquiries were frequent, but the inaccessible haunts of some of these animals, and the difficulty of procuring others, made it almost impossible for me to determine the number of species with precision. The domestic animals in Attica and Bœotia are the same as those in Cyprus, excepting the camel, which is not used in Greece; it is very common throughout Asia Minor. Pausanias mentions the bear as an inhabitant of Pendeli; about three years since one was shot in the mountains of Parnassus, and brought to Aracova. The lynx, the wild cat, the wild boar, the wild goat, the stag, the roebuck, the badger, the martin, and squirrel, inhabit the steeper rocks of Parnassus, and the thick pine-forests above Callidia. The rough mountains about Marathon are frequented by wolves, foxes, and jackalls; weasels are sometimes taken in the villages and out-houses, hares are too numerous to be particularised. The mole burrows in the rich ground of Livadea*; the hedge-hog was brought

---

* This passage does not agree with the remark of Aristotle, who says (lib. viii. c. 27), " that there are no moles at Lebadea, but many about Orchomenus." On the other hand Antigonus C (c. 10), and the author De Mirabil (c. 136), and Stephanus Byz. in v. Κορώνεια, say, that moles abound in Bœotia, but that they are not seen at Coronea, making no mention of Lebadea. See Schneider in Aris. II. A. viii. c. 27.

to me in the environs of Athens; the amphibious otter is found in
the rivers and marshes of Bœotia. The Phoca or sea-calf frequents
the rocks of Didascalo, and Ambelia in the sea of Corinth; and the
porpoise is seen often on the coast of Attica. The small species
of bat flutters about Athens late in the evening, and the larger
species inhabits the caverns and holes of the rocks in the island of
Didascalo.

The nomenclature of the birds of Attica compared with the ancient
names of Aristotle would prove a valuable commentary on that
author. The ornithologist who resided for some time at Athens
would be enabled to clear up many of the obscure passages of that
great naturalist; but he should remain there for a considerable
period, mark the migration of the different birds of passage; the
time of their arrival; then disappearance; note down the popular
observations, and the different variations in their nomenclature.
My catalogue is imperfect, but it is interesting, as being the only
one that has ever been made of the Grecian birds; it contains such
as I saw myself, and some few of the existence of which I was
assured upon the best authorities. Of the Accipitres, a large species
of vulture, called by the Greeks όgνεο, frequents the cliffs of Delphi,
and the woods and precipices of Parnassus; the smaller species,
called Aspropar os, I observed near Liacoura. Of the falcon tribe,
I saw a large species, called by our guides Aetos, and probably the
Falco Chrysaetos, soaring over the heights of Pendeli. The Falco
Ierax breeds in the islands of Didascalo and Ambelia in the sea of
Corinth. The Falco Kirkenasi, half domestic, arrives early in the
spring with the storks, in immense numbers, joint inhabitant with
them of the houses and temples of the Athenians, and retires with
these birds at the latter end of August. I observed a large grey
hawk of the Buzzard kind on the plain of Marathon; another
species brown, with a white band on the wings, flying over the
plain of Livadea; and a small dark hawk skimming the ground near
Cape Sunium. My short stay at this place not permitting me to

procure specimens, I was unable to determine the species. Of the owls, the horned owl is rare, I saw it in the island Ambelia; and I heard it hoot among the rocks near Livadea, it sometimes, though rarely, visits Athens. Dr. Chandler had kept one during his stay there, which he released on his leaving Athens; he tells us, it was visited by the Athenians as a curiosity. The little owl, Strix passerina, is the most common species in Greece, and abounds in the neighbourhood of Athens. Three distinct species of Butcher-bird are frequent among the olive grounds; the ash-coloured, the red-headed, and the small grey Butcher-bird. The two last species I do not find described by Linnæus.

Of the crow tribe, I observed the raven, the hooded crow, the jackdaw, the magpie, and the Cornish chough. The hooded crow which retires from England during the summer, is a constant inhabitant of Attica, and is probably that species noticed by the ancients under the name of κολοιός. It is the word applied at present to it by the Greek peasants, who are the best commentators on the old naturalists. Linnæus seems injudiciously to have applied it to the Carrion crow. Jackdaws abound at Athens, and are frequently seen flying round the Acropolis. The Cornish chough which generally confines itself to the mountainous parts of Greece, and inhabits the broken cliffs and caverns of Parnassus, sometimes descends into the plains; we observed it under the eastern coast of Attica. The roller frequents the fruit gardens, and the outskirts of villages and the olive grounds. The cuckoo is heard early in the spring, but its season of calling was now past. The Sitta, which I regard as a new species, distinct from the Sitta Europæa was shot on the rocks at Delphi. I saw the king's fisher flying along the eastern coast of Greece in the gulph of Negropont. The Merops invited by the bee-hives of Hymettus appears about Athens, at the latter end of summer. The hoopoe which I also observed, is here a bird of passage. Of the duck tribe, various species visit the salt lakes, and shores of the coast of Attica during the winter; these retire during the summer to more unfrequented fresh water lakes, and deep mo-

rasses to breed undisturbed   Tame geese, and ducks, are kept as
domestic birds, but are not common.   We shot two species of the
storm-finch on the Saronic Gulph; these we observed frequent on
the wing flying along the Ægæan Sea, particularly when it was
troubled   We noticed the common sea-gull, the common sea-
swallow, and a smaller species, probably the Sterna minuta

The winter and the early spring would be the most proper season
of the year for the naturalist to observe the different species of the
Grecian grallæ.   Woodcocks, and snipes, I was informed, visited the
neighbourhood of Athens during the winter in considerable quantities.   I heard the curlew and the red-shank cry along the marsh to
the right of the Piræus.   The domestic stork, a privileged bird,
arrives regularly at Athens, sometimes in the month of March, and
leaves it when the young are able to support the fatigues of a long
flight, about the middle of August.   The purple and the grey heron
frequent the marshes of Bœotia.   We observed the long-legged
plover near Marathon , the grey plover and the sand plover on the
eastern coast of Attica.   Wheler makes mention of the Charadrius
spinosus which he shot in Bœotia.   Bustards, I was assured, visited
the plain of Athens during the winter in abundance   Fowls are
the most common species of poultry, and turkeys are also kept.
The red-legged partridge abounds every where, and probably the
grey might be found in the environs of Parnassus   I heard quails
call, but could not learn the particular times of their migrations.
Wild pigeons are frequent among the rocks.   The turtle and the
wood-pigeon are found in the woods and thickets   Among the larks,
I observed the Crested-lark to be the most frequent species, with a
small sort, probably the Alauda Campestris of Linnæus.   I saw the
Alauda Calandra, but it was very rare, and a thin slender species near
the sea coast, probably the Spinoletta of Linnæus.   Blackbirds frequent the olive grounds of Pendeli , the solitary sparrow inhabits the
cliffs of Delphi, and the song thrush is heard in the pine woods of
Parnassus.   Above these, where the heights of the mountain are

covered with snow, is seen the Emberiza Nivalis, inhabitant alike of
the frozen Spitsbergen, and of the Grecian Alp.

The bunting, the yellow-hammer, and a species of Emberiza nearly
related to it, frequent the low bushes in the neighbourhood of corn
fields. Of the Finch tribe, the sparrow is the most common species;
we observed the goldfinch and the linnet; the Fringilla flaveola,
which I had seen in Cyprus, is not unfrequent about Athens. Of
the wagtail and slender-billed birds, the wheat-ear is the most general species throughout Greece, inhabitant equally of the highest
mountains, and lowest plains. The white water-wagtail we found
on the banks of rivulets, and still waters; and the redstart near the
shore on the eastern coast of Attica. Various are the species of
Motacilla, confounded under the general name of Beccafica; one
species, which I take to be the true sort, I shot in the olive grounds
of Pendeli, another sort, somewhat larger, near Athens, and a small
minute species often concealing itself among the bushes near Sunium.
Of the swallow tribe I observed all the European species, except the
Pratincola. The melba we found twittering in immense numbers over
the island of Didascalo, where it lives with the large bat in the holes
of the rocks. The sand martin burrows in the cliffs of Delphi, the
goat-sucker retains its ancient name, and still lies under the accu-
sation brought against it by Aristotle of sucking the goats.

CYPRUS

WE find in Cyprus * a much smaller number of quadrupeds than
we should expect from the size of the island. The domestic animals,

---

* Dr S. observed in Cyprus a custom which has prevailed in different parts of the East
from the earliest times, and is mentioned by sacred and profane writers. " In the Greek
village of Ipsera, five hours from Famagusta, the girls of the place, as a relief to their sun-
burnt faces, had stained their eyelids. On inquiring respecting the nature of the process,
I found that these village coquettes had used no more costly paint than lamp-black; this,
mixed with oil, was drawn through their eyelids on a small iron roller." See also Sonnini, p 170.

if we except the camel, are nearly the same as those of Crete,
and the other Greek islands; and its wild quadrupeds, when compared with the neighbouring coast of Asia, are very few. It possesses
neither the lynx, nor the wolf, nor the jackall, inhabitants of the
opposite shore of Caramania; and the weasel tribe is totally wanting,
of which we find some species in Crete. The wild boar inhabits
Cape Gatto, and the Gazella, the higher parts of Mount * Troados.
Hares are scarce, and seem to confine themselves to the mountainous
tracts of the island. The hedge-hog, I was also informed, was an inhabitant. The large bat was mentioned, but I only found the common
species. Asses, I heard on good authority, were found in a wild state
at Carpaso, and that it was permitted to any person to hunt them;
but that, when caught, they were of little value, it being almost impossible, from their natural obstinacy, to domesticate them.

The naturalist, disappointed in finding so small a number of quadrupeds, is surprised on observing the great variety of birds which
migrate to Cyprus at different seasons of the year. The birds of the
thrush tribe, inhabitants of the northern climates, visit it only during
the depth of winter. At the first appearance of spring they retire to
the higher mountains of Caramania, where, the snow preserving a
constant humidity, they find food and a proper habitation. Great

---

* A neoteric Greek, quoted by Du Cange, in the word Βουκας, says, "That the mountain Boukasa, which reaches to the foot of Troados, contains mines of gold." Mr. Hawkins, in a letter answering a question sent to him by the editor respecting this passage,
supposes the remark to be incorrect, and at variance with the more ancient authorities.
"It is not probable," he says, "that the Phœnicians who possessed Cyprus, and opened
their mines there, should have left those of gold undiscovered. I conceive the report
might have originated in this manner: at the foot of Mount Troados, on the north, about
half way to the sea coast, are some low hills bordering on the vale of Solea, where I found
immense heaps of the scoria or slags of smelting furnaces. They occur in two places,
Leíca and Skourgotisa, and appear to have been produced by the smelting of iron or of
copper. The ore must have been dug higher up. The strata of Mount Troados consist
of a kind of Trapp rock, a mixture of Hornblende and Felspar, in which rocks, as far as
my knowledge extends, no gold mines have been found in any part of the world."

numbers of Grallæ pass over in the spring from Egypt and Syria; these retreat farther, in proportion as the salt pools near Larnica are evaporated by the sun.   The Francolin and red partridge reside throughout the year; the Pardalos [*] and the quail visit the island in the spring, and retire in the autumn.   Immense flights of ortolans appear about the time of the vintage; these are taken in great quantities, preserved in vinegar, and exported as an object of commerce. The swallow, the martin, the swift, the Melba, the Pratincola, which frequent in numbers the pools of Larnica, visit also the island in spring and leave it in the autumn.   Those large birds which frequent the higher regions of Troados, called by the inhabitants Aëra, I should suppose from their flight to be a species of vulture.   The Falco Tinnunculus breeds here, but the difficulty of procuring the birds of this tribe prevented me from ascertaining the number of species with more precision.   The raven, the hooded crow, the jackdaw, the magpye, are common.   The jay is found but rarely in the pine-woods of Troados.   The little owl, though a nocturnal bird, flies frequently by day among the rocks.   The great horned owl, which I did not see, is found in the mountainous parts of the island.   The roller, the bee-bird, and the oriole are not uncommon; and we often heard the hoopoe and the cuckow.   I observed the rock-pigeon on the cliffs in the western extremity of the island; the wood-pigeon and the turtle-dove in the groves of Bel-paese.   The Calandra and the Crested-lark are the most common species of the lark tribe, and these inhabit the island probably throughout the year.   The two species of Lanius confine themselves to the pine-woods with the black titmouse.   Different species of the Motacilla are confounded under the general name of Beccafica.   Of the Fringilla tribe, the house-sparrow is the most numerous; and the beautiful Scarthalis, perhaps the Fringilla flaveola of Linnæus, rivals the nightingale in the charms of its song,

---

[*] " Near the Salines we shot a very rare bird of the Tetrao kind, Tetrao Alchata, called by the Greeks Pardalos."   Sibthorp's MS.   This bird is described in Russell's Aleppo, ii. 191.

and is sometimes confounded with it under the general name of
Ἀγέα.. Among the domestic birds, I observed a few turkeys in the
convent of the Archangel; geese and ducks are kept, but not in great
numbers Fowls and pigeons are the principal domestic birds.
During my stay in the island, I used every possible means to procure
its birds, and succeeded in obtaining the greater part of them. Of
the rarer species of these my draftsman has taken drawings. I have
been also fortunate in procuring most of the Greek names but it is
much to be regretted that Cyprus has hitherto wanted an ornithologist, who being stationary here might observe with more exactness
the migration of the different birds of the Levant.

On observing the list of amphibia, we are surprised at finding the
Testudo Caretta, mentioned by Linnæus as an inhabitant of the West
India islands, and no notice of the Testudo Aquatilis common through
Greece and Asia Minor. The genus Coluber and Lacerta are both
rich in the number of their species; of these, fortunately for the
island, the Κούφι is the only venomous species. The black snake,
whose colour is indeed suspicious, is perfectly harmless, and I was
informed by the physician of Larnica, that among the country
people it is even an object of affection; that they suffer it to twist and
twine itself in the hair round the heads of their children, as a remedy
for the Tinea capitis. * I searched in vain for the Lacerta aurea, said
by Linnæus to be the inhabitant of Cyprus, but I am perfectly convinced from a very attentive inquiry after the tribe, that it is not to be
found in the island, an inaccuracy in the information of the collectors
must probably have led Linnæus into this mistake. The Testudo
Caretta is not only an inhabitant of the Cyprian sea, but is the most
common species in the Mediterranean, and the Lacerta aurea is not

* " The skin of a snake," says Sonnini, in his Travels in Egypt, " is worn in the turban, as a preservative against diseases of the head " p 681 " The Tinea is very common
in parts of Syria, and is the natives are unwilling that the heads of girls should be shaved,
these suffer more from it than the boys." Russell, ii 304.

an inhabitant of Cyprus, but of the south of France, Germany, and Italy. Of the six species of Coluber which we find in the island, I can scarcely refer any of them to the Linnæan species.

The classical ichthyologist receives a particular pleasure from comparing the modern Greek names of the Cyprian fishes, with those of Oppian, Aristotle, and other writers. The Scarus, which the Swedish naturalist affirms to be *piscis hodie obscurus*, is known to every Cyprian boy. Belon, guided by the Cretan fishermen, found it on the rocky shores of Crete. These fishermen are much better commentators on the Greek ichthyologists than their learned editors, who, by their unfortunate conjectures, more frequently confuse than clear a doubtful text. The striking agreement of the modern Greek names with those of ancient Greece is no where so evident as in Cyprus. Here we still find the words Μόρμυρος, σπάρος, σκάρος, σαργὸς, σάλπα, μελάνουρος, πέρκα, ὀρφος, and others precisely the ancient names of Oppian and Aristotle. They are very properly retained by Linnæus for trivial names. The shores of Cyprus receive a great number of Mediterranean fishes ; some of these confine themselves to its rocks, and seldom emigrate into more northern latitudes. In river fish, it is, as we should expect to find it, deficient ; the rivulets, few in number, and inconsiderable in their size, generally dried up in summer, do not lead us to expect a large catalogue of river fish · and upon repeated inquiries I found that the eel was their only inhabitant. My list of Grecian fishes was already very considerable when I arrived at Cyprus ; the market of Constantinople had furnished me with those of the Thracian Bosphorus and the sea of Marmora. I had still, however, hopes of discovering some other species in the more southern latitude of the Mediterranean Cyprus did not deceive my expectation . I added several species of Labrus and Sparus to my collection ; among these the Labrus Cretensis, which, from its more vivid colours, and the superior elegance of its figure, carries off the palm of beauty from the L. Iulis, cited by Linnæus as *Europæorum facile pulcherrimus.*

M

The greater number of the Grecian islands have been examined by a botanist of the distinguished merit of Tournefoit. Cyprus, from its situation and its size, gives us reason to expect a peculiarity as well as a variety in its vegetables; and it is with surprise that we find an island so interesting in its natural productions has been little examined. Hasselquist visited it on his return from Egypt, at a season of the year when its annual plants, which form the greater number of its vegetables, were burnt up by the summer sun ; and Pococke, a better antiquary than botanist, has given us only a scanty account of some of them. A view of its Flora, and comparison of the modern and popular uses of the plants with those of ancient Greece, gave me hopes in an island so near to Caramania, the native country of Dioscorides, of ascertaining several of the more obscure plants of this author. My expectations have in some measure succeeded ; the modern names, though greatly corrupted, still retain sufficient resemblance to those of ancient Greece, to enable us to determine many plants with certainty ; and the superstitious and popular uses of many still remain the same. My inquiries were frequent among the Greek peasants, and the different priests whom we met. From the physician of Larnica I collected some information relative to their medical uses.

I crossed the island in different directions. Cyprus, though possessing several of the Egyptian and Syrian plants, yet, from the scarcity of water, the great heat of the sun, and the thin surface which covers the upper regions of the mountains, can scarcely be considered as rich in plants ; and when compared with Crete must appear even poor: the sides of whose mountains, those, for instance, of Ida and Sphakia, are watered with streams supplied from the perpetual snows that crown their summits Notwithstanding the character of woody given to it by Strabo, when measured by a northern eye, accustomed to the extensive woods of oak and beech that we find in some parts of England, or the sombre pine-forests of Switzerland, Cyprus appears to have little claim to the appellation of woody. The higher regions of Troados are covered with the Pinus Pinea ; this, mixed with the Ilex, and some trees scattered here and there in the valley below of the Quercus Ægilops, are the only trees that can be regarded as proper for timber. The carob, the olive, the Andrachne, the Terebinthus, the lentisc, the kermes oak, the Storax, the cypress, and oriental plane, furnish not only fuel in abundance for the inhabitants, but sufficient to supply, in some degree, those of Egypt.

ASIA MINOR.

JOURNEY FROM PARIUM TO THE TROAD — ASCENT TO THE SUMMIT OF IDA — THE SALT SPRINGS OF TOUSLA — RUINS OF ASSOS

CHAP I

Libraries at Constantinople. — *Departure from that city.* — *Sea of Marmora* — *Cephus of the ancient Greeks* — *Parium* — *Lampsacus* — *Dardanelles.*

An opinion had long been prevalent that the libraries in the palaces of the Grand Seignior, and in the city of Constantinople, contained some valuable Greek manuscripts which had escaped the destruction occasioned by the Turks in the year 1453. The imperial mosques there, particularly that of Saint Sophia, the libraries of the Patriarchs of the Eastern church, and of the Greek monasteries in the Levant, were also supposed to contain many curious medited writings. This general belief of the existence of unexplored literary treasures in Turkey induced the English government to appoint a person well versed in classical, biblical, and oriental literature, to accompany the Earl of Elgin's embassy to the Ottoman Porte in the year 1799. The plan originated with Mr. Pitt and the Bishop of Lincoln, who thought that an embassy sent at a time when Great Britain was on the most friendly terms with the Porte, would afford great facilities for ascertaining how far these hopes of literary discovery were well founded. They trusted that the ambassador's influence would obtain permission for the transcription at least, if not for the acquisition of any unpublished work that might be found.

The Rev. Mr. Carlyle, Professor of Arabic in the University of Cambridge, was prevailed upon to engage in this service, and the choice reflects great credit on the judgment of those who applied to a person so peculiarly qualified for the task. During our residence at Constantinople, Mr. Carlyle and myself visited all the monasteries of the Greek monks, or Caloyers, on the Princes' islands, in the sea of Marmora. Their names are Prinkipo, Chalke, Prote, Antigone, Oxia, Platia. The manuscripts in their libraries did not contain a single classical fragment; but there were many copies on paper and vellum of different parts of the New Testament, written apparently about the 11th, 12th, and 13th centuries; the most beautiful of these we bought from the monks, who use printed books in the service of the church, and attach little value to their ancient manuscripts. These are now deposited in the Archbishop of Canterbury's library at Lambeth.

In the collegiate-house belonging to the Greek Patriarch of Jerusalem, who resides at Constantinople*, we found a very well furnished library, including a considerable number of manuscripts, the greater part of them on subjects connected with theology and ecclesiastical history; but none of them of very high antiquity. There were also a few detached fragments of some of the Greek classics. The Patriarch behaved to us with the utmost liberality, not only sending one of his chaplains to assist us in making a catalogue of the library, but allowing us to take any of the manuscripts we might wish to send to England for the purpose of being examined and collated. Such as we thought interesting or curious were forwarded to London, along with those procured from the Princes' islands; and they are now in the archiepiscopal library at Lambeth.

We had some difficulties to overcome before admission could be obtained into the rooms attached to the mosque of Saint Sophia, the

---

* Possevin, in his Apparatus sacer, T. 2 mentions some of the works in the libraries of the Patriarch, and in different parts of Constantinople.

libraries in the Seraglio, and those belonging to the schools, mosques, and colleges of Dervises at Constantinople. The influence of Lord Elgin at length prevailed; but in none of those vast collections of books was there a single classical fragment of a Greek or Latin author, either original or translated. The volumes were in Arabic, Persian, or Turkish · and of all of them Mr. Carlyle took exact catalogues.

The result of our labours previous to his taking a final leave of Constantinople was, that we examined every library within our reach which was likely to contain any valuable manuscript; and that we sent to London twenty-seven codices of different parts of the New Testament, besides an Arabic and a Persian version. In addition to these, Mr. Carlyle procured a number of oriental manuscripts relating to history and poetry; these, since his decease, have been purchased by the East India Company. It was among his favourite pursuits to collect authentic documents for a complete history of the Crusades; and he also had it in contemplation to give a new version of the " Thousand and one Nights." *

Mr. Carlyle's health had suffered so much during his residence in Turkey, that he would not venture alone upon a journey to Macedonia, in order to examine the libraries of the Greek convents on the peninsula of Athos; he requested, therefore, that Lord Elgin would allow me to accompany him. We preferred going by sea, as we might thus have an opportunity of visiting the plain of Troy, and the islands of Tenedos and Lemnos. We procured a firman or official permission from the Porte for travelling in Asia Minor and Greece, and a recommendatory letter from the Greek Patriarch to the Council of Deputies, who govern the religious community at Mount Athos. The arms on

---

* The Arabic title is " Hakaiat Elf Leily wa Leily," *Stories, a Thousand and one Nights.* Dr. Russell, found at Aleppo two volumes; they contained only two hundred and eighty nights, but he procured a number of separate tales, some of which he thinks may possibly belong to the Elf Leily, and he remarks that many of those published at Edinburgh in 1792, as a continuation of the Arabian Nights, were to be found in his collection. i. 386.

the seal were a spread eagle and imperial crown; a sceptre and the
keys of St. Peter, with the Patriarch's name, Neophytus, Patriarch of
Constantinople.

On the 3d of March, 1801, we quitted Constantinople, and passed.
on the 4th, the island of Proconnesus *, now called Marmora, on
account of its quarries of coarse greyish marble, of which a great
quantity is sent in slabs and blocks to Constantinople for the pavement
of mosques and baths, and for making tomb-stones. The quantity
imported for this purpose from Marmora, and from the islands of the
Archipelago, is incredible; the cemeteries of the Turks, Greeks,
Armenians, and Jews, round Constantinople, could now supply marble for building a large city. But mosques and public baths and
sepulchral monuments are the only objects that most of the inhabitants of Turkey think worthy of durable materials: the possession of
private property is too precarious to induce them to build a solid
house; their residences are, in consequence, a kind of slight, but
gaudily painted wooden barrack.

The wind being against us, we beat about the entrance of the
Hellespont, where we noticed a tumulus on the European shore; but
making no progress for two days, we cast anchor in a small port on
the Asiatic shore called Camaris. Here we landed and purchased
some medals, those of silver having the letters ΠΑΡΙ round an antique

---

* This place supplied the ancient Greeks with marble for their Sarcophagi, we find
mention of a Σορὸς Προκοννήσια, and ἀγγεῖον Προκοννήσιον, in Patin 222

" Sept 1794 — The marble is a white granulated species with greyish stripes, and is
employed for the fountains, baths, and vases, which ornament the light and airy palaces of
the Sultanas on the banks of the Bosphorus   I picked up on the coast of Marmora three
sorts of sponges, the common officinal one, the oculata, and another, which, from its dense
texture, I shall call compacta   Our Greek sailors gave them the general name σπουγγάρι.
From the quantity I observed of the common sponge, I conceived a fishery might be established here with advantage.   I saw only a few shells, but picked up a stone cast on the
shore, perforated by Pholades, and two or three sorts of Serpulæ encrusted the rocks.
Some Manks Puffins flew by the side of our vessel, which our sailors called κάφας, I have
no doubt the Cephus of the ancient Greeks, though Linnæus makes it a species of Larus
or gull."   From Dr Sibthorp's Journals.

mask, and the copper the same abbreviation round an altar, on which incense is burning. As these were frequently found here, we were convinced that we were on the site of Parium, where Priapus had a temple raised to him, after his worship had been suppressed with ignominy at Lampsacus. The walls of this city, which fronted the sea, still remain, and are built of large blocks of squared marble without mortar. We saw ruins of an aqueduct, reservoirs for water, and the fallen architraves of a portico. There are also some subterranean buildings, whose arched roofs incline or dip from the horizontal level. As Καμαρα means both *arch* and *aqueduct*, we can be at no loss for the derivation of Camaris, the modern name of the town. The circuit of ancient Parium has been about four miles. The only inscriptions we found were built into the walls of the modern village, and are merely epitaphs of private individuals. We transcribe two of them

ΠΟΠΛΙΟΣ ΚΑΙ ΚΑ   ΔΙΟΦΑΝΤΗΣ
ΚΟΙΝΤΟΣ ΓΟΝΕΥΣΙΝ* ΓΑΜΕΙΝΟΝΟΣ
ΜΝΗΜΗΣ ΧΑΡΙΝ   ΧΑΙΡΕ

As the wind continued unfavourable for us, we took what articles we might want out of our ship, leaving an English servant on board to meet us with the remainder of our baggage at the Dardanelles. As this village would only furnish three horses for ourselves and our interpreter, we took the owner of one of them, as a guide, on foot, and were rejoiced at this opportunity, which unexpectedly presented itself, of viewing the shores of the Hellespont.

We set out, March 6th, from Camaris, at about half-past twelve o'clock, and in a short time came to two ruined arches of an aqueduct, which had supplied Parium with water. Here a bridge crosses the

---

* The Abbé Belley, in the 34th vol of the Mémoires de l'Académie des I observes, Je ne me souviens pas d'avoir vû sur aucune inscription l'expression καὶ τοῖς γονεῦσι, elle est singulière P. 618. See Gruter's Thes Append 1127

rivulet ; the Turkish name of the stream is Satal Tepé Sou, or the river of Mount Satal, where it rises, about five hours distance up the country, and where our guide told us there were ruins. About three hours from Camaris we came to a rich plain called Coroo Dere, or the Dry Valley, and, after crossing a hill, another vale opened upon us. The season of spring was now commencing, and every patch of grass was covered with anemones of the most vivid hues, scarlet, white, and blue ; these were intermixed with the crocus, asphodel, hyacinth, and purple orchis ; on the hills the variety of shrubs was very great. We saw the Arbutus Andrachne and Unedo, the sweet bay, the Ilex, the wild olive ; many kinds of broom, heath, the Spina Christi, wild vine and clematis.

Towards sun-set we reached a Turkish village called Jouragee. The almond trees scattered among the cottages were in full blosso m Here we found that Lampsacus was too far off for our tired horses to reach it that night. The husband of a woman, whom we had accosted, was returning from wood-cutting, he examined our appearance, and offered us the shelter of a hovel for ourselves and horses, which we were glad to accept. He then kindled a large wood fire in a corner of it, where there was a hole in the roof, and after partaking of our coffee, he gave us pipes and tobacco, and began to converse familiarly. Jouragee, he told us, contains sixty families, all Turks, each of them having a piece of land in the valley, and a few sheep and goats on the mountains. At harvest time the Aga of the district sends a person to measure the produce of each farm, and to take the tenth ; the only fixed or permanent tax which a Turk pays in this part of Anatolia. The tribute belongs to the Sultan, who sells it to some Bey or Pasha of a province for a certain sum , it is then farmed out to the Agas of smaller districts, who generally take it in kind. This tenth extends to all the fruits of the earth , but that of corn is the only one rigidly exacted a moderate composition is taken for fruit, pulse, and veget-ables, except by very sordid Agas Our host complained of the war, in which the Sultan was then engaged with the French, saying that though his land did not produce above 120 bushels of wheat, and his

N

flock was but small, yet that he paid an extraordinary war-tax last
year of 200 piastres (or 15*l*.)　He then abused the corrupt government of the Porte, and said that the Turks themselves would not be
sorry to see it overturned.　He next complained of the excesses committed by the troops on their route to the Vizier's camp in Syria,
adding that whenever news came that they were on their road towards
Jouragee, the wretched inhabitants run off to the mountains with
their little property, and live in tents there, until the soldiers have
passed.

In one of the cottages we saw the fragment of a Greek inscription,
and another on a small stone altar near it, now used as a block for
mounting on horseback; it informs us that Lucius Valerius Eutychus
consecrated or erected it to the memory of his mother and daughter.

As the accommodation for sleeping consisted only of a dirty mat
and an uneven mud floor, we were not induced to pass a long night
at Jouragee.　We therefore set off at three o'clock in the morning
by moon-light, and riding through extensive woods we again came
to the shore of the Hellespont.　On our road we met some caravans
of loaded camels; they were in strings of five, with an ass for the
leader of each division.　We now and then saw a sculptured turban,
or a heap of earth without any head-stone, by the road-side; these,
our guide told us, marked the graves of travellers who had been murdered there, probably itinerant Jews or Greeks, about whose fate no
inquiry was ever made by the Aga of the district.　The face of the
country was diversified with well wooded hills, and in every valley
was a little glittering stream, meandering into the Hellespont.　In a
large plain, we saw the huts of the herdsmen, who breed great numbers of camels here.　At this season, the males of this quiet race of
animals entirely change their character, and become so ferocious, that
it requires all the care of the herdsmen to prevent them from tearing each other to pieces.　At Smyrna, and other great towns in
Anatolia, camel fights are among the favorite amusements of the
people.

At half-past nine we reached a Turkish village called Sarthaki.
The porch of the mosque is supported by granite pillars, with marble
capitals of different orders; they appear to have originally belonged
to some church of the lower Greek empire. At the public fountain
we saw three granite sarcophagi, with inscriptions much defaced.

We did not reach Lampsacus until eleven o'clock, though it is only
six hours distant from Jouragee. On our arrival we went to the house
of the Papas or Greek priest, where we breakfasted. We could not,
however, avoid the intrusive curiosity of the Turks, and we had a perpetual succession of these troublesome visitors, who seemed glad to
shew us how much the poor Greek priest stood in awe of them.

On our going to the Bazar or market, some of them seemed disposed to insult us, but on our giving a few pieces of money to a
begging dervise, they became more civil. An Armenian shopkeeper
shewed us a small antique vase of ancient Greek, or, as some have
called it, Etruscan workmanship; he had also a few old copper medals,
but he placed so high a value on his curiosities that we declined purchasing them. Vases, similar to that which he shewed us, were often
found, he said, in old burial places in the neighbourhood. In Lampsacus we discovered not one ruin or vestige of ancient buildings.
Its wine, once so celebrated, is now among the worst that is made in
this part of Anatolia. The town contains a mixed population of
Turks, Greeks, Armenians, and Jews, amounting to about five hundred and fifty families.

At a quarter past twelve we resumed our journey. A river, called
Chiergee, runs near Lampsacus, and two hours from thence we met
another winding stream, which falls into the Hellespont at a point
projecting very far towards the European coast. We then passed a
village called Beeigan, on the banks of this river. Its situation on
a sloping hill, with clumps of trees left in picturesque spots round it,
and a clear stream running in the valley, formed a very beautiful
landscape. Indeed the whole of this shore furnishes a continual succession of the richest scenery.

Four hours from Lampsacus, and about a mile from the coast, we saw the ruined wall of some ancient Greek town. The Turks call the spot Gangerlee; we then crossed two rivulets, Yapoudak and Moosah; one of these is the ancient Rhodius, and when we reached the fertile and picturesque vale of Karajource, the promontory of Narla, on which Abydos once stood, came in view. After passing the Turkish village of Karadjo, we reached the town of the Darda-nelles about seven o'clock in the evening.

Here we lodged at the house of Signor Tarragona, a Jew, whose family has held the consulship of England for a long series of years. The Feast of the Passover had brought many members of it together. The Jews here, generally, marry at about eighteen years of age, the girls at a much younger period of life. One of the wives in this family, who was in her eighteenth year, was already mother of three children. A daughter, only fourteen years old, had been some months married, and Rachel, the youngest, a beautiful girl of thirteen, had already, as her father told us, been asked in marriage by three suitors.

The town of the Dardanelles is called by the Turks Chanak Kalesi, and by the Greeks, from the situation of the neighbouring forts, τὰ μέσα Κάστρα, The middle Castles, being about midway in the Hellespont. The only garrison we saw here consisted of three or four Topgees, or Turkish gunners, whose employment consists in re-turning the salutes of ships of war. The cannon, of which there are a great number, are on very clumsy carriages; on the battlements are light field pieces. In the great battery are guns of various calibre, and those on a level with the water are enormous; the bore of them is nearly three feet. We saw a pyramidal pile of granite shot for these huge cannon, which our Consul told us were cut out of columns found at Eski Stambol (ancient Constantinople), a name given by the Turks to Alexandria Troas. Instead of carriages, strong levers and pullies are used to work this massive artillery. At the Darda-nelles, there are about two thousand families, mostly Turks; and as it is a place of some trade, the Jews have a quarter allotted them, containing about three hundred houses and a synagogue.

Provisions of every kind are very plentiful in this neighbourhood; but we observed that within the town the price of every article of food was double of what we had paid in our journey. This arose from the exactions of the governor, who exercises a monopoly on the corn and meal sold here.

In Turkey most things are sold by weight, such as oil, wine, fruit, and corn. The oke is about 2¾lb. avoirdupoise, or 400 drachms; the cantar is 40 okes, nearly a hundred weight English; and the kilo of grain is reckoned equivalent to an English bushel. The coins are paras and piastres; a para is about the value of an English halfpenny; 40 paras make a piastre, which varies according to the exchange from 1s. 6d. to 1s. 8d. sterling. Having premised this, I may now be understood when I mention the price of provisions.

Wheat was at 100 paras per kilo at Gallipoli, a town nearly opposite to us; at the Dardanelles it was five piastres, almost eight shillings a bushel. Mutton had been also raised from 10 to 18 paras an oke, or from near 2d. per pound to 3½d.; good red wine was six paras an oke, not 2½d. a quart.

We did not here discover any traces of the ancient town of Dardanus, nor any antiquities, but what had been brought from the Troad by Jews in the hope of selling them to English travellers. Among these was a female statue from Chiblak, a few hours distant up the country. This I procured for Lord Elgin, in whose collection it now is.

CHAP. II

Hellespont — Sigean Inscription — Tombs of Achilles and Ajax — Camara Sou –Inscription of the time of the Seleucidæ. — Gheumbrek Sou — Atche Keui.

MARCH 7. — Before we commenced our tour of the Troad, we were formally introduced by our Hebrew Consul to Hadim Oglou the governor of the Dardanelles; to whom it was necessary to exhibit our firman or passport. He received us in great state, and assured us, that he would give orders to render our excursion through his territory, as comfortable as it could be made to us. Hadim Oglou has not only the important command of the entrance of the Dardanelles, but is also Pasha, and hereditary feudal chieftain of the whole district which we intended to explore. He is one of the richest individuals in Turkey; for he not only has vast estates in the neighbourhood and the adjoining parts of Anatolia, but he receives enormous bribes from the Greek merchants, who carry on the commerce of these seas under the Russian flag, while the crews are Ottoman subjects, as well as from Austrian, Ragusan, and other trading vessels, for conniving at their contraband exportation of wheat and other prohibited commodities. He however is subject, in his turn, to heavy contributions from the Capudan Pasha, who is not ignorant of the illicit traffic. Lately, in his expedition to Egypt, he anchored at the Dardanelles, where he not only made Hadim Oglou supply the whole Turkish fleet and transports with biscuit for their voyage, but levied a hundred purses on him, about 4000*l.* Indeed the Capudan Pasha, in his annual cruise to collect the tribute of the isles of the Archipelago, uniformly honors Hadim Oglou with a visit to receive his homage, accompanied with a handsome present in sequins. But these are far from being the only drains from his coffers; complaints frequently reach the Porte of his connivance at smuggling and of his monopolies; he therefore finds it his interest to have regular spies at Constantinople, to give him early intelligence of any complaints against him, and often, to preserve his wealth from confiscation and his neck from the bow-string, he is forced to send forty or fifty purses to some powerful favourite at court. And so corrupt is the administration of the Turkish exchequer, that instead of having an active and independent inspector of the customs at the Dardanelles to counteract the rapa-city and peculation of the governor, Hadim Oglou's son-in-law fills that office; and thus he is left without any real or effective control.

On presenting to him our firman, and a recommendatory letter which we had obtained from the Capudan Pasha, he not only gave us a bouyurdee or passport addressed to all the Beys and Agas of his province, but insisted on sending an officer of his guard to accompany us throughout our tour in the Troad. We hired a boat to take us to Cape Yenichei, for which we paid fifteen piastres, the force of the current aided by a fresh northern breeze, carried us to that pro-montory in less than two hours; our boat glided so swiftly down the Hellespont, that we readily believed the Reis or master, when he assured us that the current which always sets from the Black sea and sea of Marmora into the Archipelago, runs uniformly at the rate of four miles an hour. This makes it impracticable for any ship to advance against it if the wind be from the north, and renders the communication between the Mediterranean and Constantinople by sea very precarious during the whole summer, as the Etesian or annual northern wind commences in May, and continues with little intermission or change until September. The strait here is about a mile and a half over.

Both shores of the Hellespont at this spot are highly picturesque. The outline of the hills is bold; they are well wooded, and the valleys which run far up into the country are as green as in England, while, as a back ground to the landscape, the isles of Imbros and Samothrace raise their snowy tops behind the Thracian Chersonesus. The first village we passed on the Asiatic coast was Cous-Keui, inha-bited solely by Turks; then Eet Guelmess, a Greek village, which our guide at first called Ghiour-Keui, or village of infidels, a name

which we soon ascertained was indiscriminately given by Musulmans
to such villages as contain no Turkish families.

In order to give us a high idea of the strict and impartial police of
the country, Mustapha, the new guide appointed by Hadim Oglou,
told us that his lord had pursued a robber from this village to the
top of the Adramyttian gulph, where he took the culprit and had him
bastinadoed, until the nails of his feet came out; his ears were next
cut off, and he would then have hanged him if intercession had not
been made to send him to the galleys by the person robbed, who, our
guide added, was a mere Ghiour, or infidel Christian.

We next passed Ak Yar, or the *White Stains*, on the Asiatic shore,
they are abrupt limestone or chalk crags used by seamen as a land-
mark to avoid a shoal or sunken rock in this part of the strait. On
the opposite shore of the Thracian Chersonesus is a beautiful valley
winding between the mountains; it is clothed with the richest verdure, and abounds with trees of every shade. At the entrance of this
valley is an Αγίασμα, Ayasma, or Holy fountain, where the Greek
Christians have built a small chapel; to the water of this fountain
they attribute a power of counteracting witchcraft, sorcery, and dæmoniacal possession, as well as healing certain diseases. A conical barrow
near it is supposed to be the Cynossema or tomb of Hecuba.

We now came close upon the Asiatic shore, where we observed
another barrow of similar form, called by the Turks En Tepé, and
by Chevalier, Morritt, and succeeding travellers considered as the
sepulchre of Ajax. We then passed the fort of Coum-Kalé, which is
built on a projecting tongue of land, having the appearance of a
sandy shoal, and which, it is supposed, was once covered by the
waters of the Hellespont. About 200 paces to the N E of the fort
is the embouchure of the river Menderé Sou, or Scamander, the
broadest stream we had seen since leaving the sea of Marmora. We
then passed two other tumuli or conical barrows very near the shore,
they were called *Theco Tepé* (Θεο τεπη) by our guide; they have been
considered as the tombs of Achilles and Patroclus. The sun was nearly
setting when we reached the foot of Cape Yenicher, the ancient promon-

tory of Sigeum. The ascent was steep, but when we had mounted towards the top we had the gratification of a fine view of the plain of Troy, the winding course of the river through it, the island Tenedos beneath us; Samothrace, and Imbros, and Lemnos on our right, with a faint view of the Pike of Mount Athos on the opposite continent in the fading distance of the horizon.*

The objects now before our eyes, and of which we were about to take a nearer view, have been so often confronted with the scenery described in the Iliad or Odyssey, the fountains, hillocks, streamlets, nay, almost every stone on the plain beneath us, have been so minutely appropriated to some circumstance of the Trojan war, that I shall confine myself to the humble task of recording a few incidents in our tour, marking the character or manners of the present inhabitants of the Troad, and shall rely on my learned and ingenious companion for a detailed examination of the natural features and the existing monuments of the country, with the view of ascertaining their relation to the description of local scenery in the poems of Homer.

When my fellow-traveller and myself were permitted to land from the frigate which was taking the embassy to the Porte in 1799, the celebrated Sigean inscription and a fragment of exquisite sculpture were pointed out to us in the porch of the village. The first circumstance now mentioned to us by the Greek priest, in whose house we lodged, was the loss of these treasures, which, he said, had been carried off by a party of English soldiers from the Dardanelles (where they were employed in improving the forts), accompanied by their officers, and sanctioned by a Bouyurdee from Hadim Oglou, and an imperial firman from Constantinople, declaring that these marbles had been given by the Sultan to Lord Elgin, the English ambassador. The sighs and tears with which the Greek priest accompanied his story did not, however, arise from any veneration he bore to the antiquity of these marbles, from any knowledge of their remote history, or any

* " Clarè conspicitur Athos," says Vossius, " cùm cœlum est serenum, ex Hellesponto et Asiatico litore, multò autem clariùs ex Idâ monte." In Melani 119

O

supposed relation they bore to the tale of Troy divine, but because,
as he told us, his flock had thus lost an infallible remedy for many
obstinate maladies.   To explain this, it may be necessary to mention,
that during the winter and spring, a considerable part of the neighbouring plain is overflowed, thus afflicting the inhabitants with agues ;
and such is the state of superstition at present among the Greek
Christians, that when any disease becomes chronic, or beyond the
reach of common remedies, it is attributed to dæmoniacal possession.
The Papas or priest is then called in to exorcise the patient, which he
generally does in the porch of the church, by reading long portions of
Scripture over the sufferer ; sometimes, indeed, the whole of the four
gospels.   In addition to this, at Yenicher, the custom was to roll the
patient on the marble stone which contained the Sigean inscription,
the characters of which never having been decyphered by any of their
Διδάσκαλο, were supposed to contain a powerful charm.   This practice had, however, nearly obliterated the inscription. *

Exorcism is still practised by the Greek priests of the shores of the
Archipelago ; not only human beings, but cattle, silk-worms, and
even houses are supposed by them to be liable to the baneful influence of fascination, spells, and dæmoniacal possession.   In one of their
liturgies I saw a prayer to be used for counteracting the effect of a
malicious glance on silk-worms, at the season of their spinning   and
during our short stay at this village, I witnessed the ceremony of a
priest with a censer and vessel of holy water, rendering, as he pretended, the threshold, windows, and chimney of a new-built cottage.
impervious to evil spirits.

We here bought some copper coins of the Ptolemies, and some
smaller belonging to Alexandria Troas ; but we could not induce a

* The stone is in the Elgin Collection of Marbles, and a copy of this singular document
of Palæography may be seen in Chishull, Ant Asiat. and in Chandler, Ins An.   The
French letter of Bentley respecting the inscription, and the Delian Iambic, is in vol ii. of
the Acta Societatis Trajectina, 6.

peasant to sell a most beautiful little copper coin, containing on one side the full face of a female, and on the reverse two owls.

The inhabitants of this village are all Christians of the Greek church, and appeared miserably poor and squalid; and their curiosity was so obtrusive, that we almost wished for the tranquillity of a Turkish conac; however, as I had made some progress in the vernacular Greek of the Levant, I endeavoured to carry on a little conversation without the aid of our interpreter, with the Papas, our host, and he became very communicative respecting his own history and situation.

Yenicher or Ghioul-Keui, he told me, is divided into two parishes, of one of which he is officiating priest, his income amounting to about 350 piastres, or 26*l.* sterling *per annum,* out of which, however, he was forced every year to pay about 150 piastres to his Bishop and Metropolitan. His fees were, for a christening, five paras, or twopence-halfpenny, but weddings and funerals were better paid. For the latter he had seldom less than seven piastres, or half-a-guinea, for which, however, he was bound to some scores of masses for the repose of the defuncts, and to consume a few wax-lights.

The plain of Troy and its immediate vicinity he stated to produce annually from three to four thousand okes of wool, above 10,000 lbs. worth; on an average, about twelve or fourteen paras an oke, nearly twopence-halfpenny per lb. avourdupoise. Some cotton is grown in the neighbourhood, and when picked and dressed sells for about fifty to sixty paras an oke, or eleven-pence per lb.

As we proposed to ride over the plain next morning, it was necessary to procure horses, and here Mustapha began the exercise of his authority by putting four in requisition for us, but, as we observed the owners to be dissatisfied, we privately told them we would ourselves pay at the rate of two and a half piastres (four shillings) per day, for each horse, with which promise they were so satisfied, that instead of sending one boy to bring them back, each owner agreed to accompany his horse, and to act as a guide.

The first place where we halted on our route from Sigeum to the Rhœtean promontory, was at the two conical mounds, barrows, or hillocks, called the tumuli of Achilles and Patroclus, which we had anxiously viewed on our voyage to Constantinople, fearing we might not have this opportunity of examining them with leisure. Our guides concurred in calling them -ὰ δύο τεπν, the two mounds.

In 1787, M. Choiseul Gouffier, ambassador from France, hired persons to open that which is called Achilles' tomb , but the work was not carried so deep, as even to the surface of the ground on which the tumulus is raised. The remains of antiquity discovered there, proved to be, as M. Fauval himself assured me, one of those Egyptian idols of bronze so common in the times of the Ptolemies, and found frequently in the vicinity of Alexandria, having the modium or symbol of abundance on its head, and the feet placed on two horses, and a sphinx on each shoulder.

The excavation appears to have been carried on not more than one third of the perpendicular depth of the tumulus; the opening is about five or six feet in diameter, on one side of the excavation and near the top, I observed a squared block of marble in a kind of wall; this with some difficulty I raised; and on the side which had been concealed in the earth I observed an inscription in Greek letters; but on examining it, I was disappointed in finding it contained only a short epitaph, the letters, according to their form being of no high antiquity.

EPOKΛEA

ETKIOT

ΧAIPE

Heroclea, or Hieroclea, wife or daughter of Lucius, Farewel. It was brought away, and given to the Earl of Elgin.

In a field near the base of this tumulus is a slab of white marble, on which are sculptured two wreaths of laurel or olive, but it does not bear any inscription. The spot is a Jewish cemetery.

Proceeding towards En Tepé at the Rhœtean promontory we crossed a river near the fort of Coum Kalé, which our Turkish guide called Menderé Sou, and the Greeks Scamander. The wooden bridge over it was a hundred paces long; and the river itself, in comparison of the other streams that fall into the Hellespont, may be called broad and rapid. And here I cannot help remarking, that the Hellespont itself having the appearance of a large river, carrying its waters into the Ægæan sea, well merits the epithet of πλατύς given to it by Homer; for though considered as a sea, it is indeed narrow; yet as a tributary stream of the Ægæan, it may be called the broad Hellespont.* The tomb of Patroclus, near that of Achilles, and close to the road, has never been opened. It is supposed to be a cenotaph raised to his memory, as his ashes were inclosed in the same urn which held those of Achilles, and deposited in the same tumulus.

About four miles and a half from Yenicher or Sigeum, we arrived at a lofty barrow, called En Tepe, the supposed tumulus of Ajax. Before we reached it, we had crossed Camara Sou, and a salt-marsh. Our guides told us that some years ago the Turks had dug into the tomb, and taken out a great quantity of stones, with which they had made the present causeway through some oozy ground and salt marshes near it; one of these ponds is called Tous-Lazma, and the other En Tepé Lazma. to which they told us the sea sometimes reaches. This may help to confirm the opinion of those who believe that the waves of the Hellespont may have washed the base of this tumulus, subsequently to the Trojan war. To us, I confess, the ground appeared to rise gently and gradually to the base of En Tepé, so that the foundation of building in it, is probably near a hundred feet above the level of the adjoining plain, and the edge of the present shore of the Hellespont. The tumulus is raised to about twenty feet above that height, so that there is some difficulty in

---

* Herodotus calls it a river, lib. vii c. 35.

applying the account given by Pausanias in his first book to this tumulus. He there tells us, that an inhabitant of Mysia had informed him, that the sea, breaking into the tomb of Ajax on the side next the shore, made the entrance into it not difficult to any one who wished to view the gigantic remains of that hero.

The stones of which the internal building is formed are not squared or chiselled, and great masses of them roughly cemented with mortar, still adhering together, incumber the inner chamber or vault. The entrance into it in the side of the tumulus is about five feet in height, five feet broad, and the passage about six feet long, before it terminates in the vault which is lower and narrower. My fellow-traveller was extremely sceptical on the appropriation of this mound to the sepulchre of Ajax

From the top of this tumulus we had a good view of the whole line of coast, and of the Scamandrian plain, called by our guides, Menderé Sou Deresi, the valley of the Mender ; two ridges of hills, one terminating at this point (Rhœteum), and the other at Yenicher Sigeum) bound it , the breadth here is about four miles.

We had thus in a few short hours enjoyed the satisfaction of visiting the two extremities of the naval station of the Greeks, explored the tombs of Achilles, Patroclus, and Ajax, and crossed the Scamander.

We now descended to the base of that ridge of hills which terminates at En Tepé, and soon came once more to the little meandering stream, Camara Sou, or the river of the Aqueduct. We crossed it by a small bridge, and proceeded to the village of Coum Keui, the sandy village, about two miles south of En Tepé. Very near the village are extensive ruins of ancient public buildings scattered over the plain ; they are probably on the site of Ilium. The columns now fallen and broken are deeply fluted, and of the Ionic and Corinthian orders, generally about three feet and a half in diameter.

In the house of a Turk of this village I found a Greek inscription on a block of marble ; the letters were very small, and without any separation between the words. I bought it for Lord Elgin, in whose possession it now is. It is not complete, having been broken and defaced towards the conclusion. The following is the copy I took on the spot It is a decree in honour of Metrodorus a physician, for having healed a wound in the neck received by King Antiochus in battle, and it assigns him certain privileges and honours for this service as well as others performed to the Kings Antiochus and Seleucus, and to the town. Unfortunately for the topography of this part of the Troad, it does not mention the name of the city.

```
ΕΠΕΙΔΗ,Ο,ΒΑΣΙΛΕΥΣ,ΑΝΤΙΟΧΟΣ,ΕΠΕΣ          1
ΤΑΛΚΕΝ,ΟΤΙ,ΤΡΑΥΜΑΤΙΑΣ,ΓΕΝΟΜΕΝΟΣ,
ΕΝ,ΤΗΙ,ΜΑΧΗΙ,ΕΙΣ,ΤΟΝ,ΤΡΑΧΗΛΟΝ,
ΘΕΡΑΠΕΥΘ . ,ΥΠΟ,ΜΗΤΡΟΔΩΡΟΥ,ΤΟΥ,
ΙΑΤΡΟΥ,ΑΚΙΝΔΥΝΟΣ ΕΠΕΣΤΑΛΚΕΝ,            5
ΠΕΡΙ,ΕΑΥΤΟΥ,ΚΑΙ ΜΕΛΕΛΓΡΟΣ,Ο,ΣΤΡΑ.
ΤΗΓΟΣ ΠΡΟΟΡΩΜΕΝΟΣ,ΤΟ,ΤΗΣ,ΠΟ
ΛΕΩΣ ΣΥΜΦΕΡΟΝ,ΔΕΔΟΧΘΑΙ,ΤΗΙ,ΒΟΥΛΗΙ,
ΚΑΙ,ΤΩΙ,ΔΗΜΩΙ,ΕΠΑΙΝΕΣΑΙ,ΜΕΝ,
ΜΗΤΡΟΔΩΡΟΝ,ΤΙΜΟΚΛΕΟΥΣ,ΑΜΦ             10
Ε   ΙΤΗΝ ΑΡΕΤΗΣ ΕΝΕΚΕΝ,ΚΑΙ,
ΕΥΝΟΙΑΣ,ΤΗΣ,ΕΙΣ,ΤΟΥΣ ΒΑΣΙΛΕΙΣ,
ΑΝΤΙΟΧΟΝ,ΚΑΙ,ΣΕΛΕΥΚΟΝ ΚΑΙ,ΤΟΝ,
ΔΗΜΟΝ,ΕΙΝΑΙ,ΔΕ,ΑΥΤΟΝ,ΚΑΙ,ΠΡΟΞΕ
ΝΟΝ,ΚΑΙ,ΕΥΕΡΓΕΤΗΝ,ΤΗΣ ΠΟΛΕΩΣ,         15
ΔΕΔΟΣΘΑΙ,Δ,ΑΥΤΩΙ,ΚΑΙ,ΠΟΛΙΤΕΙΑΝ,
ΚΑΙ,ΚΤΗΣΙΝ,ΚΑΙ,ΕΦΟΔΟΝ,ΕΠΙ,ΤΗΝ,
ΒΟΥΛΗΝ,ΚΑΙ,ΤΟΝ,ΔΗΜΟΝ,ΠΡΩΤΟΝ,
ΜΕΤΑ,ΤΑ,ΙΕΡΑ,ΕΞΕΙΝΑΙ,Δ,ΑΥΤΩΙ,ΚΑΙ
ΕΙΣ,ΦΥΛΗΝ,ΚΑΙ,ΦΡΑΤΡΙΑΝ,ΗΝ,ΑΝ,ΒΟΥ       20
ΛΗΤΑΙ *
```

About three miles and a half to the east of Coum Keui, we found an extensive Turkish cemetery, with ruins of a mosque, the minaret of which was still standing. It belongs to the adjoining village of

---

* See the latter part of the volume, where an explanation of this and other Greek inscriptions is given.

Chali-Leui. * The sepulchral stones erected over the Mussulman graves were fragments of columns, capitals, and frizes of temples. The ground they occupied was about 260 paces in diameter ; but we could not trace the plan or foundations of any Greek or Roman buildings. The columns were of white marble fluted, about two feet six inches in diameter ; some capitals were of the Ionic, and some of the Corinthian order, the triglyphs shewed that there had been buildings in the Doric style ; one mutilated and defaced bas-relief represents a female figure in a conch-shaped chariot drawn by tritons ; on another fragment is a winged victory in a car ; on part of an entablature is a female figure with wings supporting festoons or flowers. There were other remains of sculpture, but so much defaced as to make it very difficult to discover the subject represented They have all undoubtedly belonged to the towns of New Ilium, as may be collected from the following inscriptions . —

1.
ΙΛΙΕΙΣΤΟΝ
ΠΑΤΡΙΟΝ ΘΕΟΝ
ΛΙΝΕΙΛΝ

2
ΟΙ ΝΕΟΙ
ΤΟΝΓΥΜΛΣΙΛΡΧΟΝ
ΛΣΚΛΛΠΩΝΛΚΛΛΛΙΠ
ΠΟΥΧΡΗΜΑΤΙΣΑΝ.

3.
ΗΠΑΝΘΩΙΣϴΥΛΗ
ΕΞΤΟΝΙΟΥΛΙΟΝΦΙΛ
ΟΝΚΟΣΜΟΝΤΗΣΠΟΛ
ΕΩΣΕΠΑΡΧΟΝΣΗΓΙΡΗΣ
ΦΑΒΙΑΝΗΣΓΥΜΝΑΣΙΑΡΧ
ΗΣΛΝΤΑΛΛΑΜΠΡΩΣΚΛΙ
ΦΙΛΟΤΙΜΩΣΚΛΗΠΡΩΤΟΝ
ΤΩΝΑΠΑΙΩΝΟΣΚΛΙΜΕΛΡΙ
ΛΥΝΜΟΝΟΛΕΛΛΙΟΜΕΤΡΗΣΑ
ΝΤΑΤΟΥΣΤΕΒΟΥΛΕΥΤΑΣ
ΚΑΙΠΟΛΕΙΤΑΣΠΑΝΤΑΣΚΑΙ†
ΛΛΕΙΨΑΝΤΑΕΚΛΟΥΙΗΡΩΝ
ΠΑΝΔΗΜΕΙ

About a mile and a half south-west of these ruins of Chali-Leui is the village of Chiblak. In the court-yard of the mosque and in the

---

* " The numerous architectural fragments observed near Halil Eli and Tchiblak, have been brought there to mark the graves in a Turkish burial-ground, for I could discover no foundations of buildings at either spot " Mr. Hawkins

† L 12 ἀλεὶψαντα τὴν πόλιν occurs in an inscription found at Lampsacus, see Mis Obs. T. 3 201 Respecting the office of the Aliptæ, see Van Dale's Dissertation.

walls of some cottages, we observed fragments of architectural ornaments in marble, and a number of broken capitals and shafts of
columns in the cemetery.

About a mile to the south-east of this place is a very ancient Turkish
burial-ground, filled with scattered ruins of a temple   Many inscribed marbles may be seen there.   Among them we found the
following words . *

ΡΑΣΑ ΤΗ ΘΥΓΑΤΡΙ ΚΕ ΕΑΥΤΗ ΚΕ ΤΩ

From Chali-Leui we reached Gheumbrek Sou, which falls into
Camara Sou; we crossed the former, and in an hour's time ar-
rived at the village Gheumbrek.   The valley through which the
Camara and Gheumbrek Sou run, is supposed to be the vale of
Thymbia; it is bounded by gently swelling knolls, and abounds with
beautiful shrubs.

The village of Gheumbrek is four miles from Chali-Leui, and near
it is a gloomy grove of tall pines, to which we were taken by the
peasants to see the ruins of an ancient building   It appeared to us
to be the remains of a small Doric temple; but there is not a fragment of inscription or ornamental sculpture to indicate the period of
its erection, or the name of the deity to whom it had been consecrated.

Here we were told of extensive ruins to be seen at a distance of
about four or five miles, and which, to raise our curiosity or to gain
higher pay for a guide, we were assured no traveller had ever visited.
Winding between the mountains in a southerly direction, in about an
hour and a half we came to ruins scattered among bushes and under-
wood, at a place called Palaio Atche Keui.   On our road, Mustapha,
who had now entered in some degree into the objects of our research,
with great delight took us to a block of marble he had discovered

---

* A similar mode of writing the E for AI is observable in other instances, see the remarks at the end of the volume relating to some Greek inscriptions.   We read in one,
νομισμά τε ἐπίσημον χρυσοῦν κὶ αργυρὸυν κὶ ἕτερα ἄσημα

P

with a Greek inscription on it: it had been the pedestal of a statue to Agrippa.

ΜΑΡΚΟΝ ΑΓΡΙΠΠΑΝ ΤΟΝ ΣΥΝΓΕΝΕΑ
ΚΑΙ ΠΑΤΡΩΝΑ ΤΗΣ ΠΟΛΕΩΣ ΚΑΙ
ΣΥΕΡΓΕΤΗΝ ΕΠΙ ΤΗ ΠΡΟΣ ΓΗΝ ΘΕΟΝ
ΕΥΣΕΒΕΙΑ ΚΑΙ ΕΠΙ ΤΗ ΠΡΟΣ ΤΟΝΔΗΜΟΝ
ΕΥΝΟΙΑ

Near this inscription is the statue of a female in a sitting posture; a robe is thrown gracefully over the left knee, and a zone is closely clasped beneath the breasts. On each side of the chair is represented a lion resting on his haunches A great number of broken inscriptions of different ages is scattered around The most striking object is part of the arch of a portico formed of large blocks of marble, on which are three garlands of olive with inscriptions in each ΟΙ ΝΕΟΙ in one, in another ΟΔΗΜΟΣ Ο ΜΥΤΙΛΗΝΑΙΩΝ; in a third, the words are not all of them discernible: but we saw ΙΛΙΩ ΡΩΜΑΙΩΝ. Within the arch was written ΑΠΟΛΛΩΝΟΣ ΤΟΥ ΙΛΙΓΟΣ ΕΡΜΟΚΡΑΤΟ . . Another fragment contains the name of Minerva ΤΗΑΘΗΝΑΙ.

CHAP. III

Aqueduct at Camara-Sou — Bounarbashi. — Extract from Sibthorp's Journal. — Ene.— Bairamitche. — Source and Cascade of the Mender — Summit of Ida.

WE now proceeded in a north-east direction, and came once more to the banks of the Camara-Sou, which are here very bold and picturesque. We found an ancient aqueduct, crossing the river, at a considerable height above its bed. Though much injured by time it is still so striking an object as to give the name of the " Aqueduct river" to the stream that runs beneath it. The principal arch is

about thirty-five feet in diameter, and is yet entire; this spot is about
three miles from Palaio Atche Keui, where are the ruins of the temple
of Apollo of Ilium. The rocky bed in which the river here runs, its
bold abrupt banks thus united by a lofty arched aqueduct, and crowned
with wood, form a striking scene, which I regretted my want of power
to sketch.

After remaining some time to admire the beauty of this spot, we
returned to Palaio Atche Keui, having heard from our guides that
there were more ruins of ancient buildings within a mile of those we
had just seen. But we found merely a Turkish cemetery, to which
some ancient fragments had been taken to be employed as tomb-
stones. One of the marble slabs, however, we found contained a
Greek inscription in hexameter and pentameter verses, and we decyphered the following words

TIKTE TEXNA TON APIΣTONA
ΜΥΝΤΟΡΑ ΠΑΤΡΙΔΟΣ ΑΙΙΣ
ΟΙΟΝ ZΕΥΣ ΩΡΣΕΝ ΟΙΟΝ ΟΜΗΡΟΣΕΦΥ

We now set out for Bounarbashi, where we were to halt for the
night, and going in a south-westerly direction, we passed three
tumuli, to which our guides gave the names of Mal Tepé, Asarlack Tepé, and Khama Tepé; Asarlack Tepé, near the village of New
Atche Keui, is of much larger dimensions than the others; it appeared about thirty feet high, flat at top, where it is about one hundred
feet across. It is in the form of a truncated cone.

When we had proceeded about three miles and a half from Atche
Keui, we again reached the Menderé Sou, on that broad river which
intersects the plain of Troy. We found it here very wide, though
not so deep as to prevent our fording it on horseback. This river our
guides called Menderé and Scamandros, and they here told us that its
source was in the snow-covered mountain of Kaz-Dag, which, according to their computation, was three days' journey from us, probably
about sixty miles they also said that the Camara Sou had its source
in that lofty mountain. At about a mile from the ford of the Menderé Sou, we came to the village of Bounarbashi. It is elvated

considerably above the plain, and is about twelve miles from Yenicher, and at least nine miles from the nearest point of the Hellespont. We here took up our lodging at a Tchiflick or farm-house belonging to Hadim Oglou

To the E. N. E. of this spot the ground rises during a distance of a mile and a half; we then reached the summit of a hill, the surface of which is almost flat. It has been called the Acropolis of Troy. On our road we did not discover the foundation or traces of any ancient building, or even a hewn stone or fragment of pottery to mark the site of former habitations. This high land or table-hill is about a mile in circumference, is of an oblong form, in length 650 paces, its mean breadth about 250. We noticed three barrows or conical mounds upon it; these our guides called Balah Tepé. One at the north-western boundary, now named Hector's tomb, is a heap of rough stones thrown confusedly together, as if they had been dug from the neighbouring quarry, and were placed in a heap to be ready for use. Close to it are foundations of walls; the masonry is rough, and about seven feet thick; the building, of which they mark the ground-plan, has not been of regular figure, but accommodated to the uneven surface of the rock. Its mean diameter is about forty paces. On digging among these foundations we found both tiles and mortar. About 120 paces from this heap or mound, is a second called by recent topographers the Tumulus of Priam. Remains of building appear on the top, as if an altar or some little chapel or shrine had been placed there, the foundation being about eight feet in diameter.

Continuing in the same line, we came to a rocky hillock, which we mounted, and found it flat or levelled at the summit; on this the keep or fortress of the citadel most probably was built. The position is altogether very strong, it is bounded by abrupt and nearly perpendicular cliffs and precipices. On looking down to the distant plain, we saw the river Menderé Sou, broad and rapid, nearly surrounding the base of this acropolis or Pergamus, and almost making it an island. The meanderings of the river as seen from this height appeared very numerous. It often turns back on its former course, so as to intersect the valley in various directions. Round the whole boundary of this flat space on the top of the hill, may be traced remains of walls, with heaps of stones at intervals, indicating probably the spots where towers had been raised. There are also some excavations, like quarries, whence the stones may have been dug, one of these near the first barrow is very deep; the marks of the pick-axe are discernible; many wild fig-trees grow out of its clefts.

About a quarter of a mile below the village of Bounarbashi, in a S. W. direction, is a Turkish burial-ground, on which are scattered many fragments of architecture, and columns of marble and granite. Their style precludes any pretensions to high antiquity. Neither on the hill just described, nor on the road to it, did we discover any remains of art of a Cyclopean kind similar to those seen at Tiryns, Argos, and Mycenæ, and other parts of Greece We saw no fragments of vases and pottery, so generally abundant on the sites of ancient cities in Asia Minor and Greece. We observed a few sculptured marbles in different parts of the village; one with festoons of flowers suspended from rams' heads, another with an architectural ornament.

There was also a bas-relief representing a warrior, his arm resting on another figure, this appears to have been the metope of an ancient Doric temple. Close to the mosque of the village is a marble slab, on which is an imperfect Greek inscription; mention is made in it of some act of piety towards Minerva.

About a mile below the Tchiflick of Bounarbashi and the mosque are the fountains or sources of a rivulet. They are called by the Turks, *Kirk-joss*, " Forty-eyes." One of the strongest of these springs has been formed into a reservoir or cistern, and some slabs of marble and broken pillars placed for assisting the inhabitants of the village to wash and to fill their urns The water of this fountain appeared to me of ordinary temperature, but our guides told us, that in winter it is so much warmer than the adjoining springs, as to send forth vapour or steam.

The whole of the ground near this fountain abounds with springs; and wherever there is a cleft or crevice in the rocky surface, clear water gushes out profusely. The stream formed by these fountains now goes to a Tchiflick or farm, built by the famous Hassan Pasha; here it turns some corn-mills, and then falls into the Archipelago, south of Yenicher or Sigeum, at about one-third of the distance of that promontory from Alexandria Troas. Our guides however from Yenicher assured us, that formerly it flowed in a different bed, and fell into the Menderé Sou; and that still, during the winter floods and equinoctial rains, it overflows its modern channel, and runs in its ancient bed to the Menderé· and that the precise spot of this junction of the Kirk-joss, or Bounarbashi Sou, and the Menderé is at a place called Coum Deré, and is marked by the piers of a ruined stone bridge, about three miles and a half S E. of Cape Yenicher, at about eight miles from its source in a direct line, and about three miles from Coum Kalé.

The breadth of the bed of this stream where it joins the Menderé is about seven or eight yards, and the breadth of the Menderé there about sixty yards. On visiting this spot, we found that our guides had given us a very faithful account, and that a late flood had brought some of the waters of the Kirk-joss into its old channel, and over-flowed the neighbouring part of the plain We could not find any conical barrow near this junction where the tomb of Ilus is supposed to have stood. The snowy tops of Ida or Gargarus were pointed out to us from this spot by our guides, and called by them Kaz-Dag; indeed that lofty pike may be seen from the whole extent of the plain, except near Bounarbashi; a range of hills there screens it from the spectator, as well as at the Pergamus.

The waters of the Kirk-joss at their source are very much esteemed by the natives, and our guides told us, that there is a tradition of the water having been conveyed in former times by aqueducts to ancient Troya; by which they always mean Alexandria Troas. The Menderé Sou is called by this name, from its source in Mount Gargarus or Kaz-Dag, to the place where it is discharged into the

Hellespont sometimes indeed our guides named it Scamandros, and ὁ Ποταμος, "the river," but always meant by those appellations the Menderé. It has a broad stream during its whole course, in the plain it flows over a bed generally of sand; sometimes of pebbles, but towards its source, it is full of large masses of detached granite rock, that have been rolled down by floods.

About three miles and a half west of Bounarbashi, and two miles and a half from the sea-shore, and about eight or nine miles south of Sigæum, a lofty barrow of the usual conical form rises from the plain; it is now called the tomb of Æsyetes, and mentioned by Homer as existing before the Trojan war, and as being the eminence from which Polites the son of Priam reconnoitred the forces of the Greeks. This circumstance throws much doubt on the origin of these numerous barrows or tumuli scattered over the plain and its shores. Were they raised to cover the remains of the heroes mentioned by Homer; or were the details in the Iliad adapted to the existing appearances of the country where the story is laid? Conical mounds of similar construction are to be found in all the plains of the east, bearing the name of Tepé, they are seen in Scythia, in Thrace, Macedonia, and in Greece. Our guides from Yenicher assured us that it is still the custom of the Turkish armies to raise mounds of this kind on their march; and that the standard of the Vizier or General is displayed during the encampment upon them.

Having already mentioned the situation of En Tepé, or the tumulus of Ajax, with respect to the Hellespont, I will here observe, that one of our guides informed us, that at Yenicher there is a tradition of the sea having formerly washed the foot of En Tepé; and he added, that even now the part of the plain between Coum Kalé and En Tepé (the naval station of the Greeks) is called in their old writings and title deeds, *Beyadeh Deré,* "the valley of boats," and that a village now more than a league from the shore is still called *Calafatlee,* or the "Careening place." If this tradition of the *littus relictum* be well founded, it renders much more probable many of the incidents of the Iliad, by reducing the distance between the citadel of Troy and the naval camp of the Greeks.

The master of the Tchiflick where we purposed to lodge, was so unhospitable and churlish in his manners that we left his house, and took up our abode in the cottage of an acquaintance of our guides. Here in the evening we were entertained with a rustic conceit and dancing; one of the performers played on a kind of small violin, not held to the shoulders, but supported on the knee. Another of the company played on a small guitar or lute, the body of which was simply the shell of a land-tortoise, an animal very common on the neighbouring hills. Having mentioned the use of the Testudo, we may here state two other circumstances, which in this part of our tour reminded us of more ancient times. The car or little waggon in use on the Troad has its wheels formed of solid blocks; and bears in its general appearance a striking resemblance to the chariots of Homer's heroes, as they are represented on ancient bas-reliefs, engraved gems, and Greek or Etruscan vases. The construction of the Turkish ships which are employed in the trade of the Black-sea, and parts of the Archipelago, also preserve some ancient peculiarities. The curved shape of the vessel from the poop to the prow, the lofty towering station of the pilot, the black and dusky sides of the vessel, the red-painted holes through which the hawsers or cables pass, the daubing and greasing the bottom and keel with tallow, are continued from remote times. The epithets κοίλη, μελαινα, κορωνίς, γλαφυρή, μιλτοπάρηος are as applicable to a Turkish Beyadeh. as they could have been to a Greek galley.

The Scamandrian plain in its extreme length from Yenicher to Atche Keui appears to be about ten miles, its mean breadth about five miles. It is cultivated, and said to be fertile in its whole extent, except in the neighbourhood of En Tepé, (Rhœteum,) where the ground is boggy, making about a fifth of the whole plain. The produce is from seven to ten of the seed-corn. The property here is vested in Hadim Oglou of the Dardanelles; the Sultan's tribute from the cultivator or tenant is farmed, and collected so oppressively as to make it amount to an eighth, instead of the legal tenth of the harvest.

On the 12th of March we left Bounarbashi, having the citadel and its ruins on our left, and Udjek Tepé the supposed tomb of Æsyetes on our right, or towards the west; about a mile and a half from Bounarbashi we came to a mound of earth called by our guides Arabla Tepessi. It is flat on the top; and there were traces of some former structure on it. The river Menderé runs close by Arapla, and its course here is very picturesque; the craggy precipices of Kara-Dag form one of its banks, and the adjoining valley was full of wild-flowers, and the side of the stream abounded with oleanders, olive-trees, and myrtles. An island made at this place by the divided current had many cattle grazing on it. We were still accompanied by Mustapha, who had brought with him from Bounarbashi a fine greyhound. This favourite dog had warm clothing like a trained race-horse*; the tip of his tail and ears, and some spots of his back were stained with a scarlet or deep orange colour; a dye used now, as in earlier times by the Turks. Their beards are often ornamented with it; and we see it frequently applied to the nails of the fingers and feet of the Turkish women. It is taken from the Lawsonia inermis.

Our road led us along the course of the Menderé Sou through a rich and extensive valley, a lofty wooden bridge on stone piers here crossed the river. The mountainous tract of Cebrenia was to the East. At about nine miles from Bounarbashi, the top of Kaz-Dag or Gargarus again came in view, and this nearer prospect of its snows and height made us almost despair of being able to reach its summit.

---

* Dr. Clarke observed " the dogs near Kataiina in Thessaly, making a singular appearance, wearing body-clothes." T 3

Extract from Dr. Sibthorp's Journal respecting the Plain of Troy.

" Sept. 1774. We left Coum Kale and passed by a paved road, on the sides of which were vineyards and gardens. We entered on the fertile plains of Troy, having crossed the Simois, the bed of which was dry; at Bounarbashi the steward of the Aga who had gone himself on a pilgrimage to Mecca received us, and prepared a rustic supper. The court-yard of the Aga was that of a large farmer; numerous buildings, as cow-houses, sheep-stalls, and sheds for different purposes, lined the sides of it, and instruments of husbandry were disposed in various parts. The wains were of a singular structure, and probably of very ancient origin, and had received none of the improvements of modern discoveries. A large wicker basket eight feet long, mounted on a four-wheeled machine, was supported by four lateral props, which were inserted into holes or sockets. The wheels were made of one solid piece, round, and convex on each side. The house was placed on an elevated site, commanding a view of the plain of Troy; a little to the left was the source of the Scamander marked by a poplar grove; the Simois waved to the right in a serpentine course, its bed nearly dry, edged with Tamarisk, Planes, and Agnus Castus.

" The plain of Troy, which reached almost to the village, was an extended flat of a rich fertile loamy soil, that now changed into a bed of basalt, on which the village of Bounarbashi was built. Three sorts of wheat are sown in the plain, distinguished by the titles of Cara Culchuck, Devidishi, and Sari Boulda. The country was also cultivated with cotton and sesamum. The peasants were busy in carrying home in their wicker wains their crops of Indian corn; the yellow was the most common sort.

" Having reached the point of the mountains which we judged to be the site of the ancient Acropolis, we had the broad shallow bed of the Simois immediately under us, it was now quite dry. On the declivity of the rock, which was composed of a white coarse-grained marble, and extremely steep, grew the prickly almond, the Paliurus and yellow jasmine, and from the fissures the wild fig and Conyza Candida. In the evening we walked to the source of the Scamander, and near it were shown a clear crystalline spring, said in winter to be warm, but at present (Sept.) giving no sensation of heat. We followed the river some way from its source ; the stream fed by numerous springs had been interrupted, and overflowed the neighbouring lands, forming a large tract of reedy ground frequented by ducks, coots, and snipes ; besides the chub, eels, and two other sorts of fish were caught in its stream. The marsh-mallow, the prickly-liquorice, and the goats-rue grew on its banks." — Dr. S.

We now quitted the main channel of the Mendere on our left ; and crossing one of its tributary streams *, which flows from the south, and runs through a plain called Ené Dere, we arrived at the house of Hadje Achmet, son of Hadim Oglou in the town of Ené, of which he is Aga or feudal chieftain The title of Hadje or Pilgrim, implies that he has either visited Mecca in person, or paid the expenses of a pilgrim for going thither for him The same epithet Χα-σή is assumed by Greek Christians, who have visited in this character the Holy Land. Ené is about thirteen miles from Bounarbashi ; and Hadje Achmet lives here in a kind of feudal grandeur. On entering the court of his mansion, a young page made a loud beat on a drum which hangs at the gate.

The Aga, to whom we were immediately introduced, received us with much kindness, and treated us hospitably, and though a Musulman and Hadje, he did not suffer wine to be banished from our meals. He sent one of his guards as our guide through the town and its environs in search of antiquities, but our discoveries were not

---

* This stream flowing from the south, and near Fné, is noticed in Major Rennell's map, No. vi. See his remarks on the topography of Troy.

Q 2

important.   The first Greek inscription we saw was in the wall of a
shop in the Bazar; it was broken and defaced.

. ΟΠΑΤΗΡ. . .
ΤΟΜΝΗΜΑ .
ΣΕΔΑΚΡΥΩΝ
ΓΑΙΟΣ

We crossed the Ené Deré Sou, or river of Ené, by a bridge, in the
building of which a number of ancient granite columns had been
employed.   We found a sarcophagus, now converted into the cistern
of a fountain with an imperfect inscription; the form of its letters
was not more ancient than the time of the first Cæsars.   It merely
contains the usual fine to be imposed on any one who shall dare to
put the bones of any person into it, except of him for whom it was
made.   At a public fountain near one of the mosques of Ené are two
beautiful ancient marble capitals of the Corinthian order placed beneath a sarcophagus, now used as a cistern.   There are many granite
columns in the Turkish burying ground.   These, we were told, had
been brought from some ruins about twelve miles distant.

Ené is a large town, consisting of about 800 families, mostly Turks,
who carry on a small manufactory of yellow leather.   The boys of
the town followed us in crowds, but did not behave in the least degree rudely.   At a little past three in the afternoon we left Ené and
its hospitable Aga; keeping the river on our left, we proceeded on
our journey to Mount Kaz-Dag, passing a village called Kozoul Keui.
About five miles from Ené we came to a rivulet called Baloukli Deré
Sou, and a mile further to another called Tchourmagee, both of which
fall into the Menderé Sou; we then passed a farm-house or Tchiflick
of Hadim Oglou, and about fourteen miles from Ené we reached
Bairamitché, the ancient seat of Hadim Oglou's ancestors.   Here we
were lodged and well received.   The house is so large that we counted
twenty-seven rooms opening into the principal gallery.

This town and the district for some miles round it, have the air of
riches and independence· well cultivated fields, good fences, sub-

stantial cottages, prove the comfortable state of the tenantry Fountains or wells for the use of travellers are made along the roads   It was here that the ancestors of Hadim Oglou lived in feudal dignity and patriarchal hospitality; and he is the first of his family who has suffered himself to be tempted from rural independence to accept the public employments of the Porte. I have before mentioned the heavy contributions that have lately been levied upon him at the Dardanelles, and his old tenants are beginning to fear that he must oppress them in turn, and that in no long time he will be the victim of some revolution in the ministry, and thus bring on the extinction of a family that has for ages been a blessing to the country. Bairamitché contains about six hundred families, and has a large well-built Khân or Caravanserai for the accommodation of travellers.   In this, we were told, two of our countrymen had lodged a few days before our arrival.

In one of the streets we observed a granite sarcophagus, used as a cistern of a fountain; it is six feet long and two feet deep.   There is an inscription on it in very ancient characters, but we could only decypher the following words ΚΑΙΚΟΦΑΝΓΙΝ ΞΙΝΟΦΑΕΙ. The latter is the name Xenophae, and we find a similar termination in Calliphae, a name of one of the Ionian nymphs.[*]   In the yard of a house belonging to a Greek we saw a small marble statue of a female, nearly entire, of admirable workmanship; the folds of the drapery appear a little raised by the left knee.   In the house of the same Greek was the head of a much larger statue.   [Some remarkable ruins were discovered by Dr. Clarke, about two hours distance from this place, at Kouchounlou Tepé.—E.]

The difficulty of procuring horses detained us at Bairamitché until noon.   As soon as our friendly host had provided them for us, we set out for Kaz-Dag, almost deterred by the reports we heard from the hope of being able to reach its summit, though we were resolved to proceed at least as far up as the source of the Menderé, whose wind-

---

[*] Strabo, lib. viii.

ings we had been following so many days. About five or six miles from Bairamitché we crossed the river, which our guides still occasionally called the Scamander, it was here about fifty or sixty paces wide. We saw some ruins of ancient buildings, and passed two small villages, both of which our guides called Ghiour Keui. Here the stream began to decrease rapidly in breadth, and when we forded it again, we found it not more than twenty-five paces broad. The valley here was so green, the shade so refreshing, the water dashing among masses of granite, so clear that we were induced to alight. The beauty of the scenery around us was very striking; the lofty and well wooded hills on each side prevented any glare of light, so that the outline of each object was defined with clearness. The forests, vineyards, pastures, cottages, and flocks, were blended into the most beautiful harmony of colouring; while the towering Mount Gargarus closed in the valley, and showed in the distant horizon its snowy top, reflecting a burnished light, with groves of dark pine-trees on its sides.

At a quarter past four in the afternoon, we reached Evjilah, or the village of hunters, it lies at the foot of Kaz-Dag. Here our reception was most rude and inhospitable; neither Aga nor peasant seemed disposed to receive us within their doors; and the only place of accommodation they offered to us was a ruined and uninhabited cottage of mud. On showing our firman and bouyurdee, and hinting that on our return to those who granted them, we should give an account of the treatment we had experienced, the Aga condescended to exert his authority, and ordered lodging to be prepared for us in the cottage of a peasant. In addition to some coarse cakes we were only able to procure a hare, which had been brought in from the forests of Ida by one of the villagers who had been hunting there. A large fire was made for us, as the weather was piercingly cold, and long pieces of pine-tree, saturated with turpentine, were lighted instead of lamps or candles. The inhabitants, though Turks, called these torches Δαδιὰ, a word* slightly corrupted from the ancient term.

---

* Δᾳδὶς, ligna arboris pini vel piceæ.   D'Orville, Charit. ii. 489

The Imaum of the mosque and the old men of the village came to smoke their pipes and converse round our fire in the evening, and on our offering them some of our coffee, they became sociable and communicative. The most intelligent of our visitors was a Turk, who in his youth had been a mariner, and who had visited the shores of the Black Sea and of Egypt; he had now retired to his native village, where he supported himself by the manufactory of pitch and turpentine, which are made in the extensive fir groves of Ida during a great part of the year; and in the winter he gained a livelihood by shooting the game and wild beasts of the forests of Gargarus, μητηρ θηρίων He expatiated on the wonders of Mount Kaz-Dag, telling us of its deep caverns and grottos, its streams, fountains, and cascades, and the extent of the prospect from the summit.

On informing him that the object of our journey was to reach the top of the mountain, he expressed his doubts of our being able to endure the cold and fatigue of such an undertaking at this season of the year, but finding we were resolved to make the attempt, he offered to be our guide. Accordingly at a quarter before seven o'clock the next morning we set out. The river Menderé had now decreased to about four yards in breadth, its course, however, was very strong and rapid among loose blocks of granite. Crossing its bed, we came to a ruined building, which my companion took some pains to measure. It appeared to me to have been originally a church of the later Greeks. It was about fifteen paces in length, and eight in breadth; the walls about four feet thick, of very rough stone and mortar; but there were no remains of columns or sculpture. Our guide called this and some other ruins we came to afterwards, *Klishia*, an evident corruption of ἐκκλησία; probably this has been the resort of Greek Caloyers or hermits at some former period.

We now began to climb the hills at the base of Kaz-Dag, and soon reached the region of pines In the course of our ascent we traversed very extensive forests of lofty fir-trees, which seem to be used solely for making pitch; and we saw a number of rudely constructed furnaces for boiling and thickening the turpentine. Many of these wide

forests had taken fire, and we were struck with the singular appearance of thousands of huge pines burnt as black as charcoal, standing
erect, without a branch, the white sides of the snowy hills above,
making a strong contrast with them.   The pitch furnaces and a few
huts to shelter the workmen, who at the season for extracting the
pitch came not only from the Troad, but from the island of *Salamis,
were the only vestiges of building we met with in this sequestered
region of the mountain.

At three quarters after nine o'clock, or three hours from Evjilah,
we came to the foot of a magnificent cascade of the Menderé; the
fall appeared to be about fifty feet perpendicular.   It then dashes
impetuously from rock to rock, until it reaches the plain, which is
about four or five hundred feet below this cascade.   We climbed with
difficulty over crags and broken ground to the orifice in the rock,
whence it issues.   There we found a spacious cavern, extending far
into the mountain; within it the waters of the Menderé roll from a
distance, and bring a considerable stream, making a loud and deep
noise, and bursting forth with violence into the open air.   If this be
the source of the Scamander, we are not surprised that in the days of
mythology a river issuing so nobly from so mysterious a source should
have been deified and adored under the names of the divine Xanthus
or Scamander.

On our first entrance into this spacious cavern, all was dark and
awful; and the noise of the waters coming from a distance, and dashing against their rocky channel, stunned our ears.   The guide, however, soon struck a light, and with his blazing torches of pine-wood,
δαδι as he called them, disclosed to our view the foaming waters
coming from two deeply-worn channels, which entered into the
bowels of the mountain, beyond the reach of his torches' light.   He
then bared his legs, and descended into one of these channels, desiring us to follow him up its windings, which he said might be done to

---

* See also Hobhouse's Travels, p. 384.

a considerable distance. But the water here had not been tempered by the sun and air, and was so benumbingly cold, that we declined his invitation. We then scratched our names on the roof of the cavern, and returned to day-light.

The most arduous and fatiguing part of our journey still remained to be performed, the face of the mountain being so rugged and steep as to prevent our riding. We therefore followed our guide on foot, climbing and scrambling like goats from crag to crag. Here we could not help noticing how much more secure-footed he was in his bear-skin sandals, than we in our English shoes. He told us, that the bear, of whose skin his sandals were made, had been killed by himself on this very mountain; the hair of the skin was outwards, to give a firmer hold of the ice and snow. When we had proceeded about two miles on our winding road from the cavern, we reached the beginning of the snowy district; and here it required some enthusiasm and courage to keep to our resolution, as our guide assured us that three trying hours would be employed in reaching the summit.

Reflecting however how much we might hereafter regret having been so very near the object of our wishes without accomplishing them; we halted for a short time, and then set off with renewed ardour. After climbing two hours through the snow, my feet often giving way, my strength and spirits failed, and I determined to stop here, desiring the guide and my companion to be careful in their return not to miss me, and to mark the place I made a number of crosses on the snow. However, on my friend's assuring me of my danger being greater if I should suffer myself to be overcome by sleep in consequence of my fatigue, than if I proceeded with him, I went forward; and, continuing our steep ascent, we reached in half an hour the highest point of Gargarus

On this fearful summit of Ida we found a level surface of no great extent; it was of an oblong form, with a rudely-built wall around it, in which were a few small blocks of marble. This inclosure may probably have been a Greek church, or perhaps only a sheep-pen raised for the protection of the flocks in the summer months.

Unfortunately at our first reaching the place, the snow fell so thick, and the atmosphere was so loaded with mist, that we could see little of the vast prospect it would have afforded in a clear day. One short gleam of sunshine showed us the whole Scamandrian plain extended at our feet, and watered, through its whole length, by the serpentine course of the river. At this moment our guide pointed out to us a number of places in the distant horizon, the isles of Imbros and Samothrace, Mount Athos in Macedonia, Alexandria Troas, Sigeum, and the Euxine. I drew a circle in the snow around him, noting as nearly as I could the bearings given to me by this veteran mariner. As we had no means of ascertaining the height, I can only state the calculation of Mr. Kauffer, a German engineer, who, when in the service of M. Choiseul Gouffier, estimated it at 775 toises above the level of the Archipelago.

Our guide told us that other large rivers besides the Menderé have their source in Gargarus; one he called Khshiah Sou, which falls into the Menderé; another he called Magra. And he also spoke of three great rivers called Ak-chyà, Monaster-chyà, and Gure-chyà, which discharged themselves into the Archipelago.

I here venture to record a circumstance which proves on how fanciful a foundation etymological reasonings are founded. Our guide, when he pointed expressively to the snow on the top of the mountain, repeated the words Gar, Gar, "Snow, snow," in which an enthusiastic topographer of the Iliad would easily have traced the ancient name of Gargarus.

CHAP IV

Descent from Ida — Assos — Ruins and Theatre — Salt Springs at Tousla — Great Peasantry of Neachori — Tenedos

Wᴇ now turned our steps back through the dark forests and crags of Ida, and soon reached Evjilah, where we found the villagers surprized at our having been on the summit of Kaz-Dag. We supped on the scanty fare which this place furnished, our bread was the worst we had yet seen, being unleavened cakes made of ca-lambóchi.

Evjilah contains about thirty families, all Mahometan. Their cottages are miserable; the walls are of mud, and the roof of turf or soil, laid horizontally on fir rafters. In fine weather the Turks pass more of their time on these terraces, than in the gloomy com-fortless room below, on most of these roofs we observed a fragment of a small granite column, used as a roller to smooth the surface. The only person in the place, who seemed to be above a state of indigence, was a Turk who had been in the service of the governor of the Dardanelles, and after saving a little money had retired to his native village, where he now filled the office of Aga, and seemed to act in the capacity of a mayor or justice of the peace. He had built a mosque here at his own expense, the Imaum or curate of which paid us a visit his stipend, we found, was fixed at sixty piastres, less than four pounds a year, for which he both officiated at the mosque and kept the school. To this was added an occasional present at a circumcision or a funeral. He depended, however, more on the produce of a little farm, than on his profession, for a maintenance.

The inhabitants in general live more by pasturage of cattle and the chase, than by agriculture, and seem to have few comforts of life, but we were surprised at the very extravagant price they demanded for the trifling articles with which they unwillingly

supplied us.   Our guide insisted on having seven piastres (or half
a guinea) in hand, before he set out with us to the top of Kaz-Dag ;
and told us that our countrymen had paid him double that sum

During our supper, some sooty workmen from the pitch furnaces
came to us, begging charity, and saying that they were Christians
from the island of Salamis, and that they had been impressed for
this service by the Capudan Pasha, who annually sends a ship for
some of their countrymen, that they may be employed in the forests
of Ida.

After recruiting our strength by a night's rest at Evjilah, we
proceeded next day on our return towards Yenicher ; our route led
us through part of the ancient Scepsis ; for some time we kept the
road by which we had come, and then crossed a tributary stream of
the Menderé, called Chiousluk Sou, which is dry in the summer
months.   Our road was on the western banks of the Menderé.   Four
miles from Evjilah we quitted the rich valley of Bairamitche, and
struck off towards the left.   About two miles further we crossed
another rivulet, broad but shallow, called Yaskebal-Chyà.   In a
Turkish burial-ground here, I noticed a few scattered fragments of
ancient buildings.   Four miles further we came to a lofty hill
called Kezil Tepé   We rested for a short time under an oriental
plane-tree ; and then passed through a Turkish village called
Oranjou, and soon discovered, by the frequency of fountains on the
road-side, by the goodness of the fences, and the cultivated face of
the country, that we had again reached estates belonging to Hadim
Oglou's family.   The source of the rivulet Sanderlee is extremely
beautiful, and we found the pale-green tint of the plane-trees near
it a most pleasing relief to the eye after the gloomy pine forests,
and dazzling snow of Gargarus.

In the evening we reached the town of Boyuk Bounarbashi, or the
greater Bounarbashi, so called to distinguish it from the village of the
same name at the top of the Scamandrian plain.   We found this
town very gay and noisy on account of the celebration of a Turkish
wedding ; and before we retired to rest, a band of musicians, who had
been brought to the wedding-feast from the Dardanelles came to our

lodgings with a set of dancers. The concert was composed of three instruments not unlike clarionets, and a number of drums of different sizes. The shrillness of the pipes, and the stunning noise of the drums were ill suited to the little room in which we were sitting. Both musicians and dancers were strolling gypsies in the Turkish dress; one acted the part of clown or buffoon, and the dance was altogether so indecent, that we soon dismissed them.

Boyuk Bounarbashi which Hadim Oglou told us was so much more worthy of being visited than the Bounarbashi in sight of Yenicher, is about twenty miles from Evjilah at the foot of Gargarus. It has its name like the other from the copious springs of water near it. A large modern fountain, from which three streams flow, has been built of blocks of marble, probably from some ruins in the neighbourhood; but we could detect neither inscription nor sculpture of ancient date. in the adjoining burial-ground are a few granite columns.

We proceeded hence in a S.W. direction, passing a village named Turemanly, our road was through a plain, Salkecheui Deresi, bounded by a range of hills called Kara-dag, " the black hills " there is another village, Sapooiy, at which we did not stop; and about fourteen miles from Boyuk Bounarbashi we arrived at Aivajek. This is a town of about two hundred houses, under the jurisdiction of Osman Aga, who is independent of Hadim Oglou, or at least wished to make us think so, by the contempt with which he treated that governor's Bouyurdee. At this place we were received with rudeness and insult; and were sent to a Khan with a guard to watch us, until the suspicious Aga had examined our passports and cross-questioned our guides. He would not admit us to his presence; but ordered us to leave his territory without delay; and we departed as soon as we could procure some horses. The Khan in which we halted was built by the present Aga, it has about thirty rooms besides stables; some of which are let out to pedlars, tailors, and other tradesmen, who come occasionally to reside here. From the inhospitable town of Aivajek we proceeded by a road winding

through mountains, until we reached a sluggish river, the waters of
which are concealed in many places by ridges; it is called Tousla
Chyà, or the river of the salt-marsh.   Here we had the first view of
the gulf of Adramyttium, with a groupe of little islands on it.   At
eight miles from Aivajek is the Turkish village of Beyram, adjoining
very extensive ruins of ancient buildings, whose proportions are so
great and noble, that the miserable Turkish houses of Beyram look
like the temporary huts of a travelling horde.

The next morning we eagerly began our examination of these
magnificent remains of a city which we presumed to be Assos.   We
were fortunate enough to meet with an attentive host and useful
guide at this place, whom we found waiting for us at the entrance of
the town.   He told us that he had heard of two English travellers
who proposed to explore that neighbourhood in their way to Alexandria Troas, and therefore he had prepared a lodging, and the Aga
had sent him provisions for our use.   He was a mariner, and a
native of Mytilene.   The dinner provided for us consisted of a kind
of soup thickened with barley, pancakes mixed with spinach, and a
pilaw of rice dressed with very rancid butter ; pastry made of butter
equally rancid, and swimming in honey.

March 17.—Assos has stood upon a sloping hill facing the sea,
and commanding a view of Lesbos in the Adramyttian gulf.   Its
walls have been of great strength, and are about five miles in circuit.
Three of the ancient gate-ways remain quite entire, the fourth is in
ruins, the high ground, which was originally the Ἄστυ, Acropolis
or citadel, is a rock of granite of very steep sides   Upon it are
ruins of an ancient edifice, which in the revolution of succeeding
ages has been a Genoese castle and a Greek church, and is now a
Turkish mosque.   Over its entrance on an architrave, is an inscription
in very modern Greek characters; it makes mention of Ἄνθιμος ὁ
πρόεδρος Σκαμάνδρου.*   Near the mosque are two subterranean build-

---

* It is remarkable, that throughout this district, not only on the shores of the
Hellespont but also on those of the Ægean sea, there should have been particular

ings, about thirty feet long and forty-five deep; they have probably been reservoirs or cisterns to hold water for the garrison; as a well in one of them still supplies in part the town of Beyram.

On the brow of the Acropolis are scattered some broken columns of granite, which are fluted, and among them are some bas-reliefs on blocks of granite; the figures are about twenty inches in height, one part of the subject represented seems to have been a procession to a sacrifice, there are three naked figures, with their arms extended, marching in the same direction, and another looking back to them. The style of work is Egyptian. The exposure to the sea-air has corroded the sculptured surface. On another block of granite were two bulls fighting, their horns are locked together on another were three horses running; on another two winged sphinxes, resting each of them a foot on a kind of candelabrum placed between them, and looking towards each other. A symposium or banquet is also sculptured on a block of granite; a youth is seen presenting a cup to a bearded man who is reclined on a couch, a large vase or amphora is near him; and various figures are in the back-ground, forming altogether the representation of some funeral scene or ceremony. These fragments have probably composed the frize of a granite temple which has stood on this citadel, the columns are about three feet in diameter, parts of the shafts remain on their original site, so that a person conversant with ancient architecture might easily trace the plan and different details.

---

reference made to the *Scamandros*, we find the river also mentioned on the coins of Alexandria Troas, ΑΛΕΞΑΝΔΡΕΩΝ ΣΚΑΜΑΝΔΡΟΣ (Cuper, Harpoc, 216.) Is this regard paid to the little rivulet at Bounarbashi, or to the river which rises in great majesty and beauty from the recesses and caverns of Ida? — E

* The marbles and monuments of antiquity on which are seen figures of persons reclining on couches, in the act of drinking, *genio indulgentes*, refer to the opinion, that the deceased so represented were in a state of happiness, ἐν Ἠλυσίω πεδίω, " ut beatorum conditionem exprimerent, eos accumbentes sculpserunt," says Cuper. See a remarkable passage to this purpose in Plato, l 2 de repub κάλλιστον ἀρετῆς μισθὸν μήτην αἰώνιον — E.

Descending from the Acropolis we came to a small but beautifully constructed edifice, having an arched or rather vaulted dome; the walls and roof are composed of huge blocks of granite fitted together without cement. This building had been converted into a vapour-bath by the Turks; but appeared neglected. A double wall is built against the side of the Acropolis with a space between, probably to keep the buildings free from the moisture which filters through the crevices. At a short distance towards the sea are ruins of a magnificent gate-way to the city, and part of a grand flight of steps. Blocks of an architrave with inscriptions in large Greek characters lie near this spot. This architrave seems to have belonged to the portico or Propylæa; the letters are four inches in length.

ΣΚΑΠΕΡΓΥΣΤΟΥΔΙΟΣΤ
ΟΥΟΜΟΝΩΟΥΚΑΙΓΥΜ
ΘΕΟΥΚΑΙΣΑΡΟΣΟΔΕΛΥ

This portico has been of the Doric order, as is evident by the massive triglyphs which still remain I also found another inscription in smaller characters.

ΓΚΤΗΣΠΡΟΣΟΔΟΥΤΩΝΑΓΡΩΝΑΠΕΛΙΠΕΝΕΙΣΕΠΙΣΚΕΥ
ΗΝΤΗΣΠΟΛΕΩΣΚΛΕΟΣΤΡΑΤΟΣΤΙΟΣΠΟΛΕΩΣΦΥΣΕΙΔΕ
ΑΠΕΛΛΙΚΩΝΤΟΣ

On the declivity of the hill, commanding a beautiful prospect of the gulf and island of Lesbos, stands an ancient Greek theatre, of which the remains are very considerable. The ranges of seats for the spectators remain almost perfect; they are divided into three distinct stories, and are conveniently hollowed out, for allowing the persons sitting to draw their feet a little back*, so as not to incom-

---

* This form of the seats is not uncommon, and among other instances we may refer to the theatre at Iero in Epidauria. See Des Mouceaux We find them sometimes cut out of the solid rock, as at Argos, but in all the ancient theatres the seats must have been covered with wood, πρῶτον ξύλον, *primum lignum*, was an expression used by the Greeks to signify the first seat Pollux iv. 121. The " wide walk," mentioned by Dr Hunt, is the διάζωμα, or præcinctio, which was in general equal in breadth to two steps.

mode those who are before them. Two large vaulted entrances remain by which the people entered into the area, then ascended by five flights of steps to their appropriated places. There are forty ranges of seats, and at the top of the theatre there is a broad terrace or promenade. Counting from the ground, we find the first thirty seats separated from the succeeding seven by a wide walk; there is a similar interval between them and the last three, and these are terminated by the lofty terrace.

Between the wall inclosing the theatre and the side of the acropolis against which it is built, there is a vacant space, intended, it appears, to carry off the water that trickles from the rock. Fronting the orchestra are some blocks remaining in their original place; they may probably be the ruins of the Thymele, where the musicians were placed, and which was built of stone; near them is a broken inscription, making mention of Cleostratus, the same person already recorded.

It has been ascertained, that a person sitting at the most remote extremity of some of the ancient theatres was able distinctly to hear the voice of one speaking from the part where the actors stood. Experiments of this kind have been repeatedly made in 1785 at the theatre of Saguntum, which contained 12,000 people, and Marti said (Mountfaucon, A. E. iii 237.) "that a friend reciting some verses of the Amphytrion of Plautus, on the scena, was distinctly heard by him at the top of the theatre." The distance is about 114 feet. The architect Dufourny made in Sicily, in the ancient theatre of Tauromenium, similar observations. In this the distance from the pulpitum to the most elevated extremity of the external circumference is sixty metres, or about 180 feet. He heard in every part of the theatre not only the ordinary voice of a man on the pulpitum, but the slow and gradual tearing of a piece of paper, and added in his journal a remark, which naturally suggested itself to his mind, that Echea or the sounding vases, mentioned by Vitruvius, as well as masks, could not always have been necessary for the purpose of extending and distributing the voice of the actor. See Mongez. Mem. de l'Institut. 1805. " The commentators on Vitruvius (says Schlegel) are much at variance with respect to the Echea. We may venture without hesitation to assume, that the theatres of the ancients were constructed on excellent acoustical principles."

It appears that a contrivance, similar to that described by Vitruvius, was adopted in some Christian churches to strengthen the voice of the monks and canons. " Dans le chœur du temple neuf à Strasbourg, le professeur Oberlin a découvert de pareils vases appliqués à différens endroits de la voûte." They were of Terra-cotta. Millin D. de B. A. i 478—E

s

The diameter of the whole building is seventy paces, including the thickness of the walls of the Hospitalia.* In the middle range of the seats there are two large vomitoria.

There are ruins of columns and architraves along the whole line of the wall which fronts the sea, indicating an extensive portico; in a plain beneath is the ancient cemetery of Assos, where we observed many sarcophagi Some of them are seven and eight feet high, and of a proportionate breadth and length; they have been hewn out of one massive block of grey granite, and then covers out of another. The sides are in general ornamented with festoons in relievo, and many have the remains of inscriptions, now so much defaced as to be quite illegible.

The Turks appear to have broken into them all, by making holes in their side ; this was not so difficult a task as to raise their ponderous coverings. The entrances now admit kids and lambs, glad of the shelter and shade which they find within these ancient tombs.

The view of this city in ancient times from the sea, and the approach to it from the shore must have produced a striking effect ; first, an extensive cemetery presented itself, covered with huge sarcophagi of granite; then a flight of steps leading to a terrace and porticos, and the principal gate in the city walls; then the baths and edifices of the lower town, with the theatre, acropolis, and its temples rising majestically behind.

In different parts of the ancient town we observed heaps of broken vases, of that light elegant fabric called Etruscan or Greek, beautifully varnished with black. The labours of any one who should carry

---

* For the use and position of these buildings, see D'Orville, Sicilia 259. who explains a passage of Vitruvius relating to them " Hæc ædificia," says D'Orville, "revera inservierunt variis scenicis et theatralibus usibus; hic fuerunt choragia, hic machinæ scenicæ ; hic ipsi histriones et chori parabantur." In the plan of the theatre found in Dr Hunt's papers, the foundations of the scena are marked, the λογειον, that part of it where the actors stood, being generally of wood, is not of course remaining The Λογειον answered in some respects to the pulpitum, only it was not so wide as the latter. The Romans had no Thymele; their singers and dancers were on the pulpitum — See D'Orville, 259.

on excavation in this place would be well repaid by the discovery of many valuable remains of ancient art.

Unfortunately we could not find one inscription containing the name of the city, nor one Greek coin. Our guide produced many copper coins found here, but they were of little value, having no visible device or inscription. According to the tradition preserved by the present inhabitants, the place was a fortress of the Genoese.

At half-past three o'clock in the afternoon we took our leave of these interesting ruins, and proceeding in a northerly direction, at about a mile and a half from Beyram, we crossed a stream called Tousla Chya, or the river of the Salt-wych. On our right were high hills; we then entered a plain bounded by a ridge of eminences, the highest of which is called Topal Tepessi. At six miles north of Beyram, we crossed another rivulet, Goulfà Chva, which falls into the Tousla Chya. After ascending some steep hills, and leaving the village of Beergaz on our left, about nine miles north of Beyram, we reached a small town called Tamush. It is situated in a rocky country where many herds of goats are kept, and below it is a deep dell or glen. We found the Aga of the place selfish and suspicious. Under pretence of doing us honour, he sent his supper to the cottage where we lodged; he not only questioned us very closely, but asked whether we had not a watch, or pistols, or telescopes, to leave him in return for a greyhound he would give us. To all our enquiries about the history of the place he returned evasive answers. On leaving us he said we must be careful to abstain from wine in the room in which we lodged, as there were carpets and mats on the floor used by Musulmans at the time of saying their prayers, and these might be polluted. He even ordered five or six of his attendants to pass the whole night in the room with us, however a trifling present removed these troublesome spies, except one, an old negro, who sat up the whole night by the side of the carpet on which we slept. The town consists of about fifty families, all Turks; and, with the exception of Hadje Aga, who had made a pilgrimage to Mecca, and ought to have learned hospitality, they were almost as ignorant as the goats they

tended. Next morning, accompanied by some guards of the Aga,
we were allowed to go up a hill adjoining the town ; we saw from it
the course of the river Tousla Chya, which, they told us, enters the
sea about three hours or leagues north of Baba Bournou (Cape
Lectum), and at three leagues to the south of Eski Stambol (Alexandria Troas). The plain in which the mouth of the river is situated,
is called Tchesederesi-alti.

Our road hence was by the side of a craggy glen, called Tchaytan-
deresi, or the Devil's ditch ; until we came to Tousla-Dag, a mountain which forms the western extremity of the chain of Gargarus or
Ida. We halted at a Turkish village called Babà-Deresi, seven miles
from Tamush. Here our friendly guide the sailor, who had been our
host at Beyram, gave so interesting a description of a place in the
neighbourhood called Tousla, its boiling springs, and salt works, that
when he added a visit to it would only make a deviation of an hour
from our route towards Alexandria Troas, we resolved to proceed
thither. At Babà-Deresi is a poor mosque with mud walls ; but it
has a porch supported by three ancient columns, with capitals of different orders, and of unequal workmanship. In the burial ground of
the village there are also a few ancient marbles.

Within the hour we reached the shallow ponds, in which the brine
is exposed to evaporation. The salt-springs here are so copious, that
after collecting as much of their waters as is wanted, the rest is suffered to run into the river Tousla Chya, which carries it to the sea.
About 100,000 bushels of fine white salt are thus made annually.
Hadim Oglou has the monopoly of it, which he purchases or farms of
the Sultan. At one of the hot springs a bath has been built ; the roof
is covered with locks of hair and other votive offerings, such as pieces
of cloth and ribbands from the patients who have used it. After
passing through the town of Tousla, we reached the principal hot
spring, which bursts * from the solid rock at a considerable height

* " Strabo, lib. xiii mentions the saline of Tragasea, near Hamaxitus, on the coast of
Troas. This is no doubt the one now in use at the mouth of the Tousla river, a league to

above the ground; the violence with which it issues, forms a jet of some feet before it falls towards the earth. The heat is that of boiling water; the stones, near the place, appear burnt. The taste is salt and extremely bitter. About a hundred yards from this intensely hot spring is one of cold water, unimpregnated with salt, which runs in a separate channel to the river Tousla. A plot of green turf separates the hot from the cold fountain.

The weather was so warm that our guides and servants seemed unwilling to accompany us up a high hill, that promised an extensive view. Mr. Carlyle and myself therefore ascended it together, and from its summit saw the stream which flows from the salt-springs fall into the river Tousla at about three miles distance. We noticed some slight traces of building on our road up, but on reaching the summit we found no vestiges of any edifice. The high mountains at Babà Bournou or Cape Lectum, prevented us from seeing Athos on the opposite coast of Macedonia.

After rejoining our party at Tousla we retraced our steps to the road we had quitted, and soon overtook Mustapha, whom we had sent forward to procure accommodation for us at Tchesederé. We observed in the vineyards a number of Turkish farmers working together, and found it was the custom for them to assist each other at pruning time, and at the vintage. The vineyards, however, are not cultivated here with the intention of making wine, the grapes are consumed by the Turks both as ripe fruit and when dried into raisins; a syrup is also made from the juice called Petmez, and a tough kind of dried sweet-meat, used instead of sugar in their sherbet. The Turkish town of Tchesederé consists of about three hundred houses, under the jurisdiction of the Aga of Aivajek, whose deputy, Hadje Ali Aga, resides here: he had inclosed the cemetery with a wall;

the southward of Alexandria Troas. The agency of the Etesian winds, so oddly described by Strabo, was doubtless nothing more than that of raising the level of the sea, so as to overflow the margin, and fill the hollow plain within, where in due time it crystallized."— Rennell's Troy, 18.—The words of Strabo are, ἁλοπήγιον αὐτοματον τοῖς ἐτησίαις πηγνύμενον.

we had not yet observed a burial ground in the Troad protected in this manner.

At half-past three in the afternoon we again came in sight of the sea, and entered once more into Hadım Oglou's domain, the boundary of which is here marked by a tumulus called Vizier, or Pasha Tepé Towards the shore there are many tumuli, to which our guides could give no other name than Besh Tepé, the five tumuli.

Our road now led us through forests of the Valanea oak ; the large husks which contain their acorns are used for tanning, and form a principal article of export from this part of Turkey. These trees were now (March 18th) in full foliage. The valley, which here extends to the sea, is called Olimichi Ouessi. At five o'clock we reached some ruins and observed many broken sarcophagi At a Turkish Hammaum or bathing-house, built over a natural hot-spring, is a statue of a female figure in marble. We soon reached the remains of an ancient aqueduct, called by our guide Eski Stambol Capessi, or the gates of old Constantinople, a name given by the Turks to Alexandria Troas. The day was too far advanced to allow us to visit the extensive ruins of this place, we therefore halted at Gaikli, where we slept. This village a few years ago contained a hundred and fifty Turkish families ; but the exactions of their Aga have forced most of them to emigrate to the adjacent island of Tenedos. At present there are not more than twenty-five inhabited cottages.

On mentioning to our host our wish of visiting the ruins of Eski Stambol, he told us that Hadım Oglou's flocks were feeding in the pastures near that spot ; that they were so numerous as to require fifty watch-dogs, and that it would be unsafe for strangers to venture among them. A couple of piastres, however, induced a man to go forward and inform the shepherds that some friends of their master were coming to visit the ruins. and thus the danger, real or pretended, was avoided.

Next morning, passing by the ruins of the ancient aqueduct, built originally by Herodes Atticus, and turning short to the right, we came in a short time to a vaulted building, probably in former times a bath, and coated in the inside with reticulated tile-work; adjoining to it are pedestals of stone and mortar, which once sustained perhaps the columns of a gateway. Our guides conducted us to the remains of what is called Priam's Palace, they appeared to have formed part of a gymnasium with baths, and belong to the time of Hadrian and the Antonines. The principal entrance is still a fine object, though stripped of most of the marbles with which it has been cased. Some parts of the cornice and the capitals of Ionic pilasters remain in their original positions, and the centre arch is entire. The area enclosed by this edifice has been very extensive, and all its remains indicate magnificence. Great numbers of trees and shrubs are growing amongst them.

Some of the seats of a theatre, which is not far from this spot, may be still seen; the proscenium is entirely destroyed, and the area of the orchestra is filled with bushes. We examined some vaulted sub-terranean buildings, which our guides called ancient prisons for criminals. Proceeding towards the sea we noticed the site of the stadium; some fragments of ornamental architecture are near it, of rich design, apparently of the Corinthian order. Near the ancient port we saw piles of cannon balls, formed out of granite columns by order of a late Capudan Pasha for the supply of the forts of the Dardanelles.

We now quitted the ruins of Alexandria Troas, and returned to the little hamlet of Gaikli through a forest of pines, and at one o'clock proceeded towards Yenicher. In our road we observed a lake near the shore now called Yolé, probably the Pteleos of Strabo, on the right hand was a hillock or tumulus called Devisé Tepé. We then reached the canal or bed, which, we were told, had been made to bring the waters of the Kuk-joss from Bounarbashi in order to work a corn-mill at a Tchiflick here. This, the villagers said, had been done about eighty years ago by a Sultana of the Seraglio, who was then proprietor of the estate, and that it had subsequently de-volved to Hassan Pasha who repaired it.

March 19.—We crossed this little stream by a bridge, and continued our route by the side of a fresh-water lake nearly three miles. Not far from the shore on our left was a conical mound, supposed to be the Tumulus of Peneleus, and between us and Bounarbashi arose the conspicuous barrow of Udjek-Tepé, or the tomb of Æsyetes.

On our arrival at Yeni-keui, or Neachoré as the Greeks call it, we stopped a short time to examine the church of the village, where we copied a Latin inscription.

C. MARCIVS MARSVS
V. F. SIBI ET SVIS

Here we found a communicative Greek shopkeeper, who gave us the following information respecting the state of this part of the Troad.

Neachoré contains about a hundred families, all Greek Christians; of these, seventy are land-owners and farmers, and thirty labourers and shopkeepers. Instead of the government-osour, which ought not to exceed a tenth of the produce, the rapacious Aga who buys it of the Porte, takes about an eighth from the cultivator. The charatch or capitation-tax is thus levied: Adult men pay five piastres a year or 7s. 6d.; youths three, or 4s. 6d., and boys two and a half, 3s. 10d. each. Neither women nor children are rated to this tax. At the vintage a tax of a penny an oke or about $1\frac{1}{2}d.$ a quart is paid to an officer of the Porte called the Sheraub-Emir, before it is put on board any vessel to be carried coast-wise. Husbandry servants have board, lodging, and clothes provided at their master's house, and wages varying from 60 to 115 piastres, or 4l. 10s. to eight guineas a year, besides the produce of three bushels of corn which they are suffered to sow without any expence on a piece of their master's land.

Young women are mostly employed in spinning cotton; their average work is a hundred drachms in four days, for which they receive 25 paras, about a shilling, a loaf of bread worth two-pence, and a dish of kidney beans or some other pulse, of nearly two pounds weight.

Each landholder pays a bushel and a half of wheat every year to the officiating priest, and other parishioners 60 paras, or 2s. 6d. each, the burial fee is a piastre; but generally from three to ten are given by the family to the priest for masses which he is to say for the repose of the soul of the deceased.

The poor who are disabled from work by age or infirmities are supported by a quota of grain from each farmer, which amounts to about eighteen bushels to every poor family in the year Money is also collected for them at the church on high festivals by the priest; this generally pays the rent of their cottage

As we proceeded from this place to Yenicher, our guide pointed out a dry ditch, which he pretended was once a canal, dug in ancient times for galleys, to avoid doubling the cape in bad weather. To us it appeared to be the bed of a torrent, now dry. The next object that attracted our notice was a conical mound of earth called De-metri Tepé, the supposed tumulus of Antilochus. The Greek Chris-tians have here built a small oratory or chapel at its base, where they celebrate mass on the festival of St Demetrius. We then proceeded to Yenicher, and soon arrived at the cottage of the Greek Papas which we had left twelve days before.

We had now completed our excursion through the Troad, during which I noted many objects that were remarkable as works of ancient art, or tended to illustrate the history or geography of the district. Such information as I was able to collect from guides or villagers, I have given as scrupulously as I was able; and trifling as these details may appear, they were often acquired with difficulty. The questions were generally put to our Greek servant in French or Italian; and the answers he obtained were in Turkish, in which he was not a great proficient.

Our accommodations and provisions were never of the best kind; in villages of Greeks we found that either from their extreme penury, or the fear of discovering to our Turkish guide their hard-earned pittance, we were not able to procure a meal until we had bought a kid or a lamb from a shepherd; it was then to be killed, and the

T

cooking process to be finished before we could satisfy our hunger. The olives gathered ripe and preserved in rancid oil, and the caviar, which the Greek can eat with pleasure, are disgusting to an English palate; and these with sour bread and bad wine are the only provisions a traveller can expect to meet with, unless he has sent forward some person to provide better entertainment.

In Turkish villages he meets with worse reception; and if a mattress and pillow be not among the traveller's store, he must often stretch his weary limbs on a dusty mat laid on an uneven mud floor. The provisions he generally meets with in these places are coffee and pilaw, made of boiled rice with mutton fat or suet, or rancid butter melted into it; and as it is extremely difficult to procure even two or three horses, it is impracticable to take those things which might make amends for the inconveniences of the road.

The petty Agas are sometimes insolent and suspicious of travellers, and interrupt their researches by private orders to their guides to lead them wrong, or by giving false information to travellers themselves; as they conceive all the curiosity of Franks in examining ruins and inscriptions is directed chiefly to discover concealed treasures; and if the traveller ask questions concerning the course of rivers, and the distances of towns, it is suspected that it is for the sake of facilitating some meditated invasion of their country; nor can the Sultan's firman, or even the escort of a Janissary of the Porte, always destroy such suspicions.

We now prepared to take leave of the interesting region of the Troad, the Scamandrian plain, Mount Ida, and the shores of the Hellespont. It would be an invidious task to attempt destroying any of the enthusiasm that is felt in reading some of the immortal works of the ancient writers, by showing in what instances they have deviated from geographical precision in their allusions to local scenery, and indeed it is hardly allowable to look for perfect and minute resemblance at the distance of nearly three thousand years. Natural and artificial changes must have taken place to a considerable extent in that time, in the face of the country, in the courses of the rivers through low ground, in the outline of the shores of the rapid Hellespont. But sufficient resemblance, I think, still remains to warrant the belief that the plain of Menderé and Bounarbashi is the Scamandrian plain of Homer ; the Kaz-Dag is the Ida of the poet, that Dtheo Tepé and In Tepé are the barrows alluded to as the tumuli of Achilles and Ajax ; though the names of these heroes may have been assigned to them to give a kind of local habitation to invented incidents. A citadel and walls have also existed at a remote period near Bounarbashi ; but not of a construction contemporary with the supposed æra of the Trojan war. The ten years' duration of the siege ; the numbers of ships and forces furnished by Greece ; their means of subsistence ; the names of their leaders, and the particular details of engagements and single combats must frequently have been the invention of the poet ; and perhaps he merely availed himself of some popular legend of a predatory excursion, which had ultimately led to the establishment of his fellow-countrymen on the coasts of Asia Minor, adapting the incidents of his poem as much as possible to the appearance which the plain then exhibited, and to the received traditions of its inhabitants.

March 21.—We went to Coum Kalé at the mouth of the Menderé, where we hired a Turkish boat to convey us to Tenedos. We gave the owner 13 piastres for the passage to the island.

Here we lodged at the house of a Greek, who fills the office of British Vice-Consul, and who is also Πρωτόγερος, or chief Greek magistrate. There is only one town in the island, which contains about 750 families ; 450 of them are Mahommedan, and 300 of the Greek Christian church. The harbour is small, but commodious for the trading vessels, which come to purchase wine. Fuel, corn, and most of the provisions for consumption are brought from the opposite coast of the Troad. The principal and almost sole produce of Tenedos is wine. For this the island is celebrated now as in ancient times ; we see the device of the cluster of grapes on the coins of Tenedos. The red kind is strong, and as dark and rough as port. A small quantity of muscadel is also made, which is much esteemed ;

the red sells at eight paras, or four-pence the oke of 2¼ lb. ; the white muscadel at thirty. Wine pays a custom-house duty of two paras an oke ; and rackee, the common raw spirit, pays four paras an oke on exportation.

The government exacts from the Turks one-tenth of the produce, from the Greeks an eighth : the latter pay also an annual poll-tax, or Charatch ; the men 5½ piastres, boys of ten years old and upwards about two. Besides these permanent taxes, extraordinary contributions are raised in time of war. The Vaivode or governor, the Janissaries, who are in garrison, and those who act as police guardians in the town, are paid by a tax levied on the vineyards ; from the Greeks eleven paras (or five-pence-halfpenny), are taken for every thousand vines ; from the Turks five.

The harbour was full of ships under Ragusan, Austrian, and Turkish colours ; they were taking in cargoes of wine for the English expedition under Sir R. Abercrombie, at that time in Marmorice bay, opposite to Rhodes. The government had monopolized the whole vintage of the island, giving six paras and a half for the oke

The Greek church at Tenedos has lately been rebuilt, and although the imperial firman states that the favour had been granted by the mere good will of the Sultan, yet we found that it had cost the Greeks of the town 5000 piastres in bribes and fees to officers of the Porte. There are three officiating priests for this church, each of whom derives an income of about 350 piastres a-year, a hundred of which is taken from them by their diocesan, the Bishop of Mytilene.

The Protoyero, or chief magistrate of the Greeks, is annually chosen by the inhabitants of that class ; and if his administration gives satisfaction, he is appointed a second time, or perhaps oftener.

The general appearance of the island is unpicturesque and parched ; it abounds with few trees, and presents little verdure. We could find no traces of temples or ancient edifices In the market-place near the port is a granite sarcophagus, now used as a cistern. On one side of it is an inscription, which was copied by Chandler.

REMARKS RESPECTING ATTICA,

[FROM THE JOURNALS OF THE LATE DR SIBTHORP]

—————

FROM THE HEGOUMENOS OF THE CONVENT OF PLNDLLI

THE number of sheep and goats in Attica is computed at 160,000; of these the goats are 100,000, the sheep 60,000. During the winter months a wandering tribe of Nomads drive their flocks from the mountains of Thessaly into the plains of Attica and Bœotia, and give some pecuniary consideration to the Pasha of Negropont and Vaivode of Athens. These people are much famed for their woollen manufactures, particularly the coats or cloaks worn by the Greek sailors.

Fifteen thousand goats and sheep are yearly killed in Attica; of these 10,000 are goats. All, however, are not bred in that country; many are brought from the neighbouring districts. Of the skins of the goats, those of 2000 of them are employed for sacks ὄζμακτα, for carrying wine, oil, and honey; of the remaining 8000, the skins are bought by the tanners, some of these, when tanned, are exported. The greater part is used in the country for making sandals, shoes, and boots.

A good goat gives the same quantity of milk as a good ewe. The price of a goat is 100 paras; of a kid, from 30 to 40 paras. They shear the goats at the same time with the sheep, about April or May. A goat generally gives 100 drachms of goat's hair, or the fourth part of an oke. The hair is all manufactured, and produces yearly 250 cantari, at **20** piastres the cantaro. It is worked into sacks, and bags, and carpets, of which a considerable quantity is exported.

When the wool of the sheep is exported, a duty of 4½ *per cent.* on the value is paid by the Rayah, but by a Frank only *3 per cent.* The sheep's milk is mixed with that of the goats, and used for cheese or butter, a small quantity of the latter is made principally in the month of April or May. The cows are kept chiefly for breeding. A good sheep will yield from an oke and a half to two okes of wool the price of one is three piastres; that of a lamb 60 paras. The wool is made into capots, bags, and carpets, by the Albanese. The ψώρα* or itch, to which the sheep are subject, is cured by taking the refuse of oil; this is warmed and rubbed on the animal; tar or Katrami is then applied. The sheep are particularly fond of the herbs called βρούβα, and after the grapes are gathered, the flocks are driven into the vineyards to crop the leaves, but no injury is supposed to be done to the vines.

Five shepherds are sufficient for a thousand sheep, the pay of the shepherd is 40 piastres, with board and sandals. The flocks are large; some contain 1000 sheep. Where the flock is numerous, they do not mix the sheep with the goats. During the months of January, February, and March, the sheep are kept in the Mandria, and driven out only during the day to feed. The severity of the winter some-times proves destructive to the flocks. The shepherds and the dogs are in general a sufficient protection against the wolves. The dogs of the Hegoumenos of Pendeli are remarkably fierce; they are about 60. 40 of them keep his flock, consisting of 6000 goats and sheep; the remaining 20 accompany the horses and oxen.

To make the cheese, they turn the milk with the rennet, or †·Peetya,

---

* Among the cures of the ψώρα (scabies), in the Geoponica, we find mention made of an ointment of oil and sulphur, p. 457. The wool is shorn off from the part affected, τὸ πεπονθός.

| This is the ancient word, πητύα, coagulum, ea pars viscerum qua ad densandum lac utimur. Nizolius. The best rennet according to the Geoponica, lib xviii. p 459. is from the goat but Columella mentions that of the lamb. Lac plerumque cogitur agni aut hædi coagulo, quamvis possit et agrestis cardui flore conduci. 267. I quote the latter part of the passage, because it illustrates a remark in Shaw, p. 168 " Instead of rennet,

as they call it, taken from the intestines of a lamb. The curd is separated from the whey, put into a form, and pressed; some salt is then sprinkled upon it. The cheeses will continue sound for five years. To make the butter, they take the whey separated from the curd which was used in making the cheese; this is mixed with a large quantity of milk, then scalded over the fire. The cream which rises is skimmed off, and beat or pressed in a large copper boiler, with the feet. The scalded cream is called Kaimak *

The first year the calf is called μοσχάρι, the female μοσχίτα, the male the second year is δάμαλις, which name it retains until the fourth year, when it is called βόδι; the bull is ταῦρος. Only those oxen are killed which are unfit for labour; the number may amount in the year to about 200. The labouring oxen are computed at 3000. The number of cows is something less; they are not milked, but kept only for breeding. In winter they are fed on straw. A good cow is worth 12 piastres; calves are rarely killed. † Four or eight oxen are sufficient for 100 stremata of land, according to the nature of the soil, whether it be light or heavy. They are kept out during the summer; in the winter they are put into the stalls, until the 10th of March. A good ox, at six years old, is worth 50 piastres.

Oct. 15. 1794.—At the Piræus, while I was collecting the seeds of some plants, the Haliaetos shot down with wonderful velocity, and seizing a fish, carried it in its talons high in the air, devouring it in its flight. The halcyon flew across the bay, and the sea-lark ran along the wet beach. The ground rose with a gentle ascent on a free-stone rock; the rough lands which followed were covered with Hedysarum‡ Alhagi, Passerina Hirsuta, and a beautiful species of

---

especially in the summer season, they turn the milk with the flowers of the great-headed thistle, or wild artichoke — E.

* Kaimak is the word used in all parts of the Levant. The Arabic receipt for making it is given in a translation in Russell's Aleppo, i. 370

† Veal is seldom brought to the table in any part of Turkey. Beef is sometimes killed for the market. In Syria the flesh of the buffalo is occasionally eaten.

‡ It is upon this plant that manna is found in Mesopotamia. — Russell's Aleppo, ii. 259.

Echinops a rich plain, planted with vines and olives, then extended within a mile of Athens. A narrow road conducted us through the plain on which were the evident traces of an ancient wall, occasionally fenced off with hedges of Atriplex Halimus and Lycium Europæum, the wild caper bush was also very common on the sides of the road, some fallow grounds succeeded to the olive gardens, on which a few women were busy in collecting a favourite sallad Ῥυζωμο.

Oct. 19.—We obtained from Logotheti some information concerning the present state of Attica. The country of Attica is divided into four districts, namely, Messoia, Catta Lama, Eleusina, with Mount Casha; and the territory of the city of Athens. * These districts contain about 60 towns or villages, and about 12,000 inhabitants; nearly 1000 of these are Turks, and 5000 pay Charatch, the rest are women or children under the age of twelve years. The Charatch is divided into three ratios, which are taken according to the property of the person taxed; the first includes those of the largest property, they pay eleven piastres, the next in consequence half of that sum; those of the last division, which includes the poorest persons in Attica, pay 100 paras. Among the lower class of Athenians there are many, who, notwithstanding their oppressed state, enjoy certain consequence and property, they possess each a house and garden, a vineyard containing at least a strema of land, with a score of olive trees and some bee-hives; and the olive grounds of the large proprietors furnish them during the winter months with constant employment. The season for gathering the olives begins in October, and continues until February, during which period they take at least 25,000 piastres. A man

---

* " The number of houses in the city tenanted at present (1795) is about 1600. This, at five persons to a house, makes 8000 inhabitants, which exceeds half the population of all Attica But it is necessary to remark that about 2500 persons, chiefly Turks, had been carried off in the two last plagues, and that numbers had been forced by the cruelty and exactions of Ali Aga to emigrate.

" In 1797, 250 fugitive Albanian families had returned in consequence of the execution of that person.

" The population of Athens in 1751-2, according to Stuart, was between 9 and 10,000 souls, four-fifths of whom were Christians." Note from Mr. Hawkins's Journal.

is paid 20 paras, women and boys 10 paras each, for a day's labour. The forementioned districts have a Soubashi and Scrivano attached separately to them. The Scrivano is a kind of bailiff who takes an account of what is received or due. The rights of the Vaivode are a tenth of all the corn that is reaped; the vineyards, the cotton, madder, and garden grounds, pay only a composition of eight paras the strema. The strema contains as much ground as is contained within 40 square paces. A proprietor purchases so many stremata or measures of land; he then builds cottages, in which he puts as tenants, industrious peasants. He furnishes them with cattle and seed-corn, and they supply labour. When the harvest is made, the tenth portion is taken by the Soubashi for the Vaivode, the remainder is divided into three portions, of these the οἰκούρος or proprietor, takes two, and only one goes to the tenant, but if the latter has cattle and a house of his own, which is frequently the case, he then divides with the proprietor, and takes an equal share. The villages differ much in respect to the number of houses, and the size of the farms; some farms consist only of a few zevgaria, others of several. Each zevgari contains 350 stremata; they plough with two oxen. The price of wheat, which was at present high, was five piastres the kilo; the kilo weighs about 25 okes, and the oke is 400 Greek drachms. The price of wheat is extremely variable, in plentiful years it is sold so low as two piastres the kilo*, and in great scarcity it has been sold at six piastres. But the richest produce of Attica is the oil, of which it is computed that it yields 20,000 measures annually; the measure is five okes and a half; each measure sells at present at 100 paras. A considerable quantity of madder is cultivated, and some cotton, the latter was selling in the Bazar at 15 paras the oke. The proprietors of Attica have been extremely oppressed by the tyranny of Hadje-Ali Aga. He has seized, by the most nefarious means, a fifth part of the

* Eight kilocs and a half make a quarter of wheat.

U

lands of Attica, forcing the little proprietors to sell him their possessions at his own price.

Oct. 22.—We walked to the hill of Anchesmus. The heavy rains which had fallen permitted the husbandman to stir the ground. Having passed the walls of the city we found a peasant ploughing with two oxen ; the plough, ἀλέτρι, which he held, had only one handle χέρι ; it had two earth-boards παραβολα ; a sharp iron share—. * Adjoining the handle was a piece of wood κονδύρι ; the pole consisted of two pieces, the lower one was called σταβάρι, the upper one πλάτισμα At the end of the pole was an iron ring κολλουρο, the bar ζυγός, and the two collars ζεύγεα The pieces of wood which formed the plough were fastened together by a large nail σπαθι, which was traversed by a smaller nail. The soil † was light and rich, and ploughed into small ridges and furrows, each not more than a foot broad. We advanced towards the hill ; the rain had washed away the soil, and discovered a Roman pavement composed of small cubic pieces of marble The thyme of the ancients θυμάρι, and the hairy Passerina, were the most common plants. The sweet-scented Cyclamen, and the yellow Amaryllis, were in flower. A number of Helices concealed themselves in the crevices of the rock, and I found what the conchologists consider a great rarity, the Helix decollata with the head on. From the summit of Anchesmus we had a full view of Athens ; the walls of the city did not appear more than two miles in circuit.

Oct. 23.—We walked out in the afternoon to the supposed site of the Academy, the spot is known at present by the name Acathymia ; it is a low hill about a mile to the north of the city. Among the olive groves, which are composed of large and ancient trees, we met

---

* The word in Dr S.'s journals resembles βουνι, but in Mr Hawkins it is correctly written ἐννι, corrupted from Ὕνις, Vomer The different parts of the plough of the ancient Greeks ῥυμὸς, γύης, ἐλυμα, ὕνις and ἐχέτλη are examined by Mongez Mem de l'Instit. 1815.

† The mode of threshing the corn, as practised by the people of Attica, is described in an extract from the journal of the Earl of Aberdeen See the note which follows Dr. Sibthorp's remarks.

a shepherd playing upon a pastoral flute, a single piece of the donax, about a foot long; the note was very pleasing. The husbandmen were now preparing the ground for the seed-corn, and with instruments like our pick-axes, ἀξία, pulverized the clods. We walked from the Acathymia to a small villa of the Consul's under the hill, called Turko Bouni; it was surrounded by a vineyard, contained three stremata, and was purchased for 100 piastres. We saw adjoining to it a rich piece of ground, containing nearly an acre, which had lately been bought for 50 piastres. The low price of land, and the misery every where apparent through the city and its neighbourhood, were strong evidences of the despotism which prevailed. I saw some hedges planted with the Cactus opuntia, called Ἀραβοσύκι, Arabian, or Indian fig, a sufficient proof that it is not a native plant but introduced from the east. I picked up the Aloe perfoliata in the streets of Athens; it was still called Ἀλόη[*] toasted before the fire the Albanian women applied it to swellings of the neck. The plain of Athens, if we except the olive tree, is extremely destitute of wood, and we observed on our return the peasants driving home their asses laden with Passerina hirsuta for fuel.

Oct. 24.—Logotheti called upon us in the morning, and conducted us to a tanner's, where was explained to us the process of dyeing the black and yellow leathers; the red was not made in this manufactory. The hair or wool being taken off the skin by its being soaked in a strong solution of lime-water, it was then put into a second, and afterwards into a third solution, it was next rubbed with dogs' dung. After this process, if the intention was to dye it black, it was put into a lixivium made by mixing powdered Balanida with boiling water, which is cooled by pouring in cold; the skin is then put into it, and remains steeped some time before it has acquired a due degree of astringency or toughness. It is taken out and dried, and being

---

[*] The medicinal uses of the aloe are mentioned in Dioscorides, lib. iii. c. 25 Roasted in an earthen pot it was employed for complaints in the eyes. Mixed with wine and honey it was applied to disorders in the jaws, and tonsils, and mouth.

greased with suet or animal fat is exposed to the sun. After this
process it is coloured by being rubbed with powdered martial vitriol.
The skin is polished by being stretched on a horse made of box-
wood, on which it is rubbed backwards and forwards with a roller
made of the same wood. The skin, when dressed, is worth from 40
to 50 paras the oke. The Balanida is brought from Eleusis, and sold
at three paras the oke

In dyeing the yellow colour, the leaves of the Rhus coriaria are
used as the astringent instead of the Balanida, this is called Ροῦδι, is
brought from Samos, and is sold at ten paras the oke The leaves
should be gathered before the tree ripens its fruit, as they then possess
their astringent virtue in a superior degree. The skin being prepared is put into a vat of boiling water with the powdered grains
d'Avignon, or the seeds of the Rhamnus infectorius; a sufficient
quantity is used to give to the water the consistency of a paste The
skin remains in the lixivium until the water is cold, it is then rubbed
with the hand, until it is sufficiently coloured The waters of Athens
contain a considerable quantity of salt, the rain water, and that of
the rivers, particularly the Cephissus, are preferred. In our return
home we passed by a dyer's, Βάφης, parcels of yarn, dyed of different
colours, were hanging at his door, blue, yellow, green and red; the
blue was dyed with indigo, the yellow with grains d'Avignon; an
orange colour was drawn from the Chrysoxylon. This is the wood
of the Rhus cotinus found in the mountains about Marathon and
Pendeli, and is brought to the dyers by the Albanians, of whom it is
purchased at two paras the oke. The green is made by the yarn being
first dipped in a solution of indigo, then afterwards in that of grains
d'Avignon. A violet colour is drawn from a wood called Βαλλαμιμόρικο,
and a red colour from the Βαλλαμ κό κινο, the last is sold at a high
price. Cochineal is also used in dyeing the silks; this is purchased
at forty piastres the oke. No use is here made of the Kermes,
though it is collected in small quantities in the district of Casha; it
is gathered in abundance in the Morea, where it is called πρινοκόκκι.

Nov. 3.—Leaving the hill of Anchesmus, and the monastery of Asomato on our left, we passed along the banks of the Ilissus. The bed was narrow, dry, and frequently choaked with stones, is was fringed with the Oleander and Agnus castus. Not far from the base of the mountain it divided, and one of its branches was dignified formerly with the celebrated name of Eridanus. After an hour's ride we arrived at the monastery, which presented a melancholy appearance. I took a young Caloyer for my guide to the top of the mountain. Having left the olive grounds, we found the rock at first thinly covered with the Kermes oak, the Spartium Scorpius, and Spinosum, mixed with Satureia Thymbra and Capitata, the latter of which is the celebrated thyme of the ancients, their Thymbra. I observed some strata of marble of a white colour, almost rivalling in beauty that of Pendeli. Though Hymettus was barren of plants, I had not advanced far up the mountain before I was gratified with the discovery of a new species of Colchicum, now in full flower. I saw the beautiful Persian Cyclamen under the shelves of the rocks, and towards the highest parts the vernal crocus was just opening its blossoms. The day was fine and the atmosphere remarkably clear; from the summit I commanded an extensive view of the Straits of Negropont, and various of the Cyclades; the eastern coast of Attica, with its numerous ports stretching to Cape Colonna, the Saronic gulph, with islands interspersed in it; the rich plain of Messoia and Athens, with its city and groves of olives; the mountains of Pendeli and Parnes in Attica, and of Cithaeron in Boeotia. A flock of goats and sheep appeared hanging over the cliffs, and two eagles soared over the summit. Hymettus cannot be ranked among the highest mountains of Greece, its height is less than that of Parnes, and nearly the same with that of Pendeli, not sheltered by woods, it is exposed to the winds, and has a sun-burnt appearance. The neglected state of the monastery arose from the debts which it had contracted, these, in some measure, had been lately paid by the See of Athens, to which the revenues of the monastery belonged. The honey made in it was the property of the Bishop; and the Caloyers were so poor and so strictly watched, that they could not procure me even a taste of it. The solitary sparrow flew along the walls, and thrushes and black-birds seemed almost unmolested in the olive grounds.

The following extract from Dr. Sibthorp's Journals relating to part of Attica may be inserted here.

" July 24.— We anchored in the port of Sunium. At present this famous promontory of Attica affords neither inhabitants nor cultiva-tion. I saw here partridges, hares, and a small species of black hawk flew frequent near the ground. Our sailors caught two species of the Labrus, different from the L. Iulis, which I suspect to be new; one uncommonly beautiful, with three deep transverse red stripes, called by the Greeks Ἥλις. The country about the cape was covered with low mastic bushes, and here and there some scattered trees of the Pinus Pinea, which Chandler seems to have mistaken for cedars; these, though frequently mentioned by that traveller, never grew wild in Greece."—Dr. S.

Note, from the Earl of Aberdeen's Journal, referred to in page 146.

" Barley is chiefly cultivated in Attica, and the plain of Thria is still somewhat supe-rior in fertility to the other districts of the country.

" It is the practice to turn the horses out into the green barley * This is done in the month of May, at that time the fields are seen full of horses and asses, tied each to a

---

* In the spring season, in parts of Syria, the horses are fed forty or fifty days with green bar-ley, cut as soon as the corn begins to ear   The horses of the grandees are frequently tied down in the barley-field, being confined to a certain circuit by a long tedder. Grazing is reckoned to be of great service to the health of the horses, and produces a beautiful gloss on the skin Russell's Aleppo, ii. 178   Lucerne is also cultivated for the use of the horses, oats are not given to them Some fields of this grain were observed by Russel about Antioch and on the sea-coast, but they were not cultivated near Aleppo Βρῶμι, or oats, were seen in Bœotia, by Dr Sibthorp

separate spot by the foot. They eat all the barley within the extent of their cord, and after that their position is changed thus the whole of the field is equally benefited by the manure of the animal The grain having been sown after the first rains in October or November, is at this time of considerable growth The horses continue in the fields about a month, if, at the end of that period, there remains any thing uneaten, it is plucked up, and preserved as hay.

" The field being now free, the earth is broken by a plough of the most simple construction, and is sown with cotton, to cover this seed, the labourer fastens a strait plank behind two oxen, upon which he stands, and holding the reins in his hands he is thus drawn across all the furrows, until the whole be closed up and the seed secure

" They begin to reap this cotton early in September, after which the land is again ploughed and sown with barley. In the following month of June, they either cut or pluck * up the crop, which is carried to a place more or less near to the field, sometimes paved, but more commonly the surface is only made flat, the earth in the neighbourhood of Athens being extremely hard There, when all the crop is collected, a number of mares are brought from the hills in order to thresh it, which is effected in the following manner.

" In the middle of the place a post is erected, and to it is fastened a cord, at the other end of which the heads of two, three, four, and sometimes six of these mares are fastened. A man standing in the middle of the place makes them trot in a circular direction until the cord is completely twisted round the post, and in consequence the animals brought close to it, he then makes them return, and by gradually untwisting the cord, extend the circle. By these means, the corn being kept by another man under their feet, is equally threshed, and the straw at the same time cut, for the mares are shod for this purpose The grain being separated from the chaff by throwing it in the air, it is gathered into heaps, and the guards, some of whom always watch the progress of the work, affix the seal, that is to say, each heap is surrounded by four planks, on which the name of the Aga who is the proprietor of the tythes, is cut, and until the Aga has first taken his right, none of the grain is allowed to be carried into the town or removed from the spot

" The harvest being over, the mares and a great many labourers go to Thebes, where they proceed in the same manner In the heavy and moist land of Bœotia the corn is later in ripening, and therefore many of the labourers are doubly employed

" When the whole is finished, the shoes are taken off the mares, and they, with their young, are turned loose upon the mountains, until the next year "

---

* Wheat and barley, in general, do not grow half so high as in Britain, and are therefore not reaped with the sickle like other grain, but plucked up with the root by the hand. — Russell's Aleppo, i 75

LETTERS

FROM

THE LATE PROFESSOR CARLYLE

TO

THE LORD BISHOP OF LINCOLN

LETTER I.

My Lord,   LARNICA, CYPRUS, Feb 13, 1800

I HAD hoped long before this time to have been able to communicate to your Lordship some intelligence respecting the library of the Seraglio; I had even flattered myself from the reception we met with that I should have made a considerable progress in examining its contents. But I know not how it has happened, whether from the pressure of public business, or from whatever other cause, during the first two months of my stay in Constantinople, I was not able to get any thing done towards facilitating my admission into the library. In the middle of January the plague broke out in the Seraglio with considerable violence; an entire stop was, of course, put to any investigations I might wish to make within its precincts for some time. I trust, however, as the present Sultan is extremely apprehensive of the disorder himself, and willing to take any precautions that may be thought proper for preventing its progress, that the distemper will not become general, and then I shall soon have an opportunity of prosecuting my researches in earnest. As I was thus precluded from employing myself at Constantinople to any material purpose (for I could no longer with safety frequent even the public libraries from which I had previously, I trust, drawn considerable information in Oriental literature), I resolved not to waste my time at Pera. I therefore with the greatest pleasure embraced the offer General Koeler was so good as to make me of accompanying him across Asia Minor to the coast of Syria.

Your Lordship will see from the date of this letter that we have completed our tour so far, and, I trust, a few days will now conduct me to the end of my journey. Our expedition has indeed been a most interesting one, as great part of it was through a country for many ages entirely unexplored by Europeans, and now only opened on account of the rebellions which prevail in most of the provinces through which the common route ran. The part I allude to in particular is from the ancient Iconium to the sea-port where we took shipping for Cyprus, through the countries of Lycaonia, Isauria, and Cilicia. I need scarce inform your Lordship, that we have experienced considerable difficulties in travelling; but I assure you when there were the greatest I did not for a moment regret my undertaking. In many places, especially in the neighbourhood of the ancient Laodicea Combusta, Olba, and Celenderis, we absolutely *trod* upon Grecian sculptures, columns, altars, and inscriptions, for *miles*. In different parts of our journey we found quantities of the most beautiful marble sarcophagi lying scattered on the ground. We found also the remains of several temples, with a sufficient number of their pillars remaining to ascertain the spot and dimensions of the buildings. At Celenderis a mausoleum of beautiful Corinthian architecture is still standing almost entire, surrounded by catacombs, Mosaic pavements, and sarcophagi. An aqueduct, not ill preserved, runs along the hill behind it, and the whole appears nearly in the situation it was fifteen or sixteen centuries ago. In Phrygia, too, we saw some monuments which appeared to me even more curious than these Grecian remains. They consist of excavations out of the rock, which form the most elegant mausolea one can conceive. A little romantic valley (exactly such an one as Johnson has imagined in his Rasselas) has one of its sides almost entirely covered with these sculptured and excavated rocks. Some of these monuments are very large and magnificent, and very much resemble the representations we have of the

X

tombs of the Persian Kings cut out of the rock in the vicinity of Per-
sepolis.   Upon one of those immense catacombs are two inscriptions in Greek characters, which, from the form of the letters, must
have been considerably anterior to the time of Alexander.   General
Koeler made sketches of most of the things we passed which seemed
deserving of attention, and he has been so good as to promise me
copies of all of them.   The gentlemen who were with him, Major
Fletcher and Captain Leake, together with myself, were employed in
measuring and taking those inscriptions we could get access to; so
that I trust (as I have kept a very minute journal of every thing that
took place) our three weeks tour will not be uninteresting.   But, my
Lord, while we were employed and amused with these investigations,
it was impossible not to feel melancholy at the sight of the once fertile
and populous countries we travelled over; they are now almost a
desert, and must remain in this situation as long as the present system
of government prevails amongst them.   Every little Aga of a village is
an independent prince, and generally at war with all his neighbours.
Hence the people are obliged to live in towns, and about these alone can
any cultivation take place   If by any accident one of these towns is
destroyed or depopulated, it is destroyed for ever, and the cultivation
around it immediately closes.   Thus, by degrees, all these fine plains
are becoming absolutely wastes.   We travelled over one which was
at least 200 miles in length, and from fifteen to twenty miles in
breadth, a surface, I believe, equal to one half of Yorkshire, and
consisting of the richest land that can be desired for agriculture.
The whole of the inhabitants of this large tract of country, where the
corn yields upwards of twenty for one, certainly do not amount to
above twenty-seven or twenty-eight thousand persons, of which two-
thirds are contained in the towns of Comah and Caraman.   The isle
in which we now are seems to have suffered less from the blighting
influence of Turkish power than most other parts of the empire, but
I cannot think that it contains at present one-fourth of the inhabitants
it is capable of supporting, and I fear these are rapidly diminishing in
number.   I purpose spending a couple of weeks in Palestine, where

my recommendations from the Patriarchs, together with Sir Sidney Smith's good offices, will, I trust, enable me to investigate every thing I think proper, and particularly the libraries of some of the convents of Jerusalem, which, I am informed, contain very old manuscripts of the New Testament. I shall have an opportunity also of seeing with my own eyes some of those countries which make the greatest figure in the histories of the Crusades, a period which I believe I informed your Lordship I had some thoughts of endeavouring to elucidate by means of the Oriental writers.

> I have the honor to be, &c. &c.
>
> J. D. CARLYLE.

LETTER II.

MY LORD,   JAFFA, April 10 1800

WHEN I wrote to Your Lordship from Cyprus, I trusted before this time to have been returned to Constantinople, but so many things have occurred to interrupt my journey, that it will be some weeks yet before I can arrive there; however, I do not by any means regret my having made a little longer stay in this part of the world than I originally intended, as it has given me an opportunity of judging by my own observation of the present situation of affairs here at this interesting period, and of communicating them to your Lordship. I sailed with Sir Sidney Smith soon after I wrote to your Lordship, with the hopes of being admitted by means of the supposed convention to take a transient view of Egypt, and to proceed from thence immediately to Syria. A little after we arrived off Alexandria, we received the intelligence that our government would not permit the treaty signed between the Turks and French to be carried into effect, or at least had given such orders as put a stop to it for the present. As they had both acted upon this treaty, the latter having evacuated all their frontier towns to the former, who had advanced to within seven miles of Cairo, and as the Turks demanded possession of the palace at the

x 2

day mentioned in the treaty, which the French, not being allowed to leave the country upon the terms they expected, refused to accede to. we saw that hostilities must inevitably take place between the two parties, and we were but too certain of the issue of the combat. Every thing that we feared has happened. The French, with between twelve and fifteen thousand men, attacked the Turks (who had at least four times the number) upon the morning of the 20th of March. The Turks fled in a moment without attempting to make a stand, and were pursued by the French to the confines of the Desert. The pursuit continued for three days, in the course of which and in their passage over the Desert the Turks have lost, it is said, upwards of 10,000 men the rest of the army, except about five or six thousand who are here with the Vizier, are totally, and I doubt irremediably dispersed. I do not enter into any military particulars of this melancholy event, as your Lordship will be informed of them from other quarters, where they will be sufficiently detailed, and with much more precision than I can pretend to. But as I have since been at Alexandria, and seen the French Generals and army there, I would wish to give your Lordship as just an account as I could of the situation in which I found them. I went on shore at Alexandria with a flag of truce this day se'ennight, along with an officer from Sir Sidney Smith We were received by General la Nuet, and the other *great men* there, Messrs. Julien, Tallien, Vial, &c with the utmost politeness. They gave us a very handsome dinner, in which every thing was well served, and they *seemed* (but I believe this was rather an *exhibition* to us) to have no want of wine or liquors. They appeared little elevated with their victory over the Turks, as they thought it might tend to fix them longer in the country, to leave which they made no scruple of saying was their great wish. They all, however, declared that they would never think of quitting it upon dishonorable terms. After dinner I was shown the antiquities of the place, &c ; and I had an opportunity, by crossing the parade, of seeing the greatest number of their troops. These amounted, I was told, to near 3000 . and, indeed, I never saw a finer set of men in my life They were almost all of them young, and apparently very healthy. Their clothes, however, were made chiefly of the cotton of the country, and many of them were in a ragged condition. I am informed by Captain Lacey, the only British officer who accompanied the Grand Vizier's army, that the troops of General Kleber were in no respect inferior to those I had seen at Alexandria, all of them being in the highest state of discipline, and showing every mark of activity. Against forces like these it is unnecessary to say to your Lordship that Turkish troops and Turkish commanders can have small chance of even making any head. The soldiers did not stand a single fire, and one trait will be sufficient to exemplify the ability of the Ottoman General. When the artillery was to be used, it was discovered that the ammunition had been left behind at Arish !! Your Lordship will perhaps think my account of the present situation of the French very different from what is intimated in their own intercepted letters certainly every thing there is much exaggerated. Poussielgue himself (whom I was with for ten days on board the Tigre) declared that these accounts were meant to induce the French Government to consent to the evacuation of Egypt ; but how far your Lordship may judge such a testimony to be relied on, I pretend not to say. Undoubtedly the French army is in a very formidable state , they have plenty of corn, poultry, mutton, and vegetables They now make very tolerable sugar, and of course they cannot be long at a loss for rum They already extract a spirit from dates, but it is very indifferent. They told me, they had succeeded in making gunpowder ; and they have set up manufactories of cloth, &c. Buonaparte's wild manifesto, as well as his subsequent conduct, incensed all the Christians of the country against him, without procuring him one friend amongst the Mahomedans. I fear Kleber is pursuing a more prudent line of conduct ; but I trust he will not have time to produce any permanent effect upon the minds of the inhabitants. It is very evident that he, as well as all the leaders, is beyond measure impatient to return to France, much more so, in my opinion, than any inconveniences which they suffer in Egypt can possibly justify.

They are all of them however, I think, clearly inimical to their late General, and I could not help noticing that scarce one of them at Alexandria who appeared like a gentleman, wore the three coloured cockade. I have been to-day in the Turkish camp near this place. They knew that I was an Englishman, but I am sorry to say that *at present*, they scarce either treat or consider the English as their friends. They accuse us as the cause of the defeat they have just received, and are not sparing in insult and abuse. The poor Grand Vizier is quite in despair, and means to return by land to Constantinople, thoroughly convinced that his present army is incapable of ever effecting any thing against the French. I sincerely hope he may be able to raise another which may be more efficient, I mean of Turks, for the Mamelukes have undoubtedly fought most gallantly during the whole of this contest; and I am glad to find, even from the account given by the French themselves, that their numbers are very little reduced, and that they watch every opportunity of attacking the enemy that presents itself. When Kleber marched from Cairo against the Vizier, Mourad Bey immediately rushed down from the mountains in the neighbourhood and got possession of the city, and he still remained master of it when I was at Alexandria, although the French retained the citadel in their hands. I believe this is the first letter I have written, and I trust it will be the last letter I shall write on any political subject; but I thought the information I could give upon the present occasion would not be unacceptable to Your Lordship, as there has no other Englishman been permitted to go into Egypt with so little reserve since it has been in possession of the French. Indeed they offered me an escort to conduct me to Cairo, but in the present situation of that place, they scarce thought it safe for me to make the attempt; this, together with knowing that the plague raged in most parts of the country, obliged me to decline their offer. I had an opportunity however of seeing their *Scavans*, and hearing a full and very interesting account of their discoveries. I confess I could not look at these poor men without a great deal of pity, they had been carried off by surprise, they have undergone innumerable hardships; many of them are advanced in years, and I fancy they are very poorly supplied with any comforts or conveniences. To add to all this, they are execrated by the army, (who consider them as the primary cause of all their misfortunes,) and they live in continual apprehensions from the plague, which at present is but too prevalent in Alexandria. I hope, however, they have not been idle during their stay in Egypt, they assured me that most accurate surveys and drawings had been made of all the principal Egyptian antiquities, they had spent twenty-five days at Thebes alone, guarded by a detachment of the army, during which time they had an opportunity of copying at their leisure every thing that appeared interesting. They spoke however of these remains as being trifling to what are found at Dendera. Geoffroy their naturalist has made a very complete collection of Egyptian zoology; he has promised to endeavour to obtain all the vernacular names * of the several animals, &c, and to write these along with the Linnæan. If this be performed properly it will afford us a more satisfactory Hierozoicon than any hitherto published, as I have little doubt but many of the Hebrew names still lurk undiscovered in the Coptic, Sahidic, and vulgar Arabic languages. One great object of my own journey into Syria, was to endeavour to find some intelligent person who could give me information upon this head, which I need not say to Your Lordship would throw more light upon many parts of the Levitical law, than any other species of criticism, if I may call Natural History by such a term; and I am still led to hope that I shall not be entirely disappointed in my expectations of meeting with persons of this description. My voyage has added much to my Arabic literature, as I had for my companions a prince of the Druses and

---

* " The names of animals and plants by which they are called in Eastern countries," says Shaw, " would be of great assistance, as some of them it may be presumed continue to be the very same, while others may be derivative from the originals."—Travels, p. 122.

his secretary, to whom the Arabic was then native tongue. I am very impatient however to return to Constantinople, as by this time, if at all, I trust permission may have been obtained to enter the library of the Seraglio, and the season of the year will have destroyed every appearance of plague. Most happy shall I be to protract my stay a while if we can discover any thing worthy of investigation ; but if that should not be the case, I do not imagine I shall meet with many other objects that can induce me to continue long at Constantinople. Notwithstanding the impatience which an Englishman with my long English habits must feel of returning to England, I shall not however leave that city till I have obtained all the literary information in my power. If there be any thing that strikes Your Lordship as proper for me particularly to attend to, I should be most happy to receive a hint upon the subject.

I have the honor to be, &c. &c.

J. D. CARLYLE.

LETTER III

My Lord, BOYUKDERE, near CONSTANTINOPLE, July 25 1800

I FLATTER myself you will not be wholly uninterested in hearing that I am again arrived at Lord Elgin's in health and safety. I received the letter you honored me with at Constantinople, and I need not say that I was most highly gratified in finding that what I had done, respecting the Arabian Livy, met with the approbation of Your Lordship and Mr. Pitt. I trust no exertions of my own will ever be wanting towards prosecuting the great object of my mission, but I dare not allow myself to entertain any sanguine expectations of its success. The Ministers hitherto have *denied* the *existence* of any repository of MSS., but the Reis Effendi, through whom this communication came, was a man in every respect so weak and ignorant, that no literary information could possibly be hoped for through such a channel. A few days ago he was displaced, and Chelebi Effendi, without dispute the most intelligent as well as the most enlightened man in the empire, appointed in his room. If the business, therefore, be at all practicable, this is the moment for accomplishing it; and Lord Elgin promises me that he will seriously set about bringing the matter to a conclusion without delay, being confident from Chelebi Effendi's character, that that Minister is both properly acquainted with every circumstance respecting such a library if it exists; and that he will have the candour to say fairly whether it be or be not possible to gain admittance into it. Your Lordship will suppose that I have not been deficient in making all the inquiries in my power in order to discover whatever I could relative to this mysterious library. It is impossible to conceive any thing more vague and various than the information I received. The cause of this contrariety of opinion, however, I imagine to be founded on mistake. That there does exist a library in the Seraglio is certain, but from all I can gather, *this* is only of modern formation, and consists merely of Oriental books. Into it I have little doubt of being admitted; but whether there be any *older* collection of MSS in the Seraglio is a different question. I have been informed by this very Chelebi Effendi's secretary (a person of considerable literature), that " he himself, with five others, were employed a few years ago in searching for some ancient records which were deposited in the Seraglio, they were introduced every day by the eunuchs of the palace, and they continued their search for *six months*, during all which time, though they turned over most of the papers belonging to the empire, they did not meet with any thing like a Greek or Latin MS." On the other hand there undoubtedly exists a building near St. Sophia, that is now closed up, and that, according to tradition, has been closed up ever since the conquest. Here, report says, the arms and many other things belonging to the Greek Emperors are still preserved; and here, if any where, I should hope to find the remains of their library. However, my Lord, I trust the question will soon be at issue, and we shall know both where the library is and what hopes we are to entertain of being permitted to investigate its treasures.

I hope your Lordship received the letter I wrote to you from Jaffa. It contained an account of my tour, as far as that place, with a few observations I ventured to insert, relative to my *friends* in Egypt. I was fortunate in arriving at Jaffa just before the Holy Week, by which means I was enabled to proceed to Jerusalem without much danger, in company with a caravan of Armenian pilgrims. I spent ten (I need not say to your Lordship most interesting) days in the city and neighbourhood of Jerusalem. I shall not attempt to describe scenes that have been described so often, but I cannot help saying that the city of Jerusalem is utterly unlike any other place I have ever seen. Its situation upon an immense rock, surrounded with valleys that seem cut out by the chisel, the contrast exhibited between the extremest degree of barrenness, and the extremest degree of fertility, which border upon each other here almost every yard, without one shade of mitigated character on either side, the structure of the walls, many of the stones in which are 15 or 16 feet long, by four high and four deep, the very size mentioned, by the way, of the *hewn stones* of Solomon * (1 Kings, vii. 10.); the houses where almost every one is a fortress; and the streets, where almost every one is a covered way; all together formed an appearance totally dissimilar from that of any other town I have met with either in Europe or Asia. One of my excursions from Jerusalem was to the monastery of St Saba, in order to examine the library of MSS. there. It had been often mentioned to me, and I was resolved if possible to investigate it; I believe I did run a little more hazard than was perfectly prudent, as the whole country at present swarms with banditti; however by means of a guard consisting of those very persons that I dreaded I arrived in safety, and had the pleasure to make a complete examination. Except, however, twenty-nine copies of the Gospels, and one of the

---

* " The city was intersected," says Townson, " as well as encompassed with walls of great strength, whose bases would still remain after the demolition of the city "

Epistles, this celebrated library does not contain any thing valuable; the rest of it to the number of 300 consists of Fathers, Homilies, Legends, and Rituals. I was permitted by the Superior to bring along with me six of what I judged the oldest MSS., viz. two copies of the Gospels, one of the Epistles, two books of Homilies and apostolical letters, which I took for the sake of the quotations, and a copy of the Sophist Libanius, the only work like a classic author that I met with. I hope the Patriarch will allow me to convey them to England. I was fortunate enough to attain most of the objects I hinted to your Lordship, as having in view in my visit to Palestine I saw sufficient of the country, &c., to clear up many difficulties in the Oriental writers of history which had puzzled me not a little, and above all, I obtained a dictionary of the vernacular language of the country, and established a train of enquiry, by which I shall be able in future to procure any farther intelligence I may wish for on that subject. I conceive, my Lord, *this* to be the only rational source of information by which we may hope to explain many of those passages in SS., which, depending upon local habits or vernacular dialect, are in vain to be elucidated by means of books alone. Yet this source, as far as I am acquainted, (except in Michaelis's questions to Niebuhr and his companions,) has been less resorted to than almost any other. From Jaffa I proceeded to Rhodes, where I spent near a fortnight. From thence, I sailed by Cos, Samos, Chios, to Smyrna, occasionally visiting the Continent where there was any thing worthy inspection. From Smyrna I took a Greek vessel to the Dardanelles, and from thence was conveyed in a Turkish row-boat to Constantinople.

I. D. CARLYLE.

LETTER IV.

My Lord,   BUYUKDERF, Oct 9 1800

As I did not wish to teaze Your Lordship with an account of the various delays and disappointments I have experienced in attempting to gain admission to the library of the Seraglio, I put off writing till I could say something specific upon the subject. I have been this morning informed by the Dragoman, who has managed the affair, that he has at length obtained leave for me to inspect the private library of the Sultan, and that at his audience, which is to be on Saturday, a time will be appointed for that purpose. The person with whom the Dragoman negotiated the business was Youssouf Aga, who (as perhaps Your Lordship knows), though without any ostensible title or official situation, in fact at present governs the empire, he is steward and favorite of the Valida, i e mother of the Sultan, and he possesses as complete an ascendancy over the mind of his mistress as she does over that of her son. Youssouf, from the moment of his being first applied to, seemed favorable to the request, saying that it was not only proper to be granted on account of the friendship subsisting between the two powers, but also (which I own I scarce expected) on account of the general use it might be of to literature; and he immediately promised to set on foot an enquiry respecting the existence of any collection of Greek or Latin MSS. In a subsequent conversation he assured the Dragoman "that he had made every investigation in his power, and that he found that no collection whatever of *Greek* MSS. remained at present in any part of the Seraglio." I then had a request conveyed to him to be permitted to examine the repositories of *Oriental* books that were in the palace, having previously ascertained the fact that such did exist. To this he has at length answered, "that he understands that there are two of these, one in the Treasury, the other in what is properly called the Library; that the former contains only copies of the Koran; different commentaries upon it, and treatises peculiar to the Mahomedan laws and religion, and as such, could not be subjected to my inspection, but that the library should be open to me, and on Saturday he would fix a day for my admission." This, my Lord, is the present state of the business. I dare not be too sanguine in my expectations that I shall be able to make any material discoveries, as I have received intelligence so very opposite. *Toderini*, in his *Leteratura Turchesa*, not only assures us that this library contains valuable Greek MSS. but gives us a catalogue of them, which, he says, he procured from a slave belonging to the palace. This account is in some degree confirmed by the relation of a Mr. Humphries, now dead, who declared that he, in company with a Frenchman, at present in the Castle of the Seven Towers (from whom I hope to procure farther information on the subject) had actually seen in the Library several Greek and Latin books; on the other hand an intelligent Italian surgeon (who has likewise had access to this repository) as well as all the Turks whom I have had any opportunity of consulting, affirm that it consists solely of a collection of Oriental authors. I trust, my Lord, I shall be able in a few days, to ascertain something decisive upon the question, at least with respect to *this Library*. With regard to the books preserved in the Treasury, perhaps when Youssouf Aga sees that no bad consequences result from an examination of the others, he may permit them too to be investigated; or perhaps it may be brought about by the Capudan Pasha's influence (if he return in the winter) as he has always shown the most marked attention to Lord Elgin, and is connected in the strongest manner with Youssouf. I should have been extremely happy if the time of my admission into the library could have been settled a few weeks ago, as I might then have had an opportunity of putting in execution a scheme, which I flatter myself Your Lordship would not consider as uninteresting — I meant to have coasted along the southern shores of the Black Sea, as far as Trebisond, occasionally stopping at the different places which appeared best to deserve being examined. From Trebisond I intended going over land to Erzeroum; from whence I should have returned to Constantinople, by the route of Tocat and Angora. The whole journey would not have taken up more than a couple of months (which I fear will not here have been spent very profitably); and I conceive there is no other tour of the same extent that could furnish an equal number of objects so well worthy of investigation. I need not say to Your Lordship, that I should nearly have followed the mysterious track of the Argonauts, and passed over the places where the most celebrated scenes in the retreat of the ten thousand, were transacted. Heraclea and Amastris, I understand, contain more interesting remains, and a greater quantity of inscriptions, than are to be found in any city in Asia. Sinope, the Gibraltar of the Euxine, possesses, I am assured, some valuable MSS. in one of its convents. Trebisond most likely does the same, and at any rate is curious as being the capital of an empire, which, though considerable in many respects, and existing for two centuries and an half, is scarce known to us but in romance Had I gotten to Erzeroum, I should have obtained a glimpse of Armenian manners, and perhaps of their literature, an object with which I have lately been endeavouring in some degree to become acquainted. I do not know that the country between Erzeroum and Constantinople would present any thing very remarkable, except the famous Ancyran* inscription, containing the life of Augustus (which I believe has never been very correctly taken) and the general information that must always result to a mind at all conversant in classical ideas, upon travelling through such countries as Galatia, Bithynia, and Pontus. The track I had projected investigating has never yet been examined by any Englishman. Tournefort visited it a century ago, and has given the only description of it that I have seen; he stopped at a few of the towns upon the coast, and his inquiries were principally directed to researches of a bo-

---

* The first copy of the Ancyran inscription was taken by Busbequius. Rostan, a Frenchman, is the last person who appears to have examined it a more accurate account is still wanting. Acad. des In 47. p. 89.

tanical nature. Peysonnell has merely given an account of the Black Sea in a commercial point of view; and Beauchamp, who is the latest traveller that has visited its shores (whose Memoir upon the Euxine was published in the *Egyptian Decades* of last year, and procured for me at Alexandria by Tallien), has chiefly considered them in a geographical one. Beauchamp is now confined in a castle at the mouth of the Bosphorus I have not seen him myself, but have received several accounts of his descriptions of the voyage (indet pendent of his Memoir); and he declares it to be by far the most interesting one he ever performed Your Lordship will probably have seen one of Beauchamp's essays (viz that upon the site of Babylon) detailed in Major Rennell's Geography of Herodotus.

Thus, my Lord, I conceived these countries to be in many respects almost unexplored, and I thought a journey thither would not only be curious, but might also prove useful in more essential concerns It is now fifty years since Peysonnell's materials were collected; his book is the only document that can be procured respecting the trade of the Black Sea, for, strange to tell, though we have had a commercial company established here for so long a time, and though the Black Sea is now open to English ships, yet there is not an Englishman, nor I believe any Frank to be found in Constantinople, who possesses any accurate information with regard to the geography, inhabitants or products of the regions adjoining to this sea.

But, alas, my Lord, all my fine schemes have been entirely blasted by Turkish procrastination. It is now too late for such an expedition, and no vessel will engage to navigate the Black Sea so far till spring, as there are at present only twenty-five days of fine weather to be expected before winter commences, and what is still worse, (for perhaps the former difficulty might have been gotten over,) I understand the plague has certainly spread its ravages to Angora and Tocat, and that it is suspected to have shown itself even at Sinope and Trebisond. I confess I have witnessed too much of this horrid distemper, not to feel the utmost apprehensions from it I think I did mention to Your Lordship that I had been obliged to run considerable hazard of infec-

tion in different places, but I believe I did not acquaint you with the
circumstance, which above all others, though perhaps without reason,
tended to rivet my horrors   Upon quitting Cyprus, where the plague
raged violently, the Greek captain of our little vessel was seized, as
all on board believed, with the disorder, for two days in which we
were shut up with him in the skiff, we expected his death every moment; he however recovered, and providentially no one else caught the
contagion.   I confess, my Lord, I have been much disappointed in
being thus obliged to give up a favorite scheme, from which I had
expected considerable instruction, and for which I had taken some
pains to prepare myself.   Since the time I wrote last to Your Lordship, we have been almost constantly at Boyukdere, a beautiful village
on the banks of the Bosphorus ; the room I inhabit literally overhangs
the water, and I have a view from it only to be exceeded by the lake
of Keswick.

My *amusement* when the heat of the weather would permit any exertion, (for we have had the thermometer in the shade as high as 97°,
with a sirocco besides, at which time we could only sit and try to
breathe,) has principally consisted in examining the shores of the
Bosphorus, the scenes of so much history and so much fable ; and my
employment, if I may confess it, has chiefly been reading Arabian romances.   I trust, however, that this employment appears more trifling
in the relation than it is in reality, as I conceive it affords me the most
accurate notions of Oriental manners, and certainly gives me the best
examples of familiar language.

I have the honor to be, &c.

I. D. CARLYLE.

LETTER V.

My Lord,   CONSTANTINOPLE, Nov 20 1800

I HAVE the satisfaction of acquainting Your Lordship, that at length I have been permitted to examine the library of the Seraglio, and completely to ascertain its contents. This permission was not granted me till some time after the period fixed upon for my admission, when I had last the honor of writing to Your Lordship, and I began to be apprehensive that these repeated delays would only end in disappointment, when Lord Elgin was informed by a message from Youssouf Aga, that if I called at his house the next morning, he would send an officer along with me to introduce me into the library. I fear I shall be thought tedious if I detail the minutiæ of our proceedings, but as by this means I may be able to convey to Your Lordship some ideas respecting that habitation, *alta caligine mersam*, which I visited, I shall venture to make the attempt.

The house of Youssouf Aga, like all the country houses belonging to the great men in this country, is built upon the very edge of the Bosphorus, nearly half-way between the Seraglio point and " the towers of *Oblivion*." The Dragoman who attended me and myself arrived there about *eight* o'clock. Youssouf was gone out to wait upon the Sultan, who then resided at a palace adjoining, and we found his Kiaia (steward) ready to receive us ; we were ushered into a room where that gentleman lodged, who with five others of the principal officers or attendants belonging to the Aga were still at *dinner*. We sat down upon a sofa beside them, and as soon as their repast was over and they had finished their ablutions, the Kiaia gave us a letter to the Bostangee Bashi, (chief of the guard, and in fact superintendant of the Seraglio,) which he considered as a more ready mode of procuring admission, than any person he could send to accompany us. Furnished with his passport, we rowed to the

z

Kiosk or Pavilion, where the Bostangee Bashi usually passes the day. He was engaged at the Porte, and we were shewn into a small guard-chamber in order to wait his return; a messenger however soon arrived to conduct us to him. Thus escorted, we were suffered to pass the guard and to enter the court, or rather garden of the Seraglio. This spot presented an appearance altogether new to me, the trees are neither planted in avenues nor scattered with the careless simplicity of nature, nor put in with the laboured irregularity of modern improvers; it is neither a kitchen-garden nor a flower-garden, nor an orchard, nor a court, but something composed of all these together; it seems as if it had been formed out of a large wood, principally consisting of cypresses, by scooping them into walks, sometimes straight and sometimes bending, which cross each other at different angles, and run off at different directions; the trees only that border these walks having been left and all the others cut away. A very thick paling gaudily painted, stretches itself from one tree to another; the ground between the walks is variously cultivated, some of it being appropriated to shrubs, some to fruit trees, some to flowers, and no small part laid out as a mere kitchen-garden. The lodges for the guards are placed without order at the bottom of some of the largest trees, the under boughs of which serve for the roofs of the buildings; we crossed this large space diagonally, and entered a smaller one surrounded with the habitations of the officers of the guard, into one of which we were introduced. It is inconceivable how mean these buildings appear; but indeed this is the case with most of the structures in Turkey after they have stood any time. The characteristics of Turkish architecture, (for I assure Your Lordship there exists an architecture in this country as completely *sui generis*, and as strictly confined to its own rules and proportion as the Gothic or the Grecian,) are airiness and splendor, and I think a person must be very fastidious indeed who is not struck with the light and brilliant appearance exhibited by many of the Turkish edifices, while they continue in a state of perfection; but unfortunately the frail materials of which they are composed, viz., wood painted over, render this appearance extremely transient, and the remains of magnificence thus every where blended with decay, give an idea of squalidness which the ruins of a simpler fabric can never communicate. After waiting some time for intelligence respecting the Bostangee Bashi, his deputy arrived, read the letters we had brought, and as his principal was engaged in the Seraglio, took upon himself to send for the keeper of the library, and direct him to conduct us thither; we accordingly accompanied him and three other Moulahs to a mosque at a little distance, through which the entrance to the library lies. This mosque is neither large nor elegant; but from its structure and situation is placed in the bosom of the Seraglio, surrounded with immense cypresses, and illuminated only by a few dull double windows towards the top, causing that " dim religious light" which is always aimed at in places of worship throughout the east; it possesses a silence and solemnity more imposing than I think I ever witnessed in any other building; we passed through the mosque as we were directed, without speaking, and upon tiptoe; and at length on the other side of it, arrived at the outward door of the library, which was locked, and a seal fixed upon the lock; above it is a short Arabic inscription, containing the name and titles of Sultan Mustapha, the present Emperor's father, who founded both the mosque and the library in the year 1767. The library is built in the form of a Greek cross, as in the margin; one of the arms of the cross serves as an anti-room, and the remaining three arms, together with the centre, constitute the library itself. You proceed through the anti-room by a door, over which is written in large Arabic characters, " enter in peace." The library is much smaller than Your Lordship could have any conception of; for, from the extremity of one of the arms to the extremity of the opposite one it does not measure twelve yards. Its appearance however is elegant and cheerful. The central part of the cross is covered with a dome, which is supported by four handsome marble pillars; the three arms or recesses that branch off

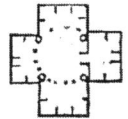

from this, have each of them six windows, three above and as many below. So small an apartment cannot but be rendered extremely light by this great number of windows, and perhaps this effect is not a little increased by the gloom of the mosque, and the darkness of the anti-room which leads to it. The book cases, four of which stand in each of the three recesses are plain but neat. They are furnished with folding wire-work doors, secured with a padlock and the seal of the librarian. The books are laid upon their sides one above another, with their ends outwards, and having their letters written upon the edges of the leaves. Your Lordship may imagine I lost no time in examining the treasures inclosed in this celebrated repository, and the disposition of the books greatly facilitated my inquiries. I am very certain that there was not one volume which I did not separately examine; but I was prevented by the jealousy of the Moulahs who accompanied me from making out a detailed catalogue of the whole. I continued however to take an account of all the writers on history and general literature, and I hope by means of a present to procure an accurate list of the remainder. The whole number of MSS. in the library amounts to 1294, much the greatest part of which are Arabic, these are however most of the best Persian and Turkish writers, but alas, not one volume in Greek, Hebrew, or Latin! The following is a short summary of my investigation, and contains a general statement of the number of books in the library, classed according to their different subjects, viz.

Copies of the Koran	17
Commentaries on ditto	143
Collections of Tradition relative to Mahomet	182
Treatises on Mahomedan Jurisprudence	324
On Logic	95
On Mystical Subjects	47
On Philosophy	86
On Physic	31
On Grammar	192

Poets, and writers on Polite Literature -   -   79
Historians   -   -   -   -   -   42
Dictionaries and Vocabularies   -   -   56

Such, my Lord, is the famous Library of the Seraglio' respecting which so many falsehoods have been advanced; but which I am now very clear, both from the manner in which it is secured, the declarations of the Turks, and the contradictory accounts of the Franks, was never before subjected to the examination of a Christian. After we had remained in the library as long as decency permitted, we took our leave of the Librarian and quitted the Seraglio. As Youssouf Aga's Kiaia had hinted that his master would wish to see me after I had finished my investigation, I waited upon him on my return. He received me with the greatest attention, and desired to know the success of my researches; but at the same time expressed his fears, that the neglect in which literature had been held by their ancestors would render every enquiry, at present, after ancient MSS. entirely fruitless. I thanked him, in the name of the ambassador, for having been permitted to enter the library at all; and assured him, that though I had not met with in it those books which were reported to have been deposited there, yet I considered it as no small satisfaction to have ascertained the negative of the question. I observed, that different nations possessed different customs; that my discovery of one of these ancient authors would be looked upon in England as very important; and I took the liberty of adding, that no person felt more interested in subjects of this kind than Mr. Pitt. Youssouf Aga replied, that nothing could give them greater pleasure than to gratify the British nation, and particularly Mr. Pitt; and that if they could give any intelligence where such books were deposited, I should not only have the liberty of inspecting them, but of carrying them along with me to England. This assurance gave me an opportunity of hinting at the other repository of books in the Seraglio, and of expressing my wish, if it were not improper, to be allowed to examine it likewise. The Aga answered in such a manner as gave

Mr. Chaubert, the dragoman who accompanied me, every reason to conclude that my request would not finally be denied. Mr. C. possesses a very considerable personal influence with Youssouf Aga; and in fact obtained leave for my admission into the library, after both Lord Elgin's presents and the request he had transmitted by others had been found ineffectual to procure that permission. I own, my Lord, I shall feel not a little hurt, if I be thus hindered from completing my enquiries; but I trust matters will be so arranged, by some means or other, as to prevent my experiencing such a disappointment.

I have the honor to be, &c. &c.

I. D. CARLYLE.

LETTER VI.

My Lord,   BRITISH PALACE, PERA, Feb 29 1801

I HAVE this moment received Your Lordship's letter, when I am upon the wing for setting out for Greece. I lament that I must be obliged to give up the favorite plan I had formed of a journey to the Black Sea, and especially as the idea has met with Your Lordship's approbation. I shall ever regret that the delays of the Turkish government, in giving an answer respecting my admission into the libraries, prevented me from undertaking my projected expedition in the autumn of last year, especially as I have not been permitted to examine the repository of books in the Khasné. It was only yesterday, my Lord, that that business was finally determined. I had been buoyed up with hopes of entering the library, by repeated promises of Youssouf Aga, and had in consequence waited with no little impatience for the termination of the Ramadan and the Bairam (during which periods the Sultan will do no business), but the message which

was received yesterday has completely put an end to every expectation. The message was from Youssouf Aga, and stated that he had
been informed by the Sehetai Aga, that "the Sultan could not think
of acceding to our request, as it might subject him to similar ones
from other persons." — I feel some disappointment, my Lord, in not
having been permitted completely to ascertain the object of my
mission, after making so long a stay in the country; but I confess I
have not the smallest idea that any Greek MSS. can exist in any part
of the Seraglio. there certainly were none in the principal library,
and from every enquiry I can make there does not appear the smallest
probability that such MSS. exist any where else. The Capudan
Pasha, (to whom I was introduced by Lord Elgin's kindness, purposely to make the inquiry,) assured me that he himself had been
brought up in the Seraglio, and had passed near thirty years in it;
that he was attached to that particular department in it called the
Khasné (Treasury); for the officers in the interior of the Seraglio are
divided into four classes, *viz.* (to speak in our language) those belonging to the *Guards,* to the *Kitchen,* to the *Bed-chamber,* and to the
Treasury. The Capudan Pasha declared that he had been in every
part of the Khasné, that he had never seen, or even heard of any
MSS. being deposited in it; that if any such did exist, they could
not but be known, as it is an invariable rule, upon the appointment
of every new Treasurer, that an inventory of the contents of the
Khasné should be made out; this inventory, his Highness informed
me, is minutely accurate, and not the smallest article which the
Khasné contains can be omitted in it. If, therefore, any manuscripts
had ever been preserved there, they must have been inserted in these
inventories, which he was certain they were not. This account of
the Capudan Pasha is entirely conformable to the information I
received upon the same subject from the venerable and excellent
Patriarch of Jerusalem; he assured me that he had not the smallest
idea that any Greek MSS. existed in the Seraglio, or in any other
repository belonging to the Sultan;—that if any had existed (such
is the veneration of the modern Greeks for what belonged to their

ancestors, and such their influence with the Ministers of the Porte), that they must have been brought to light. From these authorities, my Lord, I did not imagine that I should be able to find any thing valuable in the Khasné, but still I feel a great mortification in being debarred examining it, as, after all, I cannot but be conscious that the *re infecta rediit* must be attached to my mission. I have, however, my Lord, been more successful in my literary inquiries in other quarters. I have examined and taken a catalogue of the MSS. in the library belonging to the Patriarch of Jerusalem, the largest I believe in the empire, and have even obtained permission to carry a few of those which I judged most valuable to England. The rest consisting of 130, are made up chiefly of homilies, books of offices, and controversial writings against the Roman church. I have likewise examined the libraries (if such they may be called) contained in the convents of the Prince's Islands, as well as those in Constantinople, and have been able (and I assure Your Lordship, I have not stolen *even* one) to obtain twenty-nine Greek MSS containing the Gospels or Epistles. We have only gotten three MSS. on profane literature, viz. a Libanius, an Eutropius (with a continuation), and a history of the siege of Thessalonica by the Latins, in the time of Count Baldwin. Most of the MSS. are upon vellum, and some undoubtedly very ancient. Nor have I, my Lord, been less fortunate in my Arabic acquisitions, having ransacked the Bazars at Constantinople so frequently, that I think I have obtained all the valuable books in this language that the shops contained; at least, all those whose price was not too great for me to attempt the purchase. My Arabian MSS. amount to nearly 100, picked out of at least *forty* times that number *, and consisting (as far as my knowledge enabled me to form a judgment) of some of the best Historians, Biographers, Natural Historians, Geographers, and Poets, in the language. So that, upon the whole, my Lord, I

---

* " An European, who wishes to buy Arabic, Turkish, and Persian MSS.," says Niebuhr, " finds no where such good opportunities as at Constantinople."

cannot but flatter myself that the collection of MSS. which I have formed is one of the most valuable ever sent at one time to England. As Your Lordship will conceive I am somewhat anxious for its safe arrival, I believe I shall transmit the box to Lord Keith, to whom Lord Elgin will write, with a request to have it sent forward to England. With respect to myself, my Lord, I wished to set off immediately (in company with Mr. Hunt, who has been a zealous assistant in my researches) for Mount Athos, in order to examine the libraries in the different Greek convents there; and as we go with every recommendation that we could wish, perhaps we may not be less successful in the acquirement of MSS. at the holy mountain than in other places of the same description. From Athos, we mean to go to Salonica; and from thence, if possible, to the monasteries on the Peneus. We shall then proceed, by the most celebrated spots of Thessaly, Doris, Phocis, and Bœotia, to Attica and Athens. from thence I shall cross the Isthmus to Patras; and so get *home*, either by Malta or Trieste, by sea or by land, as circumstances may admit. I confess, my Lord, I cannot write that word *home* without feeling a sensation which all the classic grounds I have just mentioned (though I believe I shall visit them with as much enthusiasm as most persons) can never convey. with what delight shall I return to it, convinced as I always was from reasoning, and now am from experience, that it is the only country where religion, liberty, or happiness can be found '

I have the honor to be, &c. &c.

I. D. CARLYLE.

LETTERS

FROM

THE LATE PROFESSOR CARLYLE

TO

THE LORD BISHOP OF DURHAM.

LETTER I.

MY LORD, CONSTANTINOPLE, Jan 11. 1800.

As Your Lordship expressed a wish that I should endeavour to see some of the Greek Patriarchs, in order to learn the fate of the Arabic copies of the New Testament, which were sent some time ago, by the Society, to Alexandria, I took an opportunity last week of waiting upon the Patriarch of Constantinople. I was received by him with much politeness, and he seemed disposed to give me every information in his power. He assured me, however, that he had never heard of any books having been transmitted into these countries from England, and was very certain that none had ever been distributed. But as he did not understand the Arabic language himself, and as he had no personal knowledge of the East, he requested me to make a visit to the Patriarch of Jerusalem, to whom he dispatched a messenger to introduce me. I went accordingly and was immediately admitted. The Patriarch was sitting upon his sofa, and expressed great pleasure at seeing us. He is fourscore years of age, has a very pleasing countenance, and a most interesting appearance, and possesses all his faculties in their full vigor. Arabic is his native tongue, so that I was enabled to converse with him without an interpreter. Like the Patriarch of Constantinople he was entirely unacquainted that any books had ever been sent into the East, and could not conceive that they had ever arrived at Alexandria; he was very sure however, that they had never been dispersed. He was perfectly well informed with respect to the version made use of by the Society (which Your Lordship knows is the same as the Roman one, and I fear a little warped in some places in order to favor the peculiar tenets of the Roman catholic church), and he was pretty strong in his animadversions upon it. This gave me an opportunity of mentioning the new edition, which I was encouraged by Your Lordship to undertake. He immediately poured out a most pathetic benediction upon Your Lordship's head, expressing the good effects that he trusted might result from such a design, and his joy that Your Lordship was treading in the steps of those (meaning the Apostles) whose office you filled. He declared that nothing could afford him so much pleasure as to co-operate in such a work, and assured me that if it was thought fit to transmit some of the copies into those parts of the East, where he or his brethren had any influence, we might rely upon their making every effort to distribute them in the way they should judge most likely to promote the interests of religion. After being with him for an hour, I took my leave, I confess highly gratified with my visit, which he made me promise to repeat.

Both the Patriarchs are men of most respectable characters, and universally esteemed not only by the Greeks and *Turks*, but by Armenians and *Franks*. Your Lordship will perhaps wonder at this seeming anticlimax; but such is the unhappy state of things in this country, that the different sects of Christians hate each other much more than they do the Turks. The venerable Patriarch of Jerusalem has filled the chair upwards of ten years without ever being displaced. The Patriarch of Constantinople has twice been driven into exile by the intrigues of a party, and a rival placed in his cathedral, but he is thought to be now very firmly established. Both these Prelates seem to live in considerable splendor. Their mode of living is, however, entirely Turkish. The palace of the Patriarch of Constantinople is very much like what Your Lordship may perhaps remember to have read

A A 2

descriptions of in the *Arabian Nights*. One enters a large court, which is surrounded with high walls ; in the centre of this court is a terrace formed into a kind of garden, with an alcove in the middle. The walks are composed of gravel of different colours. When every thing is in bloom, the effect, I dare say, will not be displeasing. These kind of raised gardens are quite the fashion here. I saw one of the Reis Effendi's, still larger and higher than that of the Patriarch's. One cannot easily conceive why they should thus wish to elevate their gardens into the air ; but I own I had great pleasure in seeing them, as they so well explained what is meant by the hanging-gardens of Baby-lon. The interior of the palace I found constructed in the same manner as almost all the houses here. At the bottom is a large room, betwixt a stable and a hall, as it is occasionally inhabited either by men or horses. From this a staircase rises, which leads into a saloon, opening into the different apartments upon the floor. The rooms of state are exactly alike in every house ; they are nearly square, and a row of windows goes round the top on three sides. Their sole furni-ture consists of a sofa, of about eight inches in height (which likewise fills three of the sides), and a carpet. The fourth side is left for the door and a kind of recess, where, if they can procure one, they place an English clock. This is the general mode of building, from the Divan of the Capudan Pasha to the sitting-room, of the common tradesman.

We have been very much disappointed in the climate here, we find it quite as severe, and much more changeable than what it gene-rally is in England. Upon the morning of the first of this month, the thermometer (by Fahrenheit's scale) was at 15°, and eight and forty hours after it had risen to near 50°. I think Your Lordship will scarcely recollect any variation equal to this in the same time. The consequences of these sudden changes have been very uncomfortable to all of us, and particularly to myself, as I have experienced more ill-health since my arrival here than in all my former life put together. But we trust that this will only prove what the inhabitants call a *seasoning*.

As Lord Elgin has not found an opportunity of inquiring whether the libraries of the Seraglio may be opened to us, I have entirely occupied myself in my Oriental studies, and I trust the advantages I possess here will not be thrown away. I have not only the opportunities of consulting various books, but of writing and conversing in the Arabic language· and I can now do this with tolerable facility. The stores of Arabic literature in the several public libraries in Constantinople are prodigious. The histories relating to the most flourishing periods of the Khaliphat are almost innumerable; nor are the other parts of their history deficient in writers who elucidate them. I believe I mentioned to Your Lordship the idea I had formed of collecting materials for an account of that Crusade in which *Saladin* and our *Richard* the *First* were engaged. I trust I shall not be disappointed in meeting with a great deal of very curious information relative both to the history of that epoch, and also what will throw a considerable light upon the general state of manners in Europe during the middle ages, particularly with regard to chivalry and the feudal system, both of which I have no doubt originated in these countries.

The Turkish literature is at a very low ebb; were I to send Your Lordship a specimen of it you would only be too much disgusted by it. It is possible, however, I may be able to pick up something better than what I have yet seen, before my return; but I own I have little hopes upon the subject.

I fear I have tired Your Lordship with this farrago, but I trust your goodness will excuse it.

I have the honor to be, &c.

I. D. CARLYLE.

LETTER II.

My Lord,   Buyukdere, near Constantinople, July 23 1800

From the kindness I have experienced from Your Lordship, I have the vanity to think that you will not be wholly uninterested in hearing that I am once more arrived at Lord Elgin's, in health and safety, after an expedition of considerable difficulty.

The breaking out of the plague in Constantinople, at the beginning of the year, totally precluded my making any investigations in that city for some months. I was determined therefore (as I would not willingly waste any part of the time I have to spend in the East) to embrace the opportunity of General Koeler's going to join the Grand Vizier's army, to accompany him in his journey through Asia Minor. We had a most interesting *ride* through the whole of the peninsula; the latter part, from Caraman to the sea, over the ancient Lycaonia, Cilicia, and Isauria, I considered particularly curious, as I believe we were the first Europeans that had passed over it since the Turkish conquest. The whole of the country presents a melancholy picture of former magnificence, and present desolation. The desert plains we trod seemed ready to start into fertility with a touch, but that touch unhappily is wanting. At Cyprus I joined Sir Sidney Smith, and accompanied him first to Crete and afterwards to Alexandria, where, under the sanction of a flag of truce, I landed and passed a few very agreeable days with some of the French at that place. It is only justice to say that they treated me with every politeness; the *Savans* informing me of any thing I wished to inquire about, without the smallest reserve, and the military offering me every accommodation in their power to penetrate farther into the interior; but these offers I was obliged to decline on account of the situation of the country which rendered all examination of matters of curiosity totally impracticable. The moment I was there happened to be just after the battle between the Turks and French; the former kept possession of the town of Cairo, the latter of the castle, and perpetual skirmishes were taking place betwixt them. The Mamelukes, enemies to both, were masters of Upper Egypt. The Bedouin Arabs, unopposed by any, and adversaries to all, ravaged the banks of the Nile, and the plague raged throughout the whole country. Thus circumstanced, I was obliged to relinquish all idea of reaching Cairo, and content myself with what I was able to observe of Egyptian manners and antiquities in and around Alexandria. I cannot however, my Lord, regret the period at which I arrived there; if it hindered me from seeing some objects of antiquity, it showed me the country itself, in a situation as curious perhaps as any one has ever been.

From Alexandria I sailed to Jaffa, and was fortunate enough to arrive there just before the commencement of the Holy week, and thus had an opportunity of joining an Armenian caravan, and of proceeding to Jerusalem in safety; a journey which, in the present state of Syria, I could not have ventured to have undertaken at any other time, on account of the number of banditti that infest the roads I passed ten days at Jerusalem and in its neighbourhood, and I think saw most of the *Videnda* that were worthy of notice. Amongst other places, I visited the convent of St. Saba, and had an opportunity of completely examining its famous library of MSS.; except, however, 29 copies of the *Gospels* and one of the *Epistles*, there appeared nothing very valuable; the rest, amounting to about 300 volumes, consisted entirely of Fathers, Legends, Homilies, and Rituals. I was permitted to bring away with me to Constantinople six of what I judged the most curious MSS, *viz.* two of the oldest copies of the Gospels, and the only one of the Epistles and Acts; two collections of Apostolical letters, and a copy of Libanius.

I confess, my Lord, I was highly gratified with my visit to Palestine. I not only *saw* what I had much wished to *see*, but I was enabled to attain most of the objects I had in view when I undertook the journey. I was permitted to examine many libraries, by the *survey* I had of the country, &c. I shall be able to understand many parts in the

Oriental writers that have hitherto puzzled me not a little; and above all, by getting hold of a dictionary of the *vernacular* language of the country, and by putting things in such a train as to insure further information upon that subject, I trust I shall have it in my power to throw light upon many passages in the different Oriental dialects, and particularly in SS., that have not hitherto been explained for want of having recourse to such a key. I had the honor of conversing with Your Lordship upon this head in London, and was not a little gratified in finding my sentiments respecting this (I think) neglected mode of criticism, so congenial to Your Lordship's.

From Syria I proceeded by the way of Rhodes, Cos, Chios, &c. to Smyrna, occasionally touching or staying at any place where I hoped to pick up information. From Smyrna I took a vessel to the Dardanelles, and from thence was conveyed in a Turkish row-boat to Constantinople.

It will give Your Lordship pleasure to know that the idea of our proposed edition of the Arabic SS. was received with the most lively mark of gratitude and delight by every one to whom I communicated it. The different sects of Christians seemed to vie with each other in applauding the plan, and in proffers of assistance towards rendering it as completely effectual as possible. I have just heard from my friend and *neighbour*, Mr. Frederick North, governor of Ceylon, who tells me he has established in that island 150 Protestant schools, and has had the Liturgy of the Church of England translated into the different Oriental tongues there in use. It gave me the sincerest pleasure to be able to inform him of the benevolent scheme promoted by Your Lordship, in which I am an humble instrument. I trust we shall have it in our power, before he quits his government, to furnish him with the essential foundations of religious education. In the mean time, one is happy to find that he has chosen such a work to pave its way as our most admirable Liturgy. I assure Your Lordship I feel impatient to begin the work, and I am gratified in finding, by accounts from London, that every thing will be ready for my entering upon it as soon as I return.

When that may be I cannot yet precisely say. The Ottoman ministers have hitherto denied the existence of any library in the Seraglio, but as this was conveyed through the medium of the late Reis Effendi, a man in every respect feeble and ignorant, it is not greatly to be relied on. The present Reis Effendi, who was appointed a few days ago, is without controversy one of the most learned and most intelligent persons in the empire; I trust therefore in a very short time the matter will be brought to issue, when I shall be able to form some notion respecting the period of my stay in this country. Believe me, my Lord, motives of *mere* curiosity shall not detain me, when those of duty prompt my return.

I. D. CARLYLE.

LETTER III.

My Lord,

BOYUKDERL, Oct. 12 1800

I was honoured by receiving your letter to me here about the same time that I apprehend my last would reach Your Lordship. I return Your Lordship many thanks for Mr. Hawkins's interesting paper which I have perused with great satisfaction. I have the pleasure of being well acquainted with that gentleman, and have obtained much valuable information from him upon the subjects treated in his little essay, and upon similar ones previous to my departure from England. I could have wished, however, my Lord, he had been somewhat more particular in pointing out the places of smaller note where he suspects MSS. are to be discovered; as it appears to me quite as difficult to find out where they are as to gain possession of them afterwards; some of the repositories at which he hints I have already examined, and have taken steps for the examination of others as soon as I shall have finished investigating the library of the Seraglio, into which I have the pleasure of acquainting Your Lordship that I am at length to be admitted, and a day is this evening to be fixed for that purpose. The convents in the Princes Islands contain no

B B

MSS. of any value or antiquity ; a modern copy of one of the edited plays of Sophocles was the only appearance of a classical author ; nor have I as yet been able to discover any thing of consequence in the libraries of the Greek Princes here ; but I have by no means finished my investigations amongst them, nor have I seen either of the libraries of that kind mentioned by Mr. Hawkins. I trust I shall be able to make a very complete survey of the Patriarchal libraries ; I have already secured my admission into them, but I have on many accounts postponed examining them till after my being admitted to that of the Seraglio. I confess, my Lord, I have more hopes of discovering MSS. of consequence, in these libraries, than in any others in the country, both on account of their magnitude, the situation of their possessors, and their having been hitherto (as far as I understand) so little explored. I had an intention of making an excursion towards Sinope and Trebizond, both which places I have been assured contain valuable repositories of MSS., but I have been detained so long in waiting for the answer of the Divan respecting my admission to the Seraglio, that a voyage to the Black Sea is now become impracticable on account of the season of the year ; nor indeed would I venture amongst those regions at present, as the plague rages with great violence in all that part of Asia Minor. I shall endeavour, if possible, in my return, to stop a while at Mount Athos, but I fear those convents have been so often searched that there is not much hope of finding any considerable literary treasures. I perhaps however shall have more favourable opportunities of examining them than have been generally possessed. I should conceive the monasteries on the Peneus to be more likely to repay the pains of investigating them, as they certainly hitherto have been little explored, but I fear, my Lord, I shall scarce have it in my power to visit them, as I would fain get back to England and my duties there as soon as possible. I trust however, my Lord, that upon the whole I shall be able to glean some information upon these subjects that will not be uninteresting. If I do not it shall not be for want of any exertions of my own.

Your Lordship asks me about the respective numbers of the different sects of Christians in the East. I cannot say that when I was upon the spot I was able to obtain any information on the subject upon which I could much rely, as each individual always appeared to swell the number of his own community and to diminish that of others, but it will not be difficult at Constantinople to ascertain the question with tolerable accuracy. In European Turkey the Latins and Armenians (except in the town of Constantinople alone, where there are undoubtedly a very large quantity of Armenians,) bear no proportion to the Greeks. The Latins I am informed by the Vicar-General here, do not amount to more than 40,000. The Greeks in Europe certainly out-number the Turks in a ratio of three or four to one. The whole number of them according to the best information I can procure, amounting to about three millions and an half. In Asia, except upon the sea coasts and the islands, the number of the Greeks is very considerable, but the Armenians are found in every town from the confines of Tartary to Egypt, and in their habits and modes of life approach so nearly to those of the Turks that they are not easily at the first view distinguished from them. In Syria there are few persons to be found of either the Latin or the Greek communions, except those who are established in the neighbourhood of some convent. The Armenians are much more widely dispersed, and as I was informed by the Patriarch of that nation at Jerusalem, (a most respectable person who died of the plague at Jaffa, only ten days after I left that place,) constitute in Persia a very large part of the inhabitants. The population of the city of Jerusalem I believe I obtained pretty accurately; it consists of 9,000 Mahomedans, 3,000 Jews, 2,000 Greeks, 600 Latins, 300 Armenians, 100 Jacobites or Syrians, and two or three families of Copts and Maronites. Your Lordship will be surprized at the number of the Jews, and I could not gain any satisfactory account how they existed in a place where they do not cultivate the ground, and where they cannot have much commerce, as it requires a guard to go in safety even half a mile from the walls of the town, and you cannot travel to any distance without a very considerable escort ; had it not been for a caravan of Armenian pilgrims, consisting of four or five hundred persons who were going to Jerusalem to celebrate Easter, whom we joined, I should not have been able to have gotten to that city at all.

The whole of these sects at present seem to have an equal hatred to the Turks and to the French ; to the former for their constant oppression ; to the latter for their horrid cruelties they committed in their return from Acre. I myself *saw* under the walls of Jaffa the mangled and half-buried remains of 5,000 Turks, and near 500 Christians whom Buonaparte massacred upon the shore. The putrid smell was scarcely dissipated after the intervention of a year Kleber (as did several of the other officers) refused to have any hand in so shocking a transaction, but miscreants were not wanting to put in execution (with every aggravation of cruelty that could have been practised by a Nero, as I was repeatedly told by *eye-witnesses,*) the commands of the First Consul. In consequence of all this, the English are every where in Syria looked up to as preservers. When we returned to Jerusalem after a little excursion in the neighbourhood, we were met by a company of Christian women who sung in Arabic a kind of gratulatory song, the burden of which was " the English are going to the holy city, and they are the Christians after all."

With regard to the opinions of the different sects respecting the fulfilment of the prophecies, I had not, my Lord, any opportunity of learning their ideas, as, except the Superior and a few other of the monks in the convent of the Terra-Sancta, and the Patriarchs of the Armenians and Greeks, the rest of the Christians, (particularly of the two last-named sects,) seemed so deplorably ignorant, that it was hopeless to converse with any of them on such subjects.

I need not say that I was much gratified in hearing that Your Lordship found my letters at all interesting, but I must not let so flattering a declaration induce me to trespass too long upon your many other engagements.

I. D. CARLYLE.

LETTER IV.

My Lord.   Constantinople, Dec 12 1800

I have the satisfaction of acquainting Your Lordship that at length I have been permitted to examine the library of the Seraglio. I wish I could add that I had been able to make any discoveries of Latin, Greek, or Hebrew MSS. there, but, after investigating every volume, I found nothing in that boasted repository except a collection of Arabic, Persian, and Turkish authors, principally upon Mahomedan Theology and Jurisprudence. I have not, however, quite given up my inquiries in the Seraglio; I entertain hopes of being admitted into another apartment, within its precincts, which, I am *informed*, does actually contain a number of worm-eaten parchments that lie piled up upon the floor But I confess, my Lord, I have been so often deceived in the accounts that have been given me, respecting subjects of this nature, that I am by no means sanguine in my expectations of making any valuable discovery. At the same time I should wish to omit no opportunity of investigating every part of the palace where there may be the smallest chance that any ancient MSS. could either be left by negligence or deposited by design.

I see by the newspapers, that Your Lordship has been employed with your usual activity and benevolence, in endeavouring to mitigate the distresses with which we are grieved to find our poorer countrymen at present labouring, from the high price of provisions. If the evil be of a temporary nature, one has every reason to believe that such exertions, from individuals of Your Lordship's character, aided by the wisdom of Parliament, will lessen or subdue it; but, my Lord, the whole of our agricultural economy seems to be so different from what it is in most of the countries where agriculture has longest and best flourished, that one cannot but fear there may be circumstances radically improper in the system itself. I pretend not, my Lord, to be much conversant in such subjects, but I cannot help troubling Your

Lordship with a few observations I made relative to matters of this kind in my late journey through Asia Minor, Palestine, part of the Delta, and the most considerable of the islands in the Archipelago

Through all these countries I think I may affirm that I did not see one field *laid down* for hay. A narrow fringe of natural grass skirted the mouths of some of the rivers, but otherwise cultivation was entirely directed to raise human food.

After the harvest is gotten in, the straw is broken into small pieces, by a kind of harrow, and cleaned and laid up as provender. The working cattle, camels, &c. get little other food besides this. The beeves pick up what they can, for a while, on fallow grounds, and are then fattened by oil cakes. Horses, that do little, are fed with the same straw, but always when they are hard ridden, with barley. Their litter is composed entirely of their own dung, dried and sifted. The beef in the East is undoubtedly by no means so fine as some of the *best* that is sold in the London markets, but it is not very inferior to the generality of what is met with in the country towns throughout England, and from its being fed and fattened in a manner that induces little expence, it is bought for a smaller proportionate price than almost any other article of consumable commodities. At this place, while wheat is at six shillings or seven shillings per bushel, and mutton fetches three-pence-halfpenny per pound, the best beef only comes to two-pence farthing. The same *relative* difference in the prices holds good in the interior parts of the country, though the *absolute* amount of each article is not more than two-thirds of what it reaches in Constantinople. That the mode of treatment I have mentioned is not prejudicial to the horses in the East is sufficiently clear from the character they maintain; a character, to the justice of which I can bear ample testimony, as out of near six hundred, which our party used at different times in passing through Asia Minor, not more than six stumbled and fell, though great part of our roads were such as I should have imagined, if we had not travelled over them, to have been impassable. I need scarce add, my Lord, that in all these countries horses are almost solely appropriated to riding; all the cattle used for husbandry and nine-tenths of that for draught and carriages being oxen. Nor is it necessary to say that I found neither breweries to use the barley, nor distilleries to destroy the wheat.

One cannot help, I think, being struck with the different situation of Great Britain in the points I have hinted at.

1. A very great portion (Your Lordship is a much better judge what that portion is than I can be) of our cultivated land consists of *grass*, and all this, I conceive, to be nearly withdrawn from the *general* consumption; for it is appropriated either to the maintenance of horses, which are wholly useless as an article of food, or to the production of beef and cheese of so superior a quality, and consequently so high a price, as almost to preclude the common people from purchasing them.

2. Of the land that is in tillage, *that* which bears oats is almost entirely destined for *horses*, *that* which produces barley, for *brewing*.

3. Whilst the greatest part of the animals used in the east *take* little from human food for their support, and *contribute* much to increase it when they are killed, those in England *consume* much of it while alive, and when dead *contribute* nothing to add to it.

I apprehend, my Lord, that all these evils have been advancing in England, and of late years most rapidly. From the extremely small sums at which hay moduses are fixed, I believe, throughout almost the whole of the kingdom, we may judge that that article was not considered as of much consequence formerly. Indeed I have myself seen rentals of large estates, in which (160 or 170 years ago) there is no mention made of any grass lands except a *garth* or two close to the mansion. In those days, as we see from various household books, the beeves and many of the sheep were killed at the approach of winter, and pickled or dried. This practice is prevalent *here*, and it continues to be followed in most of the northern parts of Great Britain yet, as I make no doubt but Your Lordship may have heard. The seeming advantages to landlords and tenants have induced a preference for grazing farms, and the number of common fields which have of late years been inclosed has enabled them to convert no small quantity of land that was formerly arable into pasture, while the quantity of human food, has, I fear, by this means, been gradually lessening, the population of the country has undoubtedly increased, till the average produce of the land is no longer equal to the consumption; for though a number of commons and what are called waste lands have been divided and inclosed, the manner in which they have been allotted and managed has, I fear, tended to counteract much of the benefit that would otherwise have resulted from them.

In the meeting in Oxfordshire, to which I before alluded, I observe that an idea is thrown out of receiving rents in a different manner from a fixed pecuniary payment. As something of this kind is practised throughout the whole of Asia Minor, not only in paying rents but wages, perhaps Your Lordship will not dislike to have a short account of it.

Almost all the lands in Anatolia and Caramania are let from year to year; the rent of every farm is partly fixed and partly variable. The fixed part (which goes to the Seigneur of the district) is paid in money; the variable part (which belongs to the immediate landholder) differs in different places; sometimes it amounts only to a tenth of the produce, but the most general rent throughout the whole of Asia Minor is a quantity of grain equal to the quantity sown, or the *sum of money which this quantity would bring at the time of payment* This, my Lord, approaches nearer to a corn rent than I should have expected to have met with in these countries.

The mode of settling wages seems to be regulated upon similar principles. The servant hired by the year, as well as the day-labourer, receives part of his pay in money, and the rest in necessaries or an *equivalent for them*. Thus, in Anatolia the wages of a servant hired for the year amount to about forty shillings, together with a shirt and trowsers, and a claim for a couple of pounds of food, which is generally pilaw, *per diem*, i. e. boiled rice mixed up with grease. The day-labourer receives about two-pence-halfpenny a-day, together with the same quantity of pilaw as the other. In Caramania the same custom obtains, only that in that part of the country as money is more valuable, the pecuniary payments are nearly one-fifth less.

In Constantinople we have the same practice even in the palaces of the ambassadors, where every servant *of the country*, besides a certain fixed annual sum, receives a daily mess (consisting of one-half meat and one-half vegetables), weighing about 2½ lbs. which he is at liberty to make what use of he pleases.

It is singular, my Lord, that this mode of paying wages both to servants and labourers was formerly universal in England. I have had opportunities of examining and copying the *year books* of various religious houses from the twelfth century to the Reformation, preserved in the different colleges in Cambridge, and I have always found that these payments were made *partly* in money, and *partly* in corn, principally rye.

The practice is still very prevalent in Scotland, and I own I cannot but think that if something of this kind was generally enforced, it would be more likely to alleviate or prevent the distresses of the labouring poor than any thing else. To have the *whole* of their wages paid in the manner of a corn rent, would, perhaps, in times of great scarcity be subject to inconveniences, but surely they ought to receive such a proportion as would preclude anxiety for absolute subsistence. It would undoubtedly require no little consideration how to adapt these principles to the payment of the wages of the manufacturer and artizan, as well as the husbandman, but I cannot conceive that it would be wholly impracticable.

I ought to beg ten thousand pardons of Your Lordship for detaining you so long with these desultory observations, which, I fear, will only have shown my *wish* and not my *power* of communicating intelligence on subjects of this kind, but I know with Your Lordship, though it might not with others, that *wish* will serve as my apology.

I. D. C.

LETTER V.

My Lord,   Salonica, April 27 1801

Though I am not very sure that this letter may reach Your Lordship,
yet I cannot help endeavouring to communicate to you that I have
at length finished the investigation of *all the MSS.* contained on
Mount Athos.   I had always wished to make the examination of
them as it has hitherto been in some measure a desideratum in
literature, but the letter I received from Your Lordship, determined
me if possible to attempt it.

After leaving Constantinople therefore, and spending sixteen or
seventeen most interesting days upon the Troad, I proceeded by the
route of Tenedos and Lemnos to the Holy mountain.   In my voyage
between the two last places I was exposed to a most dreadful storm,
which we have every reason to believe proved fatal to several vessels
of the same size as ours, that quitted Lemnos in company with us ;
but a merciful God thought fit to preserve us ; after being buffeted
about in our little caique for upwards of twelve hours, we were
safely landed under the hospitable walls of one of the monasteries in
the peninsula of Mount Athos.   As I had previously provided myself
with letters both from the government and the Patriarch, I was
received with every mark of kindness, and introduced into every
repository that I wished to examine.   The whole number of convents
upon the mountain consists of twenty-two, and each of these is
furnished with a library of MSS., more or less numerous according
to the wealth and importance of the society to which it belongs.
The monasteries lie at different distances from each other, and in
fact with their dependencies of cells and farms, people the peninsula,
into which not one female of any kind, even to a sheep or a hen is
ever admitted.   Their situation is the most various, and at the
same time the most romantic that can be conceived.   Out of the

twenty-two convents, scarce two are placed on similar sites * ; but all are either strikingly beautiful or strikingly magnificent; and each seems designed either to soothe the tedium of solitude or to awaken

---

* *Extract from Dr. Sibthorp's MSS.*

Sep. 25, 1791. — We coasted the western shore of Athos, steep rocks covered with shrubs, traversed by deep ravines, marked with the lively verdure of evergreen trees offered the most romantic sites for the monasteries and monastic cells. Several of the latter excavated in the rock seemed to be in situations almost inaccessible, we could scarcely discover the little path that conducted the hermit to his cell. Nothing could be more picturesque than the situation of the monasteries we passed, they commanded an extensive view of the sea, and were surrounded by the finest sylvan scenery. The head of a vale or ravine laid into vineyards and olive grounds was the most general situation, the mountain itself broken grandly into ridges was ornamented with various foliage, through which was seen the slaty substance of the rock. Having cast anchor I was impatient to land on Athos and examine its shores, which from their verdure promised me a considerable addition to my Flora. On landing, I found the rock almost blue with the autumnal Scilla, and in the shade under the cover of the trees was the Cyclamen, above on the hanging cliffs, the yellow Amaryllis all in flower. This was a cheerful sight to a botanist who had just left the sun-burnt plains of Lemnos, and arid rocks of Imbros. I climbed along the shore to the port of Daphne through trees and shrubs, consisting of Arbor Judas, Alaternus, Phillyrea, Arbutus, Evergreen and Kermes oak. At Daphne, the bay mixed with the wild-olive was spread over the rocks, a rivulet flowing down, watered the roots of some huge plane trees, around which the Smilax was entwined diffusing from its flowers a grateful odour.

Oct. 1 — A caloyer had brought from a distant vineyard a basket of grapes, and I took the opportunity of having him for a conductor to visit part of the mountain, which from its height, promised to gratify my botanical researches. I mounted his mule and pursued from the beach a rugged path-way winding up the rocks; ascending for an hour this rough road through evergreen shrubs, I came to a mixture of pines and chesnuts, the latter were now laden with ripe fruit, and the crew of our boat that lay in the port of Daphne were busily employed in collecting a stock for their voyage. The pine did not appear to me different from the silver fir, but I could discover no fruit upon it. A range of mountains cloathed with these pines encircled a beautiful plain, here the convent of Xeropotamo has four Kilii or farms, where their caloyers reside. They were now busy in making their wine, and the vineyards were richly laden with the empurpled fruit, my caloyer conducted me to his Kili, and spread before me a rustic table with grapes, figs, dried cherries, walnuts, and filberds. We drunk from a chrystalline rill that flowed along wooden pipes, through the pine-grove from the mountain, the trunks of some of the pines which I observed in my walk had been pierced to draw their resin from them, and many grown old had their branches bearded with filamentous lichens.

the fervours of devotion. The scenery and the mode of life that I witnessed in the Holy mountain were certainly the most singular I ever had an opportunity of seeing before, but I trust Your Lordship will not think the observation of them diverted my attention from the more important objects of my visit, the investigation of the libraries ; during my stay, which consisted of rather more than three weeks, I think I may venture to say I did not omit examining *one MS.*, which I had an opportunity of looking at on Mount Athos. I believe their number amounted to almost 13,000. And unless there may be a few ecclesiastical authors deposited in some private hands, I do not conceive that there are any existing on the mountain which we did not inspect.   From the specimens of monastic libraries which I had before examined, I own I did not entertain much hopes of finding any of the grand desiderata in profane literature.   And to confess the truth my Lord, I have not been disappointed.   For except one copy of the Iliad, and another of the Odyssey ; a few of the edited plays of the different tragedians, a copy of Pindar and Hesiod ; the orations of Demosthenes and Æschines ; parts of Aristotle ; copies of Philo and Josephus, we did not meet with any thing during the whole of our researches, that could be called classical.   We found however a number of very valuable MSS. of the New Testament, though certainly none so old, by some centuries, as either the Alexandrian codex or the MS. of Beza ; indeed I think I have myself procured some MSS. of the N.T, from monasteries in the neighbourhood of Constantinople, as old as any I saw in the libraries of Mount Athos.   We met with only two copies of parts of the LXXII. , and not one MS. of any consequence, in either Syriac or Hebrew.   There were several very beautiful MSS. of the different Greek fathers ; and a prodigious quantity of polemical divinity.   The rest of the shelves were filled with lives of the saints, *Synaxaria, Theotocaria, Liturgies, Menaia,* &c., &c., all relating to the peculiar doctrines or offices of the Greek church.

I have, however, my Lord, made out a very detailed catalogue of the whole of the contents of these celebrated repositories which I hope to have the pleasure of subjecting to Your Lordship's perusal upon my return to England; an event that I own I long for most ardently. We leave this place to-morrow and proceed to Athens by sea, as in the present unsettled state of this country it is impossible to attempt to prosecute our journey thither by land. Indeed the passage by sea is not over secure, as most of the bays swarm with pirates, (from whom we have already had two very narrow escapes,) but as our vessel is of a pretty large size I trust we shall not be exposed to any real danger. By this arrangement, I am obliged to give up all thoughts of examining the monasteries of the Peneus, (which I had projected,) as well as the sight of the vale of Tempe. But as every person here declares that the roads are unsafe, I am obliged to submit. I shall however be able to visit the isle of Delos, (the only one of any consequence in the Archipelago which I have not seen,) and to get more expeditiously to Athens. After spending a little time at Athens I mean to proceed to Malta, and from thence, (as I have small hopes that an Englishman can travel with any safety through Italy and over the Continent,) immediately *home*.

I. D. C.

MOUNT ATHOS.

AN ACCOUNT OF THE MONASTIC INSTITUTIONS AND THE LIBRARIES ON THE HOLY MOUNTAIN

———

AFTER our tedious abode at Lemnos, and the violence of the storm which we had experienced, we were gratified in no common degree with the view of the convent of Batopaidi, embosomed in the midst of gardens, woods, and meadows. We had reached a small creek at the foot of it, but the surf was so high that we scrambled with difficulty over the rocks, and as soon as we landed we pursued a road which led through groves of lemons, oranges, and olives, to the monastery. On reaching the gate we found the approach more like that of a fortress than the peaceful abode of monks. The lofty walls were flanked with towers, and many cannon appeared at the embrasures. The outer gate was doubly plated with iron; a long dark winding passage led from it, in which were two guns on carriages, and three more gates secured by strong bolts and bars. We found all the Monks and Caloyers (or Lay Brothers) in the great church. The Principal being informed of our arrival, one of the provosts was sent to us, who, after reading our letter from the Greek Patriarch of Constantinople, desired us to wait a few minutes until the service was over, when the Abbot (or Hegoumenos) would pay his respects. The behaviour of the Monks in general was hospitable and polite, and during our residence of five days among them seemed to regret that the concourse of uncivilized and noisy pilgrims, assembled for the Holy Week, prevented them from being more attentive to us.

On Easter-day there were above fifteen hundred people who dined in the court-yard of this convent, principally Albanian, Bulgarian, and Wallachian Greeks. It appears, as soon as the oppressed Christian peasants in the neighbouring Turkish provinces have saved a little money, or when pirates and freebooters have made a successful sally, they set out on a pilgrimage to this Holy mountain, where they not only get a plenary absolution by giving up part of their gains, but enjoy the luxury of hearing a perpetual din of bells, and the sight of splendid churches, pictures of saints, and wonder-working reliques. The monastery of Batopaidi is a large irregular pile, standing on high ground, overlooking the sea, and having some lofty towers within it. as well for the purpose of watch-towers, as for a retreat in case of an attack from pirates The number of priests and friars within the walls is about two hundred and fifty, and there are about two hundred and fifty more in the farms, gardens, and vineyards of the convent. They have one large handsome church and twenty-six smaller ones. Their vineyards furnish about one thousand caricos of wine annually, of ninety okes each, but they generally buy a great deal from Negropont, Scopolo, and other islands. They bake six hundred okes of flour, half barley and half wheat, in a week, and in the hands of the congregation who attended at the great church on Easter-day, they reckoned eight hundred and sixty wax candles They are forced to give lodging and food to any stranger who presents himself at the gate, and to depend on his devotion or his ability to repay them. To defray all these expenses and such others as are incurred by keeping the buildings and aqueducts of the convent in repair, besides the interest of borrowed money and the exactions of the Porte, they seem principally to rely on the precarious offerings of pilgrims, and on the sums collected by their mendicant brethren in Russia, Moldavia, Wallachia, and such other countries as profess the Greek creed. Their own lands on Mount Athos produce little except vegetables, grapes, and fuel, and their estates in Russia and Moldavia are almost

nominal.   The Court of St. Petersburgh makes them an annual present of about two hundred rubles (30l.)

On a hill adjoining the convent, and surrounded by fine woods, is a
large school or academy where ancient Greek was taught: but in
consequence of the deficiency of the funds of the institution, this useful seminary has been shut up.   It contains a lodge for the master,
about one hundred and seventy small rooms for students; and is
supplied with water by an acqueduct carried over a long line of
arches.   If fine air, romantic scenery, and seclusion from the dissipa-
tion of the world be favorable to study, this academy should be restored.
Forty years ago, the master of it was the celebrated Eugenius, a native
of Corfu, and formerly schoolmaster at Ioannina in Epirus.   His profound knowledge of ancient Greek, as well as of different branches of
history and philosophy, soon raised the reputation of the academy at
Batopaidi; and instead of seven caloyers, whom he found on his
arrival learning to read the homilies of the Greek church, he was
able in a short time to reckon two hundred youths of respectable
families, not only from Greece, but from Germany, Venice, and Russia.   At length the envy of the caloyers raised a number of calum-
nies concerning the morals of the master and students, which ended
in his retiring with disgust, and the ruin of the school immediately
followed.   Eugenius resided sometime after this at Constantinople, as Didascalos, or Lecturer in the Patriarchal church.   The
reputation of his eloquence and learning induced the Empress Cathe-
rine to invite him to Petersburgh, and she afterwards advanced him
to the See of Chersonesus.   Of his literary productions one of the
most celebrated is his translation of the Æneid into Greek hexameter verse.

The convent paid last year to the Porte fifteen thousand piastres
(350l.) as an extraordinary contribution, besides the usual capitation
and other taxes; and it now appears to be forty thousand piastres in
debt for sums borrowed at interest.   Our principal object being to
examine the ancient manuscripts in the different convents of Mount
Athos, we found we could not have arrived at a more unpropitious

moment. The attention of the whole convent was directed to the different caravans of pilgrims, who were arriving at every instant; they were in general well mounted, each of them armed with a musket; a pair of pistols, and a sword After dinner, their mirth became extremely noisy, and my companion, Mr. Carlyle, who wished much to know the subject of their songs, found they were very similar to the old border songs in England, describing either the petty wars of neighbouring Agas, or the successful opposition on the part of the Albanians to Pashas sent from the Turkish court.

Our stay being thus delayed at Batopaidi, until the Easter festivals were over, we had an opportunity of forming some acquaintances in the convent. The Pro-Hegoumenos, the Secretary, and the Didascalos all men of letters, as well as a Bishop of Triccala, who having been exiled by the Porte from his see had chosen this convent for his residence. On our showing to him a manuscript of Josephus in the convent library, and expressing our regret that we could not recollect where the controverted passage was which speaks of Christ, he almost instantly pointed it out to us, but added, at the same time, that though such a passage, written by a Jew, would be a strong confirmation of the divine mission of Christ, yet that the manuscript we were examining* was of a date too recent to determine whether it might not be an interpolation of the original text. We also visited the venerable Ex-Patriarch of the Greek church, Procopio, who had been banished hither fifteen years ago from his throne at Constantinople. He took no share in the affairs of the convent, but I perceived he was treated with great attention, and his hand kissed with as much veneration as if he had still retained the power as well as the title of Patriarch, for he was always addressed Παναγιοτητάσας, " All Holiness." He had formerly been Bishop of Smyrna, and spoke of the

---

* The passage is in Antiq xviii. 4 798 It is found in all the copies of Josephus' work now extant, both printed and in MS , in a Hebrew translation kept in the Vatican Library, and in an Arabic translation preserved by the Maronites of Mount Libanus Hale's Chronology, vol ii. part 2 951.

English whom he had known there in terms of attachment.   He observed, that the Greek and English churches differed very little from each other in the grand articles of their creed, and regretted the causes of those divisions which broke and interrupted so much the unity of Christian worship.   He mentioned having baptized the child of an English nobleman who was visiting Smyrna, the father considering immersion more conformable to the practice of the Apostles than sprinkling.

Our inquiries respecting the library of the convent were always evaded, and at length we were told that the manuscripts were merely rituals and liturgies of the Greek church, and in very bad condition. On pressing our request to be admitted to see them, and adding that it had been the primary object of our visit, we were shown into a room where these old tattered volumes were thrown together in the greatest confusion, mostly without beginning or end, worm-eaten, damaged by mice, and mouldy with damp.   Assisted by three of those whom I have mentioned, we took an accurate catalogue, examining each mutilated volume separately and minutely.   We found copies of the New Testament, not older than the twelfth and thirteenth centuries, and a variety of theological works, of Chrysostom, Basil, Gregory of Nazianzum, and others, and an infinity of liturgies, canons, and church histories.   The only interesting manuscripts we saw were two tragedies of Æschylus, the Iliad, a copy of that very ancient poem the Batrachomyomachia* ; the works of Demosthenes, Athenæus, Lysias, Galen, some parts of Aristotle, Hippocrates, and Plato, two copies of the Apocalypse, and the Jewish history of Josephus· but none of them bore marks of remote antiquity.   We requested permission to take them to England, for the purpose of having them collated with our printed copies ; but the Hegoumenos said, he could not grant it, without express leave in writing from the Patriarch of Constantinople.

---

* Cujus carminis auctor, si non Homerus, utique vetustissimus.   Hemster in Th. Mag. 26.

The water with which this convent and its gardens are supplied is brought thither in an open canal from a distance of some miles. It is conducted along the sides of the mountains, and sometimes crosses the glens and vallies in most picturesque situations. A walk shaded by trees runs along the whole extent of this stream, which we often followed up to its source in a romantic cleft of the mountain, where there is a fine natural cascade. In one of our rambles near the monastery, we went to a small building, and to our surprise and horror found it filled with piles of skulls of such Monks and Caloyers as have died within the walls of the convent. A little church, dedicated to all the saints, is placed over this awful repository of mortality. By the canons of the order, no Caloyer or Monk can eat meat, except in case of great or extreme illness. He must also abstain from eggs, oil, and fish*, on all Mondays, Wednesdays, and Fridays. The food on those days is restricted to bread, salted olives, and vegetable soup. This is made of dried peas, beans, or other pulse; onions and leeks the latter grow to a most extraordinary size. The Hegoumenos assured us they sometimes weighed an oke (or 2¼ lbs. avoirdupois) each.

No woman is suffered to enter the gates of this, or even of any other convent on the Holy mountain†, *(gens æterna, in qua nemo nascitur,)* nor is any female animal permitted to come upon the peninsula, a prejudice to which the Turks conform by not allowing the Vaivode at Charress to have any woman with him during the period of his government. A still more whimsical regulation is, that neither cows, ewes, or hens are suffered to be brought to the peninsula; the inhabitants,

---

* On the peninsula of Athos, Belon found the river crab, *cancer fluviatilis*, it is considered a great delicacy, and is eaten by the Greeks in many parts of Turkey, in Lent time "Les Caloires les mangent cruds, et nous asseurent," says Belon, "qu'ils estoyent meilleurs que cuicts" They are found near Aleppo, and are there in perfection in the season of the white mulberries, the ripe fruit scattered on the ground under the trees is eaten by them —Russell, ii 221

† " 'Ου γυναῖκων ἐκεῖ ξυναυλία," says Nicephorus Gregoras, in his account of Mount Athos, lib xiv The words in the text are those of Pliny, when speaking of the Therapeutæ

therefore, have no milk, butter, cheese, or eggs, except when these articles are imported from Thasos and Lemnos, or from Macedonia, across the Isthmus. We saw milk sold at seven-pence an oke, when wine only cost two-pence. They use oxen for ploughing, and mules for riding. The superstitious or artful caloyers repeat gravely to every stranger who visits them, that no female animal could live three days on Mount Athos, although they see doves and other birds building their nests in the thickets, swallows hatching their young under the sheds, and vermin multiplying in their dirty cells and on their persons.

While we were walking one day on the beach, we observed that a ship had arrived, to which the priests and caloyers immediately repaired; and received from the hands of the captain a silver box, containing what was called a relic of the zone or girdle of the Virgin Mary. It appeared that it had been borrowed from the convent for a great sum, in order to stop the progress of some epidemic disorder at a town on the shores of the Black Sea, and was now brought back to be deposited in the treasury of the convent.

On Easter-Monday, after a stay of five days, we set out with mules provided for us by the convent, to the town of Chariess, in the centre of the peninsula, where the Turkish Aga, and the council of deputies from all the convents reside for the dispatch of public business. It was necessary to make this visit, in order that our imperial firman and our letter from the Greek Patriarch might be examined, and that we might be informed how to make the tour of the convents with the greatest ease and security. The distance from Batopaidi to Chariess, is two hours and three quarters. About three miles from the former we had a most striking view of the summit of Athos. This has been estimated by Delambre at 713 toises. The whole ride furnishes a succession of sublime Alpine scenery. Instead of the usual salutations which are exchanged between travellers who meet on the road, the only one we now heard was the Easter congratulation, " Christ is risen;" to which the answer is, " He is the true God." We found the deputies living together at Chariess in a very humble style . they were four in number; and after reading our letters of introduction, they assured us, that we might visit every part of the Holy mountain in perfect security without a guard. We then waited on the Turkish Aga, who had the civil jurisdiction of the peninsula, he was a young man belonging to the corps of Bostangees or life-guards of the Grand Seignior; and no situation can be conceived more ridiculous than that in which we found him. His house adjoined the great church of Chariess, called Protaton, round which a number of idle boys, and some hundreds of noisy pilgrims were assembled. The bells were ringing*, cannons and muskets incessantly firing; some were chanting the liturgy in honour of the Christian festival of Easter, while the Mahometan Aga, jovially drunk, was smoking his pipe in the midst of them.

Chariess is the only town in the peninsula; situated nearly in the centre of it, on the side of a natural amphitheatre, clothed with the richest verdure, and cultivated in a manner to render it highly picturesque. The meadows are so luxuriant as to be cut thrice in a year, owing to the richness of the soil, the complete shelter they enjoy, and the judicious manner in which the water is distributed by irrigation. The vineyards and filberd gardens are also dressed with uncommon care. Excepting the houses where the Aga and the council of deputies reside, it contains only a few shops which furnish the monasteries with cloth, shoes, watches, wooden clocks, and other articles; and the few luxuries allowed to the monks of the Holy mountain, such as coffee, sugar, tobacco, snuff, and cordials. Every Saturday a bazar or market is held here, to which the hermits repair in order to sell what they have manufactured in their solitary huts. Knit stockings, pictures of saints, a few simple oils and essences

---

* In a few places only of the Turkish dominions are the Greeks allowed the use of bells, the common mode of notifying the hour of prayer is by striking on a board. This custom is of ancient date, it was observed in the Christian monasteries before the time of Mahomet II, who at first adopted it from the Christians of Syria and Arabia. The practice of calling people to prayers from the top of the Minaret was afterwards substituted — Beckmann. H. of I. 3.

distilled from plants, common knives and forks, (on the horn handles
of which they engrave, with aqua-fortis, a series of ancient Greek
moral adages,) compose their principal labours. The trade of making
manuscripts is still practised by them, many devout pilgrims
preferring a psalter or prayer-book written by a hermit on the Holy
mountain to the clearest printed copy. Women are prevented from
coming to the town, as well as from visiting any of the convents,
nor is any Musulman permitted to have a shop there. The situation
of the Turkish governor at Charess, although certainly far from comfortable, is very lucrative. During his residence there he is deprived
of his harem, and we saw only one Turkish servant waiting on him ;
but during the two years of his superintendance, he will have amassed
a sum sufficient to give him pretensions to the post of Bostangee
Bashi, or commander of the Sultan's life-guards. The monks seem
to have been successful in converting him from one Mahometan
prejudice at least; for he now drinks wine as freely as any Greek
in the empire.

From this town, where the voice of women and the cries of
infants are never heard, we proceeded to the adjoining convent of
Coutloumoussi. It is situated in the midst of gardens, and meadows,
and the buildings are in good repair. There are about sixty caloyers
within the walls of the convent, and the principal Hegoumenos was
a polite, accomplished scholar. We visited the library the morning
after our arrival, but found it composed principally of printed books.
We took a catalogue of such manuscripts as were among them, near
forty of which are of the Gospels. One of them is in uncial
characters, but with accents; and some others seemed more ancient
than those of Batopaidi, and are beautifully illuminated. We saw
also a few copies of the Acts of the Apostles, and of some of the
works of the Greek fathers; a number of Liturgies, Menaia, and
other ecclesiastical rituals, but not a shred of a classical author.

On our leaving the convent, we were accompanied to the gate by
the principal caloyers and Hegoumenos, and saluted with a discharge
of their cannon. We were escorted by a caloyer and guards; but

rather as a mark of honour than of precaution against robbers; as caravans of well-armed Albanian and Bulgarian pilgrims were traversing the mountain in almost every direction from convent to convent. In an hour and a half's ride, we reached the monastery of Pantocratoras, built on a rock at the bottom of a small bay. After the noise and bustle of the preceding seven days, we were much pleased with the retreat afforded us by this convent. The caloyers are about forty in number, the few books which they possess are kept in the church, but among them there is not one historical or classical volume, either printed or in manuscript. They have a few copies of different parts of the sacred writings; one in the hand-writing of the Emperor Alexius Commenus their founder, who is buried here, containing the four Gospels, and another of older date, beginning with the book of Genesis, and ending with Ruth.

This convent has some lands near Salonica, and others in the island of Thasos. As we were taking leave of the Hegoumenos at the door of his church, we saw a most ferocious band approaching, firing their muskets and pistols, and shouting most riotously. They were all well-mounted, and had come from the mountains of the Balkan, the Thracian Hæmus, on a pilgrimage to the holy peninsula, a distance of fourteen conacks, averaged at twelve hours each. We staid to see their devotions, which did not seem to be less fervent on account of their ignorance of the language in which the masses were said. I observed a number of sequins and other gold coins among the offerings made by them to the church, an account of which the Epitropos entered in a book, as well as the number of masses to be said, and the names of the persons recommended by these pious travellers.

The orangeries and the groves of myrtles planted around the convent are filled with nightingales, which continued to sing incessantly, by day as well as by night, almost preventing our sleep. We left the monastery after breakfast, and went in the boat of the convent to Stavroniketa, a distance of about two miles and a half.

We lodged in an apartment which had been occupied by an exiled archbishop; the windows command a view of almost every object that a painter could wish to combine in a landscape; bold craggy rocks, which in some parts beetle over the sea, and in others, afford little nooks where the caloyers enjoy the shade and breeze; the winding shore, with hanging groves of orange and other fruit trees, broken by wild glens running up the country; and the monastery of Pantocratoras, with its walls, domes, and turrets embosomed in wood, closing the scene.

Stavronketa is a small convent of the fourth class, containing about forty monks. Its gardens are in most excellent order. A long aqueduct, which must have cost a very considerable sum, supplies them plentifully with water; and by means of this they can irrigate every spot with such nice precision, as to make their crops almost independent of rain. In the church of this convent we saw a very ancient portrait in Mosaic of the Patron Saint Nicholas; it had been much injured, the monks told us, by the rage of the barbarians; a name, I supposed, which they gave to the Turks; but on inquiry, I found they meant the partizans of their own Emperor in the eighth century, who attempted to abolish the use of images in the Greek churches. We examined the library of the convent, and took a catalogue of the manuscripts, which are wholly ecclesiastical. We then went in the boat of the convent to Iveron, a large monastery of the first class, built, as Leo Allatius informs us, *in honorem Deiparæ*. It contains about two hundred caloyers within its walls. Besides the pilgrims we found amongst the guests another exiled Patriarch of Constantinople, two archbishops, and some bishops, his brother exiles. The expences of this convent, including contributions to the Porte and borrowed money, are calculated at 6000*l*. or 7000*l*. sterling, *per annum*. The day after our arrival, we dined with the Ex-Patriarch Gregorio, who has been two years in exile here. The hour of dinner was nine o'clock in the morning; we found his table furnished in a style quite ex-conventual, with lamb, sausages, hams, and French wines. His dispensing power seems to remain although he is dethroned, and seven or eight of the sallad-fed monks who dined with us, appeared to be much pleased with their change of diet. His conversation seemed to indicate that he looked forward to be reinstated in his honors. We were told he had been banished by a cabal of rich bishops, whom he commanded to leave the luxuries and intrigues of Constantinople, and to reside in their respective dioceses; but their influence with the princely families in the Fanal, and the Dragoman of the Porte had procured his exile, and the appointment of a less rigid head of the Church. He told us, he was born in Arcadia; he appears to have made little progress in ancient Greek literature or in modern science.

Towards the close of dinner a stranger entered, who was received with much respect. He was called Methodius, and belonged to the order of caloyers, who were named Megaloschemi. A most remarkable length of beard, πώγων ποδήρης, which after unrolling a kind of shawl, he discovered to us, has probably gained him more respect from the superstitious Greeks, than if the talents and learning of a Chrysostom, or a Basil had been conferred on him in its stead. *

The library at Iveron was so large, and the printed books so much mixed with manuscripts, that we were forced to spend two fatiguing days in examining them and making a catalogue. Amidst some hundred ecclesiastical manuscripts, we found parts of Æschylus, Euripides, and Aristophanes; the Electra and Ajax Mastigophorus of Sophocles, Pindar, Hesiod, and Demosthenes; selections from Galen and Aristotle; some imperfect Greek lexicons; the works of Libanius the Sophist, and Philo Judæus. None of these bear marks of great antiquity; and from the commentary which surrounds the text, in a kind of Greek called Mixo-barbaros, they seem to have belonged to some schoolmaster.

As the road we were now about to take towards Santa Laura and the hermitages would conduct us amongst crags and mountains,

---

* Methodius with his ἄτομα πωγώνος βάθη, was at Constantinople in the year 1806, where we saw him.

and to places where there are few mules to be procured, we left the
greatest part of our baggage to be sent across the Isthmus to the
convent of Xeropotamo, there to wait our arrival; the Hegoumenos
previously requesting us to seal each parcel with our own seals.   The
road from Iveron to Philotheo, presents a succession of very
picturesque scenery; particularly the ruined convent of Mylo-
Potamos, now a kellia or farm-house belonging to Iveron; it is
placed in a little green valley near the sea, a clear glittering stream
winds its course through it; and the mountains around are covered
with overhanging woods up to their summits.   The convent of
Philotheo is small, but the church more rich and splendid than the
rest of the edifice leads us to expect.   We passed the night there,
and in the morning took a catalogue of their manuscripts.   Little is
worthy of notice amongst them, excepting a beautiful copy of the
Gospels and one of the Acts, Epistles, and Revelations; the rest
are ecclesiastical.   We rode next to the monastery of Caracalla,
which is about four miles distant.   Amongst the manuscripts, we
found a treatise in small characters, accented and contracted; the
commentary surrounding the text is in beautiful uncial letters; these
are in general supposed to be older in date than the characters
formed by the connected mode of writing; but in this instance, they
must have been subsequent to them.   A miscellaneous compilation
containing part of Demosthenes, of Justin translated into Greek, of
the Hecuba of Euripides, and the first book of Euclid, and some
verses are the only classical fragments.   The verses are from Hesiod
and from the Batrachomyomachia of Homer.   On the next day we
went in the boat of the convent to Santa Laura; and were four
hours on the passage, having the lofty snow-clad summits of Athos
continually in our view, appearing to rise perpendicularly from the
waves.   At this grand convent there are about two hundred caloyers
within the walls; they calculate their annual expences at thirty
thousand piastres, in addition to forty thousand piastres interest,
for money borrowed and funded.   The noise and confusion we
observed within the place, reminded us more of an inn than of a

convent, and instead of the attentions hitherto shewn to us, and which had almost always anticipated our wants, we were forced to send the Patriarch's letter, and afterwards the firman of the Grand Signor before we could procure a room to sleep in. When we were admitted to the library, we found the Didascalos seated there with a large book before him, in Arabic with a Latin version. Mr. Carlyle soon discovered that this important personage did not know even the Arabic alphabet, and that his acquaintance with Latin did not enable him to translate it, so that his intention of imposing himself on us as a profound scholar was severely disappointed. We had been told that the most valuable manuscripts of the convent had lately been sold, or at least concealed from strangers; but every person whom we now addressed on the subject denied the charge. The book of Job with a commentary and illuminations, of Proverbs, of the Wisdom of the son of Sirach, sixty-one copies of the Gospels, and the History of Susannah were amongst the most curious of the sacred manuscripts. Of the classical, we may mention two copies of Galen well preserved; Demosthenes, the first and second books of the Iliad; part of Pindar, some Lexicons, Apthonius the Sophist, and Photius.

The church of Santa Laura contains some fine columns and slabs of Verd-antique marble; and there is a greater appearance of splendor in every part of the establishment of this convent than in any other on Mount Athos. A caloyer was assigned us as our guide to conduct us to the hermitage of St. Anne; our ride, under a scorching sun, was rendered more fatiguing, as we were forced to dismount very frequently. At length we arrived at the romantic crags and dells where the hermitages of St. Anne are placed; and were refreshed by the oranges, which grow there in abundance. Our accommodations among the hermits were comfortless, their cells being filthy, and swarming with vermin. The library at the church of St. Anne contains a few recent manuscripts of Gregory Nazianzenus, and other ecclesiastical writers. The natural scenery here is particularly striking, and the summit of Athos, once consecrated by the fane and altars of the Athoan Jove*, rears itself with awful grandeur above the surrounding mountains The manner in which the torrents, breaking from the cliffs above St. Anne's, are distributed by a thousand little wooden aqueducts, so as to water every spot of garden or vineyard, is worthy of being remarked. Falling from terrace to terrace in cascades, they occasionally unite, to pass through tunnels of wicker-work to turn the water-mills for grinding corn. The woods and thickets in the neighbourhood are extremely luxuriant, and the Andrachne arbutus flourishes in such profusion as to supply the common fuel. The season was unfavorable for our visiting the summit of Athos, whence the monks assured us that all the islands of the Cyclades may be seen, and even Constantinople, in clear weather. They reckon it a journey of five hours from the hermitages to the top of Mount Athos.

From St. Anne's we had a hot and fatiguing walk to the monastery of St. Paul. This edifice was originally founded for Bulgarian Monks, but it is now filled solely by Greeks. In their library we examined nearly five hundred old manuscripts, but they were all in the Illyric or Servian language, except a Greek psalter of no value. The present Emperor of Russia, Paul, has been prevailed upon by some travelling caloyers to send a sum of money hither to repair and beautify the convent and church. It is thus that Russia keeps up the attachment of the Greeks; the smallest gift bestowed towards adorning or rebuilding these monasteries is certain of meeting the gratitude of thousands of pilgrims who visit the holy mountain; while they naturally draw a comparison little in favor of their own sovereign, the Grand Signor, when they hear from the monks the most exaggerated accounts of the sums levied on their convents. There are about thirty-five caloyers in this monastery; and the picturesque effect of the scenery around it is much increased by the view of a torrent which comes from the mountain, and tumbling from rock to rock, and occasionally covered by woods, here enters the sea almost in a foam.

---

* Ζεὺς Ἀθῶος, v. Hesych.

We proceeded on foot towards the convent of Dionysio, one of the first class, and containing about two hundred monks. Here we found M. Frangopolo, formerly chief interpreter to the Prussian Legation at Constantinople. As we had taken letters to him, he received us with the utmost attention. He had retired to this spot from the scenes of active life ; had assumedthe habit of a caloyer, and scrupulously conformed in almost every point to the rules of monastic discipline. He accompanied us to the library of the convent, containing, principally, writings of the fathers, and some copies of the New Testament, one of which was in uncial characters. We saw part of the Iliad with a commentary, but not very ancient, some selections from Demosthenes, Libanius, and Dionysius the Areopagite, a tragedy of Gregory Nazianzenus, and the Aphorisms of Hippocrates.

We proceeded in the boat of the monastery to the adjoining convent of St Gregorio. It is of the fourth class, and is calculated to contain about a hundred caloyers, one of whom we found well versed in ancient Greek. As this convent was burnt down a few years ago, the library had no manuscripts to detain us. We there became acquainted with Father Joachim, who had been mentioned to us as having a beard that rivalled the famous one of Methodius. We found it of a surprising length, reaching about an inch below his knees. In the venerable caloyer himself we discovered great simplicity of character. He had travelled over almost all European Turkey, and the shores of the Black Sea, begging alms for his convent. On different visits to the Fanal at Constantinople, he has paid his homage to twenty-four Patriarchs, namely, fourteen Grand Patriarchs of the Greek church ; four of Alexandria ; and six of Jerusalem. Such is the rapid succession to those envied dignities [1]

We were conveyed in the boat of the monastery to the foot of the mountain on which Simopetra is placed, and after an hour's climbing up a rock, nearly perpendicular, we reached this singular edifice. The view from its external gallery is one of the most awful and terrific

that can be conceived. * The spectator looking down, feels as if he
were suspended over a gloomy abyss ; the forests, *nox nemorum*, and
craggy rocks beneath his feet, add to the solemnity of the scene. On
turning the eyes upwards, the summit of Athos presents itself, covered
with snow. The moon and stars in this clear atmosphere seemed to
have a peculiar splendor, and the planet Venus shone with an extraordinary brilliancy of light.

The Hegoumenos or Abbot of the convent was absent, having been
sent for to Chariess, to assist at a meeting of the chiefs of the Holy
mountain, to take into consideration a firman that had just been received from the Porte, demanding a supply of ship timber for the
arsenals of the Grand Signor. As the Monks possess no means of
transporting it to the sea, they would have to make a commutation
for the required service by paying a large sum of money. We were
told that this monastery had become bankrupt during the administration of its late Hegoumenos, and had incurred a debt of thirty-five
thousand piastres : in consequence of which all its moveables, church-
plate, and other articles were sold, and the Governor and Monks
expelled After remaining some time abandoned, a new Epitropos
has been sent from Wallachia to restore it, and we had heard so high a

* *Extract from Dr Sibthorp's Journal*

" Sept 28 — We were still detained at anchor in the bay of Daphne ; we rowed in our
boat to the convent of St. Nicholas, situated on a rock projecting over the sea The monastery had been burnt down some years since, and lately rebuilt To vary the scene, we
determined to return to the bay by land ; we began our walk attended by two caloyers, a
meandering way, hewn through the rocks, which were covered with evergreen shrubs, conducted us in an hour to the convent of Simopetra. The venerable Hegoumenos stood at
the gate and bade us welcome We were led by him through many a winding path to the
tower of his castellated monastery. Romance has not figured a situation more wild and
picturesque, here was a sublimity of scenery beyond what I ever recollected to have seen.
The eye commanded a vast expanse of the Ægean sea, distinguished clearly numerous
islands that were scattered in it, surveyed the Gulf of Athos, and returning back to the
wooded region of the mountain, beheld the deepened dell, above which boldly rose to a
tremendous height the craggy precipice on which this building was raised "

character of his literature and polished manners, that we severely felt the loss we sustained by his absence. On our forwarding a note to him at Chariess for the key of the room, where the manuscripts were deposited, he sent it to us, with a polite answer, expressive of his regret at his being prevented from waiting on us. We found in the library nineteen copies of the Gospels in ancient character and in good preservation, three of the Acts and the Epistles, and a number of ecclesiastical writings.

Having descended the steep rock of Simopetra, we rowed for two hours in the fishing boat of the monastery to Xeropotamo. Here we found the spring much advanced; the roses in the garden were full-blown. The situation of this convent is very pleasing to the eye, the ground gradually rises to it in a gentle swell from the sea, and is covered with flowering shrubs, olive trees, and thickets. It commands a view of both the gulfs of Monte Santo and Cassandra, studded with islands. There are seventy caloyers within the walls, and the convent is classed among those of the third size. The buildings are in good preservation, and the great court contains a number of ancient busts and bas-reliefs on the walls, which were sent hither by a Prince of Wallachia. The church is new, and not inelegant in its construction; but the Greeks have covered it within and without with tasteless representations of the martyrdom of saints, and the visions of the Apocalypse. In the library we found a manuscript of Genesis in Hebrew, one very ancient of the Gospels in Greek; many more recent, some selections, probably by a schoolmaster of the convent, from classical authors, and many theological treatises. At the port is a broken slab of Parian marble, with an inscription containing a decree of the senate and people of Iasus in Asia Minor, bestowing privileges on some individual who had been a benefactor to them.

There now remained eight convents on the peninsula, which we had not yet examined, and five of them so small, that they could not protect us against the pirates, who, we were informed, were in some boats at anchor in the little bay of Gregorio, if they should meditate attacks upon us. But as we had already executed so large a portion

of our task and had it so much at heart to complete our examination
of all the Greek manuscripts on Mount Athos, we resolved to proceed
on foot, as the roads were impassable even for the mules, and the
risque by sea appeared to be too great. When we arrived at Russico,
we found a few monks only, and the monastery contained neither
printed nor manuscript books, except the liturgies of their church.

April 16. — After an hour's walk we reached the monastery of
Xenophou, which is reported to be placed in an unhealthy aguish air.
The inhabitants have therefore begged and borrowed money to rebuild it in a better situation, and yet have chosen a spot not fifty
paces from the walls of the present convent, pretending that it is
beyond the line of the Mal-aria. They are proceeding on a grand
scale, and in a very expensive way. We found here a Greek called
Panayotaki Baylas of Zagora in Macedonia, who had retired with fifty
thousand piastres acquired by trade in Constantinople, and has adopted
the monastic life. The rules of this convent are different from those
of any other on the holy mountain. It is called Cænobium Xenophou,
and ordains that no person belonging to the society shall possess any
semblance of property, or live in private. The caloyers therefore do
not only dine and sleep in large rooms together, instead of having
each a separate cell, as in other convents, but when any individual
wants a change of linen or any other article he must apply to the
abbot or keeper of the stock of the community. The only books in
their library were theological, and among them few of any value, except four manuscripts of the Gospels. About a quarter of an hour
further is the monastery of Docheinou, of the second class. The
rooms for receiving strangers and pilgrims of distinction are elegant.
Their library contained eighteen manuscripts of the Gospels, and a
considerable number of theological works.

The whole country now presented a beautiful appearance, looking
like a garden, and adorned with roses, hawthorns, and the Judas tree.
In a retired vale, surrounded by forests, is the little convent of Constamoneta. In their church we found a manuscript copy of a tragedy
of Æschylus, the Seven Chiefs at Thebes, and part of Hesiod.

Though the sun was setting, and the road to the next monastery long and dangerous, yet we resolved to proceed rather than pass the night with so rude and inhospitable a body of caloyers as we found at Constamoneta. Their Hegoumenos or Abbot is a native of Maina, the ancient Eleuthero-Laconia. A beggar passing some months ago by the door of this convent, asked the accustomed alms of bread and wine, on which the porter told him that the Abbot had strictly forbidden him to distribute any more, as the convent was poor, and scarcely able to support its own members. In the course of conversation the beggar asked how the convent became so poor, and on the porter's not being able to give a satisfactory answer, he replied, I will inform you. There were two brothers who dwelt in this convent at its first foundation, and on them its happiness solely depended. Your tyrannical Abbot forced one of them into exile; the other soon fled, and with them, your prosperity. But, be assured, that until you recal your elder brother, you will continue poor. What were their names? said the wondering caloyer. The expelled brother, replied the beggar, was called Δῶτε, and the name of him who followed was Δοθήσετα. (Give, and it shall be given unto you. Luke, vi. 38.)

We arrived late at Zográfou, and finding the gates locked, were told that, in the absence of the Abbot, they dared not open them at such an hour. On putting, however, the Patriarch's recommendatory letter under the door, a priest came and read it, and immediately gave us admittance. This monastery was inhabited solely by Bulgarians. They are apparently rich, as they are rebuilding the convent on so grand a scale that the cost of the church alone is estimated at fifty thousand piastres. The arches of the new colonnade are all of different diameters and heights, and the capitals of the columns more clumsy and shapeless than those of the darkest ages of the lower empire. The ritual of the Bulgarian service is exactly comformable to that of the Greek church, though the language of their liturgy and of their canonical books is ancient Bulgaric or Illyric; but as their only printing-press is at St. Petersburgh, a number of Russian letters and words have crept in, and their printed books have become very corrupt. Those who now aspire to literary attainments among them learn ancient Greek, esteeming their mother tongue not worthy of cultivation, and they assured me that all the Servic manuscripts in Mount Athos were translations from the Greek fathers.

From Zografou we proceeded to the last great convent of Mount Athos, called Chiliantári, containing about one hundred and eighty monks. This also is inhabited by Bulgarians, and its manuscripts are all in the Servic dialect except a few liturgies in Greek. The present Abbot is Gerasimos, nearly eighty years old, sixty-eight of which he has passed in the monastery. From him I obtained much information concerning the state of the religious community of Athos. He professed to know little of the early history of the convents, but seemed to think that many of them laid claim to a higher antiquity than they ought, when they referred to Constantine the Great, Arcadius and Honorius, and other early Emperors as their founders; for no records in any of the monasteries are of a date prior to Nicephorus Phocas, who reigned in the year 961. When the crafty caloyers adverted to the progress of the Turkish arms under the Sultan Orchan and his immediate successors, and conjectured what might soon be the fate of Constantinople itself, they sent a deputation to the Sultan at Brusa in Asia Minor, carrying a present of fourteen thousand sequins, and begging that when his victorious arms had taken possession of the seat of the Greek empire, the caloyers might be left in the full enjoyment of their religious privileges, and in the exclusive possession of Mount Athos. The Turk accepted the bribe, promised all they wished, and gave them a charter, which is said to be still preserved among the archives at Charies, the metropolis of the peninsula. The Turkish Sultans, however, have since made this faithless body pay dearly for their treachery to their own Christian monarch, by throwing so large a sum of money into the hands of the enemy of their religion and their country at so critical a moment; and instead of being for ever exempted from tribute as they had expected, they now pay annually one hundred and thirteen thousand piastres to the Porte, besides occasional contributions in time of war and other demands, one of which in the preceding month amounted to forty-eight purses, or twenty-four thousand piastres. In consequence of these perpetual extortions, the convents have been obliged to borrow large sums, for which they give from four to eight *per cent.*, according to the exigency of the moment, or the piety of the lender. The general debt is supposed to amount to a million of piastres, or nearly eighty thousand pounds sterling. Father Gerasimos said that some of the monasteries were unable to raise even the interest of their borrowed money, and that the whole community must soon become bankrupt.

Of the population of this peninsula we heard various accounts. It pays charatch or capitation-tax for three thousand, but the actual number of resident calovers, including the labourers, workmen, hermits, is calculated at six thousand. Each convent pays for a certain proportion of the former number, according to an old schedule; so that Batopaidi, Laura, Chiliantari, and other flourishing convents pay for fewer numbers than they actually have, while others, which have fallen into decay, pay for more than they contain. The temporal affairs of the Holy mountain are thus managed. The twenty monasteries are divided into four classes of five each, according to their respective sizes, and one convent of each class by rotation annually sends a deputy to Chariess. This council of four deputies settles all the business of the peninsula, and regulates the proportion of money which each convent is to give on extraordinary contributions. Their office is annual; they live with no external pomp, and they receive but a trifling salary for their trouble.

The vineyards, corn-fields, and gardens of Chiliantari, as well as the buildings are kept in such excellent condition, as to evince the superintendance of an able abbot. The walks around it are very beautiful, and in them Mr. Carlyle and myself frequently wandered, listening to the songs of the nightingales, almost regretting that the

r r 2

tom of the peninsula was so nearly finished. [*] During our stay at
Chiliantari, we made an excursion to the convent of Sphigmenou,
about three miles off, containing thirty caloyers. Its manuscripts
are all theological, among them are about twenty copies of the
sacred writings of the New Testament. We returned to Chiliantari
by a road that took us to another monastery called St. Basil; which
had been long in ruins, but is now inhabited by six poor caloyers. Its
proximity to the sea would at all times render it an easy prey to
pirates, but its present poverty and misery are such as to invite
neither pilgrims to enrich it nor banditti to plunder it. It is not
classed among the twenty monasteries which compose the religious
republic of Mount Athos.

We had now made a complete investigation of all the libraries
in the monasteries of this peninsula, and taken catalogues of all the
manuscripts they contain, each of which we had ourselves indi-
vidually examined. The state in which we found these tattered and
mouldy volumes, (cum blattis et tineis pugnantes,) often without
beginnings or endings, rendered the task very tedious; and our
patience was put to a very severe trial by not once discovering an
unedited fragment of any classical author. But the reflection that
we were employed on an object which had long been a desideratum in
the theological and literary world, enabled us to struggle against the
difficulties we met, and to overcome the prejudices, the jealousy,
and the ignorance which often tempted the librarians of the different
convents to thwart our views; and we endeavoured to complete our
work as accurately as our means and abilities would admit.

When the learned Greeks fled from Constantinople in 1453, they
took with them to western Europe their most valuable manuscripts;
those which they left, were probably secreted in the monasteries.
The libraries, in the islands of the sea of Marmora, and of Mount

---

Athos, of the Patriarch at Constantinople, and of St. Saba near Jerusalem, were carefully examined by Mr. Carlyle or myself —

"The convent of St. John at Patmos has been visited by French and English travellers; the manuscript of Diodorus Siculus in the library of this place appears to be only an imperfect transcript of the original, *une partie de Diodore écrite d'une main assez récente* [*] The copy of the dialogues of Plato which has been brought to England was seen by Villoison; but that learned Hellenist appears to have inspected it hastily, as he makes no mention of the marginal Scholia in it. (See Gaisford's Catalog. MSS, Clarke.) The monasteries of Meteora were visited by Biornstahl and Mr. Hawkins, and other travellers. Fourmont examined the convent of the miraculous image of the Virgin, called Megaspilæon, six miles from Calavrita [†] in the Morea; he there saw only a few copies of the Greek fathers, and some other ecclesiastical volumes. (See Not des MSS. du Roi. T. 8)"—*Ed.*

When we were setting out on our excursion to Athos, the dragomen of the English and other embassies at the Porte spoke much of the vices and gross ignorance of the Greek caloyers. This representation was very incorrect, then contempt arose more from sectarian animosity than any other cause. The dragomen or interpreters at Pera are generally Romanists, or as the Greeks call them, Latin Schismatics. Defects there certainly are in this religious republic but even in its present oppressed and degraded state the establishment is a useful one. It contributes to preserve the language of Greece from being corrupted or superseded by that of its conquerors; it checks or rather entirely prevents the defection of Christians to Mahometanism, not only in European, but Asiatic Turkey, almost all the Greek Di-

---

[*] Villoison, see the " Notice des MSS du Roi." T 8 Villoison also observed there the Anthology of Lascaris, in *literis majusculis*

[†] Calavrita is supposed by some to be the ancient Nonacris A learned Danish traveller, M Brondstedt visited the Styx, in the vicinity of this place, and learned that it was called Mavro Nero, " black water."

dascaloi school-masters, and the higher orders of their clergy are selected from this place. If it sometimes hides a culprit who has fled from public justice, yet that criminal most probably reforms his life in a residence so well calculated to bring his mind to reflection. The oath of a person who becomes caloyer on Mount Athos is very solemn and simple, it implies an absolute renunciation of the world, enjoining the person who makes it to consider himself as quite dead to its concerns. Some are so conscientiously observant of this vow, that they never afterwards use their family name, never correspond with any of their relatives or former friends, and decline informing strangers from what country or situation of life they have retired.

By the rules of the institution, every convent on Mount Athos, and indeed throughout the whole Turkish Empire is ordered to show hospitality to strangers who present themselves at their gate, whether they be Greeks, heretics or infidels; nor are they permitted to ask for payment from any pilgrim or other visitor for the provisions which they may give them. The reception we in general had experienced was polite, and apparently disinterested. In conversation with their prelates and some of the well-educated caloyers, I so often found what I judged to be religious moderation, that I was once induced to show them a Greek version of the English Liturgy; but when they saw that we kept Easter at the time affixed by the Gregorian or Romish calendar, that we laid down no precise rules about the mode of fasting, that our creed asserts the procession of the Holy Ghost from the Father *and the Son*, I saw such a disposition for controversy arise, that I ever afterwards abstained from all allusion to similar subjects. They admit the propriety of allowing the parochial clergy to marry; but a priest who has been married is never advanced to any of the dignities of the Greek Church. The Patriarchs and bishops must be ἱεροὶ μόναχοι or celibataries. They observe a number of ceremonies in their public worship. At daybreak on the morning of Easter-day, they perform a sort of dramatic representation of the Resurrection. When the bishop gives the blessing, he holds two lighted tapers crossed in one hand to signify the two-fold nature of Christ, and three tapers in the other as a symbol of the Trinity; he makes the sign of the cross, and he sprinkles holy water with three fingers in a particular form, in allusion to the same mystery; or can this be an adaptation of an ancient Pagan superstition mentioned by Ovid, *Et digitis tria thura tribus sub lumine ponit?* They burn incense, and waft it towards the pictures of the Virgin Παναγία [*], of Christ παντοκράτωρ, and of the patron saint, and kiss them with profound adoration. The clergy suffer their beard and hair to grow to great length, in imitation, as they assert, of Christ and his Apostles. They perform the ceremony of exorcism for epilepsy, and some other diseases, supposed to be the effect of dæmoniacal possession. Many more superstitious practices might be mentioned. On taking leave of Father Gerasimos of Chili- antari, we congratulated him on the peace and tranquillity which his little religious commonwealth enjoyed in the midst of the wars and revolutions of Europe; but he replied, that on the contrary, they were in a state of perpetual conflict with three most powerful ene- mies, the devil, their own lusts, and the travelling caloyers, who em- bezzle the alms by which the convents should be supported; and that these would soon produce the ruin of their community, which

* ' The Greeks of all Christians in the world seem to me Φιλο-στοκώτατοι the most zealous adorers of the mother of God The Latins in this matter are extravagant enough, but truly the Greeks far outdo them In many instances which I could give, they ascribe unto her almost as great a providence as to God himself. Taking my leave in the monasteries at Mount Athos, their last farewell to me was commonly this, Νὰ σὰς συλάγη θεὸς καὶ ἡ Παναγία, ' May God keep you and the all-holy Lady.' Infinitely more prayers are made particularly to her than to Christ, and that not only in their private devotions, but in their Euchologion or Common Prayer-book itself, and in the offices appointed for her worship. On the walls of many of their cities is this inscription Θεοτόκε παρθένε βοηθει ταύτη τε πολει, ' Virgin, mother of God, help this city,' and you will find not only in temples, but every where in private families that are of any note, and in public passages, especially at Mount Athos, lamps continually burning before her picture far oftener than before Christ himself, or any one of the saints " — Covel's Greek Church, p 376

had long been in decay. He accompanied us to the gate, and shaking us affectionately by the hand, said, he hoped he had left such an impression of himself on our hearts, that we might be mutually glad to see each other, if Providence ever brought us again together ; quoting a Turkish proverb, that mountain never approaches mountain, nor island, island ; but that man often unexpectedly meets fellow-man.

We had an escort assigned us of six well-armed Albanians, our road conducted us through the most picturesque and magnificent scenery ; but in some places so dangerous from the precipices which beetle over the sea, that a false step of our mules might have been fatal. Six miles from Chiliantari we came to the ruins of a castle called Callitze, and two miles further we halted to breakfast under the shade of some Oriental planes near a fountain, and the bed of a river filled with scarlet oleanders and Agnus castus. The spot is called Paparnitza, here we saw once more cows and ewes with their young, a proof that we had passed the holy precincts. We continued our journey towards the Isthmus, and on reaching the shore found a large fishing boat, which supplied us plentifully with fish at fifteen paras an oke, and some octopodia. [*]

We soon came to the spot on the Isthmus, now called † Problakas, where Xerxes is said to have cut a canal for his fleet of galleys. This is about a mile and a quarter long, and twenty-five yards across, a measurement not very different from that given by ‡ Herodotus

---

[*] This is the sea polypus, which we often observe beaten by the Greeks to make it tender Forskal says, ' carnem bene tusam edunt," and in older authority makes mention of this practice Πολύπους τύπτεται πολλάκις πρὸ, τὸ πέτων γίνεσθαι Suidas. — E

† " Isthmus iste a Græcis monachis montis incolis προάυλαξ hoc seculo appellatur," says Vossius in Melam, 139 It is the same word according to the Romaic pronunciation, as that given by Dr Hunt

† The length has been also stated as ἑπτασταδίος (Obs Voss ad Mel App 10.) Vestiges of the canal were visible in the time of Ælian, 1 XIII. c 20 Belon thought the ancient account of it fabulous, in opposition to Thucydides, 1 iv , who speaks of the King's canal and Pococke did not observe the remains of it Mr. Mitford (II of Greece, i 377) observes, that scarcely any circumstance of the expedition of Xerxes is

of twelve stadia. We found that it had been much filled up with mud and rushes, but is traceable in its whole extent; having its bottom in many places very little above the level of the sea; in some parts of it corn is sown, in others there are ponds of water. We saw some ruins at that end of the canal which opens into the Gulf of Athos, but our guides fearing that pirates might be lurking there, prevented us from visiting the spot, where Uranopolis is supposed to have stood. Here we saw a number of women in the fields weeding the corn and singing; the sight of female dresses, and the voices of these sun-burnt daughters of labour were most pleasing after having lived so long among the monks of Athos. At half past three in the afternoon we reached Erissos, the ancient Acanthus, about thirty miles from the convent of Chiliantari. The inhabitants are all Greeks, except the Aga, and they would even be spared the presence of this Turkish mayor or chief constable, if they would shew proper deference to their own Protogeros or Codja-Bashee, whose sentences would be disregarded unless enforced by the authority of a Musulman officer appointed by the Porte. The country around appeared remarkably well cultivated, and the sea view is beautiful. Maize and rye are the principal crops, and all the agricultural labour except holding the plough is performed by women; they are Albanian colonists, and very hardy and industrious. Their dress resembles that of the women in the Highlands of Scotland, except as to the ornament of the head-dress; the hair being braided, and the crown of the head covered with a little cap of scarlet cloth, on which is sewed a quantity of small coins, presenting the appearance of scales of fish. Their petticoats are short, and they wear neither Turkish pantaloons, nor shoes, nor stockings. A square piece of cloth is fastened behind the shoulders of those who are mothers, and in this

more strongly supported by historical testimony, than the making of this canal, and Dr Hunt's remarks are a valuable corroboration of the ancient accounts. The reference to Belon, whose authority on the occasion is worth little, should be omitted in the next edition of Mr. Mitford's excellent history.— E.

they carry a young child with such apparent ease, that they do not
relieve themselves from the burden when at the work in the fields.
in going from place to place they not only carry their infants in this
manner, but have often a lofty jar or pitcher on their heads, and a
rock and spindle in their hands, with which they spin as they walk.
The shepherds, ploughmen, and indeed every peasant without
exception had a long musket slung at his back; a pistol, and yataghan
or Turkish sword in his belt.

The price of wheat here was five piastres and a half, the kiloe, or
about eight shillings a bushel; wine three paras an oke, a measure
of two pounds and a half; a lamb weighing two okes and a quarter,
cost four piastres or six shillings; two eggs were sold for a para,
(halfpenny,) a fowl for twelve. Labourers in the vineyards have
twenty paras (ten-pence) a day, in addition to meat and drink;
common labourers fifteen paras (seven-pence halfpenny) and food.
Mules for riding cost from one hundred and fifty to two hundred
piastres each, an ox for ploughing is worth sixty piastres, a horse
for carrying burdens, sells for from fifty to sixty-five piastres. Before
we left this village we had a visit of ceremony from a bride, Νύμφη,
whose friends told us they hailed our arrival as a good omen for the
happiness of the married pair The bride was not so much veiled
as to conceal her face from us, on receiving a present she
took our hands to her mouth, kissed them, and then bowing, retired
in silence, having during the whole ceremony not uttered a syllable.
This silence we were told, was continued for eight days from her
wedding, during which period she is accompanied by her bride-
maids and husband's relations from house to house, and receives
from each male inhabitant a few paras or piastres according to the
wealth of the party Small pieces of coin were strung to the braids
of her hair, which hung down her back and over her shoulders,
nearly reaching the ground; the skull-cap was covered with larger
coins; among these were many ancient medals which we in vain
attempted to purchase at a high offer. We were told that the cap
she wore was considered as a family treasure, and that it descended

as an heir-loom, receiving occasional additions; but was never suffered to lose any of its former ornaments.

The charatch, or capitation tax, is levied at six piastres for each grown person. The Pasha of the district collects a tribute or land tax in addition, of one part out of seven and a half of every crop from Christians, whether Greeks or Albanians, and one in six from every Musulman. Besides these taxes each vineyard pays the Pasha two piastres for every two hundred okes of wine at the annual vintage; and if exported, though even to an adjoining island or port of their own country, it pays a custom-house duty of two paras an oke.

April 21.—At ten minutes past seven we proceeded on our road to Nisvoro, and crossed a rich and well-cultivated plain; at half-past nine we halted for an hour to refresh our mules. The spot was shaded by Oriental plane-trees, and near it were ruins of an old tower, which our guide called Arsinoïtche, a name it has probably preserved ever since the time of the immediate successors of Alexander, as Arsinoe, daughter of Ptolemy Lagus, married Lysimachus. The rest of our journey was along the course of a river, the waters of which were very shallow, and so strongly impregnated with some mineral solution as to be of a red colour; near its banks are frequent heaps of burnt ore. Here we met a band of Albanian pilgrims proceeding to the holy mountain, they were about sixty in number, well mounted and armed. Before we reached Nisvoro we observed a defaced inscription in the walls of a Greek church. On entering the town we immediately waited on the Bishop, whom we found to be a young man of talents and learning. In the evening we walked to the silver mines, and observed that the range of hills has been worked very extensively during a long period. Our guide told us that the ground was hollow for many miles around us. We saw about a hundred workmen employed in breaking the lead ore, drawing it from the mines, and smelting it in a very slovenly manner. The principal mine is about fifty yards beneath the surface; we observed five or six furnaces, and the double bellows used by them are worked by water-wheels. On making some inquiries concerning the plan on which they proceed, the following is the result collected by us in a conversation carried on by means of our interpreter.

A speculator who can raise a few thousand piastres, buys the right of digging a certain extent of ground for a year from the Porte, to whom the royalty belongs; a band or gang of workmen join him in the undertaking The original speculator then purchases machinery, erects furnaces, makes charcoal, and is at the whole expence of setting the gang at work. The produce of their labour is then divided; all the lead is the property of the Sultan, a fifth part of which is granted to the Aga who collects the revenue of the Sultan. The latter has also a monopoly of the silver, for which he previously stipulates to give eighty piastres per oke (not so much as three shillings an ounce) to the party who has obtained the licence to work the mine. The sum received for the silver is at the end of the year thus shared. one-seventh part to the person who advanced all the money; and the remainder to the band of workmen according to a scale previously settled

It appears, however, that the richest veins have been exhausted, and that the mines are now worked by almost compulsory means The labourers told us, with tears in their eyes, that during the last two years their division had not amounted to more than two paras a-day, but that the Sultan insisted on the works being carried on. About four or five thousand okes of lead are now produced annually, and about fifty okes of silver reach the mint at Constantinople; but we were told that one vein has been known to produce four hundred okes of silver in a year, and that ore has sometimes been found so rich as to give six drachms of silver out of an oke (four hundred drachms) of lead; though the present average is only about two drachms and a half of silver to the oke of lead.

April 22. — We left Nisvoro early in the morning, and at two miles from the town passed the residence of the Aga, who is too distant from the mines to be able personally to detect any mal-practices that may be carried on there. At 6ʰ. 40'. we reached a most beautiful plain, extending for many miles, covered with the richest verdure, and rendered picturesque by a number of spreading oak trees, standing singly and in small groupes, like the scenery of an English park. The sides of the plain are sloping, clothed with hanging woods, and its further extremity shut in by lofty mountains, rising behind each other as far as the eye can reach. The oaks here are so well adapted for naval purposes, that they have been ordered to be sent to the dock-yards at Constantinople. Some have been felled, but as it will cost fifty piastres to bring each of them to the shore, a bribe will probably be given to the government inspector for reporting them unfit for ship-building, and thus the people of the neighbourhood will escape this addition to their heavy imposts.

At 7ʰ. 20′. A. M. we passed a village called Negeshalar, beautifully placed on the side of a woody hill; and at 8ʰ. 35′. halted in the midst of a forest of oaks, many of which had been lately felled. Here our guides shewed a disposition to prolong their journey in a most tedious manner. After vainly attempting to persuade them to set off, we were forced to proceed on foot without them. In less than an hour we reached Laregovi, and with difficulty procured other muleteers, and hired a strong guard of Albanians to protect the party from robbers, who, they pretended, infested the neighbouring woods. The Codja Bashee of Laregovi has jurisdiction over eleven other towns, the largest of which contains six hundred and the smallest one hundred houses; the police of all these is superintended by him, and he gathers the government taxes. This district belongs to one of the Sultanas at Constantinople, who leaves the local government entirely to native Greeks, merely sending one of her Bostangees or life-guards to enforce the orders of the Greek Codja Bashee, when his people are refractory. Arriving at the town of Gallitze, which contains six hundred houses, without one Musulman inhabitant, we found we could procure no lodging, neither the Sultan's firman nor the Patriarch's recommendatory letter had any influence; one of our guards at length took us to an empty mud cottage, where we passed the night. At seven on the next morning we left Gallitze, and crossed an extensive plain, and at half-past nine reached the beautiful village of Basilika, containing about 150 houses. They are detached from each other, and have separate vineyards, gardens, or mulberry plantations, and the whole place breathes an air of wealth and comfort which we had not witnessed since landing at Athos. From the time of our quitting Lemnos we had seen no Turkish houses until we arrived at this place. At half-past ten we entered the immense plain, which extends as far as Salonica. We passed a Turkish burial-ground, where a number of broken granite and marble columns were scattered round us, and a few *cippi* containing defaced inscriptions, but evidently not of remote antiquity. Near this cemetery is a very large conical barrow or tumulus, and on other parts of the plain we observed similar constructions, some on circular, some on oval bases. Their shape is so regular as to leave no doubt of their being artificial mounds, and their rising abruptly from a plain as level as a lake, produces a striking effect on the eye. None of them appear to have been opened.

ADDITIONAL REMARKS ON THE SEPULCHRES OF THE EUROPEAN AND ASIATIC GREEKS

[*BY THE EDITOR.*]

MANY of a similar form may be seen in other parts of Greece; they have been observed in Thessaly by Mr. Hawkins on the road from Volo to Larissa, and in the plain north of Pharsalia. He mentions some of great size at Philippopolis, and others on the borders of the Propontis, between Silivri and Constantinople.

Adjoining to the straits of the Hellespont, and near Gallipoli, are many lofty tumuli, which were remarked by Belon. Of these Thracian barrows we may appropriate one to Lysimachus, for they are

raised near Cardia and Pactyas, and between these two places, as
Pausanias informs us, his tumulus was seen (Lib. i. p. 19.)

The most ancient form of tumuli is the simplest, namely, a heap of
earth with a stele on the top, *terreno ex aggere bustum* In parts of
Western Scythia they are found encompassed with a square wall of
large square stones. This defence or *maceria* was added to the sepulchres of Greece and Asia in early times; it surrounded that
of Opheltes at Cleonæ (Paus lib. ii.), of Alyattes in Lydia
(Herod. lib. i.); of Auge at Pergamus; of Æpytus in Arcadia (Paus.
viii); of Phocus in Ægina. (Ib. lib. ii) One with a circular wall
near the ancient Pergamus has been described by Choiseul; another
has been opened within a few years near Smyrna, in which galleries
and chambers have been found.

The custom of raising temples, altars, statues, or shrines over tombs,
attached, certainly, a greater degree of religious respect to the places
where the dead were deposited. The prevalence of it is evident from
that remarkable expression of Athenagoras, who calls the temples of
the ancients Τάφοι, tombs. (Apol c. xxv.) This name was afterwards retorted by Libanius, Julian, Eunapius, and other Pagans upon
the Christians, when they began to practise the custom of burying the
bones of martyrs in their churches.

Although one class and form of sepulchre, the raised mound, were
common both to Greece and Asia, yet there is a remarkable difference in the manner adopted by the inhabitants of the two countries in
constructing other monuments in honor of the dead. We see nothing
in Greece to equal those great and numerous excavations in the rock,
which strike the traveller's attention in Asia and Syria. They are
seen at Telmessus, at Myra*, at Antiphellos, at Amasia, where are
the supposed tombs of the Kings of Pontus, and in parts of Palestine.
Some of them are mentioned by Pococke in Phrygia, Lycia,

---

* Nunc eversæ multa vestigia extant, præcipue monumenta mortuorum in vivo saxo
cavata, quæ columnis et aliis signis ex eodem saxo incisis atque insculptis, ornata sunt.—
Coriol Cepion.

Cappadocia; others are pointed out by Le Brun, Choiseul, and Dr. Clarke. We may suppose that Gregory, who was born in Cappadocia, and had in his journies through Asia remarked these and similar monuments, alludes to them when he speaks of the " stone tombs in the mountains, the work of giants " *

That many of these great excavations in the rock were executed by the later inhabitants of Asia Minor, is evident from the inscriptions which have been discovered. Some of these in Greek were copied by Dr. Clarke, and the travellers who were sent out by the Dilettanti Society with Sir William Gell. Others are composed of characters, the meaning of which has not yet been explained. These tombs in the rocks frequently present, as we learn from the plates, in the " Voyage Pittoresque" of Choiseul, in their outward forms, pediments, Ionic pillars, and architectural ornaments resembling those used in Greek buildings. In Greece, the excavations in the rock for sepulchral purposes were generally simple, and those at Athens, and even at Delphi, are inferior in extent and grandeur to the tombs in Asia. The inhabitants of this country, from greater wealth and pride, and a love of magnificence which particularly distinguished them, were induced to form and raise monuments of a more sumptuous and laborious execution. The sarcophagi seen in Asia Minor are more numerous and of larger dimensions than those in Greece; Dr. Hunt has particularly remarked the appearance of the granite Soroi of Assos. Perhaps the most costly tomb ever raised in Greece † was that made by order of Harpalus for Pythionice; thirty talents were expended on it. *Dio. Sic.* xvii. 245.

---

* Στῆλαι, καὶ πλακόεντες ἐν οὔρεσιν, ἔργα γιγάντων, Τύμβοι —Ancc. Græca. Muratori.

† Mr. Fiott examined the Macedonian sepulchres at Vodena; but they do not appear to be distinguished by any remarkable size or form. Clarke's Travels, vol. iii. 341

NATURAL HISTORY.

A RESIDENCE in parts of Greece and Asia Minor during a period of three or four years would enable a learned and intelligent naturalist to furnish some valuable illustrations of various passages in the works of Aristotle, Theophrastus, Dioscorides, Ælian, and Pliny. The names of many birds, as well as fishes, which occur in the writings of the Greeks are difficult to be interpreted. Of the twenty-four persons who form the chorus in the comedy of the Aves, says Mr. Gray, and enter under the form of so many birds, there are ten, of which we can give no explanation in English.

We have already alluded to the great collection of materials for a Fauna and Flora Graeca procured by Dr. Sibthorp and Mr. Hawkins during their travels in the Levant. In the extracts from Dr. S.'s journals, the reader will find many remarks on the medicinal and œconomical uses of the Greek plants; the names also given to them by the modern inhabitants are annexed; and much new information is added concerning the birds, the animals of Greece, and the fishes of the Archipelago. The botany of the ancients, Beckmann observes, would be more easily explained if the names used by the modern Greeks were known, a similar remark may be applied to the ornithology and ichthyology of Greece *, and to the animals of that country. Dr. Sibthorp has noted down many of the modern appellations, but the reader will find in some instances the names of the present day very different from the ancient terms. Τυφλοπόντικος has

---

* The accentuation and mode of writing the Romaic names of the plants and animals of Greece in Dr. S.'s journals are not always correct. The editor has printed them as accurately as he could, but sometimes words occur, concerning which further information is wanting.

taken the place of Ἀσπάλαξ the former name of the mole, and the hedge-hog is no longer called ἐχῖνος, but σκαντζόχοιρος.

We have mentioned that in his various researches, Dr Sibthorp did not omit collecting information respecting the fishes of the Greek seas; and his list of them is more complete than any that has been hitherto published.   Among the lost works of the ancients, we may regret the want of those, which expressly treated of the fishes of the rivers and seas of Greece, as they would have illustrated in some degree an interesting part of the natural history of that country. The Greeks were of all people ὀψοφαγίστατοι*; the snipe, the wood-cock, the partridge held a secondary place at their tables.   *Ce me-prisement,* says Belon, *de manger chair, et estimer le poisson, a fait que les anciens Grecs et Latins, ayent moins cogneu les oiseaux, que les poissons.*   The names of some writers, who in parts of their works had examined the various sorts of fishes which frequent the rivers and shores of Greece have been preserved to us; among these we find Epicharmus the Sicilian, a poet and naturalist; Ananius a con-temporary of Hipponax, who had in his verses introduced some remarks on Ὀψο-ονία; Mithæcus mentioned in the Gorgias of Plato, and Archestratus, a writer who flourished nearly at the same time with Aristotle, and from whom the latter had probably borrowed some of those remarks respecting fishes, which are to be found in his great work. †   Of the numerous treatises on natural history written by Aristotle, a small part only has reached us.   Athenæus quotes one entitled περὶ Ζώων, ἢ περὶ ἰχθύων. ‡   Schw. ad. Ath. vii. 15.

From the Venetians, French, and Italians who have been settled at various times in parts of Greece, and the islands of the Archipelago,

---

* Qui Græcè sciunt nunquam mirabuntur ὄψον pro *pisce* dici   Quare hodieque in Græcia piscis vocitur ψάρι, voce ex ὀψάριον depravata   See Yvonis Villiomari in locos controversos Roberti Titii. 89   (A work written by Joseph Scaliger.)

† See Schneider in Aris. H. A. Epimetrum, 1

‡ The description of the Bustard from Aristotle, (in Athen. lib 9) is in no part of the extant writings of the philosopher, and in another book (lib 7) Athenæus refers to a passage of Aristotle, respecting the fleshy palate of the carp, this is not now to be found in his works — See Beckmann's History of the Invent 3

the modern inhabitants have derived a few names of fishes as well as birds. In some instances, the ancient words slightly altered have been retained, even by the Turks; the κέφαλος is still called Cephal-balluk* by them, and Scorpit-balluk is the name which they give to the Scorpæna Porcus.

PLANTS OF GREECE.

MEDICINAL AND ECONOMICAL USES

[FROM DR. SIBTHORP'S PAPERS]

1. Pinus Maritima. Πεύκος, one of the most useful trees in Greece; it furnishes a resin (ῥητίνη), tar and pitch (πίσσα), all of considerable importance for œconomical purposes. Throughout Attica the †wine is preserved from becoming acid by the means of the resin which is employed in the proportion of an oke and a half, to 20 okes of wine. The tar and pitch for ship building are taken from this tree, and the Πίτυς, the Pinus Pinea. The resinous parts of the wood of the Πεύκος are cut into small pieces and serve for candles, called Δάδια. The cones, κόννοι, are sometimes put into the wine barrels.

Notes by the Editor

1. Δάδια, a corruption of the ancient word δᾷς, see Lucian de M Pereg Ligna arboris picis, d'Orville Char. ii. 489 We find in Dr. Hunt's journal the same word δάδια, applied by the inhabitants of Mount Ida to the torches of pine-wood

* Balluk in Turkish signifies *fish*

† A practice very general throughout Greece, but which is very prevalent at Athens, may perhaps in some degree account for the connection of the fir-cone (surmounting the Thyrsus) with the worship of Bacchus Incisions are made in the fir-trees for the purpose of obtaining the turpentine which distils copiously from the wound. This juice is mixed with the new wine in large quantities the Greeks supposing that it would be impossible to keep it any length of time without this mixture The wine has in consequence a very peculiar taste, but is by no means unpleasant after a little use This, as we learn from Plutarch, was an ancient custom (Sympos. Quest. 3. and 4 p 528. Ed Wytten.), the Athenians, therefore, might naturally have placed the fir-cone in the hands of Bacchus. — (From Lord Aberdeen's Journals.)

The bark is used in tanning hides.   The wood is much employed by
the carpenters in building

I observed, says Mr. Hawkins, on Cyllene, Taygetus, and the
mountains of Thasos, a sort of fir, which, although called πεῦκος by
the inhabitants, and much resembling the πεῦκος of the lower regions,
differed from it in these particulars; the foliage was much darker,
and the growth of the tree much more regular and straight.   The
very elevated regions on which it grew leads me to suspect it must
be different from the common πεῦκος.

2. " Pinus Pinea, κουκουκαρία, −ίτυς of the ancients.   This tree and the
P. Maritima afford timber for the construction of ships, the ribs,
keel, and beams being made of the Kermes oak, and the Ilex.   These
two firs grow generally, and certainly best in sandy soils, the Pinus
Maritima, or true πεῦκος of the neo-Greeks, abounds in Attica, where
the soil is either rocky or loamy, but never here attains the same
bulk, as it does in the forests of Elis, where trees may be seen fit for
the largest ships of war, and where the soil is every where sandy.   The
timber of these two sorts of fir is much harder and tougher than
that of our northern firs, and consequently more lasting.   The seeds
of the stone pine are collected still with great industry in Elis, and
form an object of exportation to Zante and Cephallonia, and other
places."   From Mr. Hawkins.

3. Quercus Ægilops, Δρῦς, Κουπάκ   The prickly cups of the fruit
of this tree are of importance in the tanning of leather, as an
astringent, and for the purposes of dyeing.   They must be gathered

Notes by the Editor

2. The τίτυς and πεύκη are both mentioned by Plutarch, Symp lib v. 3 2. as proper
for ship building   The Pinus Pinea is still used for that purpose at Sinope and in other
parts of the Turkish empire.   The tree is common in the maritime districts of Asia
Minor and Syria   " The πίτυς," says Coray, " is now called κοκκωνάρια, from the fruit
κοκκωνάριον, anciently called στρόβιλον," κοκκώνη also was an ancient name   The kernels
of the stone pine are brought to table in Turkey, they are very common in the kitchens
of Aleppo " — Russell

3 The ἀγίλωψ of Theophrastus, Hist. iii 9. Sprengel   " The small Velani," says
Tournefort, Lett viii   " are the young fruit gathered off the tree, more valued than those
full ripe, that fall of themselves."

before the acorn is ripe, in the month of August. A quantity of this oak is planted in the plain of Eleusis, and the Valanida is sold to the tanners of Athens for two paras the oke. The wood of the Κουτσια is esteemed in ship-building and in house work, and makes good charcoal.

4. Quercus Ilex, Ἄρεος. This tree does not grow in great abundance in Attica. It may be observed on the higher parts of Pendeli, near the ancient marble quarries. The wood is preferred for the share of the plough, and for making the tyes in the walls of the Greek houses.

5. Quercus Coccifera, πρινάρι. The bark of the root is used by the tanners, particularly for tanning hides for the soles of shoes. It is powdered and mixed in equal quantity with the Valanida and the bark of the Pine. Small quantities of the grain used for dyeing scarlet are collected from this plant near Casha in Attica; but in the Morea, the collecting of it forms a considerable object of commerce. The wood being hard and durable is employed for the handles of mattocks, and for other agricultural instruments.

The plant, says Mr. Hawkins, is found stunted in its growth by the constant nibbling of the goats, of which it is the favorite food. It occasionally, however, attains the size of a small tree, and is then very fit either for timber or charcoal.

Notes by the Editor.

4. The δρῦς of Homer, according to Sprengel, and πρῖνος of Theophr. Hist. iii 16

5 It is the πρῖνος, ἡ τὸν φοινικοῦν κόκκον φέρει of Theophrastus, Hist. iii 8 and κόκκος βαφικὴ of Diosc iv. 18 The kermes are still collected in Crete and Cyprus, in the latter island the name πρῖνος is retained, according to Dr Sibthorp. The grains were found in the time of Pausanias in Phocis and in various parts of Asia Minor (Plin et Dioscor.) The colour expressed from them is the *Galaticus rubor* of Tertullian, de Pallio, p 38

The coccus is mentioned by Moses under the name Phœni Tola, the Phœnicians, according to Prof. Tychsen, having brought them into Palestine from Syria The Egyptians also were acquainted with the dye See Beckmann vol ii

Mr. Hawkins says the wood of the Q C is used for charcoal. We may add from the Schol on the Achar of Aristoph ηδε πρῖνος, ἐπιτήδειον ξύλον εἰς ἄνθρακα· Athens is still supplied with charcoal from that part of the country where Acharnæ may be supposed to have been situated, Ἀχαρνικὴ —— πρίνινοι Ach. 178

6. Arbutus Unedo, κομαριά, abounds on the mountains of Pendeli, its fruit μαράκυλά is eaten and esteemed a delicacy. The bees feeding on the flowers are said to communicate a bitter taste to the honey. The flutes of the Greek shepherds called φλόγρια are made of this wood. It is used by the turners, and is hard, though less durable than oak. In Zante a spirit is drawn from it, and a vinegar of a bright gold colour.

7. Arbutus Andrachne, ἀγριοκομαριά, grows in equal abundance with the A. Unedo on the mountains of Pendeli and Parnes. Its fruit ripens in the months of October and November, but is not eaten.

8. Erica Multiflora, 'Ρείττη, flowers in winter, and during that season furnishes the principal food of the bee. The honey, however, which they make from its flowers is little esteemed, and sells at half the price of that made during the summer season from the wild Thyme. It abounds on Pendeli and Parnes.

9. Rhus Cotinus, χρυσόξυλον. The dye of this wood is a beautiful orange-yellow. It is used to give this colour to the yarn by the Greeks and Albanians. It is brought from Pendeli and the mountains of Attica, and is sold to the dyers at Athens at two paras the oke. In Cyprus the Rhus Coriaria retains its ancient name Ροῦς. The powdered fruit called by the Turks, Sumach, is sprinkled upon the meat as seasoning.

10. Laurus Nobilis, Δάφνη, the most aromatic of the Greek shrubs grows wild about Pendeli. An oil is expressed from the berries, which is used to anoint the hair. It is used as a medicine externally in bruises and rheumatisms

Notes by the Editor

6 κομάρια in Du C the κόμαρος of Theoph. Hist 1 15.

7 Ἀνδράχνη, Theoph Hist 1. 15 ἀνδράχλι in Cyprus, Sibthorp. It suffers more from the cold (Oliver remarks), than the Ar Unedo, it is found near the Helle-pont, in the Archipelago, and in Syria

9 This use of the Sumach at meals, is mentioned by the ancient writers, Ροῦς ὁ ἐπὶ τα ὄψα. Diosc 1 c 147 The poet Antiphanes speaks of rhus and honey, among the ἀρτύματα of the table Athen Schw Lib. 11. p. 262.

11. Nerium Oleander, πικροδάφνη, a very general plant through Greece, it marks the torrent bed, and fringes the banks of the Ilissus. The flowers are used as an ornament, and cover the bazar at Athens. The leaves boiled, or the dried leaves powdered are employed as remedies for the itch; boiled in oil, they serve as a liniment for rheumatic pains. The lattice windows (Jalousies) in the Turkish houses are made of slips of this wood. In Cyprus it retains its ancient name ροδοδάφνη; and the Cypriotes adorn their churches with the flowers on feast days.

12. Salix Babylonica, 'Ιτέα. This tree is not common, and perhaps was originally introduced into Attica. I observed it near the monastery of Pendeli. The wood is made into charcoal for gun-powder, and the twigs into baskets.

13. Pistachia Lentiscus, σχῖνος This wood is much esteemed for fuel. The mastic or gum is only collected in Scio. The ashes of the wood are used by the Athenian soap-boilers for making the lye for the manufacture of soap. In Zante it is also considered as furnishing the best lixivium. The tanners employ it with Valanida in the preparation of leather. In Ithaca an oil is expressed (σχινολάδι) from the berry.

14. Vitex Agnus Castus, λαναπίττα, the constant companion of the Oleander grows by the Ilissus, and on the torrent side. The twigs are very pliable, baskets and bee-hives are made of them. The leaves are also used by the dyers to produce a yellow colour, and with indigo, green. In Zante, hoops are made of the wood of this plant; it is there called λύγεια; it bears also the same name in Cyprus as well as ἄγνεια; in Patmos it is called λυγαριά.

Notes by the Editor.

11 Νήριον of Diosc. iv 82 the Rosa laurea of Apuleius Sprengel

13 The σχῖνος of Theoph Hist iv 1 The ancient word σχινίζομαι signifies to eat mastich in order to clean and make white the teeth The substance is now much used by the women of Turkey for the same purpose We find from Dioscorides, lib i c 90 that it was employed in preparations for the teeth

14. Coray remarks, that the λύγινοι στέφανοι, of which the ancients speak, are still used by the Greeks. " It is reported," says Geraide, " that if such as journey or travel do

15. Salvia Arborea, ἐλεσφακιά. This beautiful sage I first met with on Anchesmus, afterwards on Pendeli. The wood of the stem is used in making charcoal for the manufacture of gunpowder at Athens

16. Hedera Helix, κίσσος; this tree hangs as a curtain in the picturesque scenery of the marble caves of Pendeli. The leaves are used for issues.

17. Juniperus Oxycedrus, κέδρος, grows on Pendeli and Parnes, but is not very frequent in Greece.

18. Cercis Siliquastrum, κο-ζυκιουνάρι; this beautiful shrub grows near the monastery of Pendeli, and in the forests of Sarando Potamo.

19. Anthyllis Hermanniæ, ἀλογοθυμάρ., so named from the horses feeding on it. The bees are fond of the flowers.

20. Daphne dioica, ἡμεροθερόκαλα. This plant abounds on the mountains of Pendeli and Hymettus It is used by the dyers at Athens, and Albanian women, for dyeing a yellow colour, and with indigo, green.

21. Myrtus Communis, Μυρτιά, and in Cyprus, Μυρσίνι. The varieties of the common myrtle with white fruit I observed near the monastery of Pendeli. Both this and the black fruit are eaten by the Athenians. The plant is used in garlands, and as an orna-

Notes by the Editor

carry with them a branch or rod of Agnus castus in their hand, it will keep them from merrygals and weariness. Herbal. 1202. This passage alludes to the opinion noticed by Diosc i 135 c δοκεῖ δ. κωλυτήριον εἶναι ἐν ὁδοιπορίαις παρατριμμάτων εἴτι ῥαβδον κ τ. λ. and Hasselquist observes, that "pilgrims make staffs of it" 130. In reference to the same opinion, the modern Greeks quote four lines, which are found in Dr Sibthorp's journals

ὁποῖος περάσει ἀπὸ λυγέια,
καὶ δεν κόψει κομάτι,
νὰ λυγεισθη, νὰ μαρανθη,
νὰ πέση εἰ, τὸ κραβάτι

15. A corruption of the ancient ἐλελίσφακος. Theoph Hist. vi. 2.

17. The κέδρος of Theophrastus.

21 " Et erant olim esui myrti baccæ, Plato suos cives μύρτοις tanquam bellariis vesci voluit." Lib. xi. de Rep. Wessel. Obs. 52.

ment in some of the Greek churches. In Zante they have the following distich alluding to this custom.

Μυρτιά μου χρυσοπράσινη τῆς ἐκκλησίας στολίδι,
Χωρὶς ἐσὲ δὲν γίνεται κανένα πανηγύρι.

Rubus fruticosus, Βάτος. The fruit Μοῦρα is eaten in Greece. When it is plentiful, it is a sign of a good harvest. In Zante, a syrup is made from the fruit, called βατομουρντζίδα, and is given in affections of the fauces. From it also a purple colour is drawn.

23. Ficus Carica, συκιά in Laconia; the flowers of the wild fig ἐρινὸς are still used for the caprification of the cultivated fig, in various parts of Greece.

24. Typha latifolia, βάθ. The stem and leaves are brought from the Lake of Marathon, and sold at Athens for the purpose of being made into mats.

25. Carex Riparia, Μάχαιρίτι. The name is taken from the sharp edges, and forms of the leaves. I saw a quantity of this Carex cut to serve as the covering for the bee-hives at Pendeli.

26. Arundo Donax, κάλαμο. A very important plant for various economical uses, and particularly for the employment of it in wicker-

Notes by the Editor

23. The ancient word for this practice is συκάζειν, which is explained by τὰ ἐρινα συλλέγειν καὶ περιαρτᾶν. See Pollux I. p. 113. The custom is mentioned in Aristotle, H. An. Lib. v. c. 26.

" At Athens," says Mr. Hawkins, " they take the wild figs (ὄρνοι) in June, when the insect shews itself in them, string a few and suspend them on the branches of the domestic fig tree, without which it is believed all the fruit would drop. They also engraft a shoot or two of the wild fig tree on the domestic sort, which answers the same purpose. The caprification of figs is practised in Santorini nearly in the manner described by Tournefort, except that the term ὀρίνεα must be substituted for that of ὄρνος, and the following particulars should be added. The ὀρίνεα fructifies first in December and January, when it produces the *Prodotes*, and, secondly, in March, when it produces the *Lates*, both which are used for caprifying."

24. Τύφη of Theophr. His. i. 8. and Ulva palustris of Virgil. Sprengel.

26. The δόναξ of Homer and Diosc. Sprengel 159. Mr. Hawkins observed near the lake Copais the reeds, of which the flutes are made, and saw a herdsman playing on one of them. It was formed of the Arundo D. and called φλοιέρα.

I I

work. The rural pipe of the Greek shepherd, φλκύρας, is made of the donax.—" The Donax which grows in the chasms of the rocks at Athos supplies the monks with fishing rods "—S.

27. Arundo Phragmites, καλαμότζιθρα, grows in some marshy grounds near Calandra.

28. Rubia Peregrina, ἄγριορ τάρι, grows wild in the woody part of Pendeli, also on Parnassus. The root of the plant is in Zante used as a remedy in Rachitis. The country people take from it a dye of a red colour.

29. Hyoscyamus Albus, ἱερός The leaves are applied externally to the face as an opiate, or antispasmodic in the tooth-ache. In this complaint also the fumes of its burnt seed are received into the mouth.

30. Pistachia Terebinthus, κονφέτζια. The fruit of this tree is eaten, and an oil expressed from it In Cyprus it is called τριμίθις, the ancient name, corrupted The Cyprian turpentine was formerly much esteemed, and employed for medical uses, at present the principal cultivation of the turpentine tree, as well as the mastic is in the island Scio, and the turpentine when drawn is sent to Constantinople

31. Lolium Temulentum, Ἄιρα. The seeds of this plant are often mixed with the corn, and when eaten occasion violent giddiness.

32. Smilax Aspera, in Laconia, σμίλαγγα. In Cyprus ξυλόβατος. The flowers are extremely fragrant, and are put into the wine to give it a grateful flavour. The root is used in Zante as a depurator of the blood in the room of Sarsaparella.

Notes by the Editor.

28 Rubia Tinctorum is called ριζάρι Sibthorp. See also Du Cange in v. Tournefort says that the red leather at Tocat is dyed with madder. Lett IX

29 Called also ἡ ἱερὰ βοτάνη, and δαιμονάρεα At Constantinople and in most of the Greek islands, it preserves its ancient name ὑοσκύαμος

31. Retains its ancient name In the Geoponica we find a similar observation to that of Dr Sibthorp, ἄιρα αὐτοῖς μιγνυμένη σκοτοῖ τοὺ ἐσθίοντας p 199. l. Niclas. Ed This plant is the ζιζάνιον of St Matthew, xiii., the Zuwan of the Arabian botanists, and the *Rosch* of the Old Testament. See Michaelis on the Laws of Moses, iii 357.

32 Σμίλαξ of Theophrastus and Dioscorides. The fragrancy of the flowers is alluded to in the words of Aristophanes in the Nubes, σμίλακος ὄζων, 1006

33. Asphodelus Ramosus, καραβοϊκι. This plant is very common in the plain of Athens; if it ripens into seed well it is a sign of a good harvest. In Zante the leaves are used to stuff the mattresses of the peasants. It is still called ἀσφοδελο, and in Cyprus the Turks make a sort of paste or glue which is used for various purposes.

34. Amaryllis Lutea, ἀγριοκρινα, grows abundantly on Anchesmus, and the mountain of Attica; it is used as a coronary or ornamental plant The Turks make it grow on the graves of their deceased friends.

35. Juncus Acutus βρουλα, is of great importance for various economical purposes. It is manufactured into cords and brushes, and in Zante as well as in Attica into baskets, σπυριδαc, for carrying the olives. The Zantiotes employ the stalks in the vineyard to bind the vine, and use the seeds boiled as a cathartic.

36. Cyperus Longus, κυπε... The roots are taken medicinally for the disorders of the stomach The leaves are used for stringing and bringing the roots to Athens, and for tying the wild figs on the cultivated tree.

37. Asparagus Aphyllus, ἀσπαραγγι The season for this is principally during the time of Lent, when it is boiled and eaten.

38. Rumex Pulcher, λαπαθι. Other species of docks are called by this name. The leaves are employed for making the Turkish Dolma, and are boiled and eaten with oil.

39. Capparis Spinosa, ἀππαρι, very common on the road side from Athens to the Piræus The young shoots are used as a pickle, and preserved in vinegar.

Notes by the Editor

34 " The Amaryllis lutea," Sibthorp says, " is planted by the Turks over the graves of their friends " The asphodel and myrtle were placed over tombs by the ancients and the latter I have observed to be used by the Turks for a similar purpose Myrtum tumulo imponebant antiqui Vossius de Idol v 665., and in an epigram of Porphyry, a tomb is supposed to address a passer by. " On the outside I have the mallow and the asphodel; within I enclose a dead body " — Heinsius in Hesiod, Ε και Η 11

35 Called also βουλα, see Du C. in v It is the ἐξοσχοινος of Dioscorides Prod Fl. Gr

36 Κυπειρος of Dioscorides and Hippocrates, Sprengel The recent name Ζιρχα is found in the Geoponica, Lib II

40. Cistus Creticus, λαδάνεια. Different species of Cistus which grow in Attica are distinguished by this name; but the laudanum is not collected. Crete and Cyprus are the only places at present where it is gathered. Cistus incanus is called at Constantinople λάδαιο; it is infused into the baths to give them a fragrant odour.

41. Arum Maculatum, δρακόντια, in Laconia ἄρον. It grows in great abundance about the monastery of Pendeli. The root is used by the inhabitants of the Morea in times of great scarcity for bread, being previously boiled and then pounded

42. Satureia Capitata, θυμάρι. This is the most general plant on the mountains of Pendeli and Hymettus. It is to this flower that the Hymettian honey owes its celebrity; indeed most of the honey of Attica is drawn by the bees from the flowers of this plant. Attic honey is still in high esteem, and presents of it are sent to Constantinople.

43. Satureia Thymbra, θρούβη, grows on Anchesmus, Pendeli, and Hymettus, and is mixed with the Satureia capitata, but not in large quantities. It appears to be a favorite plant with the bees. Pounded or chopped it is sprinkled on some vegetables to give them an aromatic flavour.

44. Orobanche Caryophyllacea, λύκος, a parasitic plant found frequently in the bean-fields, and very destructive to the crops. It does not appear in the first sowing, but when the beans are sown the second or

---

Notes by the Editor.

40 Κίστος of Theoph. and Hipp   Belon, lib 1. c. 7. Obser gives an account of the instrument ἐργαστῆρι with which the laud inum is collected   Tournefort describes the manner of taking it off from the shrub by whips, it is also mentioned by Dioscorides, who says " that it was combed from the beards and thighs of the goats, which browsed on the cistus." Lib 1. c 128.

41 The two names occur in Athenæus, lib. IX. δρακόντιον, ο ἔνιοι ἄρον. Gerarde says it is eaten, being sodden in two or three waters 686.

42. Θύμος of Hipp and Theophr.   Galen speaks of it as the favourite food of the bees. Sprengel.

44 See Du Cange in v λύκος.

third time. It is considered as the most detrimental weed in the bean-field.

45. Malva Sylvestris, μολώχα in Cyprus. The wild mallow is very common about Athens. The leaves are boiled and eaten as a pot-herb, and an ingredient in the Dolma.

46. Scolymus Maculatus, ασκόλυμῦρος. The young leaves of this plant are eaten as a sallad.

47. Erigeron Graveolens, κονύτζα; ψυλλίστρα in the Morea, the expressed herb gives a green colour, and is used by the Albanian women in dyeing their yarn. Powdered and applied as a cataplasm to the head it destroys lice. The gummy juice exuding from the stalk and leaves, entangles bugs, fleas, and other insects; and with this view is laid by the Greek peasants under their beds.

48. Agaricus Campestris, αμανίτης, most frequently found in the old μάνδρα, where the sheep and goats have fed. It is esteemed here as the best sort of mushroom. The Agaricus Procerus is also called by the same name, and eaten by the Greeks.

49. Scilla Officinalis, σκιλλοκρόμμυδι; this is common on Hymettus and throughout Attica. The root is used medicinally, made into an electuary.

50. Euphorbia Characias, φλόμος. This is used by the Greek fishermen to poison the fish; but caught by these means, they become putrid a short time after they are taken.

51. Osyris Alba, πλευριτόχορτο, a decoction of the root being taken in pleurisies. It is called in Zante σκρώματα, as brushes are made of it, and κοκκινοσπαρτο from the fruit which is red.

52. Punica Granatum, ρόδια, grows near Phalerus; but is here probably the outcast of the garden. It grows abundantly about Daulis, and is frequent in Bœotia.

Notes by the Editor.

47. The κόνυζα μείζων of Dioscorides

48. Μύκης of Theophrastus; αμανίτης, Botanicorum vox. See Thom. Magis. Oudend. 620.

53. Echium Italicum, γλυκό-ιττα, the name given by the Athenian shepherds; evidently a corruption of Lycopsis.

54. Carthamus Corymbosus, χαμαλέο, the χαμαιλέον of Dioscorides. It grows plentifully near the Piræus; it is called in Cyprus ὄβερος.

55. Nigella Damascena, μαθροκόκκο; in Cyprus, μαβρο.cuzάδεις; the Turks sprinkle the seeds of this plant on their caimak, a favourite dish, and the Greeks, mixed with sesamum on their bread; a very ancient custom mentioned by Dioscorides. It is also called πορλόχορτο from the crackling of the scariose capsules.

56. Amygdalus Communis Sylvestris, πικρ-αμύγδαλα. grows on the way side from Athens to the Piræus. The fruit being pounded is rubbed on the skin in coming out of the bath. Hedges are frequently formed of it for the vineyard, and the wood is employed for the tubes of pipes.

57. Conium Maculatum, μαγγούνα, and καραάκι, grows abundantly in the low grounds under the temple of Theseus. It is used like the φλόμος to poison fish.

58. Salsola Fruticosa, άλμυρία, the gathering of this in the marshes adjoining to Phalerus to make soda is farmed at 500 piastres per annum. The Cypriotes call it άλμυριά; it is esteemed by them an excellent fodder for camels; they prepare from its ashes also an alkali used in the manufacture of soap and glass.

59. Pinus Picea, ἐλάτη. The wood of the Silver fir is employed by the carpenters for various purposes. In ship-building it furnishes masts. It is found in Attica on Mount Parnes, where it grows in great abundance.

Mr. Hawkins observes that it grows in other parts of Greece on the highest mountains, it may not therefore now be much used in ship-building, the Greek navigators are able to procure very strait poles of the πεύκος from Thasos, or masts both of the Silver fir, and Spruce fir from Fiume.

Notes by the Editor

55 " Inter condimentarias herbas papaver et sesamum non postremum locum tenebant" Casaub in Athen I 34

57 See Du Cange in v Μαγγούνα.

60. Atropa Mandragora, Μανδραγόυρα, called also γεργεγαν. Used for its supposed aphrodisiac qualities.

61. Viscum Album, Μέλλα. This grows on the Silver fir on Mount Parnes. It is not the plant from which they at present make bird-lime, but from the Loranthus Europæus, which is called ὀξὸς, and grows in the mountains of Euboea, and at Athos.

62. Eryngium Campestre, τῆς ἀγάπης τὸ βοτάνι. The bruised root is applied by the Athenian shepherds to cure their asses when bitten by venomous serpents. The following verses are made on this plant.

Τῆς ἀγάπης τὸ βοτάνι
Ὅποιος τὸ ἴδει, καὶ δὲν τὸ πιάνει,
Τὴν ἀγάπην, ὁπου ἔχει, χάνει.

63. Papaver Rhoeas, παπαρούνα. A syrup is drawn in Zante from the flowers, and an infusion of them taken as a pectoral. In Cyprus it is called κτενός from the red colour of the flower resembling a cock's crest; it is worn by the Greek girls as an ornament to their head-dress. Papaver somniferum is called at Constantinople μάκων; the heads of it are bruised and drank in decoction for coughs.

Notes by the Editor.

60. The same superstitious uses are now attributed to this plant as to the mandragora of the ancients. Mandragorae putatur vis inesse amorem conciliandi. Vossius de Idol. lib. v.

"I entered into conversation," says Dr. Hume in one of his journals, " with a Russian, who had studied medicine at Padua, and was now settled at Limosol in Cyprus. In giving me an account of the curiosities which he possessed he mentioned to me a root, in some degree resembling the human body, for at one end it was forked, and had a knob at the other, which represented the head, with two sprouts immediately below it for the arms. This wonderful root he had dug up, he said, in the Holy Land with no little risque, for the instant it appeared above the ground it killed two dogs, and would have killed him also had he not been under the influence of magic." It is evident that the Russian doctor was repeating some of the absurd stories that have been circulated from very early times respecting the anthropomorphic character of the mandragora, and its supposed noxious properties. In Lambecius Bib. Vin. lib. ii. tom. 2 is an engraving from a MS. of Dioscorides, a dog, having pulled up a root of mandragora, is represented as dying. Under the print are these words, κύων ἀνασπῶν τὸν Μανδραγόραν, ἔπειτ', ἀποθνησκων. See also in Josephus, lib. vii. b. 3. the account of the root Baara.

64. Tamus Communis, ὁ βρυονίς. The shoots are gathered and boiled as asparagus in the Spring.

65. Ceratonia Siliqua, ξυλοκερ~τια, grows abundantly in the forest of Sarando-potamo. It abounds also in Cyprus, where it still retains its ancient name κερατια. The fruit is considered an object of commerce, and more than twenty loads annually are exported to the coast of Syria.

66 Rhamnus Græcus The berries of this are collected and sold to the dyers for dyeing a yellow colour.

67. Orchis Mascula, σαρ μοβοτάνι The Salep consumed in great quantity by the Turks at Constantinople is made of the bulbous roots of different species of orchis and ophrys, which grow in an open and dry soil. The ancient names are forgotten, though their aphrodisiac qualities are still held in esteem by the Turks.

68. Populus Nigra, λευκή, grows near Lebadea in Bœotia, and is called by the same name as the white poplar

69. Saccharum Ravennæ, κάλαμι, grows abundantly on the road side between Thespia and Lebadea. The peasants make use of it for covering their Callivia and hovels.

70. Sambucus Nigra, κουφόξυλο. This grows about Lebadea, and forms the hedge to the vineyards. The flowers in Zante are used in infusion as a collyrium.

ZANTE.

71. Verbena Officinalis. On the 24th June, the day of St. John, the Zantiotes carry this plant in their cincture, as an amulet to drive away evil spirits, and to preserve them from various mischief.

Notes by the Editor.

63 The ροιά; of Theophrastus and Diosc Pap somniferum is μήκων of Dioscor. " A pristinis inde temporibus, caulis largiebatur succum, opium nostrum, quod νηπενθές; dictum Odys. iv Sprengel. His R H i 25 In his route across Asia Minor, Mr Browne observed abundance of opium collected near Angora

64. Βρυωνή; of Nicander, Ther which is explained by ἄμπελος ἀγρία in the Vatican MS. See T. viii Notice des MS. du Roi.

68 "αἰγειροφορο, ἡ Βοιατία," says M. Tyrius, Diss 29

71. Now called σταυροβοτάνι, it is the ἱερὰ βοτάνη of Dioscorides. — Prod. Fl. Gr. ii. 402.

72. Salvia Officinalis. The apples, as they are called, or the tumour on this plant, φασκομηλιὰ, the effect of the puncture of a species of cynips, are made into a conserve with honey. These excrescences are also found on Salvia pomifera.

73. Dipsacus Sylvestris, νεροκράτη. The water collected in the cavity of the leaves is used as a cosmetic by the Greek girls.

74 Iris Graminea. The root of the Iris is used as a cosmetic and is dried and powdered, and rubbed on the cheek. In Cyprus it is called ζουρδιλίσι, evidently a corruption from the Italian Fior di Lis. It is sometimes called κρίνο, the name properly applied to Liliumalbum.

75. Thapsia Villosa. The young leaves are gathered among the plants that form the ἄγρια λάχανα. The expressed juice of the flowers is used with the Verbascum blattaria to dye yellow the wool which is manufactured into the coarse carpets called τζεντίαις

76. Anethum Fœniculum. The tops are used in preserving the green olives, and are chopped and served up with the Octopodia.

77. Cuscuta Europæa, one of the Greek names in Zante, imports "the thread spun by the Nereids," ἀνεραιδονέματα. From the twisting and twining of the stems, it is compared by the Greeks to the dishevelled hair of the Nereids, they also call it Μαλιὰ τῆς Παναγίας, "the hair of the Virgin." At Constantinople it is named ἐπιθύμοι, the ancient word in Dioscorides, and is given with Artemisia Pontica (ἀϐρόϑον) in fevers.

78. Verbascum Thapsus, φλόμος. The dried flower stalk is used on St. John's day, dipped in oil, as a torch. The saint from the bonfires used on this day is called Ἄγιος Ἰωάννης Λαμπαδάρης.

79. Daucus Nobilis The churches, particularly the pavements are adorned with this plant during Easter. Crosses also are made of it, and put behind the door from Easter Sunday to the Ascension. The leaves are used in culinary preparations for dressing the eels. An oil also is made from the berries.

Notes by the Editor

72. See Belon's remarks on the Pommes de Sauge in Crete, lib i. c. 17 and Tournefort, Letter ii. " In Creta ac etiam in quibusdam Apuliæ et Calabriæ locis, Salvia in cacumine gignit tubercula quædam, gallarum instar, subalbida." Dios Mathiol 378

77. See Du Cange in v Νεράϊς,

K K

80. Ruta Graveolens, ἀπήγα.ον, is externally applied in rheumatic pains, to the joints, feet, and loins

81. Ranunculus Ficaria; the name ζοχαδόχορτο comes from the use of the roots applied in the Hæmorrhoids.

82. Reseda Alba. The whole plant and the seeds also, being bruised, yield a yellow colour which is used by the Zantiotes for dyeing silk.

83. Acanthus Spinosus, ἄκανθα of Dioscorides, now called μουτρίνα. It is gathered by the Zantiotes on the first of May, and forms the central part of their garlands, which they suspend on that day in festoons.

84. Pisum Ochrus, the Zantiotes of the mountains make use of this seed mixed with their bread.

85. Lathyrus Sativus, ἀγριολαθούρι. The Zantiotes makes use of the seeds of this plant decorticated for a yellow polenta.

86. Vicia Sativa, Cίκα, used as an artificial fodder by the Zantiotes; the seeds are ground and used as a flower mixed with the bread by the Cephallonians

87. Cicer Arietinum, ῥοβίθι; the seeds are used boiled in soup.

88. Glycyrrhiza Glabra, γλυκόριζα; the root of this plant is collected and exported to Alexandria as an object of commerce to be made into sherbet and syrup.

89. Hypericum Perforatum, βάλσαμον, at Mount Athos, and σταθόχορτο at Constantinople. The flowers infused in oil are left 40 days in the sun, when the oil tinged of a red colour is used as a vulnerary.

90. Hypericum Coris, κόρις of Dioscorides; the leaves have a strong balsamic aromatic smell, a yellow colour is drawn from them.

91. Scorzonera Tenuifolia, the root being cut in pieces is used in decoction, as a sweetener of the blood.

92. Micropus Erectus; an infusion of this plant is taken for the Tinea capitis, as the Greek name κατιδοχορτο implies.

Notes by the Editor

81 See Du Cange in v κοιμαμέναι.

87. "Ἐρεβίνθοι formed a common dessert among the ancient Greeks, eaten green and tender, or, when dry, parched in the fire" See Gray on the Io of Plato. "Ἐρεβίνθοι τεφρυγμένοι," says Coray, "are now called στραγαλια." " Il y a plusieurs boutiques en Damas, qui ne font autre ouvrage, que tour des pois chiches, qu'ils appellent de nom Grec vulgaire, Erivithia."—Belon. Obs 152

92 From κατίδα, Porrigo. Du Cange in v

93. Viola Odorata, called ἴον μέλαν in Lacoma. A syrup is drawn from the flower It is an admired plant of the poets, hence the following distich.

———— 'γιούλια, καὶ μοσκαῖς, καὶ λεμονοκορφάδες,

Νὰ σοῦ τὰ βάλω, ματιάμου, εἰς ταῖς βλακομάναις.

" Hyacinths, violets, musk-roses and lemon flowers, I throw on my love to remove the marks of your small-pox."

(The first word is indistinct in the manuscript. Βλακομάναις is not found in Du Cange, but in Sommavera — E.)

94. Aristolochia Longa, is a much esteemed medicine in the Rachitis, in intermittents and other fevers. The roots for this purpose are exported to Venice and Italy. As a medicine also to puerperous women its medical powers are so great that it is considered as a specific, and called by the Zantiotes, μίζα.

95. Scilla Maritima abounds in the island of Zante; it is an object of commerce, and is exported to Holland and England. A sequin for a 1000 roots is paid for collecting them It is called ἀσκίλλα at Constantinople, and is made into paste with honey for the asthma, or applied in cataplasms to the joints affected with rheumatic pains.

96. Asparagus Acutifolius, σπαραγγούνια. The shoots appear in February, and continue until May; they are eaten boiled with oil and vinegar. In Cyprus it is called ασπαραγος, the ancient name in Dioscorides.

97. Spartium Spinosum, ἀσσαλακτος, one of the earliest flowering shrubs, and the prodromus of the spring. Spartium Villosum in Cyprus still retains its ancient name somewhat corrupted, σπάλαθος, the ἀσπάλαθος of Dioscorides.

98. Fumaria Officinalis καπνά, the herb is pounded, and an infusion is made which is taken for exanthematous complaints, and a prurient itching of the skin.

99. Mercurialis Annua, παρθενούδι, taken in infusion with Agrimonia

Notes by the Editor.

99 Called also σκαρολάχανον (see Du C. in v. παρθενούδι) from the reason assigned by Dr Sibthorp

Eupatorium, as an Emmenagogue. In Cyprus it is called σκαρόχορτο; the Labrus Scarus of Linnæus is said to be fond of the plant, and the fishermen, when they go to fish, throw quantities of it among the rocks.

100 Peucedanum Officinale, μεγαβοτάνο, in Laconia, τευκέδανον. The root of this plant is applied in cataplasms to the heads of new born infants, as a preservative against hydrocephalous and strumous swellings of the neck.

101. Matricaria Suaveolens, χαμόμιλον, an infusion of the flowers is drank in bilious and nervous fevers, and made use of also in deafness to syringe the ears

102. Lavandula Stæchas μαβρικεφάλι; an infusion of it is drank for catarrhs and head-aches. It is called in Patmos λαμπρολουλούδι; the Patmian women deck their churches with this plant on Easter Sunday ; whence its name λάμπρις, which signifies a luminous feast.

103. Nymphæa Lutea, νούφαρ, a sherbet is made of it and taken in colds, it is found in the lakes of Thessaly.

104. Cannabis Sativa, drank in infusion brings on deliquescence and delirium, it is taken by the patient previously to the operation performed by the surgeon. Boiled with oil, it serves as a liniment to remove rheumatic pains.

105 Helleborus Officin. — "We are certain, I believe (says Sir James Smith in a letter to the editor), of the ἑλλέβορος μέλας of Dioscorides only, called in modern Greek σκαρφη, which is Helleborus offici. Prodr. Fl. Gr. a species unknown to Linnæus, though near his H. niger. What the white Hellebore of the ancients was, we are not clear. Sibthorp suspected it to be Digitalis ferruginea. It is commonly thought to be Veratrum album."

Notes by the Editor

101 Used as an aphrodisiac and narcotic in Egypt (Browne, 274) The Arabs swallow a preparation of the leaves of green hemp for the purpose of exhilaration (Pococke 1. 181) Menou was obliged to prohibit strictly the use of the seeds of this plant among the French army in Egypt (Mem. de l'Instit 1805) The seeds of hemp, according to Galen, de Alim Facul 1. 31 were an ingredient in cakes served up after supper to encourage drinking; but they were apt when eaten too freely to affect the head — Russell's Aleppo, 1 378.

(Mr. Hawkins observes, that the hellebore grows only on elevated tracts, for instance on Palæovuno, Mount Helicon. Melius in Helicone. Pliny, lib. xxv. c 5. — E.)

106. Chrysanthemum Coronarium, called by the Greeks of Cyprus Λάζαρς, because the women ornament their heads with it the Sunday after the day kept to commemorate the resurrection of Lazarus. In Laconia it is called χρυσα.βίσι.

107. Lonicera Caprifolium, αγιόκ/ημα, used by the girls of Patmos for garlands, and as an ornament for their head-dress.

108. Ἐλίχρυσα, probably Gnaphallium Stæchas. The images of the Gods, says Dioscorides, were crowned with it. Lib. iv. c. 57. The Greeks still use it as a Planta Coronaria to adorn the Panagia.

PLANTS COLLECTED IN CYPRUS BY DR HUME

At Limosol in July

Gossypium hirsutum	Poterium spinosum
———— herbaceum	Juniperus
Olea Europæa	Sempervivum sediforme
Papaver rhæas	Punica granatum
Morus alba	Ononis
———— rubra	Orobanche
Rhamnus paliurus	Nicotiana pusilla
Robinia spinosa	Onosma orientalis
Hypericum repens	Jasminum grandiflorum

Notes by the Editor

107. We find the same kind of flowers, which were worn by the ancient Greeks, used now as ornaments or coronary plants, στεφανωματικὰ ἄνθη They are placed not only round the head and on the breast, but are sometimes pendant by the sides of the temples and ears " Obtinet," says Coray, " etiamnum apud Græcos mos flores solutos inter tempora et aures inserendi, ita ut pediculus quidem sub pileo teneatur lateatque, flos vero pendeat sæpe aure ima tenus " In Athen c 78 lib. 12.

At Larnica and Limosol in June and July

Convolvulus
Convolvulus repens
Lepidium latifolium
Hibiscus
Chenopodium album
Heliotropium Europæum
Amaranthus
Calendula arvensis
Solanum
S. nigrum
S lycopersicon
Polycarpon tetraphyllum
Chelidonium glaucum
Pteronia
Lavendula
Baccharis Dioscoridis
Ruta Chalepensis
Cistus crispus
C. Creticus
Ceratonia siliqua
Ricinus communis
Thymbra spicata
Plantago maritima
Carthamus Creticus
Salsola laniflora
Malva sylvestris
M Cypriana*
Mercurialis tomentosa
Eryngium pusillum
Fumaria spicata

Veronica anagallis
Lythrum hyssopifolium (collected
    near the aqueduct)
Hypericum nummularia
Statice Tartarica
Adianthum
Antirrhinum spurium
Nerium oleander
Anthemis tinctoria
Plumbago Europæa
Cyprus tusca
Rosa sempervivens
Œnothera
——————— hirta
Erigerum viscosum
Galium rubioides
Echium Creticum
Sideritis incana
Momordica elaterium
Reseda luteola
Mentha
Myrtus communis
Narcissus tazetta
Rosmarinus
Capparis spinosa
Euphorbia
Hyoscyamus
Chrysanthemum coronarium
Panicum glaucum
Inula pulicaria.

* Specific name given by Mr. Don.

BIRDS, QUADRUPEDS, AND FISHES.

[FROM DR SIBTHORP'S MSS]

PICÆ

Found in Cyprus.		*Names in parts of Greece*
1. Corvus Corax	κούρακος.	
2. C. Cornix	κορασένος.	κορόυνη.
3 C. Monedula	κολοίος.	καλλικιότη.
4. C. Pica	κατζοκοράτα	καρακάξα
5. C. Glandarius	λίτσα.	Id.
6. Coracias Garrula	γράκυλος, καρκκάξα.	χρυσοκαρακάξα.
7. Oriolus Galbula	φλωρος.	συκοφάγι.
8. Cuculus Canorus	κόκκυξ.	Id
9. Merops Apiaster	μεροψ.	μελισσόφαγος.
10. Upupa Epops	Βουβούζιοι.	ἀγριοπέτεινον

Found in parts of Greece.

11. Corvus Graculus	κολκινομίτι	

Notes by the Editor.

3 Corvus Mon   This bird retains its ancient name, κολοιος   See Schneider in H A. Arist.

9. Merops A.   Perhaps the μέροψ of Aristotle, H A. lib. IX. c 11.   See Schneider It is found in Syria also, in the woods and plains between Acre and Nazareth.—Hasselquist.

10 Upupa E.   Migratory in every part of Europe, it does not remain during the winter even in Greece and Italy —Buffon   Its name in Greece is ἀγριοπετεινον   Πετηνόν is sometimes found in ancient MSS, but probably it should be πετεινόν —Thom. Ma. Ed Ouden 765

11. Corvus G.   The Romaic name of the Cornish chough, signifies literally " Red bill."   It was seen on the mountains of Crete by Belon, it is the κορακίας φοινικόρυγχος of Aristotle.   Schn. in lib IX. c. 19

12. Sitta Europæa   τρυπόξυλο.
13. Alcedo Ispida   Βασιλόπουλι.

In Thessaly.

14. Corvus Corone   κορασένος.
15. Picus Viridis   τρυπόξυλο
16 P. Major   Id.
17. P. Medius   Id.

ACCIPITRES.

Found in Cyprus.   *Names in parts of Greece.*

1. Vultur ——   ἀετόc.
2. Falco Tinnunc.   κότζη.   ἀνεμόγατος.
3. F. Melanops.   μαβρομάτι.
4. F. Ierax   ἱεράκι.
5   Falco ——   φαλκόνι.

Notes by the Editor.

12. Sitta E. The following words of Buffon illustrate the meaning of the Romaic term, " Cet oiseau frappe de son bec l'ecorce des arbres "
15. Picus V The κελεὸς of Arist. H A. lib. viii c 15 Schn

2. Falco T. The Kestril was called κεγχρὶς by the ancient Greeks.
4 Falco Ierax, ἱεράκι The diversion of hawking is still followed by the Turks in different parts of Asia Minor and Syria The word ἱέραξ is retained by the Greeks, with a slight corruption, in the names of some birds of the genus falco and in Crete the falconer is called ἱεραχάρι. The ἱέραξ was the bird employed in ancient times in Thrace, in fowling and hunting, as we learn from Aristotle, H A Lib. ix c. 6. and a writer not much junior to him (de Mir.) informs us, that the hawks appeared when called by their names, and brought to the fowlers the prey which they had caught.—Beckman i 330.
In Syria seven different kinds of hawks are employed, they are taught to fly at herons, storks, wild geese, francolines, partridges, and quails. One sort is used in hunting the antelope, the bird strikes at the game, and thus impedes its course until the dogs come up. Russell, ii 153

Found in Cyprus		*Names in parts of Greece*
6. F. ——	τζάϊος	
7. Strix Passerina	κοκοβάϊα	ἀνεμόγαλος.

Found in Greece.

8. Vultur Orneo	ὄρνεο.	In Thessal. ὄρνεο μαυρο and ὄρνεο ἄσπρο
9. V. Aspropatos	ἀσπρόπαρος.	
10. Falco Chrysaetos	ἀετός	Id.
11. F Peregrinus	ἱεράκι	Id
12. F. Kirkenasi	κιρκενάσι.	
13 F Marathonius		
14. F. Livadiensis		
15. F. Sumensis		
16. Strix Bubo	ζέτφος.	βουφο in Thessal.
17. Strix ——	τζάϊις	
18. Lanius Collurio	κεφαλάς μέγας.	Id. in Thessal
L. Cephalas	κεφαλάς	

Found in Thessaly.

19. Falco Haliaetos
20. F Cyaneus
21. Falco —— μαβροιερακι.
22 F. Æruginosus χελα...

Found in Thessaly

23. F. Subbuteo   ἱεραχίνι.
24. Strix Otus
25. Lanius Excubitor   κεφαλάς
26. L. Cyanocephalus   Id.
27. L. Coccinocepha-
     lus   Id.
28. L. Rufus   Id.

ANSERES.

Found in Cyprus		*Names in parts of Greece*
1. Anas Anser do-mes.	χῆ α ημερα.	Id.
2. A. Boschas dom.	πατίδι ήμερα.	Id.
3. A. B Sylv.	π. ἄγρια.	Id.
4. A. Cicia	σαρσέλλα	Id. in Thessal.
5. A. Cypria	παπερόψαρς.	
6. Pelicanus Carbo	καληκατζόυ.	ιαραβάλαιο.
7. Colymbus Auritus		
8. Larus Ridibundus	λάρος	Id. in Græcia.
9. L. Canus	Id.	
10 L. Marinus	Id	Id. in Thessal.
11. Procellaria Puffi-nus	μέκω.	
12. Larus Minutus	μάρος.	
13. Sterna Minuta	χελι'όνι τῆς θαλασσης.	

Found in Thessaly

14. Anas Cygnus   κύκνος.

Notes by the Editor

24 Strix Otus, Ὠτὸς of the Greeks, seen in Cilicia by Belon.

4 Anas Cicia, σαρσέλλα   Sarcelle d' été of the French.

13 Sterna Mi. χελιδόνη, the Romaic and corrupted form of χελιδών, is found in Tzetzes and Hesiod — Heinsius, 87

Found in *Thessaly*		Names *in parts of Greece*
15 Anas Cygnus	προσοκεφάλι.	
16. A ————	κοκκινοκ φάλι.	
17 A. ————		
18 Sterna Hirundo	χελιδόι. -ης θαλασσης	καραβάλακα in Græcia.
19. Sterna Nævia	Id.	
20. S. Vulgaris	ψαρό..	

GRALLÆ.

Found in *Cyprus*		Names *in parts of Greece*
1. Ardea Purpurascens	βερκοπούλι.	ψαρόφαγος.
2 A. Nycticorax		
3 A. Alba		
4. A Major		
5 A. Minuta		
6 Scolopax Arquata		Id.
7. S. Cyprius	τρολευρίδα της θαλασσης,	
8. S. Totanus	νερολίοι.	
9. S. Gallinago	βεκκατζουν..	Id.
10. Tringa Varia	πλουμίοι.	
11. T. Cinclus		χόκι in Thessal.
12. T Littorea		

Notes by the Editor

2 Ardea Nyc called at Constantinople νυκτικόραχα, Forskal It is the βύας of Aristot. Lib. viii c 5 H A Schn

5. Ardea Minuta See a representation of this bird in Russell's Aleppo, ii

6 Scolopax Arquata The name of the curlew, says Buffon, *Combris, toutlis*, is an imitation of its voice The Romaic term is also τζούρλι

8 Scolopax Tot The Romaic name of the spotted redshank refers to its frequenting the neighbourhood of rivers, νερολίοι " Ad ripas fluviorum," says Linnæus

9. Scolopax G The snipe arrives in Egypt in November when the rice is taken off from the fields, and passes the winter there — Sonnini

Found in Cyprus		*Names in parts of Greece.*
13. Charadrius Spinosus	Ἰανιτζάρι.	καλιμάνι in Grecia.
14. C. Œdicnemus	τρολουρίδα τῆς γῆς.	
15. C. Himantopus		
16. C. Hiaticula		
17 Hæmatopus Ostra-legus		
18. Fulica Chloropus		
19. Rallus Crex		

Found in Greece

20 Ardea Ciconia	πέλαργος, καλαμόυκαιος	τελεκάνος.
21 Ardea Cinerea	ψαρόφαγος.	Id. in Thessal.
22 Scolopax Rusticola	ξυλοκότις.	ξιλόιοτα, at Athos.
23. Tringa Gambetta		
24. Otis Tarda	πτόη.	ότις, in Lemnos.

In Thessaly

25. Ardea Grus
26 A Garzetta
27. Tringa Vanellus　　　καλιμάνι.
28. Charadrius Pluvialis　νεροπόυλι.

Notes by the Editor

13 Charadrius Spinosus　This bird was shot by Wheler in Greece, and is seen, says Sonnini, in Egypt　It is found on the banks of the Aleppo river, and is represented in a plate in Russell's Aleppo, ii

14　Chara Œdic perhaps the χαραδριὸς of Aristot H A Lib ix c 12 — Schn

21　Ardea Cinerea　The Romaic name of the heron signifies "Fish-eater."

22. Scolopax Rust　The woodcock passes by Constantinople in September, in its flight to Syria, and returns in February and March　Forskal　It arrives in Egypt about November — Sonnini　Belon gives the name ξυλοριύζα

24　Otis Tarda　The Ὠτὶς of Aristotle, confounded by Pliny, and Alexander the Myndian, with otus　See Buffon, Ois ii 5　It was found in Syria and Greece (Paus Phoc), and in Thrace and Macedonia, according to Erotian, who says the word was written ὄτις and ὠτὶς　Foes Œcon Hipp in v.　The bustard is now, we find from Dr. Sibthorp, called Ὠτὶς in the Morea and in Lemnos

GALLINÆ.

Found in Cyprus		Names in parts of Greece
1. Meleagris Gallopavo		In Thessal. μέξ κα
2. Phasianus Gallus	τετεινος	In Thessal. Id.
3. Tetrao Rufus	πέρδιχ ι	περδ καλό λ ρος.

Notes by the Editor

1 Meleagris Gallopavo The turkey was entirely unknown to the ancients, America is its native country — Beckmann, ii 390.

There is no mention made of the Guinea fowl, Numida Meleagris, by Dr. Sibthorp, it was a bird well known to the ancients, and not uncommon, we may suppose, in the time of Pausanias lib x, who says that it was an offering in the mysteries of Isis, of persons in a moderate condition of life The Greeks expressed the screaming of this bird by καγκαζειν The description given by Clitus, the disciple of Aristotle (see Athen lib xiv c 71 Schn , was properly applied to the Guinea fowl by Paulmier, contrary to the explanation of Casaubon and Scaliger Nor is there any mention of peacocks as seen now in Greece, these birds were first brought into Athens by Demus, son of Pyrilampes, who bred them in his volaries See Gray on the Gorgias of Plato, they were more common in Greece after the time of Alexander, and we find them represented on the coins of Samos At Aleppo, Russell says, peacocks are sometimes seen, but they are brought from other places

3. Tetrao Rufus This is the species mentioned by Aristotle, "de perdice Græca vel rubra Aristoteles ubique loqui intelligendus est" Schn ad lib ix c 10 This bird is brought from Cephallonia to Zante, says Dr Sibthorp, where it is kept in cages to sing, or rather call (Quique refert jungens iterata vocabula perdix Stat S lib ii E 4) The red-legged and grey partridge were both seen in the vicinity of Salonica by Mr Hawkins The former frequented entirely the rocks and hills, the latter the cultivated grounds in the plains The remark of the Greek naturalist concerning the partridge, which is seen sitting sometimes on branches of trees, is only applicable, says Schneider, to the red-legged species. (In Arist H A lib ix c 10) With respect to the grey partridge, Belon thinks it probable, "qu'il n'y en a jamais eu dans la Grèce," but it appears from Dr Sibthorp that it is found in Thessaly Forskal mentions its arrival at Constantinople, in December and January Venit inter summa frigora Decemb et Januar interdum hic nidos ponit According to Ælian, the Greeks expressed the note or cry of the red-legged partridge by κακκαβιζειν, and of the grey kind, seen in Bœotia and Eubœa, by τιτυβιζειν H. A. iii 35 See also Schn in Athen lib ix c 9 But some have considered these words as denoting the different cries of the same bird (the red sort) in different parts of Greece

	Found in Cyprus	*Names in parts of Greece*
4. Tetrao Francolinus	ἀτταγινάρι	
5. Tetrao Alchata	τάρδαλος.	
6. Tet. Coturnix	ὀρτύγι.	περδικοκόκκινος in Græcia.

	In Thessaly	
7. Phasianus Colchicus	Φασαη	
8. Tetrao Perdix	περδικι καβιρες	
9. Tet. ———-	τάρδαλις	

PASSERES.

	Found in Cyprus	*Names in parts of Greece*
1. Columba Œnas. dom	περιστέρι ἥμερα.	Id.
2. C. Rupestris	π. ἄγρια.	Id.
3. C. Palumbus	φάσσα	Id.
4. C. Turtur	τρυγόνι.	Id
5. C. Risoria		δεκαιτούρις in Thessal.
6. Alauda Cristata	σκορδαλός.	Id. in Thessal.
7. A. Calandra	κάλανδρα.	Id.
8. A. Spinoletta		Id in Græcia.

Notes by the Editor

4 Tetrao Francolinus, perhaps the 'Ατταγας of ancient Greece it was a bird esteemed by the Epicures, " Tu attagenem ructas, ego faba ventrem impleo " Hierony in Epis ad Asell The bird was found in Bœotia (Acharn. 873) not in Megaris, as Athenæus states, lib ix c 40 See Schw. in locum We have seen it near Smyrna, and it is also common, Russell says, in the country round Aleppo

5 " The Greeks (says Dr. Sibthorp) have given the name of Decoctoon to this bird from its note, as the French apply the word *dixhuit* to our lapwing"

7 Phasianus Colchicus The pheasant, according to Sonnini, flies over from Thessaly to some of the contiguous islands of the Archipelago The bird was known at Athens in the time of Aristophanes (Nubes, 108) and had probably been brought into Greece from Colchis, by the companions of Jason See Beckmann de His Nat. Vet

6 Alauda Cristata, the κορυβαλλος of the ancients

Found in Cyprus		Names in parts of Greece
9. Turdus Musicus	κίχλα.	τσικοκτούρι.
10. T. Merula	κοτζυφός.	Id.
11 Emberiza Miliaria		Id.
12. E. Hortulana	αμπελόπουλ.	
13. Fringilla Domestica	στρουθί.	στουργίτης
14 F. Carduelis	καρδέλλις.	Id.
15. F Petronia		Id.
16. F. Linaria		Id
17. Muscicapa Atricapilla	καλαφούρχ.	
18. M. Grisola		
19. Fringilla Flaveola	σκαρθαλις	κρασσοπούλ.
20. Motacilla Luscinia	αηδόνι	Id.
21 M. Ficedula	συκοφάγι	βεκκαθίκι.
22. M. Œnanthe		Id.
23. M Alba		σουτουφάδα at Athos.
24. M. Flava		Id
25. M. Trochilus		
26. M. Atricapilla		

Notes by the Editor.

12 Emberiza Hortulana, αμπελόπουλ The meaning of the Romaic word will be well explained by the following passage of Buffon He states that the bird is seen in the vineyards of part of France, and adds, " ils ne touchent cependant point aux raisins, mais ils mangent les insectes qui courent sur des pampres, et sur les tiges de la vigne"

13 Fringilla Domestica, the ancient word is still retained in Cyprus

14 F. Carduelis, perhaps the θραυπι of Aristotle, lib viii c 5 — Schn

21 Motacilla Ficed When the island of Cyprus was in the possession of the Venetians 1000 or 1200 jars full of these birds were annually exported They were sent in pots filled with vinegar and odoriferous plants Buffon The bird was seen in Egypt in October, by Sonnini

24 Motacilla Flava The αλος of Aristotle, lib viii. c 5 — Schn.

Found in Cyprus		*Names in parts of Greece*
27. Parus Ater		
28. Hirundo Urbica	χελ δώνα.	σουσοφάδα.
29. H. Rustica	Id.	Id
30. H. Apus	πετροχελιδωνι.	Id.
31. H. Melba	Id.	Id.
32 H. Pratincola		
33 Caprimulgus Eu-		
ropæus	αιγιδιξυτάστρα.	Id.

Found in Greece.

34. Alauda Campestris	κατζυλάρι.	
35. Turdus Cyanus	τετροκοτζυφος	
36. Emberiza Nivalis	άσπροπούλι.	
37. E. Citrinella	στερίβρα.	εκροπούλι in Thessal.
38. Motacilla Phœni-		
curus	λοσκι σκόλλα.	στραγαλια in Thessal.
39 M Rubicola	μαιροκόλλα.	
40. Muscicapa Athe-		
mensis		
41. Hirundo Riparia		

Notes by the Editor

27 Parus Ater, perhaps the μελαγκόρυφος of Aristot lib IX c. 15

31 Hirundo Melba, πετροχελιδωνι "Ces oiseaux se plaisent dans les montagnes, et nichent dans des trous des rochers." — Buffon

33 Caprimulgus Eur from αιγίδα and βύζειν, "sugere mammam." Aristotle says, "θηλάζει τας αιγα·"

35 Turdus Cyanus The κυανος of Aristotle, lib IX c 18. Schn. Seen by Belon in Negroponte, Candia, Corfu, and Zante

36 Emberiza Nivalis The Romaic word means "White bird" "En hiver le mâle a la tête, le cou, les couvertures des ailes, et tout le dessous du corps, blanc comme de la neige" — Buffon

38 Mot Phœnicurus, the φοινίκουρος of Aristotle, lib. IX c 49

39 Mot. Rubicola, seen by Belon in Greece and Crete. The words of Linnæus "caput et collum fere nigra," will explain the Romaic μαβροκόλλα

41 Hirundo Riparia, seen by Belon on the banks of the Maritza, or Hebrus.

Found in Thessaly

42. Alauda Trivialis   κατζυλαρις.
43. Emberiza Schœ-
     niclus
44. Fringilla Cælebs   στινος.
45. Parus Major   τζινα.
46. P. Cæruleus   Id.
47.   σπίοε
48.   τζου-.

MAMMALIA

Found in Cyprus		*Names in parts of Greece*
1. Vespertilio Muri- nus	υκτερίδα.	Id
2. Canis Familiaris	σκύλος	Id.
3. C. Vulpes	ἀλῶ-ου	Id.
4. Felis Catus	γάττος.	Id.
5. Lepus Timidus	λαγός.	Id.
6. Erinaceus Euro- pæus	σχαντζόχειρος.	Id.

Notes by the Editor.

43 Emberiza Schœniclus The reed bunting is the σχοίνλος of Aristotle, lib. viii.
c 5 Schn

44 Fringilla Cœlebs The chaffinch, according to Buffon, is the ὀροσπίζης of Aristotle,
lib. viii c 3.

4. Felis Catus. γάτα in Du Cange, 249 and κάττα, ib App 98 κάττους, ἰδιωτικῶς
nominan feles, ait Callimachi Schol — Vossius de Idolol. iii lib. 382.

6. Erinaceus Eur The first part of the Romaic word is a corruption of ἄκανθα,
Acanthias vulgaris nostras. Klein The flesh of the hedge-hog is prescribed in Syria
medicinally in some disorders Russell Aleppo, ii 160 He says he saw it carrying
grapes on its prickles, as well as mulberries, and, properly, illustrates a passage in
Ælian The porcupine is not mentioned in this list by Dr Sibthorp, but he saw a quill
of that animal on the Asiatic coast opposite to Rhodes, it was probably an inhabitant of
that country. It is also found near Aleppo, and sometimes served up at the tables of the
Franks. — Russell, ii 159

	Found in Cyprus	Names in parts of Greece
7. Sus Aper sylv.	ἀγριόχοιρος.	
8. Mus Rattus	ποντ..ός	Id.
9. M. Musculus	ποντικὸς μι ρός	Id
10. Capra Gazella	ἀγρέλι.ς.	
11 Equus Caballus	ἄτπαρος.	ἄλογα.
12. E. Asinus	γάναρος	Id.
13. E Mulus	μουλάρι	Id.
14. Camelus Drome- darius	κχμέλλον.	Id. in Thessal
15. Bos Taurus	βοῦδ.	ἀγελάδα in Gracia
16 Ovis Aries	κουβέλλα	π. λι. and –ρόβατο.
17 Capra Hircus	τράγος; M. αιγα F.	κατζίκα, αιγίδι.
18. Sus Aper dom.	χοιρος ἥμερος.	

Found in Greece

19. Canis Lupus	λύ.ος	

Notes by the Editor

11 Equus Caballus, ἄτπαρος   Many Hellenic words are still retained in Cyprus, and the ancient infinitive is occasionally used in common discourse   See Leake's Researches, p 65   In no other part of the Levant do we find the word ῐ-παρος, or ἄτπαρος, signifying " a horse," except in Cyprus, ἄλογον both in common conversation and writing is always applied to that animal   We are not, however, to suppose, that ἄλογον in this sense is of the recent date which many assign to it   It was applied as early as the time of Diogenes Laertius to beasts of burden, for when he is speaking of the mules driven by Bias into the camp of Alyattes, he uses the word ἄλογα, and Menage (lib 1 sec 83) remarks τὰ ἄλογα peculiariter equi sive jumenta dicuntur   He then quotes Hesychius, καττὸν, παράβλημα ἀλόγων   See the correction of this passage in Suicer T Ecc in v ἄλογον

12 Equus Asinus, γάδαρος, γάδαρο, or ἀγίδαρος.   On consulting Du Cange we find the word explained in the following manner, ἀγίδαρος, " Asinus, quod semper cædatur," p 29 , and reference is given to the authorities whence this etymology is taken   It is needless to point out the absurdity of it   We have found no explanation so satisfactory as that which is given by Reinesius, Var Lec Lpil ad Lect   ' καλεῖ νῆσο, πλησίον Κρῆτης, ἔνθα μέγιστοι ὄναγροι γίνονται "   Suidas   Γάδαρος, therefore, in the abusive language of the mob of Constantinople, who applied it to one of their Emperors, means γαῦδόν, L Gaudo allatus asinus   Procopius says in his anecdotes, that Justinian was called Γάδαρος   Jortin Ecc Hist iv 347   The origin of the Greek name of the pheasant, φασιανός, as derived from Phasis, will occur to the reader

Found in Greece		Names in parts of Greece
20. C. Aureus	τζίαρι	
21. Phoca Vitulina	σάζια.	Id. in Thessal
22. Vespertilio Rupestris	νττερίδα.	Id. in Thessal
23. Felis Lynx	λύττος.	Id. in Thessal.
24. Felis Catus sylv.	ἀγριόγαττος.	Id. in Thessal
25. Mustela Martes	ασι ίζι.	Id. in Thessal.
26. M. Lutra	σκυλοπόταμος	βίδρα in Thessal
27. Ursus Arctos	ἀρκούδι.	
28. U. Meles	ἀσβός.	Id. in Thessal
29. Talpa Europæa	τυφλοποντίκος	Id
30. Sus Scropa dom.	γουρούνι.	Id. in Thessal
31. Sorex Europæus	ποντικ της γης.	
32. Lepus Cuniculus	λαγός.	Id. in Thessal
33. Sciurus Glis	σκίουρος	
34. Cervus Elaphus	λάφι.	λαφού in Thessal
35. C. Capreolus	ζαρκάδι.	Id. in Thessal.
36. Bos Bubalus	βουβάλι.	

Notes by the Editor

21. Phoca Vitulina, the φώκη of Aristotle and Oppian — Pennant, B Z ii.

26. Mustela Lutra, the ένυδρίς of the ancient Greeks, as is evident from the Mosaic of Præneste. "The λάταξ of Aristotle, lib viii. c 5 (says Pennant), is possibly a huge variety of otter." B Z ii. One of the Roman names of the otter, βίδρα, is very similar to the Polish Wydra.

28. Ursus Meles. "The badger (says Buffon) was not known to the Greeks, and is not mentioned by Aristotle. Le blaireau n'a pas même de nom dans la langue Grecque. This species of quadruped, an original native of the temperate climates of Europe, has never spread beyond Spain, France, Italy, Germany, Britain, Poland, Sweden." Badgers' skins are mentioned in the Pentateuch, and it was not only seen in Thessaly and other parts of Greece by Dr Sibthorp, but Mr Hawkins found it in Crete, where it bears also the name ασβός. As we now know to what animal this Greek word is applied, we may explain Du Cange in v. Ἀσβός, p 137. "Animal Trebisio incognitum," he says.

35. Cervus Capreolus, ζαρκάδι, corrupted from the ancient δορκάς, the Caprea of Pliny.

36. Bos Bubalus, "unknown to the Greeks and Romans, the bubalus of the ancients is a different animal" — Buffon.

M M 2

Found in Greece

37. Mus Terrestris   ποντικός.
38. Delphinus Del-   δελφὶν τῆς γῆς.
    phus

In Thessaly.

39. Mustela Putorius βρομοκουνάδι.
40. M. Nivalis   νυμφίτζα.
41. Sus Scrofa sylv. ἀγριογούρουνι.
42. Delphinus Pho-   δελφίς.
    cæna

AMPHIBIA REPTILIA.

Found in Cyprus		*Names in Greece*
1. Testudo Caretta	χελούνη τῆς θαλάσσης.	Id
2. Rana Temporaria	βάτραχος.	Id.
3. R. Bufo	Id.	Id.
4. R. Rubeta	Id.	Id.
5. Lacerta Cordylus	Κουρκώτας	
6. L. Stellio	Id	
7. L. Mauritanica	μεχάρους.	
8. L. Turcica		
9. L. Agilis	χιλεστρούκα.	μελινούρα.
10. L. Chameleon	χαμαιλέων.	
11. L. Chalcides		

Found in Greece

12 Testudo Lutaria	χελώνη τοῦ ποτάμου.	χελώνη τοῦ νεροῦ at Athos.
13. Testudo Græca	χ. τῆς γῆς.	Id.

Notes by the Editor.

13 Testudo Græca This is preferred as more wholesome than the T. Lutaria, the river tortoise, which is sometimes, though rarely, eaten by the Greeks. — Russell's Aleppo,
II 22

Found in Greece		*Names in Greece*
14. T. Compressa	Id.	
15. Rana Esculenta	βάθραχος	Id
16. Lacerta Aurea	καλοττάυρος	κουστερίτζα.
17. L. Uligenosa	Id.	
18. L. Delphica	σκουτουρίτζα.	

In Thessaly

19. Rana Arborea	βάτραχος

AMPHIBIA SERPENTES.

1. Coluber	κούφη.
2. ———	θηριομαύρο.
3. ———	οχενδρα.
4. ———	δρώπις.
5. ———	δισάστριχ.
6. ———	νεροφίδι

Found in Greece.

7. Coluber Astroites	αστρόιτις.
8. C. Sagitta	σαίττα.
9. C. Tuphlitis	τυφλίτις
10. C. Aparcia	απαρήα.
11. C. Dracoulia	δρακουλίο
12. C. Vittatus	λωρίτις.
13. C. Undulatus	
14. C. Parnassi	
15. Anguis Elios	ήλιος.

Notes by the Editor.

3. οχενδρα. Belon mentions the oplus, ochendra, and tuphloti, lib. 1 c 18. In Lemnos he found the cenchrity, laphiati, ochendra, sagittari, tuphlini, nerophidia.

16. Anguis Elios   δενδρακώλια.
17. ————————   πο.διλόλογος.
18. ————————   σαμάμη

PISCES

Chondropterygii

1. Raia Torpedo   μαργοτήρα.
2. R. Batis   βατί.
3. R. Oxyrinchus   βατίς.
4. Squalus Centrina   γουρουνιόψαρε.
5. Squalus Squatina   χελάρι
6. Squalus Catulus   σκυλόψ.ρο.
7. S. Mustelus   γαττόψαρο
8. Acipenser Sturio   μουρούνα.

Branchiostegi

9 Lophius Piscatorius   βατραχόψαρε.
10. Sygnathus Hippo-   άλογο τῆς θαλάσσις
    campus

Apodes

11. Muræna Anguilla   ἀχέλι

Notes by the Editor

1 μουδιάστρα in Forskal, from μουδιάζειν, *torpere*   See Du C in v
2. In another part of the journals, called ῥίνα
4. The κεντρίνη of the ancients   The Italian name " Pesce Porco" expresses the same meaning as the Romaic.
6 Dog-fish   The squalus catulus, scomber pelamis, esox belone, percalabrax, and mullus barbatus, were seen by Sonnini off the coast of Egypt
8. στυριωνι in another part of the journals.
9. Frog-fish   The βατραχος and Rana of the ancients. — Pennant, B. Z. iii.
10 Cavallo Marino of the Italians

Found in Thessaly

12. M Conger   μοῦγγρι.
13. Xiphias Gladius   ξιφίας

Jugulares

14 Uranoscopus Scaber   λύχνος.
15. Trachinus Draco   δραχίνα
16. Gadus Merlucius   βλάχος
17. Blennius Pholis   γλιδι.

Thoracici

18. Coryphæna Novacula
19. Gobius Niger   γαβιος
20. G. Iozo   γοβϊοι
21. Scorpæna Porcus   σκορπίνα
22. Zeus Faber   χριστόψαρο
23. Pleuronectes Solea   γλῶσσα
24. P. Flesus   τίσι.
25. P. Rhombus   ρόμβο
26. Sparus Sargus   σαργός.
27. S. Melanurus   μελάνουρος
28. S. Smaris   σμαρίδι.

Notes by the Editor.

12 γόγγρο. of the ancients this reading, says Schneider, is preferable to that of κόγγρο.

14 The same name is given in Forskal, it corresponds with the Lucerna of the Venetians

19 The καβίς of Aristotle, lib. ii c 17

21. The same in Forskal, it is the skorpit balluk, of the Turks

22 " Christ's Fish," in Italian, the Dorec is called Pesce San Pietro.

23 Pleuronectes, S γλῶσσα, corrupted from the βούγλωσσος. of the ancients

26 ἀτκαθάρο· in Forskal

28 σμαρίς of Aristotle, lib. viii c 30. II, A.

Found in Thessaly.

29. S. Mæna — μανάδα.
30. S. Erythrinus — ἐρυθρίνον
31. S. Boops — βοῦπα.
32. S. Cantharus
33 S. Chromis — χρομιδόψαρς.
34. S. Salpa — σάλπα.
35. S. Dentex — συναγρίδα.
36. S. Mormyrus — μορμόυρος.
37. Labrus Scarus — σκάρος.
38. L. Cretensis — ηλις.
39. L. Anthias — χάννος
40. L. Iulis — ηλιος
41. L. Merula — λαπίνα.
42. L. Turdus — λαπίνα
43. Sciæna Umbra — σκίαινα.
44. S. Cirrhosa — μελοκόπχ.
45. Perca Labrax — λαβράκι.
46. P. Marina — πέρκη.
47. Scomber Pelamis — παλαμίτις.
48. Scomber Trachurus — τραχοῦρι.
49. Mullus Barbatus — τρίγλα.
50. Trigla Cucullus — πετειόψαρο
51. T. Lucerna — ὀρνιθόψαρο

Notes by the Editor.

29. σερθυλα in Forskal.
30. In other parts of the journals, μυρσάνι.
32. Called by Forskal βοῦπα.
33 Called also χαλγερα
36 μουρμους of Forskal.
40. ἠλιοψαρο, also
47. παλαμίδα in Forskal, πηλαμὺς of the ancients.
48. Called also σταυρίδι by Dr S and by Forskal
49 βαρβούνι in Forskal, γνειῆτις τρίγλη of Eratosthenes, lib vii., Athenæ. c. 21.
50. In another part, called χελιδωνόψαρι, κόκκυξ of the ancients.
51. Gallina of the Marseillois.

Abdominales.

52	Silurus Glanis	γλάνι
53.	Esox Belone	βελονί.
54.	Esox Sphyraena	σφίρνα.
55	Atherina Hepsetus	ἀθερίνα
56.	Mugil Cephalus	κέφαλος.
57.	Clupea Alosa	θρίσσα.
58	C. Encrasicolus	χάμψι.
59.	Cyprinus Carpio	γριβάϊ

August 18.—Went to Ourangick, which is about an hour's distance from Salonica. The environs appeared more pleasant than the general scenery of Greece, and presented a cultivated corn country rising into small hills; the vales were watered by rivulets running through beds of argillaceous slate, and were planted with cotton and melon grounds. At this place are the different villas of the European merchants. From the hill above Ourangick, the view extended over a large tract of country, part of the ancient Macedonia; on one side was a plain, with the lakes of Yabasil and Beshik Seir; beyond the gulf of Salonica, was Olympus on the opposite coast of Thessaly.

Notes by the Editor

54 Caught near Smyrna and Mytilene — Belon, p. 5

55 Goumish-balluk of the Turks.

56 Called Kephal-balluk by the Turks

57. σαρδέλλα in Forskal

58. ἐγκρασίχολοι, anchoiæ, ut placet doctos, Insubrium et Massiliensium Cas ad Ath. lib vii p 301.

59. The carp is called in Ætolia, says Belon, *Cyprinus*, and Gyllius remarks, that the word is used by some of the Greeks. Beckmann, iii. 145 Norden saw it caught near Assouan in Egypt The Turks call it Sassan-balluk

N N

August 20. — Early in the morning we set out for Courtiatch, a low wooded mountain, about two hours distant from Ourangick. We left our horses at a village at the foot of it and walked to the summit. Courtiatch appeared to me a hill after the high mountains we had lately seen in Greece. We observed ice prepared in pits much below the summit, covered with dead leaves [*]

23 — Set out on an excursion to a large lake called Beshik Sen Gul by the Turks, and Robios by the Greeks, twelve hours distant from Salonica After riding two hours through a cultivated corn country, we descended into a low plain covered with marsh plants, here and there cultivated with spots of cotton and sesamum, mixed with melon beds We dined in a thick grove of oaks about three hours distant from Salonica On leaving the grove we came soon to the Lake Yabasil, rode by the side of it for two hours, then over a tract of corn land to the head of Beshik Sen Gul; we continued our journey four hours by the side of the lake, low mountains covered with wood were on the left. We arrived late in the evening at Beshik Seir, at the house of Osman Moolah, a Turk, who kept a coffee-shop.

24. — Rose in the morning early to fish. The Lake Beshik Seir Gul [†] is of very considerable extent, it is five hours in length and one in breadth, and twelve in circumference, and has several villages on its banks. The peasants were busily employed in the harvest, and we with difficulty procured horses to draw a much rent and torn drag-net. The names of seventeen different sorts of fish were obtained from Osman, of these we caught the first eleven.

1 Muraena Anguilla   Ἀχέλι.
2. Esox Lucius   Τοῦρνα.

---

[*] Ancient writers (says Beckmann, 3d vol II I) mention the custom of preserving snow in pits with branches of trees over it Athen Deip in Plutarch also, in Sympos. ii 2, speaks of chaff, and muffled or coarse cloth as employed for this purpose

[†] This is the Lake Bolbe, Βόλβη, θάλασσαν, Thucy iv 103 Belon, in going from Sideroccapsa to Cavalla, passed the stream which runs from Beshik towards the sea

3	Perca Fluviatilis	Πέρκη
4	Cyprinus Carpio	Γριβάδ.
5	Cyprinus Platanus	Πλατάνει.
6.	Cyprinus Alburnus	Σίρκα
7	Cyprinus	Σζουρνουκει.
8	Cyprinus Orfus	Id.
9	Cypr Liparis	Λιπάρε.
10.	Cypr. Minutus	Βατοῦσκα
11.	Blennius Lacustris	Γωβίδ..
12.	Silurus Glanis	Γουλιανός.
13.	—————— ——	Μαυρόψαρο.
14.	—————— ——	Μαυρογλιανός
15	—————— ——	Πλινάρι.
16.	—————— ——	Κέφαλος.
17.	—————— ——	Ρεσπώρι. *

25.—Left Beshik Seu three hours before day; and dined on the banks of the Yabasil. Different grallæ frequent this lake in winter; some yet remained; the lap-wing, the red-shank, the large grey heron and sea swallow flew along the water. We shot one which I took to be the Sterna nævia of Linnæus, and a beautiful species of a small white heron. We killed also a large black hawk, probably the moor buzzard. We observed two sorts of vulture soaring high above us, and a large falcon, that I take to be the bald buzzard.

_____

* Some of these fishes are mentioned by Belon as found in the Lake Beshik; "perchi, plesti, platanes, lipares, turnes, grivadi, schella, schurnucca, posustaria, cheronia, claria, glanos" p 52

ON THE

VARIOUS MODES OF FISHING PRACTISED BY THE MODERN GREEKS

[BY THE EDITOR]

THE modern Greeks retain with little variation some of the modes
adopted by the ancient inhabitants of their country in catching
different kinds of fish. The Scarus * we are told, was taken by the
Λαιιοζοsτις, and Dr. Sibthorp informs us that *Mercurialis annua* is
now used by the fishermen off the coast of Cyprus for the purpose
of catching the Labrus Scarus. The plant is called σκαρόχορτο and
σκαρολάχανα, and thrown in quantity among the rocks.

The Kuluriotes, Albanian inhabitants of Salamis, Mr. Hawkins
observes, are much employed in the summer months with the fishing
of Octopodia, which they take with spears affixed to poles 36 feet in
length, the surface of the water being previously smoothed with † oil
They also practise a singular method of catching the rock fish by
poisoning or intoxicating them. For this purpose they make use of
Φλόμο or Tree Euphorbia chopped and macerated, and then pushed
under the large stones or holes and caverns where these fishes lie.
After a few minutes they rise to the surface of the water, and are
either enclosed in small nets or are even taken by the hand.   Mr H.
also points out a passage in Aristotle's H. An. l. viii. 20., where mention
is made of the use of φλόμος or πλόμος in catching fish.   Schneider in
his commentary refers to Ælian, who speaks of the leaves and seeds

---

* See Belon, lib i c 8 on the mode of catching the Scarus off the coast of Crete.

† The sponge gatherers also were observed by Dr Sibthorp to throw oil upon the sea,
he saw them in their boats off the Thracian Chersonesus.   Mare commotum, si aspergatur oleo, quiescit, ut docemur ab Aristotele et Plutarcho Casaub in Athen p. 318.; add
also Pliny, Mare omne oleo tranquillatur.   Allatius mentions a dissertation of M Psellus,
entitled, διατὶ τῆς θαλασση, ἐλαίω καταρραινομένης γίνεται καταφάνεια και γαλήνη.

of the plant as being used for the same purpose. κάρυα φλόμου, where the word κάρυα, Mr. H observes, applies very well to the seeds of the tree Euphorbia.

Dioscorides' lib. iv. c 166. mentions seven different species of Tithymalus used to destroy fish, and at the present day the fishermen on the coast of Elis throw into the water the root of Tithymal which intoxicates the fish; taken in this manner, they become putrid, although salt is applied to them. (Pouqueville.) This plant is probably the Euphorbia Characias†, which according to Dr. Sibthorp is employed for the same purpose, and is now called τιθύμαλο, as well as φλόμο The latter name is also given to Verbascum sinuatum, which is used at Constantinople and Zante to catch different kinds of fish. The adjective φλομομένο is found in a Romaic poem quoted by Du Cange‡, ἐσυγκάσ ες τὸ πέλαγος σὰν φλομομένο ψάρ, "and he came up on the sea like an intoxicated fish." *Conium maculatum* is also used by the fishermen in some parts of Greece, (Sibthorp,) and the Octopodia are driven from their holes by the pounded root of κυκλαμίδα, *Cyclamen persicum*. (id.) Oppian in his Αλ iv 659., mentions the use of κυκλάμινον.§ The trout in one of the streams of Laconia are caught, Dr. Sibthorp says, with Cocculus Indicus , which is called ψαρόβοτάνι and is sold in the bazar of Tripolizza. He has also observed that the fish caught in these various manners soon become putrid Ἡ διὰ τῶν φαρμάκων θήρα ταχὺ μὲν αἱρεῖ καὶ λαμβάνει ῥαδίως τόν ἰχθὺ, ἄβρωτον δὲ τοιεῖ καὶ φαῦλον.‖ Plutarch, Conjug. Præc.

---

* See his remark περὶ Πλατυφύλλου

† Euphorbia Characias, is χαραχίας of Diosc , and τιθύμαλο of Hippoc. Verbascum sinuatum is φλόμος ἄρρην of Diosc. — Sprengel.

‡ See Du Cange in v Εὐγκάνειν.

§ Pliny speaks of a species of Cyclamen employed to kill fish (the plant was called ἰχθυόθηρο ,), lib xxv c 9 and of a species of aristolochia, used by the fishermen of Campania for the same purpose Lib. xxv. c 8.

‖ In the Red Sea the Symm El horat, *venenum piscium*, placed by Forskal among the Plantæ indeterminatæ, is used; the fishes stupefied by it, rise up, and float upon the water.

The night-fishing of the modern Greeks is similar to that of the ancients. Branches of pine, or pieces of wood steeped in pitch and lighted, or horn-lanterns with lamps in them were placed at the extremity of a boat to attract the fish. A fisherman in one of the old comedies speaks of κερατίνου τε φωσφόρου λύχνου σέλας.

The night-fishing is also mentioned by Plato, (Sophist.) and there are some verses in Oppian (Αλ l. ult.) on the same subject. At this day the inhabitants of Amorgos break pieces of the cyprus leaved cedar (cedrus folio cupressi major, Tournef. Letter vi.), and lay it over the stern of the boat at night and burn it; the fishes drawn by the light are struck with a trident.

Mr. Stanhope informs us, that there are four modes of fishing employed by the modern Greeks, 1. by beating the water and driving the fish within the nets; 2. by fire; this is lighted during the night upon a vessel, and is called περιφάνεος; the fish assemble round it, 3. by means of oil which is poured upon the sea to render it more calm; the fishermen are thus enabled to discern the fish and to spear them, 4. by means of φλόμος, great Tithymal; the water is dammed up, and some of the herb thrown in; the fish become intoxicated and float on the surface, and are easily taken by the hand. For want of phlomos, aconitum is used for the same purpose.

EXTRACTS FROM DR. SIBTHORP'S JOURNALS

SEPT. 16.—We rowed out from the coast of the Thracian Chersonesus to some small boats; the men in them were employed in searching for sponges, each of the boats had two men at least, one rowed, the other was furnished with an oil cruet and a sharp prong, with the one he smoothed the surface of the water to render the objects at the bottom more visible, with the other he reached the sponge, and took it from the rock. Most of the boats had made large captures, and were going on to Constantinople.   The sponge, when dry, was sold at three piastres the oke.   On looking among the sponges I observed some marine productions, of these the most common was a species of Star fish with five echinated radii; the prickles easily rubbed off, and the whole animal was very fragile our sailors called it Stavros. Besides these were a marine worm, σκώληκα τῆς ζωνάτης, a sea-louse, ψῆρα τοῦ ψαρίου, four sorts of small crabs, one very hairy, καβουρνάκι, a sort of shrimp, καρίδα, a third sort called τζίρα, a fourth, very small, the name of which I could not learn.   The Thracian coast afforded a few shells; the Greek limpet, perforated at the apex, called πεταλίδα, the periwinkle κογγίλι, the esculent cockle, βολβιχίνα, and the mactra stultorum, ἀχιβάδα.   The sponge gatherers had taken two sorts of fish with their spears, μελάνουρι and σαργὸ; and our own boatmen added three more to my list, πέρκα, σκάρο, and σκάδαρι, the latter is a scarce fish.

LEMNOS

The water under the rock was extremely clear and offered to the view a number of marine productions.   I saw distinctly several species of Medusa rolling themselves out with a flower-like appearance, and a very pretty Tubularia of a green colour, which looked like an Opuntia, or articulated Cactus was fixed by its base to some sponges.   The Alva pavonia was very common, and the little red Coralline covered the surface of the rock that was under the water, while the upper surface exposed to the air was encrusted with Barnacles, and two or three sorts of vermicular Serpulae.   I saw the Alcedo Ispida flying along the coast, this then is a marine as well as a river bird.   During our absence on shore, our sailors had caught a great quantity of fish, particularly of the sea perch [*], one of the best flavoured fish of the Archipelago; they had also taken some beautiful species of Labri, the Iulis called Πλία,

---

[*] Perca marina commendatur à Galeno   Vide Voss. de Idolo. lib. iv 506.

another species nearly equal in beauty, the labrus tri-maculatus of
Pennant, with a great number of χάνι

The Mousselim of Lemnos being informed that the celebrated
Lemnian earth was one of the objects of our inquiries, ordered a
number of the rolls or seals of that earth to be presented to us; he
told us, that the pit whence this earth was taken, was opened only
on the 16th day of August; that it was in great repute in curing
certain fevers; and that the earth only which was dug out before the
rising of the sun was considered as possessing any medical efficacy.
Expressing a wish to see the place where the earth was dug, he
granted us his permission.

We were invited to walk in his garden; a large square piece of
ground enclosed by four walls, it was well planted with fruit trees
and culinary herbs.   The orange trees, notwithstanding the warm
climate of Lemnos, were placed under artificial shelter   Quinces
and Pomegranates formed a principal portion of the fruit trees; the
former is a favourite tree with the Turks; and they prepare a number
of excellent dishes from its fruit.

No shores of the Levant are more productive of fish than those
of Lemnos, and we found a great variety which our servants had
purchased for dinner.   Besides the red-mullet, βαρβούνι, the grey
mullet κέφαλος, there were several excellent species of Sparus; as
the Dentex, συναγρίδα, the Salpa, σάρπα, the Melanurus, μελάνουρο, the
Sargus, σαργός, the Scorpion fish, σκορπίνα, the Sciæna umbra, a sort of
Labrus, and the shad, σταυρίδι; our cabin boys had caught, angling,
as the vessel lay in port, some little fishes, as the S. Mormyrus μόρμυρο,
a sort of Blenny φκούζα, and a small species of Gobius.

Sept. 21.—At four in the afternoon the horses arrived.   In our way
to Thermia we met with several villagers with their asses laden with
fruit.   The wine of Lemnos is cheap, but rough, and badly made.
We observed a custom that must be very prejudicial to the vine, that
of turning the goats and sheep into the vineyards as soon as the
grapes are gathered. the dry season, which this year had burnt up

the vegetation, might perhaps have induced them to try the experiment. I never saw a greater diversity of melons than in the villa of the Mousselim, they were suspended in lines along the roof of the chamber where we slept.

Sept. 22. — In the morning we walked up the mountain of St. Elias, the highest in the island; from the summit we commanded an extensive view of the country. Between the hills there was a large proportion of flat ground fit for cultivation, but the isle of Lemnos was visibly on the decline; its towns had decreased in number, and those remaining were daily going to a state of decay. Of the seventy-five towns which it contained in the time of Belon, scarcely half the number can be found. The residence of the Turks, the exaction of the new charatch, without any additional advantages from manufactures or commerce, are the evident causes of this decay. We traversed the plain of Livado-chorio, and slept at the house of the Soubashi of Baros, the miserable remains of a decayed village consisting of about fifteen houses, the inhabitants supported themselves from the flocks of goats and sheep, which scarcely enabled them to pay the charatch. The latter are a small hornless breed, frequently black, and produce a very coarse wool; a sheep was not estimated at more than sixty paras or two piasties, the horse which I rode was valued at eighteen piastres.

Sept. 23. — We set out at eight o'clock, and in half an hour arrived at the place where the Lemnian earth was dug from a small pit on a rising ground about a mile from the village. The whole had been filled up, but we observed some of the earth, which was a pale-coloured clay; before it receives the seal, the sand by means of water is filtered from it; it is then formed into figures and some pieces of cylindrical form. We had here an instance how superstition and ceremony had ennobled a thing of little or no value; it could have no real medicinal virtue; and in fevers, where the stomach is weakened, it could add only an additional burden to the peccant matter that oppressed it. We came back to Baros, more disappointed than satisfied at what we had seen. We returned by the same route of Livado-chorio and Thermia to Lemnos, the distance from which to the place where the earth is dug is about twelve miles or four hours. Upon our arrival, we were informed that the Mousselim was gone to inspect a vessel building in the bay, we went in our boat to return him thanks for the civilities which he had shewn us. The ship he was building was one of 50 guns: it had been on the stocks about six weeks; and he said the whole would be complete in six months. It was of Balanida oak, brought from Romelia, and was new and unseasoned. From this cause and other defects, the Turkish ships last but a few years. He would not suffer us to pay for our horses, he said, he was happy in the opportunity of shewing a little civility to foreigners, and did not doubt that he should receive the same if he was in our situation.

EUBŒA.

Oct. 13.—We observed in the market of Egripo, the ripe fruit of the Sorbus domestica, called here αὐγάρια and ὀυβέισι; it is one of those fruits which must be eaten in a state of decay, like the medlar, with which it agrees in flavour. A great number of wasps were collected round the fruit stalks, called Σφηγγίδες, without doubt, the Στρ of the ancients. We picked up several shells on the coast, the Gaideropus, which is here called στρίδα, different species of Murex and Buccinum, Turbo, and the Arca Noæ, and some species of Voluta. The Brain stone and some Madrepores were thrown upon the beach with a prodigious number of Medusæ. We had formerly collected here some crystals of magnetical iron ore; at present we searched in vain without discovering the least traces of it.

Feb. 26, 1795.—We embarked at Zante, and in less than four hours anchored in the harbour of Pyrgo; on the coast of the ancient Elis. We proceeded from our boat along a sandy beach covered with the shells of the Arca glycymeris and Cardium edule, mixed with the spoils of other testacea. About an hour's distance from the landing place approaching the convent we were ferried over a narrow stream, fringed with Agnus castus, into a garden belonging to the convent. A number of vernal flowers now blossomed on its banks, the garden Anemone was crimsoned with an extraordinary glow of colouring. The soil which was a sandy loam was further enlivened with the Ixia, the grass-leaved Iris, and the enamel blue of a species of Speedwell not noticed by the Swedish naturalist.

The Κίσσα of the Ancients.

The lower regions of the Arcadian mountains are covered with oaks, among which are frequently heard the hoarse screams of the Jay, still called Κίσσα. Camus in his translation of Aristotle has wrongly supposed that the Κίσσα was our magpie. These oaks produced the true misletoe of the ancients, that is the Loranthus Europæus, which is still called ὀξὸς*, and from which bird-lime is prepared. Our misletoe grows also in Greece, but is not to be found on the oak but on the silver fir, and abounds on Parnassus, where it is not called ὀξὸς but μέλλα, and is gathered by the herdsmen as food for the labouring oxen. The mountains of Arcadia supply a number of Alpine rivulets abounding in trout, called πιστέολα. Advancing near to Olono, the ancient Cyllene, we observed the Sturnus Cinclus flying along the rocky sides of these rivulets; perhaps this is the " White Blackbird," said by Aristotle H. A. lib. ix. to be found in that region.

The Murex or κάλχη of the Ancients.

At Hermione, once famous for its purple, and where that dye was particularly prepared, I had the good fortune to stumble over a vast pile of those shells, whose fish or animals had been employed for that purpose. I brought away with me a box of these exuviæ†,

---

* Viscum album is called in Lacoma ἰξιόδρυς — Sibthorp

† " They are still denominated Porphyri, the species is Murex Trunculus of Linnæus figured by Fabius Columna, under the name of *Purpura nostras violacea*." From Sir

which will establish beyond doubt, what the shell was, employed by the ancients for that purpose.

The Truffles of Laconia.

April 24th. — At Nisi, in the ancient Laconia, a basket of Truffles was brought in; my host distinguished three sorts, καλαμβοκισιὰ, σταρήσια, and συκαλίσια; the man who brought them, confirmed to me the account, that he had found them with a kind of virga divinatoria, and that by the sound of the earth from the touch of the rod, he had made this collection. I am sorry that circumstances did not admit of my going to this truffle hunt. I was assured that the Truffle * hound was unknown; and that the quantity brought to market is all collected in the manner he described to me.

CYPRUS.

The Ferula, or νάρθηξ of Prometheus.

Near the convent of the Holy Cross I observed the golden Henbane in abundance . and when we had descended, a peasant brought me a pumpkin with water; it was corked with a bush of Poterium Spinosum, which served both as a coverlid and a strainer, and prevented the entrance of flies and other insects It preserves in most of the Greek islands its ancient name Στόιβη. The stools on which we sate were made of the Ferula Græca; the stems cut into slips and placed crossways were nailed together. This is one of the most important plants of the island in respect to its economical uses. The stalks furnish the poorer Cyprian with a great part of his

---

James Smith At the taking of Susa by Alexander a great quantity of Hermione purple was found there Plut in Alex The fishery of the Murex on the coast of Laconia also is mentioned by Pliny, lib ix and Pausan in Lacon. " Blue and purple from the isles of Elisha," are referred to by the Prophet Ezek. xxvii 7 The last words, according to Bochart, designating the Peloponnesus

* A corruption of the ancient Τόνον may be traced in the ῖτνον of the modern Greeks, the name of the Lycoperdon Tuber, ὐλ/α τὰ καὶ ῖτνα ὀνομαζόμενα, Aetius See Du C. II 86

household furniture, and the pith is * used instead of tinder, for conveying fire from one place to another.   It is now called νάρθηκα, the ancient name somewhat corrupted.

Κούρι *of Cyprus.* — An veterum Aspis? †

April 17. — We left the Salines for Famagousta.   The reapers were busy in the harvest, and the tinkling of the bells fixed to their sides expressed their fears of the terrible Κούρι.   A monk of Famagousta has the reputation of preventing the fatal effects of the venom of this serpent by incantation ; and from the credulity of the people had gained a sort of universal credit through the island. We were frequently shewn as precious stones compositions fabricated by artful Jews, these were said to be taken out of the head of the Κούρι; and were worn as amulets to protect the wearers from the bite of venomous animals ‖

---

* " Cet usage est de la première antiquité, et peut servir à expliquer un endroit d'Hesiode, qui parloit du feu que Prométhée vola dans le ciel, dit, qu'il l'emporta dans une Ferule, ἐν κοίλω νάρθηκι E. xai H 52   Suivant les apparences, Prométhée se servit de moelle de Ferule au lieu de mèche, et apprit aux hommes à conserver le feu dans les tiges de cette plante." Tournefort, Lett vi   The following remark of Proclus on Hesiod (24 Ed Heins) may be added, "Εστι μὲν πυρὸς οὕτω φυλακτικὸς ὁ Νάρθηξ, ἡπίαν ἔχων μαλακότητα εἴσω, καὶ τρέφειν τὸ πῦρ, καὶ μὴ ἀποσβεννύναι δυναμένην — Ed.

† This is the Quære of Forskal " The most dangerous of the serpents in Cyprus (says Drummond, who travelled in 1745,) is the asp, the venom of which is said to be very deadly In order to frighten away these and other kinds of poisonous reptiles, the reapers, who are obliged to wear boots, always fix bells to their sickles"   A word resembling Κούρι, and applied to a species of serpent, is found in Ælian, and in Hesychius, χωρία   The latter seems to consider it improperly as the same with τυφλίας   Hasselquist (p 131.) describes a serpent called by the Greeks of Cyprus, Ἀσπις, this may be the Κούρι, and the author of the work De Mu. Aus speaks of a species of serpent in Cyprus, ὁ τὴν δύναμιν ὁμοίαν ἔχει τῇ ἐν Αἰγύπτῳ ἀσπίδι — Ld

‡ The superstition of the ancient Greeks attributed a similar efficacy to the Lapis ophites, θηρία διώκει περιαπτόμενος, says Dioscorides Ἐυπορίστ. Lib. xi. c 141.

Singular custom of making an offering of bread to the fish Melanuros.

May 2.—We weighed anchor in the port of Cephalonia; as our sailors rowed by Cape Capro, they made libations of bread, using the following words; Γιάσου, Κάπο Κάβρο, μὲ τὴ, Κάπο, Καπρένα σου, καὶ μὲ τὰ, Κάπο Κάβρο, πουλάσου. Νὰ Κάβρε, ιὰ καπρένα, νὰ τὰ, Κάπο καπρόπουλα· φάτε τὸ παξιμάδι, ἐσεῖς, ψάρια Μελαιόυρια. "Health, Cape Capro to your wife, to your children; to you Cape Capro, to your wife, (making the first libation). To your children, (making a second). You fish, Melanouros, eat the cake (making a third)." This is probably the relic of some ancient custom *; the passage by the rock was a dangerous navigation, and the fish Melanouros abounds here. †

The liver of the Scarus.

" The liver of the Scarus was not forgotten in the entertainments of the Zantiotes; the flavour and delicacy of it are mentioned in the following Romaic couplet.

Σκάρο μὲ λένε, ψητὸ μέ τρώνε,
Φάγε τὸ σκωτό μου, νὰ ἴδης τὸ φαγητό μο..

" They call me scarus; they eat me roasted; taste my liver that you may see what my flavour is. ‡

---

* This extract from Sibthorp's journal reminds us of a passage in Pliny, lib xxxii. c. 2 " In Stabiano Campaniæ ad Herculis petram, *Melanum in mari panem* abjectum rapiunt "

† Aldrovande croit, que c'est ce même poisson qu'on appelle à Rome, ochiata, en Sicile, ochiada, à Venise, ochia — Memoires de l'Instit. 1805

‡ The roasted Scarus was anciently esteemed, καὶ σκάρος ἐν παράλῳ Καρχηδόνι τὸν μέγαν ὄπτα Πλύνας. Archestrat in Athen lib vii , and the liver of it was particularly commended Unde in Vitellii patina, apud Tranquillum legimus, fuisse *Scarorum jecinora*. Imo Martialis, visceribus solum reservatis, carnem coquo reddi jubet Vossi. de Idolo lib iv. 505 The fish was one of those, according to Epicharmus, τῶν οὐδὲ τὸ σκῶς θεμιτὸν ἐκβαλεῖν θεὸις We give from Salmasius (Plin Exer p. 743), the following explanation of σκατό, or συκωτόν. Graecia infima συκωτὸν pro jecore dixit, quum antiqua jecur anseris aut porculi ficis pasti in deliciis haberet, et sic vocaret; inde recentiores συκωτόν, quodlibet jecur appellârunt, et eos imitati Latini *ficatum*.

Remarks on some of the Greek Serpents.

At Naxia, a species of serpent was killed whose eyes were singularly small; the Greeks called it Tuphlites, from Τυφλὸς; this we were told was a species highly venomous, and that the bite would prove fatal in a few hours. At Patmos, two species were killed; one having the back waved with black on a greyish ground, with a flattened head, appeared to have all the marks of a species highly venomous. The islanders called it ὀφίδ. Another which from its long slender form I judged to be perfectly harmless, they called Σαίττ. or arrow, from the manner in which it shoots or darts itself. We were told of a third species, called ποῤδοκόλογος, this was represented to us as of enormous size. The Aparea is a large serpent; another species which has the head erected, and is called κατζυλάρι, is very venomous.

July 22.—On my return from the Piræus I found a peasant waiting for me with different species of serpents, one small but beautifully waved with red lines, this he called Astroites; another, a very minute sort, a species of Anguis, called Helios; of the last the bite was said to be exceedingly venomous. Its appearance was that of the garden worm; I should, notwithstanding the report, suppose it to be innocent.

ON THE

OLIVES AND VINES OF ZANTE,

ON THE

CORN CULTIVATED IN THAT ISLAND, AND PARTS OF THE ANCIENT BŒOTIA

THE PRODUCE OF CORN IN SOME DISTRICTS OF GREECE

[FROM THE PAPERS OF THE LATE DR SIBTHORP, AND FROM SOME REMARKS
COMMUNICATED BY MR HAWKINS]

Olea Europæa, the olive of Zante, is called ἐντόπια, or natural, the first introduced into this country. It arrives at a large size, and produces a great quantity of oil, one hundred okes from a tree The wood of this variety is also the most durable, and is used for many purposes. The fruit is oval and large, and yields much clear oil.

The second sort, κορονάκι, was introduced from Coron in the Morea into Zante, at the beginning of the eighteenth century; it produces a large quantity of fruit, but the tree is small; the leaves are more attenuated at the point, the wood more fragile, the fruit smaller, the oil coarser, than that of the ἐντόπια. These two sorts are the most cultivated; part of the oil is consumed in the island, the remainder is exported.

A third sort, καρυδολιά, is so called from the large fruit which it produces resembling a walnut; it was introduced from Salona. The tree is small, the wood brittle, the leaves large and white. This variety is cultivated for the table, both ripe and green. To preserve them green and render them less bitter, the olives are taken and put unripe into a lye of lime-ashes and water, and being steeped for some hours, they are then taken out and washed in water. This washing is repeated by a change of the water, twice a-day for a week; they are then put into a pickle made of salt and water, flavoured with the tops of fennel. * To preserve them ripe, they are salted, a layer of salt being put between a layer of olives. Another way of preserving them is with oil and vinegar; a third in syrup or must, called petmez; the must is the juice of the grape boiled before fermentation to the consistence of a syrup; or lastly, simply in salt and water, the usual method adopted by the peasants. The green olives dipped in salt and water, are called κολυμζάδες. †

A fourth sort is Τραγολιά, or the goat olive; this produces very hard fruit, and is little cultivated.

A fifth sort Στραβολιά (crooked) is so called from the fruit, which is long, having the point a little curved. It ripens the latest, and remains longest on the tree; is gathered when quite ripe, and preserved as one of the former.

A sixth sort λημονλιά is termed so from the resemblance of the olive to a lemon, having a nipple-shaped fruit, of the size of a walnut. It is indeed the largest, but is little cultivated, except by some rich proprietors who have a few trees of it. The olive is preserved green

A seventh sort derives its name from the resemblance of the fruit to a hazel-nut, in shape; the skin is thin, and the pulp rich; but little cultivated.

An eighth sort is μοθιά, from Mothone in the Morea, whence it was first introduced. The fruit is either pressed into oil, or preserved ripe.

Another sort is ματσαλιά, from αἷμα blood, because the fruit, when perfectly ripe, being squeezed, gives a red colour to the hands. This is pressed into oil or preserved.

---

* We find mention in the Geoponica, ii. 631 of the μαράθρου κλωνίων, which were sometimes mixed with the olives, and Hermippus (in Athenæ. lib. ii c 47 Schw) says ἐμβάλλουσι μάραθον ἐς τὰς ἀλμάδας

† Olivas fœniculo condire etiamnum apud Græcos solenne est; has fœniculo et muria conditas olivas appellant κολυμβητὰς ἐλαίας, vocabulo paulum deflexo a veterum κολυμβάδε; — Coray in Athen lib. ii c. 47. Schw.

The north wind is considered the most favorable, with dry weather, during the flowering of the olive tree. The fruit is all picked with the hand, and not suffered to fall as in Attica.

Corn.

Hordeum sativum. Two sorts of barley are cultivated at Zante, γυμιοκριθί, and ἀλογοκριθί; the first is so called from being naked or destitute of beards; this is principally used for bread, and that of Galaxithi, a town of Phocis, is the most esteemed. The second sort is so called from being used as the food of horses.

Triticum sativum. The different sorts cultivated in Zante are,

1. γρίνεας. This is principally sown in the mountains, or at the foot of the mountains, as in the plains it is subject to the rust, and to be damaged by the south winds. To prevent its being injured by the heavy dews, two persons taking hold of each end of a long rope * draw it over the field ; by these means the water is shaken out of the husks, and the grain is preserved.

2 Another sort is the ἀσπρογρίνεας, which is also cultivated in similar situations.

3. A third sort is ρούσσιας, which grows principally in the plains, and is less subject to injury from the dews, and has the grain very hard.

4. A fourth sort, μαυρογάνι has a hard heavy grain which is much esteemed, and is sown in the plain.

5. A fifth sort γριμνίτζα is sown both in the plains and mountains ; has the spike compressed and the seeds close

---

* " Some advise, in the morning, after the mildew is fallen, and before the rising of the sun, that two men go at some convenient distance in the furrows, holding a cord stretched between them, carrying it so that it may shake off the dew from the top of the corn, before the heat of the sun hath thickened it "—— Practical Treatise of Husbandry, containing experiments collected by Du Hamel and others, p. 81. Mr Hawkins says, that ξαυλίτις is the name applied to the mildew in corn

A sixth soil, γιαλοσίτι, is like ρούσσιας, but white and shining. It is so called from γιαλίζειν to shine.

A seventh soil is διμηνιό. This is sown in the first part of March, and is a kind of spring corn; they begin sowing the other sort in the mountains in the middle of October, and in the plains in November and December, and even in some strong grounds so late as January. Weeding, νὰ βοτάνιζω, is performed by women, who are paid ten paras a-day for their labour, at least once or twice before the culmus is grown, the καλάμια. This operation is very tedious, being performed by the hand. The harvest begins early in June, first the barley, then the wheat of the mountains, then that of the plain; the return is from five to ten for one. A bacillo of land is sown with a bacillo of corn, a bacillo of land is four hundred square feet; a bacillo of corn weighs seventy pounds of Venetian measure.

BŒOTIA.

The soil of Livadea is much richer than that of Attica, the villages in Bœotia are more numerous, and in general larger; they were said to be at least 70 in number. The soil being moist and rich is not suitable to the olive, but produces wheat of an excellent quality, and great quantity of Calamboki or Indian corn. The following articles are the principal objects of cultivation. Σιτάρι, wheat*, of this there are four sorts, κοκκινοσίτι, μονολόγι, διμηνιό, and βλακοστάρι. The first of these species is the most generally cultivated; the last is sown principally in the mountains.

Αραβοσίτι Indian corn; there are two sorts; ασπροκαλαμβόκι, and κοκκινοκαλαμβόκι.

Βαμβάκι, cotton; there are two sorts, ποτιστικό and τζερικό.

Κριθάρι, barley; Κουκία, beans; Κέγχρι, millet, two sorts, κίτρινε, and

---

* Wheat retains in Laconia its ancient name, πυρό·.

μάυρο; Ρίσι, rice; Ροβίθι *, taics, Βράμι, oats; Βρίσκ, rye, ϙατόυλ, kidney-beans; φάκι; ϙόβ; Βίκια; λαθόυρι; άϙλο; ἀνύζν, anise; ϙουτάμν, Sesamum; κόμινc, cummin.

PRODUCE OF WHEAT IN DIFFERENT DISTRICTS OF GREECE

[FROM MR HAWKINS]

In the plain of Aigos, Mavrogáni (black bearded wheat) in favorable seasons gives ten for one.

In the best part of Megara and Eleusis the same sort of wheat produces in favorable seasons twelve for one.

In the plain of Vocca near Corinth, under the same circumstances, the produce of white wheat, Asprositi, is ten for one, but that of the other sort amounts to fifteen for one.

The kind of wheat called Grimas, in the rich plain of Phoneas (Pheneus in Arcadia) yields in moderately good years twelve for one. In the plains of Milias (Mantinea) and Kandila in Arcadia, where several sorts of wheat are cultivated, the produce in favorable years is twelve for one.

In the plains of Thessaly, the sort called Devedishi, or camel's tooth wheat, here cultivated almost exclusively, produces in moderately favorable years twelve for one, but in extraordinary seasons fifteen for one, and I heard of an instance of eighteen for one.

---

* Ροβι in another part of Sibthorp's journals is applied to Ervum Ervilia, and is cultivated in Cyprus for the use of camels and oxen The word άυχος is found in Du Cange under φασόυλον, perhaps it is the term which Dr S intended to use. In another part of his papers άυχο is Pisum ochrus.

Upon the mountains of Greece, the coarse sort of wheat called Vlaccostari sown on newly cleared grounds, well manured with the ashes of the plants that grew thereon, produces from twelve to twenty for one. But the greatest produce that I have heard of was an instance of wheat sown in the marshes of Topolias (Copais) in Bœotia, when the waters had retired after a similar manuring with the ashes of aquatic plants. These results however only shew what the productiveness of wheat may be under some very singular circumstances, and are by no means to be taken into general account. Upon the whole, therefore, I am disposed to estimate the produce of good soils in Greece, in favorable seasons at from ten to twelve for one, and in the very best soils, and remarkably favorable years at from fifteen to eighteen for one. It must be observed that the wheat in Greece is generally sown in unmanured ground.

ON THE DIFFERENT SPECIES OF VINE CULTIVATED IN ZANTE.

[SIBTHORP'S MSS.]

VITIS vinifera, Ἀγουστιάτης or μαυροδάφνη, of a black colour, much esteemed for the table, and makes the best wine; is cultivated in a dry soil.

2. Philaro, the fruit large, of a pale red colour, frequently of a musky smell; cultivated in the richer and moister soils of the plain.

3. Agoustolidi, a small white grape which ripens in August, and makes a sweet wine.

4. Aspiorompola, La Malvasia of Venice, a yellowish white grape, larger than the Agoustolidi; as the plant advances in age, the fruit becomes smaller, when it is much esteemed for the λιανορώγι wine, so called from λιανὸς *small*, and ῥῶγα.

The quantity of this wine is not great, and the grapes of the Agoustolidi being strewed upon the floor, and exposed to the sun are made into a wine which is sold for the Lianotogi. This vine is at present little cultivated. Previously to making the wine, the grape after being gathered is exposed to the sun, and the Rompola being a small grape is soon dried

5. Maviorompola; the racemus is remarkably close and compact, and the grape black and sweet; it makes an excellent wine, and is cultivated in a dry mountainous soil.

6. Kakotrygi or Lianovirgi; the first name is given, because the racemi are not easily gathered, and they are obliged to be cut by the pruning knife; the second name is given on account of the slender twigs. It produces a black grape with a rough sweetish taste.

7. Kondocladi, produces a large white grape; so called from its being pruned close, or *near*, κοντά, and κλαϊεύω to *prune*. The wine is strong, dry, and white.

8. Coucouliatis, an oblong grape terminating in a point; makes a white wine.

9. Chlora, produces a pale green grape, whence its name, the wine made from it is of a greenish tint. The fruit is principally cultivated for the table.

10. Petzirompola, produces a white grape with a tough skin (πετζι pellis.) It is little cultivated.

11. Papadia, a white grape somewhat flattened in its figure.

12. Tinactorogi; a white grape, so called from the grapes being easily shaken out; it is little cultivated.

13. Polypodaro, a white grape, the fruit is supported on stalks, wide from each other.

14. Τὸ κλῆμα τοῦ Βόζου The vine of the family of Bozo; a white grape; not much esteemed for the table; it makes a good wine.

15. Τὸ κλῆμα τοῦ Παύλου, a very large white grape which has been lately cultivated.

16. Kozanitis, a white firm grape, which makes a strong wine of a yellow colour, with a fragrant vinous smell; it is cultivated in

dry meagre land, and is peculiar to the island. Mixed with the Agoustiates, it keeps to a great age.

17. Mavrophilato is of a deep red colour, and makes an ordinary wine.

18. Βοιδομάτι is a large black grape.

19. Γλυκερίδα a white sweet one.

20. Laidera, of a reddish brown colour, and grows well, when planted in the shade.

21. Αμυγδάλη, of an almond shape; it is white, and is kept for the table for winter.

22. Ροιδίτις has the colour of a pomegranate, and makes an excellent clear coloured wine, and is a good table fruit.

23. Glycopati, a delicate small grape, of a reddish brown colour.

24 Asproglycopati, the same kind, of a white colour.

25. Μοσχάτε, both white and black; very sweet, and makes a rich wine much esteemed;

26. Ampelocorytho; a large white grape, so called from being trained on the espalier; it makes a good wine and is much esteemed for the table, it preserves well as a dry fruit, and is equal, if not superior, to that of Smyrna.

27. Scylopmetes, a wild vine, which produces a white grape, with an austere taste.

28. Maromtes, a large white grape; little cultivated.

29. Ἀετόνυχ, *Eagle's claw*, a large white grape; esteemed for the table.

30. Τοῦ κοκόρου τ'ἀρχίδια, a large white grape, is trained on the espalier, and is esteemed at the table.

31. Xnichi aspro, a large white grape; an inch and a half long, in great bunches of a foot and a half in length. It is trained on the espalier, and is much esteemed at table.

32. Xnichi mavro, of the same sort, of a black colour, with a still larger grape.

33. Τὸ κλῆμα τοῦ ραδικολόγου, like the last, but firmer, and of a red colour.

34. Μοσχάτο τῆς Λαρίσσης, a large white grape of a sweet musky flavour, esteemed as a table fruit.

35. Πετροκόρυθ, a red grape which keeps well, and is the last gathered , its name is probably derived from its hardness.

36. Ροζάκια, a red grape of two sorts, one oblong, the other round.

37. Ροζάκια ἄσπρα, a white grape; the sort cultivated in Smyrna for exportation under the name of Smyrna raisins.

38. Ἑπτάκοιλος, much esteemed for the table , the vine continues to ripen its fruit through the autumn In marriage ceremonies the stem of this vine is selected for the matrimonial crown, and care is taken to choose a rod of it that has forty knots or nodi, κόμποι; this is indicative of the proliferous quality of the grape, which is to be communicated to the bride.

39. Τὸ σταφύλι τῆς Ἱερουσαλὴμ, a black grape that preserves well ; has a hard seed, and a very large fruit; it is so called from its supposed resemblance to the grape found by the Jews in the land of promise.

Vitis Corinthiaca Σταφύλα; a small black grape; the famous Corinthian grape, is the principal produce of the island, the quantity produced may be computed at six millions of pounds , sometimes at more.   They are sold by a thousand weight ; the price at present is eighteen sequins of Venice , and the total produce is estimated at 54,000l sterling.   This is the most important object of cultivation in the island.   The vine continues to produce for a very long period.   The quantity of fruit in Cephallonia amounts to three millions and a half of pounds; in Ithaca to half a million ; in Turkey to six millions.   The places, in Turkey, where the fruit grows are, in the Morea, at Patras, Vostizza, Xylocastro, Camari ; in Romelia, at Lepanto, Messalungia, Natolico.   Of the whole produce

England takes twelve millions. A deep rich soil is the most proper for the cultivation of it at the root of the mountains, when the soil is irrigated and drenched by the waters which flow down from them, in the first rains that fall in October. A baccillo of tolerably good land will give, *communibus annis*, 1000 weight of currants; the poorer land, not yielding so much; the richer land more. Different attempts have been made at Corfou and Sta. Maura to introduce this grape; but such is the delicacy of it, that it will not succeed. It is eaten at the table, and makes a rich sweet wine.

REMARKS

ON

PARTS OF BŒOTIA AND PHOCIS

[FROM THE JOURNALS OF MR RAIKES]

March 5.—A ride of five hours and a half over a dull and uninteresting country, bare of wood and imperfectly cultivated, brought
me from Thebes to Negropont, which I reached at five P. M., just
before the gates were closed. The name of this place I believe was
formed from the Euripus, on which it is situated; the later Greeks,
dropping the ancient name of Chalcis, called it Egripo, by an easy
corruption from the Euripus, pronounced by them Eurïpo ; the Venetians by softening the Greek word to a sound more familiar to
their own ears, made the present name of Negropont.

The first view of the city from the hills to the westward on the
road from Thebes, is perhaps the most striking of the kind I have
seen in Greece. The double sea winding out of sight, and expand-
ing in surface on either side, the town itself surrounded by lofty walls
and towers, rising from the water, and sheltered behind by the mountains of Eubœa, which ranged along the horizon covered with snow,
formed altogether a glorious picture. Every requisite for the prosperity of a city seemed combined in the view ; advantages for commerce, strength, healthiness, all appeared to belong to the situation.
It looked dull, however, notwithstanding these advantages. No inhabitants were moving in the suburbs, not a single vessel was in the
ports ; an air of gloom and depopulation was spread over the whole
Our road descending towards the sea, passed at the foot of a hill to its
left, on which some Venetian fortifications, probably raised to defend
the approach to the bridge still remain, and are garrisoned by the

Turks. I crossed the Euripus by an old and heavy bridge of three arches, under two of which are mills worked by the current, and entered the town by a gateway between two towers.

The houses are almost universally built by the Venetians, and with a sort of gloomy solidity very different from later Turkish buildings. The streets are narrow and dark. The Turks, indeed, have made very little alteration in the town, which is filled with mementos of its Venetian possessors. The Lion of St. Mark retains his place on the gateways; and carvings of coats of arms are to be seen over the doors of some of the principal houses. Two distinguishing traits of their national character, their pride and their indolence, render them averse from abolishing these recollections of their predecessors. The first division of the city is entirely inhabited by the Turks, the Greeks and the Jews, who abound in Negropont, reside in a large suburb, separated from the town by the wall, and a broad space used as a burying-ground. In this suburb is the bazar, and the house of the Russian Consul, to whom I was recommended.

In a place which has so long been the capital of a Venetian or Turkish province, antiquities are not likely to have remained. A large subterraneous building, in which a silk manufactory is carried on, is the only object in the town bearing a date beyond the time of its modern possessors. It is vaulted with very solid masonry, and appears to be a work of the Roman empire. A large Gothic church, which burst upon me most unexpectedly, with its high roof and square tower, awakened much warmer feelings by the recollection it inspired of similar buildings in England, and by its contrast with the wretched sameness of the round-ended Greek chapels. In style of building it resembles the later Gothic churches which occur in our large towns; and is still used for divine service.

The fortifications of Negropont on the land side consist of a wall with square towers, and a shallow trench; beyond the suburb, lines are thrown up which extend from sea to sea. The same wall and towers are carried round the side of the city, which is washed by the sea, and a few small guns are mounted on it. One immense gun, haidly inferior in size to those at the Daidanelles, projects fiom a sort of gateway, not much above the level of the water, and threatens destruction to all shipping which should appioach from the southwaid.

The next moining I iode beyond the suburb into Euboea, to visit a place which had been desciibed to me as a subterraneous chuich. I descended into it by a hollow passage, wet, and not moie than three feet high, which terminated in one of those conical cisteins oi magazines which aie to be seen on the iock of the Piraeus and on the hill above Eleusis The sides of this were coveied with some coarse sculpture, and it had probably been used as a chapel oi place of devotion undei the Gieek empire, and at times when concealment in woiship was necessaiy. From this spot I iode down to the sea, which, at the distance of two miles fiom the city on the south side meets the mountains. The limestone iock, here, as at Athens, was shaped into the foundations of houses oi tombs, and a long insciiption of late date, and appaiently ielating to some private peison, is partly legible, though much effaced by the coriosion of the sea-spiay. Luxuiiant springs of fiesh water were bursting fiom the iock and falling into the sea.

Retuining thiough the town, we again crossed the Euiipus by the biidge. The channel cannot be moie than foity oi fifty yaids wide, and the passage foi the water is still furthei nariowed by the massy pieis of the biidge. The cuiient was at this moment falling with neaily as much iapidity as the tide at London-bridge, in an opposite diiection to that of the evening pieceding. I was assuied by the people of the place that the tide* changed eveiy six hours, in case no high winds inteifered with the regular couise of the waters.

---

* " Pliny, lib ii, speaks with much cleainess on the subject of tides in geneial, and paiticulaily of those in the Mediteiianean. The tides, he says, in the mouth of the straits of Messina and in the Euiipus ieturn at stated intervals, although the intervals may be different fiom those in the ocean oi in othei parts of the Mediteiianean. Modein obseivations point out a rise of about five feet at Venice, but only twelve oi thiiteen inches at Naples and the Euiipus " — Rennell's Heiodotus, 659

While the Venetians were in possession of Negropont, a Jesuit, Father Babin, studied the tides of the Euripus with attention, in order to reconcile the varying accounts of ancient authors. Seneca says it changed fourteen times in twenty-four hours.

> Septemque cursus flectit et totidem refert,
> Dum lapsa Titan mergat oceano juga

Pliny, Pomponius Mela, and Strabo, all agree in assigning seven times of flux and reflux, but F. Babin says his observations determined him to the usual tides with the exception of certain days in which the stream appeared to follow no regular order, namely, the first five days of the moon's first quarter, and the same of her last quarter.

On each side of this narrow channel, the Euripus swells into considerable breadth. Towards the south the shores project again, and form a basin of four or five miles diameter, which from the town appears land-locked; the northern part of the channel spreads uninterruptedly to the breadth of eight or ten miles, the shores of Euboea and Bœotia retreating in a number of steep sloping headlands.

Having crossed the bridge, we turned to the right, and took the road for Martino, a village which we had been assured was six hours or eighteen miles distant from Negropont. The fort on the hill was to our left. In half an hour we reached Halæ, a village situated on a cultivated plain not far from the coast. The Euripus here spreads itself into a large bay, at the northern extremity of which was a small island, with a ruined tower and church, dedicated to St. Nicholas. Fifteen years ago, a band of robbers made this place their haunt, until they were extirpated by Ali Pasha. In two hours and a half from Negropont, or at rather more than seven miles distance, we came on the side of a large ancient town; the fields were strewed with squared stones, and though no line of walls was to be traced on the land, two piers, which projected like horns, and formed a small circular har-

* Αμφικα ἔχουσα — Strabo, lib. ix.

bout, were nearly perfect in the sea below. The account given by
Strabo and Pausanias, of the distance of Anthedon from Thebes, and
other places, made it likely that this was the situation of Anthedon,
the last town of the Bœotian confederacy on this side, until Larymna
joined it. Our road continued to run at a little distance from the
sea, but parallel to the coast, over some low rising ground, for the
most part uncultivated. In four hours from Negropont, we arrived
at Potsomathi, a large deep bay, surrounded on three sides by high
and abrupt mountains. We reached a small uncultivated valley at
its head, only remarkable for some fine springs, which rose near the
sea-side. From this valley an exceedingly bad and steep *scala* formed
our road, as we ascended the side of the mountain; we toiled la-
boriously up in hopes of finding Martino at the summit, but were
mortified by hearing from a man whom we met, that we could not
reach it in five hours. As the evening came on, and we had lost
our way, we rode to some fires which were burning at a distance, but
the shepherds heard our approach, and ran off, apprehending that we
were a party of the Pasha's Albanians. We were at last fortunate
enough to find a lad who conducted us through the remainder of our
road to Martino.

This village contains about 100 houses, and is situated on a hill
commanding a view over an extensive country, cultivated only near
the town. At two hours, distance on the sea-coast, are considerable
remains of a Greek city, which, I suppose, is the ancient Larymna. The lower part of the town wall, of excellent masonry, still
remains nearly perfect, and points out the extent of the town,
which covered a considerable spot on the coast, as well as a small
peninsula, included within the circuit; on each side of the isthmus of
this peninsula, was a small harbour, formed by the projection of
piers, which left only a space for the entrance of ships. The wall,
flanked with towers, was carried along the sea-side, as well as towards
the land. The whole of the area included, is covered with remains
of building, but no foundation of public edifices, nor pieces of sculpture, could be seen. Without the walls, a large sarcophagus re-

mained unbroken, and with some vestiges of ornament on its side, but no inscription was visible

Across the neck of the peninsula, a second wall has been built, but from the rude style of its construction, it is probably the work of a later time; on each side of this place the coast forms a bay; that to the south is terminated on the opposite side by high and steep mountains, covered with wood, wherever the abrupt descent will give room for vegetation. Into this bay, at the distance of about two miles from Larymna, a river falls, which the people of the country call the Larmi*, a name retaining some traces of the ancient city.

The line of country followed by us in the road of the last night, I knew, must cross the channel through which the Cephissus of Bœotia, and the waters of the Copaic lake, were discharged into the sea, and I had been hourly expecting to arrive on the banks of the stream. The darkness had prevented all observation of the country, but the sound of a strong fall of water, had led me to suspect that we were near the river, which, still, our road never passed before we ascended the hills to Martino. From the mouth of the Larmi I rode along its banks, which near the sea had been planted with cotton, until, in about three miles, I came to a spot covered with rocks and bushes, in the middle of which the whole river burst with impetuosity from holes at the foot of a low cliff, and immediately assumed the form of a considerable stream. Above this source, there is a small plain under cultivation, bounded to the west by a range of low rocky hills. From these, a magnificent view of the Copaic lake, and the mountains of Phocis, presents itself to the eye. The lake was spread over a vast plain, into which the mountains of Bœotia jutted like bold headlands, and occasionally left some slips of cultivated land at their base. Beyond the lake, the plain of Haliartus and Orchomenus seemed hardly raised

* This is the Cephissus, Λάρυμνά τε παρ' ἣν ὁ Κηφισσὸς ἐκδίδωσι — Strabo, lib ix Larmi, is written by Meletius Λαρμι

above the level of its waters, while the ridges of Parnassus towered over all, covered with snow, and broken into the most Alpine forms.

The lake is about four miles distant from the source of the Larmi, and several circumstances corroborate the opinion of Strabo, that it has a subterranean outlet. At the foot of these hills its waters fall into a deep hollow called by the Greeks καταβόθρα, and the volume of water which rises at the source of the Larmi is so great, that it seems beyond the quantity supplied by any common spring, and to be rather the re-appearance than the commencement of a river. Near the lake, and in the supposed direction of this underground stream, square pits are cut in the rock. It is probable that these are remains of the great work undertaken in the time of Alexander, when a miner was employed to clear away some obstructions in this outlet of the waters, in order to check the inundations of the lake.

The Copaic lake is, in fact, nothing more than a lower division of the great plain which formed the territories of Haliartus, Livadea, Chæronea, Orchomenus, and other towns of Bœotia. The river Cephissus [*], flowing through this plain, stagnated in the lower extremity of it, and formed there a wide but shallow lake by the accumulation of its waters, which must have risen still higher, had not one of those fissures common in mountains of limestone received them, and carried them off through the κα-αβόθρα.

The river having no other discharge for its streams, (for the whole of the plain, like all the interior plains of Greece, is entirely surrounded by mountains [†],) every obstruction in this subterraneous

---

[*] The Permessus, Olmius, and Cephissus were the rivers that contributed to swell the Copais, (Strabo, lib ix) as well as the Melas, (Paus ix) This latter writer does not mention the lake Hylica, did he consider it, as Heyne supposes, as part of the Copais ?

[†] " The plains of Bœotia are bounded to the north by the mountains of Phocis, to the south by those of Attica, and to the west by Cithæron." — Strabo, lib ix. Cithæron is the modern Elateas, so called from the name of the silver fir, a tree which is found in many parts of it

passage endangered the safety of the tract of country, which was
situated a little above its usual level. At the time when the undertaking for clearing the καταζόθρα was proposed, the rich and
flourishing towns of the plain were reduced to a state of desolation
by the incroachments of the lake, and under the despondency
occasioned by an universal monarchy sunk into complete decay. At
present the rising of the waters in winter has turned a great portion
of the richest soil in the world into a morass, and should any
permanent internal obstruction occur in the stream, the whole of
this fertile plain might gradually become included in the limits of the
Copaic lake.

A fishery for eels is carried on at the Catavothra, and they are
salted and sold all over Greece. They have continued to retain their
celebrity from very early times, and are praised by Dorion, Aga-
tharcides, Eubulus (apud Athenæum), and Aristophanes *, and the
Byzantine writers occasionally refer to them. (Niceph. Greg. lib. iv.)

-- ------

ON THE BŒOTIAN CATABOTHRA AND COPAIC LAKE.

[BY THE EDITOR.]

These great artificial excavations were probably formed by the wealthy
Orchomenians, in very early ages, to protect the plain belonging to
their state from inundation. The people who erected the Treasury,
as it is called, of Orchomenus, wanted neither skill nor power to exca-

---

* From the Bœotian lakes the Athenian market was supplied with various articles,
which were not abundant in Attica. " The Bœotians (Irene, 1003), sold the Athenians
water fowl and wild fowl, manufactures of rush work, as mats and wicks for lamps, and
fish from the lakes — Gray on Aristoph.

vate the rock for such important purposes. The caverns (φάραγγες, Arist. Met. lib. xiii.) by which the waters were discharged from the plain were sometimes stopped by earthquakes (Strabo, lib. ix.); at other times from the same cause new fissures were occasioned. In the time of Alexander either fresh openings were made, for the sake of receiving and conducting the waters, or the old apertures were enlarged. The name of the man of Chalcis, who was employed on this occasion may have been Crates. (Compare Stephanus in v. Ἀθῆναι with Strabo, lib. ix. and consult Freret. 47 Acad. des Inscr. 13.)

The Lake Copais was known by another appellation, that of Cephissis; this was with propriety given to it, as it receives the Cephissus. A passage in Strabo may lead to a different opinion ; but that part of the geographer is corrupt, and he was not always, as Paulmier observes, αὐτόπτης.* It was known also by another name, Ἡ ἐν Ὀγχηστῷ λίμνη. Diod. S. lib. xvii. 167 The first traveller of modern times who visited the καταβόθρα was Wheeler; and the whole of the district has been since accurately surveyed by Mr. Hawkins A map† of this part of Bœotia will alone explain some of the obscure parts of the ninth book of Strabo The addition to the soil made by the river must occasion difficulties in reconciling the topography of the country with ancient accounts ; " It has added no little quantity of soil," says Diodorus, tom. i. 48.

The remarks of Mr. Raikes afford a very valuable illustration of some of the geographer's words, in which he mentions the subterraneous discharge of the waters of the Cephissus, after it had flowed through the Copaic Limne. " A chasm or gulf," says Strabo, " close to the lake, opened under ground a passage of about thirty stadia in length ; the river was received into this, and then burst into view again."‡ The

---

* Ex. in Gr auctores This reference to Paulmier is omitted in the French translation of Strabo

† Stuart in his visit to Bœotia mentions a lake distinct from that of Thebes and of Topolias, so that there are three lakes. vol iv.

‡ The words λίμνη αγχιβαθή (see Strabo, French Transl vol. iii 411) are not those of Meletius, as it is there stated, but of Pausanias, lib. ix.

distance between the lake and the rising again of the river is stated by
Mr. Raikes at about four miles; this may be considered as corresponding, though not exactly, to the distance of thirty stadia. The gulf,
into which the waters of the lake fall, is at a spot where the καταβόθρα,
the square pits mentioned by Mr. Raikes, are placed. Of the re-
appearance of the river, Strabo says ἐξέρρηξεν εἰς τὴν ἐπιφανείαν, which is
weakly rendered by the French translation, *ses eaux reparurent*, but
Mr. Raikes' words written on the spot express well and accurately the
meaning of the Greek "The whole river burst with impetuosity from
holes," &c.

In the traditions of the country, it was said, that Orchomenus was
once built in the plain; that the ground covered afterwards by the
Lake Copais, was formerly dry, that inundations caused the inhabitants to remove to a higher spot (Strabo, lib. ix.), and that Hercules,
to avenge the Thebans, stopped up a canal which had served for the
discharge of part of the lake, and thus caused the river to overflow
the territory of the Orchomenians. (Diod. Sic. iv. 158. Pausan. Bœot.
Palm. Exercit. 100.) Many of the plains of Greece, surrounded by
lofty mountains, were subject also to inundations. The Larisseans
were obliged, by dykes and mounds (παραχώμασι) to check the over-
flowing of the Lake Nesonis, the modern Caila, which, by the increase
of the Pheneus, sometimes spread itself over the adjoining districts.
(Strabo, 440. and Theophrast De C. P. p. 5) The ancient city of
Pheneus had been destroyed in this manner (Paus. lib. viii.); and
Βάραθρα or Ζέρεθρα, to use the Arcadian word, were formed in the
mountains to receive the waters of the plain.* These are described
by Pausanias as five miles distant from Pheneus. The formation of
some of the Barathra in Arcadia was attributed to Hercules, as they
were of laborious and difficult execution "et d'autant que cet exploit
étoit admirable, et surpassant les forces humaines on l'a attribué à
Hercule." (Scaliger, Discours de la jonction des mers 556.)

---

* "The Stymphalus and Ladon were absorbed by the hollow places in the earth."—
Diod S vol. ii 41

RHAMNUS

[MR RAIKES'S JOURNALS CONTINUED]

At the distance of an hour and fifty minutes from Marathon, a space answering with sufficient exactness to the sixty stadia mentioned by Pausanias, the remains of the ancient Rhamnus are still to be found under the name of Vraeo Castro The ruins of the temple of Nemesis lie at the head of a narrow glen which leads to the principal gate of the town The fall of the building seems to have been occasioned by some violent shock of an earthquake, the columns being more disjointed and broken than in any other ruin of the kind The mass of materials and their confusion are so great, that probably the contents of the temple, the statue formed by Phidias, Phidiaca Nemesis[*], may be buried under the fragments (Strabo, lib. ix) The building must have been inferior in size to those Doric temples which still remain in Attica, and the columns were only fluted in the upper part of their shaft. The diameter at the base measured two feet three inches, that at the summit one foot ten inches. The intercolumniation at a point where the lower cylinders of two adjacent columns were standing was three feet ten inches. The whole structure was of the finest Pentelic marble. The statue, as we learn from Pausanias, was formed from the Parian marble brought by Datis, for the purpose of raising a trophy, and therefore with singular propriety applied to the worship of Nemesis, according to the ideas entertained of her office by the Greeks

The town of Rhamnus was placed on a round rocky hill, about a quarter of a mile below the temple, surrounded by the sea for two-thirds of its circumference, and separated from the hills on the shore

---

[*] Rhamnus illustris, quod in ea fanum Amphiarai et Phidiaca Nemesis. — Mela.

by a broad ravine. The walls, Ραμνο͂ς τειχος, which were of the finest masonry, are still visible round the greater part of the area, and towards the land are of considerable height. The groupes of mastich which overhang them form a peculiarly picturesque view near the entrance.

Of the buildings of the town hardly a vestige remains, great heaps of marble and stone are scattered over the surface of the hill, and are partly hid by the low wood. The only fragment of which the original form can be ascertained, is the base of a large marble chair resembling those which are to be seen in the church of St. Soteera at Athens. It presents an inscription, serving, in addition to the correspondence of distances, to mark the identity of this site with Rhamnus. The words are ΡΑΜΝΟΥΣΙΟΣ ΚΩΜΩΙΔΟΙΣ, and probably they commemorate the honorary gift of the chair to some players who had contributed to the entertainment of the people. The materials of these chairs and their decoration render them objects of curiosity. Their form resembles that of the heavy arm-chair now in fashion, on those at Athens owls are sculptured under the arms, in allusion to the emblem of the city, and on the sides of the base, garlands, such as were appropriated to victors in the games, are formed in basso-relievo. Their solidity is such as to render them nearly immovable, and to this and to their strength is to be attributed their preservation. It is not likely that such masses of stone should ever have been intended for articles of furniture within the walls of a house, but all we know of the customs and way of life of the ancients suggests a different use. They were probably placed at the expense of the state, or of individuals for seats in the public places, in the popular assembly, the agora, or even the streets. Thus Homer Σ. 504, describing a judicial process, says

οἱ δὲ γέροντες

εἵατ' ἐπὶ ξεστοῖσι λίθοις, ἱερῷ ἐνὶ κύκλῳ.

Herodotus represents the citizens of Apollonia as taking the op-

---

* Scylac Perip 21 — Hudson, G. M. i.

portunity of entering into a careless and unsuspicious conversation with Evenius, κατημένου Ευηνίου εν θακω, probably on some seat of this kind in the place of general resort. The Septuagint version, which continually alludes to Grecian customs, makes Job refer to this, when in enumerating the felicities of his prosperous youth, he says, ἐν δὲ πλατείαις ἐτίθετο μου ὁ δίφρος. xxix. 7   The names of the official part of the government at Athens appear to have some connection with a distinction of this kind, the presidents for the time being were called Προεδροι; the Νομοφύλακες were said συγκαθιζεσθαι with the Proedri; but though this sort of conjecture may appear trivial, the influence of climate which invariably suggests some kind of coincidence in common habits of life to the inhabitants of any particular country, however remote in age or circumstances, and which now carries the idle Turks to the bazar, as it did the Greeks to the agora, must have then made a constant seat in the morning assembly a pleasant as well as an honourable distinction.

On the Θρόνοι and Δίφροι of the Greeks.

[Although the subject is not one of great importance, we may add some instances by way of confirming Mr. Raikes's remark.   The Νομοφύλακες sate at public spectacles ἐπὶ Θρόνων, a name given to these chairs of honour.   (Vales, in Harpoc. 55.)   They were consecrated to particular deities in ancient temples; in the vestibule of that at Olympia there was among other offerings, a *throne* presented by Arimnus king of the Etrusci. (Paus. v 12.)   In the temple of the Lycian Apollo at Argos, there was in the time of Pausanias, the throne of Danaus (II.) on the road from the Acrocorinthus, there was in a temple a column and throne of white marble, consecrated to Cybele. Id. lib. ii.)   At Naxia, a seat was appropriated as the inscription informs us to the great priest Aristarchus; one of white marble was placed at Abydos for Xerxes, when he surveyed his troops. (Herod. lib. vii.) Hypsipyle, queen of Lemnos, after haranguing the people sits down on the marble chair of her father Thoas. (Apoll.

Rhod. Arg. i 667.) On a coin of Olba in Cilicia, we see a chair represented, and on one side of the money is the name of Polemo, high priest and prince of the city. (Mem. de l'A. In. xxi. 427.) These and other examples prove that marble seats were allotted as places of distinction* to persons of eminence. They may be considered, sometimes, as forming part of the public monuments of the state. The Adulitan inscription is written on the Δίφρος Πτολεμαϊκόν. Chishull. An. As. 76. The custom we allude to was familiar to the inhabitants of Italy also. "Caius Julius Gelo is allowed to sit at the public games at Veii among the priests, called *Augustales, bisellio proprio.*" Mem. de l'Ac. xxi. 374.] — Ed.

THE CORYCIAN CAVE

[THE RAIKES'S JOURNALS CONTINUED]

March 19 — I quitted the village of Aracova at half-past seven ; the master of the cottage in which I had slept undertook to guide us to the Corycian cave, with the situation of which he appeared acquainted. We left the road to Castri which continued to run along the narrow valley between the two mountains, and turning to the right began to ascend the slope of Parnassus by a steep road immediately from the village. The declivity was cultivated with an industry worthy of Switzerland. Every spot of vegetable soil was covered with low vines ; and I remarked one attention to the value of productive ground which occurred no where else in Greece. The shallow soil was sometimes interrupted by great masses of rock which reared themselves above the surface, and the careful husbandman,

---

* On the marble chair at Lesbos, the inscription is ΠΟΛΑΜΩΝΟΣ ΤΩ ΛΕΣΒΩΝΑΚ-ΤΟΣ ΠΡΟΕΔΡΙΑ, not Τῷ, as some have erroneously copied it. At Delphi there is a chair with an inscription on the back, Clarke's Travels, T. iii who informs us, p 145. that there is one also at Chaeronea, which the Greeks still call θρόνος. A Gymnasiarch's chair in marble at Athens is mentioned in Lord Elgin's Memorandum, p 32

unwilling to lose the corner on which he must otherwise have
heaped the loose stones gathered from the rest of the field, had
raised them in pyramids on these masses   In Judea the same
causes might have led to the same economy of soil ; and perhaps
the prophet Micah alludes to some similar appearance in the vineyards of his own country, when he says, i. 6 , " I will make Samaria
as a heap of the field, and as plantings of a vineyard," or to take
the expression of the Vulgate, " I will make Samaria as a heap of
stones, when a vineyard is planted."

Aracova is famous for the quality of its wines   I had tasted some
of the grapes the night before ; they had been preserved during
the winter, by filling the jar in which the bunches were placed, with
wine   They were black, thinly scattered on the stalk, and of no particular flavour   The vineyards were soon passed, and the ascent
became more and more steep, until, in an hour's time from Aracova,
I was surprised by entering on a wide plain of considerable extent,
and under cultivation, where I expected to see nothing but rocks and
snow   High above this wide level the ridges of Parnassus rose on
the north and east, covered with snow and hid in clouds.   The plain
before me could not be less than four or five miles across ; a large
dull looking village was placed in the middle of it ; a lake,
with banks most beautifully broken, was on my left   Not having
seen the other side of Parnassus, I have no means of judging as to the
advantages of the ridge above Tithorea, which Herodotus mentions
as the retreat of the Phocians during the Persian invasion   This
plain seems peculiarly fitted for the same purpose.   The ground
would have afforded pasture for their cattle, and some proportion of
food for themselves, and the ascent to it was so steep and narrow,
that it must have been defended by a very few men.   The happy
situation of Greece protected it from the successive inroads of barbarous nations, which in Asia so repeatedly swept every thing before
them, and checked the progress of civilization.   Against the Scy-
thian tribes, the Ægæan sea, and even the Hellespont, was a sufficient
rampart, and by a fortunate chance, the emigrations from the north-

eastern part of Europe, took an easterly direction, and followed the coasts of the Euxine or the line of Caucasus, into Persia and Asia Minor. The army of Xerxes was the only foreign force which ever came with the irresistible weight of an emigration, or led them to doubt of their ability to cope with their enemy in the field.

Had these inroads occurred more frequently, the Phocians would have learned the value of their natural citadel more fully. In Syria and Judea, the wretched inhabitants became familiarized with such retreats, during the repeated invasions of the Assyrian kings. Jeremiah, in the translation of the Septuagint, expresses this dreadful necessity with great force, iv. 29., ἀπὸ φωνῆς ἱππέως, καὶ ἐντεταμένου τόξου ανεχώρησε πᾶσα ἡ χώρα, εἰσέδυσαν εἰς τὰ σπήλαια, ανέδυσαν εἰς τὰς πέτρας, πᾶσα τὸν ; καταλείφθη.

The view to the southward from this spot was extensive and very striking the mountain Cuphis on the other side of the valley of Aracova terminated in a flat table land like the recess in Parnassus, well cultivated, and studded with villages ; but the greater height of both these plains raised them above the regions of spring, which we had left below, vegetation had not yet begun to appear, and the snow lay in patches over both of them Beyond, the mountains of the Morea filled up the distance.

We rode across the plain towards the north, and leaving our horses at the foot of the ascent which bounded it, climbed up a steep and bushy slope to the mouth of the Corycian cave I had been so repeatedly disappointed with scenes of this kind, they had so generally appeared inferior to the descriptions given of them, that I expected to meet with the same reverse here, and to find nothing but a dark narrow vault. I was, however, to be for once agreeably surprised, the narrow and low entrance of the cave, spread at once into a chamber 330 feet long, by nearly 200 wide, the Stalactites from the top hung in the most graceful forms, the whole length of the roof, and fell, like drapery, down the sides. The depth of the folds was so vast and the masses thus suspended in the air were so great, that the relief and fullness of these natural hangings, were as complete as the fancy could have wished. They were not like concretions or encrustations, mere coverings of the rock, they were the gradual growth of ages, disposed in the most simple and majestic forms, and so rich and large, as to accord with the size and loftiness of the cavern. The stalagmites below and on the sides of the chamber, were still more fantastic in their forms, than the pendants above, and struck the eye with the fancied resemblance of vast human figures.

At the end of this great vault, a narrow passage leads down a wet slope of rock, with some difficulty, from the slippery nature of the ground on which I trod, I went a considerable way on, until I came to a place where the descent grew very steep, and my light being nearly exhausted, it seemed best to return. On my way back, I found, half buried in the clay, on one side of the passage, a small antique Patera, of the common black and red ware. The encrustation of the grotto had begun to appear, but it was unbroken, and I was interested in finding this simple relic of the homage once paid to the Corycian nymphs by the ancient inhabitants of the country. The stalagmitic formations on the entrance of this second passage, are wild as imagination can conceive, and of the most brilliant whiteness.

It would not require a fancy, lively, like that of the ancient Greeks, to assign this beautiful grotto, as a residence to the nymphs. The stillness which reigns through it, only broken by the gentle sound of the water, which drops from the point of the stalactites *, the ὕδατ' ἀενάοντα of the grotto of the nymphs in the Odyssey, the dim light admitted by its narrow entrance, and reflected by the white ribs of the roof, with all the miraculous decorations of the interior, would impress the most insensible with feelings of awe, and lead him to attribute the influence of the scene to the presence of some supernatural being.

---

* *Distillantes* quoque *guttæ* in lapides durescunt in antris Corycis. Pliny, lib. xxxv.

An inscription, which still remains on a mass of rock, near the entrance, marks that the cavern has been dedicated to Pan and the Nymphs

ΕΥΣΤΡΑΤΟΣ
ΔΑΚΙΔΟΜΟΥ
ΑΜΒΡΥΣΙΟΣ
ΣΥΜΠΕΡΙΠΟΛΟΙ
ΠΑΝΙ ΝΥΜΦΑΙΣ.*

The epithet applied to Pan, may perhaps allude to the share he was reputed to have in defending Delphi against the Gauls and Brennus

* Pan and the Nymphs are associated on various occasions, (see Aristoph Thesm. 987, the life of Plato by Olympiodorus, and the Attica of Pausanias Scetzen saw in Syria, a Greek inscription in which they are jointly commemorated, they are also placed together in that found in the Corycian cave, where the words allude to some act of worship rendered by " Eustratus, of Ambryssus, son of Dacidomus to Pan, who was the guardian of the place, together with the Nymphs" (περιπολος, φρουρὸ , ἔφορος Hesych.)—E.

REMARKS

RELATING TO

THE MILITARY ARCHITECTURE OF ANCIENT GREECE

[FROM THE LATE COL SQUIRE'S PAPERS]

GREECE abounding in mountains afforded an ample supply for buildings; and in different situations may be traced the progress of the military architecture of the ancient inhabitants of the country from a wall of huge irregular masses *, as they were taken from the quarry, to that magnificent style of building, where the stones always placed without cement in horizontal courses have a rectangular form, and are so adapted to each other, as to present an uniform and consolidated structure.

Among the beautiful vestiges of the ingenuity and perfection in architecture of the Greeks, four different modes of building may be observed. 1 The most ancient and simple was that in which immense masses of rock detached from the mountains are piled upon each other. Their shape being uneven, they could not be so united as to form a compact body; smaller stones therefore, as we learn from Pausanias†, were inserted between them in order that the building

---

* In the Journal des Sçavans, mention is made of a wall in Asia Minor of a most remarkable extent, it is described as enclosing a great part of the ancient Pamphylia. " C'est un rare ouvrage d'antiquité dont il est surprenant que personne n'ait encore parlé, et qui n'a été observé que depuis peu par un illustre François nommé M de Boisgien, dans un voyage qu'il a fait de Smyrne à Attalie C'est la grande et longue muraille, qui enferme toute la Pamphilie, comme celle qui est à la Chine De sorte que toute la Pamphilie est bornée ou par la mer d'un coté, ou par cette longue suite de murailles de l'autre Le consul François qui est à Attalie a assuré M de Boisgien avoir déjà fait la même remarque "

† Lib. ii λιθία δ' ἐνήρμοσται πολλὰ, instead of παλαι See the French translation of Strabo, lib viii. 235.

might be rendered more solid and secure. The walls of Mycenæ and Tiryns are constructed in this manner; the latter seem to be the most ancient, because at Mycenæ the sides of the stones are in some degree squared and adapted to each other. Many may be found in both these fortresses, equalling a cube of six feet in their bulk.* The walls of Tiryns are twenty-seven feet in thickness; Homer alludes to them in the word τειχιόεντα; and this circumstance alone might lead us to some estimate concerning their antiquity. The walls of Mycenæ could not be destroyed by the Argives; they are as well as those of Tiryns† a prodigious work, resembling the labours of giants rather than of men. They are of the class usually called Cyclopic; by which nothing more is meant than that they are constructed of large masses, in reference to the mythological accounts of the Cyclops‡, who were said to hurl rocks instead of stones

2. The most ordinary mode of building in the Greek fortresses which now exist, is that, wherein stones were used of a very irregular size and figure, differing from each other, but grooved and adapted with the most scrupulous nicety; sometimes they were of seven,

---

* See Mr. Hamilton's Memoir on the Greek fortresses, in the Archæol. vol. xv.

† See the representation of them in Sir W. Gell's Argolis. One of the earliest travellers in Greece Des Mouceaux, in 1668, thus mentions them, Les murailles ont 21 pieds d'épaisseur, les matériaux ressemblent plus à des Rochers qu' à des Pierres, elles ne sont point taillées, mais mises en œuvre comme elles se sont recontrees, les joints sont remplis d'autres Pierres plus petites. Tom v Le Bruyn

‡ The remains of what has been called Cyclopic or Pelasgic architecture may be seen in various parts of the Peloponnesus, as well as beyond the Isthmus. The Polyhedrous style of building is also observable in the islands of Candia, Cerigo, and Melos, on Mount Sipylus, near Smyrna, in Paphlagonia, near Sinope and Amisus. It was employed occasionally by the Romans at a late period. (See the remarks of Sickler, Petit Radel, and Dodwell in the Magasin Encyclop. Oct. 1809, 1810, and April 1811.) — The inscription at Ferentino proves that the Cyclopic or Polygon style of building was used by the Romans in the time of Augustus. V. Gruter 165 3. 166 1 — Ed

The Dactyli or Idean Curetes introduced various arts into Greece (Strabo, lib x.) he considers them as the same with the Cyclops of Argolis, whose works were shewn at Tiryns, and in other parts of Greece (Lib viii.)

or even eight sides, and in one instance, in a fragment of an ancient wall, forming part of the Turkish fortress of Salona, (formerly Amphissa,) of thirteen   Instead of placing them rough in the wall from the quarry, they worked the stone, according to the shape in which it happened to be detached into straight and smooth sides, so that when joined together, these stones produced a very great degree of solidity in the masonry

3. In a third method of building, the stones were placed in horizontal courses, but occasionally by descending below, or reaching above the line, they varied from regularity. The joints were sometimes at an angle with the horizon, and frequently perpendicular.

The first mode of construction seems peculiar to Mycenæ and Tiryns; the second and third are observed indiscriminately in the fortified places of Greece Proper, as well as in Peloponnesus. Phyle in Attica is built according to the fourth class; as well as the temples and other monuments at Athens, in these no cement, nor any other sort of composition has been used to unite the * masonry. In many of the fortresses of Greece, the stones have no other bond but their own elaborate workmanship; and their walls and towers present the firmness and solidity of a rock.

[The walls of Byzantium and Jerusalem, are described by Herodian and Josephus, as constructed in the same manner, the stones of a rectangular form were so adjusted to each other, as to present the most regular surface. Strict attention was paid by the military architects of antiquity to this mode of building, because their fortresses were better able to resist those engines, the sharp points of which were driven forcibly against the wall by the besieging party.

Sometimes iron cramps with lead were used to unite the stones; they were employed in the wall built by Themistocles at the Piræus, which was begun in the year 481 B. C., and finished, 477, (Dodwell.

---

* In some of the most ancient buildings of Egypt, mortar was used, " the stones of the pyramids," says Shaw, "have all been laid in mortar " See also Dr. Clarke, vol. iii.

Ann. Thucy.) This mode, as appears by inspection, was also adopted in the construction of the Parthenon. It was used by the architects of the ancient cities of the East ; at Babylon the stones were fixed by iron fastenings, and melted lead was poured in, Diod. S. lib. ii. 121. μόλιβδον ἐντήχοντες. The Turks have frequently endeavoured to extract the iron and lead from the ancient buildings of Greece and Asia Minor, by breaking the marble in pieces. In Italy, the Coliseum and other edifices have suffered in the same manner repeated injuries. In the lower ages, Maffei observes, these metals were very scarce, and the walls were destroyed for the purpose of extracting them.

The ancient architects of Egypt, Syria, and Italy, used wood also to unite and bind the stones together. The French, during their expedition to Egypt, observed at Ombos and Philæ that pieces of the Sycamore had been formed for that purpose into a dove-tail shape ; at Ombos they appear to have been covered with bitumen Fastenings made of wood, of similar forms, (*assulæ ex quolibet latere ad formam caudæ hirundinis,*) were used in some of the ancient buildings of Italy, and were seen and described by F. Vacca. The Greeks, as we learn from Jerome, expressed this mode of binding stones together * by the word ἱμαντωσις In the prophet Habakkuk, ii 11, the Hebrew term bearing a similar meaning is *Caphis*, and the passage of the original is rendered by Symmachus, σύνδεσμος ενδομήσεως ξυλινος, *Hieronym.* Opp. T. iii 1610. In the ἐκ Σύραχ, xxii. v. 16. we find ἱμά τωσις ξύλινη ενδεδεμένη εἰς οικοδομήν, which is rendered by Coverdale, in the first Bible printed in English, " Like as the *bond of wood* bound together in the foundation of an house."]—Ed.

The sites of fortified towns may be discovered in many parts of Greece ; in Phocis, the vestiges are frequent. Elatea is now occu-

---

* Codinus (de orig. Constan.) observes, that in building the walls of Sta Sophia water, in which barley had been boiled, was mixed with the lime, and that the stones were as strongly united together by the mortar, as if cramps of iron had been used See Mem de l'Ac des In. xlvii 309

pied by the little village of Turcochorio, this hamlet is at the entrance of the pass through the mountains leading from the plain of the Cephissus to Opus and Thermopylæ. Drymea was above Elatea, and some remains of an ancient fortress on a hill seem to mark its situation. On the right bank of the Cephissus, was Tithronium, and in the plain, at the roots of Parnassus, were Charadra, and Amphiclea; a palaio-castro, at the entrance of a road, across Parnassus to Delphi, appears to point out the position of the first. Between this place and Velizza, are some small remains of an ancient fort at a village called Thathia. On the road, over the tops of Parnassus, from Charadra to Delphi, may be placed Lilæa at the village now called Aghourea. Then Ledon and Velizza (Tithorea) where are walls and towers* of ancient construction The north part of the plain of Chæronea, was a portion of Phocis, the frontier town in this part was Panope, the walls of which are still in existence; the acropolis was on a rugged height; the city itself was partly in a plain, and near it is the modern village of Agios Blasios. The position of Daulis is pointed out by the modern appellation *Thaxlia* †, a village very pleasantly situated on Parnassus, and by a palaio-castro forming an acropolis, on an abrupt isolated mountain. The route from Daulis to Ambryssus, the modern Distomo, passes the όδος σχιστή, the divided way, the sacred road to Delphi. Ambryssus is on an elevated plain about an hour's distance from the sea.

Herodotus relates that the towns of Phocis were burnt, and destroyed, with their temples and public buildings, when Xerxes invaded Greece, after the battle of Thermopylæ. The remains in this country of walls and towers of the most solid construction are those probably with which the Phocian cities were surrounded after

---

* These are described in Dr Clarke's account of Tithorea See Appen. to Tomb of Alexander.

† An inscription found at Thaxlia, by the Earl of Aberdeen, and published in this volume, confirms the conjecture in the text.

the incursions of the Barbarians. On Parnassus, and in the plain of the Cephissus, at the roots of the mountain may be enumerated eight fortified places as remarkable for the strength of their position as the durability and excellence of their workmanship. These fortifications were generally placed on a rugged height naturally difficult of access; walls with square or round towers at intervals were continued along the irregular *contour* of the hill, which served as an acropolis or citadel, while the slope of the mountain with a portion of level ground at the bottom was enclosed, and contained the houses and buildings of the city. Sometimes heights are fortified for the defence of a pass in the mountains; we see an instance of this in the palaio-castro in the ἐ ἐ-σχιστη, and another on the road to Parnassus from the upper part of the plain of the Cephissus, which leads to Salona, and Delphi. The fort of Phyle on Mount Parnes, and one near a gorge in Cithæron, conducting from the plains of Eleutheræ into Bœotia, may be added. Sometimes the walled enclosures are entirely in the plain, as in the remains of Platæa, and the oval fortifications of Leuctra.

---

* Colonel Squire remarks, that the plural termination of the names of some Greek cities, as Θηβαι, Αθηναι refers to the united cities the Upper, or the Citadel, and the Lower city. This observation may be confirmed by a parallel remark of Bishop Lowth. When the prophet (Isai. lxv. 10.) speaks, he says, in the plural number of *cities*, Sion and Jerusalem may be meant, as they are divided into the Upper and Lower city.

ANTIQUITIES OF ATHENS.

This vase, which was found by Lord Aberdeen at Athens, is, unfortunately, not entire; it is remarkable for the fineness of its clay, the beauty of the varnish, and the spirit of the figures. The subject represented on it may allude to some prize obtained in a race at the public games by one or more horses; such successes were recorded on vases and marbles. An inscription in the Laconian dialect quoted by Muratori, and emended by Ruhnkenius (Greg. de D) mentions a prize gained by Damoclidas, κέλητι, *equo singulari.*

From the posture of the man who is represented as examining the foot of the horse, we are not to suppose that any conclusion can be drawn respecting the practice of nailing iron shoes to the feet of that animal.* Beckmann, with his usual industry and research, has collected almost all that has been said on this point, and infers that there is no mention of iron shoes in the ancient writers. The hoofs of the horses of Alexander were worn out by constant journies. Diod. S. xvii. Those of Mithridates are described as χωλεύοντες ἐξ ὑποτριβῆς, at the siege of Cyzicum. Appian. de B. M. To what Beckmann has said, we may add the remark of Wesseling. " *Ignotus erat solearum ferrearum quibus ungulæ equorum contra aspera et seruposa loca muniuntur, usus. Scio J. Vossius ad Catull. ex Xenophonte eas cruere, atque hinc* Χαλκοπόδας *Homeri equos illuminare conatum esse, sed irrita opera.*" D. Sic. xvii. 233.

This vase was also found by Lord Aberdeen in excavating a tomb at Athens; the ground of it is red, and the workmanship rather

* " While the Lacedæmonians were encamped at Decelea, the Athenian cavalry were to little purpose employed in endeavouring to check their ravage and destruction Many of the horses, the art of shoeing that animal being yet unknown, were lamed by unremitted service on rough and stony ground " — Mitford's Greece, ii. 498

coarse ; the figures partake of the Etruscan style. The word ΚΑΛΟΣ or ΚΑΛΕ occurs frequently on ancient vases ; in many instances a proper name is connected with it, and we may enumerate at least ten in which this is the case. Various opinions have been offered respecting the meaning of the word. Mazzochi first pointed out the true sense of it, and his conjecture has been confirmed by Lanzi, Visconti, and Bœttiger. (See Millin, Dic. de B. A.) On the finger of a statue of Jupiter made by Phidias, were the words ΠΑΝΤΑΡΚΗΣ ΚΑΛΟΣ ; one of Mr. Hope's vases bears the name Clitarchus, to whom this epithet is also given , and as it is of the most ancient style of art, we may suppose with Millin, that Phidias only imitated a custom already very prevalent and well known

In the vase before us, the word may refer to some one who had been initiated in the Dionysiac mysteries. The allusion to the rites of Bacchus is not only found on vases, lamps, and ornaments deposited in tombs, but the sides of the sepulchral Latomia are often seen sculptured with symbols and figures relating to that deity. One of these monuments may be observed at Misitra near the site of Sparta ; Bacchus is also figured on the *Mensæ sepulchrales*. These devices and symbols are explained by considering that Bacchus and Sol were in the ancient mythology one and the same god. This was the opinion of the Eleans, (see Etym. M. in v. Διονύσος) and of the Athenians* , and in one of the Orphic hymns we read

'Ηλιος ὃν Διόνυσον ἐπίκλησιν καλέουσι.

Reference is therefore made in such sepulchral monuments to Dionysius, or *Sol inferus*.

The flowing hair, the thyrsus, the spotted garment, (στικτὴ χλαμὺς,) the Ionic capital on the altar, (Vitruv. l 1) all refer to a Dionysiac procession. The figure near the altar bears a sistrum, which has

---

* See one of the arguments of the oration against Midias.

the form of a mirror.   A sistrum of similar shape is represented on a cymbalum in the Pittur. Hercol. T. i. Tav. 15.

Sigillarium.

This is one of the Sigillaria of the ancient mythology of Greece, symbolic of some deity respected by the early inhabitants of that country, (*adorare ea pro Diis* Arnob. l. 1.)   When they were of small size, they were carried about, and we find instances of this superstitious custom frequently among the ancients.   They were of different dimensions, and not always small images, as has been supposed by some writers.   See Cuper, Harp. 86.

The original figure from which the engraving is made is of stone, and is remarkable for its great antiquity; it was found by the Earl of Aberdeen in a tomb in Attica.   From its stiff and inexpressive form, (συμβεβηκως τοις ποσι,) it appears to belong to an æra preceding the time of Dædalus of Sicyon, who is said to have lived in the interval between 700 and 600 B.C.   The position of the arms plainly points it out to be a representation of some deity; in this manner the Agathodæmon, and other Egyptian idols were depicted and sculptured, *brachia decussatim composita*.   It may be a representation of Αφροδιτη a goddess whose worship was familiar to the Greeks, before even that of Jupiter.   "*Venus etiam ipso Jove antiquior sub Αφροδιτης nomine a Græcis consebatur, ut docet Schol. ad 3 Argon. Apollon.*"   See Selden, de D. Syris.

SIGILLARIEN.

Lith. Inst. v. Arnz & Co.

Evans del et sculp

ΛΗΚΥΘΟΣΑΤΤΙΚΟΣ.

EXTRACT FROM A LETTER RECEIVED BY THE EDITOR FROM S. JUSHRI DATED ATHENS, 1818

RELATING TO THE EXCAVATIONS MADE BY HIM NEAR THAT CITY, AND TO THE VASES, AND OTHER ORNAMENTS FOUND IN THE TOMBS.

Dans les excavations faites hors les murs anciens de la ville, et partout alentour, j'ai trouvé des tombeaux sans vases, et avec. On y trouve des urnes aussi, et bien souvent sans vases, elles sont de marbre Pentelique, et bien travaillées. On a bonne fortune, mais pas toutes les fois, lorsqu'on trouve des petites urnes de terre cuite, appartenant à des enfans, en général il y a des vases dans l'intérieur de l'urne, et en dehors tout alentour ; il semble que c'étoit un usage de placer à côté du mort tout ce qui lui servit d'entretenement pendant sa vie, y ayant de toutes espèces d'animaux en terre cuite, des petites figures, et de bien petits vases, en tout genre. Ce qu'il y a de singulier, c'est que j'y ai trouvé des vases au fond blanc avec des figures peintes en couleurs, qui représentent la mère d'un côté apportant au tombeau avec ses mains la petite urne ornée alentour avec des festons, ayant des feuillages peints en noir, et les petits vases et d'autres feuillages aussi en noir posés à leur place. De l'autre côté du tombeau peint sur le vase, le père de l'enfant, une main sur ses cheveux, comme s'il vouloit les arracher par l'excès de sa douleur. Ce vase a un pied et trois pouces de hauteur ; sa forme est très-élégante. Dans ces mêmes excavations j'ai trouvé de grands vases, avec des ornemens peints au dehors, fermés par une tasse de cuivre, qui contenoient des ossemens et armes brûlés, qu'on avoit pliés expressement pour les placer dans les vases. En d'autres endroits, des sarcophages placés un sur l'autre, presque tous ayant six pieds et trois pouces de longueur. En général, ces tombeaux sont situés d'orient, à l'occident, mais ce n'est pas toujours de même. On en trouve à différentes profondeurs ; j'en ai vu qui alloient à 40 pieds sous terre dans lesquels j'ai trouvé de très-beaux vases

ACCOUNT OF THE OPENING OF A TUMULUS, SITUATED ON THE ROAD FROM THE PIRÆUS TO ATHENS

[BY MR. FAUVEL —COMMUNICATED BY DR HUNT.]

Sur le chemin du Pireé à Athènes, à une demi-lieue de cette ville on apperçoit entre les longues murailles un Tumulus. L'endroit où se trouve le tumulus est nommé par les cultivateurs des vignobles voisins, Basilike. Ce tombeau est de la même forme que ceux du rivage de Troie ; il leur ressemble encore par les divers objets qu'il recelait. Notre collègue (Fauvel) y a remarqué des poteries brisées, des ossemens, des fragmens de bronze. Son élévation est de huit mètres au-dessus du sol antique, sur lequel il a trouvé les restes du Bucher, dans l'état où il fut éteint.

Le diamètre de ce bûcher étoit d'environ trois mètres et demi. Après avoir été découvert en entier par M. Fauvel, il a offert à celui-ci une couche de très-gros charbons de bois d'olivier, d'ossemens à demi-brûlés, ou totalement réduits en cendres, et entremêlés de quantité de fragmens de vases, de plats, d'amphores. Les plats sont de cette terre antique, enduite de ce même vernis noir que l'on voit sur les vases* Etrusques ; ils ne sont ornés d'aucune

---

* The word strictly appropriated to the painted vases of the ancients is λήκυθοι; they were so frequently deposited in the tombs at Athens, as we learn from some passages of the ancient writers, that we cannot be surprised at the discoveries made by some antiquaries, in their researches in that city, who have found many of them formed into various shapes, and painted with different devices. Aristophanes, in his Exxλ. alludes to them more than once "Who is that person ?" says one of the old women — "He who paints the λήκυθοι for the dead," is the answer of the young man.

ουτο, δ' ἐστι τί; ,
ὁ, τοι, νεκροῖτι, ζωγράφει τὰς ληκύθους. — v. 995

peinture, mais ils portent à leurs centres et au dedans, des empreintes de cet ornement connu aujourd'hui, et employé partout sous le nom de Palmettes. Au milieu des restes du bûcher étoient deux espèces de plateaux, ou masses cylindriques et applaties, qui paroissent avoir été formées en terre cuite sur le bûcher même; ce dont notre collégue est convaincu, en observant l'empreinte que les bûches et leur écorce y ont laissé. Ces plateaux sont colorés en bleu d'azur sur leur épaisseur; leur diamètre est d'environ trois decimêtres.

Parmi les charbons étoient des cornes de bœuf à demi consumées, des os de mouton et de chèvre; des os de poulets, des arrêtes de poisson, plusieurs autres débris du repas funèbre, et du sacrifice; enfin des plateaux à pied, propres à porter une coupe; on y voyoit aussi des lames de cuivre fort minces, et semblables à des feuilles de laurier. Il est probable qu'elles avoient été dorées, ainsi que des espèces de perles en terre cuite, de six lignes de diamètre qui paroissent avoir servi à parer des victimes.

Il y avoit encore des feuilles d'or* aussi fines, aussi bien battues

---

Again in v 537, " You went away, (says Blepyrus,) and left me, as it were dead, only you did not crown me, nor put a vase upon me," οὐδ' ἐπιθεῖσα λήκυθον.

The names of the painters of the ancient vases, are sometimes found upon them, we meet with those of Taleides, Asteas, and Kalippos The imperfect ἐποίει was, as Pliny informs us, the tense used by the ancient artists, but we meet with ἐποίησεν, as well as ἔγραψεν, the former occurs on a vase belonging to Mr Hope, the latter on one in the collection of M Valetta — (Millin, D de B A. i 550)

Among the vases found in the ancient tombs of Greece, Italy, and Sicily, are seen, those which have been termed Lacrymatories The supposition that they were intended to receive the tears of the relatives or parents of the deceased, is now rejected by the most intelligent antiquaries They contained, it is probable, substances, or oils which were poured over the ashes of the deceased — Editor

* M Fauvel in a letter to Barbié du Bocage describes the result of some excavations made by him in the ancient sepulchres. " J'y ai trouve des feuilles d'or battues en forme de langue de serpent, et des lames de cuivre, sur lesquelles on lit le nom du mort." One of the inscriptions found in these tombs was in Boustrophedon, ΥΟΙΔΙϵΜ. Among the ashes in the urns, he always observed the obolus; in one instance, the piece of money was found in the mouth of the corpse — Mag En Mars, 1812

que les nôtres ; et des portions de dome parfaitement brûlées, et employées sur un enduit à la colle.

Au bord et autour du bûcher étoient des vases de terre grossiers, semblables à nos pots à fleurs ; ces vases étoient renversés, et posés sur leurs orifices, ce sont les seuls qui se soient trouvés entiers. L'épaisseur du Tumulus, que notre collégue a ouvert par le haut, en faisant une espèce de puits, contenait quelques jolis fragmens des vases peints, sur l'un desquels on avoit représenté une jeune femme, portant une cassette sur la tête ; d'autres fragmens d'un assez grand diamétre étoient ornés des feuilles de laurier, ou d'olivier. *

---

* This kind of ornament refers to the custom of placing an olive crown on the deceased Mortuis stadio vitæ decurso tanquam victoribus corona olivæ solebat imponi   See Hemsterh.   Lucian, i. 156

THE PLAIN OF MARATHON. *

[FROM THE PAPERS OF THE LATE COLONEL SQUIRE]

Marathon, multarum magnarumque virtutum testis — P. Mela

In the year subsequent to the failure of Mardonius, a considerable force was assembled by order of the Persian monarch, and embarked from the province of Cilicia in Asia Minor. Thence the fleet coasted along the shores of that country as far as Samos; and crossing the Ægæan sea, it passed through the islands between Ionia and Greece. After the Persians had taken possession of Eubœa, where they were delayed seven days by the opposition of the inhabitants of Eretria, the army was re-embarked, and a landing immediately effected in the plain of Marathon, on the opposite shores of Attica.

There was every reason to induce the Persians to make their descent near Marathon. Along the whole extent of the Attic coast, from the frontiers of Bœotia to the bay of Phalerum, there was no other spot but Marathon, which at once united the advantages of safe anchorage, and a plain sufficiently large to contain great numbers, and to afford room for cavalry to act. The shore in this part forms a fine bay of very gradual soundings, of a good anchoring ground, and protected in some degree by the land of Eubœa from the sudden and boisterous storms of the Archipelago. The extent of the shore is upwards of seven miles, presenting a shelving, sandy beach, free from rocks and shoals, and well calculated for debarkation. The land bordering on the bay is an uninterrupted plain, about two miles and a half in width, and bounded by rocky, difficult heights

---

* Reference to the plan of the Field of Marathon. Length of base, a b, 3080 yards, D. marsh, B. Brauron, M Marathon, S C the villages of Seleeree and Bey, L. salt lake, T tumulus, H. wood of pine trees, P mountain of Pan

U U

which enclose it at either extremity; though to the south west, the mountains, which are a branch of Pentelicus, and are higher than in any other part, have a more gradual slope towards the sea, and are covered with low pine-trees and brush-wood. About the centre of the bay a small stream, which flows from the upper part of the valley of Marathon, discharges itself into the sea by three shallow channels. A narrow rocky point, projecting from the shore, forms the north east part of the bay, close to which is a salt stream connected with a shallow lake, and a great extent of marsh land. About one mile and a half south of the river of Marathon is another inconsiderable rivulet of fresh water, flowing also from a marsh by no means so extensive as the other. From the north east point of the bay, on a low narrow sandy ridge extends a wood of the Pinus Pinea for a space of two miles along the shore, in the rear of this, the plain is a continued marsh, reaching as far as the modern village Souli, probably the ancient Tricorythus, which formed with Œnoe, Probalinthus, and Marathon, the Tetrapolis of Attica.[*]

The other part of the plain, except the small marsh to the southward, consists of uninclosed and level corn land, with a few olive and wild pear-trees. The village, called Marathona, which is situated in a narrow valley of nearly uniform breadth opening into the plain, is rather more than three miles from the sea. This valley is in general three quarters of a mile in breadth, and is bounded on either side by difficult heights; on the south side it is separated from another small valley, which however is itself enclosed with rocky eminences, and appears as a bay connected with the plain; while the valley of Marathon may be compared to a creek or inlet into the interior. At the foot of the mountain, on the south side of the plain, is a small hamlet called Vrana, supposed by some to be on the

---

[*] Another town named Œnoe was near Eleutheræ, see Harpocrat. and Wesseling in D. Sic. tom. 1 305. Colonel Leake mentions the vestiges which mark the site of an ancient Demos in the valley above the village of Marathona. They are called Ninoe. — Researches, p. 420.

site of the ancient Brauron *, at the entrance of the valley of
Marathon from the plain are two small villages called Bey and Sifteri.
The modern Marathon contains a few Zevgaria, and is peopled by
about 200 inhabitants; the houses of the peasants are in the midst
of gardens, planted with apricot trees, vines, and olives. They are
watered from a copious fountain about a mile above the village,
surrounded by a circular foundation of ancient masonry; the only
remains † of antiquity which we could discover near a place once
distinguished as εὐετημένη Μαραῶα. The stream derived from the
fountain, the Macaria of Pausanias, passes down the valley parallel
to the river, to the distance of three quarters of a mile; and is then
conducted across the river in a wooden trough, and continues its
course to the village, where it is employed in the gardens. Above
the fountain is a small detached rocky height, at the summit of
which is a cavern with a low entrance, and naturally divided into
several compartments; this, according to Pausanias, may be the
mountain and grotto of Pan, though it would be difficult to conceive
the slightest resemblance in the rocks to goats or sheep, mentioned
by that author in his Grecian tour. From Marathona to Athens is a
march of about seven hours, in a S. W. direction, and the first part
of the road is through an unequal, rocky, and rather a difficult
country; over a ridge, which connects Pentelicus with the eastern
extremity of Parnes, and therefore corresponds with the situation of

---

* At the western extremity of the valley, where Brauron is placed, Col. Squire has
noticed in his plan the ruins of a marble monument. The Editor supposes that in this
portion of the plain part of a Greek inscription was found by M. Fauvel. The words he
had copied were the following

ΟΜΟΝΟΙΑΣ ΑΘΑΝΑΤ

ΠΥΛΗ

ΗΡΩΔΟΥΟΧΩΡΟΣ

ΕΙΣΟΝΡΙΣΕΡΧΕ .

There appears to be some reference to Herodes Atticus who died at Marathon

† The columns in the marsh observed by Dr. Clarke are probably part of the temple of
the Hellotian Minerva, so called from the marsh on the plain; the temple of the Delian
Apollo, and one of Hercules, are mentioned by the ancient writers.—Schol. Pind.
Olymp. xiii. Herod. vi

the ancient Brilessus. Beyond is the extensive plain of Athens, which reaches from Mount Pentelicus to the sea.

As soon as the Athenians received intelligence that the Persians had actually landed in their country they marched against them. Of the exact number on either side Herodotus makes no mention; according to Plutarch (in Parall.) and Valerius Maximus, the forces of the enemy amounted to 300,000, Justin reckons them to be 600,000; and Cornelius Nepos (in vitâ Milt.) makes them ten times the number of the Athenians, or about 100,000. The amount of the Grecian force must have been of universal notoriety; the battle of Marathon was doubtless the most important event in the history of Athens; it was ever afterwards the pride and boast of the Athenians; and might be considered no less than the fight at Artemisium, as κρηπὶς ἐλευθερίας. (Pindar) " the foundation of their freedom;" surely then the recollection of every minute circumstance of that engagement would be fondly cherished to the last hour of the republic. Although therefore Herodotus does not relate the numbers in the Grecian army, the authority of Plutarch, Cornelius Nepos, and Pausanias on this head may be accepted without hesitation; for though these authors differ with regard to the Persian army, they uniformly agree in stating the Athenian force at Marathon to have been 9000 men *, besides 1000 Platæans, who alone of the other Grecian states bore a part in the engagement. Pausanias particularly observes (in Phoc.) that in this statement of the Athenian force the slaves were also included. An army of 10,000 men was but an inconsiderable force to oppose to the Persians, unless this amazing inferiority was counterbalanced by some local advantages. The Greeks therefore when they arrived at Marathon, would not descend into the plain to expose themselves to be surrounded by numbers,

---

* Mr. Mitford in his History of Greece (i 365) supposes the regular Grecian forces engaged at the battle of Marathon to consist of greater numbers than those mentioned in the text   He *adds* some thousand slaves to the Athenian army, whereas Pausanias *includes* them in the number 9000   Ἀθηναίοι σὺν δούλοις ἐννεακισχιλίων ἀφίκοντο ὀυ πλείους.— Phoc

and afterwards destroyed by the cavalry, they would surely take a position, securing their flanks as much as possible, while they presented but a small front towards the enemy. The valley of Marathon offered to the Athenians as favourable a spot for engaging as could be desired. While they could fight the enemy on equal terms, a body so well trained and disciplined, and commanded by such able generals as the Athenians were, would have little hesitation to oppose themselves to the most spirited efforts of the barbarians. The Athenians also had powerful motives to animate and encourage them, their liberty, their existence were at stake, while the numerous hordes of the enemy, unacquainted with their officers, and prompted by different interests would easily relax in the fight, and be overpowered by the firm and daring courage of the Athenians. On the first view, indeed, the conduct of the Greeks in marching out from the city, and thus risking their country in this single engagement, appears wholly desperate; though when their situation is considered, it must be allowed that their councils were dictated by prudence and reason. To have opposed the debarkation of the Persians would have been absurd and fruitless; had they suffered the enemy to advance into the plain of Athens, their country would most probably have been lost, for no situation between the city and the place of landing could afford so many advantages for an engagement as the valley of Marathon. Had the Athenians shut themselves up in Athens, the Persians, in full possession of the open country, would soon have compelled them to surrender; so that, all things considered, the Athenians seem to have adopted the wisest measure by deciding resolutely to occupy the pass on the principal road towards the capital.

The armies of the Athenians were commanded by ten generals, according to the number of their tribes, each of whom was in his turn commander-in-chief of the day. To these was added the Polemarch, an officer who had the privilege of giving a casting vote in the event of a difference of opinion on the plan of operations. In the present instance the sentiments of the ten generals were divided, five being averse to an engagement; which the remainder strongly recommended. Miltiades, who was the youngest in rank, though highest in reputation, zealous in the cause of his country, and convinced in his own mind that the wisest course was to engage, gained Callimachus, who was then Polemarch, over to his opinion, and it was resolved to attack the enemy. Plutarch observes, that Aristides was of the same way of thinking with Miltiades, and was of great assistance in persuading the rest. When the decisive moment arrived, he disposed his forces in the following manner; Callimachus commanded the right wing; for by a law this post was always confided to the Polemarch; beginning from the right flank the tribes were placed in the line according to their order; the Plataeans were on the left. Miltiades formed his front equal to that of the Medes, weakening indeed his centre, in which were only the tribes Leontis and Antiochis (the first commanded by Themistocles, the second by Aristides), that he might strengthen the wings.

No other situation at Marathon, but in the valley itself, could have afforded him the great advantage of making his line equal to that of the enemy. The space which it is conjectured was occupied by the Greeks was about 1500 yards in length; on computing that each soldier occupied three feet, there would consequently be 1500 men in the first line. From the weakness of their numbers, and the extent of ground they were obliged to occupy, they could not afford that great depth to their line which was always customary, and would in this instance have been very important. Miltiades therefore wisely took from his centre, that he might give greater strength to his flanks.

When the sacrifices appeared favourable for commencing the engagement, the Greeks rushed forward in full charge against the barbarians. Between the van of each army there was a space of not less than eight stadia, about three quarters of a mile. The Persians when they perceived the Greeks in motion, immediately prepared to receive them, for they considered such conduct as the height of folly, and the certain cause of destruction to the Greeks, who, without cavalry or archers, pressed forward to the attack with such violent impetuosity. The latter however when they came hand to hand with the barbarians, fought in a manner most worthy to be recorded; they were the first, says the historian, of all the Greeks who advanced in full charge (Le pas de charge, *Larcher*,) against their enemies, and none before had ever sustained the Medes, and the terrific appearance of their dress. In the representation of this battle by Micon, the Persians were painted taller than the Athenians; and the artist was fined thirty minæ; but he was probably correct in his design, as the Oriental dress must have given to the Asiatics the appearance of greater height. †

In the early part of the engagement, the centre of the Greeks was obliged to fall back and was pursued up the country by the Persians and the Sacæ, but on either wing fortune favored the Greeks, and here they overcame, routed the barbarians, and compelled them to fly. Those who had turned their backs they at first allowed to retire unmolested, so that the Greeks uniting their victorious wings, attacked and defeated those of the enemy who had been successful in the centre. The rout now became general, the Persians retreated in confusion towards the beach, to regain, if possible, their shipping; and vast numbers were slain by the Greeks who constantly pursued them. Pausanias (lib 1 cap 15.) describes a painting at Athens in the Peisanactean portico by Panænus, the brother of Phidias, representing the battle of Marathon, and in which are observed the Persians flying in every direction across the plain, and driving one another into the marsh. In a second passage

* The earliest mention we find in history of cavalry in the Greek armies, is of the date 743 B C, the time of the first Messenian war. At Marathon the Athenians had no force of this kind, as Thessaly, the country from which many of the Grecian states were supplied with horses, was in the power of the Persians. — See Goguet m 151

† Sopater see Valesius in not Mauss Harpocration 123 On a frize of a temple at Athens was sculptured the representation of a battle between the Persians and Athenians, the former were distinguished by their long garments and tiaras and Phrygian bonnets — See p 20 Memorandum of Lord Elgin's Pursuits in Greece

of the Attics, Pausanias particularly mentions the marsh at Marathon, and as connected with the sea by a small stream of salt water. This description corresponds most minutely with the ground in the north east extremities of the plain.   The remainder of the Persian army embarked as hastily as possible, and doubling Cape Sunium sailed towards Phalerum with the hopes of anticipating the Athenians, and of taking the city before the army could return from Marathon.

The Athenians, however, having left the tribe Antiochis commanded by Aristides, to guard the wounded and prisoners, and to collect the spoil, marched instantly for Athens, so that the Persians being disappointed of their object, returned with their fleet to the coast of Asia.

According to the historian, there fell of the Athenians one hundred and ninety-two, while the loss on the part of the barbarians amounted to six thousand four hundred . seven of the ships were also burnt or destroyed by the Greeks.   Callimachus, the Polemarch, was among the slain, as was also the commander Cynægirus, the brother of the poet Æschylus

It was a custom with the Athenians to bury those who were slain in battle, or to erect columns to their memory, in a place called the Ceramicus, " the most beautiful suburb of their city," to use the words of Thucydides ; but as a particular mark of distinction, three monuments were erected at Marathon, in honor of the event of the battle; one was raised to the memory of the Athenians, who fell in it ; another recorded the valour of the Plateans, and the slaves who fought : a third was the monument of Miltiades. — Paus.   At this day may be seen towards the middle of the plain a large tumulus of earth, 25 feet in height, resembling those on the plain of Troy.   In a small marsh near the sea, are the vestiges of ten monuments with marble foundations, and fragments of columns, which, it may be conjectured, marked the tombs of the Athenians.

(337)

REMARKS

ON

PARTS OF THE CONTINENT OF GREECE.

[FROM THE PAPERS OF THE LATE COLONEL SQUIRE.]

THE chief communications between Athens and the neighbouring districts, were across Cithæron into Bœotia; by Decelea, through Tanagra to Lubœa; into the Peloponnesus by Eleusis and Megara.

In the first route, one traverses the plain of Athens, through the olive grounds, to the foot of Parnes, a distance of about seven miles from the city. After an hour's gentle ascent over a rugged road in the mountain, on an abrupt isolated rock, a short distance to the left, the stronghold*, Phyle, often mentioned in the history of Athens, is observed. Having crossed Parnes, you reach a small plain, in which are the ruins of Eleutheræ; then the road ascends Cithæron, through a narrow rock and winding gorge, on which are the remains of an ancient fortress in a very commanding situation. From the summit of Cithæron, by the road called the Three-heads, is the descent into the plain of Bœotia, a distance of seven hours from Athens, in a north west direction.

The Athenians derived a great part of their supplies from Eubœa; the route was to the north of Athens, between Pentelicus and Parnes; and here was the strong fort Decelea. † From Attica, there

---

* φρούριον ὀχυρόν Stephanus, see Corsini F. A. Diss. v

† "Decelea, according to Thucydides, was about 120 stadia from Athens, that is, 20 stadia further from Athens than Phyle (Diodorus, tom. i 667. Wesseling), and in a different direction, being on the other side of Parnes, for it was on the road to Oropus, and interrupted the communication by land between Athens and Eubœa. There is some

is another road to Euboea, along the sea-side from Marathon, from
this place to Athens is a distance of eight hours, three of which are
through the plain north of the city, after this, the road leads over low
and rugged heights covered with pine-trees and shrubs, until Marathon
presents itself, in a narrow valley with a plain, about three miles
wide, between the village and the sea. From Athens to the Peloponnesus, the route is through Eleusis and Megara, for the most part
along the shore of the gulf, after having traversed the plain in
an hour and a half between Corydallus and Parnes, in a small valley,
which leads immediately to the sea, is the convent Daphne, where
are two or three inscriptions, and blended with the modern building,
columns of the Ionic order, the remains of the temple of Venus.
Hence, in a quarter of an hour is the descent to the sea, called Κακή
σκάλα*, the bad road, from this point to the streams Rhiti, is the
distance of a mile and a half. The road has been formed in the rock
close to the sea, and in many places are perceived the marks made
by the carriage wheels. After the Rhiti, which are insignificant
streams, commences the plain of Thria or Eleusis, from the Rhiti to
Eleusis, is the distance of an hour and a half. The plan of the great
Temple of Ceres †, may in part be accurately traced. The plain of
Eleusis about eight miles long, and four in width, is almost entirely

---

high level ground of considerable extent in this direction, over which the road still leads
from Athens to the village of Oropo. Now the nearest distance of Athens from the foot of
Parnes is 11 English miles, or about 110 stadia. we may therefore expect to discover the
remains of Decelea at the distance of 10 stadia farther, and on the spurs of that mountain.
Here in fact Stuart has noticed some ruins of ancient Greek walls, which both he and Sir
W. Gell believe to be the walls of Decelea. The spot bears the significative appellation
of χωριο-καλύβια." — Mr. Hawkins

* Les Grecs la nomment encore aujourd'hui Kakiscala. — Des Mouceaux.

† The temple was destroyed by Alaric in 396. Ac. Ins. t. 47. The remains have
been carefully examined by the mission sent into Greece in 1812, by the Dilettanti society.
The cella was about 180 feet square, with a portico of 12 Doric columns, of more than
six feet in diameter. The fragment of the Eleusinian Goddess now at Cambridge, was
first noticed by Des Mouceaux. " L'Ouvrage," he says, speaking of the sculpture of part of
it, " où est achevé la draperie, fait des plis d'un gout merveilleux."

cultivated with barley. From Eleusis to Megara, a distance of four hours, the road traverses first a low height, until the country of Megara soon appears with the town on two small eminences, about two miles from the sea; here are few vestiges of antiquity, but it appears, that as at Athens, long walls connected the port with the town. The nearest road to the Isthmus is along the sea-shore, and the Scironian rocks, rugged and difficult; the Turks have here established a Dervent or guard-house, to prevent contraband commerce in the Morea, and no one is allowed to pass without an express order from the Pasha of Tripolizza. The ordinary route from Megara, is along the north side of the mountain, which forms the first barrier to the Isthmus, until it joins the grand line of communication from the Morea, with the northern provinces of Greece. Here is a Dervent, and hence the road traverses the mountain, through a high irregular broken country, continually descending until it meets the low, though uneven ground of the Isthmus. From Eleusis is a road into Bœotia two hours across the plain to the north, then through a part of Mount Parnes; beyond is the plain of Eleutheræ; and here the road from Eleusis joins the ordinary route from Athens by Phyle into Bœotia.

Bœotia consists for the most part of the extensive plain enclosed by Cithæron, Helicon, Parnassus, and the mountainous country of the Locrians on the sea of Eubœa. This plain is intersected by low ridges of a bare and rocky soil, so that Bœotia may be sub-divided into the plains of Platæa, Leuctra, Thebes, Lebadea, and Chæronæa. The well-watered plains of Chæronæa and Lebadea, and the land bordering on the Lake Copais are chiefly sown with rice, cotton, and doura, and a small proportion of tobacco; the other districts with wheat and barley. The soil of Bœotia is rich and productive, and from Thebes, the unworthy representative of the ancient capital, a considerable quantity of grain is annually exported.

Bœotia is well supplied with water by the numerous springs from the mountains, besides its rivers, which notwithstanding as in other parts of Greece, they are small inconsiderable streams, are more full and constant. The rapid little river Hercyna has its rise in Helicon above Lebadea, and after being augmented by the fountains Lethe and Mnemosyne, near the supposed site of the cave of Trophonius, flows through the rice grounds, and discharges itself into the Lake Copais. The Cephissus has its rise in Mount Œta, fertilizes the plain of Phocis, then entering that of Chæronæa, through a narrow gorge between a part of Parnassus and the country of the Locrians, meets the lake Copais in the neighbourhood of Orchomenus. This lake has subterranean communications with the sea: in summer, instead of a sheet of water, it has the appearance of an extensive green meadow. Topoglia, the supposed ancient Copæ, is a small insulated eminence at the north-east extremity, and is approachable from the plain by a causeway. The lake is about twelve miles in circuit. Bœotia with its rich soil, and a continual supply of water, had local advantages which Attica did not possess; there was greater opulence, more numerous cities, and a larger population than in the latter.

Lebadea, now pronounced Livadea, is placed at the entrance of a rocky ravine, on the north side of Helicon. From some small masses of ancient foundations, it is imagined that the site of the original city was a short distance from the present town, and immediately on the plain. The little river Hercyna rushes through the rocky irregular bottom of the ravine, and receives an increase of water from the fountains near the cave of Trophonius. On the left side of the river above the town, and at the foot of a rocky height surrounded by a Turkish fortress in a very ruinous state, is an artificial excavation about twelve feet square, and eight in height on the upper part are still seen the remains of an ancient coloured border similar to that which is observed on the walls of the Parthenon, and in the temple of Theseus at Athens. In front of the grotto is a powerful spring discharging itself by eleven artificial pipes into a small basin, the water of which afterwards overflows and joins the river; on the opposite side is another fountain which bubbles up from the ground, forming immediately a square reservoir, which connects also with the Hercyna

Scripoo', the ancient Orchomenus, is placed immediately on the Lake Copais, at the foot of a mountain about seven miles east of Livadea, it may contain from three to four hundred inhabitants. In the church and court of the convent of Scripoo are many long and valuable inscriptions. Immediately at the lower part of the rocky height above Scripoo, is a large block of marble, supported by two upright walls, apparently the entrance of a building.† A perfect structure on a similar design now exists at Mycenæ, so that from a comparison of the two, it may be fairly concluded, that one was the treasury of Atreus, the other of Minyas, at Mycenæ the building is of stone, at Orchomenus of marble. In consequence of the excavations made by Lord Elgin, the treasury of Atreus is a recent discovery, previously to this, Mr. Tweddell, who died at Athens in the midst of his researches‡, had ingeniously conjectured, that the large stone at Scripoo, had once formed part of the celebrated treasury of Minyas, and his opinion has been since confirmed by the examination of that at Mycenæ. On the height above the village, are vestiges of the ancient walls of Orchomenus, with a sort of citadel on the summit of the mountain; the plan of it may be very accurately traced; on the east side of the

---

* " I rode up the hill, with difficulty, to the acropolis of Orchomenus, ascending a slope which probably was the scene of Sylla's battle The walls of the citadel are well built, in the best style of masonry and without cement The citadel is long and narrow, adapted to the shape of the ridge; a long flight of steps hewn in the rock leads to the town, which extended in a triangular form down the lower part of the slope to the plain below The lake seems to have gained considerably on the land on the eastern side it came up to the foot of the mountain, and left but a small space in front "— From Mr Rakes

† The measures of the door-way and the great stone above it, were sent to the Editor, by Mr Hawkins. They are given in another part of this volume.

‡ In medio flore interceptus, fructus quos ex doctrina ejus nobis certissimos spondebamus, maturare et emittere non potuit — Salmasius Praef ad Tab Cebetis

mountain, which is here bounded by the Lake Copais, are two very copious springs.

Chæronæa, now called Caprena, is placed at the foot of that range of heights which forms the western limit of the plain traversed by the Cephissus, before it discharges itself into the Copaic Lake. Here are a few inscriptions, and on the height north of the town, are the remains of a Greek fortress, which probably was once the acropolis At the east extremity of this height, where it meets the plain, are vestiges of an ancient theatre, with several seats excavated in the rock. The site of Coronea, it is imagined, is now occupied by the little village Granizza, at the foot of Helicon, about two miles east of Livadea, here is a tower about twenty feet square, of ancient and most solid construction. North-west of Platæa, in a small plain bounded to the west by Helicon, are traced the ancient foundations of an oval enclosure, which probably was the situation of Leuctra; an insignificant village of five houses, adjoining the spot, called Lefka, in some degree confirms the conjecture; here are two inscriptions, and more in the village called Ermo Castro in the heights north of Lefka. Between Platæa and Leuctra is a considerable plain, which from two tumuli near the road, may be supposed to have been the scene of the engagement between Epaminondas and the Spartans. — On the irregular ground, the roots of Cithæron, are the remains of the ancient fortifications of Platæa, containing within them, though on level ground. a semicircular *enceinte*, (one side of the outer walls forming the chord) which perhaps was the acropolis; here are some fragments of columns and masses of masonry, and several very ancient sarcophagi, without the city. The village Kokle, containing about one hundred and fifty inhabitants, is above the remains of Platæa. — The scene of the celebrated fight at Platæa, was on the north side of Cithæron, a chain of mountains which extending from the Ægæan to the Corinthian sea, separates Attica from Bœotia. The chief road of communication between these districts passes over the summits of Cithæron, which in this part is distinguished by three remarkable points, anciently called by the Boeotians " The Heads," by the Athenians " The Heads of the Oak."

Three miles westward of the pass over Cithæron, are the vestiges of the towers and walls of the ancient Platæa; about half way between the descent from Cithæron, and the remains of the city, is a low ridge of heights extending in a north direction from the mountain, and bounding the plain of Platæa to the eastward; from either side of this ridge is a descent *, on one side towards the sea of Corinth, on the other towards the Euripus, according to the position of the country, the Asopus having its rise in Cithæron discharges itself into the sea of Eubœa, while another river which it may be conjectured was the Æroe, also flowing from Cithæron, has its course through the plain of Platæa, passes before the city, and then falls into the gulf of Corinth, near Livadostro. Both these rivers have separate branches in the mountain, and the latter precisely forms the same sort of island, so minutely described by the historian, lib ix 50 though its streams, as those of other Grecian rivers, are merely torrents in the winter; the Asopus, rather more considerable, has stagnant pools in different parts of its channel, even throughout the summer, on the left of the road leading from the Three Heads to Platæa is a copious fountain, which, during the summer months, supplies the villages Gondara and Velia with water. It is now called Vergentiani, and was perhaps the Gargaphia in Herodotus Erythræ may have been on the site of the village Pigadhia, and Hysiæ on that of Gondara and Velia On the left bank of the Asopus, consisting of perhaps thirty houses, is Scammo, which is supposed to have succeeded Tanagra in its situation, here are two inscriptions, which relate to Oropus, whereas Oropus was on the other side of the river while at Oropo, which from its situation and name may be pronounced to be the ancient Oropus, are three or four marbles on which Tanagra is mentioned

---

* Consult Mr Stanhope's Memoir and Plan relating to the country round Platæa

Helicon bounds the plain of Lebadea to the west, joins with Parnassus, and terminates to the south on the gulf of Corinth near Livadostro.   Its presents a bare and rugged appearance   but some of the
vallies are cultivated in corn, interspersed with orchards of fruit trees,
the plane, the fig, and the poplar, in abundance.

Phocis includes the plain of the Cephissus, which connects with
that of Livadea, on the north it is bounded by Œta, on the south by
Bœotia, on the east side the mountainous country of the Dorians
separates it from the sea of Eubœa, the western limit is washed by
the Corinthian or Crissean gulfs.   The soil, watered by the Cephissus,
which is joined by several smaller streams from Parnassus, is fertile
and well cultivated in rice, doura, and corn land, the plain of   Crissa
produces a small quantity of wheat and barley, though it is for the
most part planted with olive trees   An elevated plain, on which is
Thistomo, the ancient Ambryssus, seems to connect Parnassus on the
south with Helicon.   To the north the mountains join with Œta; opposite to its west side is Mount Cirphis, while its eastern slope is
presented towards the plain of the Cephissus   The outer aspect of
Parnassus is rude and without vegetation, it encloses however several
fruitful valleys, as remarkable for their natural beauties as for their
cultivation.   This mountain is intersected by several roads in different
directions, which connect the plain of Cephissus with that of Crissa,
Delphi, and the sea.   The road called Schiste, which was the sacred
way from Attica and Bœotia to Delphi, soon appears after entering
Parnassus at Daulis; it commences in a spot where three roads join,
τρίοδος, famed for the sepulchre of Œdipus.   Hence the road to
Delphi branches off to the right, and is continued through an elevated
narrow valley, either side of which is bounded by the lofty ridges of

---

* Cirrha is now called Xeropegano, the Plistus flowing between the heights of Liacoura and Cirphis passes near it   Crissa (Chriso) contains some remarkable ruins, and
near a church called Agio Sarandi, is an inscription in Boustrophedon, there is a bas-
relief in another church, and a lyre represented with 16 strings. — (From M. Gropius)

Parnassus; in this part, in the depth of summer, we observed snow in a cavity near the summit of the mountain. After an hour and a half from the τρόὸς are perceived the remains of an ancient fortress, near which is a fountain; this part of Parnassus is rugged, with little cultivation, though the sides of the mountain are much scattered with pine-trees. An hour from the palaio-castro, as this kind of ruin is always termed by the modern Greeks, is Rakova, a small village in an elevated part of the mountain, commanding a magnificent view, before us, was the valley of Delphi, which was seen in its length, confined on one side by Parnassus, on the other by Mount Cirphis, perpendicular to this valley was the plain of Crissa, clouded by its olive-yards, bounded by the rude mountainous country of the Ozolæ; the fantastic abrupt shapes of Parnassus were well contrasted with the luxuriance of the valley, which was a continued plantation of vines. Delphi is about five hours from Daulis; a small village, under the appellation of Castri, now occupies the site of this memorable spot; it presents a rugged and uneven slope, above which, the summits of Parnassus rise abrupt and perpendicular. Here are two fountains, probably those of Castalia and Cassotis [*], the " vocal streams," of which the priestess drank before she uttered her mysterious prophecies. The rock in the vicinity, has been much chisselled and excavated; near a spring, is a square artificial grotto, one of the Bacchicæ Speluncæ mentioned by Macrobius. The head of an ox, which is sculptured in a cavern or room in the rock, has a reference to Apollo. (v. Huet. D. Ev. iv. c. 8.) Some valuable inscriptions have been copied at Delphi [†] the remains of the stadium are very evident; but those of the theatre and temple, the latter of which was restored at so late a period as the time of the Emperor Julian,

---

[*] That the waters of Cassotis, as well as Castalia were used, is evident from Pausan. Lucian. Eurip See the authorities quoted by Van Dale, de Orac. 130. The " vocal streams' are mentioned in part of the response, uttered to Oribasius, Julian's physician. Cedren. 250 Ed. Bas ἀπέσβετο καὶ λάλον ὕδωρ

[†] One found by Wheler and Spon, speaks of the privileges of προεδρία, προδικία, προξενία, and προμαντεία, (or the right of consulting the oracle first) bestowed on some persons.

are not to be traced.　　Immediately above Delphi is another road into the plain of the Cephissus, over the highest part of the moun- tain, near which must have been Tithorea, and towards the descent into the plain Ledon and Charadra. From the parched plains in the summer months, the shepherds migrate with their flocks to the cooler regions of Parnassus, where a rich pasture, with springs of water abounds. The road from Delphi occasionally traverses small cultivated plains enclosed with rocky heights; sometimes detached, and continually scattered over with pine trees, affording a wild and horrid, though imposing aspect. From the western point of the plain of the Cephissus, nearer to Mount Œta, is a passage by way of Salona, the ancient Amphissa, into the plain of Crissa, and to Delphi. At the entrance of the mountain is a modern Khan, near which are the remains of a fortress, placed on an almost inaccessible rock. The descent into the plain of Salona is along a winding, arti- ficial road, formed with masonry, on the steep side of a mountain , from this town, the plain of the Cephissus is about three hours distant; it connects with that of Chæronea.

ISTHMUS OF CORINTH.

From Greece into Peloponnesus there are two roads; the one from Megara along a narrow cornice on the Saronic gulf, artificially formed in the rocks, which rise perpendicularly from the sea. The ordinary route from Bœotia and Attica into the Peloponnesus was over the summits of the mountain Gerania, which forms the first barrier of the isthmus towards Greece. You enter into a narrow gorge, near which is a Dervent, or Turkish guard-house; afterwards a good gravelly road along the slope of a mountain leads to irregular heights, covered with pines and brush-wood; hence the descent is gradual to the low, but rocky, uneven ground of the isthmus; about three miles before we arrive at Corinth may be traced the vestiges of a very ancient wall, which was built for the defence of the Peloponnesus; this is in the most narrow part of the isthmus; where it is four short miles in width; it consisted as in other Greek fortifications of a stone wall with square towers in the intervals between them. On the east side of the isthmus for a considerable distance in front of the wall, the ground appears low * and swampy, as if an excavation had been begun at some remote period to admit the sea water, and thus strengthen the position. We read in Herodotus that the Peloponnesians after the battle of Thermopylæ took post at the isthmus, and having destroyed the Scironian way, they built a wall across the isthmus. From their critical situation, under a dread of an irruption from the barbarians into the Peloponnesus, it may be concluded, as indeed Herodotus mentions, that the Greeks would lose no time in completing their fortifications, they used all sorts of materials, stones, bricks, timber, baskets filled with earth, rather temporary expedients, than the means of erecting a solid and permanent barrier. What date must we then affix to the remains of the present wall † across the isthmus? — Immediately in front of Corinth are the vestiges of some modern field works, constructed by the Venetians for the defence of the pass into the Morea; on the west side they are terminated by a square redoubt on the Corinthian gulph near Lechæum, one of the ancient ports of the city; on the east there was no necessity to continue these works to the shore, on account of a high and difficult mountain between Corinth and the sea. In front of the town is a modern village called by the modern Greeks Hexamilia, the isthmus

* Des Monceaux, who travelled in 1668, says, that in some parts it would have been necessary to dig the canal to the depth of fifteen toises, " et presque partout de dix, à l'exception des deux extremites, où le terrein se baisse vers la marine" The remains of this work will be pointed out by Mr Hawkins in his account of the survey of the isthmus, he was occupied two days in measuring it

† The wall built across the isthmus by the Greeks when they were alarmed by the Persian invasion, reached from Lechæum to Cenchreæ, a distance of five miles, as we learn from Strabo, Pliny, Agathemerus, and Diod S (See Wesseling in D S. t 1 p 116) This was in a different spot from that observed by Col. S The wall he notices is more to the north, and in a narrower part Manuel Palæologus fortified the isthmus, the wall was forced by Murat the Second, and was used again by the Venetians in 1696 — See D'Anville l'Empire Turc. pp. 33. 116.

being in this part about six Greek miles in width. On the road from Corinth to Cenchreæ the harbour of the city on the Saronic gulf, are two Roman sepulchres of masonry, and faced with tesselated brick work, the position of Lechæum, as well as of Cenchreæ is sufficiently marked by traces of stone foundation in the sea, which formed the inclosure of the harbour; these ports are now almost entirely filled up and destroyed; and capable only of admitting the very small boats of the country.

Considered in a military point of view, the isthmus renders the Morea extremely secure against any attack meditated on the land side from Greece; but on the two coasts there is a very favourable shore for debarkation, and accessible in every part; the gulf of Lepanto or Corinth indeed being very narrow and contracted at its entrance, though it afterwards expands into an extensive bay, is capable of the strongest defence; the Saronic or gulf of Ægina is more open, and an invading squadron might anchor in this sea without any fear of opposition from the land. On examining the ground, the ridge of mountains, the ancient Gerania, appears to constitute the best and most tenable barrier of the isthmus towards Greece; the Scironian road leading from Megara may readily be destroyed; an impracticable rocky height thus extends from one sea to the other, presenting only in one instance a passable gorge, the present road into the Peloponnesus, which may be defended by a handful of men against the most formidable invader. Cannon judiciously planted in this part would ensure the safety of the isthmus, for the whole ground in front, consisting of rugged uneven heights, is completely commanded by the mountain. With the Acro-Corinthus, and the ridge of heights at the south extremity of the isthmus, where are still seen the traces of Venetian field-works, may be established a second position, not so strong, and more extended than the first; the great advantage of the second post would be in the event of a debarkation on the sides of the isthmus, in the rear of the mountainous ridge Gerania. From the shore of the Corinthian gulf little may be apprehended, because the entrance into this sea may be prevented by strong batteries or towers at Lepanto That part of the shore of the Saronic bay, calculated for debarkation, is an extent of three or four miles, bounding the lowest part of the isthmus, between the Scironian rocks, and the mountains eastward of Corinth, a space which with the assistance of art might be easily defended. What has been observed with regard to the defence of the Peloponnesus relates only to an attack from Greece, or to a debarkation on the isthmus

Why did the Greeks build a wall across the isthmus, instead of fortifying the gorge in the first barrier in the mountain? It is reasonable to suppose that the last mode of defence was attended to as well as the first, and that an advanced guard would have been stationed to dispute to the last moment this important pass [*], this Thermopylæ of the Peloponnesus. But though the Greeks would take advantage of the obstacles, nature had offered for their protection against an invasion by land, they would also provide against any force, which the Persians might attempt to debark on the isthmus, in the event of a victory obtained by their naval armaments, over the allied Greeks at Salamis. Those of the Peloponnesus would therefore immediately draw the line of fortification, particularly mentioned by Herodotus, so placing their defences, as to enclose the harbour of Cenchreæ on the Saronic gulf, and at the same time to allow as little space as possible for a debarkation in their rear.

---

[*] The importance of a fortress at Gerancia was not overlooked by the Greeks, we find mention of the τεῖχος Γεράνεια in Scylax Per. 15. Hudson But the time of erecting it cannot of course be fixed

OBSERVATIONS

RELATING TO

SOME OF THE ANTIQUITIES OF EGYPT.

[FROM THE JOURNALS OF THE LATE MR DAVISON]

THE most sure and accurate method of finding the height of the great Pyramid, says Grobert, is that of measuring the steps of it, 205 were counted by some of the French Institute, and the size of each (on the side facing the N.W.) in feet, inches, and lines was taken, making 437 feet, two inches; but three steps under the apparent lowest step were uncovered; and as these add eleven feet to the measures already mentioned, the sum total is 448 feet, 2 inches; and the whole number of the tiers of stone is 208. The apparent base of the Pyramid is 718 feet, in length; the true one, is 728. —

Mr. Davison, many years before had adopted the same plan of taking the height of this Pyramid. In examining his statement, we shall find that he measured 206 tiers of stone*, and marked, separately, the dimensions of each According to this examination, the perpendicular height of the Pyramid is 460 feet, 11 inches. The base is computed by him at 746 feet. — In comparing these measures with those of the French, it should be recollected that the French foot equals 1.066 English.

The following are the particulars of Mr. Davison's Measurement.

---

* By a diligent examination, says Greaves, I and two others found the number of degrees from the bottom to the top to be 207. See vol. 1. 105

Step	F.	In.	Step	F.	In.	Step	F.	In.
1.	4	—	38.	3	0½	75.	2	5½
2	1	8	39.	2	11	76.	2	1
3	3	10	40.	2	8½	77.	2	0¼
4.	3	9½	41.	2	7¼	78.	1	11½
5.	3	4	42.	2	4¾	79	1	11½
6	3	3	43.	2	9½	80.	2	0½
7	3	4⅔	44	3	4¾	81.	1	11⅔
8.	2	11½	45.	3	2¼	82.	1	11½
9.	3	1	46.	2	3¾	83.	1	10⅓
10.	2	11⅔	47.	2	10	84.	2	4¼
11	2	9¾	48	3	1¼	85.	1	10⅓
12	2	6	49.	2	8	86.	2	2⅔
13	2	6	50	2	3¼	87.	1	10½
14	2	5⅓	51.	2	2¼	88.	1	10⅔
15.	2	6½	52.	2	2½	89.	1	11¾
16.	2	3¾	53	2	2	90.	3	2¼
17	2	4	54.	2	1½	91.	2	11½
18.	2	7⅓	55.	2	1¼	92.	2	8½
19.	3	2	56.	2	1¼	93	2	5⅓
20.	2	0	57.	2	0¾	94.	2	2¼
21.	1	11½	58.	2	3	95.	2	1¼
22.	2	11	59.	2	5⅓	96.	1	11¾
23.	2	8¾	60.	2	4	97.	1	11⅔
24.	2	8¼	61.	2	2½	98.	3	5
25.	2	8½	62.	2	1	99.	3	2⅓
26	2	7	63	2	1½	100.	2	11⅓
27.	2	5¾	64.	2	2	101.	2	8¼
28.	2	5½	65.	2	2½	102.	2	5⅓
29.	2	5	66	1	11¼	103.	2	5⅓
30.	2	3⅔	67.	2	11	104.	2	2⅔
31	2	4⅓	68.	2	7	105.	2	2⅓
32.	2	2¼	69.	2	8⅓	106.	2	1⅓
33.	2	2	70.	2	5	107.	2	0⅔
34.	2	2	71.	2	4	108.	2	5⅓
35.	4	0½	72.	2	2¾	109.	2	2⅔
36	3	7¼	73.	2	2	110.	1	11⅔
37	3	1½	74.	2	7¼	111.	1	11⅔

Step	F	In.	Step	F	In.	Step	F	In.
112.	1	11¾	144	2	5⅓	176	1	8⅔
113	1	11⅓	145.	2	2	177.	1	8⅔
114.	1	10⅔	146	2	0	178.	1	8½
115.	1	10¾	147	1	11	179.	1	9
116	2	2½	148	1	10⅓	180.	2	2½
117.	1	11¼	149.	1	9¾	181.	1	1
118.	3	0	150.	2	2⅓	182.	1	11¾
119.	2	8	151.	2	0¾	183.	1	10⅔
120.	2	6⅓	152.	2	0	184.	1	10 [illegible]
121.	2	5½	153	1	10⅔	185.	1	9
122.	2	2½	154.	1	9 [illegible]	186.	1	9⅓
123.	2	2⅓	155.	1	9⅓	187.	1	8½
124.	2	1	156	1	9½	188.	1	8½
125.	1	11½	157	1	9	189.	1	8⅔
126.	1	11¾	158	1	10	190.	1	8⅓
127.	1	11¾	159.	1	9½	191.	1	9¼
128.	1	11	160.	1	9¼	192	1	8
129.	1	10⅓	161	1	9¼	193	1	8½
130.	2	2⅔	162.	1	11⅔	194	1	8½
131.	2	1¼	163.	1	10⅓	195.	1	8⅔
132.	1	11¾	164	1	1	196.	1	11¼
133.	1	10¼	165.	1	9⅓	197.	1	11⅓
134.	1	9¾	166.	1	9¾	198.	1	10¼
135.	1	10	167.	1	8⅓	199	1	9⅓
136.	1	11¾	168.	1	9¼	200	1	9¾
137.	1	10⅓	169.	1	8¼	201.	1	10¼
138.	2	2⅔	170.	1	9	202.	1	9⅓
139	1	1½	171.	1	8	203	1	8¾
140	1	10¼	172.	1	9⅓	204	1	8⅓
141.	1	9½	173	1	8½	205.	1	8¾
142.	1	10⅔	174	1	8½	206.	3	2¼
143	1	10¼	175	1	8¾			

The perpendicular height of the large Pyramid of Giza 460 11

The square of the Pyramid is 746 feet; its perpendicular height 460 feet, 11 inches. The top consists of six stones, irregularly disposed ; 206 tiers compose the whole height of the Pyramid As the square of every tier is less than the one below it, the space of two or three feet which is left on all sides by each of them as they diminish towards the top, forms what is generally called the steps. They are of different dimensions, as may be seen on a preceding paper where the height of each is separately marked It was thought proper, by means of a level and measure, to take the height of the steps one by one from the bottom to the top, a tedious, though the most certain and satisfactory method of having the exact perpendicular height of the whole, which agrees also with that taken by the Theodolite. — The entrance is upon the sixteenth step, on the side facing the north. It is not in the middle as is generally imagined , being only 350 feet distant from the N.E. corner, whereas it is 396 feet from the N.W. corner.

Oct. 18.— Went a second time to the Pyramids, and returned the 23d of the same month. Slept in the Nizlet every night near the village of one of the principal Sheiks thence sailed before sunrise in the morning, and landed a little to the east of the large Pyramid.

Oct 19 — Left the Nizlet at sunrise, and reached the Pyramid before eight. Began immediately to level and measure every step, one by one, and did not reach the top till one in the afternoon , at three entered the pyramid, retook some of the measures, and came out

Oct 20 — Set out at six in the morning, and in three quarters of an hour landed to the east of the Pyramid*; left the boat at seven o'clock, and visited a great number of grottoes and rooms cut out of the rock , many of them are adorned with hieroglyphics, which in some places are distinct, notwithstanding the pains employed by the

---

* Mr. Davison mentions in his journal the fossil remains near the Pyramid, of which Niebuhr speaks On y trouve encore de petites pétrifications en forme de lentille, qui semblent être de la même espèce, que les petites lichees dont j'ai recueilli plusieurs à Bukir, on avoit dit à Strabon, que ces petites pétrifications s'étoient formées des miettes qu' avoient laissé tomber à terre ceux qui ont travaillé aux Pyramides. Lib 161. See also Forskal F A Testacea Fossilia Kahirensia —" Nautilus? Gizensis, ad Pyramides vulgaris, jam a Strabone memoratus."

superstitious Arabs to deface them. Thence went, and measured the
two oblong holes cut in the rock on the east of the Pyramid. Entered and took all the dimensions of the inside. In the afternoon went
in again, and descended into the pit.

Oct. 21. — Visited and took the dimensions of the second and
third Pyramid *, and the two ruined buildings to the east of them, besides three small Pyramids to the south of the third ; having measured
likewise the pyramid on a square rock. Struck down towards the
Sphinx, and arrived at the boat after sunset.

Oct. 22. — Went with the Theodolite to take the height of the
large Pyramid ; but deferred it on seeing one of the great people of
Cairo had come out to visit it. In the mean time examined the small
Pyramids and tombs to the south and east which are in a ruined state.
Having measured off a base, took the height of the Pyramid with the
Theodolite, which agreed with a former one. Thence went down to
the plain on the north side, and having taken a base, found by means
of a Theodolite, that the Pyramid stands on an elevation 163 feet
above the river.

* If we examine the measures given by the French, we shall find that the base of each
of the three Pyramids of Cheops, Cephren, and Mycerinus is to their perpendicular
height, nearly in the ratio of 8 5 , — Cheops is 448 feet H , 728 L of B , — Cephren is 398 H , 655 L. of B , Mycerinus, 162 H , 280 L. of B.

ACCOUNT OF A WELL IN THE GREAT PYRAMID

Pliny, lib xxxvi c 12 speaks of a well in the great Pyramid, which was 86 cubits in depth In this letter, Mr Davison gives an account of his descent into the pit or well, he explored it to the depth of 155 feet, and found it impossible to proceed further

LETTRE A M. VARSY.

MONSIEUR,   CAIRE, le 23 9re 1764.

EN conséquence de la promesse que je vous ai fait dans la lettre que j' ai eu l'honneur de vous écrire par la dernière ordinaire, et à fin que je puisse quitter ce sejour des morts, qui vous a déjà si fort ennuyé, je me hâte de vous dire quelque chose du puits de la grande Pyramide, où je suis descendu   Comme je m'imaginois qu'il étoit d'une extrême profondeur, je me suis pourvu d'une bonne quantité de corde, par moyen de laquelle je comptois d'aller en bas avec plus de sureté.   La precaution n'étoit pas inutile. Il est vrai qu'il y a des dégrés, ou plutôt des trous, dans l'une et l'autre côté du puits, mais il est aussi certain que ces degrés sont rompus en plusieurs endroits, et tellement usés partout, qu'en se fiant trop on couroit risque de tomber, et de se casser le col. Pour eviter une fin si funeste je liai la corde au milieu de mon corps.   Avant de me mettre en chemin, je fis descendre une lanterne attachée au bout d'une ficelle. Ayant vu qu'elle s'arrêtoit au fond, je me preparai à la suivre   Deux domestiques et trois Arabes tenoient la corde en haut.   Ils le faisoient pourtant avec beaucoup de regret   Ils m' ont dit mille sottises pour me detourner de mon dessein , " que je risquois beaucoup de descendre;" — " qu'il y avoit des Esprits en bas ; et que je ne retournerois plus." Mais quand ils ont vu que j'étois determiné de me *perdre*, et que leur remonstrances ne servoient qu'à me faire rire, ils ont pris la corde, et se sont contentés de me plaindre, et de

z z 2

me regarder comme si devoit être pour la dernière fois. Enfin ayant pris du papier, une boussole, la mesure, et une autre chandelle à la main, je commençai à descendre, m'appuyant quelque fois sur la corde, et quelque fois sur la pierre, jusqu'à ce que je fusse au fond de ce premier puits. L'ouverture en bas est du côté de midi, on marche environ huit pieds, et puis il y a une descente perpendiculaire de cinque. A quatre pieds, dix pouces delà on trouve un autre puits, ou pour mieux dire, la continuation du même. L'entrée en est presque bouchée par une grosse pierre, qui ne laisse qu' un petit trou par lequel on passe assez difficilement. Je fis descendre la lanterne ici comme en haut, non seulement pour voir où je devois aller, mais encore pour savoir, si l'air étoit mauvais. Dans cet endroit pourtant la précaution fut inutile ; parceque ce puits n'est pas comme l'autre une exacte perpendiculaire, mais étant un peu tortueux, quand la chandelle étoit en bas je ne la voyois plus. Cela ne suffisoit pas pourtant pour me rebuter. Je voulois absolument aller au fond : ma curiosité ne pouvoit pas être satisfaite d'une autre manière. Voyant qu' il seroit necessaire d'avoir quelque un pour tenir la corde à l'entrée du second puits, aussi bien qu'à celle du première, j'appellois deux des Arabes, qui étoient en haut mais au lieu de venir, ils commencèrent à me faire mille contes. Entre autres celui que vous avez lu dans ma lettre à M. Roboli, " qu'un Franc, il y a quelques années venant à l'endroit où j'étois, et ayant laissé descendre une longue corde pour savoir la profondeur, quelque Demon la lui avoit arraché des mains." Je savois très-bien à qui ils avoient l'obligation de cette histoire ; M. le Consul d'Hollande jure que la chose lui est arrivée. Il n'y a qu'une façon de faire entendre raison à cette espèce de gens , je parle des Arabes. Je promis de l'argent à celui qui viendroit, et de plus, que le trésor, s'il y en avoit un en bas, comme ils le pretendoient, seroit tout pour lui. Il sembloit que cette dernière consideration avoit son poids ; tous avoient envie de venir, mais toujours lorsque quelqu'un commençoit à descendre, la superstition l'en retiroit. Je n'étois ni d'humeur, ni dans un endroit pour attendre. Je criai longtemps en mauvais Arabe sans aucun effet. Ma patience fut poussée à bout. A la fin cependant, l'esperance d'avoir de l'argent l'emporta sur la superstition ; un Arabe se mit à descendre, temoignant pourtant toujours beacoup de repugnance. On pouvoit voir à la verité, assez clairement qu'il n'y alloit pas de tout son cœur. Il étoit dans une telle agitation qu'il ne savoit plus ce qu'il faisoit. Il tâtoit de côté et d'autre sans pouvoir trouver les trous. Je me retirai vers l'autre puits, ne le jugeant pas trop prudent de rester directement au dessous de lui. Etant venu en bas il avoit plus l'apparence d'un spectre que d'un homme. Tout pâle et tremblant il regardoit de tous côtés. Ses cheveux, s'il en avoit eu, se seroient dressés sur la tête.

Je me hâtai de descendre pour ne pas lui donner le tems de se re-pentir de ce qu'il avoit fait. J'avois la corde toujours liée au milieu du corps. Je découvris en peu de tems la lanterne en bas, qui me fit voir que ce puits étoit plus profond que le premier. Un peu plus bas que le milieu, je trouvai l'entrée d'une grotte, qui a environ 15 pieds de longueur, 4 ou 5 de largeur (car elle n'est pas regulière), et assez haut pour qu'on y puisse marcher debout. Delà je descendis à l'entrée d'un troisième puits, qui n'est pas perpendiculaire commes les autres, et dont la pente est extremement rapide. Je savois qu'il étoit profond, par une pierre que j'avois fait rouler en bas. Je criai qu'on relachât peu à peu la corde, jusqu' à ce que je leur disse de tirer. Alors laissant aller la lanterne un peu devant, et mettant les pieds dans des petits trous pratiqués dans la pierre, je descendis le mieux que je pus. Je continuai longtems de suivre la lanterne sans voir la moindre apparence de m'arrêter. J'allois toujours en ligne droite ; le puits ensuite devenoit un peut plus perpendiculaire. C'est là que j'ai trouvé le fond. Il est tout-à-fait fermé par des pierres, sable, &c. Il n'y avoit que deux choses à craindre en bas, dont l'une ou l'autre m'auroit été fort désagreable. La première étoit que les chauve-souris n' éteignissent la chandelle , et la seconde, que la grosse pierre, dont je vous ai parlé, à l'entrée du second puits, et sur laquelle l'Arabe étoit obligé de s'appuyer, ne tombât en bas, et ne le fermât pour toujours. Vous avez beau dire que j'aurois dû regarder comme honorable, d'être enseveli dans une pyramide, dans un de ces fameux monumens, qui n'ont été destiné que pour des grands rois Je vous avoue franchement, M que je n'avois pas la moindre ambition à cet égard. Bien au contraire, j'étois cent fois plus content de sortir, et de revoir le jour. J'ai trouvé une échelle de corde au fond du second puits. Quoiqu'elle y ait été plus de seize ans, elle étoit, pour ainsi dire, comme si elle avoit été faite dans l'instant, aussi forte. et l'apparence toute aussi neuve. Les dégrés sont faits de morceaux de bois, dans le goût de celle que nous avions à Sacara, mais presque trois fois plus longue. M. Wood, qui a publié les ruines de Palmyre et de Balbec, l'avoit apporté ici pour faciliter la descente, mais il n'a pas voulu aller plus bas que la grotte C'étoit dans cette occasion que M. le Consul d'Hollande dit que quelqu'un en bas lui a enlevé la corde, histoire dont les Arabes conservent encore toutes les circonstances. Par le moyen de la corde que j'avois en bas, nous avons fait monter l'échelle, mais difficilement, parce que le second puits étant comme je vous l'ai dit un peu tortueux, et le bois de l'échelle entrant de tems en tems dans les trous qui sont pratiqués dans le roc, il nous a donné par la beaucoup de peine pour la tirer en haut. Quand nous fûmes de retour au fond du premier puits, les chandelles tombèrent et s'éteignirent ; alors le pauvre Arabe se crut perdu Il saisit la corde quand je voulus monter, et protesta qu'il aimeroit mieux qu'on lui tira un coup de pistolet que de le laisser la-bas seul avec *l'affrit* (le diable). Je lui fis la grace de le laisser monter avant moi , il parut être fort sensible à cette faveur. Quoiqu'il soit beaucoup plus difficile de monter que de descendre, je ne sais comment il fit, mais il monta cent fois plus vite qu'il n'étoit descendu.

Vous auriez ri di me voir sortir du puits plus noir qu'un charbonnier. Je courus, sans m'arrêter un instant à l'entrée de la pyramide, et me jettai aussitôt dans l'eau, non pas comme nous avons fait dans la Mer Rouge, auprès de Hammam Faraoun, mais avec l'Anteri, Chemise, &c. tout ensemble. Le bateau étant à quelques distance je le gagnai à la nage.

J'ai omis jusqu' à present, mais non pas oublié de vous donner les mésures des puits Le premier a 22 pieds de profondeur , le second 29, et le troisième 99 ; et si vous voulez ajouter la descente ne cinque pieds entre le premier et le second puits, le tout fera 155.

CHAMBER IN THE GREAT PYRAMID OF EGYPT

This part of Mr Davison's Journals gives an account of the manner in which he entered a room in the Great Pyramid, over the chamber containing the Sarcophagus Maillet had been forty times in the Pyramid, and had not seen it, Niebuhr did not observe it, and after his return from Cairo, he received some information concerning it from Mr. Meynard, the person who accompanied Mr D in his visit to this Pyramid The room has never yet been explored by any other traveller , Dr Hales (Chronol. i 384) thinks the existence of it problematical, but the publication of Mr. D's remarks will satify all doubts upon the subject Bruce alludes to Mr D's discovery — Ed

M. COUSINERY, Consul at Rosetta, set out for Giza, on Monday, July 8, 1765, with an intention to make a party with some French gentlemen to visit the pyramids. The 9th in the morning I went and joined them. Having taken three Arab guides and a Janissary, we mounted our asses at midnight, and travelling by the light of the moon we arrived at the pyramids in something less than two hours. I descended the first with a carpenter and another who widened the strait passage in the first canal ; I was surprised to find that this canal which was supposed to end here continues a considerable way down the pyramid. It was formerly stopped up with stones and sand ; these have been washed in the last winter by the rain which seems to have penetrated to this part of the pyramid. At entering we contented ourselves with pushing the earth and stones into it which were taken out of the narrow passage. The chief reason of my returning now to the pyramid was to

endeavour, if possible, to mount up to the hole I had discovered at
the top of the gallery the last time I was there. For this purpose I
had made seven short ladders in such a manner as to fasten one to
another by means of four wooden pins, the whole together, when
joined, being about twenty-six feet long. As soon as the rubbish
was cleared from the strait passage at the bottom, I caused the
ladders to be brought in by two carpenters who accompanied me.
When they had conveyed them to the platform at the top of
the gallery, tying two long canes together, I placed a candle
at one end, and gave it to a servant to hold near the hole in
question. The platform being very small there was no thinking
of fixing the ladders on the ground, as it would have been very
difficult, not to say impossible to raise them. We took the only
method which seemed practicable; namely, that of placing the first
ladder against the wall; two men raising it up, a third placed another
below it, and having fastened them together by the wooden pins,
the two together were raised from the ground, and the rest in the
same manner fixed one after another. The ladder entered enough
into the hole, when all parts were joined together, to prevent it
from sliding on the side of the gallery. I then instantly mounted,
and found a passage two feet four inches square, which turned
immediately to the right. I entered a little way, with my face on
the ground, but was obliged to retire, on account of the passage
being in a great measure choaked with dust, and bats' dung,
which, in some places, was near a foot deep. I first thought of
clearing it by throwing the dirt down into the gallery, but foreseeing
that this would be a work of some time, besides the inconvenience of
filling the gallery with rubbish, and perhaps rendering the descent more difficult, I determined to make another effort to enter,
which was accompanied with more success than the first. I was enabled to creep in, though with much difficulty, not only on account
of the lowness of the passage, but likewise the quantity of dust
which I raised. When I had advanced a little way, I discovered
what I supposed to be the end of the passage. My surprize was

great, when I reached it, to find to the right a straight entrance into a long, broad, but low place, which I knew, as well by the length as the direction of the passage I had entered at, to be immediately above the large room.* The stones of granite, which are at the top of the latter, form the bottom of this, but are uneven, being of unequal thickness. This room is four feet longer than the one below ; in the latter, you see only seven stones, and a half of one, on each side of them ; but in that above, the nine are entire, the two halves resting on the wall at each end. The breadth is equal with that of the room below. The covering of this, as of the other, is of beautiful granite; but it is composed of eight stones instead of nine, the number in the room below. One of the carpenters entered with me, and Mr Meynard came into the passage, near the door, but being a good deal troubled with the dust, and want of air, he retired. Having measured and examined the different parts of it, we came out, and descended by the ladder. We then employed ourselves in digging towards the bottom of the niche in the room below, and afterwards went down and entered the first passage ; there, instead of turning to the left to go out, I descended to the right, (where an opening had been lately made,) one hundred and thirty-one feet ; the descent, except the first four and a half feet, is cut in the rock. at the end

---

* In this is the Sarcophagus. It is well observed by Greaves, that most of the authors who have spoken of the purpose for which the pyramids were erected, consider them as sepulchres. This is the express opinion of Strabo and Diodorus, and of the Arabian writers, and " if none of these authorities were extant, yet the tomb found in the great pyramid of Cheops, puts it out of controversy." i. 60.

Although the supposition, that the great pyramid was constructed as a sepulchre be generally approved, we continue to find a disagreement among different writers and travellers respecting the time of its erection. The building of some of the pyramids, is ascribed by Perizonius to the Israelites, Ego certe Josepho Israelitarum tempore factas consenti, accesserim. Æg orig Invent c. 21. See Dr Clarke's Travels, tom. iii. Dr. Hales, in his Chronology, refers them to a remote period. But it is singular, as Goguet has remarked, that although Homer mentions Thebes, and its hundred gates, he has not noticed the pyramids of Egypt. Is it probable he would have omitted to speak of them, if they had been erected in his time? Goguet l. iii. epoch. 3 —ED.

of one hundred and thirty-one feet I found it so filled up with earth, that there was no possibility of proceeding. I then came out of the pyramid at half an hour past seven, and found that all the party, except Mr. Meynard, the Arab guard, and servants, had set out on their return to Giza. Though we had but little water, I was obliged to make use of some of it, to wash my hands and face, which were all covered over with dust and bats' dung. We breakfasted in the shade of the pyramid, and went afterwards to the second pyramid, where I copied the hieroglyphics which are on the perpendicular rock facing the north side of it.

CONTINUATION OF THE LATE MR DAVISON'S PAPERS.

July 7th. — We crossed the Nile and rode on south a little to the west, and passing through a forest of date trees, reached Ummuchnan at nine o'clock in the morning. This is a large village consisting of about 1000 houses. We proceeded to visit the Sheik who had given so kind an invitation to Mr. Montagu, and found him in company with many others smoking his pipe before the door. He received Mr. M. with all marks of distinction. Remaining about half an hour here, we were conducted to a very large and handsome apartment. Some of the Sheiks, like others in the country, found it very difficult to conceive how people can have any great curiosity about a thing where interest is not concerned, and asked many questions about our journey, and why we purposed going down the pits.

The 8th. — At six in the morning, we rode W.S.W. and reached Abousir, in something less than an hour. This village is situated at the foot of the ridge of mountains running north and south, and

on which the pyramids are built. Behind this place we rode up a
rising ground, leading to an opening between the hills. In ten
minutes we reached the catacombs of birds. Mr. M. was escorted
here by above 100 Arab horsemen; most of them armed with a
long spear, some with fire arms. As men had been sent out the
night before to clear the mouth of the pit from the sand, we found
when we arrived that they had placed a tree across the top of it, to
which they fixed the rope of cords made by order of Mr. M. in
Cairo. The pit we found twenty-two feet deep; the descent was
bad, on account of the sand and stones which fell from above.
Here lighting our candles, we crept on our faces through a long
passage choked up with dirt and broken pots; we then turned to
the right, where we could easily walk without stooping. On each
side of the passage are large rooms, in which the jars containing the
bird mummies were formerly placed We found some that were
almost filled with them. We took the dimensions of all these places
foot by foot. They are entirely cut out of the rock, but less
magnificent than those at Alexandria. We then went a little further
west, where there seems to be a grand entrance to some tomb;
the mouth of it is formed of four or five very large white stones,
finely ornamented with hieroglyphics in relievo.[*] Mr. M. gave
orders to have this cleared as much as possible for the next day.

9th.—Went out this morning with Mr. Vaisy, and copied the
hieroglyphics

10th.—We went early to Sacara, which is an hour and a quarter
distant to the S.W. At ten o'clock we set out for the pyramids, and
in about an hour's time we came to the furthest but one.[†] It is no
less than 700 feet square. It is the largest of all the range of pyramids
at Sacara and Dashour The perpendicular height is 343 feet; there
are in all 154 steps. In that side which faces the north, 180 feet up,

---

* Some figures in relief on obelisks are mentioned by Niebuhr, i. 167
† Called in Pococke " The great pyramid to the north "

there is a passage which leads into it. Having lighted our candles, we descended and found it four feet five inches and a quarter high, three feet five inches and a half wide, and 200 long, at the end of 200 feet there is a passage running horizontally 24 feet four inches and a half, and leads to a large pyramidal room 27 feet four inches long, and 11 feet 11 inches broad, 43 feet four inches high, from this, a passage of 10 feet four inches conducts to another of the same dimensions. At the height of 11 feet, the stones set in six inches one over another for 11 together, each stone being three feet high. At the end of the inner room, 30 feet 10 inches from the ground, there is a passage 24 feet long, three feet five inches square, which leads to a third *, differing only from the former in being one foot eight inches broader Not only all the pavement of this room, but five tiers of stones have been forcibly taken up in search of treasure. The stones of the passage have also been taken up. There is not much of the covering preserved on this pyramid; what remains is towards the top.

11th.—Early this morning we prepared to set out for the farthest pyramid†, where we arrived in something less than an hour and a half. A little way up on the north side, there is an entrance to which one may mount, but with danger and difficulty. This pyramid has 600 feet for its base; 184 feet up to the angle, and 250 feet thence to the top, which is thirty feet broad. The passage, as far as one can advance, is 174 feet in length. It is very difficult to creep down in the lower parts, on account of the stones and rubbish with which it is at last entirely choked up. It cuts the side of the pyramid at right angles The building, as it now stands, consists of 198 steps, namely, 68 large ones from the ground to the angle; and 130 lesser ones from that point to the top. Upon measuring one of the largest of the former, I found it to be four feet two inches,

---

* Pococke saw two of these rooms only.
† The great pyramid to the south. — Pococke, lii. 1.

whereas the general size of those in the upper part is only one foot ten inches or two feet. * This pyramid is built of hard white stone; in some places you see fossil remains, but not so numerous as in the large pyramid a mile to the north of this. From the summit we had a most extensive prospect of the fertile plain towards the Nile on the east of the pyramids, which was the most probable situation of Memphis †, of Jebel Jehusi on the other side of the river, of the castle of Cairo, and of all the pyramids, both those of Giza and Sacara. On the tops of these great heights the eagles build their nests, we heard the noise of the young ones as we went up. Two of them were taken by the Arabs, and carried home with us. Pococke is mistaken in supposing that the angle near the middle only appears to be such from the covering above having slid down as we were at the summit we had an opportunity of examining it more exactly than he could possibly do below, of measuring the angle, of seeing that the covering stone is on as well above as below it; and that it is only from this station one can see the top and bottom at the same time. Having taken the bearing of this from the principal objects, we rode 20 minutes north to the largest pyramid where we had been the day before. Though the sun was extremely hot, being about mid-day we mounted this pyramid, and took its height. We descended quickly, and rode home, as the Arabs themselves were impatient, being no longer able to bear the intolerable heat. While we were employed in measuring, they sheltered themselves below the stones. In passing by the pyramid called Pharaoh's Seat we saw six Gazelles at some distance from us, there are a great number in these deserts, this animal is the Antelope of the

---

* " The following are the dimensions of one of the stones with which the pyramid is covered, ⟍ length of the side four feet seven inches "— Davison

† Mr Davison's opinion respecting the site of Memphis agrees with that of the best travellers in Egypt. Great quantities of breccia and granite are seen near Metrahenny, and extensive ruins have been found lately near this place, which escaped the researches of Shaw, Bruce, Pococke, Norden, and other travellers. — Hamilton's Egypt, 314.

Scriptures.   The mummy people came and informed us, that the pit was cleared, and that we might go when we thought proper.   We arrived there in 15 minutes; and descended by a cord with candles and two men.   It was so filled with sand that we were obliged to creep in on our faces in a passage four feet broad, as we advanced we found nothing but turnings and windings, and on all sides skulls, bones, and bandages of mummies   When we came out we found the party impatient, as the sun had been set for some time   we immediately descended from the rising ground, and rode N. E. towards Ummuchnan; in a quarter of an hour we passed over the ancient bed of the Nile

12th. — Early this morning being dressed like an Arab I rode with Mr. Varsy to the pyramid of the steps, accompanied by the Kiaiah of the Sheik.   Went up the N. W. corner and measured the height. From the top of it took the direction of all the other pyramids. The mummy pit is 300 yards to the south; to the N. E. are two smaller pyramids in a ruined state, and a little further the pit of the bird mummies.   We went then to the three pyramids a mile to the north, and having taken their dimensions and bearings, rode home. To-day the Chamseen wind was intolerable.   By the thermometer we found that the heat was ten degrees higher than human heat.

13th. — Rode out early to the west side of the palm trees of Ummuchnan, and having measured a base of 2000 feet, Mr. Montagu took the plan of all the pyramids with the Theodolite.

THE PYRAMIDS OF EGYPT.

LETTER FROM MR DAVISON TO PROFESSOR WHITE

SIR,

I AM very much obliged to you for your polite letter of the 4th of last month, and am truly ashamed of not having told you so sooner. To say I have not written a single line to any of my correspondents since it came to hand, though true, is but a lame excuse for deferring my acknowledgments so late. As I certainly might have found time to answer your letter, there remains nothing for me now but to ask your pardon, which I do very sincerely.

I have little doubt of your success in a translation of Abdallatif, of its doing credit to you, and affording amusement and information to the public; but I cannot flatter myself that any remarks of mine respecting the pyramids, particularly as I have left the greatest part of my papers at Nice, would add value to it, though, without doubt, every discovery in monuments so remarkable, which have been, and are likely to continue the wonder of ages, will be deemed of consequence by the curious in antiquities. I am now in such a disagreeable state of suspense, attendance, and hurry, as not to be able to sit down seriously to any thing, but had I even leisure, yet having left the greatest part of my papers in Italy, I could not give you so full an account as I could wish of the discovery I made of an entresol above the large room, and of the continuation of the first passage which both leads into the pyramid, and a considerable way into the rock below it. If I can possibly find time before I am sent abroad, and materials enough with me to draw up a short general account to my liking, you may depend on having it; for I am to the full as desirous as you can be of having mention made of the above circumstances in your edition of Abdallatif.

It is no reflection on other travellers that they did not make the discoveries before me, as perhaps none of them had the like advantages, excepting Maillet, who did not avail himself of them so much as he might have done. I remained long at Cairo, and had an opportunity of visiting the pyramids often, and of measuring every part over and over again, as well of the outside as of the interior of the largest, which is the only one of those of Giza into which a passage is found. Mine were not hasty visits, such as are generally paid to those noble monuments of antiquity. The merchants established in that country make a party of five or six persons to accompany a traveller, they set out early in the morning from Cairo or Giza, and return at night; they stay at the pyramids perhaps from three to four hours; suppose the visit repeated, the time is scarcely sufficient to take a general view, much less to take the dimensions with any kind of accuracy.

Besides many visits of this sort, I hired a boat to convey me there during the inundation, and staid to examine and measure them for eight days together. There is little here depending on the abilities, knowledge, or penetration of a traveller. To measure straight lines with exactness requires only leisure and labour; I grudged neither, and I so far succeeded to my own satisfaction as to think that my time and pains were not thrown away.

LETTER FROM PROFESSOR WHITE TO MR DAVISON

SIR,   OXFORD, August 15 1779

I HUMBLY beg your pardon for not having acknowledged the receipt of your very obliging letter of June 21st. Since that time I have done myself the pleasure of calling twice at your lodgings in town; but had not the good fortune to find you at home. I still flatter myself with hopes that you will find leisure to draw up some account of the pyramids to your liking, which, whatever humble opinion you may have of it yourself, will certainly add a value to my work

In Abdallatif's account of the pyramids, there are two circumstances, which I know not how to defend; the first is, that he says he saw a prodigious number of hieroglyphical inscriptions on the two great pyramids, as many, as if copied would fill perhaps 10,000 volumes. The second curious circumstance is, that he asserts the lesser of the three great pyramids was on one side considerably defaced by Al-Aziz about the year 1196

Now I cannot find by other travellers, that either of these facts has been observed, and at the same time Abdallatif is in general so accurate, that I hardly think he was mistaken. I beg the honour of a line on the subject, and am, &c.

I beg your permission to print in my edition of Abdallatif that part of the letter you have honoured me with, which relates to the entresol you discovered.

ANSWER TO PROFESSOR WHITE FROM MR DAVISON

Sir,   Lisbon, 10th October, 1779

I LAMENT exceedingly that I should have been so unfortunate, as to miss you when you took the trouble of calling twice at my lodgings in London, but as I neither found your name nor heard of it from the people of the house, it is likely, I think, that I was on a visit to my friends in Northumberland at the time. I was so much hurried before my departure from England as not to be able to thank you as I ought and intended, for your very polite letter of the 15th August. It was still less in my power to draw up any account of the pyramids, for which indeed I had not sufficient materials with me. You are welcome to make use of what I communicated to you on the subject of the entresol I discovered in the large pyramid of Giza. The

3 B

account as far as it goes may be depended upon; though had I been able to make it fuller, it would no doubt have been better deserving of a place in your edition of Abdallatif.

Finding him in general pretty accurate you are unwilling to allow your author to be mistaken in two circumstances, which at the same time you do not know how to defend, as they have not been taken notice of by other travellers. One of them is very remarkable, namely, " that he saw a prodigious number of hieroglyphical inscriptions on the two great pyramids, as many as if copied would fill perhaps 10,000 volumes." I am at a loss what to say to this. There is not now I believe a single hieroglyphic to be seen on either of them, but it may not be amiss to observe that the greater part of the outer stones or covering of the two large pyramids have been destroyed or carried away. From some of the original covering still remaining at the top of the second great one, it is more than probable that the steps of which the sides of the other now consist, were covered in the same manner, with stones of such a form as to make a smooth surface from top to bottom with a profile somewhat resembling this figure . Among the pyramids of Sacara and Dashour there is one on which the covering is still pretty entire. I do not recollect finding a single inscription upon it. Whether there be any on the covered part of the second pyramid of Giza, I cannot say from my own knowledge, as I did not succeed in my attempt to get up to it. I observed and copied two lines of hieroglyphics on a rock that is cut perpendicularly, near and opposite to the north side of this pyramid. This is the only thing of the kind I found in that neighbourhood, except in some grottoes or rooms cut out in that part of the rocks facing the east, on which the pyramids are built, and at no great distance from the largest. These appear to have been the entrance of burying places, by the pits in most of them being now filled up, down which the mummies were probably conveyed. The sides of the rooms are covered with hieroglyphics, among which I remember taking notice of human figures, some of them about as large as life.

With regard to the other circumstances he mentions, " that the lesser of the three great pyramids was on one side considerably defaced by Aziz about the year 1196," I do not think it unlikely, or even very remarkable. It is natural to suppose that it would suffer most on the north side where they would expect to find the entrance, and that they would begin to throw down the covering from that part before they touched the other sides. This pyramid appears to have been covered with red granite from some of the stones still remaining in different parts of it. Those I saw were square, and not cut like the covering I had occasion to take notice of above.

I have endeavoured to satisfy you as far as I can from memory, but fear that my letter will not reach England in time to be of any use to you in your publication. N. D.

NOTE

[Other Arabic writers prior to Abdallatif have also mentioned the hieroglyphics on the pyramids; their testimonies are cited by S de Sacy, in his translation of Abdallatif, 221. The Arabic writers do not express themselves in a manner sufficiently clear, so as to inform us, whether they mean that the characters were hieroglyphical or alphabetical. We find in Herodotus a reference to the inscription engraved on the pyramid of Cheops; it was, he says in *Egyptian* characters; but still it is doubtful, whether by these words he means *ordinary* characters or *hieroglyphics*. The former acceptation is approved by Larcher; and Dr. Hales thinks these characters could not be any other than *literal* or alphabetical, Chron. i. 381. Ebn Haukal speaks of the *Syrian* and *Greek* inscriptions which covered some part of the pyramids, the former, Quatremère supposes, were letters in the cursive characters of Egypt, of which the Rosetta stone affords a singular example. * The testimony respecting the

---

* Le plus beaux monumens de l'écriture cursive sont les Papyrus publiés par Denon et la curieuse inscription de Rosette Millin D de B. A. 189. 2 See also some remarks on the Rosetta inscription in the Museum Criticum, Cambridge, 1816.

3 B 2

Greek characters may be confirmed by Seif-ed-doulah-ben-Hamdan,
a geographer; the inscriptions were probably written by Greeks who
visited these monuments, and recorded their names and the date of
their visit.   On one of the pyramids Latin verses had been inscribed;
they were observed by Boldensleve who travelled in 1336, three of
them may be here subjoined.

> Vidi pyramidas sine te, dulcissime frater,
> Et tibi, quod potui, lacrymas hic maesta profudi,
> Et nostri memorem luctus hic sculpo querelam

The travellers who have at various times examined the pyramids
of Giza, differ in their opinion respecting the manner in which
their outward surfaces were finished   With regard to that of Cheops,
we are expressly told by the historian ἐξεταίσθη τὰ ἀνώτατα ἀυτῆς πρῶτα,
the upper part was first finished, then the remainder.   Niebuhr is
disposed to allow, that the third or that of Mycerinus might have
been partly cased with granite.   Girard, one of the French Institute,
says that the covering of the second and third pyramids, of which
there is no doubt, leads us to conclude that the first was also covered ;
and in his Mémoire on the Nilometer of Elephantine, he speaks in
the following manner of the examination of the lower part of the
great pyramid, made by some architects who accompanied the
expedition to Egypt.   " Après avoir retrouvé sur la surface du rocher
qui sert de soubassement à la grande pyramide l'emplacement des
pierres angulaires du revêtement de cet edifice, marqué par une
espèce de mortaise de deux décimètres de profondeur, pratiquée dans
le rocher, et destinée à recevoir chacune de ces pierres, ils ont
mesuré immédiatement avec la plus rigoureuse précision la ligne
terminée par les angles extérieurs de ces encastremens, et l'ont
trouvée de 716 pieds, six pouces "

Mr. D. remarks that some of the original covering remains at the
top of the *second* great pyramid.   Niebuhr climbed up to the
summit to examine it, and found the same calcareous substance
of which the rest of the building was composed   It is described also
by Grobert. " In the second pyramid," says Shaw, " which may hint

to us what was intended in them all, we see near a quarter of the whole pile very beautifully filled up and ending at the top in a point." As the upper parts are certainly not now covered with marble as some suppose, or with granite as Norden asserts, the passage of this traveller quoted by Larcher, ii. 214. should be erased in any future edition of the French Herodotus. Niebuhr supposes, that the last work of the builders was to give a smooth and regular appearance to the four sides of this pyramid, beginning at the summit.

The third pyramid, Mr Davison says, appears to have been covered with red granite. The remains of granite were seen by Niebuhr, and by some of the members of the French Institute "Les beaux morceaux de granit d'Elephantine sont dispersés et abondamment entassés prés de sa base"— Grobert. This pyramid is called by the Arabic writers the coloured pyramid, and must have preserved its covering until the time of Abdallatif, who speaks of it as, *construite en granit rouge* S. de Sacy's version, lib i. c. 4. — ED.]

CATACOMBS OF ALEXANDRIA.

[CONTINUATION OF MR DAVISON'S PAPERS]

Nov. 7th, 1763. — This morning before sunrise we rode out at Pompey's pillar gate, with a great number of Janissaries, we turned to the right leaving the column on our left, and after a ride of an hour and a half, arrived at the catacombs. At the entrance we fired three or four pistols, as well to clear the air a little as to drive out the jackalls and other animals that generally take shelter there. We were obliged to creep in on our faces for a few yards, then getting on our feet we could walk, but not upright, except in some parts. As there is no

opening above where the light can enter, we had, every one, a wax
candle. The catacombs consist of a vast number of subterranean
apartments which extend a long way. The ground is very uneven
and hilly, being filled up greatly with sand and rubbish In some
places one can stand up very well; in others there is not above four
or five feet. There is one grand door that seems to have in its architecture some resemblance to the Doric form; by this you enter into
a large rotunda of considerable height; there are three other great
doors in it, that lead to small rooms. All of these apartments are
cut out of a very hard rock. We staid there sometime to take the
plan of some part of it; but as there are no air-holes we found it very
warm and stifling, particularly with such a number of people, and all
with lights; besides, there were several bones and a dead ass that
added to the ungrateful smell. The Arabs in time of war make this
a kind of hiding place, as it is capable of containing several thousand
people. The entrance is not above twenty or thirty yards from the
sea. We came out and found the rest of the company sitting in a
large tent, that had been put up on the shore during our absence.
Just before the tent there is a convenient bathing place with a room
cut out in the rock, and open on one side, to dress and undress in.
Less than a musket-shot further there are three or four grand bathing-
rooms, cut in the rock, the water enters by doors made on purpose,
and in each there is a seat the length of the room to undress in. They
are so fine altogether, that they go by the name of Cleopatra's baths.
After dinner we went to another subterraneous place, which for the
height and grandeur of it cannot fail of surprising the spectator; it
is high and spacious, cut out of the rock, though the stone seems not
to be a hard one. They pretend that the building was used as a granary. We then went to the catacombs where the mummies had formerly been deposited. A pigeon-house may give one some idea of
the form of them. The place is large, and each hole of a size sufficient for a corpse Having measured them, we rode after the rest of the
company, who were gone to some more catacombs towards Pompey's
pillar; these we found of the same nature as the last, but much larger.

There are stairs at one end, and walking in a line for above one hundred yards we pass on both sides the entrances of ten or twelve of these burying places

Nov. 20, 21, 22, 23.—Went out to continue the measures of the walls, which we began some days before. When we arrived at the Rosetta gate some people came about us, and inquired what we were doing; they threatened to go and inform the commander, that we were some Christians taking a plan of the place. Our Janissaries advised us to desist, and we mounted and rode home.

Dec. 7.—We went without the walls towards the catacombs to see some subterranean apartments that had been lately discovered, where, they said, some ancient paintings were to be seen. We found the entrance filled up with earth, so were obliged to defer our visit to another time. To-morrow or next day four or five men will be sent out to clear away the rubbish.

Dec 8, 9, 10, 11, 12.—We went out to the catacombs, and after the rubbish was removed, we descended with lights. They are the real catacombs where they formerly buried their dead. They are of vast extent under ground, all cut in the rock; but they are now so filled with earth, that there is no way of going into them but upon one's face. In some of the apartments one can stand upright. In many of them there is no communication from one to another than by a hole, through which it is often difficult to creep. Some of the apartments are ornamented with paintings, which are so much injured that there is but little that can be distinguished. There are yet one or two figures of men to be seen, which although defaced, sufficiently show they have been the work of no great master. The mouth of each mummy's hole has a cornice round it. Before we came out, we found this inscription marked with red* over one of them. Mr. Mon-

---

* In the Hypogeum at Ægina, there is an inscription traced in a similar manner in red lines. We cannot determine the age of that which is mentioned by Mr Davidson, it is, however, no argument against the antiquity of it, that we find the omega, sigma, and epsilon, written Є C Ѡ. These characters were formed in this manner, three centuries before the Christian era.— See Villois Anecd ii 161.

tague supposed from the form of the letters that it was of the time of Alexander the Great.

HPAKΛEI.   XP. CTE XAIPE.

Over another at a small distance in the same room,

.\ΠΟΛΟΔωPOCXA . . .

Though we satisfied our curiosity in a great measure, we did not go so far under ground as we might have done. Our candles began to shorten, and we did not wish by going too far in to run the risk of losing our way back and of being left in the dark in the midst of these habitations of the dead. The catacombs are in some places no less than three stories one below another. There is a statue, but greatly defaced, in a niche in one of the apartments. The descent into the catacombs is perpendicular, and about fourteen or fifteen feet down; on one side is a rock which you may hold as you go down; we dared not touch the other side, as it is of earth, and seemed ready to fall in.

Dec. 14, 15, 16, 17, 18, 19. — Went out again to the last-discovered catacombs, and took a plan of some part of them. After dinner we rode to the pillar of Pompey; by means of a ladder we got upon the pedestal, and measured the base, though it blew so hard we could scarcely keep our feet.

Jan. 5. — Went to the further catacombs, and took the plan of a good deal more than what we had already examined. After staying in about three hours we came out, and found the company in the usual place by the sea-side under a tent. The dinner was prepared by Mr. Montague's Turkish cooks, who came by sea, and as they had done before, they converted one of the bathing rooms cut in the rock into a place to dress the victuals in. After dinner I again entered with

---

The cursive characters of C and C occur also on the marble containing a decree of the people of Gela, which Maffei assigned to the year 121 B. C. For the sigma of Æschrion, a figure applied by him to the new moon, see Ruhnk ad Long sec. 3 — En

a French captain, and two or three more, and penetrated farther under ground than I had ever yet been. The plan is very
regular and beautiful, by what we have already examined we can see
that there is yet much more wanting to complete it. The whole is
cut entirely out of the rock. There are foxes and jackalls, and other
animals which get in, and make a smell so disagreeable, that it is
enough to strike one down.

Jan. 6, 7, 8, 9.—Intended to have gone out to make some more
discoveries in the catacombs, but it was thought prudent to defer
this, as there is a caravan arrived from Barbary with about three
hundred Arabs with dates, they are all encamped near Pompey's
pillar.

Impatient to make some new discoveries at the catacombs, I set
out from the old port in a boat accompanied by Mr M.'s Janissaries,
and two men to dig and open where there should be occasion. We
reached the place in an hour's time, and having fired a gun as usual,
lighted our candles, and crept in with much difficulty into several
places which before I had thought inaccessible on account of the
quantity of earth with which they are choaked up. These were
added to the plan. There are some passages that certainly lead
to other apartments, but they are so filled up with earth, that it is
impossible to pass There is one in particular dotted out in the plan,
which seems to have been so high as to allow a man to walk upright without stooping; the roof is arched it is not more than two
feet wide; we crept in a good way, and found it turned to the right;
but the passage being too narrow to suffer us to proceed further,
we were obliged to come out with our feet first, as there was no
room to turn We took the plan of the cupola with more exactness
than before, as well as the different members of the architecture,
which, though varying in many of the proportions, comes nearest to
the Tuscan order After staying in about five hours, and seeing
every place it was possible to approach, we left the catacombs, and
took the bearing of them to the large tower in Porto Vecchio.

Jan. 16. — We set out from Alexandria for a neighbouring village, we quitted the town about nine, and after an hour's riding towards the east, crossed the Kalis; then travelled along E. S. E., having on one side of the road to the right the lake Mareotis, and to the left a lake of salt water, both close to the Kalis, which is the only separation between them. The salt water lake is formed by an inundation of the sea at the Seyd   At twenty minutes past one, turning S. E. by E we rode to Balactui, a village which we reached a quarter past four. There were many Arab tents near it, and the marks of many more all around. Then turning due east, arrived at Cafala about a quarter past five.   In the road, we past a great many ruins; on the left hand chiefly   The country is an entire flat; the villages are all situated on rising grounds, probably artificial hills raised formerly to defend the inhabitants from the annual inundation of the Nile.   Many seem to have been the ruins of ancient cities. We were kindly received by the Karmacan in a single room, where five of us slept together upon carpets spread out, with a covering over each.   The houses are all built of unburnt brick, square at the bottom, and in form of a cupola at the top without any wood, which in this country is scarce

The second morning we rode to a hill, about four miles distant; we were met by the Sheik of the Arabs encamped at the above mentioned village with his attendants.   The case of this Sheik is particularly distressing.   He has lately had his father murdered, and been robbed of 100,000 crowns.   His father had formed a friendship with one of the Beys, who was employed in suppressing the late revolt; he was sent for one day by the Bey who assured him that he had nothing to fear; and calling for the Koran, swore that nothing should happen to him.   But notwithstanding his pretended friendship and all his professions, to the sincerity of which he called his God to witness, in defiance of the sacred laws of hospitality, and indeed of all laws both human and divine, he barbarously ordered his slaves to cut his head off.   His commands were no sooner given than executed: after which he sent to seize his money and effects which amount at a moderate computation to 100,000 crowns; among other things, there were 2,000 camels, 1,800 sheep, and 30 fine Arabian horses, in addition to several purses of money. No circumstance could render the son's case more deplorable, except that the wretch should pass unpunished. This inhuman murder he endeavoured to excuse by giving out that the Sheik was cut off on account of a secret correspondence he had discovered between him and the rebels a report as false as it was needless, for every body was well apprised that his only crime was his wealth. Riches in these parts seldom or never fail of proving fatal to those who possess them. The several Pashas or commanders dispersed over the vast Ottoman empire are trusted with an absolute power, which, as men in general are less prone to good than evil, they frequently abuse. A man is no sooner known to be rich than he is marked out for destruction. The Pashas, the representatives of the Grand Signor, are in office during his pleasure, so that their chief business is to acquire the most they can, and by all accounts there are few who do not make a good use of their time; they enrich themselves by all manner of extortion and rapine, and by the destruction of those whom it is their duty to protect. But after all, they seem to be only the sponges of the Grand Signor, to whom they are obliged to recommend themselves by presents of immense value.

Jan. 21. — Returned to Alexandria, on the 23d measured the base of Pompey's pillar more exactly, having brought ladders for that purpose.

Jan. 24, 25. — Went out with the Theodolite accompanied by Mr. M's Janissary; took a base of 100 feet, and found the pillar to be 92 feet high, without reckoning the separate stones by which it is raised four feet from the ground. By means of a cord round the foot of the pillar I found the circumference to be 27 feet, four inches and a half. Le Brun and Lucas both describe the column, but do not agree in the measure.

Jan 16 — Went out with Dr. Turnbull to the pillar, removed some of the stones below, and found that the pivot of five feet square on which the pillar rests is covered with hieroglyphics. Returned the 17th with an intention to copy them.

April 11 — Yesterday was at Pompey's pillar, went in below, and copied the hieroglyphics Found them inverted, and upon measuring, saw that the stone is smaller in the lower than upper parts. The support of the column is therefore an obelisk, turned upside down. *

* The main weight of the pillar (says Pococke), rests upon the stone which has hieroglyphics on it See also De Tott, vol. II and Norry, Dec Egypt This circumstance (says Shaw) may induce us to suspect that the pillar was not erected by the Egyptians, who could not well be imagined thus to bury their sacred inscriptions, but by the Greeks or Romans, nay, later perhaps than Strabo The stone supporting the column is also mentioned by the Arabic writers See Abdallatif, p 233. S de Sacy The hieroglyphics are engraved in Dr Clarke's Travels

A few words may be added concerning the inscription on the column, and the name by which it has been hitherto known In some of the Arabic writers it is called Amoud al Sawary, "The pillars of the colonnades," alluding to the porticoes with which it was surrounded so late as the time of Saladin in the beginning of the 12th century Michaelis once thought that the words might mean "the column of Severus," but afterwards abandoned the opinion Villoison supposes the Greek inscription to refer to Pomponius, the Præfect of Egypt, who raised the column

But the common appellation of Pompey's Pillar seems to me to be properly assigned to it for this reason, *Pompeius was governor of part of lower Egypt in the time of Diocletian* He may have been governor of Alexandria, and there have raised the pillar in honour of that Emperor This information respecting a Præfect in Egypt of the name of Pompey in the time of Diocletian, which we owe entirely to M Quatremère (Mem Geog sur l'Egypte, p. 259 1) is a remarkable corroboration of the opinion of those who think the pillar was raised in honour of Diocletian by a magistrate of the name of Pompeius Major Missett informed Mr W Turner that the letters ΔΙΟΚ Η ΙΑΝΟΝ were considered by those who had lately visited Egypt, as discernible and Col Leake gives the word "Diocletian," as the result of the examination made by himself, Mr Hamilton, and Col Squire—See Classical Journal, vol. XIII p 153

Dr Clarke proposes, instead of ΔΙΟΚΛΗΤΙΑΝΟΝ, to read ΔΙΟΝΑΔΡΙΑΝΟΝ, and Pococke thought the pillar was erected in honour of Titus or Hadrian Dr C thinks, "the use of ΔΙΟΣ is perhaps unknown in Greek prose;" but we find it in a Greek inscription at Ombos in Egypt, ΥΠΕΡ ΒΑΣΙΛΕΩΣ ΠΤΟΛΕΜΑΙΟΥ ΔΙΟΥ ΚΑΙ ΒΑΣΙΛΙΣΣΗΣ ΚΛΕΟΠΑΤΡΗΣ κ τ λ. Hamilton's Ægypt, 75 —ED

THE CATACOMBS OF ALEXANDRIA.

PAINTINGS DISCOVERED IN THEM BY MR DAVISON — REMARKS ON THE CUSTOM OF PAINTING TEMPLES AND STATUES. — ILLUSTRATION OF THE SINGULAR USE OF THE WORD Γράφω

[*BY THE EDITOR.*]

THE Doric ornaments over some of the doors of the sepulchres in the Necropolis at Alexandria; the general distribution of the chambers, their resemblance in form to those in the catacombs of Milo *, and the Greek inscriptions in them first discovered and mentioned by Mr. Davison, lead us to conclude, that this great work was completed for a repository of the dead, about and a little after the time when Alexandria was built. All catacombs were originally † quarries, whence materials were extracted for some neighbouring city. The rock was afterwards formed into crypts and receptacles for the dead. The extent and magnificence of these sepulchral chambers at Alexandria were well worthy of a city distinguished for its great wealth and populousness, and described by Diodorus as ἐπιφανεστάτην. (xvii. 279.) Over one of the doors there appears in a drawing by Mr. Davison, the symbol of the globe ‡, so frequent in Egyptian monuments; but we cannot be surprised to find this in the Necropolis

---

* " Whoever has seen," says Olivier, " the catacombs at Alexandria, will discover in those of Milo, the same genius and same taste which planned the former "

† D'Orville Chart 73 75

‡ This ornament was observed by Col Squire and Dr Clarke, Travels, vol ii 289 The former speaks of a crescent, this is also seen in the drawing of Mr Davison. The winged globe, with a crescent under it, is sculptured at Kirmanschah in Persia — See S de Sacy's Mémoire, Mem. de l'Instit p 168 Year 1815.

of Alexandria, an intermixture of Greek and Egyptian rites and ceremonies, religious usages, and language, became very common under the Ptolemies in Egypt; and about the time of Alexander and his first successors, the Athenians, and probably other Greek states, began to shew a religious regard to Isis in employing her name in adjurations.

As soon as the custom of burning bodies ceased in the different parts of the Roman empire †, the Pagans buried their dead in catacombs, but in Egypt the practice of placing them in such repositories must have been at all times more frequent than that of burning, on account of the scarcity of wood in that country Mr. Davison remarks that the paintings in the catacombs appeared to him to be of ordinary execution, they probably belong to the period when the arts were declining, and might have been the works of the pagan inhabitants of the city in the sixth century; for at that time paganism was not altogether abolished, as we learn from a curious passage in Cyril. ‡ It is probable that these catacombs have also been in Alexandria, the place of resort for Christians, where, as in the crypts of Italy, they celebrated their Agapæ§; but none of the Christian symbols, the palm branch, the monogram of XP., or other devices similar to those found in the cemeteries of Italy, appear in the tombs of Alexandria.

Some sketches of the paintings found on the walls of the catacombs, are among Mr. Davison's papers; and we may observe in them the ornament of the festoon very clearly traced. This is the παγκάρπιος στέφανς, (Cuper. M A. 238.) which we find on sarcophagi and other sepulchral monuments, Dr. Hunt observed it on the huge granite Latomia at Assos. As these paintings were only seen by the light

---

* Diod S vol. i p 31 — Wessel note.

† After the time of Theodosius — Montfauc. An. Ex vol v. part i p. 20

‡ In Esaiæ, cap 18 Opp tom xi See the description of the Adonian Festival Memsius in speaking of the Adonia has omitted to refer to this passage — Valck Theoc 193.

§ Aringhi Roma Subter lib. vi. c. 27

of torches and lamps, when the relatives of the dead paid their visits to the tombs, the colour of them must have been such as admitted of a strong contrast.

The custom of painting tombs, statues, and temples was common in many parts of the east. Various animals were drawn on the bricks employed in building the city of Babylon; these were painted before they were burnt. (Diod S. vol. ii. 121.) In the sepulchres of Sidon cut out of the limestone rock, Hasselquist perceived that red colours had been used. Small statues of Isis and Osiris are frequently found in Egypt covered with a green substance. The colours which were applied to the sphinx were very plainly seen in the time of Abdallatif in the 13th century.* On voit sur la figure une teinte rougeâtre et un vernis rouge qui a tout l'éclat de la fraicheur. (C. iv. lib 1.) The painting on the walls of the temples at Tentyra, Thebes, Diospolis, and Philæ is brilliant and fresh in appearance Le coloris est si vif, si frais, et si brillant, qu'il semble, disent les habitans du pays, que l'ouvrier n'a pas encore lavé ses mains depuis son travail. (Goguet. iii. vol 68) White paint, as well as yellow, red, and green has been employed; for the white in the great temple at Philæ is not the colour of the stone, according to the remark of Lancret. The grottoes of Thebes and Eleithias have been also adorned in a similar manner. Many of the paintings in Egypt have been destroyed by the zeal of the Coptic and other Christians, who have substituted in the room of Isis and Osiris representations of the Virgin Mary, Apostles, and Saints

The custom of painting tombs and statues, and the walls of temples was also practised by the Greeks in the most flourishing periods of the arts. Strabo, lib. viii. mentions the assistance which Phidias derived from his brother Panænus in painting the statue of Jupiter. Near Tritæa in Achaia, was a tomb remarkable for its paintings, executed by Nicias, (Paus. lib. vii.) and another near

---

* See the version by S de Sacy. The colours have been also observed by Maillet, Grobert, Mr. Hamilton (.Egy) p 329) and Dr Clarke

Sicyon. (lib. ii.) Pausanias alludes to the paintings of Polygnotus on the walls of the temple of Minerva at Platæa (lib. ix.) and Plutarch (in Aristid.) speaks of them as in a state of preservation in his time. They had therefore lasted more than 550 years. Silanion and Parrhasius are called ἰκόνων Θησέας γραφὶς καὶ πλάστα. Pausanias also informs us, (lib. vii. and lib. ix.) that he saw at Ægina and Creusis three statues; two of which were of Bacchus, one was painted with cinnabar, and the other was made of gypsum and ἐπικεκοσμημένον γραφᾷ. One of Minerva was gilt and coloured.

That the encaustic process was used in some of the sacred buildings of the Greeks, we learn from that singular inscription quoted by Cuper (in Harpo.) and Le Moyne (de Melaneph.) containing a dedication of a Pastophorium, in this, mention is made of the painting of the walls, the roof, and the doors, τῶν θυρῶν ἔγκαυσιν. The persons who were employed in painting the walls were called στιλζωτοί; and the term applied to the cement or plaister is * καίασις. From an inscription in the collection of Reinesius we learn, that the same artist sometimes united in himself the professions of ἀγαλματοποιὸς and ἐγκαύστης. (lib. i. c. 9.)

It may be asked whether traces of this custom are visible in any of the monuments of ancient Greece. There are coloured ornaments on the Soffit of the Lacunaria of the temple of Theseus. † (Stuart. iii. 7.) They were also seen, the same writer informs us, on the upper fascia of the architrave within the portico of the Ionic temple on the banks of the Ilissus (i. c. 2.) The stucco in the chamber near the site of the supposed grotto of Trophonius in Bœotia, has been coloured. Garlands were seen by Olivier painted on the cement of the catacombs of Milo, as at Alexandria. M. Fauvel informed Mr. Hawkins that " he had remarked traces of painting in the frieze of the temple.

---

* Salm. in H. A. S. 451. et Plin. Exerc. 1229

† See also Chandler's Greece, 72. The painted ornaments on the roof appear to be signified by the κουρά,, of the Greeks, described by Hesychius, as, ἡ ἐν τοῖς ὀροφήμασι γραφή.

of Theseus; the ground appears to have been a sky-blue, the interior frieze of the Parthenon also had been painted, for which he accounted by the flatness of the sculpture, and the want of light from [*] above. Many architectural ornaments, (Mr. Hawkins adds,) in these temples and in the Propylea were painted; for instance the *cima recta* of the cornice of the latter, and the cieling or rather the compartments of the cieling in the Parthenon."

In some of the excavations made near Athens, Mr. Fauvel discovered the tiles or covering of tombs painted with ornaments. Il y en a de peintes avec de beaux ornemens, comme étoient aussi celles en marbre des grands temples, chose difficile à faire entendre à nos architectes, qui ne veulent pas croire aux statues, et aux bas-reliefs peints. Mag. Ency. Mars. 1812. Yet Euripides mentions in very express terms, " *the painted bas-reliefs on the pediments* [†]," γραπτούς ἐν ἀετοῖσι προσθλέπειν τύπους. Vale Diatr. c. xx.

It might be curious (says Mr Browne, the traveller, in speaking of the paintings in Egypt), to inquire of what materials these colours were composed, which have thus defied the ravages of time [‡]. With respect to the Greeks, some information may be collected from the ancient writers. Yellow ochre was found in different countries; but the most esteemed was that of Attica. (Plin. lib. xxxv.) It is stated by Vitruvius that in his time the mine which produced this substance was no longer worked. The blues brought from the mines of Egypt and Cyprus were preparations of lapis lazuli, and of

---

* Millin speaking of a bas-relief brought from the frieze of the cella of the Parthenon, observes, avant que ce marbre eut été nettoyé, il conservoit des traces, non seulement de la couleur encaustique dont, suivant l'usage des Grecs on enduisoit la sculpture, mais encore d'une véritable peinture dont quelques parties étoient couvertes.

† Templorum fastigia ἀετούς fuisse, et cur ita fuerint dicta, docuerunt P Leopardus Emen Poesius in G con Hipp in v. et imprimis lectu dignissima animadversione, P Scriverius in Martial Epig xix — Valckenaer

‡ The blue colour of some of the painted hieroglyphics is owing to copper. M Descotils a observé une couleur d'un bleu très-éclatant et vitreux sur les peintres hieroglyphiques d'un monument d'Egypte, et il s'est assuré que cette couleur étoit due au cuivre. — Mémoires de l'Instit 1808.

the blue carbonates and arseniates of copper. The greens of copper
were well known to the Greeks. Ivory black, according to Pliny,
was invented by Apelles. The ανάβαφις of Dioscor. lib v. c. 109.
called by the Romans minium, was said to have been discovered by
Callias an Athenian, and was prepared by washing ore of quicksilver.*

But a more curious part of the subject still remains to be noticed.
There is reason to believe that the word γράφω was applied by the
Greeks to express a work combining sculpture and painting.

The following passage occurs in Pliny, lib xxxv. c. 8   Fuisse Panæ-
num fratrem ejus, qui et clypeum intus *pinxit* Elide Minervæ
" Panænus, the brother of Phidias, *painted* the interior of the buckler
of Minerva at Elis." Instead of expecting to find that the concave
part of the shield was *painted*, we should have supposed, says Heyne,
that mention would have been made of some work in bas-relief; and
this we may observe from Pliny, lib. xxxvi. c. 5. was the case in the
shield of the statue of Minerva in the Parthenon ; *scuti concava parte
deorum et gigantum dimicationem cælavit.* Heyne supposes, therefore, that Pliny in the first passage, or the author from whom he
borrowed his information, wrongly understood the meaning of the
word έγραψε, which was employed to signify work in bas-relief.

The opinion of such a scholar as Heyne † is well entitled to our
attention ; but as he has given no instances of this peculiar use of the
word γράφω, I shall add some passages which will establish the truth
of his conjecture.

1. The following words occur in Ælian, lib. vi. c. 11. ώμολόγει την
πράξιν του Γέλωνος το γράμμα, the meaning of which, according to
Cuper, may be, *statua factum Gelonis ob oculos ponit,* he adds γράφειν
et γράμμα non de sola pictura sumitur, sed etiam de aliis effingendi
modis. Observ. Var. p. 39.

2. " The poets and artists feigned that Hercules sailed in a cup ," οἱ ποιηταὶ καὶ οἱ γραφεῖς πλεῖν αὐτὸν ἐν ποτηρίῳ ἐμυθολόγησ . . Athenae. lib. xi. c. 5 Casaubon in his commentary says, per *pictores*, intellige omnes simulacrorum artifices. p 498

3 Antipater in an epigram speaks of four Victories sculptured on the pediment of the house of Caius, they were represented in the act of ascending into the skies, κατ᾽ εὐόροφον γραπτὸν τέγος, " on the well roofed pediment sculptured and painted," γ. τ. says Salmasius, vocat, quod cælaturis et sculpturis domuum fastigia ornarentur, atque etiam auro pingerentur *, sicut et *templorum* Not. in H. A. S. p 423.

4. γραπτὸν τύπον, " *de sculpta imagine*," accepit Reiske in epigrammate, says Jacobs † Certe γραπτὸς hanc interpretationem non respuit. Vide Wolfium in Proleg ad Hom. xlv.

---

* An instance of *painted sculpture* is pointed out to us by Pausanias in the following passage, Attic 28 c " The battle of the Lapithæ and the Centaurs on the shield of the statue of Minerva, and whatever else is in relief there was executed, they say, by Mys, and Parrhasius painted for Mysthis and the rest of his works, ὅσα ἄλλα ἐστὶν ἐπειργασμένα λέγουσι τορεῦσαι Μῦν τὰ δὲ Μοὶ ταυτά τε καὶ τὰ λοιπὰ τῶν ἔργων Παρράσιον καταγράψαι. The four first words of this quotation are entirely omitted in the version of Amasæus. Heyne has produced some instances in which the sense of " work in relief" is given to ἐπειργασμένα, see also Pausanias, Attica, where he informs us, that on each side of the helmet of Minerva in the Parthenon, γρῦπές εἰσιν ἐπειργασμένοι. Chandler translates imperfectly the passage, ' on the sides were griffins "

† Anthol. vol. ii part i p 13

REMARKS

ON

THE MANNERS AND CUSTOMS

OF

THE MODERN INHABITANTS OF EGYPT.

[FROM THE JOURNALS OF DR HUME]

Wᴇ arrived at Rosetta, celebrated by travellers as the paradise of Egypt; but the lofty minarets of the great mosque, with those of the smaller mosques, the tombs of Arab saints, and some houses of the Franks, which are almost embosomed in woods, give the traveller as he sails up the river ideas of populousness and wealth which are strongly contrasted by the mean and ruinous buildings seen by him on landing. The situation of this town would be very advantageous for commerce were a channel sufficiently deep formed across the bar, and this might be done by an industrious and enterprising people. But as the canal of Alexandria did not allow the coasting vessels and dgerms to pass through it, Rosetta has become the entrepôt of commerce between that city and the interior of Egypt. The country being in the hands of the French, and the mouth of the Nile and Alexandria blockaded by the English, the trade had for a long time been interrupted; immense quantities of merchandize, corn, and rice were lying on the wharfs in 1801, ready for exportation.

Between the houses and the Nile is a wide space, the parade of Rosetta; in the evening I found it crowded with people, their dress consisted generally of a blue, brown, or white cotton stuff; but the prevailing colour was light blue. The longest streets or rather lanes of Rosetta, for they are extremely narrow, lie parallel to each other on a line with the river, and are irregularly intersected by others which are shorter. The houses, generally built of brick, are of two or three stories, and at the top appear nearly to touch each other; while the small latticed windows projecting into the streets, add considerably to the gloominess of the houses. The bazars, as in all Moslem towns, are covered in, and are narrow, dark, and dirty. The proximity of the Nile enables the inhabitants to water their streets with ease; some scores of Arabs are seen carrying on their backs for this purpose goat-skins containing from ten to twenty gallons of water. The great mosque is very large, and its roof is supported by a number of columns. It has two minarets of a light and beautiful construction of an unequal height. From the summit of one, the prospect on a clear day is rich and beautiful towards the Delta and the winding of the river, but to the westward the view is that of an arid and burning desert.

The shops were well filled, particularly with various kinds of grain. They are opened at day-break, the people of all eastern countries rising early, that they may transact much of their business in the cool part of the morning. The external appearance of the houses is inelegant, and if I may judge from those which I have seen, their interior is equally so, and in every respect incommodious. We ascended by a dark and dirty staircase to the upper rooms, which are lighted by windows with wooden lattices, rendering the light of day dismal.

As we walked about the town, at the southern end of a long street, we passed by an Egyptian school which was held in the open air on a kind of stage made of basket work, like our own schools, it might be easily known at a distance by the confused medley of young voices. The boys were all sitting cross-legged; in the midst of them was a young man, probably the master, reading to them.

Rosetta is nearly surrounded by gardens. A Rosetta garden is a walled inclosure, where shrubs and fruit trees are planted together without order or regularity. The rude growth of the trees affords the Arab an agreeable shelter from the intense heat; and in his garden he frequently takes his evening meal of pilau, (boiled rice and fowls,) doubly grateful from the abstinence of the day, and the refreshing shade. The gardens are watered by the Persian wheel from wells filled by the Nile during the inundation The small wheels are turned round by an ass, the larger by buffaloes The gardens of Rosetta derive their celebrity from the sudden contrast witnessed by the traveller in exchanging the barren wastes in the vicinity of Alexandria, for a tract of country round Rosetta and in the Delta, abounding in trees, and the most luxuriant vegetation.

On leaving Rosetta at nine in the morning, instead of entering the dgerm at that city, I walked to the castle of St. Julian, along the west bank of the river, and through rich fields of clover, the bersim of the Egyptians; on some parts of my road I observed pools of stagnant water, in one of which a few buffaloes had taken shelter from the mosquitoes, every part of them being covered except the nostrils. At no great distance from St. Julian near a small cottage, some women were sitting in the shade nursing a child, ill with the small-pox; this is one of the most destructive diseases in Egypt; it is the Moubarah of the Turks, and Evlogéa* of the modern Greeks.

The castle of St. Julian where the dgerm met me, consists of a tower surrounded by a wall; from the former, I believe, Poussielgue witnessed the destruction of the French fleet in Aboukir Bay. At eleven in the forenoon we passed over the Nile to a mud-built village, exactly opposite to St Julian's, where the wind being unfavourable, we were detained, until the next morning. As soon as we knew the pilot's determination we sought for a lodging, and at last fixed upon a ruined mosque, the walls of which had been shattered by the fire from St. Julian, for it appeared, that one of the English

---

* Theodorus Prodromus is the earliest writer who uses the word It is not found in Meursius See Villoison Not des MSS du Roi tom vi 539 The opinion in the text is confirmed by the observations of those who have directed their attention to the maladies of the east La petite vérole, et le carreau enlèvent presque la moitié des enfans, avant qu'ils aient atteint leur quatrieme annee —Mem sur l'Egypte —In Syria, in the neighbourhood of Aleppo, the Bedouin Arabs practise inoculation Russell, ii 317

batteries had been erected at this point against the castle. The ground upon which this village stands, is rather more elevated than the adjacent country; the houses are poor hovels, several of them being built in the form of bee-hives. The fields around are cultivated with care, and after the inundation of the Nile, and the river is confined to its proper channel, they are watered by the Persian wheel from cisterns. Where the country is in any degree shaded, not a foot of it is allowed to be waste, for even under the date trees, the cucumber and other garden fruits are seen growing; but where no shade intervenes to weaken the intense heat of the sun, the ground is hard and uncultivated, and bears nothing but thickets of brush-wood.

We found the inhabitants of the village cheerful in the midst of their poverty. The men are tall and lank; swarthy and withered. Their dress in the village is a cotton gown, like that worn by the inhabitants of Rosetta; but the few we met with in the fields were almost naked, having nothing but a cloth wrapped round their middle, and a skull-cap on their heads. The women of Rosetta, and some of those whom I saw at the village wore veils, covering every part of their face but the eyes. These were affected by a disease*, to which the inhabitants of Egypt are very subject.

The lower orders of Egyptian Arabs, appeared to me to be a quiet inoffensive people with many good qualities. They are in general tall, and well made, possessing much muscular strength; yet of a thin spare habit. Their complexion is very dark, their eyes black and sparkling, and their teeth good. Upon the whole they are a fine race of men in their persons; they are more active in agricultural employments than we should be led to imagine from seeing the better sort of them in towns smoking and passing their

---

* Les maladies des yeux sont très-fréquentes en Egypte, et difficiles à guérir.—Granger The ophthalmia in Syria attacks children and young persons, and is ascribed to sleeping in the open air, and being exposed to the night dews.—Russell, ii 299. The Egyptians are subject to psorophthalmia as well as ophthalmia.—Hasselquist. 389

time in listless indolence. The dress of the poorer Arabs, consists simply of a pair of loose blue or white cotton drawers with a long blue tunic, which serves to cover them from their neck to their ankles, and a small red woollen skull-cap, round which they occasionally wind a long strip of white woollen manufacture. They are sometimes so poor as not to be able to purchase even this last article. By means of his tunic or long loose outer garment of dyed cotton, the wealthy Arab conceals from the proud and domineering Turk, a better and a richer dress, consisting sometimes of the long and graceful Moslem habit of Damascus silk, covered by a fine cloth coat with short sleeves, and at other times, particularly among the Alexandrians and those connected with the sea, of a blue cloth short jacket, curiously and richly embroidered with gold, and white trowsers reaching just below the knee, the legs bare.

The articles of furniture in the house of an Egyptian Arab are extremely few. The rooms of all people of decent rank have a low sofa called a divan, extending completely round three sides of the room in general, and sometimes to every part of it, except the door-way; but is most commonly at the upper end of the chamber. On this divan the hours not devoted to business or exercise are passed. It is about nine inches or a foot from the floor, and is covered with mattresses; the back is formed by large square cushions placed all along the wall touching each other, and these are more or less ornamented according to the wealth of the owner. The beds are generally laid on a wicker work strongly framed, made of the branches of the date tree[*], λόιτη ἐκ τῶν σταδίων τοῦ φοίνικος, or of mattresses placed on a raised platform at the end of the room. This latter mode is the more general custom. For their meals they have a very low table, around which they squat on the mats covering the floor, and in houses of repute I have seen sometimes this table of copper thinly tinned over. They have no other furniture except

---

[*] Mentioned by Porphyry, De Abst. lib iv. in speaking of the Egyptians.

culinary utensils. The mats used in Egypt are made of straw, or the flags of the branches of the date tree, and are very neatly worked in figures, such as squares, ovals, and other forms, with fanciful borders. They are very durable, but harbour numbers of fleas, with which all the houses swarm, particularly in hot weather.

The poorer sort of these Arabs seldom can afford to eat animal food, but subsist chiefly on rice made into a pilau, and moistened with the rancid butter of the country. Their bread is made of the holcus durra * I have seen them sit down to a hearty meal of boiled horse beans steeped in oil. When the date is in season they subsist on the fruit, and in summer the vast quantities of gourds of all kinds, and melons, among which we may number the cucurbita citrullus and sativus, and the agour, and haoun of Sonnini, supply them with food The better sort eat mutton and fowls, though sparingly At a dinner given to me by an Arab in the Delta, I observed one dish was formed of a quarter of mutton stuffed with almonds and raisins Their drink is the milk of buffaloes †, and the water of the Nile preserved and purified in cisterns None but the higher orders, or those of dissolute lives ever taste wine, grapes grow in abundance at Rosetta, but little wine is made in Egypt. The Greek vessels from the Archipelago supply at a cheap rate the Franks with the quantity they want

All sorts of coin are current in Egypt; but the principal are Venetian sequins of gold and Spanish dollars; Armenians, Greeks, and Jews are employed in the mint at Cairo The mode of keeping accounts is extremely easy in piastres and paras There is a set of brokers or money changers rather, who for a very trifling brokerage

* Cereale Arabum vulgatissimum, ex quo panis conficitur Forskal

† The flesh of the buffalo is seldom eaten in the Levant, the milk is highly esteemed in Asia Minor and Syria In the time of Prosper Alpinus the tongues of this animal were salted and sent to Venice A few buffaloes are killed in the winter at Aleppo, but the meat is dried, or made into hams, and not eaten fresh Russell, 364

3 E

receive money for the merchants who employ them, and become responsible for it, and this is necessary, on account of the variety of coins in circulation, some of which may be counterfeit or light. These money changers are in general Mahometans, all of whom must be supposed descendants of the prophet; on which account they are believed to be more upright than any other class of their countrymen.

The Arabs carry on the common trades of civilized life, such as carpenters and smiths, but in a very unskilful and imperfect manner. The saw with which they used to cut a large piece of ship-timber in two, was very light and small, yet they employed it in the manner practised by our sawyers, who would in half an hour have cut through what occupied them for a long time. They have a few manufactories; the principal one is the cotton cloth, which is chain-woven, and very strong; a great part of it is dyed blue, and serves for almost general use both for men and women. There is a coarse silk manufacture, of a thin open texture, with a wide border of various colours, but generally dark, which the better sort of women and indeed men sometimes wear instead of what we call call linen, but that commonly worn by superior ranks of people is a manufacture somewhat resembling white crape, but a little thicker, with a silk border. It soon acquires a yellow colour by washing.

There are no jewellers' shops in Rosetta or Alexandria, this business is therefore carried on privately. The practitioners in medicine are the barbers, who are of course numerous in a country where every man's head is shaved; but their knowledge of physic is extremely confined. They perform a few surgical operations, and are acquainted with the virtues of mercury, and some standard medicines. The general remedy in cases of fever and other kinds of illness is a sufi from a priest, which consists of some sentence from the Koran, written on a small piece of paper, and tied round the patient's neck. This, if the patient recovers, he carefully preserves by keeping it constantly between his skull-caps, of which he generally wears two or three. My old interpreter, Mohammed, had a dozen of them. They are worn by the Mahometans, and considered to possess much efficacy [1], as were the frontals of the Jews, and phylacteries of the early Christians. An European medical man is much valued by the Arabs in general, and those of our army had plenty of practice among them, and the assistance they gave was afforded gratuitously. In every bazar some shops will be found in which a few of the most common drugs are sold, such as opium, rhubarb, and senna.

Arabic is generally spoken in Egypt; the Coptic [†] is read as a dead language, and is understood by few. The Italian is much used both by Franks and Copts. I saw no printed books in Arabic; the manuscripts are many of them beautifully written, and the notes are in red ink, or light blue. Other works are read besides the Koran; several of these I have seen in the shops of the transcribers. The natives when at school have sentences copied for them from the Koran; these they learn by heart. There are many scribes, whose employment, like that of the ancient calligraphs, consists of writing out manuscripts for sale; they also make contracts between individuals, law and justice being dispensed in a very summary manner by the basha in greater cases, and by the different sourbadjees in inferior matters. The sourbadjee is a kind of chief magistrate, like a mayor, of whom there is one in every considerable town in Egypt, he is always an Egyptian Arab. The office of sourbadjee at Alexandria was held by Sheik Gazan, a little energetic man of very good family, and some property, who was a firm and zealous adherent of the English, and who administered the duties of his station with becoming dignity. He was an active magistrate, and by means of an efficient police, kept the town and its various inhabitants in excellent order, he himself generally going the rounds once every

---

* The virtue of these scrolls and charms is supposed likewise to be so universal, that they suspend them even upon the necks of their cattle — Shaw, 243. Phylacteries are still worn by some of the Christians of the East. — Russel, ii 101.

† Aujourd'hui la langue Copte n'y est plus entendue par les Coptes mêmes, le dernier qui l'entendoit est mort en ce siècle — Maillet p 24

night at the head of a well-armed guard. The appointment is not hereditary, but is made by the government from regard to wealth or personal qualities, in fact, the office at Alexandria must always be filled by one in whom these two qualifications are united ; for there is much consequence and power attached to it. Sheik Gazan held the office at each time of our occupying Alexandria, but from his attachment to us and his consequent fear of Mohammed Ali, he emigrated to Malta when we last evacuated that city.

With respect to the economical arrangement of their families, we found that the Arabs seldom have more than two wives ; commonly but one. The second wife is always subservient to the elder in the affairs of the house. The women colour their nails, the inside of their hands, and the soles of their feet with a deep orange colour, sometimes with one of a rosy appearance. This is done by means of henna. They likewise apply a black dye to their eye-lashes, eye-brows, and the hair of their head ; a brilliancy it is supposed, is thus given to the eye, and the sight is improved. The women in general, I believe, can neither read nor write ; but the better sort are taught embroidery and ornamental needle work, in which they mostly pass their time. An Arab merchant of property made me a present of an elegantly embroidered handkerchief, worked, as he said, by his wife's hands. The women of rank are seldom seen abroad ; many of these were murdered by the Turks after we evacuated Alexandria in 1803, but some of them, and in particular two Bedouin girls succeeded in escaping to Malta.

The features of the Arab-Egyptian women are by no means

* Both these customs are of great antiquity, some of the nails of the mummies have been found dyed with henna, and Shaw saw a joint of the donax taken out of a catacomb at Saccara, containing a bodkin, and an ounce or more of powder used for the purpose of ornamenting the eyes. Bodkins, which were employed in the same manner, are found at Herculaneum, made of ivory. Dr Russell describes the kohol used for the eye-balls, or inside of the eyelids, it is a kind of lead ore, and is brought from Persia. It is so much in request that the poets of the East in allusion to the instrument used in applying it, say, " The mountains of Ispahan have been worn away with a bodkin." — Vol 1 367.

regular. In general the cheek-bones are high, the cheeks broad and flabby, the mouth large, the nose short, thick, and flat, though in some it is prominent; the eyes black, but wanting animation. The bad appearance of the eyes is in some measure owing to disease. The skin is of a disagreeable Mulatto colour. The hair, which is commonly black, is matted, and often smeared with a stinking ointment. It is formed in two or three divisions, and suffered to hang down the back. At a distance, however, the long flowing robe which covers them to the heels, though it may conceal deformity, seems, by the easiness of its drapery, to heighten their stature, and even to render them ungraceful. Indeed I have never seen any women who have displayed so much easiness of manner, or so fine a carriage, being superior in this respect even to the women of Circassia. Probably the elegance and dignity of their gait may depend upon the habit of carrying every thing on their heads. They are taller in general than our European women. From ignorance of their language I could form no opinion of their conversation, yet from their numerous and graceful gestures I supposed it might be pleasing in spite of the shrillness of their voices. As the army was passing through the villages they mounted upon the house tops, and made a confused noise like the cackling of cranes, which was interpreted to us as indicating wishes for our success.

The Ethiopian women brought to Egypt for sale though black, are exceedingly beautiful their features are regular, their eyes full of expression. A great number of them had been purchased by the French during their stay in Egypt, who were anxious to dispose of them previously to their leaving the country, and it was the custom to bring them to the common market place in the camp, sometimes in boys' clothes, at other times in the gaudiest female dress of the French fashion. The neck was in general naked, and the petticoat on one side tucked up to the knee, to show the elegant form of the limb. The price of these women was from sixty to an hundred dollars, while Arab women might be purchased at so low a price as ten.

The Circassian women, who are brought to Egypt in great num-

bers, are exposed to sale in particular markets or khans, and fetch a
price in proportion to their beauty. They have been much talked of,
and were we to give implicit faith to the eastern romances, female
beauty is no where to be met with in perfection but in Circassia.
I confess, however, that the appearances of such Circassian women
as I saw, much disappointed me, almost all their pretensions to
beauty consisting of a fair skin. I was in the harem of Hassan, a
Mameluke Kaschief, and had an opportunity of seeing three of its
inmates. They were seated in a small room, on the sides of which
was a divan or sofa covered with crimson satin; a Turkey carpet
was spread on the middle of the floor. The crimson satin was
fancifully embroidered with silver flowers; the ladies wore white
turbans of muslin, and their faces were concealed with long veils,
which in fact were only large white handkerchiefs thrown carelessly
over them. When they go abroad, they wear veils, like the Arab
women. Their trowsers were of red and white striped satin very
wide, but drawn together at the ankle with a silk cord, and tied
under their breasts with a girdle of scarlet and silver. Something like
a white silk shirt, with loose sleeves, and open at the breast, was
next the skin. Over all, was thrown a pelisse, one of them was light
blue satin, spangled with small silk leaves; the other two, pink
satin and gold. We were treated with coffee, and were fanned by
the ladies themselves with large fans, a perfume being at the same time
scattered through the room. This was composed of rose water, a
quantity of which is made in Fayum. They were reserved at first,
but after conversing with the Mameluke who attended me, they were
less careful to conceal their faces. Their beauty did not equal what
I had anticipated from the fineness of their skins. They were inclining to corpulence; their faces were round and inexpressive; but
the neck, bosom, arms, and hands were of great fairness and
delicacy. My dress seemed to amuse them very much, and they
examined every part of it, particularly my boots and spurs. When
drinking coffee with the Turkish officers, I chanced to forget my
handkerchief, and as I seemed to express a desire to find it, one of

the ladies took off a handkerchief from her head, and presented it to me, having first perfumed it.

At my return to the camp, I had a conversation on the subject of these women with a French deserter, who had become Mameluke, and belonged to the family of Hassan. I was very particular in my enquiries respecting the number of women that Hassan might have in his possession. He told me that his master had upwards of twenty, several of whom were Circassians. I expressed astonishment at his having so many wives, but the Mameluke said that Hassan in reality had but one wife, the rest of the women being her attendants, and that his wife was not among the ladies I had seen. The Mamelukes are not allowed to marry before they arrive at the rank of kaschief, but it is common for the superior to bestow a female upon his followers as the reward of eminent services. I attended Hassan while he was ill; he was extremely grateful, and would have given me his sabre, had it not been a present from Mourad Bey, whom he called Sultan Mourad.

The Moslem marriages are always regulated by the elder females, the bridegroom seldom or never seeing the bride's face, until the day of marriage. It is merely a civil contract made between their mutual friends, and signed by the young man and his father. There is a procession, consisting of many persons, male and female, who accompany the bride on a horse richly caparisoned to the house of the bridegroom, where she is received by his female friends. Some time after this, the mother of the young man informs the assembled females that the marriage has been solemnized, who immediately raise a loud and shrill cry, which they repeat at intervals during the entertainment which follows. It is the common demonstration of joy among the women, consisting of a quick guttural pronunciation of Luy, Luy, Luy*, and may be heard at some distance. After the

---

* A similar sound expressive of mirth is used by the women on the coast of Barbary, it seems to be a corruption (says Shaw) of Hallelujah 242. The ἐλολύζω of the Greeks was generally applied to the conclamation of women in affliction, but it also expressed joy. — Schultens in Job, c. 10, v. 15

first burst of joy, they make a procession through the streets, the
women all veiled, and a person mounted on a horse richly caparisoned
as before, carrying a red banner-like handkerchief fixed to the end of
a long pole.   They then return to the bridal house, and pass the remainder of the day and part of the night in feasting and carousing,
entertaining themselves with seeing dancing girls, and listening to
singing men, who are placed in an outer apartment or balcony.   I was
allowed to be present at one of these marriages, but I did not see the
bride.   Cakes, sweetmeats, coffee, and sherbet were distributed, and
wine for the Nazarani (myself).

These and similar feasts are called Fantasias ; at some which I have
attended the women were unveiled, but they were not females of good
character   At Alexandria there were very few dancing girls, but I
have seen a young man habited as a women perform all the part of
a dancing girl.   He appeared to be drunk, yet displayed many
surprising feats of agility.   At one of these entertainments, I heard
some Arabic songs, sung by singing men, and accompanied with
music.   The musicians were Jews, but the singers were Arabs.

An Egyptian coffee-house is a large open building, with a few
tables and seats within it, generally surrounded by a viranda of rude
workmanship, under which the idle and lazy, particularly the Turks,
are fond of sitting, smoking and drinking coffee.   For this, two or
three paras only are paid.   In these places we have frequently seen
two men playing at a game which consists in removing some small
shells, like cowries, from one semicircular hole to another, on a
square piece of board, counting the shells, as they remove them
This game appeared to be one of great interest ; they have also one
nearly resembling backgammon.   The higher orders of Turks and
Arabs are fond of chess, but this class is seldom seen loitering in the
coffee-houses.

The Egyptian Arabs are punctual in the performance of their religious ceremonies at the stated hours appointed by their prophet
We often beheld some of these poor men after a day's hard work for
a miserable pittance, on their knees on the sea shore, or at a seques-

tered spot on the banks of the Nile, offering up their prayers, the forehead at times touching the ground Idiots are held in great respect . whenever I have seen the Sheik el Misseri, a man renowned in Alexandria and its neighbourhood for sanctity, he has been accompanied by one of this description* of people. In a conversation once carried on by means of an interpreter between the Sheik and myself, respecting some of the religious opinions of the Mahometans, I found that he was well acquainted with the history of the creation, and with many parts of the Bible.

There is a tribe of civilized Arabs in Egypt, who pretend that they are respected by serpents, and that no sort of snake can hurt them. As a proof of this, there is an annual procession of the tribe through the streets of Rosetta, of which I was a witness, one of their number is obliged to eat a living snake† in public, or so much of it as to occasion its death Probably the snake may have been rendered harmless by some means; the people, however, suppose that for some act of piety performed by the ancestors of this tribe or family (which is by no means numerous), the Prophet protects the descendants from any injury which the snakes might occasion. The ophiophagus, who is to keep up this ridiculous farce, being no doubt well paid, begins to eat the living reptile ; a pretty large snake is held in his hands, which writhes its folds around his naked arm, as he bites at the head and body. Horror and fury are depicted in the man's

---

* Baumgarten was told that madmen and idiots were respected as saints by the Mahometans, and that tombs were erected in honour of them when they died — Peregrin in Egypt 73 Pococke at Rosetta saw two of those naked saints, he says, who are commonly natural fools, and had in great veneration in Egypt — Vol 1 14

† Antes. Observ. on Egypt, 16 , mentions the practice of eating serpents and scorpions The custom of charming serpents has prevailed in the East from a very early period, Psalm lviii 5., Ecclesiastes, x. 11 The charmers, however, were not always secure from injury " Who will pity a charmer that is bitten with a serpent ?" Eccl xii 13 Forskal says that the leaves of Aristolochia sempervirens were used for forty days by those who would wish to protect themselves against the bite of these animals At Pella the serpents, says Lucian, (Pseudom) were so tame and familiar, that they were fed by the women and slept with the children — Ed

3 F

countenance, and in a strong convulsive manner he puts the animal
to death by eating and swallowing part of it alive   This disgusting
and horrible spectacle, however, is but seldom exhibited at present.

In the house in which I lived at Alexandria, there was a room
containing a large quantity of rubbish and lumber, which had not
been removed for some years; a small snake was one day discovered
in it, on which account I resolved to have the room examined, and
the supposed nest of snakes destroyed   My interpreter persuaded
me to send for one of the family already mentioned   The snake-
charmer was an old man, and by trade a carpenter.   He prayed
fervently at the door for a quarter of an hour, and at length, pale and
trembling, ventured into the room, while an English sailor, who was
at that time my servant, proceeded to clear away the rubbish with
perfect unconcern   Two small snakes only were found, and these
were killed by the shovel of my servant.   There are many kinds of
snakes and reptiles about the ruins in the environs of Alexandria;
among them, some have fancied they discovered the asp.   I have
seen here the black scorpion, whose sting is reputed mortal; but this
is a vulgar prejudice.

A mixture of meal, wine, and honey, was the food given, as we are
informed by Ælian, N. A. lib xvii, to a species of serpent by the
ancient Egyptians.   The snake is esteemed sacred by the present
Arab inhabitants of Egypt, and I have been told that they frequently
place milk and roots for their subsistence, when it is known that any
snakes frequent the ruins of their dwellings   These house snakes grow
to a large size, and are said to be quite harmless, and even tame.

The dogs, less fortunate than the cats, have no masters; they are
left to prowl about the streets in search of whatever food they can
collect.   They are very numerous, and many hundreds were shot by
the French in different towns.   They are very savage at Alexandria,
being a mixed race of the dog and the jackal   I have been attacked
by them more than once at night, in passing by a burying-ground.
I have seen several of them at the ruins near the castle of Aboukir;
they were of a light sandy colour, and had the appearance of the

jackal. I saw one after it had been on board of the Inconstant two months; but it still retained its savage aspect, and had never become familiar.

Among the different classes of people we met with in Egypt, none struck me more forcibly that the Bedouins The desarts of Barca, or rather its oases, are inhabited by several tribes of these wanderers who are often in hostility with each other. The most formidable of them is that called Welled Ali. One of its chiefs was an inmate in the house inhabited by Osman Bey Bardisi, and to this Sheik I was introduced by Osman, who said to me aloud in Arabic, if you or I were to meet this Sheik in the desart, of which he is one of the wolves, perhaps it would not be for us a pleasant meeting. The Sheik made no reply, but smiled. Many English officers however ventured a long way into the desart in hunting parties, where they staid some days, and all the Bedouins, whom they met, behaved with civility to them. The greatest number of Bedouins to be seen at a time at Alexandria, was at a certain season of the year with their camels, when many of them assembled in the square near the Jerusalem convent gate The Bedouin, from hard living and constant exposure to the sun of the desart, is extremely lank and thin, and of a very dark complexion, his countenance wild; his eye black and penetrating, his general appearance bespeaking the half-savage, and unenlightened son of nature. His sole dress consists of a skull-cap and slippers, and a bernouse, or white woollen garment which covers the whole body, and reaches as low as the calf of the leg, having a hood to cover the head, (for he never wears a turban,) and open holes for the arms. Such is the Bedouin, whether Sheik or not The Welled Ali Sheik had a lance with a head somewhat like a tomahawk; a long rifle gun, a sabre, and a pair of pistols of superior workmanship.

The people called Levantines in Egypt are the descendants of Franks born in this country, and are thus named to distinguish them from those Franks who are natives of European countries. The Levantine women imitate the Arabs in dying their eye-lashes, eye-brows, and hair with a black colour, and they are dressed in the costume of the higher order of Arab women. I saw an example of this in the dress worn by the wife of an Italian merchant at an entertainment given in Alexandria by the English commander in chief. The dress with the ornaments was valued at two thousand pounds. Her hair was remarkably long, and was divided behind into about forty tresses, each tress was plaited, one half of it being adorned with Venetian sequins, the other half with a string of pearls; at the bottom of each tress was an emerald. The ornaments were placed at equal distances in all the tresses. When the hair is not long enough to extend to the extremity of the waist, it is lengthened by silk of the same colour. The head-dress was composed of a scarlet skull-cap with a black silk tassel in the centre, and nearly covered with different ornaments set with small rubies and emeralds. Round the head was a kind of turban formed by handkerchiefs, one placed upon another, until they projected as much as the brim of a man's hat. In the front of this turban was a handsome diamond ornament, and little gold chains with brilliants were festooned from the bottom of it over the side of the face and ears. She wore a handsome but ill-formed necklace of pearls, in the centre of which was seen an emerald valued at three hundred pounds. On her body was a close vest of superb cloth of gold with long sleeves; at the opening of which for the hands, appeared an ornament similar to ruffles, made of a manufacture common in the East of striped silk and gauze. This vest reached from the bosom to the ankles nearly, and fitted close over the trowsers, which were made of striped satin and silk of Damascus manufacture. Over the vest she wore a garment like an open gown without a train, made of very fine fawn-coloured German cloth trimmed with narrow gold lace. The whole of the dress had an elegant and singular appearance. This woman with her husband and family was then at Alexandria, going to Italy to reside there, her husband having made a handsome fortune in Cairo. It was probably the last time she would wear that dress, and she was unusually fine.

Some of the Coptic women are fair and beautiful. The features of a Copt are broader, and more inclining to plumpness than those of the Arab. These people are certainly the most intelligent in Egypt, and are better educated than the Arabs. I do not recollect to have seen a Copt absolutely poor. They are the managers, collectors, and clerks of the revenue in Egypt in general, and though at Alexandria the head of the customs was a Turk, yet the subordinate officers were Copts. Many of them are merchants and brokers. The dress of the men is the long dress of the Turks, but they and all Christian and Jewish inhabitants are not permitted to wear a green or white turban, blue being the colour substituted in general, although the better sort wear a long Cashmire shawl, twisted round the head as a turban.

I was acquainted with a Coptic merchant at Rosetta, who invited me and another Englishman to the christening of his child. We were induced to go, that we might have some insight into the manners of this people. We were received by the lady of the house on entering with great civility, she poured a little perfumed rose water into our hands, from a bottle covered with silver fillagree of very fine work, and as we passed into the room she sprinkled us all over with rose water. This I afterwards found to be a common custom in all Coptic and Levantine houses when a person makes a visit of ceremony. The room into which we were introduced was at the top of the house, where there was a table covered with all kinds of sweetmeats and fruits. The mistress of the house and her sister, also a married lady, with her husband and other guests soon made their appearance. The infant was completely swathed. The ceremony* was performed by the Coptic priest, according to a service which he read from a ritual in manuscript. As soon as the ceremony of the christening was ended, we sat down to partake of the breakfast.

---

* The Coptic form of baptism is described by Vanslcb and by Pococke. "they plunge the child three times into water and then confirm it, and give it the sacrament, that is, the wine, the priest dipping the end of his finger in it and putting it to the child's mouth."— Vol. 1 246

These two Coptic women, particularly the sister of the lady of the house, were the prettiest I had seen in Egypt. The sister was remarkably fair, and would have been reckoned handsome in any country. She was older than she appeared to be, and I was surprised to find that she had a son then in the room fourteen years of age; but marriages are made at a very early time of life in this country. The costume of these women was similar to that I have already described, as worn by the Levantines, differing only in the ornaments and jewelry.

In Egypt the unhappy Israelites, bearing with the Christians the undisguised scorn and contempt of all ranks of Moslems, drag out a miserable existence. Possessing an active and cunning mind, they contrive in many instances to over-reach their Mahometan masters, and derive their means of living from the business of money-changers and brokers They are easily distinguished both from the Copt and Arab by their prominent nose and chin, and by being darker than the Copt, but not so dark as the Arab.

The Copts and Jews are the general shop-keepers in Egypt; and in the part called the Frank town of Alexandria there is a considerable number of shops, in which cutlery of a very inferior quality, and woollen and linen drapery of various kinds are offered for sale. The muslin in these shops was very coarse. The woollen cloth was principally of German manufacture, of a thin though tolerably fine texture, narrower than English cloth, and much cheaper than the latter. Of this cloth, which is of various colours, the most esteemed being green and flesh coloured, there are many hundred bales sold annually in Cairo. There is another sort, a red cloth of a stronger manufacture, of which the Mamelukes make their trowsers, and this also is German. In the cloths and linens of that country there was formerly a considerable trade carried on between Venice and Trieste, and Alexandria, the returns being in gums, senna, corn, and rice.

JOURNAL OF A VOYAGE

UP THE NILE BETWEEN PHILÆ AND IBRIM IN NUBIA, *

IN THE MONTH OF MAY, 1811.

[BY CAPT LIGHT]

Mr Legh and his companion have communicated some valuable remarks concerning parts of Nubia, and the following journal of Captain Light will give additional information respecting the antiquities of the country, and the manners of the people

The conquests of the Mahometans and the destruction of Christianity have been followed in Nubia, as in other parts of the Turkish empire, by the most complete depopulation and barbarism Seventeen bishoprics were formerly enumerated in the different provinces of Nubia, the towns of Ibrim and Dongola were under the jurisdiction of two of them ' Mais tante de Pasteurs " (says Vansleb †), "le Christianisme est aujourd'hui entierement eteint dans tout ce royaume" The Oases also were once peopled by many Coptic Christians and the names of some of the Bishops who presided over that district are mentioned in the history of the Patriarchs of Alexandria Part of the first epistle of St Paul to the Corinthians, published by Munter and Georg in a dialect different from that of the Memphitic or Sahidic is supposed to have been written in the language of the people of the Oases

The author of the Kitab el Fehrest speaks of the Nubian characters ‡, and the Nubian language is mentioned by Macrizy (Desc de l'Eg tom ii fol 180) but Syriac, Coptic, and Greek letters were adopted by the inhabitants, when Christianity was introduced among them and we learn from Abou Selih that their liturgy and prayers were in Greek, the same thing is also stated by Abdollah of Assouan ⸗ As late as the beginning of the fifteenth century, the time when Macrizy wrote, the women and children of Upper Egypt had a perfect acquaintance with Greek The Arabic language has gradually prevailed in that country, but in Nubia, Captain Light found that a knowledge of it was of little use to the traveller A different idiom is there spoken, and this is pointed out by Leo Africanus in the following passage " Beyond Assouan are villages peopled by men of black colour, whose language is a mixture of Arabic, Egyptian, and Æthiopian "— Quatremère Rech sur l'Egypte — Ed

Assouan, May 7. — I arrived at Assouan, anciently Syene, in the usual course by a boat from Boulac. Hence I found the navigation

---

* " Le Nubie commence au bourg nommé al-Kasr, situé à 3 milles de la ville d'Assouan " — From the History of Nubia, by Abdallah native of Assouan. — See Quatremère, Mem Geog sur l'Egypte.   † Hist de l'Eg d'Alex p. 30

‡ The Bashmouric was supposed to be the language of the Nubians, by Longuerue, but this opinion has been controverted by Quatremère, who has shown that the Bashmourites were inhabitants of Lower Egypt — Rech sur l'Egy 163.

⸗ Quoted by Quatremère, p. 23. in his Mémoire sur la Nubie

stopped by the rocks, with which the river at this place is filled, and the channel so divided and reduced in the ordinary state of the stream, as not to leave sufficient breadth or depth for boats. I therefore quitted mine to proceed by land to the shore opposite Philæ, and procured asses for the journey.

On the 10th of May I left Assouan, attended by an English servant and an Arab from my boat, having two asses for riding, and three for the baggage; accompanied by Osman, the son of the Sheik of Assouan, as guide and guard, and proceeded through the ruins of the Arab town on the heights above Assouan. The desart here on every side is broken by large masses of granite, most of which had hieroglyphic characters sculptured on them. We arrived in about two hours at the shore opposite to Philæ.

This place called by the natives Selwajoud, by Norden El Heiff, merits all that has been said respecting the temples, and other structures of antiquity which are to be found there. I remained at Philæ until the evening of the 11th. It was on the morning of that day that I first saw the destruction caused by the locusts, of which an immense swarm obscured the sky. In a few hours after their arrival, the palm trees were stripped of their foliage, and the ground of its herbage. Men, women, and children employed themselves in vain attempts to prevent the locusts from settling, howling repeatedly the name of *Geraad*, the Arab and Nubian word for locusts; throwing sand in the air, beating the ground with sticks, and at night lighting fires. Yet they seemed to bear the loss of their harvests without murmur, blessing God that they had not the plague, which they said always raged at Cairo when the locusts appeared, this was actually the case at that time.

---

* " *They darkened the sun*," says the Prophet Joel, ii. 10., speaking of the flight of the locusts The word is written by Russel *girad*, Gryllus migratorius. L. In many parts of Turkey the locust-bird, Turdus Roseus, providentially appears at the same time with the locusts and destroys great numbers. In some seasons when the grain of the corn is too far advanced, these insects attack the cotton plants, mulberry, and fig leaves — Russell, ii. 230.

I hired a boat of the inhabitants of the east shore opposite to Philæ, which though of smaller size than the one I left at Assouan, was large enough to enable me to lay my bed cross-ways at the stern, four men made the crew; and a mat arched on some palm-branches served for a skreen against the sun

May 12.—Early in the morning we sailed up the river, and in consequence of the wind failing, moored at Ser Ali, on the east bank, where we observed some crocodiles. About half way between Philæ and Ser Ali on the west bank are the remains of a temple, in a village called Deboo, on the cultivated spots in the neighbourhood are many sheep and cows, with plantations of palm-trees

May 13 —Detained at Ser Ali by Kamseen winds, which set in with an obscure sky; the sun becoming pale, as seen through a dis-coloured glass.

May 14. — Arrived at Gartaas, (called by Norden, Hindau), on the west bank, where I landed to examine the architectural ruins, of which there are many at intervals, for the space of nearly two miles. The first and most southern is a square inclosure of masonry, of one hundred and fifty-three paces, its greatest height sixteen feet; its thickness about ten. In the south and north sides there are gateways; that in the north is nearly in the centre, and has a cornice, on which is a winged globe, and the outline of a symbolic figure cut on one of the stones. Beyond this, going northward, amongst some quarries of sandy free-stone, is a narrow passage open at the top, cut by art; on each side of which at intervals are hieroglyphics coarsely sculptured, and the outline of a Monolithic temple. This passage leads to a part of the rock on which is a shallow recess, here I saw the half-length figures of men in full relief; the heads are defaced, they have drapery about the shoulders and arms, and appear to have in their hands the wand and whip of the Egyptian mythology; the former being a symbol of power; the latter the Flagellum sometimes given to Osiris, at others to the genii Averrunci. They are about three feet high, and are cut out of the rock.

Above and below these figures are numerous Greek inscriptions cut in tablets, and at the bottom of the whole are rudely formed hieroglyphics. At a short distance to the north are the remains of a small temple, consisting of six columns beautifully finished with capitals : two of them facing the north engaged in a wall forming the entrance, their capitals are heads of Isis, supporting a plinth on which are cut Monolithic temples ; the other four, two on the west and two on the east, are engaged in a wall half their height ; the capitals vary ; but the opposite, or the east and west, are alike. Those at the south angles have the grape and wheat-ear worked under the volutes. The shafts are about three feet in diameter ; the distance between them about ten ; the north front is thirty feet ; the east and west thirty-six ; on the latter, towards the base, two or three symbolic figures have been sculptured On one of the columns are some Greek characters beginning with the usual form το προσκυνημα.

The west bank of the river in the neighbourhood of Gartaas is almost a desart ; a few huts scattered amongst the ruins afford shelter to the inhabitants. The opposite shore has some degree of cultivation, and the mountains are a little distant from the banks of the river.

May 15. — Arrived at Taeefa on the west bank, above which the sides of the river become bold and craggy, and near this place is the entrance to the Shellaal * or cataract of Galabshee; here Mr. Buckingham, a gentleman who had lately ascended the Nile as far as Dukkey, lays down the tropic of Cancer. Taeefa, contains several remains of ancient buildings scattered about on an open cultivated spot of more than a mile in length, and about half in breadth, bounded by the desart and its mountains. The village might contain two or three hundred inhabitants, and had a Sheik who regulated their labour and subsistence. The doom and palm-tree flourished here.

The antiquities consist of several spacious oblong enclosures of masonry of not more than three or four feet in height. In the centre of the plain, separated from each other, are two buildings, one complete, having the form of a portico, the other in ruins, seems to be

* Je sçai de divers Nubiens qu'il s'en trouve sept ou huit de remarquables cataractes, depuis Sai au dessous de Dongola, jusqu'à Assouan — Maillet p 42.

part of an early Christian church. The first is almost blocked up by a mass of mud, and is surrounded by the hovels of the natives. It is a pyramidal portico facing the south, having two columns almost engaged in a wall to the bottom of the capitals, which represent the full blown lotus, and support an entablature and cornice. Between this column and the sides are small door-ways with a cornice and frieze; and above these a second and third cornice, in each of which is the winged globe. The frieze has a bead and leaf worked on it. The front of this building is about twenty-seven feet in length; the inside is perfect, having a roof supported by four columns standing on a plain circular base, their capitals forming the full-blown lotus. On one of the walls inside is a cross of Maltese form.

The second building is open to the east; the west wall is perfect; in this is a door-way, and within, in front, are two columns with capitals of the full-blown lotus, supporting a small portion of roof. Scriptural paintings with figures as large as those of life remain on the walls, and over the cornice of the door-way is the winged globe. In front of the open side lie several capitals, broken shafts, and other fragments of buildings.

I was detained at Taeefa the 16th by the Kamseen wind, which changed in the evening to the north and west, driving the sands of the desart for many miles, with so much violence as to obscure the air, and hide from view the rocks close to the boat. The storm continued for two hours with violent gusts, attended with thunder and lightning; it ceased at last with a torrent of rain. During the tempest, my guide Osman was chaunting the praises of God and the prophet in a most discordant voice; while the boatmen trembling and shrinking from the storm, hid themselves in the bottom of the boat.

May 17. — We rowed through the Shellaal of Galabshee. This is the name given to those parts of the stream that are interrupted by rocks. Here the passage of boats is not impeded, as at Assouan, where the Nile is lost in streams of two, three, and four feet in breadth, which interrupt the navigation, except during the inundation, when, as I was informed, very small boats and rafts may pass the Shellaal. At Galabshee, the Nile flowing with a wide and beautiful course, divides itself among several rocks and uninhabited islands, the river increases in breadth, as it enters into a grand amphitheatre of bold and craggy rocks, interspersed with cultivated spots of ground extending for about a mile; then contracting itself, as it approaches Taeefa, it resumes its ordinary breadth. On the eastern bank on an elevated spot are the remains of an Arab mud-built castle, and on one of the islands those of a village and another castle, which, though of bad construction, prove that a greater degree of civilization had formerly marked this place. Beyond, the rocks recede, become lower, and the land appears cultivated. The village of Galabshee, which Norden by mistake places opposite to Taeefa, is close to the opening on the west bank, and has a larger population than Taeefa. The inhabitants live in huts round a ruined temple. They seemed more jealous of my appearance among them, than any of this country whom I had hitherto seen I was surrounded by them, and " bucksheesh, bucksheesh" (a present) echoed from all quarters, before they would allow me to look at the temple One more violent than the rest threw dust in the air *, the signal both of rage and defiance, ran for his shield, and came towards me dancing, howling, and striking the shield with the head of his javelin, to intimidate me A promise of a present pacified him and enabled me to make my remarks and sketches.

A butment of masonry rises above the bank of the river, at about one hundred and seventy or eighty feet from the front of the temple, to which a paved approach leads from the butment, on each side of this pavement there formerly had been an avenue of Sphinxes, one of which was lying headless near the pavement. At the end, steps appear to have been raised, leading to a terrace of thirty-six feet in breadth, from which rise two pyramidal moles with a gateway between

---

* " And they gave him audience unto this word, and then lifted up their voices and said, Away with such a fellow from the earth , — and as they cried out, and cast off their clothes, and *threw dust into the air*." — Acts of the Apost. xxii.

them, forming a front of about one hundred and ten feet. The upper part of the moles to within three or four layers of stone above the gateway was in ruins The moles are eighteen or twenty feet thick, of solid masonry, within is a court of about forty feet, now filled with broken shafts and capitals; it appears to have had a colonnade to the side walls joining the moles with the portico. The latter consists of four columns, a lateral wall divides this portico from a suite of four inner apartments, the door-ways to which have the winged globe in the cornice. Three of these apartments are covered with hieroglyphics and symbolic figures, there are remains of colouring very fresh and clean. All the apartments are encumbered with ruins, and have scarcely any ceiling left.

The front of the portico is plain, with the exception of a winged globe over the gateway Within are scriptural paintings, a head similar to those represented in the churches of the Greeks appears with a nimbus around it, above the ruins on the wall of the last apartment, with some Greek characters The moles have no hieroglyphics or symbolic figures excepting a few at the gateway, and these are in the first outline. The shafts of the columns are nearly six feet in diameter; the height appears to contain from five to six diameters, a common proportion in Egyptian architecture. On a column is a Greek inscription in red letters*; there are two more also which I did not copy, and one in Coptic.

May 18 — In the morning we sailed, but were obliged to moor below Abouhore on the east bank, which is enclosed by barren rocks of sand-stone and granite; I mounted to the summit of these and found the whole country to the east as far as the eye could reach broken into masses of rock presenting a most frightful and desolate appearance. On the shore I observed remains of Roman brick-work.

May 19. — We reached Abouhore, and were again obliged to stop. Here the hills recede and leave a large space of ground for cultivation

---

* See the remarks on Greek inscriptions at the end of the volume.

watered by wheels, and bearing more marks of civilization than the other villages, and the inhabitants appeared more industrious Their huts were thickly scattered among numerous palm-trees. Here there is a small Shellaal which leaves only a narrow passage to the west; on the other part there is a low ridge of rocks. Opposite to Abouhore, placed as if to command this passage, is a ruined Arab castle of unbaked bricks. At Abouhore an assembly of women was collected howling over the dead body of a child.

May 20.—We arrived by means of towing at Garsery, called by Norden, Garbe Dendoui, on the west bank, where I landed to visit the ruins Nothing can be considered more barren than the rocks and hills on each side, passed in the course of this day. The few huts I saw, were made of loose stones cemented by mud, and covered with a flat roof of straw or branches of palm-trees. The ruins at Garsery consist of a front of masonry of three sides, enclosing a portico and gateway. The longest side is about one hundred feet, and faces the river; the height above the ground is ten feet. In the centre of the enclosure is a gateway; the side stones are covered with hieroglyphics; beyond is the portico of a small temple, which consists of the usual pyramidal front, the entablature is perfect; the capitals of the columns are alike, presenting the form of the full-blown lotus; the symbol among the sacred plants of Egypt, most commonly appropriated to Osiris. A lateral wall separates this portico from two inner chambers.

May 21. — Having passed the remains of a portico at Garshee, we moored nearly opposite to Dukkey on the east side.

May 22. — Having crossed from our mooring-place, I landed and skirted the desart for the space of an hour, passing frequently over Roman tiles and brick, and arrived at the temple of Dukkey. The front faces the north close to the river, and consists of two pyramidal moles with a gateway complete; a cornice and torus surround the whole. The dimensions of the front are about seventy-five feet in length, forty in height, and fifteen in depth. The walls are without hieroglyphics.

In the cornice over the gateway is the winged globe. In each of the moles in the inside front, are small doorways ornamented in a similar manner, leading by a stone staircase to small chambers, and to the top. A court of about forty feet in depth separates the moles from a pyramidal portico, in which are two columns engaged half their height in a wall elevated in the centre, forming the entrance. The depth of the portico is about eighteen feet, the ceiling of it is almost perfect, composed of single stones, reaching from the front to the back part. Between the centre columns are winged scarabæi †, on the other part are scriptural paintings. A lateral wall divides the portico from three inner chambers; the ceiling of these are imperfect; the symbolic figures in the third room are larger than in the other parts of the building. The upper part of the side walls of the portico have the remains of some scriptural designs, representing men on horseback approaching towards angels, whose hands seem lifted up in supplication. The whole was surrounded by a wall extending from the two extremes of the moles. Over the gate of the portico are some Greek characters, in the place where the winged globe is usually seen.

ΥΠΕΡΑΣ . . .

ΘΕΟ . . .

A variety of inscriptions found about the gateway of the moles, prove that this temple was erected to Mercury. ‡ From Dukkey, where the rocks and desart begin to leave room for cultivation on the banks of the Nile, we proceeded up the river, and in a short time were hailed from the western shore by a follower of the Cashief of Deir. We were obliged to pay him a visit, and found him sitting

---

* The device so common on the temples of Egypt, and symbolical of the *anima mundi.* —Shaw, 358

† Probably of the form referred to in the Men. Is Exp. 61. Pandit alienas alas Scarabæus, Solis imago.

‡ See the remarks on Greek inscriptions at the end of the volume.

under a shady palm-tree on a carpet, surrounded by some dirty half-naked attendants. He rose on my approaching him, bade me sit down by him, and placed a cushion under my elbow. His visit to the village (named Ouffeddoonee,) was for the purpose of passing some days here with two of his wives, of whom he is said to have thirty living in different parts of his territory, and among whom he divides his time. He was dressed in a coarse linen shirt and turban ; was without slippers, he alone of the whole party held a pipe in his hand. I presented him with a telescope and small pocket-knife; these he was at first inclined to refuse, saying I was welcome without an offering. A pipe, dates, and coffee were brought to me. His attendants sat down by us in a circle, and many trifling questions were asked of me by all. My wearing apparel was examined ; I was questioned about my rank, what number of soldiers my king commanded, how many wives he had, in what garrison I was, how far off, what number of guns it contained, and whether my Pasha, meaning my commanding officer, had power of life and death.

The Cashief whose name is Hassan is one of three brothers, hereditary chiefs of the country between Philæ and Dongola He is a handsome young man of about twenty-five years of age, and his territory extends from Philæ to Deir. He has a nominal absolute power, which however he does not exercise oppressively, nor does he interfere much between the quarrels of the natives.

He gave me a letter to his son, a boy of ten years of age, left at Deir, from whom I was to receive all necessary protection and assistance ; on my leaving him he presented me with a sheep. Proceeding hence, we observed the hills to be at a considerable distance from the river, we arrived at Naboo on the west, where they again appear in rocks of sand-stone. From Naboo the river winds east and west, the hills sometimes receding on one side, and on the other bold rocks reach to the water's edge.

May 23.—Having sailed part of the night, and the wind continuing fair, we passed Seboo on the west bank, where the propyla of a temple are seen at about two hundred yards from the water-side, the rest of the temple appears to be almost buried in the sand. A few palm-trees and small strips of cultivated land, with here and there a miserable hut, serve to show that the country is not entirely abandoned. We passed El Garba on the east, where the Nile flows close to the base of the mountains, which present a wild and dreary appearance.

May 24.—We towed from our mooring-place a few miles to El Kharaba. At Songaree the Nile takes a bold turn to the west, and we continued in that direction to El Kharaba. At Croska, there is a small Shellaal on the eastern side, opposite to which at Erreiga is a mud fort.

The west bank is almost a desart; the east continues with bold rocks and hills, lined with villages of a better construction than those on the west, the buildings here consisting only of stones or of poles covered with mats or palm-branches.

May 25.—Arrived at Den, which is a long straggling village of mud cottages, situated in a thickly planted grove of palm-trees. The cashief's house, the best I had seen since I left Cairo, is built of baked and unbaked brick, in front is a rude colonnade forming a sort of caravansera. Adjoining to it is a mosque, the only one I had observed since I quitted Philæ. The village is about a mile in length; its population must be considerable, though I could never obtain any other answer to questions on this subject, than " many."

I landed and went to a mud building used as a caravansera, in which were horses; and waited until the cashief's son could be sent for.

A Mamaluke with a Greek for his attendant had lately come there from Dongola as a merchant. From him I heard that the Mamalukes had taken possession of the country on the western bank of the Nile opposite to Dongola, where they had been driven by the pasha of Egypt; that they were in force about eleven hundred, under Ibrahim Bey, the partner and competitor in power with Mourad Bey at the time when the French took possession of Egypt; that after destroying the petty chiefs of the country, they had armed five or six thousand blacks;

and that one of their beys had been able to cast cannon; and that among the Mamalukes there were eight English and ten French deserters. The Greek, who at first pretended to be a Turk, took me aside, showed me the sign of the cross upon his arm, and by way of exciting my compassion, broke out in bad English, into execrations of the Turkish government.

After waiting a short time in the caravansera, the son of the cashief, the boy before mentioned, came in, attended by a number of half-clothed inhabitants, squatted himself down in one quarter of the room, took me by the hand and welcomed me. On receiving his father's letter he got up, ran out to hear it read by the imam, and returned presently, offering me any thing I wished. He was about to order food to be brought to me, but being told that I should not eat it, he begged me to return to my boat, and in the evening visit him again. When I arrived at the boat, I found he had sent me a kid and a bowl of bread, in the centre of which was the usual preserve of dates, for which I returned him a present of a gold ring of trifling value. In the evening I went on shore, and the little cashief rather better dressed than in the morning, having the addition of a sword by his side, and my ring on his thumb, received me in the open air with an affectation of manly dignity, seated himself on the ground, and formed his divan. Having replied to his questions, and obtained a promise of horses for myself and Osman, to enable me to cross the desart that night and visit Ibrim, I took my leave, and went to the rocks behind the village, followed by a numerous party of the natives, who came in hopes of seeing me discover treasure in the ruins, which they suppose to be the object of the visits of Europeans. When I arrived at the rocks which are close behind the village, I found that the supposed temple was only a large excavation, evidently a burial-place. The approach to it was through two rows of incomplete square pillars hewn out of the rock. At the end of this approach is a rude sort of portico composed of four square pillars, with an entablature; a ceiling, the greatest part of which is fallen down, connected these pillars with the front of the excavation. On the outside front of the pillars of the portico are the lower parts of whole length statues in full relief, whose height originally extended to the top of the entablature. They appear to have been represented with a casque of a conical form, and stand on square bases. The front of the excavation is seven feet thick. There are two entrances, the largest between the two centre pillars is almost blocked up by the stones of the ceiling; on the right is a smaller entrance. The interior is divided by a lateral wall of rock into two sets of chambers. The first is the largest, is about sixty-nine feet in length, by forty in breadth; its ceiling, the rock, is supported by two rows of square pillars, three in each, with a coarse entablature. The front of the excavation and the interior have hieroglyphics and symbolic figures, there are also remains of colouring.

In the neighbourhood of this excavation are several square holes opening to vaults, the top of whose arches appear. Bones and pieces of cloth like those which are seen in mummy pits are found lying around. The sides of the openings are well finished, on one I traced a cross preceding some Greek characters, which mentioned ΤΟΥ ΑΓΙΟΥ ΑΝΤΟΝΙΟΥ. These were the first Greek inscriptions I had observed, relating to the early Christian inhabitants of this country.

Having made my remarks and sketches, I determined to set out on my expedition to Ibrim. Leaving my servants in the boat, I armed myself, and attended by Osman and two of the cashief's servants, I set off at about eight o'clock at night. We proceeded by the light of the moon over the barren and rocky mountains of the desart in continual danger from the difficulty of the road. About an hour after midnight we arrived at Ibrim*; but there was still some distance to what the natives called the temple. As the moon had gone down, and the rest of the road was over rocks by the river side,

---

* Anciently Premnis parva, Strabo, lib xvii , or, according to Pliny, Primis — See also Legh's Journey, p 79

we halted; one of the natives brought me a mat, on which I laid myself down and soon fell asleep.

May 26. — Early in the morning I proceeded by the water-side under high cliffs towards the temple, and found merely a ruined castle of considerable size, seated on a high rock separated from the rest of the hills by a ravine on each side. Square towers connected by walls of rude stones piled one on the other and strengthened by trunks of palm-trees, and shafts of columns laid transversely, compose the works. The interior presents the ruins of an Arab town, consisting of a mosque of stone, with mud and stone dwelling-houses. Shafts, capitals, and columns of grey granite are scattered about, on which I distinguished the Maltese cross. This castle is probably one erected by Selim the Second.

On my return I was shown an excavation in one of the rocks; I visited it, and found it to consist of a chamber twenty feet wide and ten deep. Opposite the door is a recess forming a seat, and above are three figures sitting sculptured in high relief; but they are much defaced. On the walls of the chamber are hieroglyphics, I distinguished also the Greek letters ΑΠΟ on one of the sides, and the form of a cross. Proceeding through the village, I was met by a venerable old man, who, I found, was called the Aga; in a friendly and hospitable manner he invited me " to tarry until the sun was gone down, to alight, refresh myself, and partake of the food he would prepare for the stranger." I gladly accepted his invitation; a clean mat was spread for me under the shade of the wall of his house, and refreshments, consisting of wheaten cake broken into small bits, and put into water, sweetened with date-juice, were brought to me in a wooden bowl; then curds, with liquid butter and preserved dates, and lastly some milk.

Having taken what I wanted, I entered the door of the Aga's house, which, like all the rest, was of mud, I found myself in a room separated from the other part of the house by a court, and covered by a simple roof of palm-tree branches. This was the place of his divan, and here my mat and cushion were brought to me, and the natives flocked around with their usual questions, whether I came to look for money, whether Christians or Moslems, English or French built the temples. They could not comprehend the use of the pencil, nor did they understand for what purpose a pocket-fork which I showed them was made; nor had they any name for it

The Aga having prepared a dinner for me, invited several of the inhabitants to sit down. Water was brought in a skin by an attendant to wash our hands. Two fowls roasted were served up on wheaten cakes in a wooden bowl, covered with a small mat, and a number of the same cakes in another, in the centre of these were liquid butter and preserved dates. These were divided, broken up, and mixed together by some of the party, while others pulled the fowls to pieces; when this was done, the party began to eat with great eagerness; rising up one after the other as soon as they had satisfied their appetites.

During my visit, I observed an old Imam attempt to perform a cure on one of the natives, who came to him on account of a head-ache from which he suffered much pain. This was done in the following manner — The patient seated himself near the Imam, who, putting his finger and thumb to the patient's forehead, closed them gradually together, pinching the skin into wrinkles as he advanced, uttering a prayer, spitting on the ground, and lastly on the part affected. This continued for about a quarter of an hour, and the patient rose up, thoroughly convinced that he should soon be well

A superstitious kind of regard seems to be paid by the Egyptians to this mode of cure, for at Erment, the ancient Hermonthis, an aged woman applied to me for a medicine for a disease in her eyes, and on my giving her some directions of which she did not seem to approve, she requested me to spit on them, I did so, and she went away, blessing me, and perfectly satisfied of the certainty of a cure.

The Aga told me that his town extended for three miles, that the government was divided between himself and another (independent of the Cashief of Deir), by a firman from the Pasha of Egypt; that it had suffered from the flight of the Mamalukes and pursuit of the

Tuiks. The whole town lies amongst palm-trees; is built without regularity, and bears marks of the ravages of war. The houses are formed in squares of mud of one story high; the roofs are of palm-branches laid flat. On passing through it the night before, I found that the inhabitants were lying on the outside of their doors, in the open air on mats, each containing five or six persons.

Having taken leave of the Aga, we returned homewards by the water-side, which was lined by rocks of considerable height, sometimes close to the river, sometimes retiring and leaving room for cultivation. I observed on some of them many hieroglyphic characters well cut, generally having the figure of some animal in the centre over the inscription. I arrived at Deir in the evening, and after receiving a visit from the little Cashief, I descended the river with the stream. The boat was now prepared for rowing, and was stripped of its masts and sails; the boatmen keeping time to their oars in a loud hoarse song.

May 27. — We arrived at Seboo, where I landed, to examine the remains of the temple there. The sand of the desart has almost covered the portico and court in front. It consists of two pyramidal moles facing the east; they are not more than thirty feet above the sand; their front is in length ninety feet; the gateway six in width, and twenty in height. A cornice and torus surround the moles, and the upper part of the gateway, which is twelve feet thick, and opens to a court almost filled with sand, in front of the portico, whose roof appears to be formed from the rock. It is oined to the moles by a colonnade of three square pillars on each side, on the front of which are disfigured statues in high relief half buried in the sand. The entablature of this colonnade is of single stones from pillar to pillar, twelve feet long, four broad, and three deep. On these and on the walls are hieroglyphics and representations of a deity receiving offerings, a subject very common in Egyptian sculpture. Two rows of sphinxes led to the temple. The first was placed at about fifty paces from the front. There are five remaining uncovered with sand; three of these are seen in full length above the ground, and the heads only of two others. The distance between each as they are placed in line, is eighteen feet; between the opposite rows, thirty feet. They are about eleven feet from the nose to the extreme parts. The two first are much decayed, or were never finished; the third, making the second in the left row, is highly finished; but the head, which lies near it, has been struck off—the work of the head in the opposite row is equally well executed. Between the two front sphinxes are gigantic figures in alto relievo on pilasters. They are about fourteen feet high, and formed the entrance to the avenue. They have the left leg advanced; they wear a breast-plate and pyramidal casque, and are four feet broad across the shoulders. On the back of the pilasters are hieroglyphics as well as on that part of the pilasters left uncovered by the statues. Similar statues, now thrown down, stood in front of the gateway of the moles; one of them is buried in the ground up to the waist, the other shows the whole length, but is half covered with sand. All these are of the same hard sandstone as the moles. I could not discover any Greek inscriptions.

May 28. — Having left Seboo the evening before, we arrived at Ouffendoonee, where there are architectural remains in the neighbourhood of a considerable village. I landed, and near the waterside found an oblong building of about fifty-four feet in length, and thirty in breadth, which seems to have been part of a Christian church. There are sixteen columns, six on the north and south sides, and four on the east and west, all perfect, of about two feet three inches in diameter. At the east end a sort of chancel projects southward at right angles with the south columns, on which are painted scriptural figures, like those in the churches of the modern Greeks. The capitals are not alike, nor do they appear to have been finished. They support a die and entablature composed of single stones from column to column, about six feet in length; the shafts are proportionably small. I saw many painted Greek inscriptions on the frieze of the interior, in small characters, which I could scarcely distinguish; the first words of all were TO ΠΡΟΣΚΥΝΗΜΑ; in the centre of the frieze at the west end on a small stone tablet was the word IOHANNI painted in red letters.

In front of the south columns are several rows of stones in regular order, apparently part of the building thrown down, on which were hieroglyphics, and on one there were Greek characters which I could not trace. A bare wall near the south-east end of this ruin, contains figures of ordinary sculpture, but evidently alluding to scriptural subjects.

Below Ouffendoonee we passed a caravan of Gelabs (slave-merchants) from Dongola on their way to Siout. I observed that they were more attentive to the forms of the Mahometan religion than the natives of these parts, of whom I had scarcely seen any attending to its ceremonies.

May 29, 30. — I continued descending the Nile to the cataracts of Galabshee, where I was tempted to land for the purpose of sketching the grand scene they presented to my view, but as we approached the shore the people of the neighbourhood ran down with their weapons dancing and howling, and appeared to be inclined to oppose my landing; I therefore continued my voyage

May 31. — Arrived at Deboo   Here, on landing to examine the ruins of the temple which I have already mentioned, I found the greatest part of the inhabitants of the village had taken refuge in its enclosure to protect themselves against the attacks of the people of a neighbouring district, who, to avenge the murder of one of their own body by an inhabitant of Deboo, committed nightly depredations on the latter village, ham-stringing cattle, which they could not carry off, plundering and murdering every male inhabitant they could find; and these atrocities were to be committed until one of the family of the murderer was sacrificed to their revenge   Not knowing how soon their enemies might appear, I contented myself with taking a general view of the ruins

They consist of three gates to pyramidal moles; of these last no traces now remain   The gates are behind each other at unequal distances, and beyond the last a portico of four columns with entablature, cornice, and side walls in high preservation

The first gate is plain, with a cornice and fillet above the door-way, which is about sixteen feet high; the masonry of it is twelve feet thick, there are openings at the top differing from any thing I had seen in other temples, and which in fortification would be called *orgues*.

The second gateway is twenty-two paces distant, and has a winged globe in the cornice; the next is nine paces distant, and the portico is fourteen paces from this.

The breadth of the latter is nearly sixty feet; the columns are plain, with the capitals of the centre differing from those on the sides, they are half engaged in a wall. The centre is raised to form a gateway; the depth of the portico is about fourteen feet, and has hieroglyphics in the interior The ceiling of the portico was composed of single stones reaching from the front to the hinder part; three of them remain The portico is divided by a lateral wall from several small rooms, which seem to be mere passages to the sanctuary; on the side walls of the first are hieroglyphics and figures; beyond is a second chamber; and last of all the sanctuary; in which are two Monolithic temples of single blocks of granite in high preservation and much ornamented. The largest is about twelve feet long and three wide, the other rather smaller The last rooms are without hieroglyphics, and the doors without cornice or ornament The second room and side chambers have ceilings, that of the sanctuary is in ruins. The whole depth from the front of the portico to the end is seventy feet The shafts of the columns are about fifteen feet high and three in diameter, and without ornament.

June 1. — I arrived at Philæ soon after sunrise. The approach to this place from the south presented a view still more sublime and magnificent than that from the north and west. If it was placed, as is generally stated, on the boundary [+] line of the ancient kingdom, and

---

* The word Philæ is not, according to M Quatremere, derived from the Greek, but from the Egyptian *Pilakh extremité*, alluding to its being the frontier town of Egypt. — Mem sur l'Egypte, 1 388. For the Greek origin of the word see Tillemont H des Em. iv.

formed an entrance to it, the sight of so much grandeur and magnificence, when the temples and other buildings were unhurt by time
or man, must have impressed a stranger with awe and admiration of
the people whom he was about to visit.

The inhabitants of the shores of the Nile between Philæ and
Ibrim, seem to be a distinct race from those of the northern districts.
The extent of this country is about one hundred and fifty miles;
according to my course on the Nile, I conceive it may be two
hundred by water, it is estimated by some travellers at much more.
They are called by the Egyptians Goobli, meaning in Arabic, the
people of the south. My boatman from Boulac applied this word
generally to them all, but called those living about the cataracts,
Berber

Their colour is black, but as we advance from Cairo, the alteration
from white to the dusky hue of the complexion is gradual, not
sudden. Their countenance approaches to that of the Negro, thick
lips, flattish nose and head; the body short and bones slender.
Those of the leg have the curve which is observed in the Negro
form The hair is curled and black, but not woolly. Men of lighter
complexion may be found among them, they may be derived from
intermarriages with the Arabs, or be descended from the followers of
Selim the Second, who were left here upon his conquest of the country.
On the other hand, at Galabshee, the people seemed to have more of
the Negro conformation of face than elsewhere, thicker lips, and
hair more tufted, as well as a more savage disposition.

The Arabic acquired from books and a teacher, had been of very
little use to me even in Egypt itself, but here not even the vulgar
dialect of the lower Nile would serve for common intercourse, except
in that district which extends from Dukkey to Den, where the
Nubian is lost and Arabic prevails again. This curious circumstance.
connected with an observation of the lighter colour of the people,
leads to a belief that they are descended from the Arabs. The
Nubian, when spoken, reminded me of what I had heard of the
clucking of the Hottentots, it seems to be a succession of mono-

syllables, accompanied with a rise and fall of voice that is not disagreeable.

In speaking of the government, law, and religion which prevailed among them, I may observe, that although the cashief claims a nominal command of the country, it extends no farther than sending his soldiers to collect the tax or rent called *mir* The pasha of Egypt was named as sovereign in all transactions from Cairo to Assouan Here and beyond, as far as I went, the reigning Sultan Mahmood was considered the sovereign, though the cashief's power was plainly feared more.

They look for redress of injuries to their own means of revenge, which in cases of blood extends from one generation to another, until blood is repaid by blood. On this account, they are obliged to be ever on the watch, and armed, and in this manner even their daily labours are carried on. The very boys go armed.

They profess to be followers of Mahomet, though I seldom observed any ritual parts of Islamism practised by them. Once, upon my endeavouring to make some of them comprehend the benefit of obedience to the rules of justice for the punishing of offences, instead of pursuing the offender to death in their usual manner, they quoted the Koran to justify their requiring blood for blood.

The dress of the men is a linen smock, commonly brown, with a red or dark coloured skull-cap, a few wear turbans and slippers. The women have a brown robe thrown gracefully over their head and body, discovering the right arm and breast, and part of one thigh and leg; they are of good shape, but have ugly features. Their necks, arms, and ankles are adorned with beads or bone rings, and one nostril with a ring of bone or metal, a kind of ornament, which has always been adopted by the women of the East. * Their hair is anointed with oil of cassia, of which every village has a plantation. It is matted or plaited in a manner similar to that observable on the heads of sphinxes, and the female figures of their ancient statues.

* Isaiah, iii. 21 speaks of the " nose jewels," and Ezek. xvi. 12 — See Lowth in locum

I found one at Elephantine, which might have been supposed to be the pattern of the mode adopted by them. The little children are naked; girls wear round the body an apron of strings of raw hides, and boys a girdle of linen.

Their arms are knives or daggers, fastened to the back of the elbows, or in the waist; javelins, tomahawks, swords of Roman shape, but longer, and slung behind them. Some have round shields of buffalo hide; and a few pistols and muskets are seen.

Their dealings with one another or strangers are carried on more by way of barter than by money, which I was informed had lately come into general use among them. The para, which they called feddâh, of forty to the piastre, (to which the Nubians as well as the Egyptians give the name goorsh,) the macboob of three piastres, and Spanish dollar called real, or fransowy, worth seven piastres and a half, were current among them. In the price of cattle, a cow sold for twenty macboobs, and from that to forty; a calf from three to seven, a sheep from two to three. Dates and senna are their chief articles of trade, and no present can be more acceptable to their chiefs than gunpowder of European manufacture. Corn is much prized by them, the bread which they eat is commonly made of durra* ; and is in form similar to the oatmeal cakes of Scotland, but thicker. Since the time of Norden, who visited the country in 1737, 1738, great changes have happened. Some places mentioned by him are no longer spoken of, and perhaps lie overwhelmed with sand. I met with less difficulties in my voyage than he seems to have encountered, yet I could not extend my researches much farther on account of the excessive heat. There was nothing in the state of the country to deter me from proceeding, if I had been inclined to

---

* The Holcus Durra has been introduced into Egypt only in modern times, the same observation may be applied to the Arum Colocassia. On the other hand, there are trees and plants of which the ancient writers speak, entirely unknown to the present inhabitants of the country. The Nymphæa Nelumbo (faba Egyptia of the Greek botanists) is one; the Persea is probably another, and a species of Amyris may be added. — See Sil. de Sacy. Abdallatif. 47

continue my route. The pasha's authority seemed established firmly enough for a traveller under his protection to proceed as far as Dongola, and the good understanding between him and the English had induced his officers to afford me every assistance. But at Dongola the Mamalukes held the country on the west bank, and perhaps would not have respected a person bearing a firman from the pasha. However I had often cause to observe that the late appearance of French and English armies in Egypt had taught the inhabitants every where to respect the Franks more than they used to do, although no opportunity seemed ever to be lost of gross cheating and imposition of every kind in all the dealings I had with them, not excepting the sheik of Assouan.

I learnt that at Wawdee Elfee, four days journey above Ibrim by water, there were *shellaals*, rendering the Nile impassable, and that no boats could be employed on the river between that place and Dongola; but I could obtain no information of the state of the river beyond that town. The names of the villages above Ibrim on the west side are, as they were given to me, Washebbuk, Toshkai, Armeenee, Forgunt, Farrey, (one day on horseback); Gustei, Andhan, Artinoa, Seriey, Deeberrey, Ishkeei (two days); Sahabbak, Dabbarosy, Wawdee Elfee, where are the shellaals, and the Nile is impassable (four by water); Wawdel-howja, Owkmee, Serkey mattoo (one day); Farkey, Wawdel-walham, Gintz, Atab, Amarra, Abbeer (two days), Tebbel, Artinoa, Korkky, Ibboundeeky, Sawada (three days); Irraoo, Oskey mattoo, Wawroey, Koyey mattoo, Irrew, Saddeefent, Delleeko, Carbaa, Wawdel-mahas, Noweei, Farreet, from which to Dongola are two days; in all, eight days from Wawdee Elfee.

In this space they said there were pictures, by which they meant hieroglyphics, on the rocks the whole way, and at a place called Absimbal on the west bank, a day and a half from Ibrim, a temple like that at Seboo, and another of the same sort at a place called Farras *,

---

* Besides the hieroglyphical tablets on the rocks between Ibrim and Dongola, the natives talked of other temples than those mentioned at Farras and Absimbal, in which were scriptural paintings The word *soorat*, or picture, they applied to hieroglyphics, they used it also in speaking of paintings which they compared with those on the walls of Dukkey, and had pointed them out to me.

three hours further on the same side.   I regretted that no more information was to be procured on this subject, because it appeared to me that the higher I advanced up the Nile, the signs of the early progress and establishment of Christianity southward on its banks became more clearly ascertained in the Greek inscriptions and other remains of antiquity.

I remarked that no buffalo, though very common north of Assouan, was to be seen between Philæ and Ibrim; crocodiles were common here, but no hippopotamus * appeared the natives spoke of it as seen during the time of the inundation in the Shellaals, particularly at Galabshee, calling it Farsh el bahr, the sea-horse My voyage was made when the Nile was nearly in its lowest state, a circumstance which must be considered in perusing the preceding journal.

---

* " Forskal nous apprend que l'hippopotame est nommé par les Egyptiens Abou-Mner Je soupçonne que ce nom est corrompu " S de Sacy, 165 Abdallatif — It appears from a passage in Themistius (Orat. x.) that the hippopotamus was rarely seen in Egypt in his time. The oration was spoken in the year 369, at Constantinople. I never saw or heard of the hippopotamus in Egypt, says Mr. Browne, but in Nubia it is said to abound.

THE MINES OF LAURIUM. — GOLD AND SILVER COINAGE OF THE
ATHENIANS — REVENUE OF ATTICA

THE Athenians had obtained silver from the mines of Laurium as
early as the time of Pisistratus (Herod. i. sec. 64.), or 561 B. C., but
in the days of Socrates, there appears to have been a deficiency in
the supply of the ore. (Xen. Mem. lib. iii. c 6. § 5.) This is perhaps to be attributed more to the want of skill in those who sought
for it than to the poverty of the mines; as from a passage in Strabo
(lib. ix.) we learn, that the smelting operations of the ancient Athenians had been very imperfect. Xenophon strongly recommends the
Republic to take the management and direction of them, and thus
derive a greater profit than by leaving them in the hands of individuals, who paid a certain sum in proportion to the metal which
they extracted (Πόροι). The district of Laurium, according to Stuart,
appears to have reached from Rafti near the ancient Prasiæ to Legre-
na; part of this tract, he says, is called Λαυρον ὄρος, and is full of
exhausted mines and scoriæ. When Mr Hawkins was on his voyage
to the Euripus, he was detained by the Etesian winds many days on
the coast of Attica, and was enabled to take during that time an
accurate examination of the mining district The result of this
mineralogical survey was, the discovery of many of the veins of
argentiferous lead ore *, with which that part of the country seems to
abound; he observed the traces of the silver-mines not far beyond
Keratia. In a paper belonging to the late Mr Tweddell, relating to
Attica, we find mention made of "Les Ateliers des Mines †," by these
Mr. Hawkins says, the site of the smelting-furnaces is indicated,

---

* Mr H. collected specimens of all the substances occurring in those veins among
which was a green stone pronounced by Werner to be chrysoprase

† Mr Hawkins mentions a remarkable allusion to the mines, still preserved in a name
given by the sailors in his boat to one of the harbours on the North-Eastern coast of
Attica, South of Thorico, εἰ, τὰ ἐργαστήρια

which may be traced to the southward of Thorico for some miles;
immense quantities of scoriæ occurring there The mines were situated much higher along the central ridge of hills * ; the smelting
operations were probably carried on near the sea-coast for the convenience of fuel, which it soon became necessary to import.

We have little information handed down to us respecting the mines
of Attica, from the time when the Romans became masters of
Greece An insurrection, in the year 135 B. C , of the slaves who were
employed in them, shews us that they were then worked (Diod. S.
Exc. lib xxiv. t. 2 528.); but the revenue they gave must have been
an object of small consideration to the Romans at this period, as
their different conquests supplied them with abundance of wealth.
In the year of the city 662, sixty millions of our money were counted
in their treasury. (Ferguson, n 121.) Large contributions were
received from Macedonia, when that country became subject to their
arms ; the conquest of it, says Polybius, brought wealth and corruption to Rome ; and the fixed and regular tribute, which the Asiatic
provinces offered to pay in the time of Julius Cæsar, was 4,100,000l.
(Gibbon, 427. *Des poids, et des monnoies des anciens.*)

In the reign of Augustus the mines of Laurium were neglected
(Strabo, lib. ix.), nor does it appear that any silver was collected there
at the time when Pausanias and Plutarch wrote. (Attica, i. De Orac.
Defectu.)

Respecting the interior management of them in the early period of
the Athenian republic, we are able to collect only a few materials
from their writers If the treatise of Theophrastus or Aristotle had
been extant (Pollux, x 149.), as well as the comedy of Phereciates,
entitled Μεταλλεῖς, we might have received many curious details
The use of our common bellows (φύσαι) was known to the Greeks ;

* According to a scholiast on Æschylus, (see Casaubon in Strabo, 380. Ox ed) there
was silver near Thoricus. Phavorinus incorrectly states that there were gold mines at
Laurium. Wheler passed over a tract where cinders in abundance lay scattered up and
down , some silver, he heard, had been secretly extracted from the ore found there —
See also Hobhouse's Travels, 117. 120.

we find mention of the σαλαγξ (Pollux, lib. x. 149. lib. vii. 99.), a sort of sieve; of the -εριδες, and the μετ αρχαις αιοιες, or pillars supporting the roof at certain intervals, the καμιος was a metallurgic furnace, on which a crucible was placed for melting and refining metals. (Beckmann, II of I ii 77.) Little progress in improvement of machinery was likely to be made, as long as slaves were easily procured; and before the hydraulic engine invented by Archimedes * was in use, the water in the pits could only have been drawn off with great labour If the remarks of Agatharides, and Diodorus S. are applicable to the general mining system of the Greeks, we may learn from them some of the various operations which were used, as the softening the rock by the application of fire; the pounding the ore in stone mortars †; the grinding it in hand-mills, and afterwards washing it, and the process of cupellation.

Although the fact of a coinage of money at Athens by Theseus be extremely improbable, yet it is remarkable that the antient writers are all agreed on this point. " *Hoc tam clare tamque perspicue* (says one of the most acute and judicious scholars of modern times) *à veteribus literis est traditum, ut si quis contra sentiat, nihil sentire videri possit.*" (Hemsterh. ad Polluc lib. x. sect 60.) Sperling attributes the first coinage in Athens to Solon. When, however, we find, that Phidon ‡, three centuries before the time of that legislator, introduced

---

* Κοχλιαις οῦ ᾿Αρχιμήδης ᾿ ὕρεν Diod Sic v 360 The earliest mention we find of water-mills is of the time of Mithridates, ὑδραλέτης is the word in Strabo, Ox ed. in I xii 801 Pumps were invented by Ctesibus, who lived at Alexandria in the second century, B C — Vitruv l x c 12 l ix c 1

† ᾿Εν ὅλμοισι λιθίνοισι πρὸς τὴν κάττω ἀλήθουσιν l iii 183 Remains of ancient mortars and mills have been found in Transylvania and in the Pyrenees Some of the smelting operations of the Greeks are mentioned by Hippoc de Vic rat l i χρυσίον εργάζονται, κόπτουσι, πλύνουσι, τηκουσι πυρί The time when quicksilver was first used in separating gold and silver from earthy particles is not known, but Vitruvius and Pliny give us a description of the manner in which gold is cleansed in cast off garments by means of quicksilver, this sufficiently proves that nothing more was wanting than the application of the same process to the separation of the ores in the smelting works

‡ Herodotus, l i says that the Lydians first struck gold and silver coins, but we find Moses, 1000 years prior to Herodotus, speaking of silver money, and 100 years

it in the Peloponnesus, it is not likely that the Athenians should have been so long unacquainted with the art. It is impossible to reconcile the opinion of Sperling with the words of Pollux; the former says that the βοῦς of Theseus must be placed *inter nummos non cusos*, it is to be considered, he says, not as money with the device of an ox upon it, though Pollux expressly says, βοῦν εἶχεν ἐντετυπωμένον The βοῦς was, in the opinion of Sperling, a piece of money which was equal in value to an ox, and δεκάβοιον was as much as would purchase ten oxen. If this interpretation be true, it is singular, as Hemsterhusius observes, that we should find no mention of an ὗς, ὄις, μόσχος, pieces of money that would purchase *swine, sheep, and heifers*. Theseus is said by the Greeks κόπτειν νόμισμα, words which have only one meaning, " striking or coining money," *certe vel secuentis adferri possit locis* κόπτειν *v. non aliter quam de signaturâ nummorum intelligi posse*. Hemst. But Sperling affixes entirely a new sense to it; *de argenti sectione sumit.** Theseus, he says, *docuit Athenienses aurum et argentum, et aes eo pondere* κόπτειν *quo bovem emere possint, talemque nummum* βοῦς *dictum, licet bovem signatum minime habuerit.* He gives a similar wrong interpretation to the word κόπτειν in Herodotus, l. i. 94. Without attempting to explain the reason that could induce the ancients to attribute the introduction of coinage into Athens to Theseus, when we find that in the time of Homer, subsequently to the age of that hero, all commerce consisted merely in exchanging different articles, we may fix upon the tenth century B C. as the period when the Greeks of Asia Minor first became acquainted with the use of coined money.[†]

---

before his time, his ancestor in the seventh generation purchased a field for silver. There is no contradiction in these statements, that of Herodotus alludes to metals formed into coins or minted, but the Hebrew money, at the period alluded to, consisted of silver pieces marked — See Michaelis on the Laws of Moses, 1 437.

* We may observe that although Pollux assigns so early a date to the coinage of Athens, he condemns those who interpret Homer Il. ς'. 236, as if the poet alluded to *money* in that verse Homerus permutationem certe antiquitùs factam non nummo autumat, sed in retributione quarundam rerum quas vicissim dabant Note 58. p. 1044. Pollux

† Knight's Proleg

The nummulary expressions in the Greek language have a reference to that period of their history, when the metals were weighed* in exchange, and not struck; thus we meet with ὁβολοστάτης, λίτρα, ταλαντον, στάτηρ.† Many centuries must have elapsed between the first introduction of money in Greece, and the period when the coins of some of her states received that spirit and form in the design and execution of them, by which they are distinguished. The alterations in the century and half which followed the age of Phidon were numerous, and some of them may be plainly traced by observing different series of coins. "Seven stages of progressive improvement or variation may be seen in the coins of Thebes, prior to the subversion of the city by Alexander the ‡Great." It is singular, that while the names of the Greek artists who were distinguished as statuaries or vase-manufacturers, or as engravers on gems and stones, are frequently recorded on their works, the names of those who were employed in the mints or ἀργυροκοπεῖα of the different republics, and in improving the dies of the money, should be so little known.§ It has been supposed that they are sometimes included in the monograms. The giving an impression or type to the coins, signifying the value of them, and thus avoiding the necessity of frequently using the scale, was a change of great importance; ὁ χαρακτὴρ ἐτέθη, says Aristotle, (Pol. 1 i c 9) τοῦ ποσοῦ σημεῖον. Another alteration, of equal consequence, was the use of the pound in tale, as well as the pound in weight; this is attributed to Solon, who raised the mina or pound, as we learn from Plutarch, (in Solone,) from 72 drachmæ to 100‖; an hundred drachmæ were given in payment

---

* The word *penny* and the Hebrew *shekel* have the same reference to weight.—Clarke on Coins, 391

†Ἱστάνω signifies *appendere*, Aristoph Pac 717, and in the LXX Jerem xxxii 9., we read ἔστησα σίκλον

‡ See Mr. Knight's remarks on the Elean tablet. Classical Journal, vol xiii p 118

§ In Crete, the coins of Cydonia bear the legend Νεύαντος ἔπεσι—Some of the characters on the coins of Attica probably refer to the different mints established in that country. The people of Marathon and Anaphlystus both struck money. Corsini Γ A xii 232

‖ Ἑκατὸν γὰς ἐποίησε δραχμὰς τὴν μνᾶν πρότερον ἐβδομήκοντα καὶ τριῶν οὖσαν, probably ἑβδμ ὑύο — See Clarke on Coins, 91

instead of having recourse to the scale. This was done to make allowance for any diminution in the weight or fineness of the money, and greatly facilitated the transaction of commercial business *

The silver-money of Attica was of seven kinds; the tetradrachm, didrachm, tetrobolus, triobolus, diobolus, obolus, and † semiobolus. The talent and mina of the Attics were merely nominal ‡ The obolus has been found at Athens in the excavations of ancient tombs, not only in the mouth of the dead, but also in urns A misconstruction of a passage in the Frogs of Aristophanes, has led D'Hancarville (2. 33.) to suppose that *two* oboli were sometimes given to the dead; but the poet, when he mentions that sum, vv. 140, 270, is ridiculing the δικαστικὸν μισθὸν, as some of the Scholiasts have remarked. § It is singular that the custom of depositing money with the dead, should have continued at Athens to so late a time as the age of the Scholiast on Juvenal (Sat 3. 267.); a practice of a similar kind is observed to prevail among some Tartar nations.

The Attic tetradrachms examined by Greaves weighed 268 grains English, or each drachm, 67 grains. ‖ We may assign 273 grains, 272 and 271, as the weight of the coins in the time of Pericles; at a later period, when the Greeks became subject to the Romans, and still retained permission to coin ¶ their own money, the drachma was made lighter, and was then equal only to 54·75 grains, or an eighth part of an ounce. The sense of the passages of some of the Greek writers, when they speak of their money, has not been always correctly ex-

---

* After Solon's time, 84 drachmæ were struck out of the pound, which was still reckoned at 100 drachmæ The pound in tale was in use also among the Romans.— See Clarke on Coins, 724

† In the Heraclean tablet we find mention of Νομοι, v 75, written in later times νούμμοι The ancient word occurs also in Epicha δέκα νόμων.—See Valck Theoc p 308

‡ Taylor ad. Mar Sand

§ Hem Polluc 1 122

‖ Mr Knight says, 65 grains Prol in Hom see 56 Of 120 tetradrachms weighed by Barthelemy, the heaviest gave 263 grains English

¶ For the time of the Peloponnesian war, we may set the drachma at ten-pence sterling, the mina of that age will be 4l 3s 4d , and the talent, 250l At a later period, the drachma may be considered as worth 8d sterling, or equal to the Roman denarius See Mitford's advertisement to the 2d vol of the H of Greece, 4to

plained by commentators and translators. Thus in Lysias, the words ὀφείλων ἀργύριον ἐπὶ τρισὶ δραχμαῖς, do not mean, as Dalecampius and the French version render them, " owing three drachmæ of silver ," but they are equivalent to this expression, " he owed three *per cent.* interest every month " ;" the sentence, when complete, being τοῦ μηνὸς τῆς μνᾶ ·   In the same writer, we find, ἴσω δέ σοι ἐπιε ὀβολοὺς τῆς μνᾶς τόκον.   " I will pay you one and a half per cent. every month." †

The Attic tetradrachms ‡ are of two kinds; the first, or more ancient, is of the rudest description, being of a globular form; the head of Minerva is covered with an ancient helmet; or sometimes there is only a radiated diadem. The face of the goddess is distinguished by the most striking deformity, a long neck and pointed chin, with an eye like that of a fish, are among the most remarkable features   The second or more modern is less rude, is much thinner, and the surface more extended; the helmet of the goddess is highly ornamented, the face is more graceful, and altogether it is executed in a much better style of work than the former; at the same

---

* The common interest at Athens was one *per cent per* month

† See Schweig in Athen. lib. xiii. c. 94.

‡ The representation of a vase is very frequently seen upon the medals of Athens, either as the principal subject, or as what the French call a contremarque on the latter tetradrachms, the owl is invariably represented as standing upon a vase reversed   The explanation of this is doubtful   Corsini and others have supposed that it refers to the perfection which the Athenians had attained in the art of fabricating earthenware   But I am inclined to think with Lekhel, that as the vase upon the medals of Corcyra, Thasos, and Chios, denoted the abundant produce of wine in those islands, so upon the later tetradrachms of Athens, it had a reference to the quantity of oil, the staple commodity, as it were of Attica   I am the more strengthened in this opinion, as I possess vases of precisely a similar form, found in the neighbourhood of Athens, where they are far from rare   From their frequency and perfect resemblance one to another, it is probable that they were designed for some one particular use, and not formed according to the fancy of the potter   nor is it probable that a vase of such an ungraceful shape and rude workmanship (as all of the kind which I have seen are), should be placed upon their medals in order to show the perfection of the Athenians in the art.

But although this supposition will account for the representation of the vase on the tetradrachms, yet the prodigious variety which we meet with upon the other medals will still remain unexplained   Perhaps some were really meant to commemorate the pretensions of the Athenians with respect to the art.—(Extract from Lord Aberdeen's Journals)

time, it bears the most evident marks of neglect and bad taste. The variations to be met with in the tetradrachm of each of these divisions are numberless, but they are so very slight, and the agreement of the general characteristics of each so universal, that they are by no means sufficient to constitute any other class than the two already described; to one of which indeed they are all easily reducible. These observations are equally applicable to the didrachm and drachm, and may be extended to nearly the whole silver coinage of Athens. It is not improbable that the head on the older tetradrachms was copied from that most ancient and most holy statue of the goddess preserved in the double temple of Neptune and Minerva; it was formed of olive-wood, and was said to have fallen from Heaven in the reign of Erecthonius. It is clear, however, that the superior beauty of the Minerva of Phidias proved more attractive than the age and sanctity of the wooden image; for on all the later tetradrachms we find precisely the same figures which adorned the head of that magnificent statue; although even in the more recent coinage, instances frequently occur, where the inscription in ancient characters is still preserved.

One of the greatest problems in numismatical difficulties, is the cause of the manifest neglect, both in design and execution, which is invariably to be met with in the silver money of Athens; in which the affectation of an archaic style of work is easily distinguished from the rudeness of remote antiquity. Different attempts have been made to elucidate the subject. De Pauw affirms, that owing to a wise economy, the magistrates whose office it was to superintend the coinage of silver, employed none but inferior artists in making the design, as well as in other branches of the process; an hypothesis wholly inconsistent with the characteristic magnificence of the republic. Pinkerton asserts, that it can only be accounted for, from the excellence of the artists being such, as to occasion all the good to be called into other countries, and none but the bad left at home. It would be somewhat difficult to explain, how Athens came to be so long honoured both by the presence and the works of Phidias and Praxiteles, Zeuxis and Apelles.

The Attic silver was of acknowledged purity, and circulated very extensively; the Athenian merchants, particularly in their commercial dealings with the more distant and barbarous nations, appear frequently to have made their payments in it. The barbarians being once impressed with these notions of its purity, the government of Athens in all probability was afraid materially to change that style and appearance, by which their money was known and valued among these people A similar proceeding in the state of Venice throws the strongest light on the practice of the Athenians. The Venetian sechin is perhaps the most unseemly of the coins of modern Europe, it has long been however the current gold of the Turkish empire, in which its purity is universally and justly esteemed, any change in its appearance on the part of the Venetian government would have tended to create distrust.

Xenophon says, that the silver of Attica in foreign countries was more valuable than the coin of other nations, because it was finer, and consequently was worth more than its own weight of any other silver, that had more alloy in it. (Davenant. See also the treatise, Πόροι.) And Zeno (Diog. L. in v.) in his allusion to the rudeness of the Attic tetradrachms, praises them at the same time, as superior in purity of metal to other coins, which were more beautiful in form and design —

Ἔφασκε δὲ τοὺς μὲν τῶν ἀτολοίκων λόγους καὶ ἀπηρτισμένους ὁμοίους εἶναι τῷ ἀργυρίῳ τῷ Ἀλεξανδρινῷ· εὐοφθάλμους μὲν καὶ περιγεγραμμένους, καθὰ καὶ τὸ νόμισμα, οὐδὲν δὲ διὰ ταῦτα βελτίονας· τοὺς δὲ τοὐναντίον ἀφομοίου τοῖς Ἀττικοῖς τετραδράχμοις, εἰκῇ μὲν κεκομμένους καὶ σολοίκους, καθέλκειν μέντοι πολλάκις τὰς κεκαλλιγραφημένας λέξεις. "He said, that the polished discourses of the learned resembled the Alexandrian money; they were beautiful to look at, and finished all round, but not the better on that account. Those of an opposite class were like the Attic tetradrachms, there was a rude and plain stamp about them; but they often outweighed the discourses of a more ornamented kind." It is evident from the nature of the commercial transactions between the Athenians and the inhabitants of some of the shores of the Euxine, that a great quantity of Attic money must have been given to the latter, in exchange for what the Athenians most wanted; namely, corn. "No

people," says Demosthenes, "require so much imported corn as we do."
C. Lept. Πλεῖστω τῶν ἀπάντων ἀνθρώπων ἐπεισάκτω σίτω χρώμεθα.   Leucon
allowed them in the year 358 B.C. to carry from the Cimmerian
Bosphorus, (now the Straits of Caffa.) and from Theudosia,
400,000 medimni of corn.   (Vales. Harpoc. 38, and Barbeyrac Anc.
Traitéz, p. 213.)   The medimnus or six pecks of wheat cost five drachm-
mæ at Athens in the time of Demosthenes, now allowing that the
Athenian ships were laden with some manufactured articles to exchange
for the corn, as well as with wine, which formed part of their export
trade, it is certain that great payments must have been made in money.

The sources of the Athenian revenue were, 1. The contributions
from allied states; the sum demanded from them in the time of
Aristides was 460 talents annually ; Pericles exacted 600 , Alcibiades
doubled the original sum (Harpoc. Vales p 58), and under Demetrius Phalerius, a further addition was made.   (Diog. L. in v.)
2. Some revenue was also derived from the customs[*], we find from
the Etymologicon, Harpocration, and Andocides. that a duty of
two *per cent.* was demanded upon imported and exported goods ,
this was called Πεντηκόστη, and was hired or farmed by a corporation,
the head of which was called Ἀρχώνης. (Valck. in Slut. Lec An.
159) 3. We may mention the confiscation of the property of different individuals ; the produce of sums arising from the sale of the
marble in the quarries of Hymettus and Pentelicus [†], the money
deposited by such as had law-suits in court , that which was paid
into the treasury by persons who worked the mines, and the capitation on the Μέτοικοι. [‡]   Some of these different sources of revenue

--- --- -   -   --   -   —   -- --—-—-—-—

[*] De Myst.   The import and export duties were farmed during the Peloponnesian
war at 36 talents, or 9000*l*   This was the 50th, if we add the profit of the farmers, we
may estimate the whole foreign trade of Athens, at more than 400,000*l*.

[†] In what request the marble of Pentelicus was held by the Greeks may be conjectured
from this circumstance, it was used at Lilæa, Stiris, Panopea, and Delphi, in Phocis ,
at Olympia for the roof of the great temple and for some statues there , it was sent into
Achaia, Arcadia, and Bœotia, and other parts of Greece — Pausanias.

[‡] The annual tax on these persons, was 12 drachmæ for a man, six for a woman —
Menage in Diog Laer ii 235

are very clearly pointed out in a passage of Aristophanes; and we learn from the poet, that at the time when the play of the Vespæ was performed, or 423 B.C., the revenue of the republic was 2000 talents, or 500,000*l.* sterling

Καὶ πρῶτον μὲν λόγισαι φαύλως, μὴ ψήφοις, ἀλλ' ἀπὸ χειρὸς
Τὸν φόρον ἡμῖν ἀπὸ τῶν πόλεων ξυλλήβδην τὸν προσιόντα·
Κᾆτα τούτου τὰ τέλη χωρὶς, καὶ τὰς πολλὰς ἑκατοστὰς,
Πρυτανεῖα, μέταλλ', ἀγορὰς, λιμένας, μισθοὺς καὶ δημιόπρατα
Τούτων πλήρωμα τάλαντ' ἐγγὺς δισχίλια γίγνεται ἡμῖν.

Vespæ. 656.

The revenue in the year mentioned by Aristophanes seems to have been unusually great; for Xenophon, Anab. lib. vii., speaks of 1000 talents as the income of the republic during the war derived from the citizens as well as foreigners. Προσόδου οὔσης κατ' ἐνιαυτὸν ἀπό τε τῶν ἐνδήμων καὶ ἐκ τῆς ὑπερορίας οὐ μεῖον χιλίων ταλάντων. In the time of Demosthenes, the sum was much smaller; the orator, Phil. iv., says it amounted to 100 talents.

The system of financial policy adopted by the Athenians (and Greeks in general) led them to amass considerable sums to meet the necessary expences of war. " The states of the ancient world," says Hume, " prepared for their contests by hoarding as much as they could. The mode adopted by modern Europe of anticipating the revenues of future generations was unknown to them." Thucydides, lib. ii., has communicated to us some particulars respecting the state of the Athenian finances at the breaking out of the Peloponnesian war. There were 6,000 talents, or 1,500,000*l.* in the treasury; a sum which had been collected from the contributions of the allies; the uncoined * gold and silver found in the religious offerings belonging

---

* Χρυσίου ἀσήμου καὶ ἀργυρίου Thuc. l. 2. Ἄσημον in modern Greek is " silver ," it is found in this sense in Cedrenus and in an epigram on a person who had placed at table before his guests some empty dishes of silver, " Seek," says the epigrammist, " for those who are fasting, if you want to make a display of your silver, you may excite their admiration by your empty dishes."

Ζήτει νηστεύοντας ἱ, ἀργυρίην ἐπίδειξιν,
Καὶ τότε θαυμάσση κοῦφον ἄσημον ἔχων — Cas. His. A S. 155.

to the state and the citizens, and the vessels used in sacred ceremonies, amounted to 125,000*l.* The gold on the statue of Minerva, which could be taken off, if the public exigencies required it, weighed 40 talents of pure metal, and was, according to the ancient proportion of one to thirteen, worth 130,000*l.*[*] A passage in Demosthenes, Περι Συμμ., gives the valuation of the property and wealth of the Athenians at 6,000 talents[†], in Polybius, lib. ii., we find the sum stated at 5,750 talents. Winkelman, as well as Meursius and Leland, consider them as speaking of revenue ; but it is contrary to all probability, that the Athenian finances should ever have been so flourishing as this statement would make them, and the passage I have already cited from Xenophon and Aristophanes is a sufficient confutation of that opinion. Mr. Wallace[‡] supposes the sum to mean a valuation of *yearly* rents and profits, according to which a tax was to be imposed on the Athenians. Mr. Hume[§] considers it as including the *whole value* of the republic, and comprehending lands, houses, commodities, and slaves ; but if we calculate the slaves at only 200,000, and at two minæ each, the lowest value which was put on any of those belonging to the father of Demosthenes, the slaves alone were worth more money.[||] Some suppose the words τίμημα τῆς χώρας to be a valuation of land ; Dr. Gillies applies them to the worth of lands and houses. The opinion of Heyne seems to be the most satisfactory, and to agree with the words of Polybius ; it was, he says, an estimate, perhaps below the real value of the general property of Attica and Athens ; and that on occasions, when an armament was to be equipped, or any contribution was required, a tax was laid on the different districts of Attica according to this estimate.

So long as the Athenians retained their command at sea, they

---

[*] For 40 talents of gold multiplied by 13, give 520 talents of silver, or 130,000*l.* Barthelemy supposes that in the time of Thucydides, as of Herodotus, this was the proportion.

[†] Τὸ τίμημά ἐστι τὸ τῆς χώρα. ἑξακισχιλίων ταλάντων

[‡] Numbers of Mankind, 289   [§] Essay V.

[||] In Aphob. 1 — See Wallace, p 189

could easily collect the tribute due to them, and protect their trade In the commencement of the Peloponnesian war, they derived from their naval superiority a great advantage in this respect; while they obtained money from the islands and Ionia *, the Spartans borrowed it on interest from the sacred funds of Delphi or Olympia. † The result of the unfortunate expedition to Sicily is well known, and the encampment of the Lacedæmonians at Decelea, added to the distress and difficulties in which the Athenians were then placed. The supplies of provisions that were usually conveyed by land from Eubœa to Athens were cut off, and were therefore sent by sea. The works in the mines could not be carried on with their usual regularity, as the slaves deserted in great numbers to the camp of the enemy. Thucyd 1 7. The poverty ‡ of the republic increased; and in the twentieth year of the war, the Athenians were obliged to spend the thousand talents §, which they had hitherto scrupulously abstained from touching; and in four years afterwards the gold coin was debased.

This metal was procured by them from Macedonia and Asia Minor. The gold mines in the vicinity of the Strymon were explored first by the Phœnicians ‖; we have little information, however, concerning the wealth or produce of them before the time of Alexander the First, who received about the year 480 B. C. ¶, the daily income of a talent from them. The revenue derived from these mines continued to be small **, until the reign of Philip the father of

---

* Προσοδον μεγίστην — Thucy 1 III.

† See the speeches of the Corinthians, and of Pericles —. Thucyd. l. 1.

‡ Thucydides informs us, that about this time they adopted a plan from which they hoped to derive an increase of revenue, l 7 Instead of exacting the usual tribute from those who were in dependence on them, they levied a duty of one-twentieth of the value, τῶν κατὰ θάλασσαν οι five per cent , τὴν ἑικοστην τῶι κατὰ θάλασσαν ἀντὶ τοῦ φόρου τοῖς ὑπηκοοις ἐποιησαν As the Greek words mean literally, "goods carried by sea," we may apply them both to exports and imports

§ Called Ἄβυσσον, Lysis 171 — See also Plato in Menon.

‖ Clem Alex. Stro 1 i. 363.

¶ Mem. de l'Ac des In 47 Some of the Macedonian coins may belong to the sixth century B. C Knight, Prol in Hom sec 78

** Diod S l xvi.

Alexander, when it amounted to 1000 talents annually. The district on both sides of the Strymon, and on Mount Pangeus furnished him with gold and silver; the former was found near Philippi The astonishing quantity of his coin which still remains, where we even without the evidence of ancient writers, would sufficiently attest the former abundance of it; in some of the more unfrequented parts of Greece the gold of Philip passes currently among the inhabitants at present. The value of one of these coins is 20 Turkish piastres, or about 25 shillings *

In addition to the sums which the mines of Philip brought into circulation, we may state that Alexander, during his progress † through Asia, sent into Greece a large quantity of money for the purpose of erecting temples and public buildings; and when we consider how much a few years before had been taken from the consecrated wealth at Delphi in the Phocic war, how many statues and vases and ornaments of gold had been melted into specie, we may fix upon this time, as the period when money must have abounded in ‡ Greece. The increase in the prices of corn and meat at different successive intervals, may be stated from some authentic documents, and will show the diminution in the value of money.—

| Wheat in 595 B C was | 1 Drachm the Medimnus, or 6 pecks § |
| ——— in 410 ———— | 2 Dr or 1s 6d the coomb ‖ |

---

* Many of the ancient coins found in Greece and Asia Minor are pierced, and through the hole a string is passed, by which they are hung, as ornaments, round the heads of women and young girls This custom is not peculiar to the modern inhabitants of these countries, we find it mentioned by Chrysostom, who particularly refers to the coins of Alexander, tom. ii 243 Ven Τι αν τις ειπει περι των νομισματα χαλκα Αλεξανδρου του Μακεδονος ται· κεφαλαι και ται: ποσι π ριεσμουντων — LD

† Plutarch, Opp Mor "Virtue of Alexander"

‡ The dresses and robes of some of the statues of the ancient deities were of gold threads, woven or knitted, such was the aureum amiculum of Jove, which Dionysius stole   (Cic. de N D 111. Beckmann, 2) In consequence of the robbery of the temples, which happened not unfrequently in the wars of Greece, many might say, as the veteran remarked to Augustus, "You see my fortune, Emperor, it was once the leg of a goddess "

§ Mem de l'Ac des In 18 391

‖ " The ancient markets," says Sir J Steuart, " were supplied partly from the surplus produce upon the lands of the great men, laboured by slaves, who, being fed from the

Wheat in 393 B C was 3 Dr the coomb
———— in 335 ————— 5 Dr. Ditto
An ox in 410 B C was 51 Dr. or 2l. 2s 6d.
———— in 374 ————— 80 Dr
———— in the same year 75 Dr   (Sand Mar.) *

It has been much doubted whether the Athenians at any period of their history ever coined money of gold ; and when we consider the few original examples of this metal which have come down to us, in proportion to those evidently forged, it is not surprising that many should have been led to suppose the whole number spurious. At the same time it appears to admit of satisfactory proof, both from the testimonies of ancient authors, and from the gold coins which still remain, of the genuineness of which we can entertain no doubt, that the Athenians occasionally made use of this metal in their coinage, although it is very probable, only on few occasions, perhaps after some victory or other great event, and even then in small quantities.

Eckhel †, who has entered pretty much at large into this subject, labours to establish a different conclusion. He rejects that passage in the Frogs of Aristophanes ‡, which mentions a new coinage as nominal, and not to be taken in its literal sense ; and at the same time adduces another from the same writer in support of his own opinion

---

lands, the surplus cost in a manner nothing to the proprietors, and as the numbers of those who had occasion to buy were very few, the surplus was sold cheap" Pol Econ i 104 This remark, though generally true, is not properly applicable to Athens, we have seen by a passage of Demosthenes already cited, that the quantity of corn imported by the Athenians was very great, the number therefore of those who had to buy was not small. From particular circumstances, indeed, the price of corn may have been sometimes cheap, for instance, the ships which brought it from the Euxine to Athens, were allowed by Leucon to export it without paying any duty, ἀτελειαν δεδωκεναι, Dem c Lept This was a great advantage to the Athenians, as the sum paid to Leucon by those who carried corn from his dominions was thirty per cent There was also a law, which, in order to prevent corn rising above its ordinary price, prohibited, under pain of death, any citizen from buying more than a certain quantity Lysias

* Mem de l Ac des In 18 356
† Doc Num Vet t ii 286
‡ V 720 Yet Corsini considers the passage as clearly pointing out the use of gold coin The comedy was acted in Olym 93 3, and the scholiast says, that gold money was introduced the year before — See Corsini Diss. xii

Ἀνέκραγ' ὁ κῆρυξ, μὴ δέχεσθ⸗ μηδένα
Χαλκοῦν τὸ λοιπόν· ἀργύρῳ γὰρ χρώμεθα.

Exr. 821.

Pollux seems to doubt whether χαλκοῦν is here to be considered as money or not, but allowing that Aristophanes is really speaking of silver, it is by no means a consequence from this supposition that gold was unknown. A little attention to the true meaning and spirit of the passage will explain this.

He is alluding to the decree respecting the use of copper *money, against which, in common with a large proportion of the Athenians, he entertained a decided aversion; and he adds, " it was proclaimed that no one should receive it, for we use silver." The mention of gold coin was here perfectly unnecessary, for such was the disproportion in Attica between silver and any other species of money, that it might with propriety be called the circulating medium of the republic; in like manner, a person might say that in England paper notes had supplied the place of specie, but this would be merely in allusion to their great abundance, without meaning to assert that the use of the latter was unknown among us. There is also another reason which induced Aristophanes to oppose silver to the copper money, which is, that, by coining pieces of less dimension, they might be so reduced in value as not to exceed that of copper, and consequently render the use of the latter unnecessary Accordingly in the silver money of the Athenians, we find some coins of incredible minuteness; several of which do not weigh more than two grains, nor were more than a farthing in value. It was obviously for these reasons that Aristophanes confined himself to the mention of silver in opposition to the latter.

The testimony of Pollux† is clear and decisive as to the existence

---

* The copper money, which was cried down this year, Olym 96. 4., had been in circulation for nine years, for it was coined in Olym 93 3., as we learn from the scholiast on the Ranæ, v 732 We find also that some copper money was in use in the time of Dionysius, in Olym. 84 4. — See Corsini, F A. Diss xii.

† Pollux, ix c. 6 Schol in Equ. 1093 Another passage of similar import may be seen in the Schol. on Aves, 1106

of Athenian gold coin; he describes the weight and value of the golden Attic stater. The scholiast on the Knights of Aristophanes, although mistaken as to the place whence the Athenians procured the metal, plainly refers to a coinage from gold.

Notwithstanding there appears to be no reasonable cause for doubting the mere fact of a coinage, yet the quantity of the material applied to this purpose in every æra of the republic was so inconsiderable, as to render the singularity of the practice scarcely less striking, and equally requiring some explanation. De Pauw attempts to elucidate the difficulty in this manner.*

Herodotus, lib. iii., in enumerating the tributes paid to Darius, makes the relative value of gold to silver as one to thirteen, and Plato in the dialogue entitled Hipparchus, as one to twelve. Now the Athenians, having to purchase their gold in Lydia, would evidently be losers in every such bargain, an Athenian merchant wishing to buy fifty pounds weight of gold at Sardes, would necessarily pay for every pound so bought one pound of silver, in addition to the price borne by the same article in his own country, and consequently could not be repaid without altering materially the nature of the gold.

We must here observe, that Herodotus is speaking of the relative value of gold to silver in the sixty-seventh olympiad, after the conquest of Babylon by Darius, and before his invasion of Greece, from which period to the birth of Plato in the eighty-seventh olympiad, there is an interval of eighty years. We cannot suppose that the value of gold at Athens should have been stationary during so long a time; nor is it credible that the circulation given to the immense quantity of this metal acquired by the plunder of the Persians, should not have operated the smallest change. Of this we may rest assured, that gold, of which there was so little in Greece before the Persian invasion, must necessarily have fallen very considerably in value after that event, and have suffered a diminution from the time

---

* Recherches, t i 366.

in which Herodotus wrote to the age of Plato, when we find it as one to twelve.

According to the testimony of Xenophon the ratio in his time was that of ten to one.[*] A great alteration, as we are informed by Athenæus, had taken place in consequence of the plunder of the temple of Apollo at Delphi, in 358, and a prodigious quantity of offerings was then turned into specie. The decuple proportion seems to have continued a long time unchanged † Menander, who lived a century after Xenophon, states the value of the two metals to be in that ratio. (Pollux, lib. ix. c 76) And the Ætolian league, a century later, proves the same thing.‡

But there is another reason, in addition to the fluctuating price of gold, which renders De Pauw's explanation of this subject inadequate For supposing that in Lydia the Athenians would have purchased gold at a disadvantage, we are by no means to conclude that they were necessarily obliged§ to repair to that market , on the contrary, the gold mines of Thasos and of Thrace in the neighbourhood of their own colonies were always ready, and to a certain degree able to afford them supplies. Besides, if this disadvantage in the purchase

---

* Mem. de l'Ac des In xlvii 202

† There is an error in the text of the third volume of Gibbon's Misc. Works, p 420., which should be corrected He there says that the proportion of gold to silver in England and Spain, is as one to fifteen in France and the rest of Europe as one to fourteen and a half. " Parmi les anciens la proportion la plus commune etoit celle *d'un a un* " It should evidently be "d'un à dix." Perhaps in Mr. G 's manuscript it is written " 1 à 10;" and the cypher, being erased, the proportion appeared to be 1 a 1 — E The difference in the proportions between the two metals in the ancient and modern world arises from the greater quantity of gold possessed by the former See Mr. Gibbon's examination of this subject, p 422

‡ See Clarke on Coins, 251.

§ In addition to what is said in the text, we may observe this fallacy in De Pauw's reasoning · he considers Herodotus, when speaking of the exchange of thirteen to one, as alluding to Asia; but there is no proof that the ratio of the two metals in that country was referred to by the historian, his observations may apply to Greece — See Larcher, Her. 1 269, and Barthelemy (Anach) c 12 note, and see 22. note

of gold existed at all, it must equally have operated against their
procuring the metal for any purpose whatever; whereas, this was so
little consonant to their practice, that we cannot estimate at less than
an hundred thousand pounds, the value of the gold which composed
the ornaments of a single statue. There must then have existed
some cause other than the difficulty or disadvantage in procuring the
metal which influenced the Athenians in their determination of so
rarely coining money from gold.

Perhaps we may look for the cause of this practice in the mode
adopted of managing the silver mines of Laurium. Every citizen of
Athens wishing to become a proprietor in the mines belonging to
the republic, first purchased from the state a permission to commence
his operations, and ever after paid the 24th part * of the annual
produce of his labour into the public treasury. Hence it was mani-
festly the interest of the government, that nothing should impede
the progress and vigour of those employed in this pursuit †; and
Xenophon, who wrote at length on the means of improving the
administration and produce of the silver mines, recommended the
number of permissions to be very much increased ‡, and approves of
the conduct of the state in allowing foreigners, denizens of Athens,
to enjoy in this respect the same privileges with their own citizens.

The currency of the silver money of Athens was almost universal,
owing to the deservedly high reputation for purity which it possessed;

---

* Meurs. Them. Att. ii. c. 26. — Suidas, Ἀγρ μετάλλου δίκη

† We find from Demosthenes (in Phænipp.) that income arising from the mines was
not considered as property, which obliged a citizen to contribute to the expenses of the
state. Some fortunes derived from this source were considerable, Nicias let out to an
adventurer in the mines 1000 slaves, for whom he received 1000 oboli a day, or 166
drachmæ, nearly 7l. — E.

‡ " Xenophon's work on the improvement of the revenues of the state is a chef-d'œuvre
of its kind, and from it more light is to be had in relation to the political economy of the
Greeks, than from any thing I have seen ancient or modern. Steuart's Political Econ. i.
460. — The object which Xenophon had in view in that work, is pointed out by Casaubon.
" Librum ab eo hoc potissimum consilio scriptum esse, ut Athenienses ad fodiendas strenuè
argenti fodinas hortaretur." Stanley ad Persas, 236 v. — E.

3 M

and on this account we find several cities of* Crete copying precisely in their coins the design, weight, and execution of the Attic tetra-drachms, in order to facilitate their intercourse with the barbarians. It is possible that the general use and estimation of the produce of the Attic mines contributed to render the Athenians averse from a coinage of another metal, which, by supplying the place of silver money at home, might in some degree tend to lessen its reputation abroad.

Having attempted to explain the circumstance which occasioned the scarcity of Athenian gold, it now remains to specify the nature of those coins which really did exist in that metal, or passed current at Athens. †

The Attic stater ‡, according to Pollux, was equal in weight to two drachmæ, but in value to twenty. This would agree with the relative proportion of gold to silver in the later times of the republic. The following citation from the same writer has occasioned some to imagine, that no other gold coin existed: ἐι μὲν χρυσοῦς ἔιποις, προσυπακούεται ὁ στατήρ. We are by no means justified in concluding from this remark, that because the stater by way of pre-eminence acquired the name of the golden attic, no other coin of this metal was in use. In the silver money we find that drachmæ, by which the Athenians usually reckoned, were frequently called, simply, attics; yet no one for an instant would suppose that because the characteristic appellation is omitted, they did not possess silver coins of various descriptions. Indeed, if we consider the observation fairly, it would appear to indicate the existence of some other species of gold money, which rendered it necessary for the author in some measure to explain this peculiar mode of expression. A coin of this metal was found in the

---

* Eckhel. in num. Gortyn. Hieropyt. Cydon.

† The reader may perhaps be inclined to agree with the Editor, in considering the remarks of the Earl of Aberdeen, respecting the rude coinage of silver money at Athens, and the scarcity of gold money among the Athenians, as affording a more satisfactory explanation of those subjects, than any which has been hitherto offered.

‡ There is a stater, undoubtedly genuine, in Lord Elgin's possession; there is one also in the Hunter collection; it weighs 134 grains English.

immediate vicinity of Athens, attended by such circumstances, as to leave no room to entertain any reasonable doubt of its being genuine. *

The stater of Cyzicum was current at Athens, but we do not know what the value of it was; at the Bosphorus it was worth 28 Attic drachmæ (Demosth. adv. Phorm.) A stater of Cyzicum is engraved in the Thes. Brand. Beger. part. i 490.

The golden staters of Phocæa are mentioned in one of the Athenian inscriptions published by Chandler, Part. ii. Ins. iv. 1.

Of the Macedonian money, we find, that the golden staters of Philip and Alexander, called φιλιππέιοι and Ἀλεξανδρέιοι, (Pollux. 9. 1024) weighed 134, 132, and 131 grains. The δίχευος, or τετράδραχμον χρυσοῦ of Alexander and Lysimachus weighed 266 and 265 grains; the τετραττατὴρ of the latter 540 grains. An engraving from a golden tetradrachm of Alexander is produced by Liebe, p. v.

---

* Respecting the value of the talent of gold, see Corsini, Diss. xii., and Hemsterhusius on Pollux, l. ix. 57., and Knight's Prol. on Hom. sec. 55. The antient globular gold coins of some of the Asiatics, are the Talent of Homer, struck and stamped, and weighing about 260 grains. Among the gold coins in circulation at Athens, we may mention the Darics, worth, as well as the stater, 20 silver drachmæ. There is no doubt respecting the value of this coin among any of the ancient writers.

REMARKS ON THE AMYCLÆAN MARBLES.

LETTER FROM LORD ABERDEEN TO THE EDITOR

DEAR WALPOLE,   ARGYLL HOUSE, May 26, 1817

ACCORDING to your request I send you a representation of the
Amyclæan marbles. They are sufficiently interesting in themselves,
but they acquire an additional importance from being instrumental in
the detection of daring imposture, and in this point of view I shall
first consider them. We may, it is true, presume that few persons
are at this time the dupes of the literary frauds so extensively practised
by the Abbé Fourmont. Mr. Knight has so ably exposed the nature
of his pretended discoveries, and from the internal evidence afforded
by his inscriptions, has so satisfactorily refuted all their claims to
authenticity *, that in England it would be difficult to find a competent judge who should now hesitate an instant in forming his
opinion respecting them. But as the inventions of the Abbé have
imposed on many estimable and learned persons, and as in France a
reluctance still exists to view them in their proper light, it is fortunate
that we are furnished by these marbles with additional proofs of his
falsehood, still more indisputable if possible than those already produced. The Abbé Barthelemy†, M. d'Hancarville, Count Caylus,
and others, have received these forgeries as authentic, and have inconsiderately adopted notions, constructed systems, and published
dissertations concerning them, which of course can have no foun-

---

* Analysis of Greek Alphabet

† It is to be lamented that in the recent editions of the Voyage d'Anacharsis, the same
idle and groundless speculations are still permitted to disfigure that admirable work.
Larcher and Valckenaer had been deceived by the forgery of Fourmont (see Theocr.
275.), but in the late edition of Greg. de Dial. by Schaefer, we find the following remark. — " Notandum est harum inscriptionum Fourmontianarum fidem esse sublestissi-
mam." P. 496.

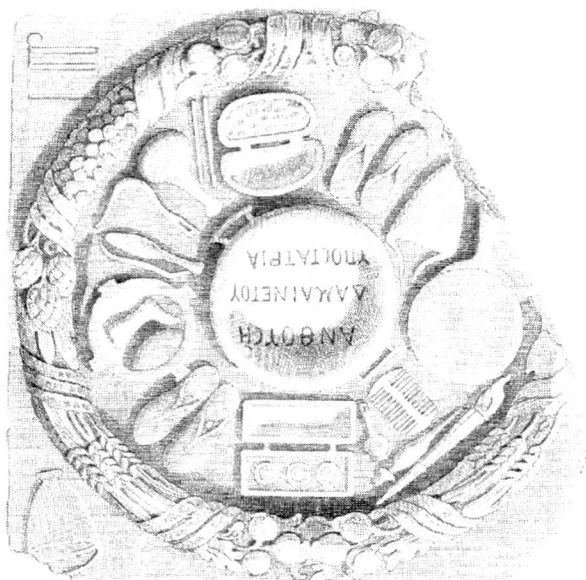

dation, thereby holding out a salutary lesson of the necessity of caution and prudence in the explanation of objects connected with remote antiquity.

I should observe, that, according to the Abbé Fourmont, the marbles in question were to be seen in a temple which he discovered near Amyclæ, of the goddess Oga or Onga, to whom, according to an inscription on the edifice, it was dedicated by King Eurotas about fifteen hundred years before Christ. Count Caylus[*] has published an engraving of these marbles from a drawing preserved among the papers of the Abbé in the king's library in Paris. In this drawing it is not very easy to recognise the originals. The subjects supposed to be represented by the sculpture are human limbs, arms, hands, feet, and legs, with knives and other instruments, denoting the sacrifice of human victims; a circumstance which very naturally puzzles the Count, considering that the inscriptions are not written in a character peculiarly antient, and that the silence of historians is uniform respecting the existence of a worship in Greece at any period, which prescribed such rites. The temple, which the Abbé describes as composed of massive blocks of stone, and whose simple and solid construction had enabled it to stand until the middle of the last century, as well as the inscription on the front, which informed him of the fact of its dedication, have all unfortunately vanished. But I apprehend, that although the temple of the goddess has disappeared, the true building, when divested of this antient and venerable character, still exists in the shape of a modern Greek chapel, in which M. Fourmont, if he was himself ever actually at Sparta, may have seen the marbles, and where I found them in the year 1803.

It cannot be necessary to detain you longer with the impudent frauds of this person You will find them in the Memoirs of the Academy of Inscriptions, where they are supported by all the parade

---

* Recueil d'Antiquités, tom. ii pl 51.

of learned disquisition.* For their full detection I refer you to the work of Mr. Knight.

Having now stated what these marbles certainly are not, we may proceed to enquire into their real nature and probable destination. The small and ruinous Greek chapel in which they were fixed, is near to the village of Slavochori. There seems no reason to doubt that this village, such as it is, was the situation of the antient Amyclæ, its position relatively with that of Sparta accords perfectly with the accounts of Greek writers †; and if further proofs were requisite, it might be afforded by the circumstance of my having discovered in the course of conducting some excavations, several inscriptions, on one of which were the letters ΑΜΥΚΛ . The precise spot on which the temple of Apollo stood cannot now be ascertained from an inspection of the ground alone, and in the endeavours which I made in two or three places, by means of digging, no satisfactory information was obtained; indeed few of the remains appeared to be of an antiquity prior to the Roman conquest.

This temple is described by Pausanias as one of the most ancient and most celebrated in the Peloponnesus. The statue of the god was a curious specimen of early sculpture by some unknown artist; it was more than forty feet high, and of the rudest workmanship, resembling in some measure a column of bronze, to which a head, feet, and hands had been affixed. He mentions several of the votive offerings, and in common with other writers, he contributes to give a high notion of the magnificence and extent of the building ‡

The question which now arises for our consideration, is, whether the marbles formerly belonged to this temple, or were in any degree connected with it; to which I am inclined to answer in the negative, and principally for this reason —The subjects of the sculpture, as you will observe, are for the most part articles of female dress or ornament; combs, bodkins, mirrors, paint-boxes, &c. Round the

---

* Mémoires de l'Academie des Inscriptions et Belles Lettres, tom. vii. xv. xvi. xxiii.
† Polyb lib v c 19.   The place is still also καλλιδενδρότατος και καλλικαρπότατος.
‡ Pausan Lacon

edge of each marble is a wreath composed of the mystic plants sacred to Ceres or to Bacchus; ears of corn, pomegranates, cones of the fir, ivy, &c. In the centre of each is the representation of a patera, in one of which is inscribed

ΑΝΘΟΥCΗ ΔΑΜΑΙΝΕΤΟΥ ΥΠΟCΤΑΤΡΙΑ

and in the other,

ΛΑΥΑΓΗΤΑ ΑΝΤΙΠΑΤΡΟΥ ΙΕΡΕΙΑ

Now I have not been able to find any authority for supposing that the custody of the temple of the Amyclæan Apollo was committed to women, or the rites performed by priestesses; and it is scarcely credible that Pausanias, who dwells so long on the subject, should omit to mention a circumstance in itself not of very frequent occurrence, and which on other occasions of less interest he does not fail to record. The Abbé Fourmont, it is true, tells us, that he found at Amyclæ an inscription containing nothing less than a list of all the priestesses, inscribed at different periods, from the date of the foundation of the temple down to the time of the Roman conquest. Among the first of these ladies, or as he calls them, the μχτερες και κεραι τε Απολλωνος, we find the name of Laodamia, the daughter of King Amyclas, who, if she ever had any existence at all, lived before the Trojan war. The boldness of this forgery can only be equalled by the author's ignorance of the language in which he attempts to write, and even of the proper forms of the letters which he employs; for he has produced a jargon unlike the Greek of any dialect, and has given us the representation of characters which are not only unknown in Greek paleography, but many of which are entirely at variance with the principles which appear universally to have regulated the mode of writing pursued throughout the widely-extended settlements of this people in the most ancient times. The silence therefore of ancient authors, and especially of Pausanias, is almost decisive on this point; indeed, I fear that the inscriptions on our marbles offer the only argument, feeble as it is, to prove that priestesses had ever belonged to the Amyclæan temple. The Abbé Fourmont observed these inscriptions near to the probable site of the ancient Amyclæ; he at once appropriated them to the temple of Apollo, and followed up this decision by the brilliant invention of the catalogue which I have mentioned Other antiquaries have also spoken of the priestesses of Apollo, but so far as I have been able to learn, on no other foundation than the pretended discoveries of this person.

Although the village of Slavo-chori appears indisputably to mark the situation of Amyclæ, and although these marbles were discovered in the immediate neighbourhood, I am inclined to believe that they originally belonged to a less celebrated spot. Pausanias speaks of a ruined town near Amyclæ, called Bryseæ, where was a temple of Bacchus and certain sculptures.   He adds, that it was permitted only to women to enter the temple; and that women only performed the sacrifices. *   The plants sacred to Bacchus, which are represented on the marbles, indicate the connection, and it appears not improbable that they were brought from this temple, which could not have been distant, for it is evident they were not in their original position when discovered in the ruined Greek chapel of Slavo-chori.

It is not easy satisfactorily to explain the purpose of these sculptures, but they seem perhaps to have been a kind of votive offering on the part of the priestess when entering on her sacred functions. The practice among the Greek women was not unfrequent of dedicating their ornaments to some deity on particular occasions, and if a lady offers her mirror to Venus when no longer young, it is not unreasonable to imagine that these articles of female decoration should be thus ostensibly abandoned on the assumption of the priesthood. If we look to the inscriptions, with a view to a more clear explanation of the marbles, I fear that we shall obtain no real solution of the difficulty.   One of these merely records the name of the priestess, the other I am not able wholly to explain. The word υποςατρια is new to me; but although the precise meaning of the title has eluded my research, we may presume that it signifies some office connected with

---

* Pausan. Lacon cap xx.

the temple. From the probable etymology of the term, it would appear to have a relation to *distribution* or *regulated measure*, this conjecture, however, is uncertain, and is liable to objections Possibly you may be more fortunate, or are already better informed on the subject.

I remain very sincerely yours,

ABERDEEN.

We may, with Lord Aberdeen, consider the marbles as offerings made *by* the priestesses * Anthusa and Laoageta ; or as consecrated, *during* the priesthood of these women In the latter case they are presented as votive offerings by the ΚΟΣΜΗΤΡΙΑΙ, or ornatrices of some deity. The office of a κοσμήτρια of any goddess, was to attend to the dress and ornaments of the statue ; the *Specula* and *Pectines*, both of which are seen on the Amyclean marbles, are mentioned by Apuleius †, as carried by women who were employed in that character. The word ΚΟΣΜΟΠΛΟΚΟΣ is used sometimes, we find it in an inscription quoted by Spanheim, Ob in H. in Pall. Callim.

ΗΡΑΚΛΕΙ ΒΑΣΙΛΕΙ
ΑΝΤΩΝΙΟΣ ΑΠΕΛΕΥ
ΣΕΒΑ ΚΟΣΜΟΠΛΟΚΟΣ
ΑΝΕΘΗΚΕΝ

" To Hercules, King ; Antonius Freed-man, ornator of Augusta, dedicated this."

---

* Caylus considers the word Ὑποστατεια in the lower marble as signifying Sous-prêtresse The name ΛΛΥΑΓΗΤΑ is probably written for ΛΛΟΑΓΗΤΑ, as ΛΛΥΔΙΚΗ for Λαοδίκη in an inscription found at Smyrna — See Boissonade in Greg de Dial Ed Schaef 179

† " Alae mulieres quae nitentibus speculis pone tergum reversis venienti deae obvium commonstrarent obsequium, et quae pectines eburneos ferentes " Lib xi. — See Tertull de Jejun c. xvi Also Hesychius in v ΣΑΡΑΧΗΡΩ

3 N

REMARKS ON SOME GREEK INSCRIPTIONS.

[BY THE EDITOR.]

Some Greek inscriptions, most of which have never yet been published, are inserted in this part of the volume; and a few remarks are added by the Editor, for the purpose of illustration. Documents of this kind are of importance, when they fix the doubtful site of some city or town, or when they throw light on the paleography and ancient dialects of Greece.* We may mention the Orchomenian inscriptions, as among the most important which have been lately discovered, if we consider them with reference to the dialect. The Elean tablet brought to England by Sir W. Gell may be added, as well as some of the Elgin inscribed marbles

Many of the numerous inscriptions copied by Cyriacus, and found in the collections of Muratori, Gruter, Hesselius, and other writers, are incorrectly transcribed. Some of these have been emended by Valckenaer, Koehn, and Bentley, but as the original marbles have been frequently destroyed, it is impossible to compare the copies with them. Of the ancient inscriptions which are sculptured on rocks, we may mention that which was found by Professor Carlyle and Colonel Leake, in their route through Asia Minor; those also which are to be seen on Mount Anchesmus, and on the south-side of the Acropolis at Athens; the Latin words in the defile of Tempe, and the Greek characters sculptured on the rock near Jerusalem, by the early Christians. †

---

* An inscription found by Col Leake in Thessaly may be here referred to as illustrating a passage in Plato it commemorates an offering, ΑΠΛΟΥΝΙ, this is the Thessalian name of Apollo, who, as we learn from Plato, was called by the same people ΑΠΛΟΣ — Craty

† ΑΓΙΑΣΙΩΝ — See Dr Clarke's Travels, vol ii.

I.

ΤΟΝ ΑΘΕΝΕΟΝ ΑΘΛΟΝ ΕΜΙ

These words are written in very ancient characters reversed, on a vase* found by Mr Burgon, in Attica. Mr Blomfield supposes that Αθηνέων is written for Αθηνῶν, and he refers to Homer, Herodotus, and Aristophanes, where this word is found. We may add two passages, one from Thales (Epist. ad Pherecy.); another from Xenophon, (see Greg. de D. ed Schaefer. 381.) The inscription may therefore imply, as he has rendered it, " I am the prize given by Athens."

Mr. Knight refers the words to a prize given at the Athenæa, Αθήναια, as we learn from Corsini, F. A. ii. Diss. 13. was a name applied to a festival once called Πάνδημον.

The use of E for AI is found in other Greek inscriptions; two instances may be observed in Chandler, Ins. xvi. p. 6. and Ins. xlviii. part 1. In the Diar. Ital. of Montfaucon, ΧΑΙΡΑΙ occurs four times for ΧΑΙΡΕ. ΧΕΡΕ for ΧΑΙΡΕ was copied by Villoison; ΚΕ for ΚΑΙ may be seen in Dr. Hunt's Journal, p. 105. An inscription found on the confines of Attica, of the date of the second century before Christ, and of which a copy was given to the Editor by M. Fauvel, has the words ΚΕ ΑΡΓΥΡΟΥΝ ΚΕ ΕΤΕΡΑ ΑΣΗΜΑ.

In consequence of the similar sound given to AI and E by the Byzantine and Neoteric Greeks, the mistakes in manuscripts are numerous; but it is evident from what has been said that the substitution of one of these letters for the others is of an older date than is generally supposed. Notat Schol. Theocriti ad Id. i. v. 12. pro γαῖα antiquos dixisse γία, unde γε λοτον, σιωγεαι, καταγεαω Lucian Ed. Reiz. vol. iii. p. 20. The time when the confusion of these letters became more general is noted by Vossius —"A Tiberii et Caligulæ temporibus tam apud Romanos quam apud Græcos, mos obtinuit, ut dipthongus AI velut E simplex pronuntiaretur." Voss. in Catull. 291.

---

* See Clarke's Travels, vol. iv part 1.

II.

Found at Carditza, near the ruins of Acræphia, in Bœotia.   From
Mr. Hawkins.

HΗΟΛΙΣ
ΑΓΛΜΗΣΤΟΡΑ
ΖΩΙΤΡΟΥ
ΗΡΩΛ

"On trouve ces trois usages du mot de HPΩΣ, l'un pour dire sim-
plement un homme de valeur, ou un brave homme, et qui fait bien
sa charge, l'autre pour un homme, qui par sa vertu et par ses
bienfaits a été mis au rang des Dieux ou demi-Dieux après sa mort;
3. pour un mort à qui on rend quelque sort d'honneur, ou qu'on
nomme ainsi κατ' εὐφημισμόν." — Spanheim, Cesars de Julien, 115.

III

Found in the island of Zante; see Chandler, Ins. Antiq.

ΑΡΧΙΚΛΗΣ ΑΡΙΣΤΟΜΕΝΕΟΣ ΚΑΙ ΛΛΚΙ
ΛΛΜΑ ΑΡΧΙΚΛΟΣ ΚΛΠΝΙΙΙΙΑΝΤΑΝΑΥ
ΓΩΝ ΘΥΓΛΤΕΡΛ ΘΓΟΚΟΛΙΣΑΣ ΛΝ ΑΡΤΕΜΙΤΙ
ΟΠΙΤΛΙΔΙ

The statue of Clemppa, a priestess, daughter of Archicles and Alci-
dama, is dedicated to Diana Opitais.* Similar forms of consecration
are met with in Greek inscriptions; in Rein. xi. Cl. v. the statue of
Minyia, a priestess, is dedicated by her brother to the celestial
Venus.

ΑΡΤΑΜΥΤΙ is seen in Chandler, Part. ii. Ins. cxlv., and in another
found in Muratori, and corrected by Ruhnkenius, in Greg. de D., we
read ΑΤΡΕΜΙΤΙ, "To Diana."

---

* Chandler translates the words, "Quae sacerdos fuit Dianæ Opitaidis" Θεοκόλος is
explained in Hesychius, by ἱέραξ.

IV.

Found on the altar of the new church at Scratho From Mr. Hawkins

ΑΥΤΟΚΡΑΤΟΡΑ
ΚΑΙCΑΡΑ ΤΡΑΙΑΝΟΝ
ΑΔΡΙΑΝΟΝ CΕΒΑC
ΤΟΝ ΟΛΥΜΠΙΟΝ
Ο ΑΡΧΙΕΡΕΥC ΑΠΟ ΠΑ
ΤΡΟC ΦΙΛΙΠΠΟC ΦΙΛΙΠ
ΠΟΥ ΑΖΗΝΙΕΥC ΕΚ ΤΩΝ
ΙΔΙΩΝ

This inscription is given here, because in the copy made by Villoison, the word ΑΔΡΙΑΝΟΝ is omitted. See Mém. de l'Acad. des Ins. xlvii. 314.

The word ΟΛΥΜΠΙΟΝ is written in the same manner in other contemporaneous inscriptions. It occurs in some copied by Captain Beaufort on the southern coast of Asia Minor We may remark, that it is also a very ancient form, as it is seen on the Elean tablet brought to England by Sir W. Gell.

Ὁ αρχ. α τ. "qui tient de son père la dignité du grand prêtre." Villoison.

Ἐκ τ. ι answers to the form S. P. F. C. of the Latins,—Sua pecunia faciendum curavit.

V.

Found at Lyttus, in Crete. From Mr. Hawkins

ΜΑΡΚΙΑΝΗΝ ΣΕΒΑ
ΣΤΗΝ ΘΕΑΝ ΑΥΤΟ
ΚΡΑΤΟΡΟΣ ΝΕΡΟΥΑ
ΤΡΑΙΑΝΟΥ ΚΑΙΣΑΡΟΣ
ΣΕΒΑΣΤΟΥ ΓΕΡΜΑ
ΝΙΚΟΥ ΔΑΚΙΚΟΥ Α
ΔΕΛΦΗΝ ΛΥΤΤΩΝ
Η ΠΟΛΙΣ ΔΙΑΠΡΩΤΟ
ΚΟΣΜΟΥ ΤΙ ΚΛΑΥΔΙ
ΟΥ ΒΟΙΝΟΒΙΟΥ

In the inscriptions found at this place, and communicated by Mr
Hawkins, we read ΑΥΓΓΩΝ and ΑΥΤΤΙΩΝ Η ΠΟΛΙΣ . in those given by
Van Dale the name is written incorrectly ΛΙΓΓΙΩΝ. (752. Diss.) The
inscriptions of Mr. Hawkins establish the reading in Strabo proposed
by the last German editors, Λύττωι, instead of Λύκτο. The city, according to Stephanus, was so called from its lofty situation , λύττοι οἱ
ὑψηλὸ τοπτοι. Hesych. Mr. H. remarks, that the situation is remarkably elevated.

The officer τρατοκόσμος designates the chief of those magistrates,
who were called Κόσμοι, and who are frequently mentioned in inscriptions. See Rem. Cl. vii. n. 22, and Chishull. Anti. Asi 123.

VI

In the church of St George, at Apollonia, in Bithynia. From
Mr. Hawkins.

```
ΓΑΙΟΣ ΙΟΥΛΙΟΣ ΚΕΛΕΡ ΕΚ
ΤΩΝ ΙΔΙΩΝ ΚΑΤΕΣΚΕΥΑ
ΣΕΝ ΔΗΜΩ ΤΩ ΑΠΟΛΛΩΝΙ
ΑΤΩΝ ΤΗΝ ΥΠΟΧΩΡΗΣΙΝ
ΚΑΙ ΓΑΙΟΣ ΙΟΥΛΙΟΣ ΕΡΜΑΣΟ
ΚΑΙ ΜΕΡΚΟΥΠΟΣ ΕΣΤΡΩΣΕΝΕΚ
ΤΩΝ ΙΔΙΩΝ ΤΗΝ ΠΛΑΤΕΙΑΝ ΑΠΟ
ΤΟΥ ΖΥΓΟΣΤΑΣΙΟΥ ΜΕΧΡΙ
ΤΗΣ ΥΠΟΧΩΡΗΣΕΩΣ
```

" Caius Julius Celer, built at his own expence for the people of
Apollonia the recess or passage ; and Caius Julius Hermas, who is
called also Mercupus, paved at his own cost the broad court leading
from the Zygostasium as far as the recess." This is the only instance
of the word ΥΠΟΧ· being applied to any building or part of a city.
It is always used in reference to the human body.

EΣT. π. line 6. and 7. We find in Lampridius, " Stravit plateas
saxis Lacedæmoniis." Heliog. 109. Salm.

VII.

Found at the Piræus, inscribed on a stone   From M. Fauvel

ΟΡΟΣ ΜΝΗΜΑΤΟΣ

The meaning of these words is well explained by Van Dale de
Cons. Ethn   " Ut autem eo minus esset periculum profanationis,
agri, luci, aut termini sive limites, aliaque loca dedicata aut con-
secrata, vel muris circumsepiebantur, vel aliter notabantur."

On a sepulchral cippus, M. Fauvel found also

ΟΡΟΣ ΣΗ
ΜΑΤΟΣ Ο
ΝΗΣΙΜΟΥ

VIII.

Found in the ruins of the temple of the Didymean Apollo.   From
the Earl of Aberdeen.

ΑΓΑΘΗ ΤΥΧΗ
ΗΒΟΥΛΗ ΚΑΙ Ο
ΔΗΜΟΣ ΕΤΕΙΜΗ
ΣΕΝ ΑΥΡΗΛΙΟΝ
ΠΟΣΙΔΩΝΙΟΝ Ε
ΡΜΙΟΥ ΝΙΚΗΣΑΝΤΑ
ΤΑ ΜΕΓΑΛΑ ΔΙΔΥ
ΜΕΙΑ ΠΑΛΗΝ ΤΡΙΣ
ΤΩ ΙΕΡΩ ΤΟΥ ΔΙ
ΔΥΜΕΩΣ ΑΠΟΛ
ΛΩΝΟΣ ΚΑΤΑ ΤΑ
ΓΡΑΦΕΝΤΑ ΑΥ .
ΨΗΦΙΣΜΑΤΑ Α
ΝΑΣΤΑΘΕΝΤΟΣ ΤΟΥ
ΤΟΥ ΑΝΔΡΙΑΝΤΟΣ
ΤΗΟ ΤΟΥ ΠΑΤΡΟΣ
ΑΥΤΟΥ ΑΥΡ ΕΡΜΙ
ΟΥ ΕΠΙ ΑΥΡ
ΑΓΑΘΟΠΟΔΟΣ
ΙΟΥ ΑΠΟΛΛΩΝΙΟΥ

" The senate and people honour Aurelius Posidonius, the son of Hermias, (who bore away the prize three times in wrestling in the great Didymean games,) in the temple of the Didymean Apollo, according to the decree proposed; the statue being raised by his father Aurelius Hermias, in the magistracy of Aurelius Agathopus, son of Apollonius."

IX.

Found near the temple of the Didymean Apollo, on the thigh of a statue. From the same.

ΣΑΤΝΙ9ΔΝΛΣΟΤ

Some more letters were found written in the Boustrophedon character on the thigh of the same statue; those we have printed contain distinctly the words τοὺς ἀιδριάντας. If they relate to the person who made this or other statues, we see an additional proof of the custom of inscribing the name of the artist on the thigh of the figure. Cicero, in one of the Verrine orations, mentions an Apollo, on whose thigh was written in letters of silver the name of Myron.

There are also representations of Etruscan Athletae, which bear characters inscribed on this part of their body. There is one of a Greek wrestler, on whose thigh are written the words ΚΑΦΙΣΟΔΩΡΟΣ and ΑΙΣΧΡΑΜΙΟΥ. It would appear therefore that inscriptions placed on this part of the body designated the persons bearing them to have been successful combatants or conquerors. Montfaucon has introduced on this subject the following remark in his great work ——
" S'il est permis de mêler la sacré avec le profane, ceci a quelque rapport avec ce passage de l'Apocalypse, où il est dit de notre Seigneur victorieux, qu'il portoit écrit sur sa cuisse, et sur son habit, le Roi des Rois. Cette écriture sur la cuisse étoit donc une marque d'honneur et de victoire." Vol. iii. part ii. 269 An Ex.

X.

Found at Daulis, by the Earl of Aberdeen. On the other side of the same stone is an inscription of equal length, which was copied by

Col. Leake. That which is subjoined contains a decree pronounced by Titus Flavius Eubulus respecting some portions of land, which are assigned to the city of Daulis, and to Memmius Antiochus. The date of the inscription is 118, anno Christi. Fuscus Salinator is mentioned in the letters of Pliny, book vi. lett. 26

ΑΓΑΘΗΙΤΥΛΗΙ
ΑΥΤΟΚΡΑΤΟΡΙ ΤΡΑΙΑΝΩ ΑΔΡΙΑΝΩ ΚΑΙ
ΣΑΡΙ ΣΕΒΑΣΤΩ ΤΟ Β ΓΝΑΙΩ ΠΕΔΑΝΙΩ ΦΟΥ
ΣΚΩ ΣΑΛΕΙΝΑΤΟΡΙ ΥΠΑΤΟΙΣ ΠΡΟ Θ •
Κ ΝΟΥΕΝΒΡΙΩΝ ΓΝ ΧΑΙΡΩΝΕΙΑ
ΖΩΠΤΡΟΣ ΑΡΙΣΤΙΩΝΟΣ ΚΑΙ ΠΑΡΜΕΝΩΝ
ΖΩΠΥΡΟΥ ΟΙ ΕΓΔΙΚΟΙΤΗΣ ΔΑΥΛΙΕΩΝ ΠΟ
ΛΕΩΣ ΕΜΑΡΤΥΡΟΠΟΙΗΣΑΝΤΟ ΑΠΟΦΑΣΙΝ†
ΑΝΤΙΓΕΓΡΑΦΘΑΙ ΤΗΝ ΔΟΘΕΙΣΑΝ ΥΠΟ Τ ΦΛΑΟΥ
ΙΟΥ ΕΥΒΟΥΛΟΥ ΤΗΝ ΥΠΟΓΕΓΡΑΜΕΝΗΝ
Τ ΦΛΑΥΙΟΣ ΕΥΒΟΥΛΟΣ Ο ΔΟΘΕΙΣ ΚΡΙΤΗΣ ΚΑΙ ΟΡΙ
ΣΤΗΣ ΥΠΟ ΚΑΣΙΟΥ ΜΑΞΙΜΟΥ ΑΝΘΥΠΑΤΟΥ ΚΑΙ ΤΗΡΗ
ΘΕΙΣ ΥΠΟ ΟΥΑΛΕΡΙΟΥ ΣΕΟΥΗΡΟΥ ΑΝΘΥΠΑΤΟΥ ΜΕΤΑ
ΞΥ ΖΩΠΥΡΟΥ ΤΟΥ ΑΡΙΣΤΙΩΝΟΣ ΚΑΙ ΠΑΡΜΕΝΩΝΟΣ
ΤΟΥ ΖΩΠΥΡΟΥ ΚΑΙ ΜΕΜΜΙΟΥ ΑΝΤΙΟΧΟΥ ΠΕΡΙΧΩΡΑΣ
ΑΜΦΙΣΒΗΤΟΥΜΕΝΗΣ ΑΚΟΥΣΑΣ ‡ ΕΚΑΤΕΡΟΥ ΜΕΡΟΥΣ
ΕΦΟΣΟΝ ΕΒΟΥΛΟΝΙΟ ΚΑΙ ΕΠΙ ΤΗΝ ΑΥΤΟΨΙΑΝ ΕΛΘΩΝ
ΚΕΛΕΥΣΑΝΤΟΣ ΜΕ ΑΠΟΦΗΝΑΘΑΙ ΚΛΩΔΙΟΥ ΓΡΑ
ΝΙΑΝΟΥ ΤΟΥ ΚΡΑΤΙΣΤΟΥ ΑΝΘΥΠΑΤΟΥ ΚΡΕΙΝΩ ΚΑΘΩΣ
ΥΠΟΓΕΓΡΑΠΤΑΙ ΑΓΡΟΥ ΔΡΥΠΠΟΥ ΟΝ ΗΓΟΡΑΣΕ
ΠΑΡΑ ΤΩΝ ΚΛΕΑΣ ΚΛΗΡΟΝΟΜΩΝ ΜΕΜΜΙΟΣ ΑΝΤΙΟ
ΧΟΣ ΚΑΤΑΛΛΑΒΟΜΕΝΟΣ ΕΚ ΤΩΝ ΕΠΙΜΕ ΚΟΜΙΣΘΕΝ
ΤΩΝ ΓΡΑΜΜΑΤΩΝ ΠΡΟΣΗΚΕΙΝ ΑΝΤΙΟΧΩ ΠΛΕΘΡΑ
ΦΩΚΙΚΑ ΤΛΕ ΟΣΑ ΑΝ ΕΥΡΕΘΗ ΠΛΕΙΩ ΤΟΥΤΩΝ
ΚΡΕΙΝΩ ΕΙΝΑΙ ΤΗΣ ΔΑΥΛΙΕΩΝ ΠΟΛΕΩΣ ΟΜΟΙ
ΩΣ ΑΓΡΟΥ ΕΥΣΤΑΛΕΙΑΣ ΠΛΕΘΡΑ ΤΑ ΚΡΕΙΝΩ
ΕΙΝΑΙ ΑΝΤΙΟΧΟΥ ΤΑ ΔΕ ΛΟΙΠΑ ΤΗΣ ΠΟΛΕΩΣ ΕΙ
ΝΑΙ ΧΩΡΙΩΝ ΠΛΑΤΑΝΟΥ ΚΑΙ ΜΟΣΧΟΤΟΜΕΩΝ

---

* ΠΡΟ ΘΚ. this is the date, πρὸ ἐννέα Καλ A similar form occurs in some inscriptions published by Montfaucon, Diar. Ital. and in Theophanes Chron. we find πρὸ ἰξ ἰδων Φεβ. and πρὸ τεσσάρων νώναν Σεπ.

† 'Αποφασις, οι αποφάσεις, as the word was sometimes written (Wytt Plut. Anim i. 206) is applied also to the Amphictyonic decrees. Diod. S. xvi. c. 24.

‡ The letters in the copy are ΑΚΟΥΣ. Mr. Elmsley proposes ΑΚΟΥΣΑΣ

ΠΛΕΘΡΑ ΣΑΚΡΕΙΝΩ ΕΙΝΑΙ ΑΝΤΙΟΧΟΥ ΤΑ ΔΕ ΛΟΙ
ΠΑ ΤΗΣ ΠΟΛΕΩΣ ΤΗΝ ΔΕ ΑΡΧΗΝ ΤΗΣ ΜΕΤΡΗΣΕΩΣ
ΚΡΕΙΝΩ ΓΕΝΕΣΘΑΙ ΤΗΣ ΧΩΡΑΣ ΟΘΕΝ ΑΝ ΒΟΥ
ΛΗΤΑΙ ΑΝΤΙΟΧΟΣ ΕΝ ΕΚΑΤΕΡΩΝ ΤΩΝ ΑΓΡΩΝ
ΔΡΥΠΠΙΩ ΚΑΙ ΕΥΣΤΑΕΙΑ ΕΝ ΔΕ ΠΛΑΤΑΝΩ
ΚΑΙ ΜΟΣΧΟΤΟΜΕΛΙΣ ΜΙΑ ΕΠ ΑΜΦΟΤΕΡΟΙΣ ΑΡ
ΧΗ ΤΗΣ ΜΕΤΡΗΣΕΩΣ ΕΣΤΑΙ ΜΕΤΡΟΥΜΕΝΩΝ
ΑΠΟ ΤΗΣ ΔΟΘΕΙΣΗΣ ΑΡΧΗΣ ΤΩΝ ΕΦΕΞΗΣ ΜΗ
ΕΛΛΟΓΟΥΜΕΝΩΝ ΤΑΙΣ ΜΕΤΡΗΣΕΣΙΝ ΑΠΑΣΑΙΣ
ΜΗΤΕ ΡΕΙΘΡΩΝ ΜΗΤΕ ΟΣΑ ΤΡΑΧΕΑ ΟΝΤΑ ΚΑΙ
ΜΗ ΔΥΝΑΜΕΝΑ ΓΕΩΡΓΕΙΣΘΑΙ ΥΠΕΡ ΔΕΚΑΣΦΥ
ΡΑΣ ΕΣΤΙΝ ΠΑΡΗΣΑΝ* Τ ΦΛΑΥΙΟΣ ΕΥΒΟΥ
ΛΟΣ ΑΠΕΦΗΝΑΜΗΝ ΚΑΙ ΕΣΦΡΑΓΙΣΜΑΙ ΑΜΕΣ
ΤΡΙΟΣ ΣΩΚΛΑΡΟΥ ΚΛΕΟΜΕΝΗΣ ΚΛΕΟΜΕΝΟΥΣ
ΝΕΙΚΩΝ ΣΥΜΦΟΡΟΥ ΛΑΜΠΡΙΑΣ ΝΕΙΚΩΝΟΣ
ΖΩΠΥΡΟΣ ΑΝΤΙΠΑΤΡΟΥ ΣΩΣΙΒΙΟΣ ΔΡΑΚΩ
ΝΟΣ ΝΕΙΚΩΝ ΑΛΕΞΑΝΔΡΟΥ ΛΕΩΝ ΘΕΟΔΟ
ΤΟΥ ΚΑΛΛΩΝ ΦΥΛΑΚΟΣ ΚΑΣΣΙΟΣ ΜΑΡΤΙΑΝΟΥ
ΨΗΦΙΣΜΑΤΙ ΤΗΣ ΠΟΛΕΩΣ

" The Emperor Trajan Hadrian Cæsar Augustus, second time Consul, and Cnæus Pedanius Fuscus Salinator being also Consul, on the 24th October, at Chæronæa, Zopyrus, son of Aristion, and Parmeno, son of Zopyrus, the magistrates of the city Daulis, testified that the underwritten decision, which was made by T. Flavius Eubulus, has been copied. ‘ I, T. Flavius Eubulus, who was appointed judge and arbiter by Casius Maximus, Proconsul, and Valerius Severus, Proconsul, between Zopyrus, son of Aristion, and Parmeno, son of Zopyrus, and Memmius Antiochus, concerning the land that was disputed; having heard each side, as far as they wished, and having come to an examination of the land, Claudius Gramianus, the chief Proconsul, ordering me to declare my opinion, I decree as is underwritten.—Judging from the writings brought to me, 436 Phocic Plethra of the field called Dryppius, which Memmius Antiochus bought from the heirs of Clea,

---

* Παρῆσαν   A similar form with the names of the persons present, is seen in an inscription in p. 604. Marm. Oxon ed. Maitt.

belong to Antiochus; whatever more than these, be found, I decree
shall belong to the city of Daulis. Also of the field called Euxyleia,
430 Plethra belong to Antiochus; the rest is the property of the city
of Daulis. Of the places called Platanus and Moschotomiæ, 230
Plethra, I decree to belong to Antiochus; the remainder is the property of the city. The beginning of the measurements in each of the
fields called Dryppius and Euxyleia shall commence at the spot where
Antiochus may wish, but in the Platanus and Moschotomiæ the
two parties shall have the same beginning for their measurements,
which shall take place from a given point, the following parts not
being reckoned in the measurements; namely, no stream, nor whatever
piece of ground there be, that is rough and incapable of tillage. * * *
There were present (I, T. Flavius Eubulus declared my opinion, and
affixed my seal); Lucius Mestrius the son of Soclarus; Cleomenes,
the son of Cleomenes; Nico, the son of Symphorus, Lampuas, the
son of Nico; Zopyrus, the son of Antipator, Sosibius, the son of
Diaco; Nico, the son of Alexander; Leo, the son of Theodotus;
Callo, the son of Phylax, Cassius, the son of Marcianus.' By the
decree of the city."

XI.

Copied by the editor at Geyra, the ancient Aphrodisias.

ZII.

O BΩMOΣ KAI H ΣOPOΣ EΣTIN OYAΠIOY ΛΑ
PITΩNOΣ IATPOY IΣHΝ ΣOPON TEΘHΣE
TAI AΥTOΣ KAI ΦΛOAΣIΑ H ΓΥΝHAΥTOY
KAI OYAΠIOΣ ΛIEΛΛAΣ O ΥIOΣ AΥTΩNE
ΠEIOΘAΨAΣ ETFPON AΠOTEIΣEI EIΣTEI
MAΣ TΩN ΣEBAΣTΩN X

The word ZH (vivat) occurs at the beginning as well as at the end
of inscriptions; see Chishull Ant. Asiat. Append. Sometimes Ζῶσι
is used.

There is nothing remarkable in this epitaph except the mode of
writing I for EI, and the reverse We may observe instances of this

3 o 2

in other inscriptions; see Falcon ad Athlet. Inscr   H, I, OI, EI, and
Υ have been for many centuries written one for the other, and the
same sound given to them by the Neoteric Greeks.   This remark
applies also to AI and E.   " *Tam captiosa pronuntiatio mendis infinitis
libros opplevit.*" (Bentl. ad I. Millium.)   What was the real power of
these different letters we shall never know, we may, however, say
with Ramirez de Prado, "*frustra distinctæ essent literæ ι, ε, οι, υ, ι, si
nihil differrent sono.*" Pentec. c. 34.   The corrupted sound of some
of them is as early as the second century of the Christian æra.   We
find ι for ει in the time of Tiberius, Mont. Palæ. 155; ει for ι in an
inscription at Ancyra of the year 180, (ib. 163.) η for υ in an epitaph
on the wife of Julius Severus, who lived about the year 155.   Montfaucon observes that few instances occur of the change of η and ι,
before the seventh century.   (Pal. 139.)

XII.

At Gheumbrek, on the Troad.   See Dr. Hunt's journal, p. 104.
" The young men honor Asclapon, the son of Callippus the Gymnasiarch, called ----." The words refer to some mark of respect
paid by the young men who were instructed in their exercises for the
public games by the Gymnasiarch.   The word ΧΡΗΜΑΤΙΣΑΝΤΑ
applies to the title or name which had been given to Asclapon.   In
Lord Aberdeen's copy, we find ΑΣΚΛΑΗΠΙΩΝΑ.

XIII.

Found on a sarcophagus on the European shore of the Propontis,
near Boyuk Chekmagee.   Communicated by Dr. Hunt.

ΑΥΡΗΛΙΑ ΒΛΟΥΚΙΑ ΖΩΣΑ ΚΑΙ ΦΡΟΝΟΥΣΑ ΚΑΤΕΣΚΕΥΑΣΕ ΤΟ
ΛΑΤΟΜΙΟΝ ΣΥΝ ΤΗΙΣΤΗΛΗΙΕΜΑΥΤΗΙ ΚΑΙ ΤΩΙΓΛΥΚΥΤΑ
ΤΩΙ ΜΟΥ ΑΝΔΡΙ ΣΑΤΥΡΩΝΙΑΩΙ ΥΠΟΜΝΕΙΑΣ ΧΑΡΙΝ ΖΗΣ
ΑΝΤΙ ΕΤΗΤΡΙΑΚΟΝΤΑΜΕΜΠΤΩΣ ΜΗΔΕΝ ΔΕΤΕΡ
ΟΝ ΕΞΕΣΤΑΙ ΒΛΗΘΗΝΛΙ ΕΣΑΥΤΟ ΕΙΜΗ ΤΑ ΤΕΚΝΑ ΜΟΥ
ΕΙΔΕΤΙΣ ΚΑΤΑΘΗΤΑΙ ΕΤΕΡΟ ΠΤΩΜΑ ΔΩΣΕΙ ΤΗ ΠΟΛΕΙ
ΧΑΦ.   ΧΛΙΡΕ ΠΑΡΘΕΝΑ

It is unusual to find the term Λατομιον used to express the stone-tomb on which the body of the deceased is placed. Σορος is generally applied in sepulchral inscriptions. We may here observe the difference between the Alexandrian use of Σορος, and that of the European and Asiatic Greeks. In the Septuagint, where mention is made of the death of Joseph, it is said his body was placed ἐν τῇ Σόρ, "in a wooden chest;" this was done in reference to the custom of the Egyptians. "When Joseph died," says Michaelis, "his brethren did not bury him, but, as was not unusual among the Egyptians, let him remain embalmed in his coffin, until their descendants, at their departure from Palestine, carried his remains along with them. The Egyptians kept the bodies of their deceased friends in an erect posture in a coffin; in some such chest were Joseph's unburied bones preserved."— On the Laws of Moses, vol. i. p. 162.

Injunctions similar to those mentioned in this inscription, forbidding the sepulchre to be used by any other persons than members of the same family are not uncommon. Fines were levied, if the prohibition was not regarded, and the money was paid to the public treasury. D. F. C. *dabit fisco centum*, is a Latin form which we sometimes meet with. Soroi and Sarcophagi were broken open for the sake of the ornaments of gold, or the money frequently placed in them with the deceased. This practice seems to have been prevalent in the fourth century of the Christian æra. "*Quarto seculo hæc impietas grassata.*" Dorv. Chal. i. 109.

XIV.

[See p. 103. of this Volume.]

The inscription is of the date of the year 196 B. C.; at that time Seleucus the Fourth was with his father Antiochus the Third on the banks of the Hellespont. "*Bello Asiatico cum patre adfuit.*" Vaillant. His. Regum Syriæ, p 112. and p 153. The inscription was also copied by Dr. Clarke.

L. 10. The name of the city of which Metrodorus was a native is not discernible in the copy of this inscription.

L. 17. Some of the honours which are bestowed on Metrodorus are mentioned in this and the two following lines. Κτᾶσιν γᾶς καὶ οἰκιᾶν occurs in the Byzantine decree in Demos. de Coron. In an inscription copied at Delos, we find ἐκκ]ᾶσιν γᾶς καὶ ο "*libertatem emendi fundos et domos* :" see Dorville in his account of Delos. In an inscription brought from the Levant by George Dousa, (Van Dale. Diss. 744.) we read, ἐφοδον ἐπὶ τὴν βουλὴν καὶ τὸν δῆμον πρώ]οις μεὶὰ τὰ ιερὰ, "*admitti statim post sacrificia* " and on a marble belonging to Burmann, we find, ἐφοδον ἐπὶ ταμ βόλλαν καὶ δάμομ μεὶὰ τὸγ χρημα]ιτμὸν τὸιυ περὶ τῶν ιρᾶι Metrodorus, therefore, was allowed admission to the senate and people immediately after the sacrifices were performed.

Valesius (Emen. 110) says, the difference between κτῆτιν and ἐγκτητιν is pointed out by Ammonius; κτῆσις τῆς γῆς is "*possessio in terra propria*," ἐγκτησις is possession "*in aliena terra.*"

XV.

[See Dr. Hunt's Journal, p. 128.]

" From his revenues derived from land, Cleostratus, adopted son of the state, but by nature son of Apellico, left for the purpose of ornamenting the city - - - - ." A mode of expression similar to that which we find in this inscription occurs in others; as, Φίλων Ἀγλάου, φύσει δὲ Νικώνος; see Mem. de l'A. des Ins. xxi. 413.

XVI.

Captain Light, in his Journal of a route through Upper Egypt and part of Nubia, says, that at Gartaas there are not less than a hundred Greek inscriptions; five were copied by him; and each contains a memorial of the act of homage and worship, τὸ προσκύνημα, paid by persons who visited the place with their wives, children, friends, and brothers. ΜΕΤΑ ΤΗΣ ΣΥΜΒΙΟΥ ΚΑΙ ΤΩΝ ΤΕΚΝΩΝ ΚΑΙ ΤΩΝ ΑΔΕΛΦΩΝ ΚΑΙ ΤΩΝ ΦΙΛΩΝ In another inscription, a person is mentioned, who ΕΠΟΙΗCΕΝ ΤΗΝ ΚΑΤΙΕΡΥCΙΝ (sic) ΤΟΥ ΙΕΡΟΥ   In the fourth inscription a priest is spoken of, Ο ΟΥΔΕΙΣ ΤΩΝ ΙΕΡΕΩΝ ΣΥΝΚΡΙΝΕ ... " with whom no other priest is compared."   In two of them, the month, Φαμενώθ *, is mentioned, in which the visit was paid by the persons coming to the temple and worshipping. The date is usually expressed, as we find from the inscriptions on the Memnonium, and from one copied by Captain Light and Mr. Legh at Dukkey, in which we find the word † ΦΑΩΦΙ.

The following inscription was copied by Captain Light at Galabshee. —

ΕΠΑΓΑΘω ΚΥΡΙC
ΤΟ ΠΡΟCΚΥ ΝΗΜΑ ΟΛ ΓΑΙΟΥ
ΚΛΕΙΟΥ ΚΕΛΕΙΡΟC ΙΠΠΕΟC
ΧαΡΤΗC ΘΗΒΑΙωΝ ΙΙΙΠΙ
ΚΗC ΤΥΡΜΗC ΚΑΛΛΙCΤΙΥ
ΚΑΙ ΤΟΥ ΠΑΙΔΙΟΥ ΑΥΤΟΥ
ΚΑΙ ΤΩΝ ΑΒΑCΚΑΝΤωΝ
ΑΔΕΛΦωΝ ΚΑΙ ΤωΝ ΑΥΤΟΥ
ΠΑΝΤωΝ ΙωΑΤω ΚΥΡΙω
ΔΟΥΛΙΚΙΟΥ ΙΠΠΟΥ ΑΥΤΟΥ

" The homage of Caius Cleius Celer, horseman or knight of the horse-troop of the Theban cohort , of Callistius and of his child, and of the Abascanti brothers , and of all who were there with the same master, — and of Hippolytus."   In the six inscriptions copied at Dukkey by Captain Light, mention is made of the god Hermes , in that which is printed in Mr Legh's travels, p. 85, relating to Apollonius, the words ΘΕΟΝ ΕΡΜΗΝ should be added after ΠΡΟC Captain Light's copy has ΘΕ - - ΕΡΜ - -

---

* Answering to March.

† 'Ος ἐστιν ὀκταβξιος. Arat. Schol. Phænom. 462.   See also Jablonski Gloss, Vocum Ægypt.

XVII.

Found at Cipaissia, in the Morea.   From Mr. Hawkins.

TO KOINON TΩN EΛEYΘEPOΛAKΩNΩN
ΓAION IOYΛION ΛΛKΩNA EYPYKΛEOYΣ
YION ΓON IΔION EYEPΓETHN ΔAMAPMENI
ΔAΣ ΣTPATHΓΩN EΠEMEΛHΘH.

This inscription occurs also in Reinesius, Cl. iv. n. 120.   Van Dale.
Diss. 295., transcribes it, but he omits the Σ in the word EYPYKΛEOYΣ.
The form EΠIMEΛHΘEN ΓOΣ ΓOY ΣTPATHΓOY occurs in many in-
scriptions.   For the meaning of ΣTPATHΓOΣ, see Van Dale, Diss. 416.

XVIII

Copied at Sunium.   " On a fallen stone of the architrave of the
temple of Minerva, some Greek had inscribed a short testimony to
the memory of his sister."   Hunt's Journal.

ONHCIMOC
EMNHCΘH
THC AΔEΛΦHC
XPHCTHC

Similar inscriptions, written by persons visiting temples or celebrated places, and commemorating their friends and relatives, are not
uncommon.   In Egypt we find on the Memnonium the following
words . —

HΛIOΔΩPOΣ ZHNΩ
NOΣ KAIΣAPEIAΣ ΠA
NIAΔOΣ HKOYΣA Δ KAI
EMNHΣΘHN ZHNΩNOΣ
KAI AIANOY AΔEΛΦΩN.

D'Orville, Charit, ii. 533. proposes in the last line, γαιανοῦ, or αιλιανοῦ:
" I heard four times (the vocal statue), and remembered my brothers
Zeno, Ælianus."
We may transcribe in this place part of another inscription on the

Memnonium *, correcting one of the verses in D'Orville's copy of it Charit. ii 532.

ΕΚΑΤΟΝ ΑΥΔΗΣΑΝΤΟΣ ΕΓΩ ΠΥΔΙΘΩ ΒΑΑΒΙΝΑ
ΦΩΝΑΣ ΤΑΣ ΘΕΙΑΣ ΜΕΜΝΟΝΟΣ Η ΦΑΜΕΝΩΘ
ΗΛΘΟΝ ΤΜΟΥ ΔΕΡΑΤΑΙ ΒΑΣΙΛΗΙΔΙ ΤΥΙΔΕ ΣΑΒΙΝΝΑ
ΩΡΑΣ ΔΕ ΠΡΩΤΑΣ ΑΛΙΟΣ ΗΚΕΔΡΟΜΟΣ

In the third line, ὁμῶυ and τᾶδε are inserted improperly in the copy of D'Orville; ὑμῶυ and τυῖδε are doubtless the proper forms, and are given in Pococke and Hamilton's Ægyptiaca. There are many instances in which the later Greeks † affected the archaisms and dialects of ancient Greece; this is one, ὑμῶυ is written for ὁμῶυ; Æoles, *quod vulgo notum, ο in υ commutant.* (Nunnes ad Proclum; see Gaisford's Hephæst. 451.) And τυῖδε is the Doric word, signifying, " Here or hither;" τυ., ὦδε, Κρῆτες, τυῖδε, Sappho. v. Maittaire

XIX.

See p. 104. Dr Hunt's Journal.

ΙΛΙΕΙΣ. κ. τ. λ.

The same term of honor, Θεὸς, was also applied, as we learn from Athenagoras, by the Ilieans to Hector· Ὁ μὲν Ἰλιεὺς θεὸν Ἕκτορα λέγει Legat. pro Xtianis.

In the same page of this volume is an inscription relating to the people of the tribe Panthois, who commemorate Sextus Julius, magistrate of the city, præfect of the Fabian cohort, who had also been gymnasiarch, and had been the first to grant some donation of

---

* On the same statue of Memnon are the following lines —

Ω ΠΟΠΟΙ Η ΜΕΓΑ ΘΑΥΜΑ - - - - - - -
Η ΜΑΛΑ ΤΙΣ ΘΕΟΣ ΕΝΔΟΝ - - - - - -
ΗΥΣΕΝ ΦΩΝΗΙ ΚΑΤΑ ΔΕΣΧΕΘΕΛΑΟΝ ΑΠΑΝΤΑ
ΟΥ ΓΑΡ ΠΩΣ ΑΝ ΘΝΗΤΟΣ ΑΝΗΡ ΤΑΔΕ ΜΗΧΑΝΟΩΤΟ

These are parts of the Iliad and Odyssey applied by the writer See Il N 99. Od Ω 529. Od Π 197.

† In another inscription found in Egypt, of the time of the Cæsars we read ΓΑΙΔΕ ΦΥΛΑΙ ΦΩΝΕΥΝΤΙ, speaking of Philæ. Ægypt. 52.

oil, and had discharged the office of Aliptes. With respect to the expression ΠΡΩΤΟΝ ΤΩΝ ΑΠΛΙΩΝΟΣ, see Muratori, Ins. ii. 632.

XX.

1. From Orchomenus.

In the Elgin collection. See also Dr Clarke's Travels, vol. iii.

ΘΥΝΑΡΧΟ ΑΡΧΟΝΤΟΣ ΜΕΙΝΟΣ ΘΕΙ
ΛΟΥΘΙΩ ΑΡΧΙΑΡΟΣ ΕΥΜΕΙΛΟ ΤΑΜΙ
ΑΣ ΕΥΒΩΛΥ ΑΡΧΕΔΑΜΩ ΦΩΚΕΗΧΗ
ΟΣ ΑΠΕΔΩΚΑ ΑΠΟ ΤΑΣ ΣΟΥΓΓΡΑΦΩ
ΠΕΔΑΓΩΝ ΠΟΛΕΜΑΡΧΩΝ ΚΗ ΤΩΝ
ΚΑΤΟΠΤΑΩΝ ΑΝΕΛΟΜΕΝΟΣ ΤΑΣ
ΣΟΥΓΓΡΑΦΩΣ ΤΑΣ ΚΙΜΕΝΑΣ ΠΑΡ ΕΥ
ΦΡΟΝΑΚΙ ΦΙΔΙΑΝ ΚΗ ΠΑΣΙΚΛΓΙΝΟΝ
ΚΗ ΤΙΜΟΜΕΛΑΟΝ ΦΩΚΕΙΑΣ ΚΗ ΔΑΜΟ
ΤΕΛΕΙΝ ΛΥΣΙΔΑΜΩ ΚΗ ΔΙΩΝΥΣΙΟΝ
ΚΑΦΙΣΟΔΩΡΩ ΧΗΡΩΝΕΙΑ ΚΑΤ ΤΟ ΨΑ
ΦΙΣΜΑ ΤΩ ΔΑΜΩ . . . .

2. From Orchomenus

ΘΥΝΑΡΧΩ ΑΡΧΟΝΤΟΣ ΜΕΙΝΟΣ ΑΛΑΛ
ΚΟΜΕΝΙΩ ΓΑΡΝΩΝ ΠΟΛΥΚΛΕΙΟΣ
ΤΑΜΙΑΣ ΑΠΕΔΩΚΕ ΕΥΒΩΛΥ ΑΡΧΕ
ΔΑΜΩ ΦΩΚΕΗ ΛΠΟ ΤΑΣ ΣΟΥΓΓΡΑ
ΦΩ ΤΟ ΚΑΤΑΛΥΠΟΝ ΚΑΤ ΤΟ ΨΑΦΙΣΜΑ
ΤΩ ΔΑΜΩ ΑΝΕΛΟΜΕΝΟΣ ΤΑΣ ΣΟΥΓ
ΓΡΑΦΩΣ ΤΑΣ ΚΙΜΕΝΑΣ ΠΑΡ ΣΩΦΙ
ΛΟΝ ΚΗ ΕΥΦΡΟΝΑ ΦΩΚΛΙΑΣ ΚΗ ΠΑΡ
ΔΙΩΝΥΣΙΟΝ ΚΑΦΙΣΟΔΩΡΩ ΧΗΡΩΝΕΙ
Λ ΚΗ ΛΥΣΙΔΑΜΟΝ ΔΑΜΟΤΕΛΙΟΣ ΠΕ
ΔΑΙΩΝ ΠΟΛΕΜΑΡΧΩΝ ΚΗ ΤΩΝ ΚΑΤΟ
ΠΤΑΩΝ - - - - - - - - - - - - - - - - - -

3. From Orchomenus.

ΑΡΧΟΝΤΟΣ ΕΝ ΕΡΧΟΜΕΝΤ ΘΥΝΑΡΧΩ ΜΕΙ
ΝΟΣ ΑΛΑΛΚΟΜΕΝΙΩ ΕΝ ΔΕ ΙΕΛΑΤΙΗ ΜΙ
ΝΟΙΤΑΟ ΑΡΧΕΛΑΩ ΜΕΙΝΟΣ ΠΡΑΤΩ ΟΜΟ
ΛΟΓΑ ΕΥΒΩΛΥ ΓΕΛΛΤΗΤ ΚΗ ΤΗ ΠΟΛΙ ΕΡ

ΧΟΜΕΝΙΩΝ ΕΠΙΔΕΙ ΚΕΚΟΜΙΣΤΗ ΕΥΒΩ
ΛΟΣ ΠΑΡ ΤΑΣ ΠΟΛΙΟΣ ΤΟ ΔΑΝΕΙΟΝ ΑΠΑΝ
ΚΑΤ ΤΑΣ ΟΜΟΛΟΓΙΑΣ ΤΑΣ ΤΕΘΕΙΣΑΣ ΘΥ
ΝΑΡΧΩ ΑΡΧΟΝΤΟΣ ΜΓΙΝΟΣ ΘΕΙΛΥΘΙΩ
ΚΗ ΟΥΤ ΟΦΕΙΛΕΤΗ ΑΥΤΥ ΕΤΙ ΟΥΘΕΝ ΠΑΡΤΑΝ
ΠΟΛΙΝ ΑΛΛ ΑΠΕΧΙ ΠΑΝΤΑ ΠΕΡΙ ΠΑΝΤΟΣ
ΚΗ ΑΠΟΔΕΔΟΛΝΘΙ ΤΗ ΠΟΛΙ ΤΥ ΕΧΟΝΤΕΣ
ΤΑΣ ΟΜΟΛΟΓΙΑΣ ΕΙΜΕΝ ΠΟΤΙ ΔΕΔΟΜΕ
ΝΟΝ ΧΡΟΝΟΝ ΕΥΒΩΛΥ ΕΠΙΝΟΜΙΑΣ ΕΤΤΙΑ
ΠΕΤΤΑΡΑ ΒΟΥΕΣΣΙ ΣΟΥΝ ΙΠΠΥΣ ΔΙΑΚΑ
ΤΙΗΣ ΓΙΚΑΤΙ ΠΡΟΒΑΤΥΣ ΣΟΥΝΗΓΥΣ ΛΕΙ
ΛΗΣ ΑΡΧΙ ΤΩ ΧΡΟΝΩ Ο ΕΝΙΑΥΤΟΣ Ο ΜΕΤΑ
ΘΥΝΑΡΧΟΝ ΑΡΧΟΝΤΑ ΕΡΧΟΜΕΝΙΥΣ ΑΠΟ
ΓΡΑΦΕΣΘΗ ΔΕ ΕΥΒΩΛΟΝ ΚΑΤΕΝΙΑΥΤΟΝ
ΕΚΑΣΤΟΝ ΠΑΡ ΤΟΝ ΤΑΜΙΑΝ ΚΗ ΤΟΝ ΝΟΜ
ΝΑΝΤΑ ΤΕΚΑΥΜΑΤΑ ΤΩΝ ΠΡΟΒΑΤΩΝ ΚΗ
ΤΑΝΗΓΩΝ ΚΗ ΤΑΝ ΒΟΥΩΝ ΚΗ ΤΑΝ ΙΠΠΩΝ Κ
ΚΑΤΙΝΑ ΑΣΑΜΛΙΩΝ ΟΙΚΙΤΩΝ ΠΛΕΙΘΟΣ ΜΕΙ
ΑΠΟΓΡΑΦΕΣΘΩ ΔΕ ΠΛΕΙΟΝΑ ΤΩΝ ΓΕΓΡΑΜ
ΜΕΝΩΝ ΕΝ ΤΗ ΣΟΥΓΧΩΡΕΙΣΙ Η ΔΕΚΑΤΙΣ

There are on the stone a few more lines, in which many of the
letters are erased

REMARKS.

The digamma occurs in the Orchomenian inscriptions. and as the
Bœotians appear to have used it to a late period on marbles, their
copies of Pindar probably continued to have this character inserted in
those parts, where the poet's verse required it, as Pyth. iv. 40, *i–í*
Γαι, 65, Χειρι Foι ; 159, ἐπιαλτα Fα αξ. As the sound of the digamma
could not have been the same in every district or colony of Greece,
it is impossible * to say in what manner it was pronounced. Sometimes it appears as Υ (in the coins of Velia†), sometimes as Β
(among the Lacedæmonians); sometimes we see it expressing the
power of S, as in *ἑ* Γ. whence comes the Latin *se*.

---

* The difficulty of arriving at any certainty on this subject is stated by Heyne — " In
lingius quæ usu populorum frequentari desierunt, de pronunciatione aliquid tuto statui ac
decerni posse, nondum mihi persuadere potui " — Excurs. ii. ad lib. xix

† In Lucania, the colonists of which, being Phoceans from Ionia, used the form familiar
to their countrymen

As the following remarks of D'Orville, Valckenaer, and I. Vossius, are omitted in the works which treat of the sound and power of this letter, we may here transcribe them.

" _Æolicum illud digamma_ in ΑΕΥΓΟΝ," says D'Orville, speaking of the Delian inscription, " _videtur nonnihil favere hodiernæ pronunciationi Græcorum_, ἀφτὲς, ἀφθέντης." Mis. Obs. vii. 27. — The Bishop of Landaff, in his _Horæ Pelasgicæ_, considers the sound of the letter to be similar to that of F, Larcher, Herod. vol. iv. l. v. 192, says that the digamma was pronounced sometimes as ou, and sometimes as v. It is impossible to understand how the word ΣοϜος should _approach_ to Σοφός, unless the digamma had the sound of F. " _Ad vocem σοφός propius accedit_ Σόος, _imprimis si vox Æolico more Laconum scribatur_ ΣοϜος." Valck. ad Theoc. 271.

The Latin _infra_ and _infera_, according to Vossius, are derived* from ἰνϜέρα, id est, ἐν ἔρα ; ἴνϜερον id est, ἔνερον. " _Veteres Atticos et complures Græciæ gentes_ ἐασυστικὰς _fuisse, et_ Ἱέρα _seu_ ἱέρα _dixisse pro_ ἔρα, _satis constat._" (In Catull. 331.)

Daps of the Roman, according to the same writer, is derived from the δαις of the Greeks the Æolians said δάϜις, and in a contracted form δαϜς, or δαί. — Id. 203.

1st Inscrip.

Line 1. The Bœotian month, Theluthius, should be added to the list in Corsini. F. A.

Ib. ΜΕΙΝΟΣ is used for ΜΗΝΟΣ ; we find ΕΠΟΕΙΣΕΝ for ΕΠΟΙΗΣΕΝ in the Sigæan inscription, and ΔΕΕΙΣΗΙ for δεήτη in Test. Dorico. Gruter. ccxix. †

" * Pro ἐν vero, Macedones, Cyprios, et alios Asiæ populos ἰν dixisse constat ex Hesychio, et aliis grammaticis " — Vossius, 331.

† On referring to Gruter's Collection, p 1036, we find an inscription given from the island of Chios. The copy which I made on the spot, enables us to correct some of the errors. Instead of the word ΑΜΠΑΔΑ read ΛΑΜΠΑΔΑ, and in another line, instead of ΛΡΤΙ ΔΕ ΦΗΒΕΙ ΘΑΛΛΩΝ, read ΑΡΤΙ Δ ΕΦΗΒΕΙΑΙΣ ΘΑΛΛΩΝ.

Line 5. AI is written H; we find instances of this change also in some of the contractions in the Doric infinitive moods, as ἀδῖν, for διδᾶι, ἀγαπῆν, and ὁρῆ· Greg 228. Ed. Schaefer

3d Inscrip.

L. 1. Υ for Ω, as χελύνη in Sappho for χελώνη, the ancient Romans also wrote *funtes* and *frundes*, for *fontes* and *frondes*

L. 5 I is written for ε, as in ΔΑΜΟΤΕΛΙΟΣ in the second inscription; and for ει, as in ἐπίδει. The Cretans, and some of the Dorians, said Θιός for Θεός. Valck. Theoc. 286.

L. 9. Ὀφείλω δ' οὐδεὶ οὐθέ.. Diog Laer. Platonis, v. 1 189.

L. 10 The sense of ἀπέχει is explained by Suidas; ἀπέχω αἰτιατικῆ ἀντὶ τοῦ ἀπέλαζον· καὶ αὖθις ἐν Ἐπιγράμματι, τὸ χρέος ἀπέχεις.

L. 11 ΑΠΟΔΕΔΟΑΝΘΙ, the common termination would be ΑΝΤΙ, as ἑστάκαιτ· for ἑστήκασι, Valck. Theoc. 374; and ἴσαντι for ἴσασι, Greg. 324.

L 14. ΣΟΥΝ for ΣΥΝ. " *Illud* ου *pro* υ *in multis scriptum est* Valck. Theoc. 279. The Lacedaemonians said ἀπέσσουα for ἀπέσσυται. Palm. Exerc. 60

Id. Πέτορες Æol *pro* πέττορες, τέτταρες *unde et pctorrita.* Hemsterh. note 59. Pollux it. 1059.

L 15. FIΚΑΤΙ, Βεικατι Hesychius, Ϛικατι, Marm. Heracl.

Translation.

1.

In the archonship of Thynarchus, in the month Theluthius, I, Archiatus, son of Eumelus, quæstor*, paid the undermentioned sums belonging to a contract, cancelling †, according to the decree of the people, with the polemarchs and inspectors ‡, the writings in the hands of Euphron, and Phidias, and Pasiclinus, and Timomelus,

---

* If the word in the third line of the original is ΧΗΟΣ, it is probably written for ΧΑΙΟΣ ἀγαθόν — Constant Lex

† Ἀναιρεῖσθαι τὴν συγγραφὴν, syngrapham irritam facere — Bud. 153.

‡ γατόπτης ἐπιτηρητής. — Const Lex.

Phocians, and Demoteles, son of Lysidemus, and Dionysius, son of Cephisodorus of Chæronea.   (Here the sum is stated.)

2.

In the archonship of Thynarchus, in the month Alalcomenius, Arnon, son of Polycles, quæstor, paid to Eubulus, Phocian, son of Archidemus, the undermentioned sums belonging to a contract, being the remainder which was due to him, cancelling according to the decree of the people, with the polemarchs and inspectors, the bonds which are in the hands of Sophilus, and Euphron, Phocians, and Dionysius the Chæronean, son of Cephisodorus, and Lysidemus, son of Demoteles.   (Here the sum is stated.)

3

In the archonship of Thynarchus at Orchomenus, in the month Alalcomenius, and in the archonship of Mencœtas, son of Archelaus at Elatea, in the first month, an agreement is made between Eubulus of Elatea and the city of Orchomenus.   Since Eubulus has received from that city all the money that was due to him, according to the contracts made while Thynarchus was archon in the month Theluthius, and nothing now is owing to him from the city, but he has received every thing; and those who are in possession of the contracts have returned them to the city,—it is agreed that for a given time, Eubulus should have the yearly right of pasturage for four cows, two hundred mares, twenty sheep, and a thousand she-goats.   The beginning of this time shall be the year following [*] the archonship of Thynarchus, at Orchomenus, and Eubulus shall give an account to the quæstor and to the - - - of the produce of the sheep, and goats, and cows, and mares; and - - - - - - - - - an account also shall be taken of any number more than those which are written down in the agreement granted to him; or ten times - - - -
- - - - - - - - - - - - - - - - - -

---

[*] A similar form of date occurs in the Corcyrean inscription, p. 415. Montf. Di Ital μηνὶ Εὐκλείῳ τῷ μετὰ πρότανιν Ἀριστομένη.

XXI.

From the Troad.   See Dr. Hunt's Journal, p. 106.

Temples and altars were raised in the provinces by the Greeks, not only to the Emperors, but also to the Governors of them.   (Mém. de l'Ac. des. Ins xviii 155.)   Even Verres in Sicily had his temples and annual festivals   This inscription commemorates Agrippa, and names him TON ΠΑΤΡΩΝΑ ΚΑΙ ΕΥΕΡΓΕΤΗΝ, these words occur also in a Corcyrean inscription published by Spon   Agrippa is styled συγγενὲς; the word applies to that relation which the inhabitants of the Troad supposed to exist between themselves and the Romans   Van Dale, Diss. 312. " *Ilienses maxime sibi gloriæ ducebant Romanos à se ortos fuisse.*"

It is not difficult to determine the period of Agrippa's life to which the inscription refers.   He went into Asia for the first time in the year of Rome 731, and having remained governor there ten years, he returned in 741. (Joseph. lib. xvi c. 4. ; Mém de l'Ac. des Ins lxii. 40)   During his residence in Asia, he remitted at the intercession of Herodes, to the inhabitants of Ilium, the payment of the sum of 100,000 drachmæ, a fine imposed on them as a punishment for the danger which, in consequence of some negligence on their part, his daughter Julia had incurred.   She was passing by night the Scamander to go to Ilium , the river had swollen suddenly, and she was with difficulty saved   (Nicol. Damas. in Excerp Vales 416)   It is probable that other people of the district of the Troad might on this occasion have expressed their gratitude to Agrippa

We may close our remarks on these Greek inscriptions by observing, that the Morley marbles brought to England from Sedgikeui, near Smyrna, in 1732, and relating to Crato, son of Zotichus, are now in the vestibule of the public library at Cambridge.   A copy of them is given by Maittaire at the end of the Mar Oxon , and he supposes them to be of the date between 158 and 151 B.C

ON THE TOPOGRAPHY OF ATHENS.

[*BY MR HAWKINS*]

The public buildings of Athens are often mentioned in the writings of the ancients, but for the most part, in so cursory a way, as to afford us very little information about their relative position. Nor is it possible, I believe, to supply this deficiency without the aid of Pausanias.* For although it be true, that there are many passages in those writings, which point out the situation of two or more buildings in respect to each other, or their general bearing from one central point, the Acropolis; yet, it is Pausanias alone, who gives us the arrangement of the whole, and conducts us in a regular succession from one object to another

Pausanias, therefore, (whose professed purpose it was to describe *the antiquities* of Athens,) must be regarded as our safest guide; and the work of Meursius, who has collected under one point of view all that relates to this subject, will prove a very useful commentary on that author.†

---

* Of the works of Heliodorus Periegetes, who gave an account of the Acropolis, of Menecles or Callistratus, who described Athens; and of Philochorus, who wrote on Attica, nothing remains but the citations that are given us by Suidas, Harpocration, Hesychius, Pausanias, and others

† There are few passages in ancient authors illustrative of the history and antiquities of Athens and Attica which have escaped the diligence of this critic, but those who consult him must exercise their own judgment in the use which they make of these materials, in proof of which I need only mention, that Meursius has quoted indiscriminately the passages which relate to the three temples of Jupiter Olympius, and that he seems never to have suspected that the temple of Bacchus, which is mentioned by Pausanias, was the same as the temple of Bacchus in Limnis. The same want of discrimination is manifest in his account of the 'Ωδεῖα.

But even Pausanias requires every assistance which can be afforded by modern information, and particularly by the best plans that have been taken of the locality of Athens, while on the other hand, these plans derive almost all their interest from the details with which he has filled them. How far they both agree, in all those points where they can be compared, or rather, with what accuracy they usually coincide; will appear in the course of the following remarks which accompany the progress of Pausanias through Athens, and are written under a conviction of the necessity of pointing out the ill consequences of deserting such a guide.

To render this view of the subject more clear and intelligible, it may be proper to give a preliminary account of the various attempts that have been made to lay down an accurate plan of Athens.

The first regular plan of Athens was published in Fanelli's Atene Attica, about the year 1704. It appears to have been engraved from an actual survey made in 1687, by the engineers who were employed at the siege of the Acropolis. The situation of the principal ruins is laid down in this plan with a tolerable degree of accuracy; and it has been copied with a few corrections and additions by Dr. Chandler, in the 2d volume of his travels, as well as by Le Roi, in his Antiquities of Athens.

The second was composed by Stuart, on the basis of a regular trigonometrical survey, made during his stay there in the years 1751, 1752, 1753, but it was not published till many years after his death.

The atlas to the travels of Anacharsis has supplied us with a third, constructed by Mon*. Barbié du Boccage, after the observations which were made on the spot by Mon*. Foucheron in 1781.

And lastly, we have a fourth by Fauvel, published in the atlas to the travels of Olivier, which is by far the most accurate of all. The long residence of this last-mentioned gentlemen at Athens, (a period of seventeen years,) had enabled him not only to make the necessary trigonometrical observations for such a work, but even to introduce most of those details which had been omitted by other topographers, (for instance the streets of the modern city); and from the examin-

ation which I made of the MS. drawing of this plan when I was last at
Athens, I have no hesitation in bearing testimony to its superior
merit.   I shall here however beg leave to observe, that although both
Stuart and Fauvel have laid down what they conceive to be the remains of the old city walls, as far as they were able to trace them
with any degree of precision, yet when we consider the account
which Thucydides gives of the hasty construction of these * walls,
the long interval which has since elapsed, together with the various
revolutions that have taken place, we can hardly expect to find any
indisputable remains of them.   Modern times, too, have witnessed
a succession of walls built round the present city, the last of which
consumed even the few remaining materials of the old; as I had an
opportunity of ascertaining, by a comparison of Stuart's plan with
the ground it represented

In the two plans of Athens, which I have pointed out as best qualified to assist our enquiries, we shall find the relative position of
those ancient buildings which still subsist, together with the form and
position of the Acropolis, and the monuments of antiquity within it.
These may be regarded as so many fixed points, by the aid of which,
and of Pausanias, we may ascertain the names of such buildings, as
are too mutilated and imperfect to afford any internal evidence of
their destination ; but unfortunately, *data* of this description are
wanting to ascertain the position, extent, and figure of that most
important part of the city, the Ceramicus ; for of all the public buildings which once adorned it, and which were so venerable on account
of their antiquity, and so interesting in respect to the history of the
arts, scarcely a vestige remains. †

---

* Ἡ οἰκοδομία κατὰ σπουδὴν ἐγένετο οἱ γὰρ θεμέλιοι παντοίων λίθων ὑποκεῖνται, καὶ οὐ ξυνειργασ-
μένων ἐστιν ᾗ, ἀλλ' ὡς ἕκαστόν ποτε προσέφερον πολλαὶ τε στῆλαι ἀπὸ σημάτων καὶ λίθοι
εἰργασμένοι ἐγκατελέγησαν.   Lib i

† I have used this qualified expression, because the single column of white marble which
is marked in Stuart's plan still remains here, and is said by M. Fauvel, who has dug to its
foundation, to be in its right place.   He found two or three other columns in the same
line with it, and is of opinion that they belonged to a Stoa or portico

We must have recourse therefore, in this instance, to written authorities alone, and we shall find that Pausanias, with the help of some occasional information from other writers of antiquity, will to a certain extent supply the deficiency.

Pausanias describes the approach to the city in two different directions. ' After mentioning very briefly what deserved notice on the road from Phalerum, he speaks of the ruins of the long walls, (that had been rebuilt by Conon,) on the road from the Piræus; and he arrives at another gate of the city, which we can have little doubt must have been the Piræan. Here it is that Pausanias begins his description of Athens, and as this is a point of so much importance in respect to what follows, I shall endeavour to ascertain its true position.

It is evident that the line of the northern long wall must point out the direction of the gate here noticed, both in respect to the Piræus and the Acropolis, and it is fortunate that so much of this wall as will serve to ascertain its general direction is still in existence. The foundations may be traced to the extent of a mile and a half along the modern road, and this portion of the wall is perfectly straight and nearly level. From the western end, which butts against a hill near the Piræus, I observed that the Parthenon bore precisely over the eastern end of the line, the Propylæa appearing to the left of it. If we advance in the same direction from the eastern end of the wall towards the Acropolis, we shall arrive by a gradual ascent at a hollow between the hills of the Museum and Pnyx, which is the modern way from the Piræus to the Acropolis, and here are still to be seen some small vestiges of a gate and of the city-walls. We must therefore regard this as the Piræan gate, which in fact it is admitted to be by many who have published their remarks on the topography of Athens; and the question next to be considered, is, in

---

' The long walls having been destroyed a century before the time of Pausanias, that traveller probably alludes to a more direct line of road from Phalerum, otherwise he would scarcely have noticed two separate roads

what new direction, Pausanias advances by the Stoæ which he describes, towards the Ceramicus. *   It is in vain to attempt ascertaining this by any remains of the public buildings which formerly stood in that quarter, for, as I have already observed, they no longer exist but there is one natural feature among the objects which engaged the attention of Pausanias beyond the Ceramicus. which may be recognised without difficulty ; I mean the fountain which he calls Enneacrunos, and which Thucydides identifies with Calliroe ; a name which, after a lapse of more than 2,000 years, it still retains. †   A little way, too, farther on, in the same direction, were the remains of the Eleusinium, when Stuart visited Athens   These have since been wholly removed, and it is no small obligation which we owe to that traveller that he had previously measured and described them with so much accuracy.   These objects suffice to ascertain the general bearing of the Ceramicus from the Piræan gate, which is south-easterly, and in some measure, too, its extent ; but the breadth of the Ceramicus, as it is limited on one side by the walls of the city, and on the other by the buildings immediately under the Acropolis, could not have exceeded one half of its length   We are not informed by Pausanias whether it extended as far as the walls, but as he notices a gate near the Stoa called the Poikile, and as it appears by a passage in Æschines ‡ that the Poikile was in the public square. and from another in Lucian, that it was in the Ceramicus, it is evident that the walls of the city must have been very near, if not contiguous to

---

* Σtoαὶ δὲ εἰσιν ἀπο των πυλῶν, ἐς τὸν Κεραμεικον   The Ceramicus, therefore, could not have been far from this point

† Stuart is the first who notices this very remarkable fact, and he speaks of Calliroe as a copious and beautiful spring which flows into the channel of the Ilissus   The Albanian women of Athens wash their clothes here, and the water is collected in a small circular bason or pit for that purpose   Near it there is a fall of several feet, in the bed of the Ilissus, and some perforations may be perceived in the face of the rock, which are supposed by Fauvel to be the traces of Enneacrunos

‡ In Ctesiph —in Piscat both quoted by Barthelemy —The words of Lucian are, Ἐνταῦθα γὰρ ἐν Κεραμεικῷ ὑτομενοῦμεν αὐτην   ἡ δὲ ἤδε που ἀφίξεται, ἐπανιοῦσα ἐξ Ἀκαδημίας, ὡς περιπατήσεις καὶ ἐν τῷ Ποικίλ-

the Ceramicus. Nor have we the means of knowing from Pausanias, whether the Phaleric gate opened directly into the Ceramicus, although it is not improbable that one of the gates in this quarter was so designated in the following passage of Philostratus, quoted by Meursius Περὶ δ᾽ εἰς τὸ τῶν τε μιῶν βουλεὶ μιν, ὁ οὶ ἀκοδόμηλαι παρὰ τὰς τῶ Κεραμικῶ ὑι ας.

Thus much may be said in regard to the breadth, extent, and direction of the Ceramicus, which comprised the Agora or public square. Pausanias, indeed, omits all mention of the latter, until he has finished his account of the Ceramicus (if we except those allusions to it which are observable in the epithet he gives to the bronze Hermes on his way to the Poikile), but as it appears from various passages of Æschines and of Lucian already quoted, that the Poikile Stoa was in the Agora as well as in the Ceramicus, we must necessarily draw the conclusion that the Agora likewise was in the Ceramicus. Barthelemy observes, that, according to Æschines, the Metroum was in the Agora, and he proves by a passage of the same author, as well as by the authority of Plutarch, Suidas, and Harpocration, that the palace of the senate, βουλευτρα, was there likewise. * The Hermes, or a Stoa so called, is moreover placed by Barthelemy in the Agora, first on the authority of Mnesimachus (*apud Athenæum*), who said in one of his comedies, "Go you into the Agora, to the Hermes !" and on that of Xenophon (*de Mag Equit.*) who says,—"At certain festivals it is proper that the horsemen render the homage which is due to the temples and the statues which are in the Agora They will commence at the Hermes, make the circuit of the Agora, and return to the Hermes "

The Agora, therefore, although not expressly named by Pausanias in his account of the public buildings which were situated in the Ceramicus, must be understood as comprehended in its periphery, and as occupying a part of the ground which he passes over

The proofs already given of the Ceramicus having been situated to the south of the Acropolis, may be regarded as conclusive, and I

* Æschin. in Ctesiph Plut s Rhet Vit t ii Suid in Μητρῳν

have only farther to observe, that this idea of its position coincides with all that we know of the early history of Athens, and the local circumstances which seem to have decided the choice of the first settlers. To illustrate this remark, I shall quote at length the words of Thucydides on this subject — " Before this period (that is, before Theseus had prevailed upon all the scattered population of the borough towns of Attica to remove to Athens), that which is now the citadel, and particularly that part which lies to *the south* of it, constituted what was called the city. This is proved, as well by the temples of the deities that are within the citadel as by those which are erected without it on this side of the city; such as the temple of the Olympian Jupiter, and the Pythium; the temple of Terra, and that of Bacchus in Limnis, in honour of whom the more ancient Bacchanalian festivals are celebrated on the twelfth day of the month Anthesterion; which custom is still retained by the Ionians of Attic descent. Other ancient temples are built in the same quarter. The public fountain too, which, since it has been fitted up [*] in the manner we now see by the tyrants, has been called Enneacrunos, but which formerly, when the springs were open, bore the name of Callirroe, being situated near, was preferred for use upon most occasions. And even now, in compliance with ancient custom, they think it necessary to make use of this water previous to the connubial rites, and upon other religious occasions. And further, it is owing to this their ancient residence in the Acropolis, that it is called the city by the Athenians to this very day."

Now, the temple of the Olympian Jupiter, which is here noticed by Thucydides, must have been that which Pausanias says was built by Deucalion, and which appears from his narrative to have stood somewhere near, if not absolutely within the peribolus of Hadrian's Olympium. An image, too, of the Pythian Apollo is noticed by Pausanias in the same quarter, although the temple itself seems to have no longer existed; and the Temple of Terra ($\Gamma\tilde{\eta}$) I suspect to be

_____

[*] Ὅυτω κατασκευασάντων, conjectura Dukeri ex Hesychio prolata et tribus Codd Pariss. confirmata

the same as that which Pausanias denominates the temple of ἡ Κουροτρόφος and Δήμητρα χλόη *, and places under the southern flanks of the Acropolis, between which and the Olympium, if we follow the order of his description, he fixes the position of the temple of Bacchus in Limnis. By the other ancient temples which stood in the same quarter, Thucydides must have meant several more of those which are placed by Pausanias on the south of the theatre, or in the Ceramicus, for instance, the Metroum, the temple of Venus Urania, &c. as well as the Leocorium, the Æacontéum, and others, which he does not notice. †

Having now proved both from the text of Pausanias, and other historical evidence, compared with existing monuments and local circumstances, that the interior Ceramicus was on the south side of the Acropolis, it follows that Barthelemy and other writers are mistaken in placing it on the north side, on the authority of a single passage in Plutarch's Life of Sylla; and it is unfortunate that this mistake has led the former to misplace almost every monument of antiquity in his plan of Athens ‖, and involuntarily to mislead his readers. But as the reputation of such a man as Barthelemy is not to be impeached upon light grounds, or without a hearing, and the authority upon which he relies is very specious, I shall devote some time to its examination

The passage to which I allude is as follows — After describing the slaughter which took place when Athens was taken by assault, Plutarch adds, " for besides those who fell in other parts of the city, the blood which was shed in the Agora alone covered the whole Cera-

---

* Κουροτρόφος ἡ Suidas But Γαῖα and Δήμητρα were originally the same, " Nec sine causa Terram eandem appellabant matrem, et Cererem " Varro

† The Leocorium is placed on the authority of Demosthenes in the Ceramicus, Demosth in Conon — and the Temple of Æacus, on that of Herodotus, Lib v c 89

‖ Barthelemy, in acknowledging his obligations for the able assistance of M Barbie de Bocage, takes upon himself the whole responsibility for these errors — " Comme nous différons sur quelques points principaux de l'intérieur, il ne doit pas répondre des erreurs qu'on trouvera dans cette partie du plan "

micus as far as Dipylon ; nay, there are several who assure us, that it ran through the gates and overspread the suburbs." Now, the position of the gate here mentioned is ascertained by the following passage in Livy. — " *Ab Dipylo accessit   Porta ea, velut in ore urbis posita, major aliquanto patentiorque quam ceteræ, est, et intra eam extraque latæ sunt viæ, ut et oppidani dirigere aciem à foro ad portam possent   et extra limes mille fermè passus, in Academiæ Gymnasium ferens, pediti equitique hostium liberum spatium præberet.*" Lib xxxi c. 24.   And its vicinity to the Academy is confirmed by the testimony of Cicero. — " *Sex illa à Dipylo stadia in Academiam confecimus.*"

The gate, therefore, called Dipylon, must have stood on the north or the north-west side of the Acropolis, for it was in this direction that the Academy was situated.   And there is a gate of the modern city in the same quarter, which leads to a spot still distinguished by the name of Kathymia, *   or Akathymia.

---

* The following extract from my Journal, Nov 1794, relates to this curious fact —
" The weather being dry and cool in consequence of the north-easterly wind, we took a walk this evening to a spot about one mile north from the city walls, which, from the circumstance of its being called Ἀκαδημία (Acathymia) by the peasants of Attica, must have been without doubt the site of the celebrated Academy   It is situated near two little hills or rather knolls of ground, one called Ἅγιο Μιλιανὸς, and the other Ἅγιος Νικολαος, from two chapels which stand on them

" All antiquaries have agreed in placing the academy on this side of the city, and at this distance from it, but as there existed no remains of the buildings which once adorned it, its position was not known with any degree of certainty, for the present Athenians are too ignorant of their own history, and too inattentive to the researches of curious travellers, to have been struck with this coincidence between the ancient and the modern name of this interesting spot.

" It was a mere accident which threw it in my way, and led to the discovery, for M Fauvel appears to have been ignorant of it

" The Consul (Procopius) not being thoroughly acquainted with the topography of the plain, we enquired of several peasants whom we met the position of the spot called Akathymia, and were thus enabled to ascertain it with more precision

" It is rather extraordinary that the spot should still be distinguished by any particular name, since it is now an open piece of ground, and presents nothing remarkable in its appearance   The name is confined to an area not exceeding five acres in the lowest and most stagnant part of the plain   The soil here is a stiff loam, which being naturally too tenacious of moisture, has been improved by drainage.   A few scattered olive trees

Unfortunately, however, for the credit of Plutarch *, on whose authority so much reliance is placed, the rise of the ground on this side of the Acropolis, towards the spot where this gate stood, points out very clearly the impossibility of the occurrence which he mentions.

This alone would lead us to suspect that the Dipylon had been substituted by mistake for some other gate which lay more to the south; and there is a story told by the same writer in his Moralia, which countenances this supposition. He is treating of the following question, — Which have the most natural sagacity, land or water animals? " When Pericles," says he, " built the Hecatompedon in the Acropolis of Athens, it so fell out, that the stones were to be fetched, every day, the distance of many stadia; and a number of carriages were made use of for that purpose. Among the rest of the mules that laboured hard in this employment, there was one that, although dismissed on account of age, would still go down to the Ceramicus, and meeting the carts that brought the stones, would be always in their company, running by their sides, as it were by way of en-

grew on it. and some paces farther west we saw a number of gardens and vineyards which contained fruit-trees of a more exuberant growth than in any other part of the plain. These gardens, in fact, chiefly supply the market of Athens with fruit and vegetables, and they are distinguished by their superior verdure from several distant points of view This is attributed to the moisture of the soil here, from which cause the air is said to be very un-wholesome in the summer months   The air of the Academy is recorded to have been of this description, and Plato on that account was advised to remove from it "

* The passage is given by Meursius —'Αυτὸ· δὲ Σύλλας το μεταξὺ τῆς Πειραικῆς πύλης και τῆ· Ἱερᾶς κατασκαψας και συνομαλύνας - - - - ὁ περι τὴν ἀγοραν φίλος ἐπέσχε παντα τὸν ἐντὸς τοῦ Διπυλου Κεραμεικόν   The gate, Ἱερά, or Sacred, was probably no other than the gate Dipylon (see a subsequent part of this enquiry). If some word, τῶν Ἡρίων for instance, could be substituted in the room of Ἱερᾶ·, referring to the gates, called Ἡρίαι by the Etymolog, and probably near the Piræum, there would be little difficulty in the passage of Plutarch The fall of the ground here would have permitted the blood to have flowed in this direc-tion, supposing the fact stated by Plutarch to have literally happened, and not to have been an exaggeration   The slight alteration also of τῶν δύο πυλῶν (referring to the two gates just mentioned), for τοῦ Διπύλου, would contribute to establish the writer's con-sistency

3 R

couragement, and to excite them to work cheerfully," &c. &c. * Now
it is highly improbable, that the road which leads to the Propylæa
from the northern part of the city, and which is naturally so much
more steep and difficult, should have been made use of for this
purpose, the Ceramicus, therefore, which is here spoken of, could
not have been on the north side of the Acropolis, but on the south;
where the ascent in fact is very gradual and wide.

Having made the tour of the Ceramicus, which, in every point of
view, first deserved the notice of an antiquary, and having led us
back to the point where he began it, Pausanias proceeds to describe
the remainder of the city, before he visits the Acropolis.

I have had occasion to remark, that Pausanias has in no part of his
description of the Ceramicus expressly mentioned the Agora. He
now however conducts us to one, which from its contiguity to other
buildings which stood there, viz. the Gymnasium of Ptolemy and
the Theseum, appears to have been situated on the north of the
Acropolis. The position of this Agora in the plan of Athens is
ascertained by a Doric portal, which both from its plan and proportions, and an edict of the Emperor Hadrian regulating the price
of oil, inscribed on the jamb of a door-case which forms a part of the
original structure, is supposed to have been the entrance into it.

This, I think, must be the same Agora that is incidentally mentioned
by Strabo, in the account which he gives of Eretria — Ἐρετρίας δ' οἱ
μὲν ἀπὸ Μακίστου τῆς Τριφυλίας ἀποικισθῆναι φασιν ὑπ' Ἐρετριέως· οἱ δ'ἀπὸ τῆς
Ἀθηνῆσιν Ἐρετρίας, ἢ νῦν ἐςιν ἀγορά. And it is not improbable that it had
been removed from the Ceramicus, where it had been polluted with
the blood of so many citizens, to a part of the city which was at
this period in every respect more central and convenient for it, and
where it is remarkable that the market of the modern Athenians still
continues to be held at the present day.

From this Agora, which, on the authority of Strabo, I shall call
the new one, and which Pausanias seems to have noticed, merely on

---

* This story is repeated in the life of Cato, it is related also by Ælian

account of the altar of pity which was in it, we pass on to the Gymnasium of Ptolemy, which he tells us was not far distant. The situation of this building is determined by some actual remains of it which were found by Stuart, compared with an inscription which had been removed from thence, recording the dedication of a statue to Ptolemy the son of Juba. Farther proofs of this appropriation have since been discovered by Fauvel and others, in the plan and dimensions of the building.

In the same direction, too, πρὸς δὲ τῷ γυμνασίῳ, was the temple of Theseus, upon which Pausanias dwells with pleasure. There can be little doubt, that this is the fine temple which is still in existence on the N. W. of the Acropolis, both on account of its vicinity to the preceding building, and the subjects of some of the sculptures on it. It is true, that Pausanias omits all mention of a ναός, calling the building simply ἱερὸν and στοάς; but this is not unusual with him, nor is he very consistent with himself in the use of any of the terms which he applies to temples * ; besides, the pictures of Micon which he here notices, imply the existence of a Naos, on the walls of which they must have been painted "Why," (to borrow the words of

---

* The following, however, is an instance of his discrimination —Τέμενος καὶ ἱερὸν καὶ ναὸν Ἀρτέμιδι ἐποιήσαντο Lib v c 6 — My readers will be glad to see how these terms are explained in Lennep's' Etymologicum Linguæ Græcæ —
"Ναὸς sive Νεὼ ,
commodè Hesychius interpretatur οἶκος, ἔδρα θεῶ. προσκυνεῖται - - - - - - - - - Ἱερὸν autem et ναὸν, sive νεὼν, quando connectuntur, veluti apud Thucyd lib. iv. § 90 ; περὶ τὸ ἱερὸν καὶ τὸν νεὼν (ubi plura notavit Dukerus) ita distingui debent, ut ἱερὸν significet τὸ τέμενος sive totam aream deo consecratam, humanisque usibus exemptam, τὸ ἱερὸν χωρίον ναὸν vero ipsum fanum vel templi ædificium Ἱερὸν autem intelligendum relinquit δῶμα, et sæpius adsciscit ἅγιον, &c &c
Σηκὸν,
- - - - - - - - - - - Porro σηκὸν in templis deorum eximiè dictam fuisse cellam, in quâ dei sedes esset, quæ pp. etiam ναὸς vocaretur, observavit cel Valck ad Herodoti, lib. vi 333. p 146 - - - - - Proprie ναὸι & ἱερὰ sunt deorum , heroum σηκοὶ, ut docuit Pollux, lib i segm 6. Ammonius et Thomas Magister in voce. Eam differentiam, etsi plerumque negligatur, sæpe tamen observavit Pausanias." Conf omnino cl D'Arnaud, Animadv. Græc p 1—3.

Stuart) " the labours of Hercules should make so considerable a part of the ornaments of this temple will appear the less extraordinary, when we recollect the respect and gratitude which Theseus professed towards that hero, who was his kinsman; had delivered him from a tedious captivity, and had restored him to his country, on his return to which, he consecrated to Hercules all the places that the gratitude of his citizens had formerly dedicated to himself, four only excepted; and changed their names from Thesea to Heraclea. V. Plut. in vit. Thes. Nor could it be esteemed a slight compliment to Theseus, when on building this temple to his honour, their labours were thus placed together." *

We are now led back by Pausanias to the foot of the Acropolis, where he places the Anacéum or ancient temple of the † Dioscuri; and just above this temple he places the second enclosure, Τέμενος, of Aglaurus. Here it appears from what he says, that the rock was very precipitous, ἔνθα ἦν μάλιστα ἄ-τομοι, although it was here that the Persians had scaled the Acropolis. The passage of Herodotus which relates to this exploit, speaks not of a Τέμενος, but of a temple, ἱρὸν, of Agraulus, leaving us in doubt, however, whether it was above or below the declivity, or whether it was within or without the Acropolis; and although it was evidently the intention of that writer to point out with some degree of precision the situation of this temple, and the spot where the Persians ascended, yet there is an ambiguity in the expression which has given rise to two very opposite and contradictory explanations, the words ὄπισθεν δὲ τῶν πυλέων, καὶ τῆς ἀνόδου, being supposed by Chandler, Larcher, Barthelemy, and others, who are supported by the authority of Ulpian, to refer to the vicinity of the entrance, while a more recent critic, Mr. Wilkins, is of opinion, that they apply to the other end of the Acropolis.

---

* Meursius seems to be of opinion that there were several temples dedicated to Theseus, but all the passages which he quotes evidently refer to one and the same temple.

† Lucian alludes in Timone to the destruction of this temple by lightning —'Ο δὲ κεραυνὸς εἰς τὸ ἀνάκειον παρασκήψας, ἐκεῖνό τε κατέφλεξε

Whatever may be the decision of grammarians in regard to the
literal meaning of this expression of Herodotus, it is certain that the
latter interpretation of it is more consistent than the former with the
general sense of the passage; for how, when the army of Xerxes is
stated to be encamped directly in front of the entrance to the Acropolis,
and so near it as the Areopagus, could this end of the citadel be
supposed to be so negligently guarded as to be taken by surprise in
the way here described?

We may be allowed therefore to place that part of the precipice,
by which the Persians ascended, at the eastern end of the platform of
the Acropolis, where in fact Pausanias evidently understood it to have
been, the Prytaneum, which he says, was not far from it, being unquestionably on this side of the hill. It follows, that what Herodotus
says of a temple, Ἱερὸν of Aglaurus, must be applied to the Τέμενος of
that personage, which Pausanias places on the eastern declivity of
the hill.

We come next to the Prytaneum, which was hard by, πλησίον δὲ
Πρυτανίου ἐστι, and on the lower slope of the hill; for according to
Pausanias, you passed from hence into the lower part of the city,
ἐντεῦθεν ἰοῦσιν ἐς τὰ κάτω τῆς πόλεως, to the temple of Serapis; near which,
he adds, was the temple of Ilythya.* All this is perfectly consistent
with the natural form of the ground on the eastern side of the
Acropolis, where the soil, as I was informed, had accumulated to the
depth of 18 feet.

The two last-mentioned temples must have been in the way from
the Prytanéum towards the Olympium, to which we are now conducted. Here Pausanias seems not to distinguish between an Ἱερὸν
and a Ναὸς, for he applies both terms to this temple. Within its
peribolus, he says, were a temple of Saturn and Rhea, and a Τέμενος
of this goddess, who is styled Olympia. All the particulars which
he, as well as Vitruvius, give us of this temple, impress us with a

---

* Vide the distinction which Pausanias makes between this goddess and Latona.

high idea of its magnificence. We have little difficulty therefore in appropriating to the Olympium those gigantic columns of the Corinthian order, which attract the notice of travellers on the south-eastern side of the Acropolis.* But as this opinion is contested, I shall briefly recapitulate the arguments upon which it is founded.

In the first place, the Peribolus of this temple agrees very nearly with the dimensions which are assigned by Pausanias, to the Peribolus of the Olympium.

Secondly, it is of the Corinthian order; which Vitruvius states the Olympium to have been, and as it was an hypæthral temple, with ten columns in each front, and a double row on each flank, it is very probably the same to which that author alludes in a very obscure, if not corrupt passage of his third book. †

Thirdly, the number and magnitude of the columns which must have belonged to this temple when entire, fully correspond with the notion that Vitruvius gives of its magnificence, and it would be

---

* These columns (of which 124 once surrounded the cell) are six feet in diameter and nearly sixty feet high. Vitruvius speaks of this temple in the following terms —" Id autem opus non modo vulgo, sed etiam in paucis a magnificentia nominatur " And afterwards he proceeds,—" In Asty vero Olympium amplo modulorum comparatu, Corinthiis symetriis et proportionibus (uti supra scriptum est) architectandum Cossutius suscepisse memoratur " It is spoken of in the same terms of admiration by Livy —" Magnificentiæ vero in deos vel Jovis Olympii templum Athenis, unum in terris inchoatum pro magnitudine dei, potest testis esse."

† Vitruvius in his third book, where he speaks of hypæthral temples, observes, that they had ten columns in each front, and a double row of columns in each flank, with other particulars, concluding what he had to say upon the subject of hypæthral temples, with the following remark —" Hujus autem exemplar Romæ non est, sed Athenis octastylos, et in templo Olympio " Ed Schneideri. Here the allusion to an octastyle temple seems to be perfectly inconsistent with what precedes it, and therefore cannot have been originally intended by Vitruvius. It is evident that he alludes to some example of what he had been speaking of, and as he makes use of the expression Olympio, it is probable that he means the Olympium at Athens. But the difficulty lies in the word octastylos, and the MSS. afford us no ground for supposing it to be a corruption We must therefore condemn it upon other grounds of criticism, and as the word contains the elements of its own correction, adopt Mr Wilkins's ingenious conjecture by substituting in asty, which at once gives it sense and consistency.

absurd to appropriate them to any other building which Pausanias has mentioned *

Fourthly, the situation of this temple is near the fountain of Enneacrunos or Callirŏe, where some old authors have placed † it, and there is reason to believe, from what Pausanias relates of the older temple built by Deucalion, that it occupies the same site as that, which we know from the passage of Thucydides already quoted to have been on this side of the Acropolis.

I am of opinion, that much of the obscurity which has hitherto attended this enquiry will be removed, if I add something on the history of this temple.

There were undoubtedly three temples erected at Athens to the Olympian Jupiter, at three very distinct and remote æras.

The first was built by Deucalion.

The second was begun by Pisistratus, and continued by his sons, but left unfinished.

The third, or the temple of which we see the remains, was begun by Perseus, or Antiochus Epiphanes, continued by the kings in alliance with Augustus, and completed by Hadrian. The first was probably a building of a very rude construction, the second, a Doric temple, the third, was Corinthian and hypæthral.

The participation of the sons of Pisistratus in the erection of the second temple, is intimated in a passage of the Politics of Aristotle (v. 11.), καὶ τῦυ Ὀλυμπίου ἡ οἰκοδόμησις ὑπὸ Πεισιστρατιδῶι, and the expression of Dicæarchus, (Ὀλύμπιον ἡμιτελες,) ‡ shows that it was left unfinished. The following passage in the ninth book of Strabo, καὶ αὐτὸ τὸ Ὀλύμπιον, ὅπερ ἡμιτελὲς κατέλιπε τελευτῶν ὁ ἀναθεὶς βασιλεὺς, as it evidently relates to the third temple, has been restored to its original reading by the learned and ingenious editors of the French

* For instance, to the Pantheon, which has the best claim

† Ταραντῖνος δὲ ἱςορεῖ τὸν τῆ Διὸς νεὼν κατασκευάζοντας Ἀθηναίης Ἐννεακρήνε πλησίον, &c Hierocles in Procemio Hippiatricorum.

‡ Vide B E.

Strabo, who substitute Ἀντίοχος for διαβᾶς. The next great effort to
finish this structure, is recorded in the following passage of Suetonius:—
Aug. "*Cuncti (reges amici et socii) simul ædem Jovis Olympii Athenis
antiquitus inchoatam perficere communi sumptu destinaverunt, Genioque
ejus dedicare.*" But it was reserved for Hadrian to put the finishing
hand to this magnificent pile of building.

Pausanias takes the opportunity in this place of mentioning what
other public buildings had been erected by that Emperor at Athens.
After which, he continues his excursion eastward, noticing, first, the
statue of Apollo Pythius, which appears to have stood in some consecrated building, Ἱερὸν, for immediately afterwards, he observes, ἐστι
καὶ ἄλλο ἱερὸν Ἀπόλλωνος ἐπίκλησιν Δελφινίου, implying the existence of
two temples; the former of which being then perhaps in a ruinous
state or absolutely destroyed, is not named. This interpretation of
the passage is, I think, supported by Thucydides, who, among the
temples enumerated on the south side of the Acropolis, mentions the
Pythium; and still more so by Strabo, who tells us that it was near
the Olympium. Of these two temples of Apollo, as well as that of
Venus in the gardens; the temple of Hercules called Cynosarges;
the Lyceum, &c. ; all which lay in the direction which Pausanias is
now taking, and attracted his notice, no remains are now extant.

Pausanias then comes to the Ilissus, which he crosses, and arrives
at the district called Agræ, where he notices the temple of Diana
Agrotéra; finishing this excursion with some account of the Stadium
of Herodes Atticus; the site of which, now correctly ascertained by
modern travellers, confirms the idea of Pausanias's general accuracy.
Nor is the consistency of his narrative less apparent, in the circumstance of his returning at once to the Prytanéum, without mentioning
either the Olympium, the Eleusinium, or Enneacrunos, which lay in
his way, or near it, but had already been noticed.

Pausanias now starts again from the Prytanéum, which had been
fixed by his narrative at the eastern base of the Acropolis hill. The
street of the Tripods, he says, commences from this building, the
same denomination being given to the quarter of the city, (τὸ χωρίον,)

in which it stood. Of this street, one vestige only remains, the choragic monument of Lysicrates, the position of which, both with respect to the Acropolis and the Olympium, enables us to fix retro-spectively with still more precision the site of the Prytaneum, which as he is now advancing towards the theatre he has left to the north.

Before his arrival at the theatre, however, Pausanias speaks of a temple of Bacchus of the highest antiquity, which seems to have been in his way towards it. This, without doubt, is the temple of Bacchus in Limnis, mentioned by Thucydides among those very ancient buildings which stood on the south-side of the Acropolis. Few of the temples at Athens have been oftener alluded to by ancient writers. The epithet evidently implies a low or marshy situation, and as there is no ground of this description in the present city, or even adjacent to it, the temple here mentioned by Pausanias has been generally supposed to be distinct from that of Bacchus in Limnis. There is, however, sufficient evidence of their identity. First, in the position assigned by Pausanias, which is in reality the lowest part of the city, and secondly, in some springs of brackish water, which, rising at the northern base of the Acropolis, and of the hill of the Areopagus, naturally flow in this direction; nor is it surprising, as the level of the ground in most parts of the city has been raised from 10 to 18 feet, that all traces of this marshy spot should have been obliterated.

After noticing the edifice in the form of Xerxes's tent, which stood between this temple and the theatre, and to which I shall presently have occasion to recur, Pausanias conducts us to the latter, the situation of which he points out with great precision, for we learn that it stood at the foot of the rock, on the southern side of the Acropolis, and that there was a grotto or cavern immediately above it. Nothing now remains of the theatre but the cavea; but this is exactly in the position here described, a grotto occurring just above it, faced with marble pilasters that support an entablature, on which are some inscriptions, proving it to have been a choragic monument. Above this entablature is a statue of marble and two columns, on each of which are the marks of the feet of a tripod, and this may be regarded

3 s

as a farther confirmation of the accuracy of Pausanias, who notices a tripod over the grotto and some statues.

Dicæarchus, too, speaks of the theatre in this position ; ὁ καλόυμενος Παρθενὼν ὑπερκείμενος τοῦ Θεάτρου, and both the Theatre and the Parthenon are represented on a bronze medal of Athens, in the same situation with respect to each other. In short, I believe it would be difficult to produce a more connected chain of topographical evidence than that which confirms and illustrates this part of Pausanias's narrative.

I shall now return to the building which has been previously mentioned, but without any denomination On the authority of Plutarch and Suidas, as well as of a false reading of Jocundus in his edition of Vitruvius, this building has been generally supposed to be the Odeum of Pericles ; but it is in reality the Odeum of Themistocles, as appears by the restoration of the text in the new and excellent edition of that author by Schneider — " *Et exeuntibus e theatro sinistra parte Odeum, quod Themistocles columnis lapideis navium malis et antennis e spoliis Persicis pertexit, idem autem incensum Mithridatico bello rex Ariobarzanes restituit*" Lib. v cap 9. *

The Odeum of Pericles, therefore, can be no other than that which is noticed by Pausanias in his excursion through the Ceramicus, and near Enneacrunos, in the following words . — Τοῦ Θεάτρου δὲ ὃ καλοῦσιν, ὠδεῖον ; and by Suidas more particularly, Ὠδεῖον Ἀθήνῃσιν ὥσπερ θέατρον, ὃ πεποίηκεν, ὥς φασί, Περικλῆς εἰς τὸ ἐπιδείκνυσθαι τοὺς μουσικούς. διὰ τοῦτο γὰρ καὶ ὠδεῖον ἐκλήθη ἀπὸ τῆς ὠδῆς, ἔστι δὲ ἐν αὐτῷ δικαστήριον τοῦ Ἄρχοντος. διεμετρεῖτο δὲ καὶ ἄλφιτα ἐκεῖ. Demosthenes informs us, that it served not only for musical contests, but for assemblies of the people. Plutarch, however, appears to have confounded

---

* This is the same building to which Appian alludes in the following words Καὶ Ἀρισίων αὐτοῖς συνέφευγεν ἐμπρήσας τὸ Ὠδεῖον, ἵνα μὴ ἑτοίμοις ξύλοις αὐτίκα ὁ Σύλλα· ἔχοι τὴν ακρόπολιν ἐνοχλεῖν He adds, that Sylla permitted his soldiers to sack the city, but not to burn it In the passage of Pausanias, ποιηθῆναι δὲ τῆς σ , — σκηνῆς is probably the true reading.

this with the other Odeum, for he tells us that in point of form it resembled the tent of Xerxes.

From the theatre Pausanias conducts us to the entrance of the Acropolis, which is about due west On his way thither, which skirts along the foot of the rock, he notices the sepulchre of Kalos, and then the temple of Æsculapius, in which there was a spring of water, which affords occasion to speak of Halirrothius, the whole story respecting whom, like that which he had before related of the origin of the term Ceramicus, shows how much the Greeks were accustomed to disguise and ennoble the most trivial circumstances.* Farther on was a temple of Themis the sepulchre of Hippolytus, and lastly, the temple which was appropriated to Tellus Curotrophus and Ceres Chloe, which are unquestionably different appellations of the same deity. And here it is, at the western end of the Acropolis, that Pausanias finishes his perambulation of the city ἄςυ In the course of his narrative there appears to be both method and selection, and we may observe that he carefully avoids any recurrence to the objects he had already noticed; for instance, he finishes his second excursion at the stadium, and in his way from the theatre, although the Ceramicus must have been pretty close on his left, he notices no one building which appertains to it, confining his observation to those which stood on a higher level, or nearer the foot of the rock, and passing over the spot, on which, soon afterwards, was erected the theatre of Regilla, which he notices when speaking of the Odeum at Patræ.

Having accompanied Pausanias thus far in his perambulation, we shall not follow him into the Acropolis, because there is no difficulty in recognizing in the remains which are extant there, almost every one of the public buildings which he describes. It is in this part of his narrative, however, that he incidentally mentions the hill of the

---

* Such as a spring of brackish water and a place for the manufactory of tiles. Pausanias mentions a spring within the sacred enclosure, we may conclude it was not potable, from the nature of the two springs on the opposite side of the Acropolis, and the silence both of Pausanias and Strabo, when they speak of Enneacrunos. The true and ignoble origin of the term Ceramicus is given by Pliny, lib. xxxv c 12 Suidas in Κεραμ.

Museum, on which was the monument to a certain Syrian (Philopappus), which still crowns the summit of a hill at no great distance from
the Propylæa, on the south-west   This hill, too, he says, was within
the old walls of the city, ἐντος τοῦ περιβόλε ἀρχαίε, which is literally
true in respect to the building here spoken of, the foundations of the
old walls forming an angle on the summit of the hill, and enclosing it.

On his return from the Propylæa, Pausanias points out a few more
objects of curiosity on this side, before his final departure.   Of these,
the first in order is a grotto consecrated to Apollo and Pan, which
was situated a little below the Propylæa, and near to a spring of
water.   Here, precisely in the situation pointed out by Pausanias, a
grotto and a spring of brackish water are still observable, and a representation of the former, with all the circumstances which are
requisite to fix its identity, may be seen on a bronze medal of Athens,
which is engraved in the Atlas to the Anacharsis.

Pausanias next conducts us to the Areopagus, which was in the
vicinity of the Propylæa, and there is a rocky eminence just opposite
to that object, which, although no vestiges of a building are observable on it, is generally supposed to have been the site of this venerable
tribunal.   But there is a passage in the *Bis Accus.* of Lucian *, which,
as it fixes its position with respect to the cave of Pan, the Propylæa,
and Pnyx, and notices the ascent to it, removes nearly all doubt of its
situation   It is remarkable, that Pausanias makes no mention of
Pnyx ; but his silence may, I think, be accounted for, as Pnyx had
long ceased to be the place of assembly at the period when he visited
Athens, the Romans having then nearly abolished the forms of an independent government. † Nor is it probable that any thing in the

---

* The passage is rather too long for insertion, but a part of it, which more particularly
regards the cave of Pan, has been already quoted   The ascent to the Areopagus is
noticed in that speech of Pan, which begins with the words, Βαβαὶ τοῦ Σοφιδου

† The complaint of Athemon (vide Athenæum, lib v) closes with the words, καὶ τὴν
θεῶν χρησμοῖς καθωσιωμένην Πνύκα, ἀπηργμένην τοῦ Δημου   According to Pollux and Hesychius, it continued to be made use of only when certain magistrates were to be elected
The pulpitum looks towards the city

shape of a public building had ever existed here, for Aristophanes speaks of the people, when assembled, as seating themselves on a rock. There is a circumstance, however, mentioned in Plutarch's Life of Themistocles, which helps us to fix its situation, for he tells us it commanded a view of the sea. Now, there is a rocky eminence between the last-mentioned spot and the Museum, which answers to this description, and I know of no other within the old walls that does. The surface of the rock is there cut into a form which appears to be not ill calculated for the purpose to which Pnyx was appropriated. According to Plutarch, Pnyx must have been near the Museum, for he speaks of the hottest part of the combat of Theseus with the Amazons as having taken place between these two places; and Pnyx appears to have given its denomination to a quarter of the city, χωρίον, (vide Pollux,) which was inhabited, for Cimon dwelt there. Moreover, it was bounded by the city wall, for Suidas, in Μετα, says, Προ Πυθοδωρε ὸ ἠλ στροπιον ἦν ἐν τῆ νῦν ἔστιν ἐκκλητία πρὸς τῶ τείχει τῶ ἐν Πνυκί; and the scholiast on Aristophanes (in Avibus) tells us, on the authority of Philochorus, Ἡλιστρότιον Metonis extare πρὸς τῶ τείχει τῶ ἐν τὴ Πνυκί. (Salmas.) Enough, I believe, has been said, to fix the site of the Areopagus, Pnyx, and the Museum. The Piræan gate, as I have already mentioned, lay between the two last.

We are now arrived at the end of the topography of Athens, as it is given us by Pausanias, and in the course of these remarks, I have endeavoured to explain that topography by the help of the existing remains; but, as the progress of the narrative has been much interrupted, it may be useful to pass once more under review the whole series of positions that have been fixed by this enquiry.

The first point thus fixed, with reference to the plan of the ruins, is the Piræan gate; where Pausanias begins his description of the city. By the second, which was Enneacrunos and the Eleusinium, we obtained the general direction of the Ceramicus on the right, or to the south of the Acropolis, and thus acquired some idea of its extent. The third fixed point, is the situation of the new Agora, which is determined both by the order of the narrative, and by the remains of the Doric portal, which forms the entrance to it. The Gymnasium of Ptolemy and the Theseum are the two next. The situation of the Temenos of Aglaurus on the eastern declivity of the Acropolis, which I have taken some pains to ascertain, determines pretty nearly that of the Anacéum and the Prytanéum, as well as the site of the temple of Ilithya; all which are fixed with still more precision by the positions of the Olympium and the theatre; the last, and perhaps the least equivocal points in the topography of Athens.

Having thus established the claims of Pausanias to the merit of veracity and correctness, I shall beg leave to make some remarks on the method which is observable in his description of the antiquities of Athens, and on his omissions.

Proceeding directly from the Piræus in the direction of the northern long wall, Pausanias enters by the gate which was nearest to the Acropolis, when, turning to the right, he soon reaches the most ancient, most important, and most frequented part of the city, the Ceramicus. After making the tour of this quarter, and noticing some objects beyond it, he returns to the spot where he began, for the purpose, as it would appear, of mentioning a few buildings which he had omitted; and from thence he proceeds with the Piræan gate on his left, to the north. His course however, on this side of the Acropolis, is more desultory, for when he has noticed the new Agora, (incidentally,) the Gymnasium of Ptolemy, and the Theséum, which two last lead him far to the left, he turns suddenly round, and retraces his steps towards the Acropolis, for the purpose of visiting the Anacéum, the sacred portion of Aglaurus and the Prytanéum. From hence, he continues his course easterly to the temples of Serapis and Ilithya, the Olympium, the Delphinium, the temple of Venus in the gardens, Cynosarges, the Lycéum, the Ilissus, and the Stadium, where, in a direction about due south from the Prytanéum, he finishes his second excursion.

He starts again from the Prytanéum to commence his third excursion; and at first proceeds due south along the street of the Tripods; from whence he turns to the right, and approaches the eastern base of the hill of the Acropolis, describing some very remarkable edifices in this quarter, (the quarter of the Tripods, ἀφ' οὗ δὲ καλοῦσι τὸ χωρίον,) and then continues his march round the upper slope of the hill, until he reaches the entrance of the Acropolis; without touching the line of his first excursion through the Ceramicus, which was on his left. It is proper to remark, that the term *excursion* which I have here made use of, cannot be applied in a literal sense, because Pausanias merely describes what objects were to be seen, without expressly mentioning that he had visited them.

Before Pausanias begins his account of Sparta, he thinks it necessary to observe, that he should follow the same rule as he had laid down in his description of Attica; not to describe every object that occurred without distinction; but to select what best deserved notice

We may collect from this observation, that he had passed over a number of objects unnoticed in his description of Athens, but not without motives for such an omission.

Meursius has collected with much learning and industry, all that has been said by ancient writers on the subject of the public buildings which are thus omitted. Of these, many were no longer in existence at the period when Pausanias visited Athens, among which, I suspect, were the Pythium and the Leocorium, which from their celebrity he was not likely to have passed over unnoticed. Some, too, are of his own, or even of a later age. Pausanias, therefore, is responsible only for having omitted what he saw, and as the buildings which may be referred to this head, were, as far as we know, of a Macedonian-Greek or a Roman origin, it is probable, that his omission of these was deemed more consistent with the object he had in view, a description of the antiquities, and not, generally speaking, of the public buildings of Athens. Thus, for instance, he passes over without notice the temple of the Winds, because it was a modern structure, while he dwells with feelings of interest on the Anacéum and the sacred portion of Aglaurus. He dispatches, too, in a few words, and as it were in a parenthesis, the great additions which had been made to the city by Hadrian. For the same reason, Pausanias barely and incidentally

notices the new Agora, the Gymnasium of Ptolemy, and the monument of Philopappus, and if he deigns to expatiate on the Olympium
and the Stadium ; it is, because they were classed among the greatest
works then in existence

Again, it appears that more than three-fourths of all the original
public buildings at Athens, were either on the south, south-east, or
south-western side of the Acropolis Of the remainder, viz the
Theseum, the Dioscuréum, the Anacéum, the sacred portion of
Aglaurus, the Prytanéum, and the temple of Ilithya, the first stood
at some distance on the north-west, the second, third, and fourth on
the north-eastern slope of the Acropolis hill, and the fifth and sixth
at a short distance from the eastern angle of the Acropolis The
space therefore on the north of the Acropolis within the city walls,
which contained no genuine monument whatever of Athenian origin,
was above one half of the entire area of the city. In short, previous
to the final subjugation of Athens by the Macedonians, and even long
after that period, the whole northern half of the city seems to have
been appropriated to private buildings.

Nor is there any difficulty in explaining how this came to pass. I
have already quoted a passage from Thucydides, which points out the
situation and extent of the original city previous to the time of
Theseus The choice of the spot had been already determined, first,
by the convenience of a neighbouring spring and rivulet, and next by
the natural strength of the hill of the Acropolis, to which all could
speedily retire in case of alarm. In the progress of time, the habitations extended to a greater distance from both, and when Theseus
prevailed on all the Demoi to assemble in one city ; the space on the
south of the Acropolis being no longer sufficient for so many inhabitants, the new settlers were obliged to erect their dwellings farther
eastward, and to occupy the vacant portion of the periphery of the
hill on the east and on the north.* The Prytanéum was built at this
period, and precisely on the same spot, where the building described

---

* Vide Platonem in Critia.

by Pausanias under this name then stood*, and to this early extension of the city round the Acropolis, we may refer the rest of the ancient buildings, which he describes at the base of the hill or near it. No other public buildings, however, appear to have been erected on this side until after the Persian invasion, when the Theséum was built, for which in all probability no space that was sufficiently large, could be found unoccupied in the more ancient part of the city. The same reason must have induced the Macedonian conquerors and Hadrian, where the site was not already chosen, (as in the instance of the Olympium,) to decorate the northern part of the city with those public buildings, which were designed to commemorate their munificence, and consequently, it is in that quarter that we must look for their remains. The style of sculpture and architecture observable in these buildings, bear witness to the decline and corruption of the arts, and they have occupied perhaps more of the public attention than they deserved. †

If I am correct in the historical view which I have just taken of the antiquities of Athens, as well as in my opinion of their local disposition; my readers will not be inclined to admit a very fanciful, although ingenious application, of the inscriptions on the arch of Hadrian, which has been lately brought forward by ‡ Mr. Wilkins. The arch here spoken of, which stands at the north-western angle of the Peribolus of the Olympium, and appears to have had no connection with any wall of the city, has been generally considered as a monument of adulation, erected by the citizens of Athens to the

---

* Thucydides says only, that the Prytaneum was built by Theseus, but Plutarch tells us that Theseus erected it precisely on the spot where it then stood, ἐπὶ τοῦ θέρεται

† I allude here to the Stoa or Portico, as it is called by Stuart. Upon this building I find the following observation in my Journal —"The uncertainty of antiquarians respecting this ruin is less to be regretted since there is so little to admire in its style of architecture, the swollen flutings in the lower half of the shafts of the columns, the sharp-pointed abacuses and the insulated and starting entablatures, producing a very bad effect, and proving it to have been built in the decline of Greek architecture, and not in the best period of the Roman."

‡ Athemensia, or Remarks on the Topography and Buildings of Athens, p. 15

Emperor Hadrian, who indeed had done much for their city, but in no instance so much, as in completing that magnificent structure the Olympium.

This opinion is confirmed by the two inscriptions on the entablature of the arch, the idea of which seems to have been borrowed from the celebrated column on the isthmus of Corinth, which pointed out the boundaries between Ionia and the Peloponnesus. In the same way, these two inscriptions were intended to point out the distinction between New and Old Athens, the former of which is here called the city of Hadrian, as it is called New Athens in the inscription over the aqueduct.

The compliment, however, was not wholly unmerited; for if the Athenians had more reason to be proud of the edifice which this arch directly faces, than of any other which had been for some ages erected; it is certain, that Hadrian had contributed in a material degree to its completion; as may be collected both from the testimony of Pausanias, and from some unequivocal proofs of the Roman school of architecture in this building, which are pointed out by Mr. Wilkins himself. (p 159.) How much, too, the vanity of Hadrian was flattered by the connection of his name with this temple, may be seen by the title of Olympius, which was given him in a dedicatory inscription published by Stuart. Moreover, we are told by Pausanias, that the whole enclosure was full of statues dedicated to that Emperor; besides four which were within the temple, and a colossal statue and an altar, which were erected to him by the citizens of Athens.

I have already stated what has been the received opinion concerning these inscriptions, I mean their application; for some variation of the sense arises from the different collocation of the Greek letters. But according to Mr. Wilkins, these inscriptions refer to what is seen through the arch, and not from it; the arch itself being intended, as he says, to guide the reader of these inscriptions to the objects which they refer to. The result of this hypothesis is, that the Olympium forms a portion of the city of Theseus, while the greater part of Athens bears the new denomination of Hadrianopolis [1]

Now admitting that this mode of interpretation is not constrained and artificial, and that it does not ill accord with the genius of those times; it will be found by no means to correspond with the local circumstances that are connected with the arch, which it pretends to illustrate. " On reading the southern inscription," says Mr. W., "ΑΙΔΕΙΣ ΑΔΡΙΑΝΟΥ ΚΑΙ ΟΥΧΙ ΘΗΣΕΩΣ ΠΟΛΙΣ, the eye is immediately directed to the picture seen beyond the arched opening, over which it is placed, and of which it forms the frame. Through this, the greater part of the modern town presents itself lying in the plain, on the north-east side of the citadel, whilst the Acropolis itself is on the left, without the field of view." On consulting the plan of Athens which is prefixed to Mr. W's work, we find a line drawn at right angles to the plan of the arch, which is evidently intended to mark the centre of the view here alluded to. This line nearly touches the eastern angle of the Acropolis, the Acropolis therefore is on the left, not as he says, without the field of view, but within it, or rather near the centre. That part of the city, too, which is on the left of this line, and which is the more ancient, has full as much claim to the distinction here conferred as that which lies to the right; and, if we apply the rule which has just been laid down, must equally bear the name of Hadrianopolis. But the position to the right of the line actually includes the Prytanéum, which we know to have been erected by Theseus, and consequently it includes that very city of Theseus, which it is the object of this new interpretation to exclude from it.

Equal inconsistencies arise on the other hand, from the application of the inscription on the north side of the arch, ΑΙΔΕΙΣ ΑΘΗΝΑΙ ΘΠΣΕΩΣ Η ΠΡΙΝ ΠΟΛΙΣ, to the objects on the south; for, waiving the objection that might be made to a modern building on this side, which occupies so much of the ground, as being an argument equally available against the position of the old city on the north side of the arch; it will be seen by a reference to Mr. W.'s map, that the city of Theseus is removed to a very inconvenient distance from the citadel to which it owed its protection; while a very considerable space directly to the south of the Acropolis remains wholly unoccupied.

Mr. W. seems to have been aware of this objection, and has endeavoured to obviate it; first, by removing the Pelasgicum from the
north side of the Acropolis to the south, and secondly, by occupying
as much of the vacant space as he could on this side, with the
southern extremity of the Ceramicus, and the left wing of his city of
Theseus, which is thus conveniently made to extend beyond that
line to which it was before limited. But that the situation of the enclosure called the Pelasgicum was on the northern side of the
Acropolis, is proved by its connection with the cave of Pan, as it is
stated in the following passage of Lucian — καὶ τὸ ἀπ᾽ ἐκείνου τὴν ὑπὸ τῇ
ἀκροπόλει στήλυγγα ταύτην ἀπολαβόμενος οἰκεῖ μικρὸν ὑπὸ τοῦ Πελασγικοῦ.
and the cave here alluded to, is represented on this side of the
Propylæa, on a bronze medal of Athens, which I have already mentioned. Besides, we learn from Plutarch, that the Κιμώνιον τεῖχος was
the southern wall of the Acropolis, so that the Pelasgic wall which
overlooked the enclosure, must have been the northern.

It is therefore clear, that if the author of this hypothesis means to
be consistent, he must abandon the ground which he has thus
endeavoured to occupy; the consequence of which is, that all that
portion of the city which I have proved from Pausanias and other
writers, to have comprehended the most ancient and most important
part of it, and to have been best situated both in regard to security
and a supply of water; will present in Mr. W.'s plan a blank space of
ground, unaccountably interposed between the city and that fortress
to which it looked for protection. But enough has been said to prove
the weakness of this new hypothesis, and we may safely revert to the
old explanation of these adulatory inscriptions, which are evidently
intended to feed the vanity of the Emperor Hadrian; a proof of
which, is the negation which is introduced into the southern inscription, showing that the northern is to be read first, and that the
reader is supposed to be advancing from the old city towards the
Olympium *

---

* In Stuart's plan of Athens the aqueduct of Hadrian lies to the south of the line of the
arch, which stands, he says, nearly north east and south-west. The inscription over the

In the preceding enquiry, (the necessity for which in my opinion ought long ago to have been superseded,) an attempt has been made to settle some of the most leading and important points in the topography of Athens.

The enquiry may now be extended to the walls of that city, although with less prospect of success, for here unfortunately our intelligent guide forsakes us, and the information which we must now glean from a variety of other sources, is too scanty to afford us a competent idea of the plan of these walls, either in respect to the ground which they occupied, or the number and position of the gates.

As Thucydides was almost an eye-witness to their construction, we may justly regard whatever he says upon the subject as authentic; I shall therefore avail myself to the utmost of his information, and have recourse only to other writers when they are not in opposition to him.

We are told by that historian, that the inhabitants of Athens returned to the city immediately after the departure of the † Persians, and in the same year began to rebuild the walls, after which they proceeded to fortify the Piræus. An interval, however, of some years elapsed, before they began to erect the long walls which united the city with the Piræus, and completed the general plan of fortification recommended by Themistocles.

The length of the northern long wall, or the Piræan, according to Thucydides, was forty stadia, and that of the southern or Phaleric, thirty-five, which measures agree pretty well with the respective distances of the Piræus and Phalerum from Athens ‡.

The new walls round the city comprehended a greater space of

---

aqueduct shows it to have been in New Athens.   The Olympium, therefore, even according to this hypothesis, must be in New Athens.

† A. C. 478, Olymp. lxxv. 2-3 Dodw.

‡ It is necessary for me to observe in this place, that I argue on the hypothesis of two long walls, one connecting the city with the Piræus, the other with Phalerum. I have therefore called one of these walls the Piræan, and the other the Phaleric. It will be seen by an inquiry into the subject of the long walls, which is printed in this edition, that both these walls joined the city to the Piræus. The conclusions therefore in respect to a single gate between the long walls and Athens, remain unaltered, for which reason I have not thought it necessary to correct the text.

ground than the old, and the part which it was necessary to guard, measured forty-three stadia.* Of the remainder, which we may conclude was the part shut up between the long walls, he does not give the measure, probably because it was insignificant. His scholiast, however, informs us, that it was seventeen stadia, which is highly improbable; the strength of the long walls, considered as lines of fortification, much depending upon the shortness of their distance from each other and their parallelism But the position of the Piræan gate, which may now be regarded as fixed, and that of the Ilissus, fully demonstrate the impossibility of this wide † interval.

That it comprehended the Museum hill, might be inferred from the importance attached to this spot after it was fortified, both by Antigonus and his son Demetrius; who, by means of the garrison which they placed here, kept the city effectually under subjection. On the other hand, the vestiges of the city walls, (if they can be depended upon,) which inclose the monument of Philopappus, evidently terminate on the summit of this pointed hill southwards, striking off nearly in a right angle to the east; so that the junction of the Phaleric with the city wall, must necessarily have taken place within this distance from the Piræan. ‡

The space thus left between the long walls, would admit of one gate of communication only between the city and the sea-ports, which some will think improbable. I am inclined, nevertheless, to adopt

---

* It would appear from some passages in the writings of Xenophon and Thucydides, that the walls of the city had been extended farther than was necessary for the accommodation of the inhabitants, in consequence of which there was a considerable space of vacant ground   This must have been to the north of the Acropolis. Here, then, was room for the garden of Epicurus, and for all the public buildings which were subsequently added to the city by the Macedonian Greeks and the Romans   Ὁι δὲ πολλαὶ τά τε ἔρημα τῆς πόλεως ᾤκησαν, καὶ τὰ ιερὰ, καὶ τὰ ἡρῶα παντα, &c &c. Thucyd Hist   Εἰτα ἐπειδὴ καὶ πολλὰ οἰκιῶν ἔρημα ἐστιν ἐντὸς τῶν τειχῶν καὶ οἰκόπεδα.   Xenoph de Redit

† The bed of the Ilissus bends so much to the north, after it has passed by the Museum hill, as to reduce this space very considerably   Chandler crossed it in his way to the town

‡ Xenophon represents the long walls at Corinth as being at some distance from each other , but their length, according to Strabo, did not exceed twelve stadia.

this supposition, and for the following reasons, which it will be proper to state at some length.

In the first place, I must observe, that we have proofs of the existence of a Pyraean gate, but none of a Phaleric, (at least of a gate so denominated,) which, if it had ever existed, must have been somewhere between the long walls, and probably as close to the Phaleric wall as the other was to the Pyraean, and although Pausanias speaks of a gate as you entered the city from Phalerum; yet, it will be recollected, that he is silent with respect to the southern long wall which had been long demolished, and that it is the more direct as well as shorter road, which he is describing from that sea-port to the city

In the next place, it is a circumstance well known, that the northern long wall was principally efficient in keeping open the communication between Athens and the Piræus, and it appears upon all occasions to have secured Athens from being closely invested. It was therefore of the most essential importance in either point of view, and not only the first of the two walls which was constructed*, but in all probability the strongest; and this will explain the reason why so great a part of its foundations are still visible, while nearly all the traces of the Phaleric wall have disappeared. †

I conceive too that the northern long wall was provided with some watch towers, while few or none were necessary to the southern. ‡ For the same reason, gates which would have impaired the strength of one of these walls, might not have been incompatible with the use of the other; and thus it is possible that the city which was least exposed to an attack on the south side, may have had the

---

* Vide Andocid de Pace.

† Of the southern long wall a small fragment or two only remains, which M. Fauvel discovered by accident in the vineyards. These walls, he says, were parallel, except near Phalerum, and about forty paces asunder, as well as he could recollect without his notes. MS. Journal

‡ I think this may be fairly concluded from the expression of Thucydides, — Τὰ δὲ μακρὰ τείχη πρὸς τὸν Πειραιᾶ τεσσαρακοντα σταδίων, ὡς τὸ ἔξωθεν ἐτηρεῖτο

hoice of some points of communication with the interior of the long walls, besides that which the Piraean gate afforded. For instance, there were two, if not more gates, which opened into the Ceramicus, and the use of these might have been safely combined with that of a gate in the Phaleric wall, which was at a short distance.

The periphery of the city walls, according to the above supposition, could not much have exceeded the measure given by Thucydides, which is forty-three stadia *, and if we take that of the distance between Athens and the Piraeus, as a scale for computing the length of the stadium here made use of, it would appear that there were about ten of these to a geographic mile. On applying this scale of measurement to the traces of the old walls of the city, as they are represented in Fauvel's plan, we shall find them not to exceed 30 stadia in circumference.

I have already observed, that no reliance is to be placed on what are called the vestiges of the ancient walls, with the exception of such as are perceivable on the Museum hill and near Pnyx; for these, besides something of a regular plan and connection, have historical evidence in favour of their antiquity. And although the very near approach of these walls to the entrance of the Acropolis might justly excite some suspicion of the validity of their claims, yet it will be recollected that this was a most vital point in the general system of defence, and that Themistocles has probably adapted the plan of the walls on this side to the natural strength of the position. In like manner, it is evident that the bed of the Ilissus must have set some inconvenient limits to the extension of the walls on the southern side of the Acropolis, so that the fountain of Enneacrunos, which was probably not within, although immediately under the protection of the walls, may be regarded as the farthest point to which they advanced in that direction. And thus, after admitting as

---

* It is remarkable, that Dicaearchus, in his Metrical Fragment, gives the same measure to the walls of Thebes

genuine those traces of the walls, which Fauvel and Stuart have laid down on this side of the Acropolis, and which amount to about one-third of their periphery, we may suspend the labour of further enquiry, for all beyond is doubt or conjecture. *

It is on account of these insuperable difficulties, in ascertaining the plan of the walls, that we are unable to fix the exact position of the gates. We have even no precise information respecting their number or denomination, and it is only by carefully comparing whatever may be gleaned from ancient authorities, with a few fixed points in the plan of Athens, that we can hope to satisfy our curiosity. The result, however, of this investigation has been more successful than I had anticipated.

To begin with Dipylon. The first object which Pausanias takes notice of, on the sacred way leading from Athens to Eleusis, is the tomb of Anthemocritus. Now, we are told by Plutarch that this personage was interred near the Thriasian gate, which was then called Dipylon†, a circumstance which derives some confirmation, if it needed any, from a passage in the oration of Isæus, πρὸς ‡ Καλυδῶνα. From which we may conclude, first, that the Θριασίαι Πύλαι and Δίπυλον were only different denominations of the same gate, and secondly, that the Ἱεραὶ Πύλαι (if they ever existed) could have been no other than this gate. It is remarkable that the two roads which lead at present from Eleusis and the site of the Academy, met at one and the same gate of the modern town.

I have expressed a doubt, whether the denomination of Ἱεραὶ Πύλαι was ever given to Dipylon; for the sole authority for it is in a passage of Plutarch. I am inclined to believe, that Ἱεραὶ has been substituted

---

* We may collect from the following passage of Strabo, how far they extended towards the south-east. Ἔστι δ᾽ αὐτὴ ἐν τῷ τείχει μεταξὺ τοῦ Πυθίου καὶ τοῦ Ὀλυμπίου Lib. ix. Vitruvius says, that the walls on this side were of brick — "Nonnullis civitatibus publica opera, et privatas domos, etiam regias, e latere, structas licet videre, et primum Athenis murum qui spectat ad Hymettum montem" Lib. xi. Pliny repeats this account, lib. xxxv c. 14

† Ταφῆναι δὲ Ἀνθεμόκριτον παρὰ τὰ Θριασίας πύλας, αἳ νῦν Δίπυλον ὁ ὀμάζονται

‡ Quoted by Harpocratio.

in it by mistake for Ἡρίαι or the Sepulchral gate, which probably stood at the foot of the Muséum hill, and was the next in succession to the Piraean, for some sepulchres are still observable in the side of the rock which forms the base of that hill [*] Here, too, the funereal rites might have been performed with less danger of interruption than on the other side, while the city was pressed by a besieging enemy. The evidence however, which results from all this, is far from being conclusive, and it amounts only to a high degree of probability, that the Sepulchral gate of the city stood in the situation which I have described.

That which is called by Philostratus [†] the gate of the Ceramicus, was, without doubt, the next in succession eastward; and either this or the preceding must have borne the denomination of Ἱππάδες or the Equestrian. The expression ἐ πόρρω τῶν Ἱππέων in the passage of Philostratus which I have just referred to, would lead to the conclusion that it was the Ceramic; and the πύλαι ἐν πόρρω τῶν ἱππεων seem to be the same gate noticed by Pausanias in the following passage ἰοῦσι δὲ πρὸς τὴν στοὰν ἣν Ποικίλην ὀνομάζουσιν ἀπὸ τῶν γραφῶν, ἔστιν Ἑρμῆς χαλκοῦς καλούμενος Ἀγοραῖος, καὶ πύλη πλησιον ἐπεστι δὲ οἱ τρόπαιον Ἀθηναίων ἱππομαχίᾳ κρατησάντων Πλέσταρχον. On the other hand, there is a passage in Plutarch's life of Hyperides, which seems to show the connection of the Equestrian gate with the Sepulchral [‡]

The Ceramic gate must have been the same as that which has already been noticed near the Mercury of the Agora, and it is pro-

---

[*] " On our left," says Chandler, ' were the door-ways of ancient sepulchres, hewn out in the rock." By a law of Solon the dead were not permitted to be interred within the city, and although many sepulchral monuments of persons of distinction are noticed by Pausanias both on the road to the Academy and to Eleusis, yet it is not improbable that persons of inferior note were deposited in one particular situation, the gate leading to which was called Sepulchral. The author of the Etymologicon says, Ἡρίαι, πύλαι Ἀθήνησι, διὰ τὸ τὰς νεκρὰ, ἐκφέρεσθαι ἐκεῖ ἐπὶ τὰ ἡρία, ὅ ἐστι τὰς τάφε The choice of a western gate for this purpose seems to have been consistent with their mythology

[†] Παρῆλθεν ἡ, τὸ τῶν τεχνιτῶν βουλευτήριον, ὃ δὲ ᾠκοδόμηται πάρα τὰς τοῦ κεραμεικὲ πύλας, ἐ τορόω τῶν Ἱππέων — Philostratus in Philagro Soph lib xi

[‡] Τὰς δὲ οἰκείας, τὰ ὀξ ὑπάρχοντα, θάψαι τε ἅμα τοῖς γονεῦσι, πρὸ τῶν Ἱππάδων πυλῶν The ἅμα τοῖς γονεῦσι, probably referring to a place of common interment.

bably the same gate through which, at certain festivals, Xenophon recommends that the Athenian cavalry should issue, after they had made a procession round the Agora, and thence gallop off in squadrons as far as the Eleusinium. As the Ceramic gate appears, from this passage of Xenophon, to have been at some distance from Enneacrunos, we must conclude that there was a point of communication with that public fountain through some gate which was nearer to it, if not directly opposite, although no such gate is expressly mentioned by any ancient author. A gate, however, called Diochares, is mentioned by Strabo in this quarter; which I suspect to have been situated precisely in the spot where it was so much wanted. The passage is as follows —Ἐπὶ μὲν οὖν αἱ πηγαὶ ἀθρξ καὶ πετίμ ὕδατος, ὡς Φασιν, ἐκτὸς τῶν Διοχάρους καλουμένων πυλῶν, πλησίον τοῦ Λυκείου. This is the only fountain which Strabo speaks of at Athens. How improbable, therefore, is it, that he should have passed over in silence so important an object as Enneacrunos, while he mentions a fountain which must have been comparatively insignificant? Besides, I know of no springs (πηγαὶ) to the eastward of Enneacrunos, except one which is about a mile above the Stadium. But the words which follow my quotation more particularly designate Enneacrunos:—Πρότερον δὲ καὶ κρήνη κατασκεύαστο τις πλησίον πολλῆ καὶ καλῆ ὕδατος. Nor could this be the fountain which is so commended in the Phædrus of Plato, for Strabo expressly mentions that fountain in another part of his narrative, and in a manner which shews that they were very distant from each other. †

* " When we had passed these columns (of Jupiter Olympius)," says Stuart, "and the eastern end of the Peribolus, of which we found two hundred and thirty feet not utterly demolished, we arrived immediately at the vestiges of the city wall and of one of its gates, probably that called Diochares. We were now on the side of the Ilissus, hence we descended to a copious and beautiful spring, at present called Calliroe, flowing into the channel of the river." Vol. iii p. 23.—Chandler, too, speaking of the foundations of this gate and Calliroe, expresses his opinion that the passage of Strabo above quoted refers to the latter.

† See the passage in the Phædrus relating to these springs or fountains, and their situation.

3 u 2

The Itonian gate was probably the next as we advance in this direction. It is mentioned by Æschines the philosopher *, in the following words — Ὡς δὲ θᾶττον τὴν παρὰ τὸ τεῖχος ᾔειμεν, ταῖς Ἰτωνίαις (πλησίον γὰρ ᾤκει τῶν πυλῶν, πρὸς τῇ Ἀμαζονίδι στήλη,) καταλαμβάνομεν αὐτόι. Now, Plutarch gives us pretty accurate information where this column was situated , for speaking of Hippolyta, the Amazon who was slain by Molpadia, in the battle between Theseus and the Amazons, he adds,—καὶ τὴν στήλην, τὴν παρὰ τὸ τῆς Γῆς τῆς Ὀλυμπίας, ἐπὶ ταύτη κεῖσθαι. The Itonian gate therefore must have stood on the eastern side of the Peribolus of the Olympium, or between that and the Pythium , for Strabo speaks of a wall, probably the wall of the city, in that situation †

I must now conduct my readers back to the western side of the city, where the situation of the Melitensian gate seems to be clearly pointed out in the following passage of the life of Thucydides by Marcellinus — Πρὸς γὰρ ταῖς Μελιτίσι πύλαις καλουμέναις ἐστὶν ἐν Κοίλῃ τὰ καλούμενα Κίμωνος μνήματα. According to Herodotus, the sepulchre of Cimon, the father of Miltiades, was in front of the Acropolis, beyond the way called *through Coele*. We are told by an anonymous author, who is quoted by Meursius, that the dwelling of Cimon was in Pnyx, which would lead us to suppose that the monuments of that family, and consequently the gate which stood in their vicinity, could not have been very distant ; and in reality, the form of the ground between Pnyx and the Areopagus, (a very remarkable hollow, and the only one at Athens,) fully confirms this supposition. ‡

The Melitensian gate was, therefore, the first as you advance northward from the Piræan gate, and probably at no great distance

* In Axiocho

† Ἔστι δ᾽ αὐτή (ἡ ἐσχάρα τῆ Διὸς Ἀστραπαία) ἐν τῷ τείχει μεταξὺ τοῦ Πυθίου καὶ τοῦ Ὀλυμπίου Lib ix

‡ Chandler describes this spot very accurately —" We now enter a valley," says he, " at the foot of the hill of the Acropolis, in which is a track leading between Pnyx and the Areopagus, toward the temple of Theseus   This region was called Coele or the Hollow On the left hand is a gap in the mountain, where, it is believed, was the Melitensian gate, and within is a sepulchre or two in the rock   Going on, other sepulchres hewn in the side of the mountain like those first mentioned occur "

from it, then followed Dipylon, beyond which must have stood the Acharnian, for such was the direction of Acharnæ in respect to Athens. The space now left for the remaining gates, supposing the intervals between them to be like the others, or nearly so, will admit of three more, one of which was probably the Dioméian. The other gates enumerated by Potter, are the πύλαι Θρακαι or Thracian, the authority for which is taken by mistake from a passage of Thucydides relating to Amphipolis[*], the πύλαι Σκαιαι[†], which is mentioned only in a monkish legend quoted by Meursius, Αγραι πύλαι, which was unquestionably no gate of the city; and the gate of Hadrian, of which I have already treated.

But a question of some importance remains to be answered,—How was Athens supplied with water?

The first settlers were undoubtedly influenced in the choice of their situation, by the proximity of Callirroe and the Ilissus; and until the time of Theseus, it is probable that these were sufficient for the supply of the inhabitants. But the great addition which was then made to the population of the city, by causing the buildings to extend considerably to the north of the Ilissus, must have suggested other means of supply, and those inhabitants who dwelt at the greatest distance from Callirroe and the Ilissus, doubtless, had recourse to wells.

Plutarch mentions a police law of Solon, respecting the use of wells. According to this law, every one who dwelt within the space defined by Hippicon or four stadia around a well, might make use of it. Others, not within that distance, were enjoined to provide one of their own, and in case they should meet with no water at the depth of ten fathoms, they were allowed daily to fetch a limited quantity from their next neighbours' well. Plutarch says, that Solon enacted this law, because he thought it right to provide against the want of water, without holding out any encouragement to indolence; but, it is evident, that in such a country as Attica, it was necessary

---

[*] This is a most extraordinary instance of carelessness in such a writer as Meursius.
[†] Between the walls and Anchesmus is a little Greek church called Agra Sota

thus to limit the distance of the wells from each other, or they would have been very soon drawn dry.

This law, the very provisions of which demonstrate the insufficiency of such a resource for a condensed population, has, nevertheless, been very absurdly applied to the city alone, and the question seems never to have occurred, how Athens could have been better supplied? For the Athenians, at an early period, are known to have indulged in the luxury of baths , and were not less nice than the Romans or even the present inhabitants of those countries, in the discrimination of water, nor could the practicability of conveying it by an aqueduct have escaped the observation of that ingenious and enterprising people. On the contrary, there are some plain indications, I think, of this art having been understood and practised here at an early period, in the following passage of Phrynichus, Μέτων ὁ Λευκονεὺς, ὃς ὁ τὰς κρήνας ἄγων. Upon which Salmasius (to whom I am indebted for this authority) observes, " *Metonem per ista, planè designavit, qui etiam aquilex fuit, non tantum astronomus,*" for according to the testimony of the same writer (Phrynichus,) which is quoted by Suidas, it appears, that a fountain was constructed by Meton within the walls of Athens Ἐν τῷ Κολώνῳ κρήνην τινὰ (ὁ Μέτων) κατασκευάσατο, φησὶν ὁ Φρύνιχος, Μειοτρόπα. (Meurs. Reliq. Att) The Colonus here mentioned is supposed to have been an eminence somewhere near the Agora, and therefore called Ἀγοραῖος, to distinguish it from the Ἵππιος, which was situated near the academy. But we have the positive testimony of Thucydides that Athens was supplied in this way, in the following passage of his description of the plague which prevailed there καὶ ἐν ταῖς ὁδοῖς ἐκαλινδοῦντο, καὶ περὶ τὰς κρήνας ἁπάσας τῇ τοῦ ὕδατος ἐπιθυμίᾳ. L. 2.

In the Lysis of Plato, Socrates says, " I was going out of the Academy directly towards the Lycéum, by the way which lies without

---

* It is said in one of the comedies of Aristophanes, " that the Gymnasia were empty, but the baths were always full " Demosthenes complains of the degree to which this usage had spread among the manners of the fleet.

the city walls; but when I got to the gate where the fountain of Panops is, I there met with Hippothales." Now, when we recollect the position of the Academy from whence he started, and the intervention of the long walls which stopped his passage on the right, no doubt can remain of the fountain of Panops having been situated on the north-eastern side of the city, where it could have had no communication with the Enneacrunos.

We have evidence of the existence of an aqueduct soon after this period in the Lycéum. It is mentioned by several writers [*]; but as Theophrastus seems to have been the original authority, I shall give it in his words — Ἡ γε οὖν ἐν τῷ Λυκείῳ ἡ πλάτανος, ἡ κατὰ τὸν ὀχετὸν ἔτι νέα οὖσα περὶ τρεῖς καὶ τριάκοντα πήχεις ἀφῆκεν (ῥίζας) ἐχετα τόπον τε ἅμα καὶ τροφή. Pliny repeats this wonderful account of the plane-tree with some variations; noticing a fountain here — "Nunc est clara (Platanus) in Lycéo, geldi fontis, socia amoenitate," &c. It was, probably, one of those trees which Plato in the dialogue above quoted mentions as having been planted in the new Palæstra, the formation of which, as well as the planting of the trees [†], is ascribed by Plutarch to the orator Lycurgus [‡].

It is remarkable, that at this very period, Dicæarchus, in the words, ἡ δὲ πόλις, ξηρὰ πᾶσα ἐκ ἐνυδρος, appears to represent the city as very ill supplied with water. But according to Gataker [§], the word πόλις here applies to the district or country of Attica χώρα, and not to the city.

We have another proof of the existence of these public works for the supply of the city, in the offices of Κρηνάρχη and Κρηνοφύλαξ. In the Politics of Aristotle, he is called ἐπιμελητὴς κρηνῶν. Themistocles seems at one period of his life, to have held an office, perhaps a superior one of this sort; for Plutarch says, ὁ αὐτὸς, ὅτε τῶν Ἀθηναίων

---

[*] Theophrastus, Hist. Plant. lib. i. c. x. Varro, lib. i. c. 37, and Pliny, lib. xii. c. 1.

[†] It is impossible that any tree, except the Pinus maritima or the olive, could have grown in such a dry and rocky soil as that of the Lyceum, without constant irrigation.

[‡] Vide his Life in the X. Rhet.

[§] Adv. Post. cxiv.

ὑδάτων ἐπιστάτης ἦι, εὑρὼν τοὺς ὑφρημένους τὸ ὕδωρ καὶ παρωχετεύσατο; ἀνέθηκεν. An instance is given by Thucydides, in his account of the siege of Syracuse, how sensible the Athenians were of the importance of these works. Οἱ δὲ Ἀθηναῖοι τοὺς δὲ ὀχετοὺς αὐτῶι, οἳ δὲ ἐς τὴν πόλιν ὑπονομηδὸν ποτοῦ ὕδατος ηγμένοι ἦσαν, διέφθειρα. And it is not improbable, that the mischief thus described, was afterwards retaliated upon themselves, either on the invasion of Philip or the capture of the city by Sylla.

Whether it was in consequence of a violence like this, that the aqueducts were abandoned, or they had become useless by long neglect; we find that Athens at a subsequent period had relapsed into her former state, for Pausanias, who visited that city in the latter half of the second century, speaking of Enneacrunos, informs us, that Φρέατα μὲν καὶ ὀα πάσης τῆς πόλεως ἐστι, πηγὴ δὲ αὕτη μόνη. Soon after this, however, as we learn from an inscription over the Ionic arcade at the foot of Mount Anchesmus, Athens was provided with an aqueduct, by the munificence of the Emperors Hadrian and Antonine. *

The modern city is abundantly supplied in the same way by a subterranean canal, which conveys to it the whole perennial stream of the Ilissus. It is, therefore, no wonder, that the bed of that river should present an appearance, at this time, so little corresponding with its poetical character; and that travellers should complain so feelingly of its degradation. †

---

* It was begun by Hadrian and finished by Antonine in his third consulate.

† The following extracts from my Journal will convey some information respecting the present state of the Ilissus —

"Oct. 21. — Notwithstanding the heavy rains of the preceding evening, the bed of the Ilissus was quite dry, but as we were tracing its course upwards towards Enneacrunos, I discovered a subterranean canal immediately beneath it, which contained a small stream of clear water. It was about six feet below the bed of the river, hewn out of the solid micaceous rock, and measured about three feet six inches by two feet six inches."

"Nov. 14 — I observed in my walk this day, that notwithstanding the heavy rains which we had lately experienced here, a very small rivulet ran along the gravelly bed of the Ilissus. Fauvel informed me, that he had found the traces of seven or eight pipes belong-

The principal source of the Ilissus is near the monastery of Cyriani, just below the higher region of Mount Hymettus. The stream bursts forth there from the cavities of the marble rock, and soon loses itself in a deep ravine, which it has worn in the schistous basis of the mountain. At some distance below, the old bed of the river turns to the left, and is joined by several other ravines, which convey to it in the rainy season an additional supply of water. The stream, however, before it reaches the Eridanus, is turned off in a more straight direction towards the city, and conveyed during the remainder of its course under ground. This must have been an enterprize of considerable labour and expence, not unworthy of the better days of Greece; for a little to the north of Ampelokipo, I took notice of a number of shafts by the road side, sunk in the hard rock, which proved upon enquiry to belong to the city-aqueduct there, at a considerable depth under ground.

Stuart was of opinion, that the reservoir of Hadrian's aqueduct had been supplied with water by a raised aqueduct of no mean length; for he passed some ruined arches of it in several places, at a considerable distance from each other in his way to Cephissia; which is between six and seven miles from Athens. He supposes it to have led from that place. Chandler likewise noticed these remains of an aqueduct, and accounts for them in the same way. It appears extraordinary, however, that Athens should have been supplied in this direction, since the distance from which the water is conveyed by the present aqueduct is comparatively much shorter.

---

ing to Enneacrunos in the face of the rock, where the great fall is in the bed of the Ilissus and that the subterranean canal which I observed draws off all the water, and has a stream the whole year. The source of this stream is probably the original Calliroe"

Fourmont (Acad Inscrip xvi) says, " that Enneacrunos and Calliroe were not sufficient to supply the city with water " On signa l'Ilissus dès sa source, à deux lieues et demie de la ville" They also formed, he adds, subterraneous aqueducts, of which two remain now, distributing water to the town. Fourmont thought them of high antiquity

ON THE LONG WALLS OF ATHENS

[BY MR HAWKINS]

In the course of the preceding enquiry into the topography of Athens, some reference has been made to the long walls which connected that city with the Piræus, and I have adopted without scruple the opinion which has prevailed both in ancient and in modern times, respecting their number.

But it would be improper not to notice in this place, an opinion adopted by some critics, whose judgment is entitled to every respect, that there was a third or middle wall in the same direction. I shall therefore proceed to its examination.

The first authority for this opinion is derived from Thucydides, who notices the commencement of these walls and their completion as well as their respective measures and direction, but who unfortunately expresses himself in such a manner concerning their number, as to lead his readers to two very opposite conclusions.

In the following passage of his history, "Ἥρξαντο δὲ κατὰ τοὺς χρόνους " τούτους καὶ τὰ μάκρα τείχη Ἀθηναῖοι ἐς θάλασσαν οἰκοδομεῖν, τό, τε Φαληρόνδε, " καὶ τὸ ἐς Πειραῖα,"* two walls only are mentioned under the denomination of the Long Walls; one joining the sea at Phalerum, the other at the Piræus.

In a subsequent passage, Thucydides confirms this idea of their number and direction in the following words . " Τοῦ τε γὰρ Φαληρικοῦ " τείχους στάδιοι ἦσαν πέντε καὶ τριάκοντα πρὸς τὸν κύκλον τοῦ ἄστεως καὶ αὐτοῦ τοῦ " κύκλου τὸ φυλασσόμενον τρεῖς καὶ τεσσαράκοντα· ἔστι δὲ αὐτοῦ ὃ καὶ ἀφύλακτον ἦν, " τὸ μεταξὺ τοῦ τε μακροῦ καὶ τοῦ Φαληρικοῦ."† Here we have the positive measure of the Phaleric wall, which agrees with the actual distance; and

* L 1   † L. ii.

it is plainly intimated that there were two walls only in contact with that of the city, one of which is called the Phaleric, the other simply the Long Wall. In the next sentence, however, we unexpectedly find two long walls expressly noticed in the direction of the Piræus, and exceeding the length of the Phaleric by one eighth; " τὰ δὲ " μακρὰ τείχη πρὸς τὸν Πειραῖα, τεσσαράκοντα σταδίων;" and that no doubt might exist of two walls being here understood, (τείχη being often applied to the single wall of a town,) he has added " ὧν τὸ ἔξωθεν ἐτη- " ρεῖτο."

The sense of the entire passage therefore is inconsistent and contradictory, for the parts taken separately authorize very different conclusions. Nevertheless there are two distinct points of information which I think may be fairly deduced from it; and they are of no small importance in settling the object of this enquiry, namely, that whatever might be the number of these long walls at the period alluded to, two only joined those of the city, and two only were in the direction of the Piræus.

But the authority upon which the notion of a third wall principally rests, is taken from the following passage in the Gorgias of Plato. " Περικλέους δὲ αὐτὸς ἤκουσι, ὅτε συνεβούλευεν ἡμῖν περὶ τοῦ διαμέσου τείχους." Plutarch, alluding to this passage, in his life of Pericles, informs us that the wall here spoken of was one of the long walls, for he says, " τὸ δὲ μακρὸν τεῖχος, περὶ οὗ Σωκράτης ἀκοῦσαι φησὶν αὐτὸν εἰσηγουμένου ' γνώμην Περικλέους, ἠργολάβησε Καλλικράτης." Now if we take διαμέσου strictly in the sense of an adjective, and understand by this expression a middle wall, the notion of a third seems to be necessarily connected with it; but if we take it in the sense which is intended in the following passage of St. Chrysostom, where it is synonymous with ἐν τῷ μέσῳ, " Καί τοι διακοσίων σταδίων εἶναι τὴν περίμετρον τῶν Αθηνῶν, " τοῦ Πειραιέως συντεθεμένου, καὶ τῶν διὰ μέσου τειχῶν," we are at liberty to give it a more enlarged interpretation, the meaning here being evidently that of the walls between the city and the Piræus.

Whatever part might have been taken by Cimon in this great

3 x 2

national work*, the erection and completion of the long walls appear to have principally taken place under the administration of Pericles; and as the southern long wall was built according to the testimony of Andocides, subsequently to the northern, it is probable that this last is the very wall which Pericles here recommends.

The sense, then, in which we are to understand this passage in the Gorgias, must depend, as I have already observed, on the existence or the non-existence of a third wall, which can be no other than the Phaleric; and as this is a question of so much importance, it is necessary that we should examine it very rigidly.

I have already stated the very positive information which is derived from the sense of two detached passages of Thucydides, and shewn how much that sense is weakened, if not wholly destroyed by what immediately follows; insomuch that had Thucydides only spoken of a Phaleric wall, and not given us its precise length and direction, we should feel little or no scruple in rejecting the idea altogether of a wall which connected the city with Phalerum.

I shall therefore proceed to observe that with the exception of Harpocration †, Thucydides seems to be the only authority for this wall, and that Pausanias has noticed no traces of it on the road from Phalerum to Athens; whereas he expressly mentions the ruins of the long walls on the road from the Piræus. In the next place it is evident that after the ships and the docks, and probably the greater part of the inhabitants, had been removed to the Piræus, Phalerum must have lost all its importance as a sea-port, and as it does not appear that it was ever fortified, I am at a loss to conceive what could have been the use of a wall connecting it with Athens

On the other hand we know that the Piræus was most strongly

---

* Plutarch says that he laid at his own expence a firm foundation for the long walls in the swampy grounds near the Piræus, and that they were erected some time afterwards.

† Harpocration says there were three long walls, the northern, the southern, and the Phaleric, the middle one being called the Southern. He refers to the authority of a lost comedy of Aristophanes. My readers will judge what credit is due to his testimony.

fortified, and that the very existence of Athens as a great state depended upon its being connected in this manner with its ships and its arsenal.

It may be said that this is merely presumptive evidence against a third wall I shall now therefore bring forward what may be regarded as a direct proof of its non-existence.

Thucydides observes that the circumference of the walls of Syracuse was not less (εδει ελασσονα) than that of the walls of Athens. Now we learn from Strabo[*], that the old walls of Syracuse measured 180 stadia we must therefore conclude that there were two long walls only, not three, for under the first supposition the number of stadia would be 183, and according to the other 218.[†] And it follows from what has been said before on the passage of Thucydides, that both these walls connected Athens in a straight line with the Piraeus.

It has been already remarked that the notion of two walls in this direction is that which was generally adopted by the ancients. The very general appellation of σκελη and brachia which they bestowed on these walls, very clearly denote this; nor is there, I believe, a single passage except those which I have cited, in which they are not understood to be joined to the Piraeus. " Τειχει ταυτα," says Strabo, when speaking of the wall of this town, " συνηττε τα καθειλκυσμενα " εκ του αξεις σκελη· ταυτα δ' ην μακρα τειχη, τετταρακοντα ςαδιων το μηκος, " συναπτιντα το αςυ τω Πειραιει." And the same precise information is given by Livy, " Inter angustias semiruti muri, qui duobus " brachiis Piraeum Athenis jungit."

---

[*] Πενταπολις ην το παλαιον, εκατον και ογδοηκοντα ςαδιων εχουσα το τειχος. L II.
[†] The measures, according to Thucydides, are as follows —

The walls of Athens	43 Stadia.
The northern long wall	10
The southern	40
The Piraeus including Munychia	60

183

We are told by Andocides*, that after the Piræus had been fortified, the northern long wall was erected, and that after the completion of the arsenal, the southern. Æschines † too speaks of the erection of the northern, and assigns to it the same period of time but neither Æschines nor Andocides hint at the existence of a third wall either in this or in any other direction.

It has been already shewn, that the long walls could not have been very far asunder at the point where they joined those of Athens; but it is not improbable that they diverged a little as they approached the Piræus; for this was by no means inconsistent with the system of defence, and must have greatly facilitated the intercourse between such a crowded mart as the Piræus and Athens Plato ‡ speaks of Leontius as going up from the Piræus under the northern long wall, which seems to confirm this notion of their divergence; for he would hardly have particularized the line of march upon this occasion, had not the long walls been here at some distance from each other, one perhaps in a direct line from the shore of the haven, the other more to the south and in a line with Munychia.

When we compare the hasty and very faulty construction of the walls of Athens, as they are represented by Thucydides, with the great care which was taken by Themistocles in erecting those of the Piræus, as well as with the prodigious height which he intended to give them §, no doubt can be entertained which of the two was

---

deemed by him of the greater importance, in respect to the vital interests of his country; nor can we be at a loss to account for what Plutarch says of him upon this occasion, "*that he had rather joined* "*Athens to the Piræus than the Piræus to Athens.*" The same view of the subject is taken by C. Nepos in his life of Themistocles " Hujus consilio triplex Piraei portus constitutus est, isque mœnibus " circumdatus, *ut ipsam urbem dignitate aequiparaet, utilitate superaret.*" Appian, speaking of the walls of the Piræus, calls them "Ἡρακλέου " ἔργα, ὅτι τοῖς Ἀθηναίοις ἐπὶ Πελοποννησίοις ϛρατηγᾶ., καὶ τὴν ἐλπὶ α τῆς " νίκης τῶ Πραεῖ τιθέμενος;" and Corn. Nepos in his life of Phocion repeats his opinion of their importance " Neque ita multo post, " Nicanor Piræo est potitus, *sine quo Athenæ esse omnino non possunt.*"

The object, in fact, both of the fortifications of the Piræus and of the long walls, was to combine the very existence of Athens as a state, with that of its great naval arsenal, or in other words, to found its greatness on its maritime power. This policy of Themistocles is very plainly set forth by Thucydides " Ταῖς γὰρ ναυσὶ μάλιϛα " προσέκειτο, ἰδὼν ὡς ἐμοὶ δοκεῖ, τῆς βασιλεως ϛρατιᾶς τὴν κατὰ θάλασσαν " ἔφοδον εὐπορωτέραν τῆς κατὰ γῆν οὖσαι· τὸν τε Πειραῖα ὠφελιμώτερον ἐνόμιζε " τῆς ἄνω πόλεως καὶ πολλάκις τοῖς Ἀθηναίοις παρῄνει, ἤν ἄρα ποτὲ κατὰ γῆν " βιασθῶσι, καταβάντας ἐς αὐτὸν, τας ναυσὶ πρὸς ἅπαντας ἀντίστατθαι." And it was pursued by Pericles, under circumstances somewhat different, when all apprehension of a Persian invasion, either by land or by sea, had subsided. According to this policy, the empire of the land in any case of extremity which might happen, was to be abandoned; but that of the sea, ἡ θαλασσοκρατία, was to be retained, because the greater part of the revenue of Athens, which was at this period derived from the island subsidies, (to the amount of 600 talents,) depended upon this naval dominion.

ON THE VALE OF TEMPE.

[*BY MR. HAWKINS.*]

THE Vale of Tempe is generally known in Thessaly by the name of the Bogaz. *

It is a pass of great natural as well as political importance ; for it affords an outlet for the accumulated waters of a large province, and forms the only road into it; the pass by Velestin (the antient Pheræ) excepted, which is not exceedingly difficult.

It has therefore been celebrated in all ages as the scene of great events ; and has excited in modern times no small degree of curiosity.

And yet, in spite of its superior claims to our attention, I know few objects in this part of the world which have been so seldom visited or described; and I recollect no traveller before myself, who has deviated from his route, and made an excursion on purpose to view it. †

This circumstance may be ascribed, in some measure, to the wild and insecure state of the country in which it is situated ; and in part, to the excessive heats which prevail there during the summer and

---

* In the middle ages it was called the pass of Lycostomo The title of the bishop of the diocese is Ἐπίσκοπος Πλαταμόνης καὶ Λυκοστόμου

† Gyllius is, I believe, the first modern traveller who has visited Tempe. He says of it, " Vidi Penei ripas, quas amœnas efficiunt illa nobilia Tempe Thessalica, in nemorosa convalle inter Ossam et Olympum sita, per quæ media Peneus viridis labitur, amœna, ut dicuntur, sed angusta et brevis, undique montibus in altitudinem immensam elatis coarctata, ut terror adsit prætereuntibus " — De Bosph. Thr lib 1

autumn, when it is scarcely possible to escape those dreadful intermittent fevers, which are the natural consequences of heat, fatigue, and marsh effluvia.

Such was the result of the first attempt which I made to visit Thessaly in July 1795, when I had nearly fallen a victim to my temerity *

But in the year 1797, being more fortunate in the choice of the season, I was enabled most fully to gratify my curiosity. I landed at Volo on the 21st of May, and proceeded directly across the great plains of Thessaly to the vale of Tempe. The heat even now raised the thermometer at noon to 85°, but was not intolerable, nor was the air in any part of our route insalubrious

We spent six days at Ambelakia, a large Greek town which overlooks Tempe, after which we ascended the summits of Pelion and Ossa, visiting the plains of Pharsalia on our return to Volo. We had been prevented by the fear of the plague from proceeding to Larissa, and the ruins of some old towns beyond it, a circumstance which we much regretted.

My fellow-traveller, Mr Randle Wilbraham, who had recently returned from Persia, was struck with the resemblance which the general aspect of Thessaly bore to the provinces of Ispahan and Hamadan. This resemblance, he said, was most conspicuous in the vast extent of these open plains, in the bold rise as well as the bare and rocky surface of the mountains around them, and in the numerous hills which emerge like so many islands out of their stagnant level.

From the summit of Mount Ossa, (now called Kissavo,) we observed, how all the rivers of Thessaly poured themselves into the Peneus, and in what manner the collected stream, in its course towards the gulf, forced its way through the high ridge on which we were seated On its appearance again to the right of the mountains, we saw it

---

* I mention this for the benefit of others No English traveller can perambulate Greece with impunity in the months of July, August, and September.

meandering slowly through a plain of great fertility, which had been evidently formed by its alluvions, and which it seemed to quit with reluctance.

The very hospitable reception which we met with at Ambelakia, as it enabled us to make four successive visits to the vale of Tempe beneath, afforded us ample leisure to survey this curious spot, and to make a series of accurate drawings.

The Turkish word Bogaz, which signifies a pass or strait, is limited to that part of the course of the Peneus, where the vale is reduced to very narrow dimensions.

This part, I think, answers to our idea of a rocky dell, and is in length about two miles.* Travellers are prepared for their approach to it, by the gradual closing in of the mountains on each side of the river, and by a greater severity of character, which the scenery assumes around it.

At a short distance from the mouth of the dell, some groves of the oriental plane-tree adorn the banks of the river ; and were the stream here as limpid as that of the Thames, or many other rivers in England, and the vegetation on either side of it as luxuriant, we might justly admit the truth of Ælian's description.† Not far beyond this spot, which has some degree of beauty, the river is seen to strike into the body of the ridge, where it is soon lost between the successive folds of the mountains.

---

* This distance was computed by time and the rate of motion

† The breadth of the Peneus is generally about fifty yards Its water was at this time very muddy, but is said to be much clearer in the latter part of the summer, and Brown, who was at Larissa in September, says, that Homer's epithet of ἀργυροδίνη is very applicable to this river, which has a clear stream. On the other hand, the Swedish traveller Biornstahl, who visited Larissa twice in the spring of the year, says, that the Peneus resembles the Tiber in its yellow colour, and that the inhabitants of that city, who have no other water, drink it after it has been kept a week in cisterns, where it deposits a sediment Biornstahl is certainly mistaken in the colour of the water, and I cannot give credit to the assertion of Brown that it is ever clear.

It contains several sorts of fish, one of which, the Κολεανος, the Collanus of Belon, or Accipenser Huso of Linnæus, is much esteemed for its delicate flavour, and grows to a very considerable size.

The following extract from my Journal describes the remainder of the vale, or as it may be termed with more propriety, the Defile of Tempe

" The road through the Bogaz is chiefly the work of art, nature having left only sufficient room for the channel of the river. This road is, nevertheless, broad enough for the use of wheel-carriages ; and in some parts of its course consists of a paved causeway, which has been laid on the bank of the river, whilst in others, it is a solid terrace of rock, hewn out of the base of the mountain. It is carried on for a great way, at the height of 20 or 30 feet above the river ; but towards the eastern end of the vale it rises much higher, in order to surmount the brows of some promontories which fall there precipitately, and without any basement, into the water. In short, it appears to have been conducted with as much attention to the ease and safety of passengers, as the nature of the ground would admit of, and even, in its present neglected state, inspires a traveller with sufficient confidence, to contemplate the various features of the scenery

" This scenery, of which every reader of classical literature has formed so lively a picture in his imagination, consists of a dell or deep glen, the opposite sides of which rise* very steeply from the bed of the river. The towering height of these rocky and well-wooded acclivities above the spectator, the contrast of lines exhibited by their folding successively over one another ; and the winding of the Peneus between them, produce a very striking effect, which is

---

* The Editor is obliged to Professor Gaisford for a copy of the following passage relating to Tempe, and now published for the first time from a manuscript of Nicetas, in the Bodleian library The passage occurs in fol. 116 of the MS and corresponds with p 658 of Wolfius's edition, Genev 1593 It follows the word τίμπσιν

ᾺΑ τον πηγειὸν πόταμον ὃ· τὸν σαλαβρίας ὡ/μασται ᾿ τὸ παντη στενοτατον συναγουσιν ω· καὶ καχλάζειν ἐν πολλοῖς ἐστι μέγα τὸ ρόθιον και τὰς ὄχθας τῇ τῶν ὑστων ἀντιπέμψει συνεπηχεῖν περὶ δὲ τὰς τῶν ὀρῶν ὑποβασεις. μίαν παρανοίγουσιν ἀτραπον συνεπτυγμένην και ταύτην και χαλεπὴν τοῖς βαδίζουσιν ωστε πη μηδ' ἐπὶ τεσσαρων ἀσπίδων αυτὴν ἀναπτυσθαι ὑπὸ πετρῶν λισσάδων και τοταμίου ρεύματος ἐς τὸ παντελῶς συνιοῦσαν στενόπορον.

heightened by the wildness of the whole view, and the deep shadows of the mountains. The eye, however, dwells with pleasure only on the Peneus. The full but silent stream of that river is bordered nearly in all its course through the dell by the Oriental plane-tree, which supports the wild-vine thickly interlaced among its branches, and dropping in festoons to the surface of the water. This beautiful parasite was at the season when we visited Tempe in full bloom, and scented the air with a delightful odour. About midway, a fountain of the coldest water gushes out at the foot of a rock, which forms the base of the causeway. Here travellers usually halt to refresh themselves and their cavalry; while many repose here; or devour, as we did, the contents of their wallets; cooling their wine in the chrystal fountain.

"Just beyond this spot and adjoining to the road, are the ruins of a fortress of no very ancient date, which once, perhaps, guarded the pass, but the peasants conceive it to be the monument of a princess, who met here with an untimely death, and in memory of whom, it is called τὸ ὡραῖο κάστρο or τῆς ὡραίης τὸ κάστρο. The remains of this old castle are situated at the mouth of a small dell, which is rendered in some degree remarkable by a ruined tower on the brow of a lofty cliff. One or two dells, of less magnitude, diversify this side of the river, as we proceed eastwards.

"On the north side of the Peneus, the mass of rock is more entire, and the objects which strike the eye are altogether more bold, but perhaps less picturesque.

"It is here, however, that the exposure of the strata suggests to the imagination some violent convulsion, which, in a period of the most remote antiquity, may have severed the ridge and drained the great basin of Thessaly."

The above account of Tempe, which was written almost immediately after visiting that celebrated spot, will convey to my readers a faint, but no unfaithful representation of the scenery which I observed there. It is scarcely necessary for me to add, that the scenery itself by no means corresponds with the idea that has been generally conceived of it; and that the eloquence of Ælian has given rise to expectations which the traveller will not find realised. In the fine description, which that writer has given us of Tempe, he seems to have misconceived the general character of its scenery, which is distinguished by an air of savage grandeur rather than by its beauty and amenity, the aspect of the whole defile impressing the spectator with a sense of danger and difficulty, not of security and indulgence. In short, it is mortifying to be obliged to confess, that the highly-finished picture which Ælian has left us of Tempe, is almost wholly an imaginary one; and that even those which are sketched with so much force by Livy and Pliny bear no very marked resemblance * Were it possible to set aside the impression made by these writers, and to divest this celebrated spot of all the historical importance which is attached to it, I even doubt, whether it would attract that notice, which has been bestowed on many vales of the same wild character in the west of Europe

But Tempe, had it even fewer pretensions to grandeur or beauty than it in reality possesses, would still be viewed with interest, for it has been in all ages the theme of poetic encomium, and it is moreover connected with some of the greatest events in ancient history

We are told by Herodotus, that Xerxes advanced some way before his army, on purpose to survey this remarkable spot. Having enquired of his guides, how far it were practicable to turn the course of the Peneus; and being assured there was no other passage by which that river could find an issue towards the sea, Thessaly being surrounded by mountains — " The Thessalians," said he, " act with

* " Sunt Tempe saltus, etiamsi non bello fiat infestus, transitu difficilis, nam praeter angustias per quinque millia, qua exiguum jumento onusto iter est, rupes utrimque ita abscissae sunt, ut despici vix sine vertigine quadam simul oculorum animique possit terret et sonitus et altitudo per mediam vallem fluentis Penei amnis" Liv His — " In eo cursu Tempe vocantur quinque mill. passuum longitudine, et ferme sesquijugeri latitudine, ultra visum hominis attollentibus se dextera laevaque leniter convexis jugis Intus sui luce viridante adlabitur Peneus, viridis calculo, amoenus circa ripis gramine, canorus avium concentu" Plin lib iv c 8

prudence in not offering any resistance; they seem to be aware of
their own weakness, for, by filling up this valley, I could lay their
whole country under water."

This boast, so hyperbolically expressive of the might of Xerxes,
conveys a pretty accurate idea of the physical geography of Thessaly;
for the closure of Tempe alone, whether effected by the labour of an
immense army, or by an earthquake, would undoubtedly cause an
inundation so extensive, as to cover the whole eastern half of that
country.* In this state of things, (if I may be allowed to carry on
the supposition,) the first draught of the waters would be towards the
Pagasæan gulf + But were they to rise so much higher, as to
spread over the plains on the western side of Thessaly ‡, they would
ultimately find an issue between Pelion and Ossa, near the modern
town of Aia. In this case, I conceive, that a range of hills which
separates the two great level districts, would be the only part of the
interior above water. §

In reality, it is not possible to view the dead level of these extensive plains, and the very compact barrier of mountains which
surround them, without forming some idea of the existence of such
a primæval lake, which, as it has been evidently drained off by the
opening of Tempe, might be restored again by the closure of that
passage. Nor would it be easy to explain the formation of Tempe
itself, without attributing it, as the most ancient inhabitants of this
country did, to the effect of some violent convulsion. And in this
way, I think, we may account for all the traditional relations of such
an event, to which Herodotus alludes. ‖

---

* That is, Perihæbia and Pelasgiotis.

† Now the gulf of Volo   ‡ Estiæotis

§ This range of hills connects Pheræ and Pharsalia with Tricca and the towns which
lie on the south-western borders of Macedonia   The battles of Cynocephalæ and Pharsalia were fought on the skirts of these hills.

‖ Strabo, who loves to dwell upon subjects of this kind, repeats these very ancient
traditions

I am further confirmed in this opinion on the origin of Tempe,
by the marks of similar revolutions, which I observed in other
mountainous districts of Greece. For instance, several of the
rivers of Arcadia run through deep and narrow glens, which must
have been formed in the same manner. One of these, the Ladon,
bursts its way through a vast chasm; which is reported to be several
miles in length, and has the appearance of being inaccessible to a
human being.* The Gortynius and the Neda, two other Arcadian
rivers, run through glens, the steep and lofty sides of which almost
conceal their course from the view of the traveller. But the most
remarkable chasm of this description, which occurred to my notice,
is that, which is known in Crete by the name of the Pharangi,
Φαράγγι (from the old word Φόραγξ). The whole body of a mountain
there, appears to have been rent asunder from the top to the bottom,
the two sides of the fissure which form a narrow pass of four miles in
length, threatening to close over the head of the adventurous
traveller. It was by this formidable defile that I visited Sfackia, and
I still feel the impression which it made upon me †

To recur to the history of Tempe, which has been necessarily interrupted by these reflections on its origin. Whatever may have been
the motive which induced Xerxes to view in person the defile of
Tempe, it does not appear from what Herodotus says, that he had
any intention of making use of it for the passage of his army; and
indeed, it would be absurd to suppose this ‡; but the line of his
march had been already settled; he was to cross the mountains into
the country of the Perrhæbians, in the direction of the town of
Gonnos; for that, says Herodotus, had been pointed out to him as
the best route. On his return from Tempe, Xerxes remained some

* It is at a short distance above the ruins of Telphusa
† I was above two hours immured in the Pharangi, the ascent being in some places
very rapid and much encumbered every where with the fragments of the fallen rock. It
is mentioned by Pococke, who passed through it
‡ When the very confined breadth of the road is considered.

time in Pieria; whilst one-third of his army were employed as
pioneers, in clearing the way over the mountains.

The Thessalians, however, some time before this, when Xerxes was
preparing to cross the Hellespont, seem to have been of opinion
that he would attempt to penetrate into their country by the pass of
Tempe; and the confederated army of the Greeks whom they had
invoked to their assistance, had, in compliance with their advice,
actually taken post in that situation. They remained there but a few
days, for being secretly apprised by the son of the King of Macedonia,
of the overwhelming force which would be brought to act against
them, and hearing at the same time, that there was another practicable
way into Thessaly across the mountains, they judged the attempt to
defend it would prove both useless and unavailing, and retreated to
Thermopylæ, upon which the Thessalians reluctantly joined the
standard of the invader.

It was accordingly by this route across the mountains that Xerxes
marched into Thessaly; and there are two passages of Herodotus
which point out the line of his march. Both of these mention
Gonnos, as the point to which it led, and Macedonia, as the country
from which it proceeded. But in one of these passages, we find the
designation of Upper Macedonia, which creates some difficulty, for
if Gonnos was the same town as the Gonni of a later period, of
which, I think, there can be little doubt, the army must have
began their march from the Lower, not the Upper Macedonia Now
Gonni is often mentioned by Livy, and the following passage of his
36th book describes the march of a Roman army, (if I am not
greatly mistaken,) by the same route as is pointed out by Herodotus.
After mentioning the irruption of Antiochus and the Ætolians into
Thessaly, and then arrival before the walls of Larissa, which was
then in the interest of Philip and the Romans, " M. bæbius *interim,
cum Philippo in Dassaretis congressus, Ap. Claudium ei communi
consilio ad præsidium Larissæ misit, qui per Macedoniam magnis
itineribus in Jugum montium, quod super Gonnos est, pervenit. Oppidum
Gonni viginti millia ab Larissa abest, in ipsis faucibus saltus, quæ Tempe*

appellantur, situm" The object of the Roman general being to relieve Larissa, it is evident, that no time was to be lost ; and whatever may have been his reason for not taking a shorter road towards that city, or for not passing through the defile of Tempe, when he was so near it; (Gonni, which commanded the pass, being at that time in the possession of the Romans or their allies,) yet, it is plain that he reached Perrhæbia at the same point, and must have crossed the ridge of mountains in the same direction as Xerxes.

In the subsequent war with Perseus, the Romans seem to have acquired the knowledge of several practicable roads across the mountains, to the north as well as the south of Olympus; and by one of these Quinctius Flamininus was fortunate enough to penetrate into that country, but the narrative of this transaction is so obscure, that it is impossible to fix with any degree of precision the line of his march It appears, however, to have been a very difficult and desultory one

At the present day, travellers, instead of passing through Tempe, not unfrequently take the road over the mountains to the north of that pass, which leads through the populous Greek town of Rápsiani (Ραψιάνη).

I shall conclude these remarks on the history of Tempe, with observing, that the ruins of a fortified town, which I suppose to be Gonni, are still visible on the brow of a rocky hill, which commands the western entrance of the defile. It is hardly necessary for me to observe that these ruins are on the road side of the river, that is, on the right; and not on the left, where a fortified post would have been useless, but where nevertheless, on the authority of the above passage of Livy, it has been generally placed in the maps of ancient Greece.

As there is a classical interest attached to every thing which belongs to Tempe. I shall subjoin a list of some of the plants which I observed there.

Laurus nobilis, the Bay.

Punica granatum, the Pomegranate.

Jasminum fruticans, the yellow Jasmine.

Vitex Agnus castus, the Chaste-tree.

Cercis siliquastrum, the Judas-tree.

Quercus Ilex, the evergreen Oak.

Quercus coccifera, the Kermes Oak.

Olea Europæa, the wild Olive.

Arbutus Andrachne, the smooth-barked Strawberry-tree

Arbutus unedo, the common Strawberry-tree.

Vitis vinifera, the wild Vine.

Platanus orientalis, the oriental Plane-tree.

Pistacia terebinthus, Turpentine-tree.

Fraxinus Ornus, the true Manna Ash.

Phillyrea, (the several varieties).

Zizyphus Paliurus, Christ's-thorn.

Spartium junceum, Spanish-broom.

Colutea arborescens, Bladder-Senna.

Coronilla Emerus, Scorpion-Senna.

Coronilla glauca or *Securidaca*.

A species of *Lonicera*, ditto of *Clematis*, and the white garden-lilly, which had not then expanded its petals, but flowered completely in my tin box eight days afterwards.

I found neither the myrtle nor the oleander. What Ælian says of the κιττός or ivy, and the σμίλαξ, (the Smilax aspera of Linnæus,) is untrue, for the former does not grow there, and the latter grows in a very different way from what he represents.

ON THE

SYRINX OF STRABO,

AND

THE PASSAGE OF THE EURIPUS.

[BY MR HAWKINS.]

In the very short description which Strabo has transmitted to us of the celebrated Straits of the Euripus, there is an expression which has long exercised the ingenuity of critics, without having received any very clear or satisfactory explanation. The words of the geographer are the following — Ἐστι δ' ἐπ' αὐτῶ γεφύρα δι-λεθρος *, ὡς εἴρηκα· -ὑργος δ' εκατέρωθεν ἐξεστηκε, ὁ μὲν εκ τῆς Χαλκιδος, ὁ δ' εκ τῆς Βοιωτίας διωκοδομηται δ' εἰς αὐτὸν σύριγξ. Here, I believe, with the exception of αὐτὸν, for which some critics have substituted αὐτοὺς, the purity of the text has been generally admitted, but the meaning is nevertheless obscure, because the term σύριγξ seems not to be used in its ordinary acceptation; the passage accordingly has been variously rendered by translators, nearly all of whom have avoided giving any precise interpretation of the term σύριγξ, without which the whole is unintelligible.

We are indebted to Isaac Vossius † for the first successful attempt to remove this obscurity, by pointing out the true meaning of the verb which is here put in connection with σύριγξ. " Διωκοδομει," he

---

* Two plethra amount to one hundred and seventy-one French feet, which may be stated as about twice the present breadth of the Euripus; according to Spons's evaluation it is ninety-one French feet, while Gyllius estimates it at seventy-three French feet only. No dependence can be placed on the accuracy of these measurements, which are unfortunately the only ones that have been taken by modern travellers.

† Observ. ad P. Melam. lib. xi. c. 7.

says, " *proprie est ædificationem separare et dividere, locumque intermedium vacuum relinquere. Dicit itaque Strabo, pontem istum Euripi non esse continuum, neque perpetuis fulciri fornicibus, sed ab ea parte qua est turris litori Bœotico vicina, habere unum canalem, qui sit apertus, quemque præsidiarii turris ponte pensili soleant tegere, tum securitatis gratiâ, tum etiam ut navibus pateat transitus*"

The two towers of Strabo are thus very properly disposed opposite to each other, and with a navigable passage between them, instead of one being placed on the shore of Bœotia and the other on that of Eubœa, with the mole or long bridge between, as some commentators and translators have conceived ; but why this fortified passage should be assigned to the Bœotian side in preference to the other, we are left to conjecture, nor is a word said to account for the very singular use which is here made of the term σύριγξ to designate a navigable canal between two towers

It appears then that the passage thus simply considered by itself, is susceptible of no farther explanation than what Vossius has given to it, and it is only by examining it in an historical point of view, with all the aids which may be derived from a local acquaintance with the spot, that we can hope for any success.

Most fortunately there is a passage in Diodorus[*] which supplies in a great measure this deficiency ; for it relates upon what particular occasion this work was constructed, the immediate purpose which it was designed to answer, and the manner in which it was executed   After his account of the naval engagement in the Hellespont, and the victory gained there by the Athenians, Diodorus proceeds as follows ·
" The Chalcidians, however, and almost all the inhabitants of Eubœa, had separated themselves in the mean while 'from the Athenian alliance, on which account they were very fearful lest their towns might be besieged and taken by the Athenians, who were now again become masters of the sea.   A proposal therefore was made to the Bœotians to unite with them in the enterprize of damming up the Euripus, and

---

[*] Lib. xiii. 173.

connecting Eubœa with Bœotia. To this the Bœotians, who felt how much it was for their interest that Euboea should be an island to all others but themselves, assented. Wherefore all the cities around concurred cheerfully in this undertaking, animating each other by their mutual example, and not only were all the natives called out upon this occasion, but even the strangers who sojourned with them, so that by means of the multitude employed about it the work was soon completed A mole ($\chi\tilde{\alpha}\mu\alpha$), therefore, was formed on the side of Euboea near Chalcis, and on the side of Bœotia near Aulis, for this was the narrowest part.

" It is to be observed that there had been always a current in this place and frequent changes of the tides, but now the violence of these became much greater, the sea being confined within a narrow space, for a passage was left for one vessel only.

" They constructed likewise high towers on the ends of the two moles, and laid wooden bridges over the currents between."*

The above narrative would convey to us a very clear idea of the construction of the mole, were it not for the inconsistency observable in the last sentence of the description. This arises from the use of the plural in the words " bridges and currents;" when from all that precedes it is evident that there could have been only one bridge and one current or passage for the water. Nor can we get rid of this difficulty by a conjectural emendation, for the text bears no marks of corruption

We are left, therefore, to the choice of two meanings, and in adopting that which naturally results from the former part of the narrative, we shall best reconcile Diodorus with himself as well as with Strabo

I shall therefore take for granted that the $\chi\tilde{\alpha}\mu\alpha$ or mole, in reality, left only one passage for vessels between the two opposite shores, and that this passage was fortified by two towers, between which there was a bridge of wood.

---

* Ὠκοδ́μησαν δε καὶ πύργους ὑψηλους ἐπ' ἀμφοτέραι τῶν ἄκρων, καὶ ξυλίνας τοῖς διάρροι: ἐπέστησαν γεφύρας.

Such was the original plan of this great work, which was executed in the second year of the ninety-second olympiad, and in the twenty-first year of the Peloponnesian war (Dodwell) Some alterations, we are told by Strabo, lib x., were made by the Chalcidians at the period when Alexander marched into Asia, both in the fortifications of the town and in those of the mole; but in Strabo's time, or about four hundred years afterwards, it appears, from the very short description which he gives, to have been pretty much in the same state as when it was first constructed, although the term γεφύρα is substituted for ζεῦγμα in both passages, and the new and very unusual term σύριγξ is made use of to designate a part of the work which I shall now proceed to consider

In the first place, then, we must admit that the term σύριγξ evidently applies to the navigable passage described by Diodorus, which Strabo would not have passed over unnoticed. In the next place, taking it in its usual acceptation, it conveys an idea of a circular or cylindrical passage of some kind or other.

The obvious result of this is, that the Syrinx must have been a sort of tunnel, which is precisely the form which a civil engineer in these days would have recommended for this purpose.

Nor is there any difficulty in supposing that such must have been the construction of this passage in the time of Strabo, when the use of the arch was well known, although it may be necessary, with a view to establish this hypothesis, to point out in a practical way the mode of its application. Let us suppose, then, that two towers are to be built at the two opposite ends of such a mole, and that a navigable passage is to be left between, while some mode of communication is required above. It is evident that the foundation of the two walls contiguous to the passage ought to be laid on an inverted arch, there being no other effectual mode of giving it any stability. The communication above might be effected by the means of a moveable or an immoveable bridge The Romans would undoubtedly in most cases have chosen the latter, and when we consider the importance which they attributed to this passage in a military point of view, it is probable that such was the construction which they adopted It is hardly necessary to add that the two opposite arches would form a tunnel

The term Syrinx, however, could not with propriety have been applied to a passage which was not truly cylindrical, i e where the length of the passage was not greater than its diamete , and we have no other way of getting over this difficulty than by supposing that a more than usual breadth was given to the two towers in this direction, which is by no means inconsistent with the purpose for which they were built

After all, however, that can be said upon this subject, I confess that it amounts to no more than a plausible hypothesis, which every critic is at liberty to adopt or reject, although the form of the present bridge over the Euripus tends rather to confirm it

This bridge is evidently built on the χῶμα of Diodorus, and although of a barbarous style of construction, suggests an idea of its ancient plan. The western end, or that which is contiguous to Bœotia, has five small ill-shaped arches, which give a passage to the shallow part of the current. The navigable passage is at the eastern end, and this is flanked as well as fortified by two opposite square towers, between which there is a communication by means of a draw-bridge.

The tower on the eastern side of this canal projects far beyond the line of the city wall; but as this wall is washed by the current, and the ground within it is very low, it is not improbable that the west side of the city covers the eastern segment of the χῶμα, which will account for the canal or navigable passage being now no longer in the middle of the Euripus†, although I am inclined to think that it must always have been nearer to the walls of Chalcis than to the shore of Bœotia, for the purpose of a better system of defence.

I shall conclude with observing that the tower supporting the western half of the draw-bridge is connected with a small fort, which extends in length far to the southward of the line described by the two bridges.‡

---

* See the engraved plan which follows.   † Vide note * in p 539

‡ I find the history of this fort in the following passage of the Latin version of Nicetas   " Postremo Eubœa quoque omissa defensione, supplices ad Marchionem mia-

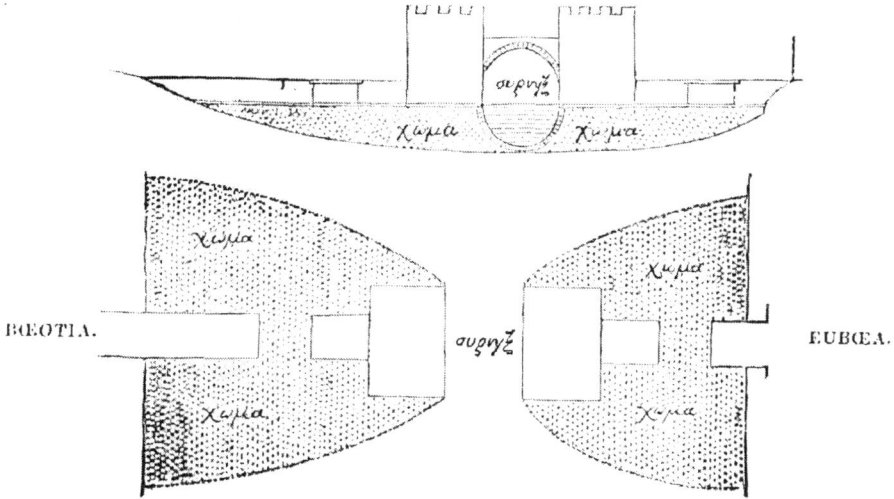

In the preceding attempt to explain the Syrinx of Strabo, I have noticed only such particulars in the passage of Diodorus, as might assist in explaining the meaning of that term. I shall now observe that Diodorus has not very clearly or fully expressed what were the reasons for constructing the mole. The Chalcidians, he says, together with almost all the inhabitants of Euboea, had abandoned the Athenian interest, but upon the unexpected restoration of the naval superiority of that power, in consequence of their victory over the Lacedæmonian fleet in the Hellespont, they became justly apprehensive of measures of hostility. A proposal therefore was made to the Boeotians to concur with them in closing the passage of the Euripus, and in joining the island by these means to the opposite continent.

The proposal, he adds, appeared to be so advantageous to the common interest, that the work was immediately begun and carried on with so much spirit, that in a short time it was completed.

nus tendit; et exercitui Euripo concitatiori pontem substernit, et in ipso freto castellum ædificatum, in eoque sedentem exercitum cernit." He is relating the rapid successes of Boniface, Marquis of Montferrat, in Greece, at the commencement of the 13th century.

Now, it is evident that the closing of the passage of the Euripus alone, could not prevent the Athenians from over-running the island, at least, that portion of it which lay to the south of Chalcis, nor could it prevent Chalcis itself from being invested by land. We must therefore conclude the meaning of Diodorus to have been, that when a communication of this kind was opened between the island and the main, it would be impossible for the Athenians to prevent the Bœotians from succouring their allies in Eubœa, as they had hitherto done. And this I conceive to have been the direct and immediate object in view when the work was undertaken. There was another object however of infinite importance, which could not have been overlooked when the work was projected, and this was the interception of all communication between Athens and the north of Greece, Thessaly, and Macedonia, during a great part of the year.

To explain this supposition, it will be necessary to state some peculiar circumstances in the navigation of the Ægean, which have been little attended to by the ancient as well as modern writers on the affairs of Greece.

There were two seasons of the year when the open navigation of this sea must have been either subject to great obstructions, or wholly interdicted to the Greeks, namely, the season of the Etesian winds, which prevail about four months of the summer and autumn, when all attempts to proceed northwards must have been fruitless; and the season of winter which was deemed too perilous.

These remarks however, apply *only* to the open navigation of the Ægean, for there was still a very practicable passage in the worst seasons for vessels, between the main land and the neighbouring island of Eubœa, where the smoothness of the water enabled them to take every advantage of local winds and the land breezes. I speak here from personal experience, having myself navigated the two Eubœan gulfs in all seasons, the spring excepted, without any material obstacle or impediment.

On the other hand, the ancients appear to have had a singular dread of the passage round the Caphareau promontory*, and they

---

* " Et Eubœæ cautes, ultorque Caphareus " Æneid, lib. xi.

4 A

must have regarded the whole eastern coast of Euboea, while the Etesian winds blowed, as a most dangerous lee-shore. For here, if I mistake not, were the tremendous hollows (κοῖλα, Coela) of Euboea, where a detachment of the Persian fleet were wrecked; and even at this day, the navigators of these seas carefully avoid all approach to an iron-bound coast, which in a line of about thirty leagues presents only one place of shelter for a ship in distress. *

The harbour† which is thus situated, being little frequented by the Greeks, was wholly unknown to navigators from the west of Europe, before I visited this inhospitable coast in the autumn of 1797, for the purpose of carrying on a series of triangles along the eastern side of Greece. After surveying this harbour, I was anxious to proceed round Cavo d'Oro (Caphareus), but such was the hollow form of the coast on my right, and so great the danger of being forced on a lee-shore, that the captain of the vessel (a polacre of Ipsera) thought it not adviseable to attempt weathering that cape, until, at the end of two days, the violence of the northerly wind (Etesian) had a little abated ‡

In proposing a new explanation of the Coela of Euboea, I have ventured to differ from some of the latest and best writers on ancient geography, such as D'Anville, Larcher, and Barbié du Boccage; but when it is considered how greatly the actual examination of a country must assist in clearing up the obscurities of its ancient geography, I trust I shall be acquitted of presumption; more especially when we observe how much the reports of ancient geographers are at variance with each other, and how many corruptions have been introduced into the text of their works. Even Strabo and his epitomiser are at variance upon this point, the former assigning to

---

* Kingsbergen observes, that, " on the whole north-eastern coast there is no landing-place. It is even dangerous to approach that shore " This is the observation of a seaman, but it is not strictly correct

† Now called by the Greeks Πετρίαι,

‡ On my return to England I communicated to Mr Arrowsmith the corrected form of this coast and the situation of this unknown harbour, which were engraved in his new map of the Ottoman empire.

the Cœla a situation between Aulis and Geræstus, and the latter placing them between Geræstus and Caphareus.

To prove how groundless the former supposition is, it will be only necessary to remark, that the coast of Eubœa on this side presents a series of noble harbours and roadsteads, without a shoal or sunken rock, and that in most winds it is distinguished by the smoothness of its water

There is a passage indeed, in Valerius Maximus (lib. i. c. 8) which countenances the idea of the Cœla having been on this side. " *In eam regionem successit, quæ inter Rhamnunta nobilem Atticæ soli partem, Caristumque Chalcidis freto vicinam interjacens, Cœlæ Eubœæ nomen obtinet.*" But the situation here assigned, as I have already observed, so far from being dangerous to shipping, which was the character of the Cœla, affords every where the securest anchorage-ground.

The epitomiser of Strabo, too, must be equally mistaken ; for the Cœla could not have been on a coast of so convex a form as that between the the promontories of Geræstus and Caphareus. A much better authority in favour of this hypothesis is adduced by Larcher, in a passage of the Troad of Euripides, v 84 Πλῆσον δε νεκρῶν κοῖλον Ἐυβοίας μυχόν ; in allusion to the vessels of Ajax, which, on their return from Troy, were shipwrecked on the promontory of Caphareus[*] ; and in the words cited by him from the scholia of Tzetzes on Lycophron, we find the Cœla actually placed in the neighbourhood of [†] Caphareus. It is remarkable that both Philostratus and Euripides, make use of the expressions, τὴν κοίλην Ἐυβοιαν and κοῖλον Ἐυβοίας μυχὸν, which are more agreeable to the hypothesis that I have ventured to propose. Having now proved how ungrounded every other idea of their position has been, I shall produce two ancient authorities which place the Cœla in that which I have assigned to them.

The first is Ptolemy, who in his description of the coast of Eubœa

---

[*] Homer says only on the Gyræ, without mentioning where they were situated Odyss lib iv. The coast of Cavo d'Oro is bristled with rocks and islets

[†] Ἤψε ερυκται περὶ τὰ κοῖλα τῆς Εὐβοίας καὶ ὃν εἴομεν Καφηρέα. Scholia Tzetzæ, Fd. Muller p. 573

mentions next after the port of Geræstus the promontory of Caphareus, and then the Cœla of Eubœa. The other is Livy, who after describing the capture of Oreus by Attalus and the Romans, observes, " that as the autumnal equinox was drawing near, and as that bay of Eubœa, which they call Cœla, was by sailors reputed dangerous, it was judged expedient to return without delay to the Piræus." * By the context it appears that at this time Chalcis was in the possession of their enemies, their fleet therefore could not pass through the Euripus, and as no other course remained towards the Piræus, but along the eastern coast of Eubœa, it is there, and there only, that we must look for the bay denominated Cœla.

The near connection of the Cœla with the promontory of Caphareus, has been already proved by a series of quotations, for which I am indebted to Larcher, but I am sorry to differ as to the meaning which he has assigned to the term Τὰ ἄκρα τῆς Εὐδίας; instead of designating the rocks near the promontory of Caphareus, the words more probably refer to the heights of Eubœa.

Having now explained what I conceive to have been the main object of the fortification of the Euripus, I shall produce some further proofs of its importance.

We learn from history, with what vigilance the Athenians for a long series of years maintained their sovereign influence over the vassal states of Eubœa ; and of what importance they regarded this connection, we have two most convincing proofs in the popular feeling at Athens, excited at two different periods by the news of its rupture. The first happened upon the occasion already mentioned, or rather just before it, when, after the destruction of the Athenian fleet at Eretria, the Lacedæmonians caused all the cities of Eubœa to revolt. † Thucydides informs us that the consternation produced at

---

* Jam autumnale æquinoctium instabat, et est sinus Euboicus quem Cœla vocant, suspectus nautis, itaque ante hyemales motus evadere inde cupientes, Piræum, unde profecti ad bellum erant, repetunt — Liv. lib. xxxi. c. 17

† In the twenty-first year of the war, the departure of the Lacedæmonian force exposed the cities of Eubœa to the vengeance of the Athenians, and suggested the immediate necessity of fortifying the Euripus

Athens by the news of this disaster was greater than had ever before been known there. greater even than that which was occasioned by the destruction of nearly all their forces, both naval and military in Sicily ; " not only," says he, " on account of their fleet. but what was of more importance, *the loss of Euboea*, ἐξ ἧς πλείω ἢ τῆς Ἀττικῆς ὠφελοῦντο, on which they were more dependent for their supplies of provisions than even on Attica." L. viii. c. xcvi. The second happened in the 105th olympiad, when in consequence of the revolt of Rhodes, Chios, Byzantium, Cos, and Caria, from the sovereignty of Athens, Euboea entered into a close connection with Thebes, and renounced her alliance with Athens, the receipt of which intelligence there produced such an effect on the public spirit, as stimulated it to make an exertion till then unparalleled, with a view to re-establish its dominion.

Now, the loss of subsidies and of a supply of provisions from the single island of Euboea, will not sufficiently account for the feeling here described, unless we add to these assigned causes. the prospect of having all communication cut off between Athens and the northern parts of Greece and Macedonia ; that is, all power of co-operating with their allies in those parts, and of procuring from them any farther supplies of grain, naval stores*, &c † In this enlarged sense, then, I take the passage above quoted from Thucydides ‡, the loss of Euboea alone, unconnected with the free navigation of the Euboean gulfs and of the Euripus, not being sufficient to account for the

---

* Vide Thucyd. l. iv. 108. with regard to ship timber

† And in this way its importance appears to have been estimated in subsequent times by the Romans. " Ut terra Thermopylarum angustiae Graeciam, *ita mare fretum Euripi claudit*." Liv. lib. xxxi. c. 23. Chalcis, Corinth, and Demetrias were called by Philip the fetters of Greece

‡ There is another remarkable passage in this History relating to Euboea, it is that (l. 3.) wherein he mentions the planting the colony of Heraclea in Trachinia by the Lacedemonians, who among other objects, intended to intercept the communication between Athens, Thrace, and Macedonia. Καὶ ἅμα τοῦ πρὸς Ἀθηναίους πολέμου καλῶς αὐτοῖς ἐδόκει ἡ πόλις καθίστασθαι· ἐπί τε γὰρ τῇ Εὐβοίᾳ ναυτικὸν παρασκευασθῆναι ἄν, ὥστ᾽ ἐκ βραχέος τὴν διάβασιν γίγνεσθαι, τῇ, τε ἐπὶ Θράκῃ παρόδου χρησίμως ἕξειν.

alarm * occasioned by the news of its defection. In confirmation
of which, I shall observe that Euboea, if we except the two plains of
Oreus and Lelantus, could never have been a fruitful island, nor could
the produce of the plain of Lelantus alone, or even that of the two
plains, have been sufficient for the main supply of such a population
as that of Attica.

If we take this view of the Euripus, we shall be at no loss to
account for the importance attached by the Athenians at all periods,
to the possession of a fortified sea-port, on so remote a part of their
frontier as Oropus, or for the reasons which induced the Thebans,
when they had captured that town, to remove it seven stadia from
the sea.

PANORAMIC VIEW OF ATHENS ILLUSTRATED

BY W. HAYGARTH, ESQ.

THE hill of Musæus is a rocky ridge of land to the S. W. of the
Acropolis; Athens with the most celebrated of its ruins, the Saronic
gulf, the shores of Argolis, the citadel of Corinth, and the distant
mountains of the Peloponnesus, names awakening a thousand
interesting associations, are visible from its summit. During my
residence at Athens, I employed some of my time in making a sketch
of the surrounding scene. The plates containing the panoramic view
are faithful copies of it. Beginning on the right hand of plate first,
I shall proceed in my description towards the left. The reader will
be able to find every place very exactly by marking the intersection

* It is true indeed that the defection of Euboea took place at a time when the Lacedæmonians, by having gained the ascendancy on the sea, were able to intercept the supplies of
corn which the Athenians drew from the Thracian Chersonesus and the Euxine, and this
may have rendered the loss even of a small supply from Euboea very sensible, but their
chief supply on this side of the Ægæan, as I have observed, must have been derived
through the Euripus, from Macedonia.

of two imaginary lines, one drawn from the figures at the side, the other from the letters at the top of the plate. The right side of Plate II. connects with the left of Plate I., and continues the subject.

Plate I. *Aspect from N. E. to N. W.*

A. 1. Part of Hymettus This mountain is now famous, as it was formerly, for the honey produced from the flowers on it. Strabo, 1 ix 580. Its quarries also were equal to those of Pentelicus. Paus. 1.

B. 2 Entrance to the Stadium Panathenaicum It was built of Pentelican marble, Paus. 1 i. The form is tolerably perfect, but the seats are destroyed; and of the prodigious quantity of marble used, according to Pausanias, in its construction, only some broken fragments remain.

A. 3. The situation of the fountain Enneakrounos. Thucyd. 1. ii.

A. 4. The bed of the Ilissus It is now quite dry, except after the storms of winter It was not very deep anciently, for Socrates and his companion, and Plato, speak of walking through it barefoot. Plato, Phæd The banks of the Ilissus are now almost entirely destitute of buildings, although anciently adorned with temples, nor are they overshadowed, as formerly, with planes. See Paus. i., and consult Plato's beautiful description of the scenery in its vicinity, in Phædo.

[The manner in which the Ilissus is mentioned by the ancient writers, does not lead us to suppose that it was a constant or regular stream. " What a flow of words is here;" (says Cratinus, speaking of an orator,) " Ilissus is in his throat." These expressions refer rather to a torrent, than an equable current of water. As however the rocky channel near the town, according to Mr. Raike's observation, seems to have been widened and formed by art, the stream anciently may have been more abundant than it is at present.

Wheler in three different parts of his work mentions the waters of the Eridanus and Ilissus being collected together, and carried under ground to supply the city; 352. 378. 450. Thucydides speaks of the κρήναι* or artificial fountains, as well as of the φρέατα of Athens; and the former must have been supplied from the waters of the neighbouring mountains. Dicæarchus indeed says, ἡ δὲ πόλις οὐκ ἐνύδρος; but his words may refer to the *country* of Attica; and not to the *city*, as Gataker † has remarked; and applied in that sense, his observation is true; for Attica has few streams of water.

It is singular that the word Callirhoe should still be retained; τί πρᾶγμα ἔναι ‡ Καλλιρρόη! said some of the inhabitants of Athens to an English traveller, when a greater quantity of water than usual was running at the spot, after a heavy rain.

We may here notice the wrong application made by Chandler, p. 111., of a passage in Statius, (Theb. l. iv) to the Ilissus of *Attica, anfractu riparum incurvus Ilissus* The poet is speaking of a river in the *Peloponnesus* See Hemsterh ad Plutum, p. 182.] ED.

D. 2. The ruins of the temple of Jupiter Olympius From Pausanias's description, l. i, I should infer that there was a large precinct in this quarter occupied by several other buildings.

E. 6. The arch of Hadrian connecting New with Old Athens.

E. 7. Course of the Eridanus, which falls into the Ilissus a little below. Paus. and Plato in Crit.

F. 8. The situations of the gardens, and temple of Venus   (Paus. l. i.) The modern village Ἀμπελόκητο, which stands nearly on the site of the gardens, retains in its present name a memorial of the ancient ΚΗΠΟΙ.

G. 5. The Lycæum. It was formerly laid out in groves and gardens, (Ovid. Meta xi. 710) and was also used as a place for

---

* Meto is said in Phrynichus, ἄγειν τας κρήνας. Μέτων ο Λευκονοεὺς ὅδ' ὁ τὰς κρήνας ἄγων — See Heringa, Observ. Crit 34

† Regio (ita πολιν, capio, πολιν, χώραν, Hesych) arida tota est, nec aquis irrigata — Adv. Post cxiv.

‡ I have written ἔναι (used by the modern Greek for ἐστι), instead of εἶναι, ἔναι occurs in Bessarion's letter, for the singular number, and ἔναι for the plural, and in the catalogue of the Madrid MSS in Cod lvi. p 184 ἔναι is written by Lascaris's own hand, ἔναι ἡ εὐεργεσία. But in the Prolegomena of Longinus to the Enchirid of Hephæstio, c 2., we find εἶναι, which the scribe has inadvertently placed in the text for ἐστί. — See Gaisford's Hephæs 143.

military exercises. Aristoph Pax. 351. Close to Lycæum was the gate of Diocharis, and fountains of water. (Strabo, l. ix) We may here remark, that the situation of the Lycæum may assist us in finding the frontier town of Decelea; the Lycæum was in a direct line between that place and Athens, Agis leading out his troops from Decelea against the Athenians, was met by the army of the latter under under Thrasylus at the Lyceum. Xenop Hell. i. c. 1.

II. 8. The site probably of Cynosarges Diog. Laer. l vi c. 1. There was a temple sacred to Hercules in it, Paus. l. i, near which the Athenians, after the battle of Marathon, encamped in their way to Athens. Herod. l. vii.

F. 9. The road to Marathon, passing at the foot of Mount Hymettus.

F. 1. The beginning of the range of Pentelicus

F. 2 Part of the modern town of Athens. The whole space to the south of the Acropolis, between it and the Ilissus, was formerly covered with temples and other edifices, as well as the part to the north of the rock. Thucy. l. 2. Plato in Crit. Dion. Chrys. Orat. vi.

I. 6. Round this point of the rock is the site of an ancient theatre, supposed by Chandler to be the theatre of Bacchus. At a short distance to the right in the town is the Choragic monument of Lysicrates.

[A representation of this theatre is given on a painted vase belonging to Yianachi Logotheti, it was found thirty years ago near Aulis; the eastern end of the Acropolis is there depicted; the corresponding part of the Parthenon above, below it is the cavern of Apollo and Diana, and beneath, the Theatre.] En.

K. 8. The Choragic monument of Thrasyllus, placed before a grotto, which is at present a church dedicated to the Holy Lady of the Cave. Over it was a female figure clothed in a lion's skin; now in the possession of Lord Elgin.

[It has been considered under various denominations; and Visconti shows clearly that it represented the female Bacchus In addition to what he has said respecting the character of this Deity, we may state the following references. Porphyry calls Bacchus, Θηλυμόρφος. Theodoret, H. Eccl. l. iii c 7, says that the Gentiles of Emesa consecrated a building Διι ὑπω τῷ χλανι, and

Isidore, in Orig., remarks that he was depicted *mulicbri et delicato corpore*] Ed.

K. 10. The remains of an ancient portico supposed by Stuart to be either part of the peribolus of the temple of Bacchus, or the portico of Eumenes

L. 11 The Parthenon, west front. *

M. 10. Ruins of a theatre. Wheler, Pococke, and Stuart, suppose it to have been the theatre of Bacchus, Chandler and Barthelemy call it the Odeum of Herodes Atticus. From the situation of it, I should certainly conclude that it was the theatre of Bacchus. It appears from Pausanias that the theatre of Bacchus, the Cave of Pan, the Propylæa, and Areopagus were all near each other. If we allow the ruins to belong to the theatre of Bacchus, these particulars agree with Pausanias; they are irreconcilable, if we place it at the S E. angle of the Acropolis. Pausanias says, there was a cave above the theatre, and a tripod upon it, such a cave is still seen at the S. E corner of the citadel; and this Barthelemy adduces as a strong argument for placing the theatre of Bacchus in that situation. But this is not sufficient to outweigh the rest of Pausanias's narrative, especially as there is another cave not far from the ruins of the S W. point, on which Wheler supposes a tripod to have been placed

N. 11. Modern tower, built near the site of the temple of Victory Apteros. Paus. 1 i. From this part of the citadel Ægeus threw himself down in a fit of despair for the supposed death of Theseus. Paus ib.

O. 1. An ancient building of white marble, and formerly a gallery for pictures. Paus. 1 i. This and the temple of Victory Apteros were connected by a range of Doric columns, placed at the top of the steps of the Propylæa; and through this portico was the chief entrance into the Acropolis. The space between the columns has been filled up by a modern wall; and a very short time before my arrival

---

* Concerning the front or proper entrance of the Parthenon, see Visconti's Memoir Theodosius Zygomalas in a letter to Martin Crusius, speaking of the ancient buildings remaining in the year 1575 at Athens, refers to what he calls the Πάνθεον, and mentions ἐπάνω τῆς μεγάλης πύλης ἵππους δύο φρυκσσομένους ἀνδρηπίαν εἰς σάρκα A head of one of the horses now in the Elgin collection, and brought from the west tympanum of the Parthenon, is probably alluded to It is a piece of sculpture of the highest merit. — Ed

at Athens, the Turks had knocked off the capitals of the columns, in order to erect one of their batteries on the summits. In front of the picture gallery and temple of Victory were anciently two equestrian statues. Paus. l. i.

L. L. Intersected by A. 12. That part of the city called Coele or the Hollow. In this spot were shown the tombs of Cimon, Herodotus, and Thucydides.

P. 1. The beginning of the range of the Icarian mountains, which terminates at the sea near Salamis

Q 4. Turkish burying-ground.

R. 10. Part of the Areopagus. This place is a rugged rock of small elevation, situated at the distance of about a furlong from the Acropolis at the N. W. extremity. The steps cut in the rock are still remaining. Pausanias describes it as being nearer the cave of Pan; and gives the etymology of the word, l. i See also Æsch Eum. 682. Eurip. Elec. 1258.

Plate II. Aspect from N. W. to S. W.

A. 1. Part of the modern town.

C. 3. The Ceramicus *within* the city. Paus. l. i.

D. 4. The temple of Theseus ; a little beyond, to the right. in the modern town, are the ruins of the Gymnasium of Ptolemy, and the Pantheon.

E 4. Road to the Academy, beginning at the gate Dipylon. Cic. de Fin. l. v. c. 1. It passed through the suburb called Ceramicus *without* the city, and was covered with the sepulchres of the illustrious dead. Thucy. l ii It has been supposed that the tomb of Pericles was in that direction ; but it appears from Cicero, (De Fin. v. c. 2.) that it was on the road to Phalerum. The accumulation of earth is not the only cause of the destruction of the Athenian sepulchres it is one of the accusations brought against Demosthenes by his rival, that when appointed to repair the walls of the city after the battle of Chæronea, he used the stones of the tombs for that purpose. Æsch. in Ctes.

F. 1 Via Sacra, leading from the Sacred Gate to Eleusis, as it is seen ascending the distant hills, G. 5

E. 6. The Collis Coloneus, the birth-place and residence of Sophocles, and the scene of one of his tragedies Suidas. and Cic de Fin. 1 v. 1. It was ten stadia from Athens. See Corsini, F. A. Diss. v. 207.

K. 6. The Academy*; a road passing from the gate Dipylon through the Ceramicus, and near the tombs of statesmen and warriors, led to the Academy, distant six stadia from the gate The site of the Academy is now laid out in gardens. It is overshadowed with woods of olive, a few planes and cypresses, and watered by the Cephissus. We meet with many illustrations of the scenery of the Academy and Colonæan hill in the writers of the ancient drama. See particularly Œdip. Col. 671. 700. and Aristoph. Nub. 1005.

The Lacedæmonians in their invasions of Attica always spared the olive woods of the Academy. Plut. in Thes.

I. 3. Lycabettus, a low rocky knoll, joining the hill of Musæus.

G. 5. The Via Sacra, ascending the mountain between Ægaleos and Corydalus. Acharnæ was situated near this place, as appears from Thucydides Archidamus leading the Peloponnesians from Eleusis to Athens came to Acharnæ, where he fortified himself, but did not descend into the plain Thucy. l. ii. c. 20. Stuart is mistaken in placing Ægaleos to the N. of Corydalus. Thucydides expressly says that it was on the right of the road from Eleusis to Athens; and that it was near the sea, we know from Xerxes having taken his position under it to view the battle of Salamis. Herod viii.

[The Via Sacra crosses the Cephissus in a direction nearly west of Athens. This river, says Strabo, flowing through the plain where the bridge is, δί τε τᾶν σκελᾶν τῶν ἀπὸ τοῦ ἄστεος εἰς τὸν Πειραιᾶ καθηκόντων, ἐκδίδωσιν εἰς τὸ Φαληρικόν †

It is evident from this passage that the long walls were destroyed in the time of Strabo; for if they had been entire, the river could

---

* The forest of olive-trees seen in this direction is one of the most striking features in the plain of Athens The groves and plantations in and about the city in ancient times, intermixed with the public and religious edifices, must have justified the application of the epithet παγχαλη to Athens. (Ælian, V H. iii. 26.) "Ἄση δὲ τίς πα τοιαδ' ἐσχ' ἄλλη πολι," says a comic poet, (apud D. Chrysos. Orat. 61) speaking of the city. — Ed.

† Strabo, lib. ix.

not have pursued its course to Phalerum ; it must have continued its direction towards Piræus. In fact, Strabo observes in the same book, that the walls were no longer standing.] ED.

L. 7. Distant summit of Cithæron. Strabo, l. ix.

Plate III Aspect from S. W. to S. E

A. 1 Distant summit of Cithæron.

B. 2. The old road to the Piræus, with the marks of the ancient chariot-wheels worn in the rock.

C 3. Mount Ægaleos It was not on the summit of this mountain, as some suppose, but at the foot of it, that Xerxes sat. Herod. l viii.

D. 4. Distant mountain of the Peloponnesus, perhaps Cyllene, on the confines of Arcadia.

E 5. The Acro-Corinthus.

F. 6. The island Salamis, the birth-place of Ajax, Strabo, l. ix. Æschyl. Pers 566.

H. 8. The Piræus, distant five miles from Athens. This is also the distance given by Thucy. l. ii. and Strabo, l ix. In different parts of the road, the ruins of the long walls* are visible, consisting of large blocks of stone, scattered loosely around. The marks of the chariot-wheels in the rock are evident also. Of the former splendour and busy throng of the Piræus, nothing now remains A monastery dedicated to St. Spiridion, and a Turkish custom-house, are the only buildings there. One or two small merchant vessels and a few boats frequent the harbour, once filled with the numerous galleys of Athens. The remains of the outer walls near the sea are considerable ; in some places four tiers of stones may be counted The port is a beautiful bay, well landlocked. †

---

* See Note, p 559

† Although some of the excavations in the rock at the Piræus and near the Museum hill may have served as sepulchres, yet it is more probable that they were places in which the Athenians were forced to dwell, when, during the Peloponnesian war, they quitted " their beautiful and ornamented country-residences," and were straightened for room in the city The words of Thucydides are, — Καλὰ κτηματα κατὰ τὴν χώραν οἰκοδομίαις τε και πολυτελέσι κατασκευαῖς. Lib ii The scholiast on the Equit of Aristoph. mentions the want of room in the city, and then dwelling in caves,— ἐν τοῖς σπηλαίοι ῷκουν τῇ σπανει τῶν οἰκημάτων. — ED.

K. 9. On a rocky point of land stretching to a considerable distance on the outside of the bay, is the tomb of Themistocles. Large blocks of a broken column, and an oblong excavation in the rock about six feet in length, which is occasionally covered by the waves of the sea, mark the position. The accounts of Plutarch and Pausanias agree that the tomb was placed near the Piræus. The former says, that as you come from Alimus, which is to the east of the port, after doubling a promontory, the tomb of Themistocles is seen near the harbour, close to the calm water, he cites some verses by Plato, the comic poet, which he supposes were composed for the tomb of the hero.

I. 5. Mount Arachnæus in Argolis, between Epidaurus and Argos. Its summit was the last post in the line of communication between Troy and Argos; and a fire blazing on it announced to Clytemnestra the destruction of the former city. (Æschyl. Agam. l. 319.) Between Arachnæus and Cithæron, l 22., there was only one other post for the signal. It is called Ægeplanctus by the poet, and was probably part of that high range which we ascend in leaving Megara on the road to Corinth.

Plate IV.   Aspect from S. E. to N. E.

A. 1. Port of Munychia.

B. 2. Port of Phalerum. Here Xerxes stationed his fleet previous to the battle of Salamis. (Herod. lib. viii c. 67.)

C. 3. The isles Eleusa and Belbina, near Ægina.

C. 4. The Sinus Saronicus.

D. 5. Isle of Ægina. The distant mountains beyond it are in Argolis.

E. The monument of Philopappus, on the summit of the hill of Musæus. (Pausan. lib. i.)

F. 5. I have here lowered the hill of Musæus a little, in order to introduce the point of Scyllæum, near which the Saronic Gulph enters the Ægæan Sea. Near the point is a small island anciently called Calauria, where Demosthenes ended his life by poison. (Plutarch. vit. Demos. Pausan. lib. i. Strabo, lib. viii. p. 542.)

G. 7. The remains of an ancient building on the Ilissus. The foundation-stones are large blocks of white marble. It is the ruin of a temple, but it is uncertain to whom it was dedicated. Stuart has given a drawing of it. (Antiq. vol i. c. 2) It has suffered much in its appearance since his time; he calls it the temple of Panops.

H. 8. Hymettus It joins on to the right side of Plate I., and completes the Panorama.

NOTE

[Many tombs and sepulchres have been cut out of the rock on the eastern side of the Piræan harbour, as well as numerous niches or shrines in the face of them; and here votive offerings to Neptune were placed. Among the ruins of the town of Piræus, some of the ancient streets may yet be traced; and the remains of two theatres, and of a Doric temple, marked by the capitals and triglyphs now scattered near its site.

The construction of part of the ancient walls here is remarkable; they are not built in horizontal courses, but formed of huge polygonal blocks of stone with smooth joints.

The masonry of the long walls is very coarse, and materials of every kind seem to have been used. There have been towers at certain distances all the way from the Piræus to Athens; but the wall on the side of Munychia is not so easily traced as the other. The foundations are about twelve feet thick. In the space between the long walls, over which the road to Athens conducted us, we observed in many places the foundations of houses, built on terraces, for which the rocky ground had been levelled, with the utmost regard to economy of space; staircases had also been cut in the rock. We here noticed some remains of tessellated pavements and many ancient wells. Some of these have a hollow cylindrical stone at their mouth, about three feet high above the surface of the ground, others have a moulding round the top, and look like circular altars; and I believe it was not uncommon to have bas reliefs on them. The stones were deeply indented by the frequent friction of the ropes to which the bucket was hung. One of these wells, if it be a well, is of a very singular form*; A. B. is an inclined plane; the mouth B. C. is about three feet in diameter; steps lead to the bottom.

I descended until heaps of stones and rubbish that choaked up the shaft prevented my advancing beyond fifteen feet. We observed some sepulchral chambers as we proceeded towards the city; and marks of chariot-wheels worn into the rocky soil are to be seen on the road; they are about four feet and a half asunder. While I was examining one of the wells, our guide Logotheti informed us, that lately some person employed by him in cleaning out a well near his house, found a bas relief in the soil at the bottom of it. This we afterwards saw; it is well executed; and represents a warrior in a chariot drawn by horses; a winged Victory stands near him; it was covered by a calcareous incrustation; but was afterwards cleaned, and is now in Lord Elgin's possession.

The approach to Athens is rendered very striking by the surrounding scenery; on the left the plain is enclosed by a chain of hills, part of Parnes and Brilessus; on the right by Hymettus; and it is terminated by the distant summit of Pentelicus. From the centre of the plain, Mount Anchesmus rises majestically; the Acropolis is contiguous to it; and at the northern side of its base are seen the houses of the modern Athens. The summit of the Acropolis is crowned with the remains of the temple of Minerva and other religious edifices; these, together with the Propylæa, must have produced in their entire state a sensation on the mind of a stranger arriving from the Piræus, most impressive and sublime.]—From Dr. Hunt's Journal.

---

* Dr. Clarke mentions the discoveries often made, at the bottom of the wells of Athens, of vases and other monuments of antiquity. We may add that coins may probably be found there, as in the time of civil wars money was concealed in them. Aristio, who had amassed much wealth by plunder, hid it, we are told, in the wells of Athens. — See Athenæ, lib. v. c. 5. Schw — Ed.

REMARKS ON THE THESAURI OF THE GREEKS

[BY THE EDITOR]

THE style of building adopted in the heroic ages of Greece for the construction of the ancient Thesauri may be seen by consulting the plates in Sir W. Gell's Argolis, which represent the treasury of Atreus at Mycenæ. We find this edifice described in Col. Squire's Journals in the following manner.

" Among the remarkable monuments of antiquity at Mycenæ, is a large conical subterraneous building of stone. From what we read in Pausanias *, respecting the Thesaurus of Minyas, and from the large stone over the entrance, compared with that now seen at Orchomenus in Bœotia, it may be fairly presumed that this underground building was the treasury of Atreus, a conjecture in some degree confirmed by small hooks of brass † which are still seen in the walls, and on which were probably suspended ornaments or articles of value belonging to the King of Mycenæ. The building is of a bee-hive form, 45 feet in diameter in the lower part; and on entering

---

* M Bartholdy has since examined this singular structure, and has drawn the same conclusion as Colonel Squire respecting the purpose for which it was erected, from comparing Pausanias's account of the Treasury at Minyas, with the actual building at Mycenæ. Une preuve plus que suffisante est celle qui se tire de la parfaite analogie de ce monument avec le tresor de Minyas à Orchomène. Pausanias dit, "que ce tresor est en pierre, et de forme ronde, la coupole ne s'élève pas fort en pointe, la pierre la plus élevée paraît servir de clef à toute la voûte," toutes circonstances qui cadrent textuellement avec la voûte de Mycènes — Voyage en Grèce, i 268

† Pausanias dit que l'on voit à Mycènes des chambres souterraines où Atree et ses fils gardoient leurs tresors Ces clous de bronze pourroient même avoir servi à suspendre des écus et des armes, ou des tapis et de riches habits. — Bartholdy

4 c

it, you find on the right hand, an adjoining chamber excavated in the rock about 20 feet square. The whole of the large building was lined or rivetted with masonry; in the adjoining chamber the solidity of the natural rock precluded the necessity of an artificial substitute The principal building is nearly 60 feet high; the top is enclosed by a single stone, and is level with the surface of a low height, on the east side of which is the entrance into the treasury through a passage lately opened by the means of Lord Elgin, leading to a gateway eleven feet wide, and eighteen feet in height; over the entrance is a triangular opening for the admission of light; the sides of which rest on a stone shaped like that at Orchomenus. Its dimensions are 27 feet long, 16 wide, and four feet six inches in height.

With respect to the treasury of Minyas at Orchomenus, mentioned by Pausanias as a wonder of art, we find the form and structure of it described by him in these words " It was made of marble; the shape was round; the building was not very much pointed at the summit, and the uppermost stone was said to bind or keep together the whole edifice." Λίθου μὲν εἴργασ]αι, σχῆμα δὲ περιφερὲς ἐσ]ιν αὐτῷ, κορυφῇ δὲ οὐκ ἐς α,αν ὀξὺ ἀνηγμένη, τὸν δὲ ἀνω]α]ω τᾶν λίθων φασὶν ἁρμονίαν παν]ὶ ἴναι τῷ οἰκοδ μήμα]ι From the version of Amasæus of the last part of this passage no meaning can be collected; " supremum lapidem toti ædificio modulum convenientiæ esse dicunt;" but the sense I have given to ἁρμονία may be determined by the commentary of Ruhnkenius on Longinus, sect. x.

We collect from Pausanias the purposes for which these ancient Thesauri were erected; they were built ἐς ὑποδοχὴν χρημά]ων (lib. IX.), and that of Minyas, now in ruins at Orchomenus, was the first, he says which was raised in Greece. From some circumstances belonging to the history of this state in very early times, a considerable quantity of wealth of different kinds was collected; πρόσοδοι ἐγίνον]ο τῷ Μινύᾳ μέγεθος, and the Thesaurus was built to receive these revenues. A distinction is clearly laid down by Pausanias between sacred edifices and Θησαυροί. he says, " that Agamedes and Trophonius were skilled in building θεοῖς τε ἱερὰ, καὶ βασίλεια ἀνθρώποις; therefore they erected a shrine for Apollo at Delphi, and a Thesaurus for Hyrieus." We may suppose that in early times when no temples * (in the sense we usually attach to that word) were erected in Greece, religious offerings as well as the treasures of the monarch were preserved in Thesauri, and places of greater security and strength can hardly be conceived.

There is nothing more curious in the history of ancient art in Greece, than the existence, at so remote an æra, of the Thesaurus of Orchomenus (a work, according to Pausanias, which was as worthy of admiration as the Pyramids of Egypt), and the great Καταβόθρα, excavated in the vicinity, for the purpose of receiving the waters of the Copaic Lake, and conducting them by subterraneous canals to the sea. The wealth of Orchomenus in the time of Homer was such as to justify particular mention of it; Il. i. 381., Ουδ' όσ' ές Ορχομενον προτινίσσεται; and we must suppose with Heyne that the last word indicates the wealth to have been *brought* to Orchomenus, probably by persons who visited that place with religious views, and carried with them offerings of value " What is most surprising," as Barthelemy observes, c. 34. V. d'Anach. " is, that the canals and pits, the καταβόθρα, in the neighbourhood of Orchomenus, of which neither history nor tradition have preserved any remembrance, must be attributed to the most remote antiquity, and that in those distant ages we have no knowledge of any power in Bœotia capable of forming and executing so vast a project." The time when Minyas lived, the builder of the Thesaurus, belongs to a very remote and obscure æra in the history of Greece; he is placed by Pausanias four generations before Hercules, or a century; allowing twenty-five years to each generation, and must have lived 1377 years B. C.

The Greek Thesauri of a later age are of very different dimensions

---

* On ne voit point qu' Homère ait eu la moindre idée de ce qu'on appelle ordre d'architecture, il parle des temples consacrés à Minerve et à Neptune, et cependant il n'en fait aucune description. The columns in his palaces are not ΣΤΗΛΑΙ, a word which would indicate stone, but Κίονες qui ne peut s'entendre que de poteaux de bois — Goguet, lib ii cp ii. 192

and construction; we may infer that they were small buildings, for
no less than ten are enumerated by Pausanias as erected at Olympia;
and as many, we learn from the same writer, and from Herodotus,
Strabo, and Xenophon, were seen at Delphi. *   In describing one
raised by the people of Megara, at Olympia, Pausanias mentions a
circumstance which leads us in some degree to a knowledge of the
form of these buildings; he says, " the war of the gods and giants
was worked in relief on the pediment of the Thesaurus," Τοῦ θησαυροῦ
δὲ ἐπείργασται τῷ ἀετῷ ὁ γιγάντων καὶ θεῶν πόλεμος.   We have no word in
English by which we can properly designate the Thesauri of this
second class, unless we adopt " sacred chambers or chapels." The
expression οἶκος, as well as ναὸς, is applied by the Greeks to them.
(Wytten. Anim. in Plut. ii. 990.)   The French use the term, " espèce
de chapelles ou salles, Larcher, Herod. 1. 200. Chapelles occurs in the
French translation of Strabo, lib. ix. 454., and in the Mémoires de
l'Acad des Inscrip 47. 84.   The Greek word is sometimes rendered
by Sacrarium †, and Schweighæuser, in his commentary on Athenæus, lib. xiii. c. 84., says, " varias fuisse Delphis cellas quas Thesauros
vocabant," a similar meaning is affixed to the word by ‡ D'Orville.
We learn from different testimonies that religious anathemata or the
offerings of states and individuals of a sacred nature (καθιερωμένα) were
preserved in them (Strabo, 607.); in one, at Delphi, called by
Polemo ὁ πινάκων θησαυρός, there were two statues of marble, and the
name implies that tablets were placed in it.   (See Schwei in l. supra
citato.)

---

* See Pausanias, lib x , Herodotus, lib 1. and iii , Xenophon Anab lib v , Strabo,
pp. 607 301. 312., for the mention of the Thesauri of the Clazomenians, Corinthians,
Siphnians, Athenians, and of the people of Spina and Agylla

† See Wesseling ad Diod Sic t i 744

‡ Sicil 74 Thesauri vocabantur cellæ separatæ et seclusæ circa templa in quibus singulæ
civitates donaria sua dedicabant, non aliter fere ac hodie Romanæ Hierarchiæ illustriores
sæpe subditi suam quisque, quam vocant capellam, in ipsis templis habent In an Oscan
inscription, we find TESAVR, which is Thesaurus, locus sacelli Herculis — See Passeri
Pitt. Etrus 3 vol lxii.

It appears that the word Thesauri was also applied by the Greeks to places formed or excavated under their temples; for the term Favissæ used by the Romans corresponded, we are told, to the Thesauri of the Greeks. Aulus Gellius, lib. xi. c. 10. Now the former were subterraneous apartments or recesses in which things of value pertaining to the temple, or connected with religious ceremonies, were preserved. When Livy, lib. v. c. 50. speaks of money deposited, "*sub cella Jovis*," he alludes to money placed in one of these Favissæ. Hence we may explain the expression which occurs sometimes in inscriptions, *Signa translata ex abditis locis* (Fabretti, 280.), that is, the statues or images were taken out from the Thesauri in which they had been deposited.

It remains that we should point out another meaning of the word θησαυρός; it was used to signify a granary, or place dug in the rock, in which grain was preserved. The city of Cyzicum had three Thesauri, τὸν μὲν ὅπλων, τὸν δὲ ὀργάνων, τὸν δὲ ΣΙΤΟΥ. Strabo, lib. xii. And in Aristotle, Œcon., lib. ii., we find mention made of θησαυροὶ παρὰ τὰς ὁδούς. This mode was adopted in early times, and is still used for preserving corn in the East, and in one of these magazines Philopœmen was confined, as we learn from Plutarch and Livy, lib. xxxix. c. 50 "Conveying him," says the Greek writer, "to what was called the Thesaurus, a subterranean building, receiving neither air nor light from without, and having no doors, but closed by a great stone, which was rolled against it by some mechanical power, there they placed him." Κομίσαντες αὐτὸν εἰς τὸν καλούμενον θησαυρὸ, οἴκημα κατάγειν, οὔτε πνεῦμα λαμβάνον, οὔτε φῶς ἔξωθεν, οὔτε θύρας ἔχον, ἀλλὰ μεγάλῳ λίθῳ περιαγομένῳ † κατακλειόμενον ἐνταῦθα κατέθεντο. A similar punishment was inflicted on Antigenes, he was put into one of these excavations made under ground for the purpose of receiving corn, and was burnt alive. Diod. S. T. ii. 351

---

* The Thracian word for these excavations was ΣΕΙΡΟΙ τοὺς θησαυροὺς καὶ τὰ ὀρύγματα ἐν οἷς κατετίθεντο τὰ σπέρματα σιτοῦ, ἐκάλουν οἱ Θρᾷκες. — Schol. in Demos. Orat. de Cherson.

† The word περιαγομένῳ in Plutarch is explained, as Gronovius observes, by the phrase in Livy, saxum quod machina sive tormento movetur.

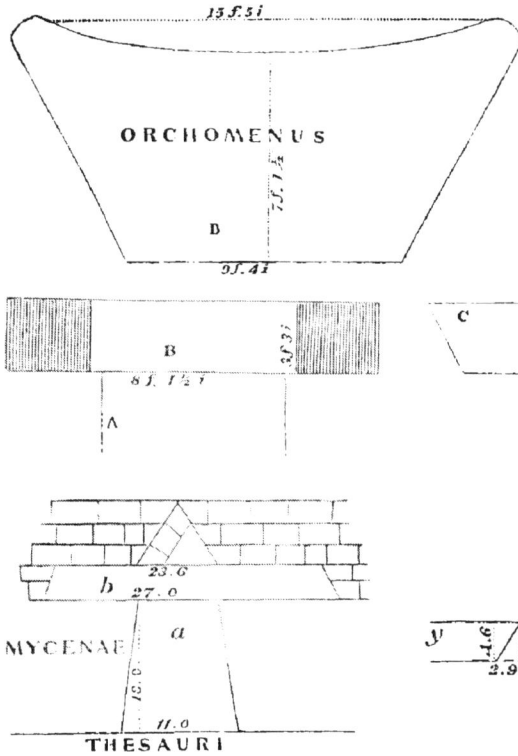

A. is the door-way of the Treasury at Orchomenus.

B. is the great stone over the door-way, of granular marble.

C. the inside slope.

a. is the door-way of the Treasury of Mycenæ.

b. is the great stone over the door-way, having above it a triangular opening for the admission of light. The stone is twenty-seven feet long; four feet six inches high; one foot six inches broad.

y. is a section of the large stone.

The measures of the Orchomenian Treasury are from Mr. Hawkins; those of the Thesaurus of Mycenæ are taken from Colonel Squire's papers.

REMARKS ON THE TROAD

CONTAINED IN A LETTER ADDRESSED BY MR. MORRITT TO DR. CLARKE
AUGUST 1812;

DEAR SIR,

WHEN, like you, I first visited the ruins of Tchiblak, then coincidence with the description given by Strabo of the Pagus Iliensium, struck me so strongly, that I hesitated for some time whether I should not adopt the system which they have led you to pursue, and suppose this to be the situation which Homer assigned to Troy. Had I found the ruins you describe at Palæo Califat, the coincidence would have struck me still more forcibly, and the remains you describe as the Callicolone, and the tombs of Ilus and Myrinna, would have been powerful corroborations of my opinion. I confess it is more than probable that Strabo adopted it, and yet it is so inconsistent with Homer's poem, that after comparing them I should have been compelled to doubt extremely the accuracy of his information. I cannot lay any stress on the traditions which in Strabo's time continued to identify the different objects in the plain with the features of the poem. The Troad was consecrated ground, travellers of the greatest celebrity, kings and warriors, stopped in their career to contemplate its remains, and the natives of Ilium and Alexandria appear to have been no less officious in gratifying their curiosity than the monks of Jerusalem now are, in pointing out their scenes and situations to the veneration of the pilgrims. There are some difficulties which perhaps you may remove (or which may be left to future visitors of the plain,) in reconciling Strabo's description with your system and first with regard to the position of New Ilium This you consider as situated at Palæo Califat, to the north of the stream now called Califat Osmack, and supposed by you to have been the Simois of Homer and of Strabo. " It is *surrounded on*

all sides by a level plain," which you conjecture to have been the
Simoisian plain, and from the medals which are said by the Turks to
have been found there, certainly it appears to have existed here.
But in Strabo's description of New Ilium it appears to me to have
stood *between the two rivers*, which he considered as the Simois and
Scamander ; for his description of the country is as follows (Strabo,
p 597. lib xiii.) " The two rivers, the Scamander and the Simois,
the first having approached Sigæum, and the latter Rhæteum, join
their waters at a little distance in front of New Ilium, and then fall
into the sea near Sigæum, and form what is called the Stomalimne
A large neck of land divides the two plains from each other (the
Scamandrian and Simoisian plains,) beginning immediately where
the modern town of Ilium stands, and συμφυὴς αὐτῇ, '*connected with
it,*' but extending to Cebrenia, and completing the form of Υ, till it
reaches the ridges on either side ;" which ridges he had before described as enclosing the plain in a semicircle. If New Ilium *stood at
the end of a neck of land* between the Simois and Scamander, and the
junction of the two took place *in front* of the town, it would seem as
if Strabo considered the *front* as the side next the shore, from whence
and not from Ilium he seems to have taken his survey. The city of
New Ilium also in the time of Strabo had another peculiarity which I
candidly confess agrees neither with the situation in which I looked
for it between the Mender and the stream of Bournasbashi, nor
with that which you assign it for it could not admit, he says, of the
flight of Hector round its walls (which he considers as essential to the
situation of ancient Troy), διὰ συνεχῆ ῥάχιν on account of the *continued
ridge* on which it stood In this confusion it appears to me impossible to reconcile Strabo's description to the places now discoverable
in the plain. I found some old work and broken inscriptions between
the two rivers, which I supposed the Simois and Scamander. Should
a city have existed in that situation, it would, from Strabo's account,
dispute the title of Ilium with your ruins at Kalifat, as they are so
contiguous, that Ilium medals would be found by the Turks at either
place. Where Kauffer gets his name for it of Ville de Constantine,

I do not know; but if Constantine built near Ilium these ruins may certainly have belonged to him.

Another point still left to be ascertained from Strabo is the ναύσταθμος, or *position of the Grecian fleet and camp during the siege.* He mentions it first in p. 595.—" Beyond Rhœteum is Sigæum, a city in ruins, and the station of the ships, and the port of the Grecians, and the Greek camp, and the marsh called Stomalimne, and the mouths of the Scamander." In p. 598. he adds, " The ναύσταθμος (station of the ships) is *at Sigæum,* and near it the Scamander discharges its waters at the distance of twenty stadia from New Ilium. But if any one should insist that the place now called the ΛΙΜΗΝ ΑΧΑΙΩΝ, the *port of the Grecians,* was the *station of the ships,* he will fix it at a place twelve stadia distant from the city (of New Ilium), for all the plain between the city and the sea is an alluvial plain, formed by the river, so that the interval, which is now twelve stadia, was formerly less than the half." This passage appears to me of great importance in ascertaining not only the situation of the Grecian camp, but the relative positions of the rivers and the city, as I will endeavour to convince you. For, first, the description of the shore is such as precludes all possibility of deriving from its present form any argument as to its ancient windings, next, the little bay which you mark as the harbour of the Grecian fleet is indeed nearly in the position of the place called in Strabo's time the λίμην Ἀχαιῶν, the *port of the Greeks,* which he expressly asserts to have been different from the ναύσταθμος, or *station,* assigned by Homer; for this was *at Sigæum,* and consequently on *the other side* of the Mendere river. I should lay less stress on this position assigned by Strabo, were it not confirmed in many respects by Homer, and did it not account also for the straitness and crowding of the Grecian quarters, for which, under the other supposition, it would be difficult to assign any reason.

The source of the Scamander was, according to the account of Demetrius, in a hill of Ida called Cotylus, at one hundred and twenty stadia from Scepsis; from whence also rose the Æsepus and the Granicus, the Scamander alone flowing to the west. Strabo, p. 602.

It is then apparent that Demetrius and Strabo considered the Mendere as the Scamander, and though I doubt the justice of that conclusion, yet your researches have completely satisfied me as to the accuracy of their description.

Allow me, then, at last, to revert to Homer, from whom alone I think the clue is to be obtained which will guide us out of the labyrinth in which we have wandered. And, first, with regard to the situation of the Grecian camp and fleet. I am led to place it at Sigæum, from the following circumstances. All the tombs, except the Aianteum, are to the west of the Mendere river ; and that one of these at Sigæum was always celebrated as the tomb of Achilles, we have the concurrent testimony of ancient history, the tomb of Patroclus, whether a cenotaph as described in the Iliad, or that in which his ashes, mixed with those of his friend, were deposited according to the Odyssey, must also have been in this part of the plain. That these tombs were at no great distance from Achilles's station, we may, I think, gather from the description, given in the twenty-third book of the Iliad, of the funeral rites of Patroclus. I think, too, that the situation of the tomb of Patroclus at the Sigæan promontory is marked by the arrival and return of the winds Boreas and Zephyrus over "the Thracian sea" Il. Ψ. v. 230. This position of the sea to the north and west agrees remarkably with the situation of the tombs at the Sigæan promontory, which appear, I think, also to have been in or immediately adjacent to the camp. That the camp was here, appears farther from the inimitable picture of Achilles in the first book. "sitting apart from his friends," ἐπ' ἐφ' ἁλὸς πολιῆς ὁρόων ἐπὶ οἴνοπα πόντον. This *surfy shore*, and *black sea beyond it*, I have always considered as applicable to the *Ægean*, and not to the bounded view across the *Hellespont*. If the Grecian camp was *at Sigæum*, and the tents of Achilles and the Myrmidons at the *western extremity* of that camp, I need not point out to you how exactly the position would agree with the circumstances thus alluded to. Here, too, we have the θῖνα πολυφλοίσβοιο θαλάσσης, where Chryses addressed Apollo, the *patron of Tenedos*, a picture surely made more natural on this supposition, as the *island and fane of Tenedos* would here be within his view. Il A. v. 38. Such are the circumstances which induce me to adopt the opinion sanctioned by Strabo, that the ιάυττάβμος, or station of the Grecians, was on the *western side* of the mouth of the Mendere, and not at the harbour called in after-times the ΛΙΜΗΝ ΑΧΑΙΩΝ From the nature of the alluvial plain described by Strabo, and existing at this moment near the mouth of the Mendere, we cannot now expect to point out with precision the spot to which Homer alludes; we know that it was not extensive, from the crowded manner in which the Grecians ranged their ships, the Mendere, however, at different times must have varied the direction of its course, before it formed the point on which the modern castle of Koumkalé is situate. No argument drawn, therefore, from the present form of this sandy and alluvial shore, would induce me to reject Strabo's position of the Naustathmus, as it is confirmed by Homer.

Between this camp too, and the city of Troy, we find repeated mention of the *fords of the Scamander* Il Φ. l. 1. and subsequently Ω. l. 350 and 692 Whether, then, the Mendere or the stream of Bounarbachi be looked on as the Scamander of Homer, the camp and the city were on *different sides* of the river; and in assigning to Troy the position of Tchiblak, we should still come to the same conclusion that the camp was *at Sigæum*. When the Trojans were encamped near the walls and ships of the Grecians, their fires were lighted between the ships and the Scamander, Μεσηγὺ νεῶν ἦδε Ξανθοιο ῥοάων Ἰλιόθι πρὸ, *in front of Ilium*. Now, in the position assigned by you to the post of the Grecians, and to the ancient city at Tchiblak *no river intervenes except the* *Thymbrius*. If Hector also and the Trojans were "between the river and the ships" in this memorable night, the tomb of Ilus, where the council of the Trojan chiefs assembled, was in this *Scamandrian plain*, and, as Heyne justly observes, the ὑψ᾽ σμὸς πεδίοιο was probably on the side of the river *next the ships*, αγχι νεῶν We must then look for it on the other side of the Mendere, to that which you seem to have discovered, and which was probably pointed out to Strabo. That the monument of Ilus was near the ford, and probably close to the Scamander. but on the other side of the ford, appears from the twenty-fourth book, v 349, in the account of Priam's journey to the tents of Achilles.   My own opinion was, that the ancient mouth of the Mendere had probably been altered, and that the Stomalimne and marshes nearer to Rhæteum had at some time received it.   The difficulties already mentioned induced me to adopt Chevalier's system, which places Troy at Bounarbachi in preference to Tchiblak, where, however, I conceive that Strabo found the *Pagus Iliensium.*   The rocks of the Acropolis alluded to in the Odyssey, Θ. 507., exist only (if they exist at all) in that direction.   The station of the scout Polites upon the tomb of Æsyetes corresponds with this view of the subject.   If Troy was at Bounarbachi, it would not only be the point from whence a survey of the Grecian position would naturally be taken, but one from which his swiftness of foot would secure him a retreat, but if we place the city at Tchiblak, the banks and waters of the Mendere would intervene, and his distance from the city would be nearly equal to that of the Greeks themselves.

Of the nature of the rivers in question, and of the plain, I would observe, that you have, perhaps too hastily, adopted an idea that the principal battles were fought in the *Simoisian plain,* in contradiction to Homer, who, though he places the scene of action for several books between the Simois and Scamander, or between the Scamander and the ships, always, I think, designates it by the title of the *Scamandrian plain,* which also was nearest to the camp and ships. B v. 469. The Grecians are described as issuing from the camp, and forming their army, ἐν λειμῶνι Σκαμανδρίω ἀνθμόις., and the Trojans at the sepulchre of Myrinna (Ibid 815.)   The subsequent battle was fought between the Simois and Scamander (Ζ. v. 4.), and nearer to the Scamander than to the Simois, if Heyne be correct in his note on the Il. E. v. 775 vol. ı. p. 297., where Juno and Minerva descend at the confluence of the two rivers.   Indeed they leave their car and horses on the banks of *Simois,* before they proceed to the plain, v. 777. This is the scene of the first battle, and the second begins in the same position; but the Grecians being driven to their ships, the Trojan are, we find, in the eighth book, Il. Θ. v. 556., between the ships and the Xanthus, or Scamander, which last river of course they *must have crossed.* The relative situation of the two rivers you very justly lay down as Homer describes them, the Scamander to the left of the Trojan army, and consequently to the right of the Grecian, when both armies were between the rivers; and after the Scamander had been crossed by both armies, of course that relative position would be reversed. In the seventh book, Il. Η. v. 329., the bloodshed is all stated by Nestor to have been Έυρροον αμφι Σ αωκαντος, on the *banks of Scamander*, nor do I recollect any mention of the *Simois*, or the *Simoisian plain*, except where the river is incidentally named in the passage I have already quoted, and where Xanthus calls on him for assistance against Achilles in the twenty-first book, Il. Φ. v 307. There is another passage indeed which I should wish to lay before you, and which goes far to prove that the *Simois* was certainly the river now called the Mendere, for it is quite clear that the Simois *descended from Ida*, whatever was the case of the Scamander, which I will presently consider. In the fourth book, Il. Δ. v. 473., Simoisius, the son of Anthemion, is slain by Ajax — Simoisius, " whom his mother, as she was descending from Ida, brought forth on *the banks of the Simois.*" This passage I look on as conclusive against any system that places the whole course of the Simois in the plain below Troy. The Simois, too, ill accords with your description of the Califat Osmak, which, as you justly state, can " hardly be said to flow towards the Mendere " It is indeed most accurately designated by you as a " small and almost stagnant river," but the Simois was of a totally different description ; it descended from Ida, and raised on occasion πολυν ορυνγον, φιτεων και λας ι. L. 21 Surely, therefore, the Mendere has a title to be the Simois of Homer. But the claim of the Scamander is very dubious. Great stress has been laid upon the relative size of the rivers, of which, if you will for a while tolerate the assertion, which, I think, I can support, Homer no where makes any mention. He describes the Simois, as we have seen, as a mountain-river descending from Ida, and sometimes with great violence. I have been severely reprehended, as well as Sir W. Gell, for misstating the nature of the Mendere river, and Chevalier's conjecture, that it was in summer inconsiderable, has met with equal severity.

In November it was, when I visited it, a *very considerable river.* You
have, with Sir W. Gell, borne testimony, which *I can confirm,* to the
strength of its stream and the depth of its fords; but in spite of all
this, I must continue to give credit, not to Chevalier, indeed, but to
Chandler, who expressly states ('Travels in Asia, chap. xiii.) that
" he passed the stream where the bed of the river was wide, and the
bank steep, *several times without being wet shod,*" though when I was
there, if he had attempted to pass on foot at the same place he would
probably have been drowned With respect to the Scamander of
Homer, we are not *singular* in conceiving it to have had its rise from
the two fountains near the city, for though, as you judiciously observe.
the πηγαὶ Σκαμανδρου do not *necessarily* imply in all cases the *sources* of
the river, yet it is by so much the *most usual* acceptation that Strabo
himself understood Homer in that sense, for, he says, that Homer's
description affords room for discussion, " because no warm springs
are now found in the place (that is, at New Ilium), and the source
(πηγή) of the Scamander is not there but in the mountain, and is only
one source, *not two,*" though at the same time he admits, that, by supposing the cold water he found there (probably the Califat Osmak) to
have flowed in a subterraneous passage from the Scamander, and
to rise here; or, perhaps, on account of *the vicinity* to the Scamander, it might be called Σκαμάνδρου πηγή; and that the hot
spring had probably failed.   Strabo, lib. xii. p. 602.   The first, therefore, was the *usual and obvious* sense of Homer's expression, and the
only objection that has been made against it, is the passage in the
twelfth book, Il. M. v 20. where the Scamander is mentioned as one
of the rivers that flow from Ida to the sea.   The *Simois* is also mentioned in the very next line, so that, if this passage be genuine, we
must look for *both* these rivers in the mountains; and the Califat
Osmak, as well as the river of Bounarbachi, would lose all claim to
either designation.   It is, however, more than suspected, I should be
inclined to say that it is *nearly certain,* that the whole of this passage
in the twelfth book is spurious.   In Heyne's notes on the place, he
mentions many grounds to support this opinion, some of which are
very strong.   The reason assigned for the Grecians building the wall

is inconsistent with the account given of it in the seventh book, the disappearance of the wall (which itself was in all probability an invention of the poet) was accounted for already in the seventh book, where it would naturally occur. In the twelfth it has no connection whatever with the narration, to which I would add that the absurdity of bringing all the rivers of Ida to co-operate in the work of destruction is so great and obvious, that it could only be the addition of some subsequent rhapsodist unacquainted with the nature of the country.*

There may be other passages, but there are none in my recollection where Homer describes Scamander as *issuing from Ida*, or descending from *Idæan* Jove. It is true, as I have already shown, that *Simois* descended from the mountain, but we are at full liberty to look elsewhere for the Scamander. Being ignorant of the geography of Ida near Bairamitche, and finding in Wood's Map a continued chain of hills from Bounarbachi southwards to Scepsis, and the sources of the river that flows past it, and which he mistook for the Scamander, I certainly consider the hills behind Bounarbachi as part of the ὑπώρεια, or roots of Ida, as that name includes in Strabo the whole of the mountain-district, as it did in Homer's time; and indeed as the plain of Bairamitche, though it extends between this range and the summit of Kasdaghi, does not cut through the chain behind Scepsis, the hills of Bounarbachi, seem still to be only the claws of the large Scolopendra, to which it was likened by the ancient writers. Supposing, however, that the hills at Bounarbachi are " *no part of Ida,*" they do not therefore become less likely to have been the seat of Troy. I do not remember in the Iliad any passage where Troy is said to have been situated on that mountain, though it stood near the fountains of Scamander. The only remaining objection to our Scamander is its size, which has been thought inconsistent with the

---

* Though the passage supposed to be interpolated is unquestionably ancient, I still should think it not genuine from the mention of the ἡμίθεον γένος ἀνδ͂ῶν, demi-gods, a race of beings with which the old bard himself seems to have been totally unacquainted. I question if they are alluded to in any *genuine* passage of Homer. Castor, Pollux, and even Hercules, are always represented as men and as mortal.

epithets assigned to it by Homer   He certainly was the son of
Jupiter, and in the 21st book his epithets would lead us to expect a
considerable river, but after the Trojans in that book had arrived at
the ford of the Scamander (Il. φ. v. 1.), and one part of them fled
towards the city, those whom Achilles pursued fled to the left, and
the slaughter continued below, and at the confluence of the two rivers.
Below that point the united stream retained always the name of the
Scamander; I have elsewhere given reasons for this supposition, for
were not the battle between Achilles and the Scamander at least
near the confluence, the demigod could not be so silly as to invoke
the assistance of his kinsman the Simois.   At that point all the
epithets are certainly applicable, and they are but sparingly used if
at all in other parts of the poem, where the Scamander is more
appropriately complimented as εὔρροος, καὶ ἔρριος, and on his ἄγλαον ὕδαρ,
and καλὰ ῥέεθρα.   Indeed in after-times the Mendere received all the
honours due to the Scamander, and probably the alteration arose
from the diversion of the original stream; for notwithstanding the
story of the drain made by a Turkish governor, I strongly suspect
the present channel of the stream of Bounarbachi to have been a
much more ancient work.   The *amnis navigabilis* of Pliny is marked
in your maps, and Mr. Walpole's research has completely accounted
for the epithet; but you seem to forget that Pliny expressly calls it
the Scamander.   A Turkish governor, as you know, was not likely to
originate an improvement of this nature, and it is not possible to
account for Pliny's expression, but by supposing the new channel of
the Scamander, as it is called, to have existed when he wrote.   Nor
even does the modern name of Mendere appear to have been
uniformly applied to the larger river.

I agree, therefore, with Chevalier, that after the deflection of this

---

* I should suppose the entreaty of the Scamander to the Simois most naturally timed
when he was driving the hero down his stream to the point of confluence   It should
never be forgotten that near this point a single elm pulled down by Achilles formed a
bridge across it, a circumstance which can only be applied to such a stream as that of
Bounarbachi

stream, subsequent geographers continued to the larger river the name which in Homer's time it only bore below the confluence, and looked for the Simois where they could not find it. This alteration in the course of the Scamander, if it was very early (which I strongly suspect it was), accounts for the variance we find between Homer and even the best of the ancient geographers. This system, which Chevalier first adopted, still appears to me so far from being a "wild theory," that it seems to remove the chief difficulties which stand in the way of every other. It is strongly borne out not only by the existence of the two fountains, which, according to the obvious, though not the necessary sense of the only genuine passage relating to the sources of the Scamander in Homer, appear to have been those sources, but also by the tumuli on the hill behind Bounarbachi, which agree with the probable position of the Trojan tombs, and were certainly near the city. As to the nature and heat of these springs and the number of them, they have given rise to more minute researches than when I was there; and my only excuse for this and many other omissions is, that when I visited the plain, Bryant had not written, and I never dreamt of controversy. The survey I took was merely to satisfy a classical curiosity with respect to Homer, and I neither used a thermometer to the springs, nor took more of a map than just to mark with a pencil some of the incorrect delineations of Chevalier's. You who have been on the spot, will appreciate what I did, and not wonder at what I omitted, under such circumstances. Every traveller has confirmed what I originally stated with respect to the tradition of one of the springs being hot and the other cold. I call the Kirk Geuse one spring, for though the water issues from a number of small orifices in the rock, yet being all so near together and forming only one large pool, it is refining far too much to suppose a poet would necessarily speak, as Shakspeare says, by the card, and count every separate crevice. To the touch when I was there, the water of the marble fountain, in which only one spring rises, was warmer than in the larger and more exposed pool formed by the Kirk Geuse. If Homer had heard by a similar inaccurate report what we all heard from the tradition of the country, such an

opinion would be quite foundation sufficient for the incidental description with which he has ornamented his 22d book. The tombs
are another striking feature of this system. They of course were near
Troy, for the same reason that those of the Greeks were near the
shore. Hector's was made τυμβο͂ ιν λᾱέσσι, and all those you found
there were of stones heaped together, like the Scotch cairns, of
which we ourselves have numbers in each part of the island   It
would perhaps be difficult to point out that of Hector after your
observation, that the same description would apply to all; but it by
no means follows that the same did not apply to all, as the poem
closes without mentioning the other tombs. Not only the tombs however, but the rocks mark the Acropolis of Troy, for they, too, are
mentioned in Odyss. Θ. v. 508 —'Η κατὰ τέτράιν βαλέειν . . a circumstance not sufficiently weighed by many who have written on
the subject. Nay, I am almost inclined to insist on this situation
the more, from its explaining, I own, to my own satisfaction, a very
curious passage which has been much discussed by the commentators.
In the 21st book, Il. Φ. 555, after the Trojans, pursued by Achilles, had
entered the city, and Priam had closed the Scæan gate to stop pursuit,
Agenor, incited by Apollo, remained on the outside of the wall   In
his alarm at the approach of Achilles, he meditates on flight, and says,
Il. Φ. 556, — " What, if leaving the others to destruction from Achilles
I fly from the wall elsewhere, πρὸς πεδίον Ἰλήιον, till I come to the
forests of Ida, and lurk in the dingles? In the evening, after washing
in the river, I can return refreshed to Ilium." By some commentators the πεδίον Ἰλήιο. is translated, the Ilian plain; but surely the
absurdity of flying towards the plain, when Achilles had driven the
army to the town, need not be pointed out, and the plain which extended to the sea could not lead Agenor to the recesses of Ida.
Neither, I think, can any form of Greek derivation deduce Ἰλήιον
from Ἴλιος, of which the possessive adjective would be Ἰλίεον or
Ἰλιακοι. Other commentators have on this account read the word
Ἰδήιον, and supposed it the plain of Ida, to which Agenor might
naturally go. I believe it myself to be a genuine and uncorrupted
passage, and that Ἰλήιοι, or more anciently ΦιλΦηιον, is derived from

Ἴλη or Εἴλη, " turma," a troop ; that it was the place of exercise, the Campus Martius, beyond the city, and that in that situation it exists in the opening plain about Arablar. This interpretation was suggested to me by my friend Mr. Payne Knight, and strongly confirms our system Be this as it may, the plain alluded to must be sought in the direction of Ida, and the real geography of the country round Bounarbachi appears to me to explain that of Agenor's meditation. The dingle which intervenes between Bounarbachi and the tombs need not create a difficulty in assigning that situation to the Acropolis. If I recollect right, it does not cut off entirely Bounarbachi from the hill ; and if it did, there is no proof in Homer that such an interruption did not intervene. It was so in other ancient cities, as for instance, between the Acropolis of Argos and the lower town on the Aspis or Phoronean hill.

I have now gone through what I thought might throw light on this intricate subject, and have, I fear, tired you with a twice-told tale. I have reconsidered a subject I once paid much attention to, and am not sorry for an opportunity to retract some of my former errors, as, I assure you, I attach no vanity to the maintaining contrary to conviction one word that I have inconsiderately written. I will conclude then, as you have done, with a view of the present state of our united discoveries.

The river Mendere is the Scamander of Strabo, and Xanthus of Pliny, who however gives the name of Scamander to a small river now flowing into the Ægæan, south of the Sigæan promontory. The Scamander of Homer was that small river which in his time flowed into the Mendere, and gave its name to it The Mendere above the junction was Homer's Simois, and descends from Ida

The plain on the north-east side of the Mendere was the Simoisian plain, that on the south-west the Scamandrian, in which the battles were chiefly fought.

The ruins of Palæo Califat I believe to have been those of the Ilium of Strabo, but his description is attended with some obscurity. Eastward is Strabo's Thiosmos, which however disagrees completely with Homer's description of that mound.

The hills near Tchiblak probably mark the site of the Pagus Iliensium and the Callicolone of Strabo, but do not agree with Homer's position of Troy.

The springs of Bounarbachi are warm springs, but tradition only makes one of them warm, and Homer might adopt it. They were probably the ΘΕΑΙ ΠΗΓΑΙ; and if so, near the Scæan gate.

The source of Mendere is in Gargarus, and so was that of Simois; the position of that of the Scamander is no where mentioned, unless the two fountains near Troy were the sources.

The Πεδίον Ἴλιον was behind Troy in the way to Ida.

Troy stood at a considerable distance from Ida, properly so called, τηλόθεν ἐν πεδίῳ. The Acropolis stood on a rock Odyss 507. The situation of Bounarbachi has nothing irreconcilable with these suppositions; it is on a low elevation above the Scamandrian plain, backed by higher mountains. Homer describes such a situation by the epithet ὀφρυόεσσα.

REMARKS

ON THE

ARCHITECTURAL INSCRIPTION BROUGHT FROM ATHENS,

AND NOW PRESERVED IN THE BRITISH MUSEUM

[BY MR WILKINS]

IN the annexed inscription, which is six years older than the date of the archonship of Euclid, the H occurs with the power of an aspirate; instead of Ψ and Ξ, we have ΦΣ and ΧΣ respectively; and for the diphthong ΟΥ, O alone is written, as well in the genitive case of the singular number, and the accusative of the plural, as in the words ΒΟΤΑΗΣ and ΟΥΣ, the diphthong is, however, retained in the first syllable of the pronoun ΟΥΤΟΣ throughout all the cases. The dative cases ending in Α, Η, Ο, are distinguished by the iota adscript.

A fac-simile of the inscription was engraved at the expence of the Dilettanti Society, and was submitted to the learned of the age for observation and remark. It seems, however, to have elicited little or no illustration, for it is introduced with a few scanty notes in the volume of inscriptions subsequently published by Chandler.

In attempting the translation of this remarkable piece of early writing, Chandler has failed in many instances, through the want of that architectural knowledge which those intimately acquainted with the details of Grecian buildings alone possess. In transcribing the inscription he has likewise erred in many important points, besides omitting several passages he was unable to decipher.

The errors and omissions of that learned author chiefly occur in the terms of art, and in passages relating to the particulars of the building; and hence it is that one who possesses a competent knowledge of ancient architecture, although professing to have but a moderate acquaintance with the Greek language, may hope, by availing himself of the labours of a more learned precursor, to give an interpretation of this technical inscription with better success, and to transcribe it with fewer errors.

The transcript would have been less perfect but for the assistance of an eminent scholar, who, possessing a profound knowledge of Attic Greek, was enabled to decipher some passages of importance. To Mr. Elmsley I am indebted for the latter part of the forty-second line in the first column, and part of the ninety-first in the second, besides some other readings of less moment, which are noticed as they occur.

I purpose dividing the inscription into its several passages, and at the same time to introduce such corrections as a laborious and attentive examination of the original marble, and a cast I caused to be taken, enable me to state with confidence. In doing this, I shall divest the original of those archaisms which belong to an early period of the Greek language.

The temple to which allusion is made, is mentioned by no particular designation; it is stated to be situated in the *city*, the original appellation of the Acropolis, and to be that in which the ancient statue was kept. This object of Athenian veneration is mentioned by Pausanias, amongst the relics preserved in the temple of Minerva-Polias. The statue was carved in wood of the olive, and was probably one of those described by the traveller as still black from the effects of the conflagration with which the Acropolis was visited, amongst the other acts of violence inflicted upon Athens, after the Persians had obtained possession of the citadel.

A little to the north of the Parthenon stand the ruins of the Erectheum, a double temple of the Ionic order of architecture. The two divisions of the building, although under one continued roof, are distinctly marked, the level of the one being eight feet below that of the other; the difference in the levels commences at the transverse wall, separating the two cellæ.

Each division had its particular approach, the higher by an hexastyle portico at the east end, and the other by a portico of four columns, attached to the north-west angle of the building. There was also another approach to the lower division by a small staircase from the higher ground within a portico, which is remarkable from the circumstance of having statues instead of columns. The columns of the west were closed by a wall, excepting where three windows afforded light to the pronaos

The building has erroneously been termed a triple temple, dedicated to Erectheus, Minerva-Polias, and Pandrosus. the portico, where statues are introduced instead of columns, being supposed by modern travellers to be the Pandroseum of Pausanias. This author, however, calls the building a *double* temple, dedicated to Minerva-Polias and the nymph Pandrosus; although when he speaks of it collectively, he calls it the Erectheum, from the circumstance of its occupying the site of the ancient temple of Erectheus, whose altar was still preserved in the entrance.

Pausanias gives no information respecting the origin of the building, and none being furnished by earlier writers, the period of its commencement has been referred to a time subsequent to the burning of a temple of Minerva, which is recorded to have happened in the ninety-third olympiad. * The accident is erroneously thought by Stuart to have befallen the building in question, whereas the words of Xenophon describe the edifice to be the old temple of Minerva; that is to say, the Hecatompedon, which the Greeks, in conformity with their general policy, suffered to remain unrepaired, as a monument of the sacrilegious violence of the barbarians who invaded Greece. Pausanias mentions several instances of this intentional neglect, and speaks of two temples in the vicinity of Athens which were suffered to remain, as he expresses it, ἡμίκαυτοι, for the reason assigned. The Erectheum was burned by the Persians, together with the whole of the Acropolis, but Herodotus alludes to it as still standing in the third year of the eighty-third olympiad. viii. 55.

Pericles, who entertained the idea of rebuilding all the temples injured by the Persians, began with those of the Acropolis. The Parthenon was in all probability first undertaken, and completed before any progress was made in erecting the Propylæa; for he only survived the completion of the latter building five years. Eleven years had elapsed before its commencement, since the death of Cimon insured to Pericles the sole control of the Athenian people. in this interval the Parthenon was probably erected. The Erectheum may have been begun after the Propylæa were finished, a short time before his death; although the inscription describes it as unfinished in the archonship of Diocles, twenty-one years subsequent to that event, and two years before the conclusion of the Peloponnesian war. But the interruption given to the progress of all works of ornament during that contention will sufficiently account for the delay in finishing it.

The Erectheum was erected upon the site of the ancient temple, and in this instance the Greeks departed from their usual practice, by

---

* Xenoph. Hist. Græc. i 6

removing the ruins of the violated fane to make way for the new building. But in doing so, they were directed by a necessity which existed in no other instance. The sacred spring which their fore-fathers regarded with holy reverence, and the olive which the pro-tectress of Athens had caused to be created and to take root in the soil, were within this sanctuary, and identified with the spot, the site of the temple might be changed, but the sacred objects, for whose protection the temple had been reared, could not be re-moved. It is not possible that the present building should be a restoration of the ancient Erectheum, for the inscription enters into the detail of too many particulars to permit of any other application than that to a recent and entirely new structure, approaching towards completion by a gradual progress. The basis of all the columns, the wall towards the west, upon which the columns of that are front elevated, the substructure of the portico towards the south, and other particulars in the lower part of the edifice, are described as still unfinished; hence it is evident that the building was not undergoing that kind of repair which a conflagration would have rendered necessary, for in this case, the new and unfinished work would have been almost exclusively confined to the upper parts.

In the inscription the statues in the portico facing the south, are simply termed Κοραὶ, *the virgins,* perhaps they were representations of those called *Canephoræ,* who assisted at the great Panathenean festival; two of them are said by Pausanias to have their residence near to the temple. Vitruvius calls statues so introduced, *Caryatides,* and relates a fanciful story of their supposed introduction, as objects of architectural embellishment.

The survey begins at the angle of the building nearest to the Cecropium, or tomb of Cecrops. It is manifest from the context that this monument was situated to the south of the temple; for in the 56th line, it is said that " the wall facing the south wind is unpolished

---

* Ἄνω γ: ἐν τῇ Ἀκροπόλει Κέκροπο· ὅτι τάφος, παρὰ τὴν Πολιοῦχον αὐτήν   Theodoret. l viii Therap

throughout, excepting within the portico near the Cecropium." This point established, we know where to look for the unfinished parts, which the inscription begins with enumerating. *

The preceding Inscription divested of its Archaisms.

[The figures refer to different readings in Chandler's copy, — see the end of the Inscription]

ΕΠΙΣΤΑΤΑΙ(1) ΤΟΥ ΝΕΩ ΤΟΥ ΕΝ ΠΟΛΕΙ, ΕΝ ΩΙ ΤΟ ΑΡΧΑΙΟΝ ΑΓΛΑΜΑ, ΒΡΟΣΥΝ ΗΣ ΚΗΦΙΣΙΕΥΣ, ΛΑΡΙΑΔΗΣ ΑΓΡΥΛΗΘΕΝ (2), ΔΙΟΔΗΣ ΚΗΦΙΣΙΕΥΣ ΑΡΧΙΤΕΚΤΩΝ ΦΙΛΟΚΛΗΣ (3) ΑΧΑΡΝΕΥΣ, ΓΡΑΜΜΑΤΕΥΣ ΕΤΕΑΡΧΟΣ (4) ΚΥΔΑΘΗΝΑΙΕΥΣ, ΤΑΔΕ(5) ΑΝΕΓΡΑΨΑΝ ΕΡΓΑ ΤΟΥ ΝΕΩ, ΩΣ (6) ΚΑΤΕΛΑΒΟΝ ΕΧΟΝΤΑ ΚΑΤΑ ΤΟ ΨΗΦΙΣΜΑ ΤΟΥ ΔΗΜΟΥ, Ο ΕΠΙΓΕΝΗΣ ΕΙΠΕΝ ΕΞΕΙΡΓΑΣΜΕΝΑ (7) ΚΑΙ ΗΜΙΕΡΓΑ ΕΠΙ ΔΙΟΚΛΕΟΣ ΑΡΧΟΝΤΟΣ ΚΕΚΡΟΠΙΔΟΣ ΠΡΥΤΑΝΕΥΟΥΣΗΣ ΠΡΩΤΗΣ ΕΠΙ ΤΗΣ ΒΟΥΛΗΣ (8) ΗΙ ΝΙΚΟΦΑΝΗΣ ΜΑΡΑΘΩΝΙΟΣ ΠΡΩΤΟΣ ΕΓΡΑΜΜΑΤΕΥΣΕΝ.

ΤΟΥ ΝΕΩ ΤΑΔΕ ΚΑΤΕΛΑΒΟΜΕΝ ΗΜΙΕΡΓΑ .
ΕΠΙ ΤΗΙ ΓΩΝΙΑΙ ΤΗΙ (9) ΠΡΟΣ ΤΟΥ ΚΕΚΡΟΠΙΟΥ
ΗΙ ΠΛΙΝΘΟΥΣ ᵃ ΑΘΕΤΟΥΣ, ΜΗΚΟΣ ΤΕΤΡΑΠΟΔΑΣ
ΠΛΑΤΟΣΔΙΠΟΔΑΣ, ΠΑΧΟΣ
ΤΡΙΗΜΙΠΟΔΙΟΥΣ .
ΜΑΣΛΑΛΑΙΑΝ (10) ᵇ ΜΗΚΟΣ ΤΕΤΡΑΠΟΔΑ
ΠΛΑΤΟΣ ΤΡΙΠΟΔΑ, ΠΑΧΟΣ ΤΡΙΩΝ
ΗΜΙΠΟΔΙΩΝ
Η ΕΠΙΚΡΑΝΙΤΙΔΑΣ ᶜ ΜΗΚΟΣ ΤΕΤΡΑΠΟ
ΔΑΣ, ΠΛΑΓΟΣ ΤΡΙΠΟΔΑΣ, ΠΑΧΟΣ
ΤΡΙΩΝ ΗΜΙΠΟΔΙΩΝ .
ΓΩΝΙΑΙΑΝ ᵈ, ΜΗΚΟΣ ΕΠΤΑΠΟΔΑ,
ΠΛΑΤΟΣ ΤΕΤΡΑΠΟΔΑ ΠΑΧΟΣ
ΤΡΙΩΝ ΗΜΙΠΟΔΙΩΝ .
ΓΟΓΓΥΛΟΥΣ ΛΙΘΟΥΣ ᵉ ΑΘΕΤΟΥΣ ΑΝΤΙΜΟ
ΡΟΣ ΤΑΙΣ ΕΠΙΚΡΑΝΙΤΙΣΙΝ (11), ΜΗΚΟΣ
ΔΕΚΑΠΟΥΣ, ΥΨΟΣ ΤΡΙΩΝ
ΗΜΙΠΟΔΙΩΝ .

---

* The angle of the building nearest to the Cecropium is marked F. in the plan and view The portico of the temple of Minerva-Polias is marked H.

A, The temple of Minerva-Polias B, the Pandroseum. C, The *stylagalmatic* portico G, The entrance into the Pandroseum.

The parts of the building distinguished by crossed lines, as well as the ground without, at N. and W , are eight feet lower than the rest of the building. Two walls, D,D, supported the higher ground.

II ΑΝΤΙΜΟΡΩ ΤΟΙΣ ΕΠΙΣΤΥΛΙΟΙΣ,
     ΜΙΚΟΣ ΤΕΤΡΑΠΟΔΕ, ΠΛΑΤΟΣ ΠΕΝ
     ΤΕΠΑΛΑΣΤΩ

I ΚΙΟΚΡΑΝΟΝ ^f ΑΘΕΤΟΝ
     ΜΕΤΩΠΟΝ ΤΟ ΕΣΟΜΕΝΟΝ
     ΠΛΑΤΟΣ ΤΡΙΩΝ ΗΜΙΠΟΔΙΩΝ ΠΑΧΟΣ
     ΤΡΙΩΝ ΗΜΙΠΟΔΙΩΝ

II ΕΠΙΣΤΥΛΙΑ ^g ΑΘΕΤΑ, ΜΗΚΟΣ ΟΚΤΩ
     ΠΟΔΑ, ΠΛΑΤΟΣ ΔΥΟΙΝ ΠΟΔΟΙΝ
     ΚΑΙ ΠΑΛΑΣΤΗΣ, ΠΑΧΟΣ ΔΙΠΟΔΑ .

III ΕΠΙΣΤΥΛΙΑ ^h ΑΝΩ ΟΝΤΑ ΕΔΕΙ
     ΕΠΕΡΓΑΣΑΣΘΑΙ ΜΗΚΟΣ ΟΚΤΩΠΟ
     ΔΑ ΠΛΑΤΟΣ ΔΥΟΙΝ ΠΟΔΟΙΝ ΚΑΙ ΠΑ
     ΛΑΣΤΗΣ ΠΑΧΟΣ ΔΙΠΟΔΑ
     ΤΟΥ ΔΕ ΛΟΙΠΟΥ ΕΡΓΟΥ ΑΠΑΝΤΟΣ
     ΕΝ ΚΥΚΛΩΙ ΑΡΧΕΙ Ο ΕΛΕΥΣΙΝΙΑΚΟΣ
     ΛΙΘΟΣ ⁱ ΠΡΟΣ ΩΙ ΤΑ ΖΩΙΑ (12) ΚΑΙ ΕΤΕΘΗ
     ΕΠΙ ΤΩΝ ΕΠΙΣΤΑΤΩΝ ΤΟΥΤΩΝ
     ΤΩΝ ΚΙΟΝΩΝ ^k, ΤΩΝ ΕΠΙ ΤΟΥ ΤΟΙΧΟΥ
     ΤΟΥ ΠΡΟΣ ΤΟΥ ΠΑΝΔΡΟΣΕΙΟΥ

IIII ΚΕΙΜΕΝΩΝ ΚΙΟΝΩΝ
     ΑΤΜΗΤΑ ΕΚ ΤΟΥ ΕΝΤΟΣ ΑΝΘΕ
     ΜΙΟΥ ΕΚΑΣΤΟΥ ΤΟΥ ΚΙΟΝΟΣ ΤΡΙΑ
     ΗΜΙΠΟΔΙΑ
     ΕΠΙΣΤΥΛΙΟΥ ΟΚΤΩΠΟΔΟΣ
     ΕΠΙ ΤΟΥ ΤΟΙΧΟΥ ΤΟΥ ΠΡΟΣ ΝΟΤΟΝ
     ΚΥΜΑΤΙΟΝ ΕΣ ΤΟ ΕΣΩ ΕΔΕΙ (13)
     ΕΠΙΘΕΙΝΑΙ
     ΤΑΔΕ ΑΚΑΤΑΞΕΣΤΑ ΚΑΙ
     ΑΡΑΒΔΩΤΑ (14)
     ΤΟΝ ΤΟΙΧΟΝ ^l ΤΟΝ ΠΡΟΣ ΝΟΤΟΥ
     ΑΝΕΜΟΥ ΑΚΑΤΑΞΕΣ ΤΟΝ,
     ΠΛΗΝ ΤΟΥ ^m ΕΝ ΤΗΙ ΠΡΟΣΤΑΣΕΙ
     ΤΗΙ ΠΡΟΣ ΤΩΙ ΚΕΚΡΟΠΙΩΙ
     ΤΟΥΣ ΟΡΘΟΣΤΑΤΑΣ ⁿ ΑΚΑΤΑ
     ΞΕΣΤΟΥΣ ΕΚ ΤΟΥ ΕΞΩΘΕΝ ΕΝ ΚΥΚΛΩΙ
     ΠΛΗΝ ΤΩΝ ^o ΕΝ ΤΗΙ ΠΡΟΣΤΑ
     ΣΕΙ ΤΗΙ ΠΡΟΣ ΤΩΙ ΚΕΚΡΟΠΙΩΙ .
     ΤΑΣ ΣΠΕΙΡΑΣ ^p ΑΠΑΣΑΣ
     ΑΡΡΑΒΔΩΤΟΥΣ (15) ΤΑ ΑΝΩΘΕΝ
     ΤΟΥΣ ΚΙΟΝΑΣ ΑΡΑΒΔΩΤΟΥΣ ΑΠΑΝΤΑΣ,

ΠΛΗΝ ΤΩΝ ΕΠΙ ΤΟΥ ΤΟΙΧΟΥ ΤΗΝ ΚΡΗΠΙΔΑ[9] ΕΝ
ΚΥΚΛΩΙ ΑΠΑΣΑΝ ΑΚΑΤΑΞΕΣΤΟΝ
ΤΟΥ ΤΟΙΧΟΥ ΤΟΥ ΕΚΤΟΣ ΑΚΑΤΑΞΕΣΤΑ,
ΤΟΥ ΓΑΥΛΟΥ (16) ΛΙΘΟΥ[1] ΤΕΤΡΑΠΟΔΙΑΣ ΗΗΗ
ΤΟΥ ΕΝ ΤΩΙ ΠΡΟΣΤΟΜΙ (17)
ΤΕΤΡΑΠΟΔΙΑΣ
ΤΗΣ ΠΑΡΑΣΤΑΔΟΣ
ΤΕΤΡΑΠΟΔΙΑΣ
ΤΟΥ ΠΡΟΣ ΤΟΥ ΓΑΛΜΑΤΟΣ (18)
ΤΕΤΡΑΠΟΔΙΑΣ
ΕΝ ΤΗΙ ΠΡΟΣΤΑΣΕΙ ΠΡΟΣ
ΤΟΥ ΘΥΡΩΜΑΤΟΣ
ΤΟΝ ΒΩΜΟΝ ΤΟΥ ΘΥΗΛΟΥ (19)
ΑΘΕΙΟΝ
ΤΗΣ ΕΠΟΡΟΦΙΑΣ ΣΦΗΚΙΣΚΟΥΣ (20)
ΚΑΙ ΙΜΑΝΤΑΣ ΑΘΕΤΟΥΣ
ΕΠΙ ΤΗΙ ΠΡΟΣΤΑΣΕΙ ΤΗΙ ΠΡΟΣ ΤΩΙ
ΚΕΚΡΟΠΙΩΙ ΕΔΕΙ (21)

III ΤΟΥΣ ΛΙΘΟΥΣ ΤΟΥΣ ΟΡΟΦΙΑΙΟΥΣ[1] ΤΟΥΣ
ΕΠΙ ΤΩΝ ΚΟΡΩΝ[1] ΕΠΕΡΓΑΣΑ
ΣΘΑΙ ΑΝΩΘΕΝ, ΜΗΚΟΣ ΤΡΙΩΝ
ΚΑΙ ΔΕΚΑ ΠΟΔΩΝ ΠΛΑΤΟΣ ΠΕΝΤΕ
ΠΟΔΩΝ
ΤΑΣ ΚΑΛΛΑΣ[1] ΤΑΣ ΕΠΙ ΤΟΙΣ ΕΠΙ
ΣΤΥΛΙΟΙΣ ΕΞΕΡΓΑΣΑΣΘΑΙ
ΕΔΕΙ
ΛΙΘΙΝΑ (22) ΠΑΝΤΕΛΩΣ ΕΞΕΙΡΓΑΣΜΕΝΑ
Α ΧΑΜΑΙ
ΠΛΙΝΘΟΙ ΤΕΤΡΑΠΟΔΕΣ ΜΗΚΟΣ

ΔΙ ΠΛΑΤΟΣ ΔΙΠΟΔΕΣ, ΠΑΧΟΣ
ΤΡΙΩΝ ΗΜΙΠΟΔΙΩΝ ΑΠΩΜΑΤΑΙ·
Ι ΜΑΣΧΑΛΙΑΙΑ ΜΗΚΟΣ ΓΕΙΡΑ
ΠΟΥΣ ΠΛΑΤΟΣ ΤΡΙΠΟΥΣ ΠΑΧΟΣ
ΤΡΙΩΝ ΗΜΙΠΟΔΙΩΝ
ΤΟΥΤΩΝ ΕΚΑΣΤΟΥ, ΟΥΚ ΕΞΕΙΡΓΑ
ΣΤΑΙ Ο ΑΡΜΟΣ Ο ΕΤΕΡΟΣ ΟΥΔΕ
ΟΙ ΟΠΙΣΘΕΝ ΑΡΜΟΙ.

ΔΙΙ ΜΗΚΟΣ ΕΚΠΟΔΕΣ ΠΛΑΤΟΣ ΔΙΠΟ
ΔΕΣ, ΠΑΧΟΣ ΠΟΔΙΑΙΟΙ,
ΤΟΥΤΩΝ ΕΚΑΣΤΟΥ, ΟΥΚ ΕΞΕΙΡΓΑ
ΣΤΑΙ Ο ΑΡΜΟΣ Ο ΕΤΕΡΟΣ, ΟΥΔΕ

ΟΙ ΟΠΙΣΘΕΝ ΑΡΜΟΙ

Π ΤΕΤΡΑΠΟΔΕΣ ΜΗΚΟΣ ΠΛΑΤΟΣ ΔΙΠΟ
ΔΕΣ ΠΑΧΟΣ ΠΟΔΙΑΙΟΙ,
ΤΟΥΤΩΝ ΕΚΑΣΤΟΥ ΟΥΚ ΕΞΕΙΡΓΑ
ΣΤΑΙ Ο ΑΡΜΟΣ Ο ΕΤΕΡΟΣ ΟΥΔΕ
ΟΙ ΟΠΙΣΘΕΝ ΑΡΜΟΙ·

Ι ΠΕΝΤΕΠΟΥΣ ΜΗΚΟΣ, ΠΛΑΤΟΣ ΔΙΠΟΥΣ.
ΠΑΧΟΣ ΠΟΔΙΑΙΟΣ,
ΤΟΥΤΟΥ ΑΡΓΟΣ Ο ΑΡΜΟΣ Ο ΕΤΕ
ΡΟΣ ΚΑΙ ΟΙ ΟΠΙΣΘΕΝ ΑΡΜΟΙ
ΓΕΙΣΑ ˣ ΜΗΚΟΣ ΤΕΤΡΑΠΟΔΑ ΠΛΑΤΟΣ

ΙΙΙΙ ΤΡΙΠΟΔΑ ΠΑΧΟΣ ΠΕΝΤΕΠΑΛΑΣΤΑ,
ΛΕΙΑ ΕΚΠΕΠΟΙΗΜΕΝΑ ΑΝΕΥ ΚΑΤΑ
ΤΟΜΗΣ

Π ΕΤΕΡΩΝ ΜΕΓΕΘΟΣ ΤΟ ΑΥΤΟΝ,
ΚΥΜΑΤΙΟΥ ΚΑΙ ΑΣΤΡΑΓΑΛΟΥ ΕΚΑΤΕΡΟΥ
ΑΤΜΗΤΟΙ (23) ΗΣΑΝ ΤΕΤΤΑΡΕΣ ΠΟΔΕΣ   ·
ΕΚΑΣΤΟΥ

ΙΙ ΕΤΕΡΟΙΝ,
ΑΤΜΗΤΟΙ ΗΣΑΝ ΤΟΥ ΚΥΜΑΤΙΟΥ, ΤΕΤΤΑΡΕΣ
ΠΟΔΕΣ, ΤΟΥ ΔΕ ΑΣΤΡΑΓΑΛΟΥΟΚΤΩ ΠΟΔΕΣ

Ι ΕΤΕΡΟΥ,
ΤΟΥ ΚΥΜΑΤΙΟΥ ΤΡΙΑ ΗΜΙΠΟΔΙΑ ΑΤΜΗΤΑ,
ΑΣΤΡΑΓΑΛΟΥ ΤΕΤΤΑΡΕΣ ΠΟΔΕΣ

Ι ΕΤΕΡΟΝ,
ΤΗΝ ΜΕΝ ΛΕΙΑΝ ΕΡΓΑΣΙΑΝ (24) ΕΙΡΓΑΣΤΟ

ΙΙΙ ΤΟΥ ΔΕ ΚΥΜΑΤΙΟΥ, ΑΡΓΟΙ ΠΟΔΕΣ ΗΣΑΝ ΕΞ (25)
ΚΑΙ ΗΜΙΠΟΔΙΟΝ, ΑΣΤΡΑΓΑΛΟΥ, ΑΡΓΟΙ
ΠΟΔΕΣ ΟΚΤΩ.
ΕΤΕΡΩΝ
ΚΥΜΑΤΙΟΥ ΕΞ ΠΟΔΕΣ ΑΡΓΟΙ
ΑΣΤΡΑΓΑΛΟΥ ΟΚΤΩ ΠΟΔΕΣ .

Ι ΕΤΕΡΟΝ
ΗΜΙΕΡΓΟΝ ΤΗΣ ΛΕΙΑΣ ΕΡΓΑΣΙΑΣ

ΙΙΙΙ ΤΩΝ ΑΠΟ ΤΗΣ ΣΤΟΑΣ ΜΗΚΟΣ ΤΕΤΡΑΠΟ
ΔΑ ΠΛΑΤΟΣ ΤΡΙΠΟΔΑ ΠΑΧΟΣ ΠΕΝΤΕ
ΠΑΛΑΣΤΑ ΛΕΙΑ ΕΚΠΕΠΟΙΗΜΕΝΑ
ΑΝΕΥ ΚΑΤΑΤΟΜΗΣ
ΓΩΝΙΑΙΑ ʸ ΕΠΙ ΤΗΝ ΠΡΟΣΤΑΞΙΝ ΤΗΝ

ΙΙ ΠΡΟΣ ΕΩ, ΜΗΚΟΣ ΕΚΠΟΔΕ, ΠΛΑΤΟΣ
ΤΕΤΑΡΤΟΥ ΗΜΙΠΟΔΙΟΥ, ΠΑΧΟΣ

ΠΕΝΤΕΠΑΛΑΣΤΑ
ΤΟΥΤΩΝ ΤΟΥ ΕΤΕΡΟΥ, Η ΛΕΙΑ ΜΕΝ ΕΡΓΑ
ΣΙΑΣ (26) ΕΝΕΙΡΓΑΣΤΟ, ΤΟ ΔΕ ΚΥΜΑΤΙΟΝ
ΑΡΓΟΝ (27) ΟΛΟΝ, ΚΑΙ Ο ΑΣΤΡΑΓΑΛΟΣ,
ΤΟΥ ΔΕ ΕΤΕΡΟΥ, ΑΡΓΟΝ ΚΥΜΑΤΙΟΥ ΤΡΕΙΣ
ΠΟΔΕΣ ΚΑΙ ΗΜΙΠΟΔΙΟΝ, ΤΟΥ ΔΕ ΑΣΤΡΑ
ΓΑΛΟΥ, ΑΡΓΟΙ ΠΟΔΕΣ ΠΕΝΤΕ
ΕΠΙ ΤΟΝ ΤΟΙΧΟΝ ΤΟΝ ΠΡΟΣ ΤΟΥ ΠΑΝΔΡΟΣΕΙΟΥ
ΜΗΚΟΣ ΕΠΤΑΠΟΔΩΝ, ΚΑΙ ΗΜΙΠΟΔΙΟΥ,
ΠΛΑΤΟΣ ΤΡΙΩΝ ΠΟΔΩΝ ΚΑΙΗΜΙΠΟΔΙΟΥ,
ΗΜΙΕΡΓΟΝ ΤΗΣ ΑΛΙΑΣ ΕΡΓΑΣΙΑΣ
ΜΗΚΟΣ ΕΚΠΟΔΩΝ ΠΛΑΤΟΣ ΤΡΙΩΝ
I ΠΟΔΩΝ ΚΑΙ ΠΑΛΑΣΤΗΣ ΠΑΧΟΣ ΠΕΝΤΕ
ΠΑΛΑΣΤΩΝ (28) ΚΑΙ ΤΟΝ ΤΟΙΧΟΝ ΤΟΝ ΠΡΟΣ
ΤΟΥ ΠΑΝΔΡΟΣΕΙΟΥ,
ΤΟΥΤΟΥΑΣΤΡΑΓΑΛΟΥ, ΑΤΜΗΤΟΙ ΠΟΔΕΣ
ΠΕΝΤΕ
ΛΙΕΤΙΛΙΟΙ ₐ ΤΩΝ ΑΠΟ ΤΗΣ ΣΤΟΑΣ, ΜΗΚΟΣ
III ΕΠΤΑΠΟΔΕΣ, ΠΛΑΤΟΣ ΤΡΙΩΝ ΠΟΔΩΝ
ΚΑΙ ΗΜΙΠΟΔΙΟΥ ΠΑΧΟΣ ΠΟΔΙΑΙΟΙ
ΟΥΤΟΙ ΗΜΙΕΡΓΟΙ .
II ΕΤΕΡΩ ΜΗΚΟΣ ΠΕΝΤΕΠΟΔΕ ΠΛΑΤΟΣ
ΤΡΙΩΝ ΠΟΔΩΝ ΚΑΙ ΗΜΙΠΟΔΙΟΥ ΠΑΧΟΣ
ΠΟΔΙΑΟΙ ΗΜΙΕΡΓΟΙ
ΓΕΙΣΑ ΕΠΙ ΤΟΥΣ ΛΙΣΤΟΥΣ ᵇ, ΠΛΑΤΟΣ
ΠΕΝΤΕ ΗΜΙΠΟΔΙΩΝ, ΜΗΚΟΣ ΤΕΤΤΑ
ΡΩΝ ΠΟΔΩΝ ΚΑΙ ΗΜΙΠΟΔΙΟΥ ΠΑΧΟΣ
ΠΟΔΙΑΙΑ, ΤΗΝ ΛΕΙΑΝ ΕΡΓΑΣΙΑΝ
ΕΚΠΕΠ ΟΙΗΜΕΝ · ·
I ΕΤΕΡΟΝ ΗΜΙΕΡΓΟΝ ΤΗΣ
ΛΕΙΑΣ ΕΡΓΑΣΙΑΣ
II ΘΥΡΑΙ ΛΙΘΙΝΑΙ, ΜΗΚΟΣ ΟΚΤΩ ΠΟΔΩΝ
ΚΑΙ ΠΑΛΑΣΤΗΣ, ΠΛΑΤΟΣ ΠΕΝΤΕ
ΗΜΙΠΟΔΙΩΝ
IIII ΤΟΥΤΩΝ ΤΑ ΜΕΝ ΑΛΛΑ ΕΞΕΠΕΠΟΙ
ΗΤΟ ΕΙΣ ΤΑ ΖΥΓΑ (29) ΔΕ ΕΔΕΙ ΤΟΥΣ ΛΙΘ ΟΥΣ
ΤΟΥΣ ΜΕΛΑΝΑΣ ΕΝΘΕΙΝΑΙ .
I ΟΥΣ ΤΩΙ ΥΠΕΡΩΤΡΩΙ (30) ΤΩΙ ΠΡΟΣ ΕΩ
ΗΜΙΕΡΓΟΝ .
III ΤΩΙ ΒΩΜΩΙ ΤΩΙ ΤΟΥ ΘΥΗΛΟΥ (31) ΛΙΘΟΙ ΠΕΝ

TEΛEIKOI, MHKOΣ TETPAΠOΔEΣ,
ΥΨΟΣ ΔΥΟΙΝ ΠΟΔΟΙΝ ΚΑΙ ΠΑΛΑΣΤΗΣ,
ΠΑΧΟΣ ΠΟΔΙΑΙΟΙ
Ι ΕΤΕΡΟΣ ΤΡΗΠΟΥΣ

The following are some of the different readings in CHANDLER's *copy*

(1.) ΟΙ ΕΠΙΣΤΑΤΑΙ

(2) ΑΑΡΥΛΕΘΕΝ.

(3.) This name is omitted in Chandler.

(4.) ΕΠΑΡΧΟΣ

(5) Ch. omits this word.

(6.) ΗΟΣΑ

(7.) ΕΝΕΡΛΑΣΜΕΝΑ

(8.) ΠΟΛΕΣ, Ch Mr. Elmsley reads BOLEΣ

(9.) ΕΛΕΙΠΟΝΤΑΙ

(10) ΜΑΣΧΑΛΙΑΝ.

(11.) ΕΠΙΚΡΑΝΤΙΣΙΝ

(12.) ΖΟΛΑ ΚΑΙ ΕΡΛΟΣ, Ch. Mr. Elmsley reads ΖΟΙΑ ΚΑΙ ΕΤΕΘΕ

(13.) ΕΛΣ. Ch.

(14) ΑΡΑΡΔΟΤΑ. Ch.

(15.) ΑΡΑΡΔΟΤΟΣ Ch.

(16) ΖΟΛΛΥΛΟ ΛΙΟΣ. Ch.

(17.) ΗΡΟΣ ΓΟ. Ch.

(18.) ΤΟ ΑΛΔΟΜΑΤΟΣ. Ch.

(19.) ΤΟΜ ΒΟΜ. Ch.

(20.) This line is not given by Chandler.

(21.) ΚΛΕΙ. Ch.

(22.) ΑΔΕΛΟΙΠΑ Ch.

(23.) ΑΙΜΗΤΟ.

(24.) ΤΕΣ ΜΕΝ ΛΕΙΑΣ ΕΡΛΑΣΙΑΣ. Ch.

(25.) ΕΛΣΙΣ

(26) ΗΟ ΛΕΙΑΣ ΕΝΕΡΛΑΣΙΑΣ. Ch

(27.) ΠΟΔΙΑΙΟΝ. Ch.

(28.) ΗΑΛΑΣΤΟΙ. Ch

(29.) ΑΔΕΤΑ ΕΙ. Ch. ΔΕ ΕΔΕΙ, Elmsley.

(30.) ΡΟΥΤΡΟΙ. Ch.

(31) ΤΟΙ ΤΟΜΟΙ ΤΟΙ ΤΟ ΟΥ ΕΣΟ. Ch.

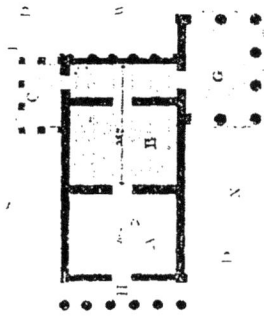

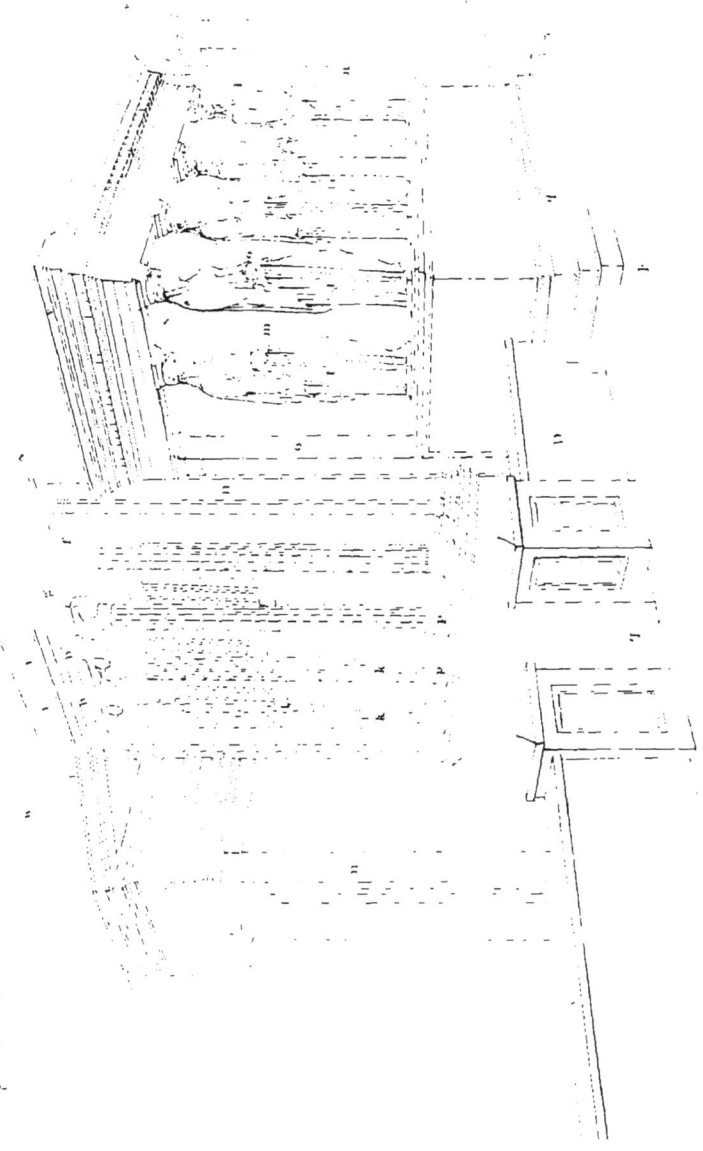

Section through the wall

Translation.

Bro͞syn͞͞es of Cephisia, Chariades of Agryle, Diodes of Cephisia, the epistatæ of the temple in the citadel, in which is the antient statue; Philocles of Acharnæ the architect, Etearchus of Cydathenæum the secretary, have reported the works completed and half-finished, as they found them to be, according to the decree of the people proposed by Epigenes, in the archonship of Diocles, the Cecropic tribe presiding in the council, in which Nicophanes of Marathon was secretary of the first prytany.

We have found these parts of the temple half-finished at the angle nearest the Cecropium.

IV   Tiles [*] not placed, four feet in length, two feet in width, a foot and a half in thickness

I   Shoulder tile [†] four feet in length, three feet in width, a foot and a half in thickness

---

* The tiles were slabs of marble wrought with great precision, every precaution calculated to keep out the wet being adopted in the mode of their formation. The meeting joints of the tiles in the same line were saddled, as it is now termed; that is, a rim, raised above the surface, was left on each side, so that if any wet found admission under the narrow strips that covered the meeting joint of two contiguous tiles, its further progress was prevented. A similar kind of rim was left at the top of each tile, and the under side of the one next above it was throated, or grooved, where it overlapped the other. The tiles usually varied in length and breadth according to the scale of the building. In temples of no great magnitude, such as the Erectheum, they were about two feet wide. The tiles at the eaves of the roof were formed out of the sloping blocks immediately above the cornice, which were almost invariably equal in width to two tiles. These are the tiles alluded to in the beginning of the survey. The common tiles were seldom more than four inches thick, they were sometimes made with clay, although every other part of the building was marble. Where gutters were introduced at the eaves, they were hollowed out of these blocks the front of such gutters were formed into a molding, which Vitruvius calls the *sima*. Whether or not gutters were carried along the eaves, the sima was made to surmount the cornice of the pediments, and was returned for a short distance round the angle of the cornice

† The tile here alluded to was probably that at the point or extremity of the pediment, which was returned along the flank. It might be so termed, because here they were placed immediately upon the *humeri*, as Vitruvius, speaking of this temple, calls the returns of the building at the angles of the front

V.   Epicranitides*ᶜ four feet in length, three feet in width, a foot
     and a half in thickness.

I   Angular ┃ᵈ (epicranitis) seven feet in length, four feet wide, a
     foot and a half in thickness.
     Eaves joint-titles ‡ᵉ not placed.

I   Continuation § of the epicranitides, ten feet in length, a foot and
     a half in height.

II   Portions in continuation of the epistylia ‖, four feet in length,
     five palms in width

I   Capital of a column', to be above the window-jamb¶, not
     placed; a foot and a half wide; a foot and a half in thickness.

V   Epistylia⁺ˢ not placed, eight feet long, two feet and a palm wide,
     two feet in thickness.

---

* The Epicranitides were tiles forming the *sima*, or top-bed of the cornice belonging to
the pediments Ἐπίκρανον, from which the term is derived, signifies *fastigium* and *vertex*
— Poll. lib. ii. c. 1 3

† The angular Epicranitis was that at the vertex of the fastigium, or pediment

‡ Γογγύλοι λίθοι, I imagine to be the upright circular pieces, terminating the *joint-tiles*
at the eaves or gutters of the roof By joint-tiles I mean those which were placed over
the meeting joints of the flat tiles, they were equal to them in length, but narrow, resembling in their outward form an hexagonal prism cut in two They extended from the
ridge of the roof down to the eaves, or gutters. In some temples, these, as well as the
common, or flat tiles, were made of clay. The *imbrex*, or eaves-tile, of potter's earth,
was termed by the Greeks στογγυλοειδὴ·, or γογγυλοειδὴς, κέραμος when made of marble,
the word λίθος would probably be substituted for κέραμος. The joint-tiles are mentioned
in a subsequent part of the inscription.

§ Ἀντίμορος; means, I presume, a corresponding portion, or continuation, of the member
of the building with which the term is conjoined, perhaps the contiguous piece.

‖ The epistylia were blocks extending from centre to centre of two adjoining columns.
In temples where columns were not employed to form a peristyle round the building, as in
the example before us, the epistylia were nevertheless continued along the flanks The
two portions alluded to in this passage are said to be adjoining or contiguous, probably to
the five mentioned almost immediately afterwards.

¶ Μέτωπον, that part of the forehead immediately above the interval between the eyes
In this place it means part of the building above the interval, or jamb, between two
windows

** The epistylia here alluded to, seem to be those upon the wall, beginning from the
angle of the building. The length of each piece being eight feet, the extent of all five
together would have been greater than the length of the building in front. One described

III Epistylia which are up" (in their places) require to be worked
on the surface, eight feet in length, two feet and a palm in width
two feet in thickness   The Eleusinian stone', against which are
the sculptures *, surmounts the rest of the work all around, and
is placed above the epistylia † of those columns ' which are upon
the wall next the Pandroseum.

Of IV engaged columns ‡, a foot and a half of each column is
left unsculptured, measured from the volute § within

It is necessary to place the inner cymatium of I epistylium.
eight feet long, upon the wall towards the south —These are

---

in a subsequent passage, of equal length, is said to have been upon the south wall
whence it is probable that these also were part of the same range in the flank of the
temple.

* A remarkable singularity is to be observed in the construction of the Erectheum
The facing of the frize, and of the tympanum of the remaining pediment, is formed of a
hard stone, similar to that found in the neighbourhood of Eleusis   It is studded with
iron clamps, which formerly served to fasten either bronze or marble sculptures   The
word ζῶα signifies, as Facius observes, small statues   " Mihi quidem ζῶα et ζωδια minu-
tiora varii generis simulacra denotare videntur "— Ad Pausan v. 11

† The word ἐπιστατόν is one of rare occurrence, it is found in the Sigean inscription,
where it seems to allude to the base or stand of the consecrated vase   On this account,
Chandler supposed it to signify, in this place, the bases of the columns   These, however,
are mentioned in a subsequent passage, under the common denomination σπείραι

In another Athenian inscription (given in Chandler's work, pp. xviii. 43.), which is
nearly coeval with that under discussion, the base or stand of a consecrated vase is termed
ὑποστατόν, whence it seems evident that ἐπιστατόν is an Attic word, and signifies here,
something placed over the columns

Mr. Elmsley supposes the sentence to end with the words ἐπιστατων τουτων.   The
epistatæ are, however, speaking in the first person, and the works in the preamble are
said to be done under Diocles the archon, and not under the epistatæ   Besides, the
actual existence of Eleusinian stone in the frize of the temple, makes it evident that the
ἐπιστατά, over which it is described as placed, must be synonymous with the epistylia

‡ The blocks of marble out of which the capitals of the four columns of this front are
formed, constitute part of the wall in which they appear inserted   The parts of them thus
immured were consequently unsculptured.

§ Chandler, from Hesychius, supposes the word ἀνθέμιον to signify some place in the
Acropolis, but in the same lexicon we find another explanation, ἡ γραμμη τις ἑλικοειδη,
εν τοῖς κίοσι, some spiral shaped line in columns, that is to say, the volute   Vitruvius
terms the volutes of the Corinthian capital, helices

4 G

unpolished and unfluted. * The wall¹ facing the south wind is unpolished, excepting in the portico ᵐ opposite the Cecropium. The antæ ⁿ without are unpolished throughout, excepting in the portico ° opposite the Cecropium.

The bases †ᵖ of all the columns are unfluted in the upper part.

All the columns are unfluted excepting those upon the wall.

The whole plinth ¦ ˢ is unpolished all around

Parts unpolished of the exterior wall. Four feet lengths of the gutter-stone §,ᵗ VIII in the entrance ‖ . . . four feet lengths next the pilaster . . four feet lengths near the statue . . four feet lengths in the portico in front of the door-way

The altar of the Thyecus ¶ is not placed

---

* Ἀραβδωτος and ἀρραβδωτος, for it is written both ways, signifies *not fluted*. Chandler reads αραχδοτος, in which he has been followed by the learned author of the *Prolegomena in Homerum*. Upon submitting my reading of the word to that profound and elegant scholar, he expressed his conviction of its propriety

† The upper torus of the bases are found to have been fluted in a manner similar to the shafts of the columns

‡ The columns of the western front, and the statues supporting the south portico of the building, are raised upon a podium or low wall, the κρηπις is the footing, or plinth, of this wall.

§ Chandler here reads ΞΟ ΛΥΤΛΟΛΙΟΣ, but the true reading is, ΤΟ ΛΑΥΛΟ ΛΙΘΟ, sc τοῦ γαυλου λιθου The first letter has a mark below it such as is found below the initial letters in many of the lines of the inscription, which gives it the appearance of the ancient ξ The γαυλος λιθος was, perhaps, the stone forming the cistern or trough, into which the water from the salt-spring, or well, in the Pandroseum, flowed, or, more probably, the gutter-stone which conveyed the water rising from the spring away from the building, because of its being under the head of the parts unpolished of the exterior wall Along the wall in the flank of the temple of Diana-Propylæa at Eleusis, there is a gutter-stone of the kind here alluded to.

‖ Προστομιον, the opening between the door-jambs. As the windows of the building were metaphorically termed the eyes, so the door-way was called the mouth Vitruvius, who preserves the same kind of metaphor, calls the passage leading from the door-way to the atrium, or court of the house, *fauces* vi 4

¶ This word, of which the two first letters are wanting, was in all probability ΘΥΕΧΟ This may be inferred from a passage towards the end of the inscription in which all the letters remain perfect. Τῷ βωμῷ τῷ τοῦ θυηχόου λιθοι πεντελέικοι, κ τ λ.

Of the coping * over the portico opposite the Cecropium the dovetails † and clamps are not placed, it was necessary that III ceiling stones¹ supported by the statues ‡,¹ should have the upper surface tooled, thirteen feet in length, five feet in width. It is necessary that the echinus molding §,¹ above the epistylia, should be finished.

From Photius we learn that the θυηχόοι were οἱ ἱερεῖς οἱ ὑπερ ἄλλων θύοντε. τοῖς θεοῖς. Some of the MSS. of this author write the word θύηχοοι, that of Beckius, quoted by Herman, gives it with the χ.

* The επορατία is the inclined and outward surface of the roof. This portico is covered with four blocks of marble extending from the south wall of the temple over the epistylia or marble beams, supported by the statues. The cornice of the portico is worked in these blocks. The gentle inclination given to the upper surface was for the purpose of throwing off the rain. The under surface of the same blocks formed the ceiling, it is divided into pannels deeply sunk in the marble.

The numerals of the inscription make the number of blocks to be tooled three. Each block measures twelve feet ten inches in length they are not all of equal width, two of them exceed, and two of them fall something short of five feet. The width of the four together is somewhat less than twenty feet six inches, so that they may be said to average five feet one inch and a half.

† Στηχίσκοι were small tenons of metal in the shape of two wedges, united at the points. Vitruvius calls them securicula, iv 7. They were likewise termed γόμφοι.

‡ The word KOPON is one of those which Chandler was at a loss to explain, under the impression that its nominative must be κορο. It here alludes to the statues of females, which, in this portico, supply the place of columns. By the modern Greeks they are still called κορίτσια, the damsels.

§ Κάλχη, the word here applied to the ornament over the epistylia of the stylagalmatic portico, signifies the shell fish which produced the scarlet dye of the Tyrians. Κάλχη γαρ εστιν ο κόχλος τῆς πορφύρα, Schol in Hesych He thus likewise explains it to denote some part of the capital of a column, μέρος κεφαλῆ κίονο that part probably of the Ionic capital which is now termed the ovolo Vitruvius calls this molding the Echinus, because, perhaps, it was a type of the shell fish of the same name, the shell and its spines being represented in a continued ornament, to which has been given the vulgar name of Egg and dart.

It was the practice of the Greeks to paint with red the moldings of the cornice and other parts of the building. This has been done in the Propylæa at Athens. At Rhamnus the cornice of the temple of Nemesis has been thus ornamented all around. The parts tinted with red stand out beyond the rest, the colour having resisted the corrosion which attacked the natural surface. A solution of dragon's blood is found to harden the surface of marble to such a degree, that if a piece partially stained be exposed to the action

      Stone-work lying upon the ground wholly finished

XI   Tiles four feet long, two feet wide, a foot and a half in thickness, without the covers. ⸭

I   Shoulder tile ", four feet long, three feet wide, a foot and a half in thickness.

    Of each of these, the alternate joint is not finished, nor the joints behind.

XII Six feet long, two feet wide, a foot in thickness; of each of these the alternate joint is not finished, nor the joints behind.

V   Four feet long, two feet wide, a foot in thickness; of each of these the alternate joint is not finished, nor the joints behind.

I   Five feet long, two feet wide, a foot in thickness; of this the alternate joint is not worked, nor the joints behind.

VII Eaves †⸭ four feet long, three feet wide, five palms in thickness, worked smooth without the carving.

    Of V others the size was the same, of both the cymatium and astragal, four feet were not carved of each

    Of II others there were uncarved, of the cymatium four feet, of the astragal eight feet.

    Of I other a foot and a half of the cymatium, and four feet of the astragal were not carved.

I   Other, the smooth work was done, but of the cymatium of III

---

of a strong acid, the part which is not covered will be eaten away to a considerable depth, and the tinted part will have the appearance of being in relief.

    I should have supposed that these painted ornaments were intended by the word κάλχαι, but for the word ἐξεργασάσθαι, which is applied in other parts of the inscription, to signify some operation performed by the masons upon the marble.

    " The word ἀπαμάται, which I have lately corrected from an inspection of the inscription, alludes to the absence of the tiles covering the joints of the flat tiles

    † Γεῖσα, the eaves or cornice   Upon this member of the entablature the moldings are carved   The eaves are here said to be λεῖα ἐκπεποιημένα ἄνευ κατατομῆς, by which is probably meant that they were, at the time of the survey, worked as plain moldings, preparatory to the enrichment, or carving upon them.   The lower moldings of the cornice were a cymatium and astragal.

there was unwrought six feet and a half; of the astragal eight feet unwrought.

Of . . others, six feet of the cymatium unwrought, of the astragal eight feet

I   Other, half worked, as to the smooth work.

IV belonging to the portico four feet in length, three feet in width, five palms in thickness; of these the smooth work is finished with out the carving. II angular ' (eaves) upon the portico facing the east, six feet in length, three feet and a half in width, five palms in thickness Of the one of these the smooth work is done, but the cymatium is wholly unwrought, and the astragal; of the other — of the cymatium three feet and a half are unwrought, and of the astragal five feet are unwrought.

Upon the wall next the Pandroseum, seven feet and a half in length, three feet and a half in width, are half finished.

Of smooth work, six feet in length, three feet and a palm in width, five palms in thickness.

And I upon the wall next the Pandroseum, the astragal of this has five feet uncarved

VI Stones of the fastigium * α belonging to the portico, seven feet long, three feet and a half wide, a foot in thickness; these half finished.

II   Others five feet long, three feet and a half wide, a foot in thickness; half finished.

The eaves upon the pediment ſ, two feet and a half in width, four feet and a half in length, a foot in thickness, the smooth work finished

I   Other half finished as to the smooth work

---

* Ἀετίαιοι, sc. λίθοι, are the slabs forming the face of the tympanum of the pediment The facing of this part of the building is done with vertical joints, one course of stone in height Like the facing of the frize, the stone is that called Eleusinian

V   Stone door-frames eight feet and a palm in length, two feet and
     a half in width, of IV of these, some were wholly completed,
     but it was necessary to place the black marble* against the
     supercilia. †

I   Consol ‡ to the hyperthyrum facing the east, half finished.

III Pentelican stones to the altar of the Thyecus, four feet in length,
     two feet and a palm in height, a foot in thickness.

I   Other, three feet .   .

Remarks on the preceding Anagraphe, by the Editor

It is well known that many of the public edifices of Greece were
built by contract, those who undertook the work were called
ἐργολαβοὶ, those who placed it out to them were ἐργεπιστάτοι, and the
δοκιμασταὶ were the persons who examined it, when it was § finished.
The title of ἐπιστάτοι was peculiarly applied to those who inspected

---

* The situation of the black marble between the ζύγα, or transverse pieces of the door-
frame, and the hyperthyra, or cornices above it, is analogous to that of the marble frize
between the epistylia and cornice   The black marble was therefore the same, probably,
as that mentioned in the forty-second line, under the epithet Eleusinian   Pausanias mentions a black stone or marble found under Parnassus, of which the walls of the city of
Ambryssus were built.   The temple and statue of Diana at the same place were also of the
same material, it was remarkable for its hardness. Pausan x. 36   The stone found
around Parnassus is of similar formation with that produced by the quarries of Eleusis.

The numeral letter prefixed to this sentence, was probably II, although it has now the
appearance of two units, this, as well as the one next above and below it, are all placed too
high up in the inscription, each should have ranged one line lower

† The upright pieces of a door-frame were called by the Romans, *antepagmenta*, and
those placed across them, *supercilia* The latter are the ζύγα of the Greeks In some instances, nothing intervened between the supercilium and hyperthyrum, although very
often a sculptured frize was intermediately placed

‡ Ὀῦς is the handle of a vase, so called from its resemblance to the human ear   Ears
of the kind alluded to here, are something similar in shape to the Greek letter ζ   Vitruvius
calls these ornaments *ancones* and *parotides*   The last word I have corrected from the
edition of Vitruvius, published by Schneider, which has only very lately fallen into my
hands   The ὠτίδι, are termed by us *consols*, from the French *console*

§ Dodwell, Ann Thuc 135 , Athenæ, lib. vi., Herod vi c 62.

the public works (Pollux. lib. vii. c. 33.) The word occurs in the first line of the preceding inscription, which is a report of the survey of the temple, partly finished, made by the Epistatæ, whose names are mentioned, and by the architect Philocles Τάδε οἱ ἐπεμελήθην ἔργα τοῦ νεώ, " they took an account of the work of the temple ;" the inscription therefore is properly an ἀναγραφή, recensio, it was made in the archonship of Diocles, 409 B.C., in that meeting of the senate in which Nicophanes was the secretary of the first prytany.† The inscription was written six years before the archonship of Euclid, and is about fifty years posterior to the celebrated marble ‡ relating to those of the tribe Erectheis who had perished in battle, a copy of which is given by Montfauçon, Palæ. l. ii., and by Maffei, Mus. Veron. After the archonship of Euclid, ε was no longer written Λ, nor the lambda L, in which form they both appear in the Athenian marble. The use of ο for ω seems to have been retained to a later age, until the time of the Macedonian æra.§ Although H occurs as an aspirate in the inscription, yet it is certain that this character, used as a letter, as well as Θ, was known in the time of Euripides, who died before the archonship of Euclid, and Callias, a poet prior both to Sophocles and Euripides, has described the form of ✝ and Ω; and H as well as Ω occur on some of the Macedonian coins of the fifth century B C.‖

L. 1 Ἐν πόλει. This expression has not always been properly understood, see Larcher, Herodotus, i. 453.——Ib. ἄγαλμα. It is re-

---

* Ἀναγράφειν, proprie de iis rebus, quæ solenniter describuntur et in tabulas referuntur Sluiter, Lec Andoc. 201.

† Πρῶτος ἐγραμμάτευσεν, Greffier de la première Prytanie See Barthelemy, Mém de l'Acad xlviii 107

‡ The true date of this inscription is fixed by Barbeyrac Anci Traités, p 110 Montfauçon referred it to the year 449 B.C, when Cimon died, but the war of Egypt mentioned in it, is of the date 463, and that of Ægina, of 457

§ Taylor, Sand Marm viii

‖ Knight, Proleg ad Homerum, sect 78 See also Valesius in Not Mauss Harpocrat, who supposes the Ionic letters were used privately, but not publicly received before the archonship of Euclid, Oly xcv 2.

markable that the rude statue of Minerva-Polias was preserved by the Athenians to so late a period as the age of Plutarch. See Euseb Præp. E. l. iii. c. 8., and Wessel. Prob. p. 310.

L. 2. Ἀγρυλῆσι. See Harpocrates in v. Ἀγρυλή This word and Ἀγραυλή have been improperly confounded by some writers; see Corsini, F. A. Diss. v.

L. 6. The archonship of Diocles does not commence before July in the year 409 B.C., for the archonship of Glaucippus finished at the end of June in that year. Barthelemy, Mém. des In. xlviii. 407.

L. 23. Γογγύλους λίθους. There is some difficulty in pointing out the part of the building to which these words refer. The scholiast on the Pax of Aristophanes, v. 28., merely uses the expression, ἔστι δὲ καὶ γογγύλος λίθος, without giving any elucidation.

L. 29. Παλαστή τὸ μέτρον, says Phrynichus, ἄνευ τοῦ ι In this form it always occurs in the inscription It is also found without the iota in one of the MSS. of Herodotus, Cod. Med.; see Oudendorp ad Thom M. 674. On the Nilometer of Elephantine we find παλάιστοι, (see Girard's Mémoire,) but the inscription there is of the age of Severus.

L. 30. As διόκρανον occurs in the inscription, it may be sufficient authority for the word in those places, where some propose to alter it to κιονόκρανον Pollux, l. vii. 121.

L. 34. The expression used by Euripides to denote this part of a building, is λάινα κίοσιν ἔμβολα, Bacch. 591., lapideæ trabes columnis impositæ See D'Orville, Charit. ii. 626.

L. 38. Ἔ-εργ. This word, as Heyne remarks, is applied by Pausanias to work in relief, καθ᾿ ἑκάτερον δὲ τοῦ κράνους γρυπές εἰσιν ἐπειργασμένοι, " on each side of the helmet are griffins worked in relief," L. i. In the language of the Greek artists, περιφανῆ ζώδια, are " figures in high relief," πρόστυπα *, " those in low relief." See Schweigh. in Athenæ l. v. c. 38.

---

* Τύπος is the word applied to sculpture in relief in general, see the passage already cited, p 380. of this volume, from the Hypsipyle of Euripides

L. 12. Πρὸς ὦ τὰ ζῶα, or, as the inscription gives it, ΖΟΙΑ, and in this manner the word is properly written (ζωΐον, i. e. ζώων) in a MS. of Antigonus Carystius. See Bast. Epis. Crit. p. 82 ΖΩΙΑ also occurs in an inscription in the Mus. Veron. p. xviii. Ζῶα is the certain reading of Mr. Elmsley, instead of ΖΟΛΑ, which Chandler gives in his copy of the Inscription Ζῶα signifies the figures in relief on the temple, in this sense the word occurs in Empedocles, γραπτοῖς δὲ ζωΐοις., not *pictis animalibus*. but painted figures, see Athen. Schweigh. lib. xii. c. 3.; and in Diodorus S. Excer. 606. ζῶον signifies a figure; " Antiochus employed himself with pieces of mechanism, and with moving by means of them figures of five cubits in height, silvered and gilded, ζῶα τετάτηχα."

L. 45. The sacred olive is said by Apollodorus, (lib. iii.) to be in the Pandroseum ; by Herodotus, (lib. viii.) in the temple of Erectheus ; by Pausanias, (lib. i.) in the temple of Minerva. All these passages are reconciled by considering, that the chapels or buildings were connected together.

L. 64. Σπείρας This word is solely applied to the bases of *Ionic* columns. See I. Pollux.

L. 65. 'Αραβδώτους, "unfluted." ῥάβδωσις is the word used by Aristotle to denote the fluting of a column , (see Schneider in His. An. iv. c. iv) In Diodorus S we find διαξύσματα employed in the same sense ; they are the *strigiles* of Vitruvius. See Wesseling, in lib. xiii. 607 " The body of a man, says the historian, when speaking of the temple of Jupiter Olympius at Agrigentum, might be fitted in the fluted parts of the columns."

At this day, we may still see at Girgenti, a portion of the entablature, with a Triglyph, and the upper part of one of the columns ; and if we take 18 inches (French), as the breadth of one of the flutes at this portion of the column, and add a sixth for the breadth of one in the lower part, we shall find more than sufficient space for the body of a man. See Quatremère, Mem. 1815.

In an inscription on one of the Oxford marbles, some columns are called κίονες κυμβελλέται, these words are translated by Selden,

I II

columnœ striatœ, but Remesius proposes another interpretation.   Mar.
Ox. 512. Ed. Maittaire.

L. 81. Σφηνίσκος, "the dove tails, tenons of metal," Wilkins
σφήκωμα ὁ δεσμός, Hesychius τάντα συνεσφήκωσει, "*omnia compegit
simul*" Diog. L. in v. Anax.

L. 85. Ὀροφιαίους, λ. "ceiling stones." This word is only found in the
present inscription, and in a dialogue of the 12th century, entitled
Timario, which may be seen in the Notice des MSS. du Roi. ix.

L. 86. Lessing objects to the origin given by Vitruvius, lib. i. to the
name Caryatides, (the ΚΟΡΑΙ of the inscription,) as applied to
columns, he does not think the town of Caryæ was of consideration
enough to join the Persians in their invasion of Greece.   But we are
expressly told by Herodotus, lib. viii. "that some Arcadians sided with
the Persians; and there was Caryæ, a town in Arcadia, a borough of
the Pheneatæ, as well as in Laconia.   The fact, therefore, mentioned by Vitruvius may be true, only we should read with Larcher,
(ad Herod. lib. viii.) *civitas Pheneatarum*, instead of *civitas Peloponnesi*.

The Caryatides of Praxiteles are mentioned by Pliny, lib. xxxvi. c. 5.,
as well as those which were placed by the sculptor Diogenes on
columns to decorate the Pantheon of Agrippa; but no instance remains of any building, belonging to the pure age of Athenian
architecture, in which we find them used, except in the Pandroseum
of Athens.

L. 120. Ἐκπεποιημένα.   This word implies "finished work."   "The
Propylæa were finished, ἐξεποιήθη," Heliodorus in Harpocratio in v. Προ.
Herodotus says, "the stones of the Pyramids were *finished off*."
This is the translation of Dr. Hales.

L. 148 Τετάρτου ἡμιποδίου, "three feet and a half" The meaning of
this numeral form among the Greeks has not always been correctly
explained; thus, τέταρτον ἡμιτάλαντον, is three talents and a half; but
πέντε ἡμιτάλαντα, are not four talents and a half, as Kuhnius translates
the words; they mean only two talents and a half.   See Hemster. in
Poll. ix. c. 6. note 88. and the Addenda.

L. 166. Ἀετίλιοι, "the stones of the pediment," the Ἀετό. It is worthy of remark, that this word is found in an inscription on the entablature of a temple at Antæopolis in Egypt; it is not therefore appropriated solely to the triangular form. Hamilton's *Ægyp.* 395.

L. 186. ΟΣ ΤΟΙ ΗΥΠΕΡΘΥΡΟΙ. The ὑπερθυρον is described by Kuhnius as that part, "*supra supercilium sub corona, vicem quodammodo zophori gerens.*" Pollux. i. c. 8. Mr. Howes translates it "lintel" in Odys. vii. in the description of the palace of Alcinous. (On Books, t. i.) A balcony over the door was called τὸ προῦχον τοῦ ὑπερθύρου; it is the στηλζο of the later Greeks. See Salm. H. A. 155.

Ægypti operculum.

London, Published Oct.r 1, 1827, by Longman, Hurst, Rees, Orme, & Brown, Paternoster Row.

4 H 2

REFERENCES TO MR. LESLIE FOSTER'S MAP OF THE TROAD.

THE annexed map does not lay claim to perfect accuracy; but on a subject which has given rise to so much controversy every degree of evidence may be of some value.

It was constructed by observations of angles made from a variety of stations; principally the hill of Yenicher, the tomb of Ajax, the tomb of Æsyetes, and the Pergamus. The instrument with which they were observed was merely a small mariner's compass with sights adapted to it.

A. The plain of Troy perfectly level, in general dry and tolerably well cultivated. Its produce corn and pasturage.

1. The fortress of Koum Kalé.

2. The town of Koum Kalé, supposed to contain about 2000 inhabitants, all Turks.

3. Seven Windmills.

4. The village of Yenicher, inhabited by Greeks. The hill on which it stands was probably the Sigæan promontory in the time of the Trojan war. From hence to the fort is sand, different from the soil of the plain, and seems to have been formed by the river.

C. A shoal of sand.

d. Here probably was the line of shore formerly.

5. A tumulus on the brow of the hill, 24 feet high towards the plain, supposed to be the tomb of Achilles.

6. A tumulus in the plain.

7. A Turkish cemetery, on a rising heap of earth, but whether natural or artificial it seems difficult to determine.

8. A wooden bridge, the river is here 465 feet broad

M. A perpendicular chalk cliff about 100 feet high.

9 The ancient confluence of the Simois and Scamander.

10. A stone bridge of four arches and 60 feet long, built over the ancient bed of the Scamander issuing from the marsh (12). The water was barely moving in this channel in May 1803. The channel was no where less than 20 feet broad.

11. A rising heap of earth; it may be doubted whether it is natural or the remains of a tumulus.

12. Deep marshes, and pools of water.

13. A tumulus 24 feet high.

14. A narrow drain through which the water issues from the marsh rapidly.

15. The river Simois. The channel filled with water was no less than 200 feet broad in May 1803.

16. Kallifatli, village.

17 Marshes on each side of the ancient bed of the Scamander. It is impossible in this part to distinguish the channel.

18. Village of Yeni Keui.

19. A tumulus.

20. A singular shaped chalk cliff

21. An artificial canal which diverts the greater part of the waters of the Scamander; this canal, at the place marked 22, where it branches off from the river, is carried along the brow of the hill to preserve the level; a proof that it is artificial.

23. The river Scamander.

24. A Turkish village.

25. The tomb of Æsyetes, about 100 feet high.

26. Marshes full of the Arundo donax about the bed of the Scamander.

27, 28. The sources of the Scamander, both cold in May, 1803; but reported by the Turks to be hot, and to smoke in winter.

29. A gently rising hill, insulated in the plain.

30. A rough rocky hill, at the bottom, above the sources producing wild fig-trees. Quære the 'Ερινεός.

31. *Qnære* whether the place thus marked is not the site of the ancient Scæan gate.

32. Turkish village of Bournabashi, containing about 20 houses.

33 A Turkish cemetery full of fragments of granite and marble of rude workmanship, and very great antiquity.

34. A valley between the Erineos and the site of Troy.

35. This dotted line marks what was possibly the boundary of the city on the north.

36. A tumulus of stones and earth.

37. A tumulus of stones, probably the tomb of Hector. It stands on a naked rocky hill, on the brow of a precipice rising immediately from the river, at least 300 feet perpendicular.

38. Dubious remains of a tumulus.

39. A tumulus. *Quære*, did the wall of Troy enclose this hill?

40. The precipice, on the brow of which was the Pergamus.

41. A most beautiful romantic valley; in spring the river overflows its whole breadth.

42. A deep ravine between the Pergamus and the city.

43. A steep rocky mountain.

44. A gently swelling hill, probably Callicolone.

45. Tchiblak, a Turkish village

46 The village and valley of Thimbrek.

47. Halel Eli; in the cemetery, there are remains of a temple

48. Koum Kem, in the cemetery considerable remains.

49. The tomb of Ajax.

50. A tumulus.

51. Marshes overflowed by the Hellespont. This seems to have been the station of the fleet.

52. Mouth of the river.

53 Steep rocky mountains extending to the Dardanelles.

The dotted line denotes the track pursued by the drawer of the map.

Remarks on the Demetrian System of the Troad, by the Editor

(The references are made to Mr. Leslie Foster's map.)

1. COURSE OF THE SIMOIS. It is plainly stated by Demetrius when speaking of the two rivers, Scamander and Simois, that the former *approaches* Sigæum, the latter Rhœteum; ὅ τε Σκάμανδρος καὶ ὁ Σιμόϊς· ὁ μὲν τῷ Σιγείῳ —ργμάτως, ὁ δὲ —ῷ Ῥοίτῃ. L. XIII. There is no other stream in the whole plain, to which the words alluding to the Simois apply, but that in the valley of Gheumbrek. The course of it may be seen* in Sir W. Gell's map., and it may be said to pass to the south of fig. 46., in Mr. Foster's map. to continue to run by fig. 47., and then to the north of fig. 48. The stream is called in Dr. Hunt's journal Kamára Sou †, or the aqueduct river, from a building of this nature which crosses the stream at another part of the Troad.

2. The Shimar of Professor Carlyle, (the Kalefath of Dr. Clarke,) flows in a direction south of fig. 41. 45, 44. towards fig. 46, where is

---

* At the season of the year, in the month of May, when Mr. Foster visited the Troad, the course of the stream is not very observable. Mr. Frere, in a letter to the editor dated from Pera, speaks in the following manner of it.— 'Descending from the southward the hills into the plain of the Thymbrius, we came to the left bank of that river, a little below Halel Eli (fig. 17.) and following its course upwards, crossed it at a ford at the eastern extremity of the village, and, winding to the left through an extensive tract of ruins, then riding some time west, or north-west, along a plain of pasture, we began to ascend some gravelly hills connected with the promontory of Aian. In traversing this pasture we crossed a river, or rather a water, (for it seemed nearly stagnant, whereas the Thymbrius is a clear and rapid stream,) which must, I should say from the position of the ground, fall into the Thymbrius, but I cannot say that it does certainly.'

† The Kamara of Dr. Hunt is the Shimar mentioned in the Journal of his fellow-traveller, Professor Carlyle. See Major Rennell's Topography of Troy. Dr. Hunt says the word is written in his own papers Kamara and Tchamara. Kamara is an *arch* in modern Greek, hence applied to an aqueduct. K is pronounced in many parts of the Levant as *tch*; the word Tchamara the Professor writes Shimar.

the village of Kalefatli ; consequently it cannot be the Simois, or the Scamander of Demetrius, as it neither approaches Sigæum at fig. 1. and 2., nor Rhæteum at fig. 49.

3. In the valley of Gheumbrek, D'Anville places the Simois; (see Rennell's Observations on the Plain of Troy, 44) Sandys the traveller, also, supposes it was to be found in that part of the plain, " nearer Sigæum was the station for the Grecian navy ; but nearer Rhæteum, the river Simois, now called Simoes, discharges itself into the Hellespont."

4. If we suppose the Simois to flow in the valley of Gheumbrek, we may easily explain the words of Ptolemy, who notices, in order, the following places, — Δάρδανον· Σιμοέντος ποταμοῦ ἐκϹιλαὶ Σκαμάνδρου ποταμοῦ ἐκϹολαὶ Σίγειον ἄκρα. L. 5.

5. We may ask on what authority the Thymbrius and plain of Thymbria have been placed at fig. 46, 47, 48 There is no mention of Thymbra but once in Homer, Il. κ. 430. It is there only said, " that the Carians and troops of other nations are *towards the sea ;* but *towards Thymbra* are the Lycians, Mysians, Phrygians, and Mæonians.

Πρὸς μὲν ἁλὸς Κᾶρες. .

Πρὸς ΘύμϹρης δ' ἔλαχον Λύκιοι

We learn nothing from this passage concerning the situation of Thymbra, except that instead of being *near the sea,* as it has been generally placed, the opposition expressed in the words of the poet would lead us to seek for it at a distance *from the sea.*

And if we examine the words of Demetrius, we shall also see that Thymbra cannot be placed where we are generally directed to look for it, at fig 47, 48. These figures are not distant, at the utmost, two miles from New Ilium, which stood between fig. 48. and 15. , but Thymbra was five English miles from New Ilium, or fifty stadia. This is the obvious deduction from the words in Strabo.—Πλησίον ἐστι (τῷ παλαιῷ κιτίσματι) τὸ πεδίον ἡ ΘύμϹρα, καὶ ὁ δι' αὐτοῦ ῥέων ποτάμος ΘύμϹριος, ἐμϹάλλων εἰς τὸν Σκάμανδρο, κατὰ τὸ ΟυμϹραίου Ἀπόλλωνος ἱερόν του δὲ νῦν Ἰλιοῦ πεντήκοντα σταδίους διέχει. Lib. xiii. Ox. ed. 862. " The plain Thymbra and the river flowing through it (which joins the Scamander near the temple of Apollo) are in the vicinity of the ancient city, but distant fifty stadia from New Ilium."* If we suppose with Bryant, that the words apply to the conflux of the Thymbrius and Sca- mander, the conclusion is the same

If, then, Thymbra was *near* to the site of Old Troy, according to Demetrius (and in Homer we find nothing to the contrary), on what authority, we may repeat, has it ever been placed by those who con- sider Bournabashi, as representing the situation of old Troy, at a con- siderable distance from this village?

6. At Thymbra was a Temple of Apollo, as we learn from Strabo; by the Scholiast on Homer, Il. χ. 430, we are told it was ἱερον ἐπιφανές. Dr. Hunt found at Atché-keui, to the S. E. of Tchiblak (fig. 45. in Mr. Foster's map), some ruins and Greek inscriptions, one of the latter mentions Apollo In this very part of the plain we are about five miles from New Ilium, the distance of Thymbra from that place as given by Demetrius. A stream flowing near Atché-keui is noticed in Kauffer's map ; the same is also observed by Mr. Hob- house, 153 In this district of the Troad he was inclined to seek the plain of Thymbra and the river Thymbrius ; and Dr. Hunt's disco- very of the ruins there, and the inscription mentioning the name of Apollo, may be considered as pointing out the site of the temple of that deity, and confirming Mr. Hobhouse's opinion

7. Demetrius, when speaking of the Simoisian and Scamandrian plains, uses these words·—" A certain ridge or hilly tract of consider- able size separates each of these mentioned plains one from the other. It takes its beginning straight from New Ilium , is connected with (or attached to) it, and reaches to Cebrenia." Διείργει δ᾽ ἑκάτερον τῶν λεχθέντων πεδίων ἀπὸ θατέρου μέγας τις αὐχὴν † τῶν εἰρημένων ἀγκώιων ἐπ᾽

---

* For the site of New Ilium, see Dr Clarke's Travels, vol iii, and Sir W Gell's Topo- graphy, p 117 "The discovery of inscriptions ascertaining the site of New Ilium," &c.

† Ἀυχὴν, collis, τὸν αὐχένα διαζώσας, Plut in Pericle, *collem cingens* Constant. Lexic. The αὐχὴν τῶν ι. α. implies, that the ridge of land stretches out from the two bending hills which he had before mentioned

εὐθέιας ἀπὸ τοῦ νῦν Ἰλίου τὴν ἀρχὴν ἔχων, συμφυὴς * αὐτῷ, γινόμενος δ᾽ ἕως τῆς Κεβρηνίας. Now there is *no other* ridge or elevation in the whole Troad to which these words can be applied, but that marked 44, 44. in Mr. Foster's map, there is *no other* commencing from New Ilium, *no other* connected with it, and running towards Cebrenia. If, then, the plain of the Mender be one of the plains separated by this ridge from the other plain, namely, that in which the Gheumbrek runs, we have found the Scamander and Simois of Demetrius; for the Scamandrian plain is, he says, the " broader" of the two ; and that expression only applies to the plain A, A, where the Mender flows, consequently the other is the Simoisian, and the Simois is in the Gheumbrek valley.

8. In Major Rennell's Observations on the Topography of Troy, p. 29., the passage we have quoted from Demetrius is thus rendered — " A narrow ridge divides each of the above plains from the other, beginning near the present Ilium ;" but μέγας τις αὐχὴν is not a *narrow* ridge ; ἐπ᾽ εὐθείας ἀπὸ τ. ν. Ι., does not mean " beginning *near* the present Ilium ," but *from* the present Ilium , and the words συμφυὴς αὐτῷ are *omitted*. We shall make no other remark than this , that if the passage had been properly translated, it would not have suited Major Rennell's hypothesis. See the plate in his work, No. 2., where the ridge of land which he considers as corresponding to the αὐχὴν of Strabo, is not represented as beginning *from* New Ilium, and is *not* connected with it.

9. With respect to the πηγαὶ of the Scamander, mentioned by the poet, Il 22., it is evident that Demetrius thought one of them was to be found, namely, the cold source, and not in the mountain but in the plain ; he interprets the word πηγὴ in the sense of " source near the river ," διὰ τὸ πλησίον εἶναι τοῦ Σκαμανδρου; instead of " source of the river." The hot spring he thought had failed. We mention this, because it is generally supposed that the words in Strabo are the ex-

---

* Συμφυὴς, is the reading of four MSS., it means *adherens*. See Steph. in voc.

planation given by the geographer, but, by referring to the first book
we shall find that they are the words of Demetrius.

These few remarks may show, that notwithstanding the diligence
and curiosity of some preceding travellers who have visited the Troad,
there remains still much to be done. The ruins and inscriptions
found at Atché-keui by Dr Hunt were never yet mentioned, and more
documents may be found which will inform us of the names of some
of the cities of the Troad, and guide us more surely in our investigation of the antiquities of the country.

---

* Those who have attended to the controversy respecting the Troad, will recollect the
attempts which have been made to appropriate the Throsmos of the poet to some particular feature in the plain. But may we not adopt the plain and simple explanation given by
an excellent scholar and critic? " Ἐπὶ θρωσμῷ πεδίοιο, in campo bellico, in campi planitie
ad pugnam apta." Wyttenbach Anim. in Plut. ii. 1412. Mr Hobhouse (see his Travels,
p. 758.) will be glad to see his opinion confirmed by such good authority.

NOTES.

Page 475. *The Orchomenian Inscription.*

Mr. Dobree has lately communicated to Dr. Clarke some observations on the Orchomenian marbles they are printed in the new edition of that volume of Clarke's Travels which contains the inscriptions; and they are now inserted in this work, as they supply the deficiencies in the translation which has been given of the third inscription.

"Inscription III., line 13. —I put a comma after ἐπινομίας. Let Eubulus have a right of pasturage for a given time, that is to say, the right of grazing, for four years, 220 head of cattle, including horses, and 1000 sheep, including goats, *i. e.* a horse to reckon as an ox, and a goat as a sheep.

"Line 19. Νομώνης is the contractor who farms the public pasture land: thus τελώνης, ἐργώνης, (Chandler. Marm Ox xlix), &c Eubulus enters his cattle at the offices of the treasurer and of the contractor, that their accounts may check each other.

"Line 20 Κάυμα, or ἔγκαυμα, is a burnt-in mark, see Scaliger on Varro de L. L. p. 107. ed. 1619, and the Notes on Hesychius, vv χυπατίας and τρυσίππιον Eubulus is to register, 1st, the marks of his cattle, horses, &c. specifying any that may be unmarked, 2d, the number of each sort.

"Line 22. Ιωνδι is for ὦσι (ἔωσι), Ι being put for Ε, as in ΑΙΩΝΟΘΕΤΙΟΝΤΟΣ and ΔΟΚΙΕΙ, in the Orchomenian inscriptions, and ΙΟΣΑΣ for ὥσας, in one at Thebes, which Pococke has given with his characteristic inaccuracy.

In the first inscription, lines 3. and 4 the marble seems rather to have ΧΡΙΟΣ than ΧΙΟΣ. This was pointed out to me by one of the gentlemen at the Museum. May it not be right, taking it for ΧΡΕΟΣ, a debt?" — Mr Dobree's Note

The third inscription, beginning with line 19. may be thus written, according to Mr Dobree, in the common dialect —

> εκαστον παρα τιν ταμιαι και τον νομα-
> ναν τα τε καυματα των προβατων και
> τιν αιγων και των βοων και των ιππων, καν
> τινα ασημα ωσι, και το πληθος μη
> απογραψ σθω ο πλεονα των γεγραμ-
> μενων εν τη συγγραφη. Εαν δε τι
> εμπρατтη το εναωμον Ευβωλω, οφειλ-
> ετω η πολι των Ορχομενιων αργυριω
> μνα. τετταρακοντα Ευβωλω καθ' εκα-
> στον ενιαυτον και τοκον φερετω δραχ-
> μας . τη μνας εκαστη κατα μηνα
> εκαστον, και εμπρακτος εστω Ευβωλω
> κατα τους των Ορχομενιων νομους

Page 199 line 5.

For " Kalos," substitute " Talos , ' and add, " The authority for Talos rests not so much on the passage from Lucian's Piscator, quoted in a subsequent note, as on those readings and authorities which are cited by Wesseling ad Diod. S. and others, V not ad pag. 160, in the Annotationes in Piscat. Bipont Ed."

Page 199 line 13.

This idea of the position of the Sepulchre of Talos and the Temple of Æsculapius is confirmed by a passage in the Piscator of Lucian, where Parrhesiades, after proclaiming from the Acropolis the invitation to the philosophers, and the promise of a bonus of two minæ, some figs, and a Sesamus cake, cries out, Βαβαί, ω πληρης μεν η Ακρος αθιζομενων, επι τας δυο μνας ως ηκουσαν μονα. Παρα δε το Πελασγικον αλλοι και κατα το Ασκληπιειον ετεροι, και περι τον Άρειον παγον ετι πλειον, εισι δ. και κατα τον του Ταλου ταφον οι δε και προς το Ανακειον προθεμενοι κλιμακας ανεπουσι βομβηδον η Δια και βοτρυσιν, εσωω δικην, ινα και καθ Όμηρον ειπω Whoever has been at Athens, and has not been inattentive to the manners and customs of the present inhabitants, will be at no loss to comprehend what is here meant by the two eatable presents which allured the philosophers, namely, the παλαθη ισχαδων, and the σησαμιους πλακους. How often he must have noticed the strings of dried figs in the market, and the surface of the cakes there strewed with sesamum seeds

Page 501 line 18

It appears, from what occurs in Lucian's Dialogue, entitled "The Ship," that although Pausanias, as an antiquary, thinks proper to enter the city by the Piraean gate, yet the usual road from the Piraeus at this time was towards Dipylon, where it is at present. As the long walls were then demolished, and the principal part of the city on the north of the Acropolis, the road must have been obviously in this direction

THE END

Printed by A Strahan,
Printers-Street, London

OCT 3 0

REC'D YRL

Form L0–Scr

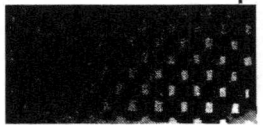

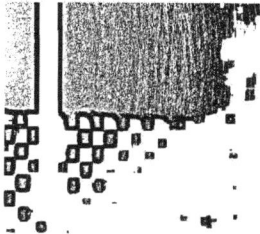

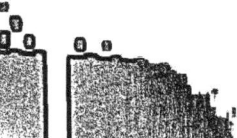

Lightning Source UK Ltd.
Milton Keynes UK
UKHW052039040621
384870UK00013B/963

9 781363 841905